INSIDERS' GUIDE TO
SOUTH DAKOTA'S BLACK HILLS AND BADLANDS

Help Us Keep This Guide Up to Date

Every effort has been made by the authors and editors to make this guide as accurate and useful as possible. However, many things can change after a guide is published—establishments close, phone numbers change, hiking trails are rerouted, facilities come under new management, etc.

We would love to hear from you concerning your experiences with this guide and how you feel it could be improved and be kept up to date. While we may not be able to respond to all comments and suggestions, we'll take them to heart and we'll also make certain to share them with the authors. Please send your comments and suggestions to the following address:

The Globe Pequot Press
Reader Response/Editorial Department
P.O. Box 480
Guilford, CT 06437

Or you may e-mail us at:

editorial@globe-pequot.com

Thanks for your input, and happy travels!

INSIDERS' GUIDE® SERIES

Insiders' Guide®
to South Dakota's
Black Hills and Badlands

SECOND EDITION

Barbara Tomovick and Kimberly Metz
Revised and updated by Bert and Jane Gildart

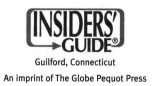

Guilford, Connecticut

An imprint of The Globe Pequot Press

Copyright © 2002 by The Globe Pequot Press
The previous edition of this book was published by Falcon Publishing, Inc. in 2000.

Insiders' Guide is a registered trademark of The Globe Pequot Press.

Cover photo: Steven A. Page
Back cover photos (from left to right): Steven A. Page (angler); courtesy South Dakota Tourism (climber, church, bicyclist); Steven A. Page (Needle's Eye)
Maps created by Brandon Ray; © The Globe Pequot Press

ISSN 1539-3542
ISBN 0-7627-2259-2

Manufactured in the United States of America
Second Edition/Third Printing

Contents

Directory of Maps

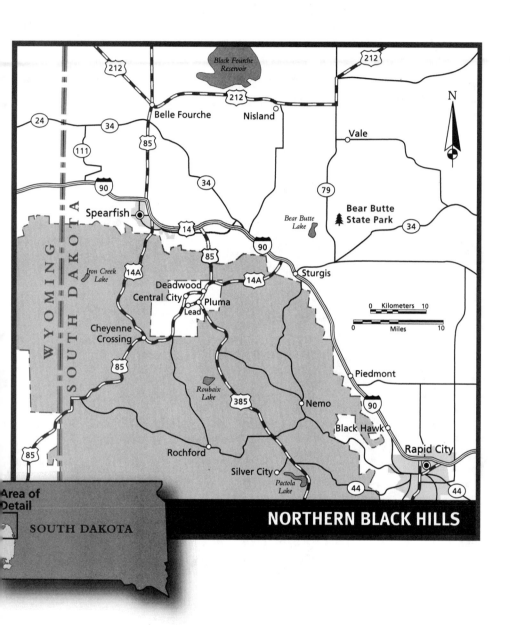

NORTHERN BLACK HILLS

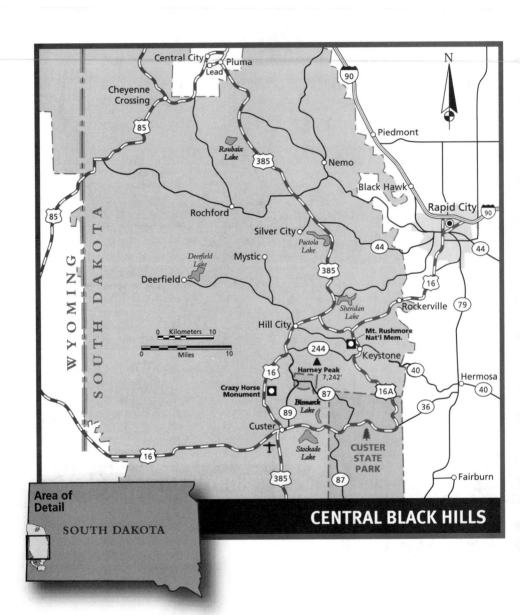

CENTRAL BLACK HILLS

Area of Detail

SOUTH DAKOTA

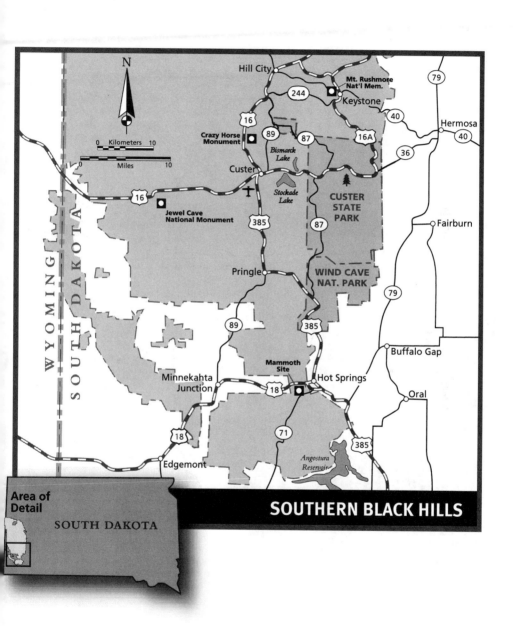

SOUTHERN BLACK HILLS

Area of
Detail

SOUTH DAKOTA

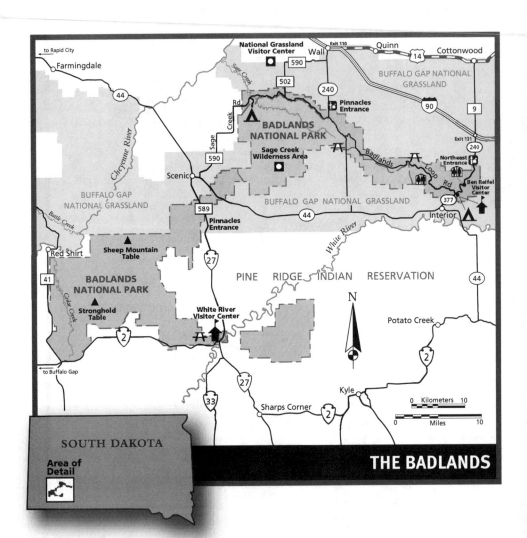

to Rapid City

Farmingdale

National Grassland
Visitor Center

Wall   Quinn   Cottonwood

Exit 110

14

BUFFALO GAP NATIONAL
GRASSLAND

590

502

44

240

90

9

Rd

Pinnacles
Entrance

240

Exit 131

BADLANDS
NATIONAL PARK

Sage Creek
Wilderness Area

Badlands

Loop

Rd

Northeast
Entrance

590

Scenic

BUFFALO GAP NATIONAL GRASSLAND

377

Ben Reifel
Visitor
Center

BUFFALO GAP
NATIONAL GRASSLAND

589

Pinnacles
Entrance

44

Interior

Battle Creek

Cheyenne River

Red Shirt

Sheep Mountain
Table

White River

27

PINE   RIDGE   INDIAN   RESERVATION

41

BADLANDS
NATIONAL PARK

Cedar Creek

Stronghold
Table

N

44

2

White River
Visitor Center

Potato Creek

to Buffalo Gap

2

27

33

Sharps Corner

2

Kyle

0   Kilometers   10

0   Miles   10

SOUTH DAKOTA

Area of
Detail

THE BADLANDS

Preface

The Black Hills and Badlands form a region of contrasts. The Hills are an uplifted island of mountains in the middle of prairie flatland, and the Badlands resemble a sometimes spooky, prehistoric moonscape. Considered together, as they are in this book, they form a place that is welcoming, accessible, and quietly magnificent.

The Black Hills and Badlands are bounteous and beautiful, but sometimes tough and challenging, too. You'll find natural beauty of great power here: craggy mountains, mysterious geologic formations, sudden weather changes, towering evergreens, grassy prairie, and vistas that will make your heart ache. This is still a homey kind of place where the goodhearted residents look you in the eye and say hello, and where visitors are welcomed with smiles, questions, and helpful hints.

In addition to the natural wonders and welcoming atmosphere, the contrasts, we believe, are what make life here so very interesting. You'll find ghost towns and modern towns, commerce and country life, and a taste of the combined Old West, Midwest, and New West. We have trendy restaurants and rustic bars, sophisticated art galleries and quaint attractions, and cowboys and businesspeople and artists. Recreation ranges from rough-and-tumble rodeos to skiing, skating, and mountain hiking. In some areas you can still view century-old wagon trail ruts from modern highways. Life has changed quickly here in our relatively short history of settlement; yet, in other ways, it has hardly changed at all.

We've filled this book with places to visit, eat and shop, fun activities for children, sights to see, trails to hike, history to discover, and much more. The Table of Contents will direct you to specific chapters, and the How to Use This Book chapter will help you use and enjoy some of the unique tidbits we've sprinkled throughout this book.

Whether you're an armchair traveler or tourist or new resident, we're glad for the opportunity to contribute to your enjoyment of our beloved Black Hills and Badlands. We think you'll love this place, too, and that you'll take pleasure in its delightful contrasts. We hope you'll feel at home here, just as we do.

Welcome. The Black Hills and Badlands await your exploration.

Sunset casts a bison in silhouette in the Badlands. PHOTO: STEVEN A. PAGE

The Needle's Eye is a well-known Black Hills landmark and a favorite spot for rock climbers.
PHOTO: STEVEN A. PAGE

Acknowledgments

Writing my share of this book proved to be equal parts giant undertaking and labor of love, but it goes without saying that I could not have done it without the generosity and support of countless others. To all the friends and acquaintances, both old and new, who provided information for my chapters, I extend my heartfelt appreciation for your assistance, enthusiasm, patience, and good wishes. To those who went above and beyond the call of duty, here is the acknowledgment you so deserve.

Because I also was the book's photo gatherer, I have several people to thank for providing top-notch slides, beginning with Chad Coppess, senior photographer for the South Dakota Tourism Department, and the exceptionally openhanded Steve Page. Other local photographers who generously shared their work are Jerry Boyer, Robb DeWall (with help from David Melmer), Jon Frost, Roxanne Heizler, Dick Kettlewell, David Sandvik, Johnny Sundby, Ken Tomovick, and Mark Wanek.

I am indebted to my colleagues at the *Rapid City Journal,* who made time in their own hectic schedules to assist me: Erin and Mark Andersen, who lent me their adorable son, Dylan; Ron Bender, who accepted my numerous phone calls with his usual good humor; Ted Brockish; Eric Bursch; Dan Daly; Steve McEnroe; Hugh O'Gara; Dick Rebbeck; Denise Ross; Sheri Sponder; and Roger Toland, who guided me through Spectator Sports with unfailing good will.

To those who spent an inordinate amount of time patiently feeding me information or helped in other ways, many, many thanks: Suki Brinkman, restaurant manager at Miss Kitty's; Gordon Brownlee, former executive director of the Mount Rushmore National Memorial Society; Jacki Conlon, special events coordinator for the Custer County Chamber of Commerce; Terri Davis, Deadwood Public Library director and diligent researcher; Dallas Dietrich and Tedd Stymiest, formerly of Adventure Sport—always helpful and upbeat; Dave Gray and Ron Sieg at the state Game, Fish & Parks Department; Dick Fort, cross-county ski guru; Bill Grant, affable bank vice president; George Guest, Chris Niewold, and Steve Thede at Badlands National Park; Roxanne Heizler, whose knowledge of hors d'oeuvres and other matters proved invaluable; Carolee Hoekman at the Office of Child Care Services; Bill Honerkamp, president of Black Hills, Badlands & Lakes Association, whose cheerful assistance has endured through the years; Audrey Howard, information specialist with the Black Hills Parent Resource Network; Mick Jenniges, special agent at the state Department of Revenue; Don Kennedy of the American Association of Retired Persons; Sammi Kenzy, willing adventurer and fearless driver; Jim Langer, creator of Langers Original Black Hills Silver; Larry Lewis, proud father of an Olympic champion; Principal Janet Luce and teacher Rhonda Schier at Rapid Valley Elementary School; Frank Mason, Hot Springs Chamber of Commerce volunteer; Don Mueller, community development specialist for the city of Spearfish; Harley Noem at the state Division of Forestry; Bill O'Dea, Belle Fourche school superintendent; Dale Ostyn, Beth Peters, Beulah Donnell, and Carl Bockert, Hot Springs preservation champions; Todd Phillipe, Loren Poppert, Gene Singsaas, Scott Spleiss, and Lois Ziemann of the U.S.D.A. Forest Service; Dave Ploof, who introduced me to American Legion baseball; Jim Popovich, chief of interpretations at Mount Rushmore National Memorial; Craig Pugsley, visitor services coordinator at Custer State Park; Danielle Routhier at the National Cowgirl Museum and Hall of Fame; Susan Scheirbeck, rock climber extraordinaire; Tim Schnabel, resort manager and recipe procurer at Spearfish Canyon Resort; Wes Shelton, marketing director at Mount Rushmore Black Hills Gold; Mark "Spiro" Speirs, who taught me everything I know about golf—that is, just enough to write the entries in this book; Rod and Terry Stamper, owners of Stamper Black Hills Gold Jewelry

A pronghorn antelope surveys the landscape in Custer State Park. PHOTO: STEVEN A. PAGE

Manufacturing Inc.; Charlie Sunde, true believer at Nutrition Coalition; Janelle Toman at the state Department of Education and Cultural Affairs; Don Toms of the Black Hills Mining Museum; and Tom Troxel, director of the Black Hills Forest Resource Association.

My thanks go to real estate agents too numerous to name but including Linette Batterman, John Gerken, Rich Harr, Greg Klein, Marianne Knutson, Marv Matkins, Gil and Vel Raben, Connie Ruebel, and Johnny Sundby.

I am grateful to my editors, Annie Kao, Rebecca Swinehart, and Carol Kopec, who were more than generous with their time and guidance.

I would be remiss if I didn't pay tribute to the family members who tolerated my virtual exile for the better part of a year without complaint: my wise and wonderful husband, Ken, who has been my best friend, helpmate, and source of laughter through this and much more; my sons, Garrett and Ethan Grover, who appear to have overcome their embarrassment at having a mother who writes and actually bragged about the book to their friends; and my mother, Elizabeth Lee Richter, who has accomplished much in her own right while cheering me on and patiently waiting for me to have time to write letters again.

Finally, to all the friends I did not invite over for dinner, ski with, write to, or call for almost nine months, thank you for not forgetting me. I'm back now.

—Barbara Tomovick

No author is an island, and no book is written in a vacuum. From the beginning, this project had a synchronicity that still astounds me. I learned about it from someone I barely knew, and it quickly became clear that it would teach me some fine lessons about writing and other important matters and lead me down some interesting paths.

I was amazed and humbled by all the treasures that came my way: information that was pleasantly serendipitous, and strangers, friends, and colleagues who helped and participated, sometimes in ways they didn't even realize. So many times important facts, which I despaired of finding, came along at the last minute in snatches of overheard conversation or as tidbits in unrelated articles and books.

I was delighted by the opportunity to learn more about my adopted and beloved state of South Dakota. I am grateful to have had the chance to explore this beautiful state and meet its feisty but friendly residents and for the knowledge, resources, people, challenges, and experiences it brought my way.

Publisher Beth Storie and editors Theresa Chavez and Annie Kao were consistently kind, calm, and professional. Editors Dave McCarter, Becki Swinehart, and Carol Kopec came late to the project; I commend them for jumping in and taking charge in their capable way.

Friends were thrilled when I got this assignment and never failed to jokingly ask if they could say they knew me "when." These friends also provided tips on their favorite places off the beaten path, ones I otherwise wouldn't have known about.

Thanks to my loyal cyberspace friend, Marty Severe, whom I've never met but greatly admire and appreciate; and to Ed Metz, Valerie Dresslar, Joy Heutzenroeder, and Linda Embrock, who were so supportive. Thanks to Molly Abeln, the consummate authority on nightlife and local color, and Kate Schlenker, who has an enviable knowledge of the Hills. And special thanks to my star-crossed best friend, John Zabrocki, for being himself and for YK2.

My humble appreciation goes to the hundreds of South Dakotans—at museums, attractions, galleries, airports, hospitals, casinos, motels, and houses of worship—who patiently and pleasantly provided information. Very special gratitude goes to the talented local and regional authors whose wonderful books on the Black Hills became rich sources for this one. My fond gratitude also goes to the readers of this book. May you have as much fun reading and using it as I did writing it, and may you come to love the Black Hills and Badlands and their residents as much as I do.

—Kimberly Metz

Even the littlest dancers get involved in powwows. PHOTO: STEVEN A. PAGE

How to Use This Book

Let's say you've just opened this book for the first time. The cover is glossy and smooth, the page corners sharp, the spine a bit stiff. So you've opened it somewhat gingerly, wondering where to begin.

The fact is, we think you'll get hooked on the Black Hills and Badlands no matter where you start your armchair journey. Naturally, the table of contents near the front will give you an idea of the sort of information you'll find here. The comprehensive index at the back will help you zero in on specific things you'd like to learn more about. But maybe you just want to chapter surf and get a feel for what this guide is all about. Go right ahead. The ride's on us.

To make it more fun, we've sprinkled interesting little "factoids" throughout the text, flagged as Insiders' Tips. And because we wanted to make our book unique among the dozens of other Insiders' Guides, we borrowed from the South Dakota state slogan, "Great Faces, Great Places" (a reference to the faces of Mount Rushmore National Memorial) to bring you vignettes about some outstanding people and places you might not otherwise hear about. You'll find those stories under the headings "Great Faces" and "Great Places." We've also included some Legends and Lore we thought you might enjoy and a dozen Close-up features for an in-depth look at some of what makes this a special place.

Most of our chapters are arranged geographically, from north to south. Since Insiders customarily refer to various sections of the Black Hills as the Northern Hills, the Central Hills, and the Southern Hills, we've done that, too. The boundaries aren't necessarily hard and fast, so for our purposes we've divided the area up as follows:

The Northern Hills include Belle Fourche in Butte County, all of Lawrence County (primarily Deadwood, Lead, and Spearfish) and Sturgis and Bear Butte State Park in Meade County.

Piedmont and Black Hawk, in southwestern Meade County, come under Central Hills listings because those communities tend to be closely tied to Rapid City (in Pennington County) and are even listed under Rapid City in the phone book. Hill City, Keystone, Mount Rushmore National Memorial, and Harney Peak, all of which are in Pennington County, also come under the Central Hills umbrella.

The Southern Hills, at least in this book, encompass Custer and Fall River counties, which include the towns of Custer and Hot Springs, respectively, plus Custer State Park, Wind Cave National Park, Crazy Horse Memorial, and Jewel Cave National Monument.

Some might argue with our geography, and we would agree there's a certain amount of latitude in defining these locations. Nevertheless, we think our divisions will help you plan and navigate your trip and perhaps come to a better understanding of the area. You'll get better acquainted in our Area Overview chapter, which describes each region in more detail.

In our chapters on Attractions, Kidstuff, Gaming and Casinos, and Annual Events and Festivals, you'll learn about fun and fascinating things to see and do. In Campgrounds and RV Sites, Bed-and-Breakfast Inns and Ranches, and Accommodations you'll find out where to rough it and where to relax in comfort. Our Restaurants chapter will point you toward the best places to eat, whether you want a plain bagel, a homemade pizza with the works, or an elegant multicourse dinner. You'll get a closer look at our Insiders' lifestyle in our Education, Childcare, Real Estate, Retirement, Healthcare, The Arts, and Worship and Spirituality chapters. And in our chapters on History, Recreation,

Parks and Grasslands, The Badlands and Nearby, and Daytrips and Weekend Getaways you'll find out why we and so many others choose to make this our home.

We've done our best to be thorough in every chapter, but chances are you're still going to have to make some phone calls while you're here. Luckily, South Dakota is still "small" enough to have just one area code, 605. Unfortunately, we can't give you a hard and fast rule for determining whether a call is local or long distance.

To avoid overloading you with information, we haven't specified which of our attractions include sales tax in their admission prices and which ones add tax at the time of purchase, so you'll need to inquire. Tax rates vary depending on where you are and what you're buying, but be prepared to pay sales tax on groceries everywhere in South Dakota. Many out-of-staters are surprised, and not a little indignant, the first time they meet a check-out clerk who adds on those extra few cents for a loaf of bread.

We've included general credit card information in our chapters that have to do with accommodations and dining, but when shopping or visiting our attractions you should ask whether plastic is accepted.

You'll notice that we do a lot of cross-referencing among chapters, and that's because we want to make sure you don't miss anything.

You'll find, too, that we've used both the terms Native American and American Indian or Indian in references to the aboriginal peoples of North America in an effort to accommodate those who prefer one title or the other. You'll also see that we use both Sioux and Lakota in writing about the tribes of western South Dakota because although all Lakota people are Sioux, not all Sioux are Lakota. We've explained the distinction in a Great Faces section in our History chapter.

We hope you'll have as much fun reading about and exploring the Black Hills and Badlands as we did in putting this book together. But if you think we've left something out or made a mistake, let us know. You can write to us at Insiders' Guides, P.O. Box 480, Guilford, CT 06437. Or contact us on the Internet at www.globe-pequot.com. Of course, you can tell us what you like, too.

Soon, we hope, the volume you hold in your hands will begin to look a bit dog-eared, and the pages will carry your underlines and notes. We hope the spine becomes creased from constant use, like a set of well-earned laugh lines.

Area Overview

The Black Hills are ancient, some of the oldest mountains in North America. Although they don't claim the same attention as younger, taller mountain ranges, they're recognized, like wise and aged matriarchs, for their quiet splendor.

But mountains they are, nevertheless; they could as easily have been christened the Black Mountains as the Black Hills. The Lakota Sioux named them *Paha Sapa—paha* meaning any "height," whether mountains or hills, and *sapa* meaning "black." It seems likely that early translators settled on Black Hills for this, the only mountain range in Dakota Territory, to avoid confusion with North Carolina's Black Mountains, a range of the rolling Blue Ridge.

But why black when the Hills are covered with thick stands of evergreens? Quite simply because from a distance these pine-covered slopes loom like a backlit silhouette against the vastness of the Great Plains. The Black Hills have been called an oasis in a sea of grass, a description you're likely to appreciate after a long drive across the boundless prairie (which has its own lilting poetry) to reach us.

We are no longer surprised to meet people who don't know where the Black Hills are or who think all of South Dakota is flat. Yet the Hills claim a substantial number of distinctions. For starters, this is one of the richest gold-producing areas in the United States. As the burial place for legendary Wild Bill Hickok and Calamity Jane, and as the site of an apocalyptic expedition by Lt. Col. George Armstrong Custer (see our History chapter) and a reverberating vision by Oglala Lakota holy man Black Elk, we have what one friend calls "name-brand history."

The Hills are home to the nation's first national forest (also covered in our History chapter) and to one of our country's most prominent and defining symbols, Mount Rushmore National Memorial (see Attractions). Yet even among those who easily recognize Mount Rushmore, many don't know that the famous mountain carving is in the Black Hills, in South Dakota.

Nevertheless, some four million people from around the world find their way here each year, making tourism one of our top industries (again, see History), along with agriculture and mining. Visits to Mount Rushmore, Custer State Park (see our Parks and Grasslands chapter), and Deadwood (see our Gaming and Casinos and Attractions chapters) are likely to capture your imagination. A climb to the top of Harney Peak or a trek in the Black Hills National Forest (outlined in our Recreation chapter), could very well make you want to stay forever. But to understand the nuances of life here takes more time.

For in some ways Black Hills Insiders have a bit of an identity crisis. We cherish and brag about our area's natural beauty and fascinating sights while tolerating a profusion of billboards that mar the view and a fair number of embarrassingly tacky roadside attractions. We want to continue to live in the slow lane while crying out for wider, faster roads and new industry.

We call ourselves South Dakotans while professing deep philosophical differences with our neighbors in East River, that portion of our state east of the Missouri River where the bulk of our population lives. West River South Dakota, which includes the Hills, is the more politically conservative half of an already conservative state, yet we like to think of ourselves as rugged individualists. And we're never quite certain whether to call ourselves Westerners or Midwesterners. On one hand, the semiarid climate and rocky peaks of the Black Hills, which spill over into northeastern Wyoming (a bona fide Western state), make us feel and often dress like Westerners. Not only that, we relish our

3

Insiders' Tip

Phone book listings for Rapid City and Keystone alone include some 70 businesses that start with Rushmore, and another 10 that include Mount Rushmore in their names.

wild-and-woolly gold rush past. Our closest metropolis is Denver, a certifiable Western city that occupies the same mountain time zone we do. On the other hand, we are in South Dakota, which is undeniably a Northern Plains state in the nation's heartland. To confuse us even further, in between the protected Hills and the open plains lie the mysterious Badlands (described in our chapter on The Badlands and Nearby), which seem to belong on another planet altogether.

Some Insiders like to call the Black Hills "God's country," but like any earthly paradise, this one has its imperfections. For instance, most of us work hard for dishearteningly low wages, and although some argue that our cost of living is lower than in many other places, few families here can survive on a single paycheck (more about that in our Childcare chapter). For too many would-be home owners, "affordable housing" is an oxymoron, and for all of us property taxes are high. Limited career options and low pay drive many of our best and brightest young people to other states. So when Insiders say they live here for the quality of life the area offers, they're talking less about material objectives and more about intangibles such as neighborliness, clean air, elbow room, and a sense of safety.

Add the fact that only a portion of the Black Hills is privately owned. The rest is public land and, for the most part, unspoiled. The Black Hills National Forest takes up 1.2 million acres, or about 2,000 square miles—that's about one-third of our total area. National and state parks, monuments, and recreation areas make still more of the land

Lumbering is an important industry in the Black Hills, as well as a source of conflict between timber interests and environmentalists. PHOTO: COURTESY OF SOUTH DAKOTA TOURISM

surface off limits to expansive development. All of this makes the Hills an extraordinarily unfettered playground (see our Recreation chapter).

The Hills are remarkable in other ways as well. There is a strong Native American presence here, particularly in Rapid City, that manifests itself in our public art (see our Arts chapter), museums, interior design, local products, and even our architecture. The same holds true for our Scandinavian pioneer heritage. Jokes about Norwegian bachelor farmers abound, as do surnames that end in -son or -sen, -ahl or -al.

Our place names are revealing, too, often summoning images of land formations and wildlife. Many of our towns were named for their natural features, straightforward descriptions consisting of the plainest word combinations: Belle Fourche (French for "beautiful fork"), Spearfish, Deadwood, Rapid City, Hill City, Hot Springs.

Our roads meander as if they had minds of their own, seeking out the irregular more than the smooth spots. It's not uncommon to see riders sweeping across the foothills on horseback as we drive along. And only in the harshest winter weather do we fail to pass roadside bicyclists or joggers on even our most mundane jaunt into town.

Nestled within the Hills are a couple of dozen small towns, each with a personality all its own. Rapid City, with a population nearing 60,000, is the largest by far. Yet even in Rapid City it's practically impossible to go anywhere without pausing to talk to someone you know. To our way of thinking, that's one of the best reasons to live here.

The information below is meant to serve as an introduction, a verbal handshake from Insiders all over the Black Hills. Not every community is included, though, so we urge you to check a map, explore on your own, and get acquainted with us face to face. And be sure to check other chapters in this book such as Real Estate, Education, Healthcare, and The Arts for additional information about our Black Hills hometowns.

> ## Insiders' Tip
>
> Many Black Hills towns post signs at their city limits proclaiming "GOLD Community." In this context, GOLD stands for Guide to Opportunities for Local Development, a resource every bit as precious as the yellow metal that is mined here. The program is administered by the Governor's Office of Economic Development.

Northern Hills

Northern Hills residents enjoy small-town life enhanced by the presence of a four-year liberal-arts college (see our Education chapter) centrally located in Spearfish. To the north is Belle Fourche, to the east is Sturgis, and to the south are the twin cities of Deadwood and Lead. Each of these communities is unique in character and contributes something in the way of goods, services, and employment to the area as a whole.

Belle Fourche

As the northern gateway to the Black Hills, Belle Fourche, the Butte County seat, is a prairie town with close ties to the Northern Hills community. Near the fork of the Belle Fourche and Redwater rivers, it's home to about 5,000 people, small enough that one longtime resident described it this way: "Even if you dial the wrong number, you still know who you're talking to." With its railroad tracks and rodeo grounds, it's not hard to imagine

GREAT FACES

Saga of Sue

In some ways the saga of Sue is a classic, the tale of a simple country girl transformed into a superstar worth millions of dollars. Thrust unwillingly into the spotlight, she quickly became world famous. Men fought over her, and one even went to prison. Today Sue is in Chicago, a skeleton of her former self—just as she has been for millions of years. Sue, you see, is a nearly complete set of Tyrannosaurus rex bones and for now, anyway, the largest, most complete T. rex ever found.

Sue the dinosaur fossil was named for Sue Hendrickson, a field-worker for the Black Hills Institute of Geological Research in Hill City. After Hendrickson found the giant skeleton on land belonging to rancher Maurice Williams in 1990, the institute paid Williams $5,000, and workers removed Sue's remains for restoration. But before long there were allegations that institute President Pete Larson, his brother, Neal, and their partner, Bob Farrar, had been stealing fossils from public land. An investigation started.

In 1992 the FBI confiscated Sue along with other fossils and records from the institute, and a federal indictment charged the Larsons and Farrar, among others, with 153 crimes. None of the charges had to do with Sue, but the institute couldn't get her back. The courts said Williams couldn't sell the fossil without government permission because his land, which is on the Cheyenne River Indian Reservation northeast of the Black Hills, was held in trust. So the government kept custody of Sue, and Williams kept the institute's money, saying it was payment for disturbing his land. A federal jury ultimately rejected most of the charges in the federal case against the fossil hunters, but Pete Larson spent 18 months in federal prison for transporting undeclared travelers checks through customs.

Meanwhile, Williams asked the government to sell Sue for him, and in October 1997 the 65-million-year-old fossil went on the auction block at Sotheby's in New York. In less than nine minutes she was sold to the highest bidder for $8.3 million. Williams became a multimillionaire, and the Field Museum of Natural History in Chicago became Sue's new owner. However, Walt Disney World Resort and McDonald's had put up most of the money to buy Sue. So, although the fossil will be properly curated and exhibited at the museum, a full-size cast of Sue eventually will be on display at DinoLand USA. McDonald's-sponsored DinoLand is part of Disney's Animal Kingdom, a new feature of Walt Disney World in Florida.

After the auction, the Black Hills Institute kept the rights to the registered trademark name "Sue," and "Dakota" was chosen as the winning entry in a contest to rename the fossil. The institute later relented so Sue could keep her name, but paleontologist Bob Bakker (who is not affiliated with the institute) already had figuratively pinned a new tag on the world's most famous T. rex. Because of her star power, Bakker called Sue "the Marlene Dietrich of dinosaurs."

Belle Fourche when it was a dusty cow town. Although tamer now than in its heyday as a cattle shipping center (see our History chapter), the downtown business district retains a strong ranching flavor with stores that cater to folks who work on the land.

The sugar-beet fields of the early twentieth century are gone now, but agriculture remains the town's backbone; grain companies, The Belle Fourche Livestock Exchange, and three wool warehouses help producers get their goods to market. The bentonite industry runs a close second, with American Colloid Company and Bentonite Corporation as major employers. Medical facilities and the school district also provide a number of jobs.

The school district and the community tend to work closely with each other. In 1992 the Governor's Office of Economic Development named Belle Fourche South Dakota's Small Community of the Year—thanks in large part to efforts by Belle Fourche High School students, who were instrumental in getting the town involved with the state's GOLD (Guide to Opportunities for Local Development) Program.

Deadwood and Lead

The Lawrence County towns of Deadwood and Lead (with about 1,800 and 3,500 people, respectively) are so closely associated with each other that it seems appropriate to couple them here. Through the years their list of cooperative efforts has included anything from a school district to a street sweeper. The mountainous twin cities were at the heart of the Black Hills gold rush and quickly prospered after San Francisco–based Homestake Mining Co. acquired the area's richest gold deposit in Lead in 1877 (see our History chapter).

Homestake Gold Mine, 8,000 feet deep and the nation's longest-running underground gold mine, has been the community's lifeblood for more than 120 years. Homestake pumps millions of dollars into the local and state economy through property and severance taxes, purchases of goods and services, and excellent wages that help support all manner of regional businesses. Even after Deadwood became a gambling resort in 1989 (see our Gaming and Casinos chapter), its gaming halls courted well-paid Homestake miners to help round out tourist and retiree business. But as one lifelong Lead resident told us recently, "We've been living on borrowed time," knowing the golden lode is finite. The ticking of the clock got much

louder when Homestake abruptly shut down for 60 days in early 1998 to streamline its operation, then announced it would lay off about 500 of its 850 employees. Although not entirely unexpected due to dropping gold prices, the blow hit hard, and its impact will be felt throughout the Hills for some time.

Smaller, surface-mining operations in the Deadwood-Lead area also have laid off workers as ore bodies diminish and gold prices slump (see our History chapter). With no place for a viable industrial park, earnest efforts to diversify Lead's economy have been slow to bear fruit; a bowling alley and an electronics store are recent additions.

Gambling remains the primary employer in Deadwood (the county seat). However, despite its continued success and a truly impressive downtown facelift funded by wagering—the Paint Quality Institute named Deadwood, with its entrancing Victorian architecture, one of the "prettiest painted places" in 1997—the town is still struggling to bring in retail and other businesses to make visitors stay longer.

Insiders' Tip

The original name of the town of Deadwood was "Dead Wood Gulch." The hills around the mining camp had suffered a forest fire years before the first prospectors arrived, and dead trees were everywhere. It wasn't long before enterprising entrepreneurs were selling firewood and the town had become known simply as "Deadwood."

One longtime businessman speculates that Deadwood-Lead's ace in the hole could very well be its proximity to the Hills' two downhill ski areas and to premier cross-country skiing and snowmobiling trails (turn to our Recreation chapter for information). Those assets will continue to attract vacationers and vacation-property owners. It's also reasonable to expect that as high-tech innovations allow more and more people to telecommute long distances, a certain number will choose to live here, bringing their jobs and new ideas—and paychecks—with them.

Spearfish

Black Hills State University and an accessible location off I-90 have provided Spearfish with some priceless advantages. The town has grown quickly in recent years, boosted to a population of nearly 8,000 (with another 3,500 in the surrounding 3-mile area) in part by retirees who succumb to its charms: a progressive outlook, tidy appearance (notice the pretty porches on houses along Main Street), convenient shopping, assorted medical facilities, and handy recreational opportunities. The Donald E. Young Sports and Fitness Center on the BHSU campus is open to community members, and an 18-hole golf course and outdoor swimming pool (see our Recreation chapter) are situated at the mouth of beautiful Spearfish Canyon. The unspoiled canyon, which beckons with stunning views of cliffs and streams, also offers excellent trout fishing in Spearfish Creek (see our Recreation chapter for information about licenses and regulations).

The creek also runs through town, not far from the attractive new $3.4 million city hall–library and a paved mile-long bike path scheduled for a second mile-long extension. With a small strip mall (see our Shopping chapter) and a vital downtown, Spearfish is the subregional shopping center for the Northern Hills, and Black Hills Healthcare Network helps make it the local medical hub as well.

Ranching, the timber industry, retail stores, healthcare, light manufacturing, and the school district are top employers, along with the university. Pope & Talbot Sawmill has operated here for close to two decades; OEM Worldwide, which manufactures electronics primarily for the healthcare industry, is in one of three industrial parks on the southeast edge of town. Many people see Spearfish for the first time when they attend a summer performance of the Black Hills Passion Play, a premiere visitor draw you can read about in our Attractions chapter. But for those familiar with the town, Spearfish has long been a favorite place to conduct meetings, and that has meant plenty of business for a new convention center that opened in 1998.

Sturgis

Although best known as the home of the annual Sturgis Rally & Races motorcycle gathering (see Annual Events and Festivals), Sturgis is much more. The Meade County seat of about 7,000 residents is a retail and service center for those who live on outlying farms and ranches. Located roughly a half-hour's drive from both Spearfish and Rapid City, it's also home to a number of professional couples who go their separate ways to work each day. Sturgis citizens are active in their community, planting thousands of petunias in the spring and attending weekly chamber of commerce meetings at Bob's Family Restaurant (see our Restaurants chapter) to hear speakers on a variety of topics.

We don't know of any town that gets more use out its community center, either. Everything, it seems, takes place at the center, from recreation and meetings to concerts and school plays. Fort Meade Veterans Administration Medical Center (in our Healthcare chapter) is the town's top employer, with the school district, the local hospital, and Black Hills Special Services Cooperative also providing jobs. Majestic Bear Butte (turn to our Parks and Grasslands chapter for details) rises from the prairie northeast of town, a landmark for recreation and Native American spiritual rites.

Central Hills

Hill City

After the national magazine *Men's Journal* recently declared Hill City one of the country's 25 "truly cool" places, the little village that accurately calls itself the Heart of the Hills seemed poised for a population boom—and soaring property values. But a scarcity of available houses and building sites made the town's "cool" phase short-lived, no doubt to the relief of many of the 700 or so people already living here (and worried about their property taxes).

Part of the town's charm is its ready access to hiking and snowmobile trails and some of the Hills' most popular bodies of water: Sheridan Lake and Deerfield and Pactola reservoirs. Sylvan Rocks Climbing School & Guide Service, an accredited climbing school, is located here, convenient to some of the area's foremost climbing spots (see our Recreation chapter).

As seasonal shops along Main Street attest, a certain number of residents rely on tourism for their livelihood, and Black Hills Central Railroad/The 1880 Train (see our Attractions chapter) has long been the main tourist draw. Some residents find year-round work at the Rushmore Forest Products sawmill, the Black Hills Institute of Geological Research, the school district, and the Forest Service; others commute to jobs in Rapid City. The new Railroad Avenue truck bypass and the new, inviting Old World Plaza boutique mall on Main Street show that Hill City is on the move; further proof comes from the infusion of excellent art galleries showcasing regional talent in many forms.

Insiders' Tip

Outside magazine's March 1998 issue listed Spearfish Canyon among the 50 best bicycle rides in America. The publication recommends biking from the town of Spearfish to Spearfish Canyon Lodge at Savoy and back. That makes the 25-mile round-trip doable with one vehicle but ignores the scenic riches of the stretch from Savoy to Cheyenne Crossing.

Along the Deerfield Trail in Black Hills National Forest, sunlight streams through a stand of pines.
PHOTO: BERT GILDART

Keystone

Mount Rushmore is the *raison d'être* for Keystone, a town that at first glance looks like a T-shirt mecca but bears a closer look. True, you could probably fill several pickup trucks with logo-emblazoned shirts, fudge, and Black Hills Gold jewelry (see the Close-up in our Shopping chapter) from the 40-plus summer tourist shops that line Winter Street—known as the Strip.

But there are major attractions here, too (as you'll see in our Attractions chapter), such as Borglum Historical Center (Rushmore-Borglum Story), Big Thunder Gold Mine, and Beautiful Rushmore Cave. And although fewer than 250 people live in Keystone year-round, a keen interest in local history—gold and tin oxide were among the minerals mined here decades ago—has spawned the impressive West River History Conference, held each September at the Keystone Community Center.

Rapid City

Rapid City, with more than 57,000 residents, is the largest community in the Black Hills—and all of western South Dakota for that matter. Not surprisingly, then, this gateway to the Hills off I-90 is also the medical, educational, cultural, air-transportation, and shopping hub for the entire region. But even in the face of ongoing expansion, Rapid City remains a low-key place with friendly shopkeepers and minimal traffic hassles. Its 22 parks (one of which surrounds Canyon Lake) and the paved 13.5-mile bike path that runs beside Rapid Creek are some of its most attractive features. The bike path is symbolic of the city's ability to survive tragedy: After a 1972 flash flood killed 238 people and injured more than 3,000 others, the city established a parklike floodway along the creek so no one could build there and live in harm's way again. But even today, Rapid City and its longtime residents continue to define themselves in terms of "before the flood" and "after the flood."

While Rapid Creek divides the city into north and south, the forested ridge known as Skyline Drive (see the Dinosaur Park listing in Kidstuff) splits it the other way. To the east lie the oldest development, the downtown core, and Central High School; the west side, with its newer housing, golf courses, expansive Sioux Park, and Stevens High School, is almost a community unto itself. In early 1998 the Rapid City Common Council ended years of discussion aimed at building the controversial Road Over the Hill in the Skyline Drive area. Such a road would have connected the east and west sides of town and alleviated traffic congestion in the adjacent area known as the Gap. Efforts shifted to an alternate connector more to the southwest, which opened in 1999.

The Rapid City economy depends heavily on Ellsworth Air Force Base (read about the base in our History chapter) to the northeast of the city. Ellsworth employs some 3,000 military personnel and another 500 or so civilians, injecting about $140 million a year into the local economy in wages alone. Other major employers include several Black Hills Gold manufacturers, Merillat Industries (makers of particleboard), Rapid City Regional Hospital, the school district, Conseco (formerly Green Tree Financial Corp.), SCI Systems Inc. (an electronic-components

Insiders' Tip

The nonprofit InterTribal Bison Cooperative in Rapid City, (605) 394-9730, provides financial and technical assistance and other services to Indian tribes that want to restore bison to tribal lands, primarily for cultural and spiritual purposes. At last count 47 tribes in 17 states belonged to ITBC.

With its golden onion dome, the historic Buell Building at Seventh and St. Joseph Streets is a distinctive feature of downtown Rapid City. PHOTO: STEVEN A. PAGE

manufacturer), Federal Beef Processors Inc., the federal government, and the state of South Dakota, to name just a few.

When not working, Rapid citizens enjoy recreational opportunities at the newly expanded YMCA (see our Healthcare chapter), cultural events and entertainment at Rushmore Plaza Civic Center (listed in the Annual Events and Festivals chapter), and artistic expression at the Dahl Arts Center (see The Arts chapter). Other advantages include The Journey Museum (written up in our Attractions chapter), South Dakota School of Mines and Technology (see our Education chapter), Rapid City Regional Airport (see our Getting Here, Getting Around chapter), and easy access to I-90.

Southern Hills

Like the Northern Hills, the Southern Hills are characterized by small towns, but the pace might be even a step slower.

Custer

Custer is home to fewer than 2,000 people despite the extraordinary landmarks that lie right outside its borders. Incomparable Custer State Park (see our Parks and Grasslands chapter)—at approximately 73,000 acres one the nation's largest state parks—is just minutes east of town; inspirational Crazy Horse Memorial (see our Attractions chapter) is to the north. Although summer brings a flood of visitors to both, as well as to Flintstones Bedrock City and other attractions (see our Kidstuff chapter), Custer lacks the spit and shine and amenities of, say, Cody, Wyoming, a sophisticated tourist town that has made the most of its location near Yellowstone National Park.

Indeed, when the visitors vanish in the fall, Custer emerges as what it really is: a tightly knit community whose citizens are united by their love of high school basketball and who faithfully attend games whether they have a relative on the team or not (read about the team's accolades in our Education chapter). Social life revolves largely around school and youth activities, banquets, and church events. The Custer Youth Corrections Center, a state-run boot camp for juvenile offenders, is south of town; headquarters for the Black Hills National Forest is on the north end. Both are major employers, as are the school district, Colonial Manor nursing facility, Custer Community Hospital, Crazy Horse Memorial, and the park. Ranching, lumbering, and mining (primarily feldspar, mica, and quartz) also add to the town's economy.

Hot Springs

When desirable attributes were being handed out, Hot Springs must have been near the front of the line. For starters, our southernmost town brags that it has the best climate in the Hills, and we wouldn't argue to the contrary. Pick a day, any day, and it's likely to be warmer and drier here than anywhere else nearby. Other marvels of this city include the thermal waters that made it a health resort for buttoned-up Victorians with or without physical complaints. They probably walked right over the top of what is now Mammoth Site of Hot Springs, the serendipitously discovered spot where ancient elephant-like mammals succumbed to the forces of nature and were preserved for all time (see our Attractions chapter). Visitors and residents alike must have delighted in the area's lovely pink sandstone that positively begged to be turned into eye-catching buildings in the town and, in fact, was (see the Close-up in our Attractions chapter).

Award-winning Southern Hills Municipal Golf Course, historic Evans Plunge warm-water swimming pool, and nearby Angostura State Recreation Area are other bright gems in the crown of this prom queen called Hot Springs. So it makes sense that the Miss South Dakota pageant takes place here the third weekend of June each year. Likewise, it seems fitting that the healthcare industry is a key employer for Hot Springs' 4,300-plus citizens, along with the school district. Hot Springs Veterans Administration Medical Center and the State Veterans Home are here.

A sense of well-being is furthered by well-placed city parks and the Freedom

Each change in light and weather transforms the appearance of Bear Butte. PHOTO: STEVEN A. PAGE

Trail hiking and biking path beside the Fall River, which runs through town. If you can tear yourself away, you'll find unspoiled, uncrowded recreational spots in just about any direction, including Wind Cave National Park to the north (see our Parks and Grasslands chapter) and Cascade Falls to the southwest, on the way to the Black Hills Wild Horse Sanctuary (described in our Attractions chapter).

Getting Here, Getting Around

Getting to the Hills
Getting around the Hills
Specialty Transportation

Whether you're planning a trip to the Black Hills or you've already arrived, this chapter will give you all the transportation information you need. Set in the middle of the country, the Hills are landlocked, a bit remote and far from any huge metropolitan area, so you won't find a lot of options for your journey here. Still, getting here is easy enough and not too inconvenient, and we do think their relative remoteness allows the not-yet-spoiled Black Hills to remain their charming selves. Most of us who live here wouldn't want it any other way, and you'll understand why when you've looked around awhile.

Once you get here, however, you have quite a variety of options for getting around. There are bus, van, airplane, helicopter, and balloon tours—if you'd rather let someone else do the driving or flying—as well as some great bike paths and rentals. Of course, there are taxis and rental cars, too. Still, your best bet is to drive and see the Hills at your own pace. Although the Black Hills encompass 6,000 square miles, it's easy to get around quickly via I-90 and some well-maintained U.S. and state highways. But because the fastest way isn't usually the most interesting way, we've included some of the lesser-known scenic roads, too. These more lightly traveled routes meander through some of the most pleasant scenery in the Hills. Although it may take you twice as long to get where you're going via these routes, you'll have twice as much fun getting there. And fun is why you're here, isn't it?

You'll be delighted to know that South Dakota drivers are generally courteous and patient, even laid-back. Irate horn honking is rare, even if you make a mistake or day-dream right through a red light into a green one.

But—a word of caution—many Insiders drive over the speed limit. It's probably part of the nationwide trend toward faster driving for faster lifestyles, but do be careful.

We're happy to report that parking shouldn't be a problem in most places in the Black Hills, unless you're attending a popular event that draws a big crowd and lots of cars. Most towns have plenty of parking available, both on-street and in lots. Even Rapid City, the largest town in the Hills, doesn't have much of a parking problem—though you may occasionally have to park 1 or 2 blocks away from your desired destination.

And rush hour? Well, if you're from a big city or either coast, you'll probably laugh at what we call rush hour. But, just in case you worry about such matters, we'll tell you that traffic on many streets and roads becomes heavy between approximately 7:30 and 8:30 A.M. and 4:30 and 5:30 P.M. on weekdays. Rapid City experiences a lunch-hour rush between about 11:30 A.M. and 1:00 P.M. during workdays as people dash out to restaurants, then dash back to work.

Relax, this is an easy place to get around, and have fun traveling the beautiful Black Hills.

Getting to the Hills

By Air

If you fly in on a commercial flight, you'll be landing at Rapid City Regional Airport. If you're flying your own plane, you have more choices.

Northern Hills

Black Hills Airport
U.S 14A, Spearfish
(605) 642–4112, (800) 843–8010

Planes both small and large land here. The airport can handle large corporate craft such as Lear jets; in fact, Kevin Costner's big private jet occasionally sets down here. There are three grass strips, two of which are 4,000 feet long, one 5,600-foot asphalt strip, two overnight hangars, and four county hangars. The airport also has an instrument approach. Fuel, maintenance, and repair services are available (though no food service), and you can even camp on the grounds. Rent a car at the Rent-A-Wreck office, (605) 642–4112, (800) 843–8010. The airport is 3 miles east of Spearfish on U.S. Highway 14A. It is managed by Star Aviation, which also offers Adventure Air Tours (see listing under Star Aviation) and provides aircraft rental, flight instruction, and Cessna service and parts.

Sturgis Municipal Airport
Alkali Rd., Sturgis
(605) 347–3356

This small, city-owned airport is 5 miles east of Sturgis on Highway 34, then another mile down Alkali Road (turn right off the highway onto Alkali). The airport has 4,600 feet of asphaltic concrete runway; fuel, hangars, and maintenance service are available. You can't buy food or rent a car here, but for a lift into town you can call Courtesy Taxi, (605) 347–4253. C&B Aviation manages the airport, which can accommodate small planes and jets, turbo props, and twin-engine craft.

Aspen trees catch the sun on a fall day in Spearfish Canyon. PHOTO: COURTESY OF SOUTH DAKOTA TOURISM

Insiders' Tip

The Black Hills Visitor Information Center (at Elk Vale Road and exit 61 off I-90, east of Rapid City) has displays, picnic and pet exercise areas, information hosts, video theater, a gift shop, and the office of the Black Hills, Badlands, and Lakes Association. The telephone number is (605) 355-3600.

Central Hills

Rapid City Regional Airport
U.S. 44, Rapid City
(605) 394-4195

This city-managed regional airport is a user-friendly and family-oriented facility. Inside the 90,000-square-foot terminal, which is cozy and pleasant, you'll find thoughtful services. The airport is one of only two in the country originally built with nurseries. The unattended nursery room—furnished with sink, chairs, and diapers—gives moms and dads a chance to let a child nap, change a baby's diaper, or find a moment of peace and quiet for themselves. Each elevator, escalator, and rest room has information in Braille, and there are two TDD phones in the terminal. The public-address system broadcasts outside the terminal entrance, so you won't miss important information if you leave the terminal.

The airport, 10 miles from downtown Rapid City, has a recently installed concrete runway for commercial flights and another for general aviation use. Jets the size of 747s and 757s can land here, but larger jets and international flights are not accommodated.

One hint that may save you money: It pays to shop for airline tickets and, some-times, to give up a bit of convenience. Some Rapid City travelers find that occasionally it is considerably less expensive to drive to a larger hub, such as Omaha, Nebraska; Denver; or Sioux Falls, South Dakota. This will add hours to your traveling time, but you might consider the inconvenience worth the savings. Ask your travel agent.

Five car rental agencies have desks at the terminal: Avis, (605) 393-0740, (800) 831-2847; Budget, (605) 393-0488, (800) 678-0488; Hertz, (605) 393-0160, (800) 654-3131; National, (605) 393-2664, (800) 227-7368; and Thrifty, (605) 393-0663, (800) 367-2277. Listings of additional car rental agencies are in the Getting Around the Hills by Rental Car section of this chapter.

Airport Express Shuttle, (605) 399-9999 or (800) 357-9998, serves the airport. Other shuttle and taxi services are available, but you must call them to schedule service. All are listed later in this chapter in the Getting Around the Hills by Taxi, Shuttle, and Limo section.

If you fly your own plane into Rapid City Regional Airport, two fixed-base operators can service your plane while you tour the Hills. General Aviation, 3900 Airport Road, Rapid City, (605) 393-0000, (888) 754-1220, has both tie-downs and hangars and offers full service for your airplane. It's open 24 hours, and the staff can help with almost anything you might need during your stay, including catering and lodging arrangements. They even provide a tourist information center. Westjet Air Center, 4160 Fire Station Road, Rapid City, (605) 393-2500, (800) 888-4270, provides full maintenance services and aircraft sales. Both fixed-base operators offer charter flights, though not air tours of the Hills.

Southern Hills

Custer State Park Airstrip
Custer State Park, Custer
(605) 255-4515

You can fly your small plane into Custer State Park, land on the paved runway, park, and tie down your plane (no hangars are available). No car rentals or pickup services are available, however, and whoever picks you up must purchase a state park entrance license. The airstrip is in the east-central portion of the park, off Wildlife Loop Road.

Hot Springs Municipal Airport
Hwy. 79 S., Hot Springs
(605) 745–3555
The city of Hot Springs manages this airport, which has one asphalt runway (4,500 feet) and one turf runway (4,000 feet). It can handle aircraft weighing up to 11,000 pounds, including small jets. The airport has no hangars or maintenance service, but it does have tie-downs, fuel, car rentals, a lunch counter, and a customer lounge area. The airport is 7 miles from Hot Springs.

By Bus

The Black Hills are apparently considered so remote that Greyhound buses don't serve the area. Fortunately, if you favor traveling by bus, you can make connections from Greyhound routes to two regional bus services, which operate out of Milo Barber Transportation Center in Rapid City and share a local telephone number and ticketing staff. The small transportation center terminal has a pleasant waiting area and vending machines but no food service.

Insiders' Tip
Temperature differences in the Northern, Central, and Southern Hills can be as much as 10 to 15 degrees. You may leave Rapid City, for example, on a warm afternoon only to find it much cooler in Deadwood or windier in Hot Springs. Pack the proper clothing for your drive.

Jack Rabbit Charters and Tours
Milo Barber Transportation Ctr.,
333 Sixth St., Rapid City
(605) 348–3300 and (800) 678–6543
(charters and tours), (800) 556–0519
(schedules)
Jack Rabbit offers bus service to points east of Rapid City. The staff can schedule your entire trip, even the portions you'll travel by Greyhound. Rapid City is the only Black Hills town at which Jack Rabbit buses make scheduled stops. The company also offers charters and sightseeing tours for groups.

Powder River Coach USA
Milo Barber Transportation Ctr.,
333 Sixth St., Rapid City
(605) 348–3300, (800) 442–3682
1700 East U.S. 14, Rapid City
(307) 682–0960
Powder River has service to points west of Rapid City. You can schedule your complete route, even the Greyhound connections, through the Powder River office. In addition to stops in Rapid City, buses make scheduled stops in Sturgis and Spearfish. Powder River also provides charters and sightseeing tours to groups.

By Car

Denver is about 400 miles from the Black Hills; Kansas City, Missouri, is nearly 700 miles away; the Twin Cities of Minneapolis and St. Paul are about 600 miles distant; and Omaha, Nebraska, is some 500 miles away.

The major (and easiest) route to the Hills is I-90, which crosses the United States from one coast to the other and skirts the northern and northeastern boundaries of the Black Hills. I-80 has convenient exits to Rapid City, Sturgis, and Spearfish. Alternatively, if you're crossing the northern Midwest on I-94, you can exit at Belfield, North Dakota (near Dickinson), onto U.S. 85, which goes south to Belle Fourche. I-80 runs through the midsection of the Midwest, where you can catch U.S. 26 at Ogallala, Nebraska, then U.S. 385 at Northport, Nebraska, and head north to Hot Springs, South Dakota, at the southern edge of the Black Hills.

Check out the rules of the road in the Getting Around the Hills by Car section that follows, so you'll be aware of South Dakota's traffic regulations as soon as you cross the state line.

Getting around the Hills

By Air

If you're a fan of flying, try an air tour or a balloon or helicopter ride. For those who fly a private plane into the Hills, there are several places mentioned in the Getting to the Hills By Air section to park your aircraft, have it serviced, and leave it safely while you go off to sightsee. Two balloon companies in the Hills can take you for a very special ride. Dakota Balloon in Rapid City, (605) 393–8808, and Black Hills Balloons in Custer, (605) 673–2520, are listed in our Recreation chapter under Ballooning. A helicopter ride is another thrilling way to see the Black Hills. Rushmore Helicopters in Keystone, (605) 666–4461, is listed in our Attractions chapter.

Insiders' Tip

It's a good idea to fill your gas tank before touring the Black Hills, especially if you're using back roads and scenic routes. Gas stations are sometimes few and far between, and you'll be driving for miles, possibly quite far from the nearest town. You don't want worries about running out of gas to spoil your enjoyment of the scenery.

And if you're really fearless and want to see the Hills from the air—*without* an aircraft—read about Black Hills Air Sports and its skydiving opportunities in our Recreation chapter.

Northern Hills

Star Aviation
Rte. 2, Spearfish
(605) 642–4112, (800) 843–8010

Star Aviation, which is based at and also manages Black Hills Airport, offers Adventure Air Tours for two to five people in a Cessna high-wing aircraft (the wings are above the windows for unobstructed views). Fly over gold country (Lead, Deadwood, Spearfish Canyon, and the Homestake mines) or Devils Tower, Mount Rushmore, and Crazy Horse Memorial on 20- to 120-minute tours. Upon request, pilots can even fly you over some of the attractions in Wyoming and Montana. Star Aviation also has a charter service.

By Bicycle

Bicycling is a great way to see the Hills up close, at a more leisurely pace. If you didn't bring your own, you'll find bike rental information in the Bike Tours and Rentals section of the Recreation chapter.

Rapid City has a wonderful bike path that meanders 13.5 miles through the city, following sparkling Rapid Creek and bisecting the city's extensive park system. This foresighted city's policy is that all new streets will incorporate bike paths in their construction. The town of Sturgis has a Centennial Bike Path that runs from Brown High School, east of town, to Route 34 on the south side of town. Spearfish has a short bike path that runs in sections (some are concrete-paved, others are sections of streets) from the northwest side of town to the south side. Even the streets of most small towns that lack official bike paths are usually lightly traveled, which makes biking them a treat.

The best-known bike paths in the Black Hills, however, are our recreational gems: the George S. Mickelson Trail and the Centennial Trail (both multiuse and open to bicyclists, hikers, horseback riders, and cross-country skiers). You'll find more about both in our Recreation chapter.

By Bus and Van Tour

Many of these companies will customize your tour; just tell them what you'd like to see and they'll take you there. We recommend you write or call for a brochure to determine if the tour fits your plans, then call to schedule before you arrive. Some companies may adjust their operating hours for winter weather.

Northern Hills

Alkali Ike Tours
Deadwood
(605) 578-3147

These are history-packed, narrated, one-hour tours of Deadwood and Mount Moriah Cemetery. Look for the ticket booth in front of Old Style Saloon No.10 at 657 Main Street. Tours begin at that location, five times per day. Alkali Ike Tours' 46-passenger buses operate from May through October 1, weather permitting.

Boot Hill Tours
11 Jackson St., Deadwood
(605) 578-3758

This tour company provides one-hour narrated tours of Deadwood and the

Mount Moriah historic cemetery in a 45-passenger bus. Tours start at the Bodega Cafe, 662 Main Street, five times each day.

Dakota Bus Service
631 S. 32nd St., Spearfish
(605) 642-2353

This service offers shuttles to Deadwood as well as charters and customized sightseeing tours to destinations in the Black Hills and throughout the country. It accommodates only groups.

Original Deadwood Tour
Deadwood
(605) 578-2091

Since 1974, the Original Deadwood Tour has provided factual, entertaining, and humorous one-hour narrated tours of Deadwood and Mount Moriah Cemetery conducted in 40-passenger buses. The ticket booth is located in front of the Midnight Star at 677 Main Street, where the tours begin.

Western Transportation, Inc.
Sturgis
(605) 347-5066

Take a sightseeing tour around the Hills or a chartered trip across the country. Customized and escorted tours are offered in 47-passenger coaches. Step-on guide service is available, too, which means a Western Transportation guide will accompany and narrate any tour. If you wish to write for tour information, send a request to P.O. Box 700, Sturgis, South Dakota 57785.

Central Hills

Affordable Adventures
Rapid City
(605) 342-7691

A very flexible tour company, Affordable Adventures offers jaunts all over western South Dakota, including the Pine Ridge Reservation, and to national and international destinations. The owner is a "receptive operator," which means she can customize your tour to your needs and specifications. Vehicles are 7-and 11-passenger vans, but larger vehicles are available, too. The tours are informative, are conducted by knowledgeable guides, and accommodate parties from two up to several hundred people. To write for information use P.O. Box 546, Rapid City, South Dakota 57709.

Gray Line of the Black Hills
Rapid City
(605) 342-4461, (800) 456-4461

Gray Line is a worldwide company, and this locally owned franchise has 50 years of experience. It offers four- to eight-hour narrated sightseeing tours around the Hills and customized package tours that include accommodations and attractions. Gray Line also has a nationwide charter service. Many campgrounds, motels, and hotels can arrange a tour for you, so inquire where you're lodging.

Stagecoach West
Rapid City
(605) 343-3113, (888) 343-3113

Groups of 10 or more can take both standard and customized narrated tours with Stagecoach West. The company also offers nationwide charters. If you'd like to write, send queries to P.O. Box 264, Rapid City, South Dakota 57709.

Southern Hills

L & J Golden Circle Tours
Custer
(605) 673-4349, (877) 811-4349

Golden Circle's owners say their 14-passenger vans travel roads that large buses can't. They add that their drivers are experienced and knowledgeable and that their tours (including available narrated tours) are flexible. For more information write to P.O. Box 454, Custer, South Dakota 57730.

Plenty Star Ranches
U.S. 385, Pringle
(605) 673-3012

You'll find more information about Plenty Star Ranches in the Horse Camps section of our Campgrounds and RV Sites chapter. Guests at Plenty Star can sign up for customized tours around the Hills and to the Pine Ridge Reservation. The wildlife tours around Custer State Park

are especially popular because drivers follow little-used county roads as well as the more heavily traveled Wildlife Loop. The owners conduct tours in cars, small buses, or large coaches, depending on the size of the group. They also provide step-on guide service and can even direct you on a self-guided tour, if you prefer.

By Car

If you're driving around the Hills, you'll need to know and observe South Dakota's traffic laws. We'll caution here that all drivers should be alert for the many motorcycles that frequent this area. They can be difficult to see at times and, if you're used to watching for the bulky outlines of cars and trucks, it's easy to overlook the smaller, shorter shapes of motorcycles. Four-wheelers (that's what motorcyclists call the drivers of more conventional vehicles) should watch out for two-wheelers.

Another word of caution: from dusk to dawn (and even, less frequently, in the daytime) deer cross the interstate, the highways, and city streets. Be alert, slow down, and use extra caution because deer are very hard to see and tend to dart into the roads, often in groups of two or more. Collisions with deer cause tremendous destruction to vehicles, their human occupants, and, of course, the animals.

South Dakota's mandatory seat belt law was approved by voters in 1994. It states that the driver and front-seat passenger are required to wear a seat belt. Backseat passengers (and backseat drivers!) are not required to buckle up. However, this is a secondary law; that is, drivers cannot be stopped specifically for not wearing a seat belt. If you're stopped for a traffic offense or accident and are not buckled up, though, the fine is $20.

A related law concerns child safety restraints. State law requires that children ages two and younger be strapped into a car seat and that children ages three to five be buckled into a car safety belt. After the age of five, the mandatory seat belt law (as detailed above) applies.

Drinking and driving is not taken lightly in our state. A person is legally intoxicated with a blood-alcohol content

Back roads are one of the best ways to see the Black Hills. PHOTO: COURTESY OF SOUTH DAKOTA TOURISM

of .10 or more. Highway patrol officers carry digital breath-analyzer devices. If you're suspected of driving under the influence, you'll be asked to take the test. If you are arrested for DWI and refuse, your driver's license will be confiscated at the time of arrest. And if the officer smells alcohol on your breath, you can be taken directly to jail.

The speed limit on South Dakota interstate highways is 75 MPH, except through cities, where it is reduced to 65 MPH. Most state and U.S. highways have a speed limit of 55 through the Black Hills.

Right turns on red are permitted in South Dakota unless otherwise posted.

If you're traveling on school days, you may meet school buses on the roads. When the yellow lights of a bus flash, prepare to stop. When the red lights flash, all drivers (in all directions) must stop at least 15 feet from the bus and remain stopped until the lights no longer flash. When the bus's yellow hazard lights flash (for example, at a railroad crossing), motorists must stop and then proceed with caution. Bus drivers are authorized to turn in the license numbers of offenders.

South Dakota has a few more rules of the road for motorcycles. An amazing number of motorcycle riders visit our beautiful Black Hills, especially during the Sturgis Rally & Races in August (see our Annual Events and Festivals chapter). This area is perfect for motorcycle touring and has been popular with cyclists for decades. Motorcyclists, however, should know the applicable laws. Helmets are not mandatory for adults, but are required for riders younger than 18. Eye protection must be worn, unless your motorcycle has a windshield, and clear eye-protection is required at night. Daytime headlights are not required, but a rear-view mirror is mandatory. A motorcycle's handlebar grips must be below the shoulders of the driver. Do use caution on our scenic graveled roads, which can be less than stable under the wheels of a motorcycle. And watch out for four-wheelers; they aren't always watching out for you.

The Faster Routes

Northern Hills

If you need to get where you're going in a hurry, I–90 is the route to travel. It follows the boundaries of the north and northeastern Black Hills and, thus, is the ideal route to Sturgis (exits 30 or 32) and Spearfish (exits 10, 12, or 14). From those towns you can pick up routes to take you farther north to Belle Fourche or south to the towns of Lead, Deadwood, Nemo, Rapid City, and others.

Insiders' Tip

Some highways in the Black Hills are paved with concrete, and you may experience the "singing highway" phenomenon when you drive on them. When the roads are constructed, finishers add a textured surface. This and the nature of concrete make your tires "sing" as you drive. The high-pitched tones change as you speed up or slow down, an interesting accompaniment to your sightseeing. Statewide, just 25 percent of our highways are paved with concrete, which highway officials believe holds up better through freezes and thaws and has a longer life than asphalt.

Tunnels along the Needles Highway (Highway 87) are a tight fit. PHOTO: COURTESY OF SOUTH DAKOTA TOURISM

Central Hills

From I-90, use exits 55 through 61 to reach Rapid City. If you're heading to the Central Hills, U.S. 16 South has four lanes from Rapid City to Keystone. U.S. 16A to Mount Rushmore, which branches off U.S. 16 near Keystone, is also a four-lane highway. From that area, U.S. 16 South becomes a two-lane road.

Southern Hills

The fastest route to the Southern Hills is Highway 79, which runs from Rapid City, past Hermosa, to the Hot Springs area. Highway 79 rolls through prairie hills and Buffalo Gap (where legend says the buffalo entered the Black Hills). It intersects U.S. 385, which will take you 3 miles west

into Hot Springs. There you can journey farther south on Highway 71 to Angostura State Recreation Area or use U.S. 18 to go farther west or east.

The Scenic Routes

Ah, the scenery! That's what you came here to see, and there's no better way to view it than on our scenic routes. We can truthfully say there are no un-scenic highways in the Black Hills, but we've listed our favorites below. Take a leisurely drive through some of the most picturesque landscape west of the Mississippi, with plenty of opportunities to pull over, park, and look around.

If you favor quiet, little-traveled routes known only to Insiders, we have plenty to offer. The Black Hills National Forest is positively laced with county and Forest Service roads—most graveled and rather narrow—where you'll see sights only locals usually see. A friend of ours says her favorite activity is heading down one of these little roads just to see where it leads. She swears you can't get lost because, as she puts it, "you always come out somewhere." We don't particularly advise that for our readers because, after all, she grew up here. Still, if you're feeling brave and have a good sense of direction and an adventurous spirit, you'll love exploring these roads. Get a detailed road map and plenty of gasoline first, and be prepared for emergencies or car trouble, because you may not meet another car, and you'll be far from help should you need it.

Northern Hills

The 19-mile Spearfish Canyon Scenic Byway, U.S. 14A, is one of the best drives around. It runs between Spearfish and Cheyenne Crossing, and you'll meander along the paved road, following pretty Spearfish Creek past towering limestone cliffs and evergreen and aspen forests. There are some great places to hike just off the highway, including Roughlock Falls and Spearfish Peak, and there's information about biking, climbing, and cross-country skiing in Spearfish Canyon in our Recreation chapter. Here in the Black Hills the scenery is the main attraction, so you'll find more information on the Spearfish Canyon Scenic Byway in our Attractions chapter.

U.S. 14A also runs east and west between Deadwood and Sturgis, through beautiful Boulder Canyon. Traveling west, you'll reach a wide valley that is being developed with houses and businesses, then the road enters the canyon again and twists, turns, and climbs. The last mile or so is a steep grade that drops down into the town of Deadwood.

Central Hills

A great Central Hills drive is along Highway 44 (Jackson Boulevard west from Rapid City), then U.S. 385 North. Highway 44 is known as the Rimrock Highway. It passes Cleghorn Springs State Fish Hatchery, Thunder Head Underground Falls, and other attractions (there's information about these in the Attractions chapter). It runs through spectacular canyons, where rimrock cliffs tower above you, and the little town of Johnson Siding. Rimrock Highway dead-ends into U.S. 385, the Black Hills Parkway, from which you can head north to Deadwood and Lead, taking side trips on county roads to the little towns of Rochford, Silver City, or Mystic. You can also follow the road south to Hill City, Custer, and Hot Springs. The Black Hills Parkway bisects the Hills, north to south, from Deadwood/Lead to Hot Springs.

Nemo Road (Pennington/Lawrence County Road 234) begins at West Chicago Street in Rapid City and winds first through the site of a past forest fire, then through lovely woods to the quaint town of Nemo. The road ends at U.S. 385 south of Deadwood and Lead.

Pennington County Road 323, the Old Hill City Road, will take you from Keystone to Hill City through some pleasing scenery. The narrow road follows Battle Creek and crosses and re-crosses (several times) the tracks used by The 1880 Train (there's information in our Attractions chapter). Watch out for the train in the summer. You'll see some gorgeous rock formations along this quaint route, too.

One of our favorite drives is Forest Service Road 17 from Hill City to Deerfield Lake. The road occasionally runs parallel to the George S. Mickelson Trail, which is detailed in our Recreation chapter. This area has some interesting and surprising examples of rolling prairie in the middle of the pine-covered Black Hills. From Deerfield, F.S. 17 (this section is unpaved) turns north and intersects with F.S. 231, which leads to the whimsical mountain town of Rochford, founded in 1878.

Insiders' Tip

In Rapid City, Main Street runs one way west and St. Joseph Street (locally known as "St. Joe") runs one way east. West Boulevard and East Boulevard mark the west and east borders of downtown, and numbered streets from First to Ninth run north and south between them. Mount Rushmore Road is sometimes called Eighth Street by longtime residents. Since it is between Seventh and Ninth, that's quite accurate. And if you hear residents say "Rushmore Road," they really mean Mount Rushmore Road, which is also U.S. 16. Follow it south of Rapid City and it will indeed lead you to Mount Rushmore.

Highway 40 travels from the subtle prairie plains of the Hermosa area to the wooded foothills around the little town of Hayward, then into the higher hills of Keystone. As you drive toward Hayward, look to your left (the south side of the road) to see Mount Rushmore in the distance.

Southern Hills

You simply must not miss the exquisite Peter Norbeck Scenic Byway, 70 miles of road that loops through the Black Hills National Forest, Norbeck Wildlife Preserve, and Custer State Park. The byway includes the Needles Highway (Highway 87/89), Horse Thief Lake Road (Highway 244), and Iron Mountain Road (U.S. 16A). You'll see historic sites, wild animals, nifty switchbacks, pigtail bridges, lakes, and towering granite spires as you pass through tiny tunnels (dimensions are listed in an Insiders' Tip in our Parks and Grasslands chapter). Because we consider the byway a major attraction, you'll find complete information in our Attractions chapter, but note that sections of Iron Mountain Road and the Needles Highway close during the winter.

Custer State Park's Wildlife Loop is another drive you mustn't miss. Its 18 miles of paved road literally loop through the beautiful park. You will probably see deer, hawks, pronghorn antelope, prairie dogs, and the park's begging burros. If you're really lucky, you'll also spot Rocky Mountain goats, bighorn sheep, elk, and coyotes. There's more about Custer State Park and its wonderful roads in our Parks and Grasslands chapter. We also recommend Highway 36 from Hermosa to Custer State Park, a delightful road that winds through pretty farm and ranch country. The landscape becomes increasingly beautiful as you approach the park. Near the park entrance, Highway 36 becomes U.S. 16A.

By Public Transportation

Unfortunately, the Hills lack public transportation systems, except for the two below.

Bus tours allow visitors to enjoy the scenery and leave the driving to someone else. PHOTO: COURTESY OF SOUTH DAKOTA TOURISM

GREAT PLACES

South Dakota's Low Profile

In 1987, Frank and Deborah Popper of Rutgers University in New Jersey proposed turning parts of the Great Plains (which include South Dakota) into a Buffalo Commons—a game preserve of sorts. They predicted that climatic and economic hardship, and even the landscape, would drive away what remained of the already sparse population. Two years later an article in *Newsweek* magazine included our fair state in what it called "America's Outback," a region on the brink of decay.

At the same time, publisher Rand McNally omitted South Dakota, North Dakota, and parts of other apparently insignificant states from portions of its *Photographic World Atlas* for lack of space. Insulting? Not really. The truth is, we kind of like it when others think we live in a throwaway state. As Custer State Park once noted in a promotional piece, "Out Here" a traffic jam is when the buffalo herd crosses the highway in the park.

Northern Hills

Deadwood Trolley
Deadwood Visitors Bureau
3 Siever St., Deadwood
(605) 578–1876, (605) 578–2600 (City Hall)

The town of Deadwood operates this trolley service. You'll spot the trolleys by their pretty green paint, mock locomotive front-ends, and the wooden benches inside. This is a transportation service, not a tour service, but it's a great way to get around Deadwood in style. Tickets are 50 cents for a round-trip ride. In both summer and winter, the trolley runs seven days a week and from one end of town to the other, stopping at nearly every hotel and casino. In the summer, trolleys arrive at each stop about three times per hour. In the winter, service hours are shortened, and you'll see a trolley at each stop about once per hour. Because this schedule is subject to change, however, it's best to call ahead or pick up a schedule at the Deadwood Visitors Bureau in the old railroad depot.

Central Hills

Rapid Ride/Dial-A-Ride
333 Sixth St., Rapid City
(605) 394–6631

These small buses operate Monday through Friday, 6:15 A.M. to 6:30 P.M. Fares are $1.00 for adults and students and 50 cents for seniors 60 and older, children younger than five accompanied by an adult, and disabled individuals. Those with transfers from another route and children younger than two (with adults) ride for free. The Rapid Ride office is in the Milo Barber Transportation Center. Its four designated routes cover schools, the hospital, the mall, the library, and popular shopping areas rather than visitor attractions, so it's more a service for residents than for tourists. If you want to try it, however, get a schedule at the transportation center so you'll know where the buses stop.

By Rental Car

We've listed the nationally recognized companies plus some local businesses. Some automobile dealerships also rent vehicles (look under Auto Renting in the Yellow Pages). Many rental car companies have Suburbans, pickup trucks, four-wheel drives, and vans, too; inquire if you need something bigger and more rugged than a passenger car.

In the Black Hills you'll find Avis Rent A Car, (605) 393–0740, (800) 831–2847; Budget Rent-A-Car, (605) 393–0488, (800) 676–0488; Dollar Rent A Car, (605) 342–7071, (800) 800–4000; Enterprise Rent-A-

Nellie Zabel Willhite, Pioneer Aviatrix

In the early days of aviation it took a courageous person to fly those "orange crates"—rickety biplanes that would never pass the aircraft safety standards of today. That's why the pilots were called daredevils, for only truly daring people risked life and limb to soar through the air, betting skill and wild courage against the high odds they'd never make it safely back to the ground.

In the 1920s, in the midst of excitement over aviation's arrival in the area—which brought wing-walkers, barnstormers, stunt flyers, and ride-for-a-dollar pilots—came Nellie Zabel Willhite. She was skilled and adventurous, brave and strikingly pretty, with determined eyes and a bright smile... and she was deaf.

Nellie was born in a log cabin in Box Elder in 1892. Her father, Charley "Pard" Zabel, was also a pioneer. He left Wisconsin for the Black Hills when he was 17 and took up freighting: driving oxen teams loaded with merchandise over the Fort Pierre-to-Deadwood route. Nellie's uncle was the famous Russ Madison, known as Mr. Rodeo for his role in founding many rodeo events as well as the organization that would later become today's Professional Rodeo Cowboys Association.

When Nellie was two, a bout with measles robbed her of her hearing. When she was eight, her mother died. She was unable to communicate, so her grieving father took her to the State School for the Deaf, where she was taken in by a kindly doctor and his wife, who taught her lip reading and other skills. She later studied drawing at Yankton College and music at the Boston Conservatory.

But it was another talent that changed Nellie's life in a most dramatic way. In late 1927 she learned to fly, just five days before her 35th birthday. She was the 13th student at the Dakota Airlines Flying School in Sioux Falls. She soloed on Friday, Janu-

Nellie Zabel Willhite was the first licensed woman pilot in South Dakota. PHOTO: COURTESY OF MR. AND MRS. STANLEY MADISON

ary 13, 1928, after 13 hours of instruction, then landed smack-dab in a mud puddle. Thereafter, 13 was her lucky number.

The first licensed woman pilot in South Dakota, and probably the first woman in the state to pilot an airplane, Nellie told her father of her dreams to fly. He promptly bought an old Eaglerock biplane, which she christened with the number 13 and the nickname "Pard" in Charley's honor. He returned the compliment by joyfully telling her she had "the instincts of a wild goose" when she found her way, using road maps and with Charley aboard, to Wisconsin.

Nellie and winged Pard barnstormed the country, racing, stunt-flying, and giving rides to awed onlookers. Once they were swept up into a tornado and went from 2,000 to 8,000 feet in a matter of seconds. Keeping her head, Nellie pushed Pard into a downward 3,000-foot-spiral and restarted the stalled engine, escaping with only badly shaken nerves. Her most memorable experience, however, was the time "at the top of a loop-the-loop maneuver two or three mice fell out from somewhere in the floor of my plane—and I hoped there wouldn't be any more of them."

Nellie belonged to the "99s," the prestigious club of women pilots of which Amelia Earhart was the first president. She was a friend and student of Clyde Ice, another early South Dakota Aviation pioneer for whom the field at Black Hills Airport in Spearfish is named.

Nellie Willhite passed away at the age of 99 in 1991. Before she died, however, she was inducted into the South Dakota Hall of Fame and the state's Aviation Hall of Fame in recognition of her achievements as both a pioneer aviatrix and a woman whose handicap never got in her way.

Car, (605) 399-9939, (800) 325-8007; Hertz Rent A Car, (605) 393-0160, (800) 654-3131; National Car Rental, (605) 393-2664, (800) 227-7368; Sears Rent A Car, (605) 393-1411, (800) 527-0700 and Thrifty Car Rental, (605) 393-0663, (800) 367-2277. Budget also has a second location at the Rushmore Plaza Holiday Inn and Conference Center, near downtown at 505 North Fifth Street, (605) 343-8499.

Local rental car companies include Rent-A-Wreck in Spearfish and Rapid City and Rent-Rite car rentals in Rapid City. The Spearfish Rent-A-Wreck is at the Black Hills Airport, (605) 642-4112, (800) 843-8010; you can fly into the airport and pick up your Rent-A-Wreck at Star Aviation (which owns the rental car service). Pickup service is available within a limited area. The Rapid City location, 1318 Fifth Street, (605) 348-3050, (800) 733-WREK, provides pickup and return service if you rent for three days or more. Rent-Rite car rentals, 926 Main Street, (605) 348-0611, (800) 722-0207, offers its customers pickup and delivery service, as do some of the national companies.

By Taxi, Shuttle, and Limo

Many of these services also offer customized sightseeing tours; please call ahead if you're interested.

Northern Hills

Courtesy Taxi
Sturgis
(605) 347-4253
Courtesy Taxi serves the Sturgis Municipal Airport and the Northern Hills.

Central Hills

Airport Express Shuttle
Rapid City
(605) 399-9999, (800) 357-9998
You'll find drivers waiting at Rapid City Regional Airport during scheduled flight arrivals, or you can call them for a pickup.

They'll take you where you want to go, whether that's from the airport to downtown Rapid City, to your hotel, to Deadwood, or on a tour.

City Cab
Rapid City
(605) 341–4141, (605) 388–0123

These taxis make trips to and from the airport, and out of town or around Rapid City.

Dakota Limo
Rapid City
(605) 787–9658

Rent a stretch limo here for 6 to 10 people. Dakota Limo specializes in special occasions, such as anniversaries, weddings, and trips to Deadwood, but also provides shuttles to Rapid City Regional Airport. You can go to the airport in style!

Rapid Taxi
Rapid City
(605) 348–8080

This taxi service will take you around town or out of town.

By Train

Black Hills Central Railroad/The 1880 Train
222 Railroad Ave., Hill City
(605) 574–2222

You can take an old-fashioned train ride from Keystone to Hill City and back again on this delightful train. There's information in our Attractions chapter on these 20-mile round-trip train rides, which are a terrific way to see the Black Hills the way the old-timers used to.

Specialty Transportation

Wheelchair Service of the Black Hills
(605) 341–2577, (605) 348–7544

This company specializes in nonemergency transportation for people both in wheelchairs and on stretchers. Although its drivers usually transport people on errands and to appointments, the service also offers sightseeing tours around the Hills. Its vans with lifts have a capacity of five to six wheelchairs. Operating hours are 6:00 A.M. to 6:00 P.M., Monday through Saturday. Call ahead to ask about arranging a customized tour.

History

In geologic terms, Black Hills history dates back millions of years. Because that part of our past is covered in our Natural World chapter, this chapter focuses on what is known about humans' presence here. (For a history of the Badlands, please see our Badlands and Nearby chapter.) It's an abbreviated account, however, because so much took place in a very short time. Scores of books have been written on the subject, and you'll find many of them in our libraries (see our Arts chapter), bookstores (see our Shopping chapter), and gift shops.

South Dakota attained statehood on November 2, 1889, more than a decade after pioneer settlement of the Hills had begun in earnest in 1875-76. From that time forward the story has been one of boom and bust, fire and flood, hunger and plenty—but always one of diligent efforts toward the building of strong, enduring communities.

Black Hills history, however, isn't just about the spread of European civilization on the Western frontier. For the native inhabitants, white encroachment on the Black Hills region was an invasion of a bountiful and cherished domain, and the struggle for its control was long and bloody. Although American Indians and non-Indians later learned to coexist, bridging the ideological and cultural chasm between the two groups is still a work in progress.

Tensions flared anew in 1973 when members of the American Indian Movement (AIM) rioted and set the Custer County Courthouse on fire to protest the killing of an Indian by a white man. The conflict soon grabbed national headlines when AIM members occupied Wounded Knee village on the Pine Ridge Indian Reservation, staging a symbolic 71-day standoff to protest the treatment of American Indians in general. Wounded Knee II, as it came to be called, is considered a turning point in modern American Indian life, but it took almost another two decades before Indians and non-Indians in South Dakota reached out their hands in friendship. Accepting a challenge by then *Indian Country Today* newspaper publisher Tim Giago (see our Media chapter), the late Governor George S. Mickelson declared a Year of Reconciliation in 1990, the 100th anniversary of the infamous Wounded Knee Massacre (see our Daytrips and Weekend Getaways chapter). It was the first step of a long journey.

Who Was Here First?

Archaeological evidence indicates the presence of prehistoric hunters called Paleo-Indians in the area as early as 11,000 years ago. Believed to have originated in Asia and crossed the Bering Land Bridge to the New World, these nomads and their successors left a record over the course of several millennia. Their ancient petroglyphs have been found carved, painted, and pecked into the rock at various places in the southern Black Hills; you'll get to examine some of them if you tour the Black Hills Wild Horse Sanctuary near Hot Springs (see our Attractions chapter). More recently, roughly between 200 and 500 years ago, aboriginal peoples left evidence of hunting activity at the Vore Buffalo Jump west of nearby Beulah, Wyoming (again, see Daytrips and Weekend Getaways).

That American Indians were here when the first Euro-Americans arrived is undisputed, but there is broad disagreement about so much else. According to a Sioux creation story, the Lakota (Western, or Teton, Sioux) tribes have lived here since the beginning of time. They entered the world through Wind Cave, lured from their subterranean home by a trickster who falsely promised them material riches. However, historians and scientists state that the Lakota were relative newcomers, having been driven west from Wisconsin and Minnesota by their enemies. When they reached the Black Hills (*Paha Sapa,* or "hills that are black" in Lakota) in the mid-1700s, they found other tribes had preceded them.

Whatever the date of their arrival, events from the last quarter of the nineteenth century are clearly documented. The United States' last great gold rush forever changed the Black Hills and ended a way of life for a proud, powerful people who found themselves confined on desolate reservations and reduced to poverty and government dependence.

We might never know the name of the first person who set foot in the Black Hills, but we do know that a white man traveled through during the late summer of 1823—it was none other than fearless, pious Jedediah Smith, on his way west. But while Smith's presence is little more than a footnote in our history, the unfinished chapter on the ultimate battle for control of the Black Hills begins with the name of bold, brash Lt. Col. George Armstrong Custer. For Custer it was who led an 1874 expedition authorized by the War Department to gather information but also, and perhaps above all, to confirm rumors of gold in the streams and soil of *Paha Sapa.*

Treaties and Land Claims

As the westward push brought competition for land, the U.S. government devised treaties that set aside territory for exclusive use by Indian tribes in exchange for promises that westering pioneers and settlers would not be harmed. The Fort Laramie Treaty of 1868 was one such agreement; it ceded western Dakota Territory (which includes the Black Hills) and parts of neighboring states to the Sioux—oblivious to claims that might legitimately have been made by other tribes.

Enter Custer and a series of events that changed minds in the nation's capital. First, the Custer expedition confirmed and greatly exaggerated the presence of gold in the Black Hills. That left the government powerless, and soon unwilling, to turn aside the wave of prospectors counting on quick wealth. In addition, the gold rush of 1876 coincided not only with the nation's centennial but with Custer's death at the hands of Indian tribes in the Battle of the Little Big Horn in Montana. We can assume that federal officials and the nation as a whole did not look kindly on Indians after that. Congress, determined to annex the Black Hills, demanded in 1877 that they be sold and opened the area for settlement in spite of Sioux resistance. Refusing to accept the terms, the tribes filed suit in 1923, claiming that the Black Hills had been seized unlawfully.

More than half a century later, in 1979, the U.S. Court of Claims agreed, awarding the tribes compensation and damages in excess of $100 million, a decision upheld by the U.S. Supreme Court the next year. However, as of this writing the Sioux have refused to take the money, which has approximately tripled in interest-bearing accounts in the Sioux Nation's name. Now there are demands for the return of

Insiders' Tip

Some early-day denizens of the Black Hills had pretty colorful nicknames. Cold Deck Johnny, Swill Barrel Jimmy, Three Sixes Joe, Slippery Sam, Bummer Dan, Mineral Jack, Bedrock Tom, and Madame Mustachio are monikers that arouse conjecture about their owners.

the land itself in accordance with the Fort Laramie Treaty.

Former U.S. Sen. Bill Bradley of New Jersey tried to settle the controversy in 1985 with a bill that would have given the Sioux all federal land in western South Dakota except Mount Rushmore National Memorial, along with natural-resource and jurisdictional rights as well as the settlement money. The Bradley Bill never made it to the Senate floor, however, and a second attempt failed as well.

There is understandably a great deal of opposition to the concept of conveying the Black Hills to Native American ownership, for several reasons. To many in the wider society, this concept appears as a threat to the social and economic order that has taken hold over the last century. In addition, there are those who argue that the Fort Laramie Treaty was broken by both sides and is no longer valid or even relevant; that whites acted no differently from Lakotas in displacing prior occupants of the land.

There is also disagreement over the role of the Black Hills in American Indian life. Plains-dwelling Indian tribes are not known to have lived within the boundaries of the Hills but did enter the area at times for various purposes and do consider them sacred.

If consensus about who can rightfully claim the Black Hills is ever reached, it's not likely to happen any time soon.

Black Hills or Bust

Once word of the Custer expedition's discovery of gold in French Creek was out, adventurers began organizing illegal forays to the Black Hills. The first group to evade the military units assigned to keep fortune hunters out was the Gordon Party, which departed from Sioux City, Iowa, in late 1874. Among the party were Annie Tallent, the first white woman known to enter the Black Hills, and her nine-year-old son, Robert. Arriving at French Creek on Christmas Eve, the invaders set about building a sturdy log stockade. Their presence was soon detected, however, and the next April they were escorted out of the Hills by blue-

Old mines and "glory holes" pay silent testimony to those who toiled after riches during the gold rush—and who were often disappointed.

PHOTO: STEVEN A. PAGE

coated soldiers. Today you can visit a recreation of the Gordon Stockade in Custer State Park (see our Parks and Grasslands chapter).

The escapade made headlines, and soon prospectors were entering the Hills in a brazen fashion. By 1876 a full-blown gold rush was under way. Although early efforts to find treasure focused on the French Creek and Custer areas in the Southern Hills, news of a gold strike in Deadwood Gulch quickly shifted the action north—so quickly, in fact, that the population of Custer City dropped from an estimated 6,000 or more to just 14 in a mere two weeks.

Potato Creek Johnny was credited with finding the largest gold nugget in the Black Hills; but some accounts say it wasn't the largest, and some folks even believe it was a hoax.

The first workings were placer (rhymes with Vassar) deposits that could be washed out of the gravel where gold had been dropped by slow-moving streams. As the easy diggings played out, miners began looking for rich hard-rock lodes on which to patent claims. The most famous of these was the Homestake (see our Area Overview chapter), discovered in 1876 by brothers Fred and Moses Manuel and sold to George Hearst for $70,000 in 1877. By that time, the Hills were teeming with tens of thousands of prospectors, many of whom eventually returned home with empty pockets. Others successfully developed mining properties, harvesting gold, silver, or other minerals; in time, many of the deposits were mined out and once-thriving towns decayed into ghosts of their former selves.

The Homestake Gold Mine in Lead had a different fate, continuing to produce gold decade after decade and ensuring that mining would remain the cornerstone of the Northern Hills economy for generations. Mining and related business opportunities provided secure jobs and cash flow for the area, attracting immigrants of many nationalities who often formed their own ethnic neighborhoods in the new country.

The roster of early-day citizenry also included many characters whose names and exploits are legendary. James Butler "Wild Bill" Hickok, dubbed the "Prince of Pistoleers," was an early arrival in Deadwood. So was Martha Jane Cannary (or Canary) Burke—Calamity Jane. Wild Bill, already famous as a lawman and a dead shot, made a grand exit when he was murdered during a card game by drifter Jack McCall (see our Attractions chapter for more information). Salty-tongued Calamity, who often wore buckskins and carried six-guns, was reputed to be a down-and-out, not altogether honest, but kindly drunk who nursed the sick during a smallpox epidemic before succumbing to alcoholism in 1903. The origin of her nickname is uncertain, but many accounts attribute it to a venereal calamity that befell the gentlemen with whom she consorted. She and Wild Bill ("the only man I ever loved," she claimed after his death in 1876, although the then-recently wed Hickok doesn't seem to have returned the

Calamity Jane is one of the early-day Deadwood characters who achieved immortality just by being colorful. PHOTO: COURTESY OF SOUTH DAKOTA TOURISM

compliment) are buried along with other Deadwood notables in Mount Moriah Cemetery in Deadwood (see our Attractions chapter). Elfin 4-foot, 3-inch prospector Potato Creek Johnny, martyrized Preacher Smith, and quick-witted Sheriff Seth Bullock also found their final resting place there, and a considerable tourist industry quickly took hold around all their legends. You can learn more about them at the Adams Museum in Deadwood, which you'll find listed in our Attractions chapter.

Tourism has become a top industry in the Black Hills, but it was mining that helped sustain the area during the Great Depression, when the federal government promised to pay top dollar for all the gold

GREAT FACES

The Sioux

Tepees. Buffalo hunts. Beadwork. Feather headdresses. The movie Dances with Wolves. This is how the Sioux are most often portrayed. Is it an accurate picture? Yes, and no.

The term "Sioux" refers to a group of American Indian tribes originally united by a common language, Siouan. The name is a French-English corruption of the Ojibwa (Chippewa) *nadow-is-iw,* a derisive term meaning "adders," or "snakelike." But many don't realize that the people known today as the Sioux are made up of three divisions that have distinct dialects and cultural attributes. The primary divisions are Dakota (Santee, or Eastern), Nakota (Yankton, or Middle) and Lakota (Teton, or Western), and each of these has further subdivisions.

Dakota and Nakota tribes, who settled in woodland and river areas respectively, often lived in bark dwellings or earth lodges and grew crops. The largest and most powerful division, the Lakota, was made up of nomadic, tepee-dwelling, horse-mounted bands that dominated the Great Plains when white settlers arrived. The Lakota came to represent the quintessential Plains Indians.

Lakota subdivisions, known as the "Seven Tents," are Oglala (Red Cloud was a famous chief), Hunkpapa (Sitting Bull's people), Minneconjou (Big Foot's followers), Sicangu (also called Brule), Sans Arcs, Sihasapa (Blackfeet, distinct from the Algonquian Blackfeet), and Oohenanpa (Two Kettle). The Pine Ridge Indian Reservation east of the Black Hills is home to many members of the Oglala Lakota tribe.

Skilled buffalo hunters, the Lakota also became well known for their bold geometric quillwork and beadwork. Today, many examples of traditional Lakota artwork, both old and new, can be seen in Black Hills museums and stores (see our Attractions, Arts, and Shopping chapters).

By the way, the book *Dances with Wolves* is about a Comanche tribe. The multiple-award-winning movie is about a Lakota tribe because, according to author Michael Blake, it was hard to find anyone who spoke fluent Comanche. (Native Americans in the film speak Lakota with English subtitles.) And anyway, the movie was filmed in South Dakota, including several locations in the Black Hills.

that was produced. Many who had lost their livelihoods found work as miners, and the value of Homestake stock soared. The company continued to prosper and pay good wages, and a new gold rush began after the price of gold reached $800 in the early 1980s. New heap-leach technology and the development of giant earth-moving machines led to the resurrection of mines that had closed decades before, and in the mid-1980s modern-day surface mining was introduced to the Black Hills. State permits were granted for operations that would dig deep pits totaling hundreds of acres and use cyanide solution to treat huge piles of crushed ore—as well as provide good jobs and substantial tax revenues.

Those developments produced a passionate, bitter conflict between environmentalists and mining supporters that ruptured the community and ruined friendships. Statewide citizen-initiated ballot measures failed to win support for halting the operations, but opponents have continued efforts to limit surface mining in the Black Hills. Occasional cyanide spills, for which mines pay heavy fines to the state, are among their concerns.

At this writing the price of gold was well below $300 an ounce, the lowest in more than a decade. That raises questions about the future of the local mining industry, at least in the short term. However, gold continues to be a valuable commodity with important applications in technology and industry in addition to its ornamental and monetary worth. Aerospace products, medicine, architecture, and electronics are just a few of the areas in which ongoing research has found new uses for gold.

Law and Order

A shooting a night was the rule when a tent city sprang up in Deadwood Gulch in 1876. In no time at all there were 75 saloons in the town, and the local newspaper deplored the presence of claim-jumpers and dance-hall girls. "The summer air is filled with profanity and curses," an editorial protested. Was Deadwood much different from any other Western mining camp? Likely not. Things began to settle down, though, when court was called to order on May 10, 1877. (One account says it was the first court session held in the Hills; another has the first session taking place about the same time in now-defunct Sheridan.)

Meanwhile, a Canadian hardware dealer who had come to Deadwood by way of Montana had become the first officially appointed sheriff in the Black Hills. An imposing figure, mustachioed Seth Bullock gained a reputation as the lawman who never killed anyone. He went on to success in many ventures including a stint as the first Black Hills forest supervisor. He also became a close friend of Theodore Roosevelt, who was his frequent guest. A Belle Fourche rancher, he's even credited with introducing alfalfa to South Dakota.

Law officers in Belle Fourche probably could have used Bullock's help when handsome Harry Longabaugh—the Sundance Kid—and a group of outlaws tried to hold up the Butte County Bank there on June 28, 1897. The bungled job netted a trifling $97, but most of the bandits were quick enough to get as far as Red Lodge, Montana, before they were captured. They later escaped from the Deadwood jail and were never prosecuted for their crime.

History books recount many hair-raising stories of drunken judges and astonishing jury verdicts in the region's early days. But on some occasions irate citizens took the law into their own hands, as when masked vigilantes broke into a temporary jail in Rapid City and hanged three alleged horse thieves the night of June 21, 1877. Many people believed one of the executed men, 19-year-old Jas. (presumably James) "Kid" Hall, was innocent. The incident caused a rift among the citizenry and earned Rapid City the unflattering nickname Strangle Town. A dead tree on

Insiders' Tip

The Homestake Gold Mine has caused the city of Lead to be rearranged several times. In the early days, before mined-out tunnels were properly backfilled, streets and buildings had to be moved as the ground above the mine gradually sank. In the 1990s the mine rerouted U.S. 85, the city's Main Street, and moved buildings to allow expansion of the Open Cut surface mine.

James Butler Hickok—the legendary "Wild Bill"—put Deadwood on the map for all time when he was murdered there in 1876. His grave is in Mount Moriah Cemetery in Deadwood. PHOTO: COURTESY OF SOUTH DAKOTA TOURISM

Hangman's Hill on Skyline Drive in Rapid City may or may not be the actual tree used in the lynching, but, rooted in cement, it serves today as a grizzly reminder of do-it-yourself frontier justice.

Nowadays, judgment is handed down in hushed courtrooms according to uniform, codified laws that take up many volumes on our law library shelves. But even after the law became more organized and orderly, a wild streak persisted in the Black Hills for many years. Brothels like Pam's Purple Door continued to operate in Deadwood until an FBI raid closed them down in 1980. The bust made national news, and Deadwood once more made headlines as a sinful city.

Ranching

While others were busy with the pursuit of shiny yellow metal, would-be cattle barons had their sights set on green gold. To them, the waving grass on the fringes of the Black Hills looked like a giant pasture for fattening livestock. Soon cattle herds that plodded up the dusty trails from Texas were grazing on vast spreads where, not long before, huge bison herds had roamed. White hunters, eager for buffalo robes, had decimated those native herds and by so doing, driven a stake into the heart of Plains Indian life.

The first herd of cattle turned loose on the range was driven away by the Sioux, but in 1875 a Coloradan named Joe Reynolds brought Hereford stock to the Central Hills and established the area's oldest ranch. Historic Reynolds Stage Stop is still a working ranch.

Once settlers arrived for good in the Black Hills and it became clear that there weren't enough gold mines to go around, some turned their attention north to the wide-open grasslands of what is now Butte County. Ranching flourished there, and so did the city of Belle Fourche in its southwest corner. By the end of the nineteenth century, Belle Fourche had become the cattle shipping capital of the world, with herds lined up for miles waiting to be loaded into railroad cars bound for Eastern markets.

Early on, however, in the 1880s, an enterprising Minnesota judge noticed that the short-grass prairie would also be ideal for raising sheep. H. J. Grant brought the first sheep to western Dakota Territory from Texas in the 1880s, much to the indignation of the cattle ranchers. They listed all kinds of ways sheep would ruin their grazing land and contaminate their water. They were wrong, it turned out, and when they discovered that wool could be at least as profitable as beef, some either switched altogether or added sheep to their operations. Today, three wool warehouses in Belle Fourche buy wool from ranchers in a wide area and sell it to mills all over the country.

Ranching is still important to the Belle Fourche economy, and its heritage is celebrated each year during the Black Hills Roundup. You can read about this three-day festival in our Annual Events chapter.

Between 1898 and 1910 the granddaddy of local ranching celebrations took place in Rapid City. Cowboys from all over the region as well as dignitaries from Chicago and other faraway places looked forward to April each year so they could attend the three-day meeting of the South Dakota Stock Growers Association there. Stockmen's Days was their time to buy supplies and have fun as they raced their horses down Main Street, played games, danced, and generally made a racket.

The celebration died out, some say because the ladies of Rapid City found it too boisterous, but the Stock Growers Association is still headquartered in the foothills town staked out by energetic

Insiders' Tip

The community of Hisega west of Rapid City is said to have been named for six young ladies who had a picnic there: Helen, Ida, Sadie, Ethel, Grace, and Ada.

Babe the Blue Ox and the Beginning of the Black Hills

Geologists will argue, but we think this whimsical tale of mythological giant lumberjack Paul Bunyan and his beloved blue ox, Babe, offers a perfectly good explanation for the creation of the Black Hills.

One morning, so the story goes, Babe spied a batch of pancakes baking for the logging crew's breakfast. The sight made her so hungry that she gobbled up all 400 flapjacks, but even that wasn't enough to quiet her rumbling stomach. So with one bite, Babe devoured the scorching hot griddle and then gulped down the cook stove, flames and all. Suffering from the worst case of indigestion ever known, Babe galloped off with a mighty bellow, tearing up the prairie in her distress. When Paul finally found her, poor Babe was flat on her back, feet sticking straight up in the air, dead as a post. Grieving, Paul started to dig a grave but changed his mind and instead covered his pet with a layer of dirt and rocks. Babe's burial mound became the Black Hills, and if you don't believe it, we have proof: The Belle Fourche River and South Fork of the Cheyenne River still flow all the way to the Missouri with the tears Paul shed while performing this sad task.

Denver hotelier John Brennan. Brennan, who quickly gave up a hard miner's life in favor of civic development, envisioned a new Denver when he chose a town site near the banks of Rapid Creek. Rapid City began life as a hay camp where freight crews could revive themselves and their animals before pushing on to the mining camps deep within the Hills. The town quickly became the area's commercial center, a role it continues to play today (see our Shopping chapter) while retaining a good deal of its cowboy flavor.

Timber and the Forest

Once prospectors arrived in the Hills, primitive lumbering operations couldn't produce board feet fast enough to meet the demand for mine shafts, buildings, and fuel. It didn't take long for steam-powered sawmills to get up and running just about everywhere, but by the mid-1880s, railroad construction increased the need for timber still further. Much of the area was clear-cut as a result. The situation was exacerbated by a rash of major forest

fires in 1893, moving President Grover Cleveland to establish the 1.2-million-acre Black Hills Forest Reserve in 1897. The next year the nation's first commercial timber sale on federal forested land was authorized here, with Homestake Mining Company as buyer. In 1907 the reserve was renamed the Black Hills National Forest, having come under the jurisdiction of the U.S.D.A. Forest Service two years earlier.

During the Depression, the forest provided jobs for Civilian Conservation Corps laborers who worked at improving timber stands, preventing and fighting forest fires, and numerous other tasks. Historical markers along many of our roads remind us of the CCC's many contributions during those tough times. Its legacy remains intact at the Black Hills Playhouse, a once-abandoned CCC camp in Custer State Park where theatrical performances are staged each summer (please see The Arts chapter).

The Black Hills National Forest has been a leader in the concept of multiple use, a practice that became law with the 1960 Multiple Use–Sustained Yield Act. This law ensures that national forests are managed for a variety of public uses, from logging to wildlife habitat and recreation, while maintaining productivity of land and harvestable resources. Logging and the manufacture of wood products remain important industries in the Black Hills today, employing more than 1,800 people in logging and milling alone. In addition, timber sales provide 97 percent of income from the forest (25 percent of those receipts go to counties with national forest acreage). But in recent years timber sales have come under a barrage of challenges by environmentalists who think too many trees are being cut and too many roads are being built for logging.

The Railroad

Because the Black Hills were part of the Great Sioux Reservation and off-limits to the railroads, iron horses bypassed the area during the height of the nineteenth-century rail boom. In the first decades of white settlement, people came on horseback, in ox-drawn wagons, and, later, in stagecoaches.

Nevertheless, narrow-gauge rail lines were used within the Hills to carry fuel and materials to the mines. Homestake Mining Company built the first such railroad in 1881. The first outside train arrived in Rapid City during the 1886 Fourth of July celebration after the Fremont, Elkhorn & Missouri Valley Railroad built a branch from Chadron, Nebraska, to the Black Hills. The Elkhorn soon laid track to the Northern Hills, reaching Whitewood in 1887, Belle Fourche in 1889, and Deadwood in 1890. Other lines such as the Chicago, Milwaukee & St. Paul Railway Co., the Grand Island Railroad, and the Chicago, Burlington & Quincy Railroad brought supplies and tourists to the area. You can still ride part of the old CB&Q route on the Black Hills Central Railroad (The 1880 Train) in Hill City (see our Attractions chapter).

Because it was a destination resort, Hot Springs had two rail lines that delivered visitors eager to soak in its mineral baths, starting in 1892. Ironically, though, western South Dakota didn't connect via rail to the eastern part of the state until the next century, and one historian has speculated that the continued isolation may help to account for ongoing political and other differences between "East River" and "West River" South Dakota (see our Area Overview chapter).

Competition for invaluable rail service was stiff and often underhanded. In the push for the first train, Rapid City got the upper hand when citizens executed a legal maneuver that skirted a ban on financial aid to railroads while raising money for a depot and other improvements. To the north, Seth Bullock cut a deal granting the Elkhorn a right-of-way across his acreage in exchange for a station that would give rise to the town of Belle Fourche, even as residents of nearby Minnesela were attempting negotiations for a depot in their town. (Belle Fourche later "stole" the county seat away from Minnesela, too.) It just goes to show how vital rail service was for economic and social progress.

Railroads declined in importance as interstate highways and airlines provided efficient alternatives. Many miles of track were abandoned and now, through a rails-to-trails project, a 114-mile section that belonged to the Burlington Northern Railroad has new life as a recreational trail. You can read about the George S. Mickelson Trail in our Recreation chapter.

The Burlington Northern Santa Fe Railway still has a crew change point in Edgemont, and the Dakota, Minnesota & Eastern Railroad chugs along the eastern slope of the Hills. Sometimes it stops traffic on its way through Rapid City. As this chapter was being written, DM&E was proposing to extend its main east-west line into the coal fields of northeast Wyoming and rebuild its existing line to the Mississippi River in Minnesota at an estimated cost of $1.2 billion.

Education and Refinement

The first business to get a foothold in any rough-and-tumble mining camp was generally a saloon, but a newspaper often followed on its heels. Once respectable women and children arrived, settlers lost little time in starting schools, churches, and other cultural institutions.

At first many of these activities took place in crude shared or rented quarters, but within a few years pupils were attending classes in schools built just for them. The area's first teacher arrived long before that, though: Annie Tallent, the first white woman in the Hills, was a teacher. After she and the rest of the Gordon Party were expelled from their stockade in 1875, she returned to the Black Hills and, after being deserted by her husband, taught school and later became a school superintendent. She also wrote a book, *The Black Hills, or Last Hunting Grounds of the Dakotahs*. Her typically nineteenth-century views on Native Americans later branded Annie Tallent a bigot in some people's minds, and a Rapid City elementary school named for her was recently rechristened South Park Elementary School.

A prevailing philosophy in Tallent's day was that Native Americans' best interests would be served through acculturation. With that in mind, the federal government chose Rapid City as the site for an Indian school much like the one at Carlisle, Pennsylvania, where students were forced to cast off their native dress, language, and religion and try to become Christian farmers and ranchers. Rapid City Indian School opened in 1887 and operated for several decades.

Perhaps some of the teachers at the Indian school were trained at Spearfish Normal School, which opened in 1883. And perhaps some of their students went on to study at Dakota School of Mines, where classes were offered for the first time in 1885. Both schools have grown and undergone name changes over the last century-plus, and you can read about Black Hills State University and South Dakota School of Mines and Technology in our Education chapter.

Many early settlers must have gone to school and learned to read before arriving here, because newspapers were in demand from the beginning. Not surprisingly, the first paper was published in Deadwood, where the action was. Deadwood was first, that is, if you don't count the single issue published in Custer by W. A. Laughlin and A. W. Merrick before they packed up their press and headed north. Before long their *Black Hills Pioneer*, founded in 1876, had lots of competition, and at one point Deadwood had three dailies and three weeklies.

In 1878 pioneer newspaperman Joseph Gossage arrived from Nebraska to start the *Black Hills Weekly Journal* in Rapid City. But Gossage's industrious, intelligent wife, Alice, gets much of the credit for the newspaper's success and longevity as well as for breaking ground for other early women reporters. Together, and with help from the talented reporter Richard B. Hughes, the Gossages built the paper into an outstanding daily publication. Today the *Rapid City Journal*, as it's now called, is the largest newspaper in all of western South Dakota. You can read more about local media in our Media chapter.

News on the spiritual front showed notorious Deadwood to be a leader, a reassuring achievement given the town's early reputation as a wicked place. Congregationalists founded the area's first religious institution there in 1876, although they didn't get a church building until almost a year later—and then they shared it with two other Protestant sects. Catholic worship also came first to Deadwood in 1877 as did Baptist church services in 1881. The Black Hills' first religious martyr, Methodist preacher Henry Weston Smith, was found shot to death a few miles outside Deadwood not long after the death of Wild Bill Hickok, and although Preacher Smith's murder was initially attributed to Indians, to this day the crime is unsolved. Worship remains an important part of life

Insiders' Tip

Pactola Reservoir and Sheridan Lake bear the names of gold-rush towns that were flooded when the lakes were built.

The Lawrence County Courthouse

The fight to save the Lawrence County Courthouse in Deadwood didn't provoke gun play, but it had all the intrigue of a full-blown range war.

The Beaux-Arts style courthouse, with a cupola on top and hand-painted murals on the walls inside, opened for business in 1908. Three years later President William Howard Taft came for a visit, and the courthouse was decorated in his honor.

As time went by, county offices grew cramped, and in the 1970s a new public safety center was added on. But a decade later the original part of the courthouse was declared structurally unsafe, and everybody had to move out. That's when the fighting started.

At first, the Lawrence County Board of Commissioners couldn't decide whether to fix the building or demolish it. So a citizens group, Save the Courthouse, held a rally on the front steps and got up a petition to have county voters decide. Then the commissioners voted to tear the building down, but the public vote went the other way. That meant the commissioners had to figure out how to renovate the building and accommodate ongoing expansion in county government at the same time, and also how to pay for the mandated work. The discussion lasted more than three years. In the meantime there were efforts to stop the county from issuing bonds to pay for the project, a proposal to move the county seat to Spearfish, a dispute over land for a new courthouse annex, and an attempt to block the annex project altogether. In addition, a leader of Save the Courthouse was convicted of arson for setting fire to her own restored Victorian home in an attempt to collect insurance money.

Fortunately, though, the courthouse was repaired, and while the job was in progress, workers uncovered all kinds of beautiful artwork that for decades had been hidden under false ceilings and behind wall panels. Restoration experts cleaned and touched up murals and refurbished original stenciling with paint and gold leaf. When the building reopened in 1991, the citizens of Lawrence County reaffirmed what they'd known all along—that they had saved a national treasure.

---

in this part of the country, though, and you can read about its diverse forms in our Worship and Spirituality chapter.

For entertainment, settlers joined fraternal organizations such as the Masons and Oddfellows, and many immigrant groups had their own ethnic societies. Theater troupes were often among the first to arrive in a new settlement, and as cities gained a foothold, elaborate theaters were built. Historic Matthews Opera House in Spearfish, now beautifully restored and hosting productions (see The Arts chapter), was considered the most handsome of its kind in South Dakota when it opened in 1906. Its red, ivory,

gold, and blue interior seated 800. Soon, however, it was upstaged by the ornate Homestake Opera House in Lead, which could accommodate 1,000 spectators when it opened in 1914.

By 1881 Rapid City had its first public building, Library Hall, and the townspeople used it for all kinds of civic and social activities. As the city became the area's population center, it also became the cultural center, and today western South Dakota's largest city, with a population of close to 60,000, hosts most of our major cultural events. Please turn to The Arts chapter for an in-depth look at the local cultural scene.

Not surprisingly, the Black Hills today are home to many talented artisans who appreciate living in such an aesthetically pleasing environment. Two of the most conspicuously inspired pieces wrought by local artists, however, can't be seen in any gallery. Mount Rushmore National Memorial near Keystone and Crazy Horse Memorial near Custer are monumental works whose very existence makes their creators themselves seem larger than life. You can read about both of them in our Attractions chapter.

The Military

From the arrival of the first warrior society to the present, the Black Hills have had a military presence. It wasn't until 1878, however, that Fort Meade, east of Sturgis, became the first official military post in the area. By then, there was little fighting left to do on the frontier, and the soldiers' role was largely one of peacekeeping and community service. What remained of the Seventh Cavalry after Custer's defeat built Fort Meade, and many of the regiment's major players were in service there. Among them was Maj. Marcus Reno, the senior surviving officer of the Little Big Horn. Reno's troubled career ended in an 1880 court-martial at Fort Meade after he was accused, unjustly it is now believed, of window-peeping at the home of his commander, Col. Samuel Sturgis. Another renowned Little Big Horn survivor, the horse Comanche, lived out his life as a pampered mascot at Fort Meade (see our Retirement chapter for a write-up on Comanche).

Relations between the fort and the nearby town of Sturgis were not always amicable. Racial tensions arose when a black soldier from the 25th Infantry, Cpl. Ross Hallon, was hanged by vigilantes for allegedly killing a Sturgis doctor in 1885. And in 1924 citizens were shaken when two soldiers fired machine guns on a burning cross erected by the Ku Klux Klan. The Klan was so well organized in the Black Hills at that time that newspapers reported on the activities of its eerily hooded members, which included giving money to churches and marching in parades.

Overall, though, Fort Meade was a community asset where civilian girls attended dances and military operations continued for 66 years, far longer than the average Army fort. During World War I, South Dakota National Guard troops trained there, and during the Depression the facility was headquarters for all South Dakota CCC camps. In 1942 the Fourth Cavalry's horses were retired and exchanged for motorcycles and light tanks. The next year, Fort Meade became a training ground for glider troops, and then, in 1944, it ceased to be a military post and in 1945 became a prisoner-of-war camp for German soldiers. Today Fort Meade is the site of a Veterans Administration primary care facility (see our Healthcare chapter) and houses a fine museum.

The same year Fort Meade soldiers turned their horses out to pasture, the Army gained a new foothold in the isolated southwestern corner of South Dakota. Work began in 1942 on the Black Hills Ordnance Depot (later called the Black Hills Army Depot), a long-term storage facility for weapons and supplies, and soon a whole new community had sprung up near the tiny hamlet of Provo. The new town called itself Igloo, after the igloo-shaped concrete bunkers used for storing ordnance at the site. The depot brought a degree of prosperity to the area, where the agriculture-based economy had suffered tremendous losses during the Dust Bowl years. The depot closed in 1967, and much of the land reverted to livestock grazing. Igloo is now deserted, a veritable ghost town.

About the same time that work first started on the depot, the Army also established an air base near Rapid City as a place to train B-17 bomber crews. Unlike the depot, Rapid City Army Air Base shut down for about six months after World War II, but it soon reopened under the auspices of the U.S. Air Force. It became a permanent installation in 1948 and after a series of name changes was dedicated to the memory of Brig. Gen. Richard E. Ellsworth in 1953. Ellsworth, commander of the 28th Strategic Reconnaissance Wing, and a crew of 23 died in a plane crash while returning from a routine mission in Europe.

A study of Ellsworth Air Force Base prompts contemplation about some of the critical developments in modern-day world events. For example, during the Cold War a series of increasingly sophisticated weapons, from surface-to-air missiles to intercontinental ballistic missiles (ICBMs) was assigned to the base. Nuclear warheads were stored in 150 heavily guarded underground silos under base command. A new age dawned, however, with the toppling of the Berlin Wall (see our Attractions chapter for information about an exhibit in Rapid City) and the Strategic Arms Reduction Treaties (START) between the United States and Russia. Ellsworth began deactivating its missile silos in 1991 and finished destroying them in 1996. One deactivated silo and launch capsule east of Wall were preserved with plans to make them into a historical site. Currently, a former training silo is open to the public during the summer; please check the South Dakota Air and Space Museum listing in our Attractions chapter for more information.

As recently as 1992 Ellsworth was considered the "Showplace of Strategic Air Command," home to four wings plus two squadrons with separate missions of their own. It's a smaller operation now, due to general military cuts, but the base remains a key heavy-bomber facility. The 28th Bomb wing, which started at Ellsworth and fought in World War II, is still based there, in charge of a fleet of B-1B bombers and still adapting to the nation's military needs. Today it stands ready for conventional rather than nuclear warfare.

Ellsworth is the largest, but not the only, military presence in the Black Hills today. The South Dakota Army National Guard established itself in Rapid City and other Black Hills towns almost two decades before Ellsworth was built, in fact. Camp Rapid, the Army Guard's state headquarters, was established in the mid-1920s.

The South Dakota National Guard itself formed in 1862 to protect settlers while regular troops were busy with the Civil War. Under the command of the state governor, today's Guard fulfills a threefold mission that includes providing reserve forces for federal service, helping local agencies during emergencies, and

being active in community service. Local units, which are based in Belle Fourche, Spearfish, Sturgis, and Custer, as well as Rapid City, have helped quell forest fires, served in overseas conflicts, completed construction projects, and performed numerous other vital tasks. Along with Ellsworth, the Guard also provides government jobs and purchasing power that have a significant impact on the local economy (see our Area Overview chapter).

Tourism

When it came to attracting tourists to the Black Hills, Hot Springs had a natural advantage: thermal waters along the Fall River that were reputed to cure any number of ailments.

Indian tribes used the springs long before white settlers arrived, and the Sioux continued to visit them after the town sprang up. (You can read about Hot Springs' historic sandstone buildings in the Close-up in our Attractions chapter.) Travelers came from all over the country to soak their aching joints or simply relax in the spas of Hot Springs, and it wasn't long before the rest of the Hills began making bids for tourist business. Sylvan Lake, in what is now Custer State Park, was created in 1890 and a hotel built on its shore. The next year the first automobile rattled and huffed into Deadwood. The ensuing years brought roads, and the roads brought visitors looking for a place to spend their summer vacation.

However, President Calvin Coolidge—"Silent Cal"—gets much of the credit for bringing widespread tourism to the Black

Hills in the twentieth century. The reticent Vermonter decided to make Custer State Park his summer home in 1927, and while he was here he took time out from trout fishing and running the country to dedicate Mount Rushmore (see our Attractions chapter). Newsreels of the day gave untold numbers of Americans—many of whom apparently didn't know where or even what the Black Hills were—their first glimpse of the area's pine-covered mountains and dramatic rock outcroppings.

Today summer visitors flock to our national and state parks (see our Parks and Grasslands chapter) to enjoy wildlife and explore underground caves (see our Attractions chapter). They crowd into Sturgis each August for a big motorcycle rally (see our Annual Events chapter), "take the waters" in Hot Springs, and tour the sights of Rapid City and Keystone (see our Attractions chapter). They tread the cobblestone streets of Deadwood to see where Wild Bill Hickok played his last

hand of poker and to try their own luck in the town's gaming halls (see our Gaming and Casinos chapter). Throughout the year, they take to our forest trails for hiking, biking, snowmobiling, and skiing (see our Recreation chapter).

Tourism has become an important part of the Black Hills economy, and with 55 percent of the state's visitor dollars being spent here, it's obvious that the Hills are the most important tourist draw in South Dakota. We're betting that the more than four million people who visit us each year think so.

The Natural World

For most visitors, the natural world of the Black Hills is the awe-inspiring main attraction, their main reason for coming. And this delightful aspect of the Black Hills makes so many other activities and attractions possible. For example, camping and recreational opportunities abound here. We also have some great art as well as geology- and paleontology-based museums and sites. Many accommodations boast gorgeous locations; some restaurants serve Black Hills trout. All of these are inspired and sustained by our natural world.

We talk a lot about nature and its many facets throughout this book—it's so integral to our way of life—and we'll make a point here of directing you to our Recreation chapter, which provides thorough information on outdoor activities. In this chapter, however, we'll tell you a bit about our natural history: the Hills' elements and how they came to be; the animals, birds, fish, and flora you can expect to see; the insects you'll likely swat; and the weather you will alternately bask in and curse (sometimes all in the same day).

There's just something about these Hills. First-time visitors often remark on their gentleness, intimacy, and accessibility. Returning natives speak of coming home to a place they could never forget. Recently arrived residents tell of falling in love with the landscape. As best we can describe it, entering the Hills is like walking gratefully into the welcoming arms of a loved one who is so very glad to see us. We think you'll experience this feeling, too.

Geology

The Black Hills are a unique geologic formation. They rise out of the Great Plains like an oasis and are unlike the landscape of the rest of South Dakota. Do know, however, that Hills is a misnomer; they're definitely mountains, smaller than the Rocky Mountains but higher than the Appalachians. From a distance, they look black—the effect of dense pine and spruce cover—although they also sometimes appear purple or deep blue, or, in a snowstorm, gray.

The Precambrian formations here have been estimated at 1.7 billion to 2.5 billion years old. During the Cambrian period the area was covered by ancient seas, and changes during the Mississippian period left the lower deposits of limestone, sandstone, and shale some 300 million years ago. Younger rocks cover and surround these deposits, including a purple limestone at least 230 million years old. Higher layers are composed of more sandstone, limestone, and shale, including Pierre shale and Niobrara chalk, remnants from the bottom of a Cretaceous sea.

The Black Hills were uplifted during the Paleocene epoch, some 63 million years ago, by the same geologic forces that created the Rocky Mountains. Although the mind envisions this as a noisy, cataclysmic, cinematic event, it actually happened very slowly, and over the span of eons, the Hills changed many times.

Over the slow millions of years, the area was arid, then subtropical, and then nearly buried in volcanic ash. New rivers and streams carved their own paths, and rain and wind carried away surface particles. Toward the end of the Eocene era, the climate became arid once again, turning South Dakota into a windy desert. Hundreds of feet of clay and sand nearly covered the Hills and buried the Badlands.

The Needles rock formation attracts both climbers and sightseers. PHOTO: COURTESY OF SOUTH DAKOTA TOURISM

Nature sculpted the eerie Badlands formations through erosion by wind and water, then supplemented them with sediments washing and blowing eastward from the Black Hills.

During those days, so long ago we can barely fathom them, the Black Hills formation became elliptical, and today the area is approximately 50 miles wide and 120 miles long. Much of it is now the Black Hills National Forest. But the land hasn't changed much since Lt. Col. Richard Irving Dodge viewed it. Dodge accompanied the Jenney-Newton expedition here in 1875; it was the second government-sanctioned visit to the mysterious and then-unknown territory. He wrote:

"There can scarcely be a country where the scenery is more varied. From the top of some lofty peak the explorer gazes in wonder at the infinite variety at his feet. Grand mountains, frowning crags, gloomy abysses, dense forests, and intricate jungles alternate with lovely parks, smooth lawns [grasslands], and gentle slopes. Each portion of the Hills has its own especial peculiarities of scenery. One struggles through dense, apparently interminable thickets, over masses of broken rocks, up and down steep ravines, to emerge at the most unexpected moment upon a smooth, well-kept flower-covered lawn, as varied and beautiful in form... as was ever conceived by the most enthusiastic landscape gardener. One finds himself continually saying, 'What perfect taste.'" More than 123 years later, visitors and residents still agree with his assessment.

The geologic island that is the Hills is made up of four distinct subregions. The Great Hogbacks form the outer ring. These sandstone ridges were turned upward when the dome of the Hills broke through the surface of the earth and pushed skyward. They got their name because their sharp ridges look like the backs of razorback hogs. The best-known break in the Hogbacks is at Buffalo Gap, where Highway 79 cuts through it.

Just inside the Hogbacks is the Red Valley, or Red Racetrack, a lower, narrow feature composed of the red sandstone of the Spearfish Red Beds. It drops down sharply from the Hogbacks and is from a

Insiders' Tip
Rose quartz is the South Dakota state mineral. You can find large and small specimens and gifts made from the pretty pink mineral in our local rock and gift shops.

quarter-mile to 2 miles in width. The Lakota knew this valley, and their mythology includes a wonderful legend about its formation, which you'll find in this chapter's Legends and Lore.

A limestone plateau lies inside the Red Valley, circling the core of the Hills. The western portion of this plateau is wider and higher than the eastern, in places reaching some 7,000 feet above sea level and rivaling only Harney Peak—the Hills' tallest mountain—in height. Within this plateau lies our famous network of caves and caverns, although no one knows for sure if they are actually connected to each other. The soft limestone was deeply carved by water and time, resulting in modern-day Wind Cave National Park, Jewel Cave National Monument, and many privately owned and operated caverns (they're listed in our Attractions chapter).

The fourth region, the inner core of the Black Hills, is crystalline. This is where the oldest rocks and the tallest mountains can be found. Eighteen peaks higher than 7,000 feet are here, including Harney Peak at 7,242 feet above sea level and Terry Peak at 7,064 feet. Harney, by the way, is the highest mountain east of the Rockies and west of the Spanish Pyrenees.

The crystalline core was formed from volcanic magma about 1.7 billion years ago, and it's estimated that the crystallization occurred some 8 miles deep in the bowels of the earth. This core was later transformed during the geologic uplift into quartzite, granite, schist, and mica.

The soft schist and mica eroded away, leaving the tougher granite to form craggy mountain peaks (some geologists believe that if Harney Peak had never eroded, it would be 15,000 feet above sea level). This area also contains our famous veins and deposits of gold, silver, and other minerals as well as the less financially valuable but more accessible granite Needles, which are the result of erosion.

The bones and fossils of many prehistoric creatures have been discovered in the Black Hills and Badlands regions. The most famous is Sue, the Tyrannosaurus rex who has her own Great Faces in our Area Overview chapter. Another is a genus of dinosaur discovered by paleontologist O. C. Marsh of Yale University on Piedmont Butte. In 1889 Marsh spotted a bone fragment displayed at the Piedmont Post Office, visited the site where it was found, and named his new find Barosaurus. Mammoth Site of Hot Springs is an ancient sinkhole; you can visit its mammoth graveyard (it's listed in our Attractions chapter). The remains of a "big pig," an archeotherium or wild boar, were found in the Badlands, which has its own abundance of fossils and finds. If you're fascinated by paleontology, you'll thoroughly enjoy a visit to the Museum of Geology at South Dakota School of Mines and Technology in Rapid City (also in our Attractions chapter) and to the Black Hills Institute of Geological Research in Hill City.

Rock hunters will enjoy searching for clear and white quartz and, less often found, rose and smoky quartz as well as feldspar, apatite, mica, columbite, agate, jasper, tourmaline, petrified wood, and beryl. Near the town of Keystone, you may find pieces of schist containing tiny but lovely rough garnets. Just make sure you're on land where collecting is allowed before you dig or take anything away with you.

If you'd like to further explore the geology of this area and see the natural roadside (and off-road) attractions most visitors whiz right past, we recommend John Paul Gries's fine book, *Roadside Geology of South Dakota*. You'll find other books in our local bookstores, too, on dinosaurs, fossils, rock-hounding, and natural history. We also urge you to read our Badlands and Nearby chapter to learn more about the geologically wondrous Badlands and the natural treasures you will discover there.

Wildlife

Here in the Hills, perhaps more often than in many other states, you're likely to come across animals you've never seen in the wild and those you've always wanted to see. Perhaps it's because they are abundant here, or perhaps it's because the wilderness areas that are their homes are so close to our towns and cities. Just outside any municipality, you're back in the "real" Hills and likely to see all manner of critters in their natural environments.

If you want to meet some of these animals up close and personal, where they can't run too far away, try Bear Country U.S.A., Black Hills Wild Horse Sanctuary, or Reptile Gardens, all detailed in our Attractions chapter. It's more difficult, but also more rewarding, to get out into the Hills and find these animals on your own, on their turf, and under more natural conditions.

Do remember to keep your distance (the animal's reaction will tell you if you're too close), and never feed a wild animal. Use extra caution during rut (mating season) and when viewing mother animals with their young. Keep your camera and plenty of film handy, and we recommend a telephoto lens so you don't have to get too close. If you come upon a wild animal while hiking, stop immediately and back away slowly, making some noise and avoiding direct eye contact. Like you, most animals prefer to avoid a confrontation and will do so unless they feel threatened. Please also watch out for wildlife while you're driving; many species cross our roads at all times of the day and night.

The early morning and evening feeding hours are the best times to see wildlife. Most species virtually disappear during broad daylight, preferring to rest and conserve energy before resuming their quest for food.

Nothing quite defines South Dakota like the buffalo, pounding across the

Once extirpated, sheep have been reintroduced to Custer State Park and to the Badlands. Today, visitors frequently encounter these animals. PHOTO: JANE GILDART

plains and hills the way their ancestors did so long ago. Actually, so you can speak with authority, the critters you see today are bison (North American bison, to be exact), but most everyone calls them buffalo, and you won't be laughed at if you do, too. We've written about these immense creatures in our Parks and Grasslands chapter, where we extol the beauty of Custer State Park, home of a fine and easily viewable herd. Small groups also live at Bear Butte State Park and Wind Cave National Park (also detailed in that chapter) and in the Badlands. When driving through these areas, you may come upon shaggy buffalo standing in the road. It's best to just enjoy the awesome view and wait until they move—you wouldn't want your car gored by a perturbed buffalo. You're on their turf, after all. We'll say this several times in this book: Buffalo are wild and unpredictable. If harassed, they will attack quicker than you can turn around and hightail it back to your car.

Custer State Park and Wind Cave National Park are probably the best places to see elk, although they are more shy than buffalo. Elk were reintroduced here from Yellowstone National Park in the early 1900s, after being exterminated by overhunting. You may need to hike off the road a ways, at sunset or sunrise, to see a herd moving down into a valley to feed. If they see you first, which they likely will, they will move away. It's best to carry binoculars to get a better view. And here we'll express our personal opinion that you haven't lived until you've heard an elk bugle. During the fall rut, males call females with a strange hooting, echoing sound that really can't be described, but it will give you goose bumps.

You may see shaggy white mountain goats standing precariously on the rocks above you at Mount Rushmore National Memorial and the Needles area. Their ancestors came to Custer State Park from Canada as a wildlife display, but the wily

Prairie Dog

If you stop in certain grass-clipped prairie areas of Wind Cave, Custer State Park, or the Badlands and hear a barking sound, chances are you've stopped at the home of the prairie dog, one of the most social of all mammals. Once entire "cities" stretched thousands of miles across the prairies of the West. Because prairie dogs cut all plants growing within 100 feet of their burrows, and because their "towns" required such expansive areas, these communities eventually had to give way to agriculture.

As social animals, prairie dogs communicate with one another in a variety of ways, using body language and often calls. As well, you might see them grooming one another, for they are fastidious. Wait long enough and you might also see them standing erect and whistling or "throwing" themselves backwards. Gestures such as these have evolved as survival techniques, serving as warnings that their homes are about to be invaded by a hawk, coyote, snake, or ferret, and that it may be time to seek refuge in their burrow.

Life for the prairie dog centers around these burrows. Invariably, each member in the community has a guardroom located about 3 to 6 feet below the entrance. Though the room itself may be little more than a shelf, nevertheless, it is adequate as a sanctuary from predators. From the guardroom a tunnel turns horizontally and leads to a bathroom and a separate bedroom. To prevent flooding during times of heavy rainfall, generally, these two chambers are elevated above the level of the guardroom.

For increased surveillance, prairie dogs reduce grass heights around the burrows to about 6 inches, which in turn serves to attract other species of animals. Bison are

Prairie dogs constructed a system of burrows in the Badlands. PHOTO: BERT GILDART

The burrows constructed by prairie dogs attract burrowing owls. Owls are just one of the twenty different species that prairie dogs attract in this area. PHOTO: BERT GILDART

attracted to the barren grounds to wallow in the dust on hot summer days. The short grass and burrows also attract one of the most interesting species of owls, the diminutive burrowing owl, which you might well see should you stake yourself out for an early morning watch. All in all, biologists say prairie dog communities attract more than 26 different species of animals, to now include the much-endangered black-footed ferret, which preys on the prairie dog.

Because these "dogs" serve as such wildlife magnets, we are indeed fortunate the Black Hills provides a safe haven for these remarkable creatures.

creatures escaped and made their way to the Northern and Central Hills, where their progeny live happily today. They consider these high, rocky areas safe and cozy, but it makes us dizzy just to watch them. We still relish the time we saw—at first glance—what appeared to be a large white dog standing beside a parked motor home at Mount Rushmore. A second glance made us gasp with delight: It was instead a mountain goat, nibbling delicately at the grass and posing nonchalantly for excited tourists with cameras.

The Audubon bighorn sheep native to the Black Hills unfortunately became extinct in the 1920s. Rocky Mountain bighorn sheep were introduced years later to the Badlands, the area around the Stratosphere Bowl near Rockerville, and Custer State Park. They have done well,

Bull snakes, like rattlesnakes, are fairly common in the region and are easily identifiable. Unlike rattlesnakes, however, they are not poisonous. PHOTO: BERT GILDART

despite an early die-off caused by disease. At a Moonwalk at the Stratobowl (we highly recommend these nighttime moon-lit hikes, listed in our Annual Events chapter), we learned that some of the sheep had strolled down to Hill City (several miles away) where, we presume, the grass was greener. That wildlife can still make pilgrimages at their own whim, and find the room and freedom to do so, is further evidence of the Black Hills' abiding wildness.

Unfortunately (although ranchers and farmers wouldn't agree), grizzly bears and wolves were eliminated from this area by the early 1900s, although rare sightings of black bears, wolves, and wolf-dog crossbreeds are still reported.

Mountain lions and bobcats are more prevalent, both species making a comeback. You probably won't see them, as they are solitary, shy animals that hunt at night. You'll be lucky if you find tracks or scat to mark their passage. However, we do know a resident of the area near Hermosa who, while on a morning walk, saw a mountain

lion; she wisely went home immediately. Neighbors told her the big cat is a long-time resident that makes a regular circuit around the Hills every few years.

We're delighted to say we've seen coyotes in Custer State Park, and we hope you do, too. It's unusual to spot them and, thus, a special treat. They usually appear nervous, slinking, shy, and a bit raggedy. Get a good look while you can, because coyotes will disappear as quickly as they emerge from cover.

Delicately beautiful creatures you'll see plenty of are mule deer, white-tailed deer, and pronghorn antelope. The deer, with their ghostly gray-brown coloring, are easy to miss, especially in low light. Antelope, with their bold splashes of white, are easier to spot. You'll often see both grazing on distant hillsides, even in the middle of the day, and you can see them close up at our state and national parks, especially Custer State Park.

We'd be remiss if we didn't mention the begging burro population that also

Black-Footed Ferret Reintroduction Project

The rarest mammal in North America is making a comeback in South Dakota. Endangered black-footed ferrets, once common in the Black Hills and Badlands, are being reintroduced here through a project of the National Park Service and the Forest Service.

Ferrets live in prairie dog towns, because their required diet, prairie dogs, live there, too. Decades ago, poisoning and shooting were common means of exterminating prairie dogs to prevent them from burrowing on ranch land. With their decimation came a decline in their predators, the ferrets, until the only known group of black-footed ferrets in the world survived in Mellette County, South Dakota.

Captive breeding of black-footed ferrets was attempted unsuccessfully, and eventually they disappeared. The species was considered extinct in the late 1970s. Then one day in 1981 near Meeteetse, Wyoming, a rancher's dog brought him a black-footed ferret, and the human race had a second chance to save the species. The total population of the Meeteetse group was estimated at 129. The group was monitored for four years, until an outbreak of deadly canine distemper struck in 1985 and 1986; officials then captured 24 animals, of which 18 survived to become the core of the reintroduction program.

Black-footed ferrets have been successfully bred and released into Badlands National Park and Buffalo Gap National Grassland since 1994. More litters of wild kits are born each year, including five during the terrible winter of 1996–97 when prairie dog burrows were plugged with ice and snow. During the mild 1997 fall, when 63 juvenile kits (120 to 130 days old and preconditioned for their new lives in the wild)

Black-footed ferrets are the rarest animal in North America. PHOTO: COURTESY OF CANATA BASIN/BADLANDS
BLACK-FOOTED FERRET REINTRODUCTION PROJECT

were released, program administrators were able to claim a 70 percent survival rate for their charges.

Ferret breeding season begins in March, and kits are born in May and early June. In July and August, mother ferrets take their offspring above ground to learn, explore, and play. Nighttime spotlight surveys by volunteers estimate the range and size of the population. Volunteers stay awake from 8:00 P.M. to 6:00 A.M., sidestepping prairie rattlers and watching for buffalo, and wield high-powered spotlights that reveal animals by their eye-shine. A ferret's eyes glow emerald green due to a corneal film that reflects that color. (A rabbit's eyes shine red, an antelope's glow green-yellow, and a coyote's reflect green, but not that distinct ferret-emerald.) Since ferrets are solitary, several dancing emerald-green eyes mean a mother and her kits—and success for the program.

Bill Perry, district ranger for Buffalo Gap National Grassland and the regional black-footed ferret coordinator for the U.S.D.A. Forest Service, says the reintroduction program is the most exciting he has participated in during his career. He has helped reintroduce big-game animals such as Rocky Mountain bighorn sheep and mountain goats, but he has a special fondness for the ferrets, which he calls "enchanting." We're dealing with an animal threatened with extinction," he says. "If we can't make this program work, there's very little hope for the ferret."

On a visit to the Black Hills and Badlands, you'll see plenty of prairie dogs. You probably won't see a ferret, though, because they've adapted to nocturnal hunting in order to capture their diurnal prey. Sleeping prairie dogs are perfect targets for wily ferrets, and—despite their enchanting faces—a fight between the two is anything but cute. "Pound for pound," Perry says, "the only fighter more vicious than a ferret is a wolverine." This is especially impressive when you consider that prairie dogs are more than twice the size of ferrets.

Please read The Badlands and Nearby chapter and about Buffalo Gap National Grassland in our Parks and Grasslands chapter; at the National Grassland Visitor Center in Wall, you can watch a ferret from the captive-breeding program. And if you'd like to participate in a spotlight survey (volunteers are especially needed during July and August), call the National Park Service at (605) 279–2464 or the Forest Service at (605) 279–2125.

populates Custer State Park, although there's more about them in our Parks and Grasslands chapter. Not technically wild animals and introduced in the 1920s, they are nonetheless great fun to watch (from your car, because they can be aggressive). Park officials don't want you to feed them, which will annoy the burros very much, but your consolation is an almost-assured sighting of the shy little foals that hang back from the group and watch you with their big, dark eyes.

Kids and grown-ups alike will love the prairie dog towns at Custer State Park, Wind Cave National Park, and Badlands National Park. These little critters chirp, whistle, and bark (but not like a dog does);

dive underground and poke their heads up again; and sit up to nibble at food held in their paws. You'll swear they're performing and long to feed the cute little fellows, but don't do it. They're wild, and their cute little teeth are uncommonly sharp.

You may also see jackrabbits and cottontails, foxes, squirrels and chipmunks (great photo subjects), skunks, badgers, marmots, porcupines, raccoons, mink, and beavers (along with their beautifully engineered dams and the pointed stumps of the trees used to build them)

Bird species that populate the Black Hills include wild turkey, turkey vulture, golden and bald eagle, hawk, great horned owl, crow, ruffed and sharp-tailed grouse, mountain blue bird, ring-necked pheasant, red-tailed hawk, magpie, meadowlark, burrowing owl (at prairie dog towns), and many songbirds common elsewhere.

Amphibians and reptiles to watch for include prairie rattlesnakes, bull snakes, western painted turtles, snapping turtles, and various lizards and toads. If you're hiking or climbing, watch out for the prairie rattler, the only poisonous reptile in the Black Hills and very common. To avoid rattlers, a good rule is to never put your fingers or feet where you can't see what you're touching, especially behind logs and rocks. If you are bitten, get help immediately.

To learn about the species of fish you'll find here, we'll refer you to our Recreation chapter (we're assuming you want to catch these fish). The streams in the Hills afford blue-ribbon fishing, and that includes Rapid Creek, which winds its way through Rapid City. We don't know about you, but we can't name many cities where people can fly-fish near downtown.

Trout are the big draw here, including brown and brook trout, rainbows and splake, but you'll also find some walleye, perch, crappie, bluegill, and bass. The trout aren't native, but they have been raised and stocked here since the late 1800s. Anglers can visit the D.C. Booth Historic Fish Hatchery and the National Fish Culture Hall of Fame and Museum in Spearfish, or the Cleghorn Springs State Fish Hatchery west of Rapid City (all discussed in our Attractions chapter) to learn about the process of stocking our sparkling streams with healthy, hearty, feisty trout.

Flora

The Black Hills are home to a great variety of wildflowers, plants, trees, and native grasses. The Hills are, in fact, unique due to the combined effects of climate, geology, topography, relative isolation, and location where several botanical zones meet and overlap, creating interesting diversity not seen elsewhere.

Some of the magnificent trees and fascinating shrubs you'll see here include ponderosa pine, white spruce (recognizable by its drapery of lichen on the lower branches), ground juniper, quaking aspen (which turns a beautiful yellow in the fall against a backdrop of dark spruce), western red cedar, mountain mahogany, currant, buffalo berry, and sumac. Ponderosas grow above the 4,000-foot elevation mark, preferring rocky soil and drier growing conditions. Spruce prefers moist, northern exposures. At lower elevations you'll see burr oak, box elder, American elm, cottonwood, willow, and much more.

Insiders' Tip

Noxious weeds, a real problem for farmers, ranchers, and wildlife, can be spread when people pick the pretty flowers and take them home or to their next campsite. Weed seeds can even stick in the tread of your automobile tires or boots, or lodge on your sleeping bag or tent. What can you do to contain the spread of noxious weeds that choke out necessary plants and sometimes poison livestock? Drive and walk only on established roads and trails, don't pick unknown flowers, and feed your horse only certified weed-free hay and feed.

Celebrating a Species of Pine

Essentially, because of a species of tree rare in the Black Hills, in 1977 Congress proclaimed the Cathedral Spires Trail a registered National Landmark. Limber pine—a five-needled pine tree—grows a ways in from the trail and to find this same species elsewhere, one must travel hundreds of miles north or go west to the Big Horn Mountains.

Core samplings indicate that the limber pines here are hundreds of years old. The question is: How did they ever establish themselves along this remote trail deep within the Black Hills of South Dakota? Glaciologists say that some ten thousand years ago, massive ice fields isolated these stands of *Pinus flexilus,* generating the questions of just how so many of its kind have established a toehold in the Black Hills.

Not to prolong the mystery, botanists theorize that the trees' seeds could have been transported into the area in bird droppings. Whatever happened, limber pine now grows along this trail as an isolated that remains peculiar to the Black Hills. By hiking the Cathedral Spires Trail, you'll have an opportunity to see stands of this beautiful species as well as a multitude of other aspects such as the area's unique geological features. Still, it's the trees for which Congress designated the trail, and it's the trees that will make you want to take the short hike of less than one hour.

A small population of lodgepole pines grows on 150 acres in Lawrence County, some 150 miles from the nearest stands in Wyoming's Bighorn Mountains, where it commonly occurs. A tiny population of limber pines grows near Harney Peak; again, the nearest stands of this species are in the Bighorns. Botanists believe both have been growing in the Black Hills for more than 200 years, but no one knows for sure how they mysteriously arrived and came to thrive here in relative isolation from their kin.

Just outside the Great Hogbacks that surround the Hills are grasslands, with mixed grasses and shrubs such as prairie June grass, buffalo grass, blue grama, little bluestem, and western wheatgrass, plus prickly pear cactus and yucca. Inside the Hills, however, you can see examples of high-elevation prairie. Gillette Prairie and Reynolds Prairie are west of Deerfield, in the Central Hills, and beautifully illustrate a striking transition from coniferous forest to grassland. Another high-elevation prairie is in Danby Park, west of Custer in the Southern Hills. Although their exis-

tence is a bit of a mystery, these small prairies are beautiful examples of nature's unaccountable whims and fancies.

There's an incredible variety of landscapes to view here—at all seasons of the year—but we hope you won't overlook the understated but lovely changes on our prairies and plains. Native grasses and plants put on subtle shows all the time: in fertile spring, high summer, winter, and chilly fall, when grasses as well as trees change color. Mountain sunsets are wonderful, but prairie sunsets are, too; we think you'll love watching pastel evening light flood over the prairie, sinking every hollow and draw into deep shadow.

Romantically named wildflowers and herbs you'll enjoy are prairie coneflower, Indian paintbrush, black-eyed Susan, wood lily, yarrow, wild bergamot, fleabane, yellow lady slipper, blue larkspur, Rocky Mountain iris, and aster. There are many more, but our favorite is that harbinger of spring, the pasqueflower, South Dakota's state flower (also called wild crocus or mayflower). This dainty, tuliplike, white-to-purple beauty pops up through

Pasqueflower, a white-to-purple member of the buttercup family, is the South Dakota state bloom.
PHOTO: DAVID SANDVIK

the melting snow in late winter and early spring, determined to share news of the coming warm season.

Because the climate of the Hills varies so drastically from region to region, and because elevations range from high mountains to low valleys, with the varied moisture and light levels that accompany such differences, we can't tell you here where to find all these examples of flora (and the many more we haven't room to list). Instead, we recommend a good field guide, which you can find at our local bookstores. Put on some sturdy shoes, long pants, a light heart, and a sense of adventure, and take an exploratory trip into the Black Hills.

Weather

This is a region of weather extremes that swing wildly from one end of the spectrum to the other. Our weather has something for everyone's taste, often at the same time. The Southern Hills are usually warmer and drier than the Central or Northern Hills, which receive more snow in the winter and thunderstorms, hail, and rain in the summer. However, anywhere in the Hills, summer temperatures in the 90s are not unusual and winter sometimes brings temperatures well below zero and windchill factors considerably lower than that. On the other hand, the Rapid City area is sometimes called "The Banana Belt" because of its relatively mild climate compared with other parts of the Hills. It's known for an average of 300 days of sunshine each year and snowfalls that often melt before the next ones arrive. January thaws usually occur throughout the Hills, bringing warmer temperatures and a few days of blessed relief from winter's cold—as well as lots of mud.

Many first-time visitors have heard all about nearly mythical South Dakota weather: raging blizzards, howling prairie winds, dust storms, intense heat. Generally speaking, however, the Black Hills don't experience those events on a regular basis, although our weather is indeed

Bear Butte: A Lakota Legend

In Lakota mythology, Maka is the Earth spirit. second only to Inyan, who created her. Inyan's spirit is Wakan Tanka (The Great Mystery) and Maka's is Makaakan (Earth Goddess). Their home is the Black Hills, The Heart of Everything That Is.

Long, long ago, Maka became deeply disappointed by the behavior of her children, whose many nations had grown away from her and who had begun to fight among themselves. She called to them, but most ignored her, so she shook herself, causing earthquakes, floods, and volcanoes, breaking the surface of the Hills, and changing life for all the inhabitants.

The four-legged creatures held a meeting to discuss this disaster, and Buffalo declared that the two-legs should be destroyed, since they had caused all the trouble. Magpie heard this discussion and flew back to the winged creatures, who held a meeting of their own. Owl made the point that Bear was a two-legged creature and the symbol of wisdom, which must be spared at all costs. The winged creatures declared that the two-legs must, therefore, be saved. A great race was proposed; the winners would decide the fate of the two-legs.

Four times, over many days, the creatures ran and flew clockwise around the sacred Black Hills. The Magpie didn't stop except to sleep for a bit at night; many times he passed exhausted animals who were forced to rest. The pounding feet, hooves, and paws left a red trail of blood on the racetrack, and the earth shook with the running. With Buffalo nearing the finish line at Bear Butte, clever Magpie hitched a ride on his back, then flew ahead at the last moment to win the race and save the two-legs.

Visitors are allowed to photograph ceremonial areas at Bear Butte only with permission.
PHOTO: BERT GILDART

During the contest, a strange swelling had risen from beside Bear Butte, which you can still see there today. They opened it and found Inyan's sacred staff there. In commemoration of Bear, whose wisdom was spared that day, Maka named Bear Butte his home. She left the trail of blood, the Red Racetrack, in place to mark the sacrifice of her children and to remind all the creatures—the four-legs, the two-legs, the winged, and the growing things—to always live in peace as equals and to remember that we are all relatives.

variable due to our elevation and location near the center of North America.

Gardening isn't always easy here, with an average frost-free date of May 20, a short growing season, and the possibility of a frost or freeze every month in the Northern Hills. Damaging hailstorms can occur during any summer month. However—and this points up the differences in regions—Hot Springs has a growing season a full 35 days longer than Deadwood's.

Usually winters are relatively mild (compared to the rest of South Dakota), although blizzards come through occasionally. Spring is often wet and wild, with fluctuating temperatures and snow as late as May and June (again, depending on the region). Summer is warm and sunny, with chilly nights, thunderstorms, and frequent hail. Fall arrives in September with pleasant, warm days and cool nights, sometimes with temperatures dipping into freezing. Tornadoes don't occur often, but high winds are frequent (although they're nothing like the winds the plains withstand). Statistically, Rapid City is windier than Chicago, the Windy City.

If you're visiting in the summer, watch out for thunderstorms, lightning, and some pretty large hailstones. Our storms

A rainbow makes a colorful counterpoint to a streak of dangerous lightning as a spring storm approaches the Badlands. PHOTO: DAVID SANDVIK

are spectacular, but hail hurts (it can even cause concussions), so take shelter under a covered area, preferably in a hard-topped vehicle.

If you're outdoors and see lightning, find shelter in a low spot, not under a tree, and away from water and metal objects. If you feel a tingling and your hair stands up, lightning is about to strike. Make yourself as small as possible—immediately—by squatting down, keeping as much of your feet from touching the ground as possible (stay on the balls of your feet) and minimizing your contact with the ground. Indoors you won't be much safer than outdoors if you're talking on the phone, showering, or using an electrical appliance.

Accommodations

Cabins and Cottages

Hotels

Resorts and Lodges

Vacation Homes and Condominiums

Alternative Accommodations

Whether you're visiting the Black Hills for pleasure or business, whether you're staying awhile or just passing through, your accommodations are an important component of a pleasant visit. In this chapter you'll find a selection of accommodations that includes hotels, cottages, vacation homes, and cabins—both housekeeping cabins (with kitchens) and sleeping cabins (without kitchens). Although the Hills have literally hundreds of lodging possibilities—including inexpensive chain or mom and pop motels and single rooms in private homes—we've selected only those we think you'll find most interesting, comfortable, and enjoyable.

If you're looking for a bed-and-breakfast inn or seeking a taste of the Western experience at a guest ranch, please read our Bed-and-Breakfast Inns and Ranches chapter. If you prefer camping or brought along your favorite riding horse, check out our Campgrounds and RV Sites chapter; it has a Horse Camps section, too.

You may assume the accommodations in this chapter do not allow indoor smoking or accept pets and are not wheelchair accessible. If these issues are of concern to you, read the write-ups closely, because we'll indicate all exceptions. You may also assume that each accepts credit cards, requires an advance deposit, and expects advance notice of cancellation.

Do keep in mind that the Black Hills tourist season runs from Memorial Day weekend through Labor Day weekend. Some accommodations are open before and after those holidays, and some close as soon as the season ends and never, ever open early. Others remain open most of the year, catering to fall travelers and winter recreation enthusiasts.

We'll give you the approximate dates of operation but these dates are not set in stone, as they sometimes change with the weather.

You should also be aware that many lodging operators raise their rates during tourist season and lower them in the off-season, and some raise their rates during the Sturgis Rally & Races (more about that in our Annual Events and Festivals chapter). During rally time, the first two weeks of August or so, the Hills are pretty much filled to the brim with visitors and available accommodations are scarce, even if the rates are higher than usual.

Use this chapter to find pleasant accommodations while you're visiting the Black Hills—so you can relax, sleep well, feel safe and comfortable, and thoroughly enjoy your stay.

Price Code

Each listing has a dollar sign code that serves as a price guide. The code is based on the cost of one night's lodging for two people (double occupancy). The ranges cover the in-season rates. However, some businesses lower their rates during the off-season; inquire when you call. there is often an extra charge (not included in this code) for each extra person or child.

$	Less than $50
$$	$50 to $75
$$$	$76 to $100
$$$$	$101 and higher

Cabins and Cottages

Northern Hills

Cheyenne Crossing $$$
U.S. 14A and 85, Cheyenne Crossing, Lead
(605) 584–3510, (800) 529–0105

Built near the site of one of the old Deadwood-Cheyenne stage stops and locally known for home cooking, Cheyenne Crossing offers a three-bedroom lodge and a creekside rental cabin by Spearfish Creek that sleeps four people and has a whirlpool and deck. Fish for trout right out the back door.

Wickiup Village $$–$$$$
U.S. 85 Cheyenne Crossing, Lead
(605) 584–3382, (800) 505–8218

The setting is the best amenity here. These 19 log housekeeping cabins are surrounded by Black Hills spruce and near lovely Spearfish Creek. They are heated by gas log fireplaces and furnished with everything you'll need, except groceries. Each cabin has its own bathroom and shower. Three cabins remain open in the winter. Leashed pets are allowed. Here you'll be within just a few miles of Lead, Deadwood, and Spearfish. All major credit cards are accepted.

Central Hills

Bode's Abode $$$
U.S. 385, Rapid City
(605) 578–3054

This chalet-style cabin, with wooden beams and knotty pine interior, is operated by the nice folks who own Black Hills Hideaway Bed-and-Breakfast near Deadwood (find more information about the Hideaway in our Bed-and-Breakfast Inns and Ranches chapter). The cabin is south of Pactola Reservoir and off the highway at Edelweiss Mountain. It sleeps up to six people with two full beds and a sleeper sofa, and has one-and-a-half-baths, a fully furnished kitchen, washer and dryer, TV and VCR, and a deck. Unlike the bed-and-breakfast inn, meals are not provided at the cabin. A minimum of two nights' stay is required.

Elk Creek Camping Resort and Lodge $–$$$
Elk Creek Rd., Piedmont
(605) 787–4884, (800) 846–2267

This 11-acre resort has four cabins and five ranch-style houses that enclose 17 "cottage rooms." Each motel-style cottage room shares only a wall with adjoining rooms and has a private bath, coffeepot, and refrigerator. Some rooms have kitchens, too. Cabins have one main room and a small bunk room that sleep up to eight people. The cabins have no plumbing (shower facilities are nearby), but they do have air conditioning and refrigerators. An outdoor shared hot tub

is on the premises, as is a heated pool. Breakfast is available for purchase on summer weekends. Your pet is welcome, but an additional deposit is required. One cottage is wheelchair accessible. Elk Creek Resort is open year-round, and a campground is also on the property. To get there, take I-90 to exit 46.

Harney Camp Cabins $–$$$
24345 Hwy. 87, Hill City
(605) 574–2594

Seventeen housekeeping cabins share this quiet, secluded property in the tall pines. Each has a private bath and sleeps from two to eight people. Sunday Creek runs through the property and you can select a cabin that is accessible by a little bridge across the creek. Fire pits, grills, and a playground are available, and pets are allowed (please inquire). There's a hot tub and sundeck by the creek, and you can hike on the Forest Service land that surrounds Harney Camp. The cabins are open from April through October. We recommend that you call to make reservations; the address above is not a mailing address.

High Country Guest Ranch $$$–$$$$
12172 Deerfield Rd., Hill City
(605) 574–9003, (888) CABIN28
www.highcountryranch.com

We've written about this ranch in our Bed-and-Breakfast Inns and Ranches chapter. We mention it here, too, because of its seventeen cabins, some of which have furnished kitchens, vaulted ceilings, bay windows, hot tubs, decks, and fireplaces. No credit cards are accepted.

Holy Smoke Resort $$–$$$
U.S. 16A, Keystone
(605) 666–4616

This great place is nestled off the highway in Buckeye Gulch, the site of old gold, silver, and copper mining operations. Stay in one of 13 cabins, including an 1893 mining camp cabin, soak in the outdoor hot tub, and stable your horse in the stalls for $10 per day (bring your own feed). You can ride your horse (or rent one here) or hike on the fire roads that lace the 75-acre property. The cabins have one or two bedrooms. A duplex unit is perfect for two couples traveling together, or you can stay in the one guest room in the charming 1920 main lodge. The Holy Smoke is open from May 1 to September 30. Register at the nearby Holy Smoke Restaurant and Lounge (see our Restaurants chapter), just down the road.

Little Elk Canyon Cabin $$$–$$$$
100 Dalton Lake Rd., Nemo
(605) 578–2012

This beautiful 1930s cabin was built by the Civilian Conservation Corps and moved to its present site in Vanocker Canyon. It's just 3.5 miles from the little town of Nemo, close to Dalton Lake and great hiking in Little Elk Canyon, yet right off Lawrence County Road 26 for convenience. Set in a pleasant meadow and surrounded by tall pines, it feels quite secluded and you may see deer, elk, or eagles during your stay. The cabin was lovingly restored by its talented owners and is charming, modern, and comfortable. It sleeps several people in the one bedroom, a loft with two twin beds, and a sofa bed in the living room. It has a warmly glowing wood interior, furnished kitchen, full bathroom, microwave, telephone, VCR, two woodstoves, baseboard heat, and a picnic table and grill outside. Bedding and towels are furnished. The friendly owners live just "over the hill and through the woods."

The Lodge at Palmer Gulch Resort $$$–$$$$
Hwy. 244, Hill City
(605) 574–2525, (800) 562–8503

Palmer Gulch Resort has a lovely 62-room lodge and 30 cabins. Some of the one- to three-bedroom cabins have kitchens of various sizes and some are sleeping cabins. All have private baths. Outdoor and indoor hot tubs and two outdoor pools are available for use. The cabins are open only from May 1 through October.

The lodge has both rooms and mini-suites, which have fireplaces (some mini-suites also have kitchenettes and balconies). It's a popular place for family reunions, as it has meeting facilities, a

> ## Insiders' Tip
> If you're traveling with your pet, it's best to ask in advance (when you make reservations) if your pet will be allowed to stay in your room. If the accommodation has a pets-allowed policy, restrictions on the pet's size and weight may apply, and there may also be requirements for carriers and leashes.

conference room, indoor sauna and hot tub, a reunion hall with kitchen, a picnic shelter outside, and a restaurant and lounge across the parking lot. Pets are allowed, and the lodge is wheelchair accessible (one room has a roll-in shower). The lodge is open from April 15 through October 15. Smoking is permitted in the cabins, but there are designated no-smoking rooms in the lodge.

The resort is 5 miles west of Mount Rushmore. Please see our Campgrounds and RV Sites chapter for information about the Mount Rushmore KOA, which is located at Palmer Gulch, and the many activities available there.

Mountain Meadow Resort $
11321 Gillette Prairie Rd., Hill City
(605) 574–2636

Mountain Meadow Resort has four heated cabins that each have one large room, two double beds and one rollaway bed, a kitchenette, and private bath. It's a year-round resort and there's always something to do here. Deerfield Reservoir is next door, with great fishing in both summer and winter, and Hill City is just 14 miles away. Winter, however, is the resort's busiest season, as the property is adjacent to popular snowmobile trails; you can even rent a snowmobile here. From November through March breakfast is available. You can camp at the resort, too, and that information is in our Campgrounds and RV Sites chapter.

Mystery Mountain Resort $$$-$$$$
13752 S. U.S. 16W., Rapid City
(605) 342-5368, (800) 658-CAMP

You have your choice of 22 lodging facilities that offer seven different kinds of accommodations. There are camping cabins (one room, no bathroom, and lower rates than those designated by the above price code), guest houses, and the big reunion cottage with three bedrooms, one-and-a-half baths, and kitchen with microwave and dishwasher. All remain open throughout the year, except for the camping cabins and one small cabin. Pets are allowed. You can enjoy the rest of Mystery Mountain while you're there, too: pool, hot tub, playground, camp store, and laundry. There's also a campground, which you can read about in our Campgrounds and RV Sites chapter.

Nemo Guest Ranch $$$-$$$$
Main St., Nemo
(605) 578-2708, (800) 699-NEMO

There are 13 cabins and houses at the Nemo Guest Ranch, with private baths and one to five bedrooms that sleep 4 to 13 people. Some have kitchens or kitchenettes. The Ox Yoke Motel, 2 miles southeast of the main ranch, has motel rooms with lower rates, plus two cabins that sleep four to six people. Pets on leashes are allowed, as is smoking. The motel is open from Mother's Day until October 1 and the cabins are open from mid-April until December 1. The ranch is rustic and designed for outdoor fun; there are no televisions or phones (except pay phones). Campground and horse accommodations are available (see our Campgrounds and RV Sites chapter for information). You can shop for supplies at the late-1800s general store, dine at the Brandin' Iron Café, or have a drink at the Ponderosa Bar, all nearby. The ranch is on Lawrence County Road 234, which is also called Nemo Road, and is 16 miles northwest of Rapid City and 30 minutes from Deadwood.

Pine Rest Cabins $$-$$$
P.O. Box 377, Hill City
(605) 574-2416, (800) 333-5306

You can get your rest here in these rustic little cabins with their backdrop of pine forest, yet they're only 1 mile south of Hill City. There are seven one-bedroom cabins, one guest room and four two-bedroom cabins to choose from. Some have kitchenettes with basic utensils, coffeepot, toaster, and outside grill and picnic table. Linens and towels are provided, too. Your pet is welcome in some rooms at an additional charge. There is cable television and a playground for the kids while you soak in the hot tub. The George S. Mickelson Trail is across the highway (see our Recreation chapter). We suggest that you call for reservations.

Robins Roost Cabins $$
12630 Robins Roost Rd., Hill City
(605) 574-2252

Eight housekeeping cabins are on the property—these are fully furnished cabins with private baths and showers, fireplaces, two double beds, and furnished bedding and towels. Some of the cabins have been set aside for smokers and pet owners; please inquire. Robins Roost is in a pretty pine setting, close to Hill City, just 12 miles from Mount Rushmore and near tiny Mitchell Lake, which is reported to have great fishing.

Spokane Creek Resort $$-$$$$
U.S. 16A, Keystone
(605) 666-4609

This family-oriented resort is just a mile from Custer State Park and has some fine amenities, too, such as laundry facilities, trout fishing, a deli/general store, heated outdoor pool, miniature golf, fresh cinnamon rolls each morning, and a playground for kids. There are 17 cabins, two of which have no bathrooms or kitchens but do have electricity and use of the nearby shower. The 15 housekeeping cabins have private baths and from one to four rooms that sleep two to eight people. The resort is open from mid-May to mid-September, and there's information about the resort's campground in our Campgrounds and RV Sites chapter.

Spring Creek Inn $$$-$$$$
23900 Hwy. 385, Hill City
(605) 574-2591, (800) 456-2755

This pretty property is just off the highway and a short distance from Hill City. You can rent the cottage house or one of three chalets. The cottage house has three bedrooms, two bathrooms, kitchen, air-conditioning, and outside picnic tables. The chalets have three bedrooms, one or two bathrooms, living rooms, decks, kitchenettes, and air-conditioning. The facility is open year-round and motel units are also available. Spring Creek runs through the property, which is surrounded on three sides by Forest Service land. Barbecue grills and a playground are available for use. Smoking is permitted, but you should inquire before bringing your pet along.

Whispering Pines Campground & Lodging $
22700 Silver City Rd., Rapid City
(605) 341-3667

Four camping cabins are for rent here. These are simple one- and two-bedroom cabins without bathrooms (facilities are nearby). A campground is on the property, too, with a general store and snack bar where breakfast specials are served. Nightly cookouts and movies are also offered to campers and cabin-renters. Whispering Pines also has two luxury vacation homes, which you can read about in the Vacation Homes and Condominiums section of this chapter. The property is on the Centennial Trail (see our Recreation chapter) and close to Pactola Reservoir and Central Hills attractions.

Southern Hills

American Presidents Cabins & Camp
$$-$$$$
U.S. 16A, Custer
(605) 673-3373
www.presidentsresort.com

A serene country setting makes American Presidents a popular place for family reunions. There are 45 cabins, all with private bathrooms, although a few are sleeping cabins. The more luxurious cabins sleep from 10 to 12 people, have several bedrooms, two bathrooms, and their own decks. Other cabins vary in size; ask which will best suit you. Guests can use the 60-foot-by-40-foot heated pool and hot tub then hit the convenience store for snacks. There are some nonsmoking cabins, but most allow smoking, and pets are permitted. A few cabins are wheelchair accessible, as is the shower house on the grounds. American Presidents also has a campground (there's information in our Campgrounds and RV Sites chapter), and the facility is open from approximately April through November.

Blue Bell Lodge and Resort $$$$
Custer State Park, Custer
(605) 255-4531, (605) 255-4772
(800) 658-3530 (reservations)

The Blue Bell Lodge houses the Tatanka Dining Room, with family-style dinners (see our Restaurants chapter), the Buffalo Wallow Lounge, and the White Buffalo meeting room. Around the lodge are log cabins, including sleeping cabins, a honeymoon cabin with one room and fireplace, and housekeeping cabins that accommodate four, six, or eight people. The Commissioner's Cabin is also on the grounds; it has four rooms, a full kitchen, and sleeps eight. Some cabins are open in winter.

Calamity Peak Lodge $$-$$$$
U.S. 16A, Custer
(605) 673-2357, (800) 591-5949
www.blackhills.com/calamitypeak

If you stay here, you'll be just 2 miles east of the town of Custer and look out on both French Creek and Calamity Peak, a craggy granite mountain across the highway. You have your choice of accommodations here. A house that sleeps ten is available. One cabin sleeps four people, the other sleeps six; both have a kitchen and private bath. Motel units are also available, including two that sleep six people and have fully furnished kitchens. Grills and picnic tables are outside. Calamity Peak Lodge is open only from May through September.

Custer Mountain Cabins & Campground $-$$
U.S. 16A, Custer
(605) 673-5440, (800) 239-5505

The eight log housekeeping cabins here have two or three bedrooms, private baths, and decks. You can hike on the adjoining Forest Service land, and you'll be near both the city of Custer and Custer State Park (see our Parks and Grasslands chapter). There's a campground on the property, too, and you'll find information about it in our Campgrounds and RV Sites chapter.

Fobaire Ranch $$$-$$$$
Little Italy Rd., Custer
(605) 673-5592

This 241-acre cattle ranch has several cabins. One is a rustic log cabin, styled after an 1880s miner's shack, but with modern amenities except for television. Another is cedar-sided and more modern-looking; it has a television and microwave. Both have woodstoves, sleep four to six people, and are fully furnished; fire grates and picnic tables are outside. Fresh eggs are delivered to the cabin kitchens each day, ranch-raised beef is for sale, and laundry facilities are on the premises. Kids will find plenty to do: fishing for trout in the pond, petting the begging burros, and watching the antics of the resident marmot colony. Your horse is welcome, and so is your RV—two sites with full hookups are on the property. The rustic cabin is closed in the winter; the others are open year-round. The Fobaire Ranch is quiet and secluded—1.5 miles off the highway and up a canyon—yet the town of Custer is only 2 miles away.

Larive Lake Resort & Campground $-$$
1802 Evans St., Hot Springs
(605) 745-3993

This lakeside resort has nine cabins—some are very simple (without kitchens) and others have one to two bedrooms, kitchens, and decks. All have air-conditioning, private bathrooms, and color cable television. Larive Lake has plenty of amenities, too: fishing, swimming, and boating (nonmotorized) as well as a store, playground, and laundry. RV and tent sites are available, too, and there's information about those facilities in our Campgrounds and RV Sites chapter. The resort is open from May 1 through October 1.

Legion Lake Resort $$$-$$$$
Custer State Park, Custer
(605) 255-4521, (605) 255-4772
(800) 658-3530 (reservations)

Another pretty little spot in Custer State Park (see our Parks and Grasslands chapter), Legion Lake has a store, a gift shop, and dining room, plus 25 cottages, some with kitchens.

The log cabins at Blue Bell Lodge and Resort in Custer State Park offer a variety of amenities, from basic sleeping quarters to fully equipped kitchens and a romantic honeymoon hideaway. PHOTO: COURTESY OF SOUTH DAKOTA TOURISM

South Dakota State Parks Camping Cabins
$
Angostura Recreation Area, Hot Springs
(605) 745–6996, (800) 710–CAMP

Six one-room cabins are available at Cascade Campground at Angostura. These are the only cabins operated by the state parks in the Black Hills, although the park system operates others in recreation areas and parks elsewhere in the state. These simple cabins are available year-round, and guests use outside vault toilets and nearby shower facilities (shower buildings are closed in the winter). Each has electricity, beds, table, and benches. Food concessions at Angostura are open only in the summer. Reservations in advance are required, but the above toll-free number is not answered in the winter (call the local number instead). Out-of-staters pay an extra $5.00. Leashed pets are allowed.

State Game Lodge and Resort $$$–$$$$
Custer State Park, Custer
(605) 255–4541, (605) 255–4772
(800) 658–3530

The charming State Game Lodge and Resort offers cottages or motel units on its grounds. The motel rooms accommodate up to four people. Cottages range in size from one room with two double beds to the Creekside Cabin and Bunkhouse or the Gamekeeper's Cabin, both of which accommodate up to 16 people. Some of the cabins have kitchens or kitchenettes and fireplaces. If you'd prefer to stay in the lodge, you can read about it in the Resorts and Lodges section below.

Sylvan Lake Resort $$$–$$$$
Custer State Park, Custer
(605) 574–2561, (605) 255–4772
(800) 658–3530 (reservations)

Thirty-one one-room sleeping cabins on the lodge grounds have fireplaces and television, but no kitchens. Housekeeping cabins have televisions, and the Senator's Cabin accommodates up to 10 people. It has four rooms, full kitchen, fireplace, three beds, and two sofa-beds. You can also stay in the lodge's guest rooms; there's information on those accommodations in the section called Resorts and Lodges in this chapter.

Northern Hills

Bullock Hotel $$$$
633 Main St., Deadwood
(605) 578–1745, (800) 336–1876
www.bullock-hotel.com

Deadwood legend Seth Bullock, the town's first sheriff and a friend of Teddy Roosevelt, built this elegant and charming hotel in 1895. It soon became known as one of the finest hotels in the region. When Deadwood's renovation began, the Bullock was meticulously restored to its early grandeur. Today, you can bask in the fascinating history of the building while enjoying some very modern luxuries. The old ballroom is now a casino (see our Gaming and Casinos chapter), and you can dine beside the ornate fireplace in Bully's Restaurant and Lounge (named in Teddy's honor). Seth's Cellar can accommodate your private party or banquet. Like many Deadwood hotels, the Bullock offers tour packages (food, lodging, and gaming) for groups. The hotel also operates the Branch House, 37 Sherman Street (about a block away), which offers mostly suites; rates are slightly higher than the Bullock's.

First Gold Hotel and Gaming $$$–$$$$
270 Main St., Deadwood
(605) 578–9777, (800) 274–1876

Although not a historic hotel, First Gold has a lot to offer, including two restaurants (one with a bar), four casinos (one with a bar), and a motel. The hotel has three suites with Jacuzzis; two of the suites have kitchens. An entire floor is set aside for smokers, and pets are permitted (deposit required).

Historic Franklin Hotel/Motor Inn $$$–$$$$
700 Main St., Deadwood
(605) 578–2241, (800) 688–1876

The Franklin has a rich and lively Deadwood-style history. Built in 1903, it was the site of the first South Dakota radio broadcast, and its Star of the West Casino is the oldest live gaming hall in town. It also has a great second-floor veranda and comfort-

Cal slept here: President Calvin Coolidge occupied this room when he stayed at the State Game Lodge in Custer State Park in 1927. PHOTO: STEVEN A. PAGE

able rocking chairs on the front steps—a great place to sit and watch historic Main Street. Durty Nelly's Irish Pub and Callahan's Sports Bar, also in the hotel, are discussed in our Nightlife chapter.

Some famous folks have stayed at the Franklin: Babe Ruth, Teddy Roosevelt (who gave a campaign speech on the veranda), John Wayne, Will Rogers, Jack Dempsey, Mary Hart (a South Dakota native), and Kevin Costner. You can even stay in the rooms and suites named for these visitors. The 1903 Dining Room (see our Restaurants chapter) and banquet rooms are on the premises. The hotel is open year-round.

Historic Town Hall Inn $$$
215 W. Main St., Lead
(605) 584-2147, (800) 265-9992

We were quite taken with this Italianate building, renovated into a charming and unusual hotel after serving as Lead's first city hall, the police headquarters, municipal courtrooms, and Homestake Mining Company's payroll offices. The two-story inn was built in 1912 and is listed on the National Register of Historic Places. The rooms, named for their former purposes, have been beautifully decorated with floral themes and oak reproduction furniture, including lovely dressers and armoires. Stay in the Auditor's Office, the Vault Room, the Jury Room, or the Municipal Judge's Chambers. The 13-foot ceilings and 10-foot windows are still in place, as is the open stairway and its oak banister, but private bathrooms, phones, and televisions have been added for modern visitors. Private parking and shuttle service to and from Deadwood are available. There are just 12 rooms in the inn, so you should call ahead. Refunds are not possible should you need to cancel during the Sturgis Rally & Races (the first two weeks or so of August).

Mineral Palace Hotel $$$-$$$$
610 Main St., Deadwood
(605) 578-2036, (800) 847-2522

The Mineral Palace is a new hotel, at least compared to others in town that are housed in historic buildings. Each of its rooms and suites has a big bathroom, television, and clock-radio. Some rooms are wheelchair accessible, and you can also request a nonsmoking room. The Royal Suite has a Jacuzzi, wet bar, and fireplace. The multiroom casino and restaurant are on the first floor of the hotel.

Central Hills

Alex Johnson Hotel $$-$$$$
523 Sixth St., Rapid City
(605) 342-1210, (800) 886-2539

The Alex was built in the 1920s by the businessman whose name it carries. The hotel is one of the treasures of Rapid City's historic downtown (Franklin Roosevelt once stayed there), and its lobby is beautifully furnished with Lakota art and artifacts. Here you'll be in the heart of town, yet within an hour or so of every attraction in the Black Hills. The 143 rooms are elegantly furnished and two suites (the Presidential and the Bridal) have hot tubs. Some rooms are wheelchair accessible and one floor is reserved for smokers. The Landmark Restaurant is on the first floor, as is Paddy O'Neill's Pub and Casino (in our Nightlife chapter), and meeting and banquet facilities are available.

Radisson Hotel $$$-$$$$
445 Mt. Rushmore Rd., Rapid City
(605) 348-8300, (800) 333-3333

We've included this chain hotel here because it's in the heart of Rapid City and has some special accommodations for business travelers. Located on the corner of busy Mount Rushmore Road and Main Street, the hotel's rooms have coffeemakers, microwaves, and data ports. Other amenities include free shuttle to and from Rapid City Regional Airport (see our Getting Here, Getting Around chapter); coffee shop, hair salon, and rental car service just off the lobby; restaurant, lounge, and comedy club; banquet facilities; indoor pool and hot tub; exercise area; and business center with fax, copier, and computer. Two floors are for smokers, four floors are strictly for nonsmokers, and four rooms are wheelchair accessible.

The Alex Johnson Hotel offers lodging, dining, and nightlife in the heart of downtown Rapid City. Photo:
Steven A. Page

**Rushmore Plaza Holiday Inn and Conference
Center $$$–$$$$**
Rushmore Plaza Civic Center, 505 N. Fifth St.
Rapid City
(605) 348–4000, (800) HOLIDAY
This eight-story chain hotel is adjacent to
the Rushmore Plaza Civic Center and,
thus, quite convenient for those attend-
ing conventions, meetings, or events
there. The hotel's amenities include a
lovely atrium, indoor pool, sauna,
whirlpool/hot tub, exercise room, cable
television and HBO, the Tiffany Grill
restaurant (see our Restaurants chapter),
and the Fountain Court piano lounge.
The Presidential Suite has its own Jacuzzi.
Some rooms and floors are nonsmoking
and pets are allowed (please ask, deposit
required). Rapid City also has two Holi-
day Inn Express hotels (750 Cathedral
Drive and 645 Disk Drive), which have no
restaurant or lounge but do offer free
continental breakfast.

Resorts and Lodges

Northern Hills

Deadwood Gulch Resort $$$
U.S. 85 S., Deadwood
(605) 578–1294, (800) 695–1876
Deadwood Gulch is a complete resort,
with something for everyone, including
98 motel rooms of various sizes and
styles. The resort is on the Mickelson
Trail—the part that can be accessed by
snowmobiles. It has a convenience store,
convention center, two casinos, restaurants, outdoor pool, indoor hot tub, and
restaurant.

**Spearfish Canyon Lodge at Latchstring
Village $$$–$$$$**
U.S. 14A, Spearfish
(605) 584–3435, (800) 439–8544
This 54-room resort in glorious Spearfish
Canyon offers lodging, conference facili-

ties, gift shop, restaurant (see our Restaurants chapter), a lounge, and a sports center. The accommodations vary in size from guest rooms to suites, with amenities like coffeemakers, fireplaces, balconies, and microwaves. At adjacent Latchstring Village you'll also find trails, fishing, a botanical garden, and snowmobile rentals. Although you'll be close to Deadwood, Spearfish, and Northern Hills attractions, the incredible scenery may entice you to stay right here.

Southern Hills

State Game Lodge and Resort $$$–$$$$
Custer State Park, Custer
(605) 255–4541, (605) 255–4772
(800) 658–3530

This beautiful structure was President Coolidge's summer White House in 1927, and you'll enjoy it as much as he did. The charming lodge is listed on the National Register of Historic Places and is one of the treasures of Custer State Park (see our Parks and Grasslands chapter). You can stay in one of the lodge's seven guest rooms, which come in a variety of styles and sizes and accommodate up to four people. While you're there, dine in the Pheasant Dining Room (listed in our Restaurants chapter) or have a drink in the lounge. Meeting and banquet facilities are available, too. Cabins and motel rooms are also for rent; there's information in the Cabins and Cottages section near the beginning of this chapter.

Sylvan Lake Resort $$$–$$$$
Custer State Park, Custer
(605) 574–2561, (605) 255–4772
(800) 658–3530 (reservations)

This is a cozy lodge next to picturesque Sylvan Lake, close to the trails to Harney Peak (see our Recreation chapter), and on the way to both Mount Rushmore National Memorial and Crazy Horse Memorial. Sit by the pleasant fireplace in the lobby or have dinner in the Lakota Dining Room (details in our Restaurants chapter). The lodge has thirty-five rooms that vary in configuration and size, and accommodate from one to six people.

Please read about the cabins on the grounds in the Cabins and Cottages section of this chapter.

Vacation Homes and Condominiums

Northern Hills

Barefoot Resort $$$$
HC 37, Lead
(605) 584–1577, (800) 424–0225

Located on the site of the historic Barefoot mining claim, and (at 6,400 feet) higher than any other lodge east of the Rockies, these 27 condos are across the road from the Terry Peak Ski Lodge and 15 minutes from Deadwood. One- to four-bedroom units are available and each has a private bath, kitchen, living and dining room, fireplace, and a great view from the balcony. A pool and hot tub are on the premises. Timeshare programs are also available, as is one four-bed cabin.

Mountain Stream Estates $$$$
Rockford Rd., Lead
(605) 229–1619

These three luxurious vacation homes are near Cheyenne Crossing, deep in the Hills and close to Deadwood, Spearfish, skiing, snowmobile trails, and hiking. A stream

Spearfish Canyon Lodge at Latchstring Village lures both vacationers and conference-goers with its rustic ambience. PHOTO: COURTESY OF SOUTH DAKOTA TOURISM

runs close by, and there's a trout pond near the houses. Each fully furnished house has five bedrooms, three baths, and kitchen with dishwasher and microwave. One house has a jet-spray tub and garage. No credit cards are accepted.

Terry Peak Condos $$$–$$$$
HC 37, Lead
(605) 584–2723, (888) 584–2723

These 18 condos are attached to the main lodge, which faces the Terry Peak Ski Area. Each has its own private entrance. Seven of the condos have two bedrooms and two baths; the remainder have one bedroom and bath. This is nice but simple lodging for people who are more interested in being outdoors—the condos have no phones, cable television service, or air-conditioning, but they do have fully equipped kitchens. Guests have access to an indoor pool, hot tub, and game room.

Central Hills

Edelweiss Mountain Lodging $$$–$$$$
U.S. 385, Rapid City
(605) 574–2430

More than 25 vacation homes are available through Edelweiss Mountain Lodging in the summer, and 15 of those are available in the winter. The office is off the highway, between Sheridan Lake and Pactola Reservoir; the homes are all in the immediate area. Homes with one to four bedrooms and private baths are available. Some have hot tubs and pool tables, and all but one have fully furnished kitchens. Some of the homes are accessible to the disabled. All have great views of the pine-covered surrounding hills.

Whispering Pines Campground & Lodging
$$$$
22700 Silver City Rd., Rapid City
(605) 341–3667

Two lovely vacation homes here will give you the chance to relax in luxury. One is a four-bedroom, two-and-a-half-bath home and it's open all year. The other has three bedrooms and two baths and, like the rest of the facilities here, is open only from May 1 through September. Both homes

are fully furnished and include a kitchen, living room, dining room, deck with grill, two-car garage, woodstove with furnished firewood, and private driveway. Both smoking and pets are allowed and the three-bedroom home is wheelchair accessible. Whispering Pines is in the midst of some great attractions, close to Hill City and Rapid City, 2 miles north of Pactola Reservoir and right on the Centennial Trail (the Deer Creek trailhead is on the property; see our Recreation chapter). Camping cabins are also available and that information is in this chapter under the Cabins and Cottages section.

Alternative Accommodations

These don't quite fit into our categories—they're not cabins, not cottages, not quite bed-and-breakfast inns either. Looking for an inexpensive, yet interesting, place to stay? Try these.

Northern Hills

Deadwood Knotty Pine B&B $–$$
788 Main St., Deadwood
(605) 578–1995

This is a private little place to stay if you're visiting Deadwood on a budget. It's just a small room with bath and porch on the second floor of the friendly owner's home, but it's clean and cute and accessible via its own outside stairway. It has air-conditioning and off-street parking, but there's no telephone and few other amenities. However, you may get to see owner/artist David Young's wonderful sculptures decorating the house. Breakfast is included in your room rate, via a voucher that entitles you to the breakfast buffet at the Gold Dust Gambling Hall and Restaurant on historic Main Street, not far away.

Poker Alice House $$–$$$$
1802 ½ Junction Ave., I–90, exit 32, Sturgis
(605) 347–2506

Notorious Poker Alice Tubbs's historic house (a former brothel) is next to the National 9 Junction Inn motel. The little house is bigger than it looks but does not have separate apartments, so it is best rented to one party at a time. It has a full kitchen, two bedrooms downstairs, four upstairs, and another in the basement. The basement also has a kitchenette and bathroom with shower. The full kitchen and the Poker Room—with player piano—are on the first floor, which is the common area. The house has old-fashioned decor (you'll think Poker Alice might still live here) and it can be used for meetings or reunions. Pets and smoking are allowed (Alice, with her ever-present cigar, would approve). The house is rented monthly during the winter and nightly during the summer season.

Insiders' Tip

Tourist season in the Black Hills and Badlands begins Memorial Day weekend and ends Labor Day weekend. But spring, fall, and winter are great seasons in which to visit and enjoy the scenery and recreation (although many attractions are closed), as well as to take advantage of lighter traffic and smaller crowds.

Bed-and-Breakfast Inns and Ranches

Northern Hills
Central Hills
Southern Hills

No single definition exists for Black Hills bed-and-breakfast inns and ranches. Instead, each is wonderfully idiosyncratic because each reflects the strong individuality and character of its South Dakota owners.

Here you'll find a selection of classic inns (where you'll have access to the facilities of the house), inns with rooms set apart (in a separate wing, for example, with common areas for guests), and some that are actually cabins and cottages, though they serve breakfast in the classic style. You'll also find guest ranches and working ranches listed here as well as ranches that are also bed-and-breakfast inns. We've described each carefully, but if you aren't sure if an inn or ranch is for you, call ahead and talk to the proprietors.

In the listings we'll discuss the very special amenities that set each inn or ranch apart from others. We'll touch briefly on the basics, too, but you may assume that the listed businesses are not wheelchair-accessible (most are renovated homes) and do not allow pets or smoking (except outside), but do allow children. Assume, too, that the inns listed permit guests to bring their own alcohol and have private baths for each room. Exceptions to these assumptions will be noted.

Most bed-and-breakfast inns and ranches require a deposit to secure your accommodations, paid either by credit card or mailed check. Most also require advance notice of cancellation (usually two weeks or so) for the return of your deposit (less, sometimes, an administrative fee).

The owners of the inns and ranches listed here started their businesses because they enjoy meeting new people and making their guests feel welcome. During our interviews with these owners, the same amenities were stressed again and again: At each of these places, you will be pampered exceedingly well and made to feel comfortably at home. You may even become part of the family. These accommodating people specialize in family and home, and they're willing to share both with you.

Price Code

Each listing in this chapter has a dollar-sign code that serves as a price guide. The code is based on the cost of one night's lodging for two people (double occupancy). These ranges denote higher in-season rates. Many businesses maintain the same rates throughout the year, but some lower rates during the off-season; be sure to inquire. In addition, many offer various accommodation choices, and the price ranges also reflect those options. There is usually an additional charge (not included in this code) for each extra person or child. Assume that each business accepts credit cards; exceptions will be noted.

$	less than $50
$$	$50 to $75
$$$	$76 to 100
$$$$	$101 and more

Northern Hills

Aunt Sophia's Bed & Breakfast $$$–$$$$
15 Washington St., Deadwood
(605) 578-3257, (800) 377-1516

Spend a night or two in this 1903 Victorian home that's within walking distance of historic downtown Deadwood. The full and ample breakfast (that will sustain you during a morning's stroll through town or a rest on the front porch) always includes a fruit bowl, eggs, and meat. Sometimes it includes French toast and other goodies. Breakfast is served on different "company dishes" every day in the Oriental-themed dining room, and the house is furnished with original art and antiques.

The owners like to pamper their guests and will entertain requests for special foods or treats for special occasions (extra charge). Aunt Sophia's is open from May 15 until January, so do make reservations in advance for your choice of one of the four suites or two single rooms. Children are welcome, as are weddings, receptions, and reunions.

Bear Butte Bed & Breakfast $$$
Hwy. 79 N., Sturgis
(605) 347–2137, (800) 347–2137

This pleasant century-old farmhouse is on 50 acres, yet right off the highway and within sight of awe-inspiring Bear Butte. There's only one guest room, but it has a private entrance, parking space, and its own porch overlooking the tranquil backyard. It is peaceful and pretty and furnished with a rocking chair, where you are invited to rock your troubles away. There's a piano you can play in the living room, too.

The owner enjoys making her "scrumptious full" breakfast, and her specialties are buttermilk pancakes, breakfast pizza, omelettes, apple muffins, and cinnamon rolls. Cold drinks will be served when you arrive and during your stay.

This is a down-to-earth home on a working ranch where you'll especially enjoy the kind hosts, who say, "Our home is your home." Stroll over to Bear Butte Creek, which runs through the property, pet the cats and dog, feed the chickens, and watch the calving in the spring. There are horses and sometimes Limousin cows (a breed from France) to observe. The owners can't let you help with the chores, but you can always just sit in that rocking chair and soak up the atmosphere.

You'll be close to Sturgis, Bear Butte State Park, Deadwood, and Lead, and not far from most Northern Hills attractions. In Sturgis, take Highway 34 East to Highway 79 North. Watch for the fourth right turn, where you'll see the Bear Butte Bed & Breakfast sign. No credit cards are accepted.

Black Hills Hideaway Bed-and-Breakfast
$$$$
11744 Hideaway Rd., Deadwood
(605) 578–3054

It's a tribute to the tranquility of this property that it was selected by the owners, two corporate dropouts from the East who, after vacationing in the Hills 10 years, "downsized" themselves and created their hideaway in the forest. Now it's your turn. You can downsize your hectic life here, at least for a while, and bask in the peaceful mountain air. Once the site of a 1904 mining claim, these 67 acres are bordered by the Black Hills National Forest.

The owners invite you to "come and be pampered" in one of their eight guest rooms. They offer turndown service with chocolates on your pillow and a full, hot country breakfast that features their trademark dishes: homemade blueberry coffee cake and egg skillets. Hot and cold hors d'oeuvres are served in the evenings, and cookies and fruit are available during the day. A light sandwich menu is available upon request, and the commercial kitchen can accommodate small parties (both at extra charge).

You can hike and mountain bike on the premises; snowmobile, ski, and golf nearby; and drive to Deadwood and Lead for gaming and sightseeing. But you may want to stay right here, soak in the hot tub or whirlpool, and just listen to the silence. Please inquire about bringing children along.

Black Hills Hideaway is 7 miles south of Deadwood off U.S. 385. Watch for the Tomahawk Country Club, then turn onto Forest Service Road 247 and follow the signs.

Castle Rock Bed-N-Breakfast $$
HC 66, Box 60, Newell
(605) 866–4604

If you've never visited South Dakota's high plains, you're in for a treat. The Smeenk Ranch is an authentic cattle and sheep operation on more than 10,000 subtly spectacular acres. This is ranch country, and if you like you can help with the chores. Help move the cattle, brand calves, or watch the lambing and calving operations in the spring. You can participate or observe as much as you like. The owners will board your horse in their barn, too.

If you prefer, you can hike and look for old tepee rings, fish in the bass dam, or hunt. You can climb rugged Castle Rock Butte (the highest peak in Butte County) or stand at the geographical center of the nation, both of which are on the property. Or you can dig for dinosaur bones on the butte, at the site where a duck-billed dino was found.

A country-style, home-cooked breakfast is served each morning, and you'll be treated to homemade cake or pie upon your arrival. Additional meals are served upon request for an extra charge.

The two comfortable rooms are simply furnished and share a bathroom. You can watch satellite television or listen to the stereo, but you may prefer to just make yourself at home and enjoy the peace and quiet.

Castle Rock Bed-N-Breakfast is 17 miles north of Newell, geographically outside the Black Hills but philosophically part of them. From Newell, follow Highway 79 North, turn west on Highway 168, then right on the unmarked gravel road (a good landmark is the Wendt Indoor Arena sign on the left). It's 2 miles farther to the ranch house. No credit cards are accepted.

Lown House Bed & Breakfast $$$
745 Fifth St., Spearfish
(605) 642-5663, (888) 642-5663
(800) 529-0105 Black Hills Central Reservations

This is a charming, historic Victorian house built by a local merchant in 1893. Your breakfast will be served in the formal dining room.

The house has some interesting architectural features, and each of the four rooms is named for a past owner. The third-floor suite has a cupola and whirlpool, and two rooms have fireplaces.

The owners like to accommodate their guests' special requests for flowers, balloons, wine, chocolates, shuttles to Deadwood, and customized packages.

Old Stone House Bed & Breakfast
$$$–$$$$
1513 Jackson St., Sturgis
(605) 347-3007, (888) 447-3007
www.bbonline.com/sd/stonehouse

If you like lounging on a big, high, shady verandah and whiling away the hours, knowing you're close enough to everything to drive there if you want, this is the place for you.

The house is historic, built in 1885 of local sandstone. It's been beautifully restored, and the three rooms are furnished with antiques and quilts. In the 1930s it was used as the county poor farm. Today's amenities, however, are modern and lovely.

A four-course, hearty, family-style breakfast is served on antique china with elegant linens, either on the verandah or in the kitchen. The owner requests that guests inquire before bringing children. Alcohol is not permitted.

Old Stone House is close to Fort Meade, Bear Butte State Park (see our Parks and Grasslands chapter), and the local bike/hike trail as well as Deadwood/Lead.

Central Hills

The Anchorage Bed & Breakfast $$$–$$$$
24110 Leaky Valley Rd., Keystone
(605) 574-4740, (800) 318-7018
www.anchoragebb.com

Jim Gogolin promised his wife, Lin, that in return for her sacrifices during his years as a Naval officer and their travels around the world, she could choose their retirement home. Although she could have selected Majorca, the Philippines, or other lovely places, Lin chose the Black Hills and announced that she wanted to open a bed-and-breakfast inn. Thus the name The Anchorage and the Navy-eclectic decor.

Some accommodations are in a separate, private building called The Chart

House. It sleeps up to eight people and is rented to just one party at a time. The kitchen is fully equipped, even supplied with some staple items, and there's a hot tub on the deck where you can watch the stars and the deer that come out of the woods. It's a real home with a handmade quilt, books, and a game table, but it doesn't have a television or telephone. You're on vacation, after all.

Then there are four rooms in the main quarters, each with private bath, fireplace, and access to a hot tub.

The houses sit on the rim of a lovely valley with a view of Harney Peak. You may see bobcats and coyotes and hear the whistle of the Black Hills Central Railroad/The 1880 Train (see our Attractions chapter) as it chugs past. The Centennial Trail is just over the hill (see our Recreation chapter). There are 20 acres to play on here; if you need more room, you can go next door to national forestland.

The most-used word in the guest book is "wonderful," but that is hardly adequate for Anchorage breakfasts. "Spectacular" may be more apt. The specialty breakfast is pumpkin waffles with hot apple butter, smoked turkey sausage, rhubarb cake, and a compote of mango and fresh blueberries. Other delights include seafood quiche, wild raspberry crepes, and huge pecan caramel rolls. You might get to try Jim's Baked Pancakes, filled with apples, nutmeg, pecans, and sour cream, served with ham and muffins. Breakfast is served in the main house.

Anemarie's Bed & Breakfast $$$–$$$$
10430 Big Piney Rd., Rapid City
(605) 343-9234
www.bbonline.com/sd/anemarie

This is a bed-and-breakfast inn locals like to use as a getaway. The owners describe it as having European styling with contemporary convenience. Each of the four suites has a hot tub, television, VCR, and small refrigerator. All the rooms look out on peaceful views, and one room is wheelchair-accessible.

Breakfast is served in the rooms, and the menu varies daily. Coffee is available in the rooms. When you wake in the morning, you may see deer, rabbits, squirrels, and chipmunks outside.

Anemarie's is centrally located near Rapid City, 30 miles from Deadwood, across the road from a fine restaurant and lounge, The Fireside Inn (see our Restaurants chapter).

Audrie's Bed and Breakfast and das Abend Haus Cottages $$$$
23029 Thunderhead Falls Rd., Rapid City
(605) 342-7788
www.audriesbb.com

This glorious Old World estate was the Black Hills' first bed-and-breakfast; it was founded in 1985 and is still owned and operated by the same family. Its handsome antique furniture, purchased while the family was in Europe, adorns each room.

The beautiful buildings on the property are the Cranbury House, the Old Powerhouse (built in 1910 for water-generated electricity), and the chalet-style das Abend Haus (German for "The Evening House") Cottage. Each has two suites. You can also stay in one of seven big, high-ceilinged log

> ## Insiders' Tip
> Many of the businesses listed in this chapter are members of the Bed & Breakfast Innkeepers of South Dakota (BBISD). Members must meet certain standards for hospitality, cleanliness, and safety, and must pass an association inspection conducted by state-trained inspectors. For additional information, or to request a member directory, call (888) 500-INNS.

Bed-and-breakfast inns such as Audrie's Bed and Breakfast and das Abend Haus Cottages in Rapid City are perfect for getaways. PHOTO: COURTESY OF SOUTH DAKOTA TOURISM

cottages, each of which is delightfully decorated.

The rooms, suites, and cottages are elegant and luxurious. They're beautifully furnished in rich colors, fabrics, and woods. Each has a private bath and entrance, latticed deck or porch, hot tub, cable television and VCR, refrigerator, and microwave.

Breakfast is placed in each refrigerator so guests can heat and enjoy it in privacy. It includes bacon-and-egg quiche for two, homemade baked goods, fruit, cereal, and juice.

Audrie's is in a pretty, quiet, and secluded canyon 7 miles west of Rapid City. You can easily drive to any Central Hills attraction, or you can take a walk, explore the Black Hills National Forest around the property, fish for trout in Rapid Creek, which flows right through the estate (you'll need a license—see our Recreation chapter), or bicycle up the road. Fishing poles and bicycles are provided for guests.

Dedicated to comfort and privacy, Audrie's does not allow children or pets, and guests are asked not to bring visitors. The hot tubs can't be used after 11:00 P.M. or before 7:00 A.M., so everyone can enjoy the nighttime peace and silence.

Black Forest Inn $$$–$$$$
Bed & Breakfast Lodge
23191 U.S. 385, Rapid City
(605) 574–2000, (800) 888–1607
www.blackforest.net

You'll love the spaciousness here (10,000 square feet and 10 rooms), especially the huge great room with its rock fireplace. A wonderful deck overlooks the lawn and surrounding forest and holds a hot tub that's waiting just for you. Or, settle into the game room, where you can read, play pool or games, or watch television.

A homemade breakfast is served in courses on silver and crystal. Meeting rooms are available for retreats and workshops, and this is an especially lovely place for reunions, weddings, and anniversary celebrations.

Black Forest Inn is centrally located: It's near Pactola Reservoir, Sheridan Lake, Mount Rushmore, and Rapid City, as well as within a 30-minute drive of every attraction in the Central Hills.

Carriage House Bed & Breakfast $$$$
721 West Blvd., Rapid City
(605) 343–6415, (888) 343–6415

If you're a fan of historic houses, you'll love this graceful three-story 1900s home in the West Boulevard Historic District. In fact, take a walking tour up and down The Boulevard and view the historic houses there, then come back and explore this one. Today it maintains its historic integrity with some delightful design features and antiques, yet it offers comfortable, modern amenities in the five suites.

The full homemade breakfast varies daily, and romantic candlelight dinners called "Affairs of the Heart" are available. The house is in the middle of Rapid City and thus close to Central Hills attractions. It is open April 1 through Thanksgiving.

Country Manor Bed & Breakfast $$$–$$$$
12670 Robins Roost Rd., Hill City
(605) 574–2196, (888) 560–5508
www.countrymanorbb.com

These pleasant accommodations are in a separate building next to the main house: The four rooms and one family suite have private entrances.

Other amenities include television, air-conditioning, and a theme for each room that honors an aspect of our American heritage. The three-room suite, which accommodates eight people, has a Wild West motif and features a double Jacuzzi bath, minikitchen, microwave, and refrigerator.

The full breakfast is served on the dining porch in the main house, and the hospitable owner describes it as a classic "Sunday morning breakfast." Her specialties include bacon quiche and strawberry waffles.

Here you'll be close to lovely Spring Creek and only a few minutes from Hill City, in the heart of the Black Hills. No credit cards are accepted.

Coyote Blues Village Bed & Breakfast $$–$$$$
P.O. Box 966, Hill City
(605) 574–4477, (888) 253–4477
www.coyotebluesvillage.com

The Swiss owners have given their bed-and-breakfast inn a contemporary, European flavor. "Experience a piece of Europe in the Black Hills," they like to say. You'll love the original art scattered throughout the house, the huge deck, and the wonderful views across open land and forest.

Breakfast includes home-baked breads such as brioche, chocolate croissants or gugelhopf (an Austrian yeast cake), and other culinary delights including fruit, French toast, eggs, and, another specialty, Swiss muesli.

When they purchased the property, the owners were intrigued by the nocturnal howling of coyotes, which they decided was coyote singing; thus the Coyote Blues name. You'll still hear the coyotes, nearly every night, but that's about all; the peace and quiet will astound you.

The owners offer three rooms, one suite, and a conference room. There's an exercise area and a piano (for those who want to exercise only their fingers). The guest sitting room has a large-screen TV and VCR.

Coyote Blues Village is 12 miles from Hill City and 22 miles from Rapid City, just south of Pactola Lake off Highway 385.

Creekside Cottage Bed & Breakfast $$$–$$$$
23934 U.S. 385, Hill City
(605) 348–9835
www.bbonline.com/sd/creekside

Creekside Cottage is situated on three pretty acres that are bisected by Spring Creek and bordered by national forest. It's also conveniently right off the highway and within five minutes or so of Hill City, but while you enjoy the view from your choice of two accommodations, you'll forget you're so near civilization.

The sunny Garden Suite is on the second floor of the main house and has its own deck. The Creekside Cottage is a separate building, beautifully decorated in a fish theme (it's rumored there are at least 45 decorative fish throughout—count them!). It has a kitchen, fireplace, and deck and shares the hot tub with the Garden Suite.

The owners enjoy making their guests comfortable, and that includes nourishing them with a great breakfast. Specialties include chili cheese squares, buttermilk pancakes with pecans, and pineapple cream French toast, accompanied by fresh-ground coffee.

After breakfast, explore the Black Hills (you'll be in the heart of the region), take a hike, go fly-fishing in the creek (catch and release only), pet the family dog, or just bask on the deck and watch for deer.

Creekside Cottage is open from May through September.

Deerview Bed & Breakfast $$$–$$$$
12110 Deerfield Rd., Hill City
(605) 574–4204, (888) 622–5274

Deerview is a beautifully appointed and carefully designed bed-and-breakfast that

GREAT PLACES

Deciding on a Bed-and-Breakfast

If you've never stayed at a bed-and-breakfast inn or ranch, you're in for a treat. But there are a few things you should understand in advance. You'll be staying in someone's home, which precludes total privacy. Hotel-style anonymity is impossible. Although most innkeepers will respect your wishes if you prefer to be left alone, the beauty of the inn and ranch experience is the family-style mingling (if that's what you want).

Business travelers who are weary of sterile hotel rooms can bask in an inn's comfortable, attentive atmosphere. Some female travelers appreciate the sense of safety they don't find in hotels.

You'll meet some fascinating innkeepers and their guests, each of whom has a tale to tell and a story to share. You may eat together, pass each other in hallways, watch television together, and maybe share the hot tub. If this sounds like fun to you, you'll do fine. Best of all, you might make some new friends.

reflects the owners' attention to detail. The pine-studded property is bordered by national forest, where you can hike, snowmobile, look for old gold mines, or fish at Deerfield Reservoir, just 9 miles away. It's only 5 miles to Hill City along scenic Deerfield Road.

The cottage is set in the pines, apart from the main house, and has two rooms. A separate space between the rooms houses the shared hot tub. A third room is in the main house but has its own entrance and a private hot tub outside. Each room has a microwave (with complimentary popcorn), small refrigerator, satellite television, and a coffeemaker.

The owners are proud of their hearty Hungry Man Breakfast, which is served in your room.

Flying B Ranch Bed-and-Breakfast $$$$
RR 10, Box 2640, Rapid City
(605) 342–5324

Immerse yourself in Western ranch living. This 3,500-acre cattle ranch has been in the family since the 1940s. Three horse thieves were captured on the land in 1877, and two have suites named for them. Another, McClintock's Suite, is named for the owner of the last Deadwood stage line and has a secret passageway for kids to explore.

The house is beautifully decorated in Western themes. Each large and comfortable suite has its own hot tub on a private deck and a loft where children can sleep (well-behaved children are welcome).

Old Man Wright's Keeping Room is a grown-ups-only common room with an open-hearth fireplace and antique cookstove. You can sit on the deck and look out over Box Elder Creek, or get comfortable on the sofa and listen to the owner tell some delightful tall tales. His stories are always free—just don't believe everything you hear!

The owners live on the property and will arrive each morning to fix your breakfast, which is served buffet style. The fixings are authentic ranch-style food because, as the owner says, "Real cowboys don't eat quiche."

You can swim in the pool, sit in Uncle Bill's Cowboy Cabaña, hike on the property, fish in the creek, and listen to the nocturnal coyotes and morning meadowlarks. You'll hardly believe you're only five minutes from the Rushmore Mall in Rapid City (see our Shopping chapter).

If you like, you can participate in the ranch chores. The Flying B is a working ranch, and the owners stress, "We don't do things just for show." There's always real work to be done, and you're welcome to help out. Guests who bring their own horses can help move cattle on a 10-mile trail drive on Mother's Day. Kids love to bottle-feed the calves in the spring. But the owners confide that a favorite guest activity is the CPCPC, Cow Pie Chip Pitching Contest, held in dry years only. Participants can experiment with throwing techniques—which is better, Frisbee-style or the good old heave?

Horse accommodations include hay and feed and use of the barn, corral, and pasture. The Flying B is open from Memorial Day to Labor Day.

In Rapid City, take I-90, exit 58, and follow Haines Avenue north and out of town. The ranch is 3 miles from the exit.

High Country Guest Ranch $$$-$$$$
12172 Deerfield Rd., Hill City
(605) 574-9003, (888) CABIN28
www.highcountryranch.com

This one's not a dude ranch or a working ranch, but a real guest ranch where you can spend a few nights, relax, ride horses, eat a ranch breakfast, and still do your sightseeing. You can help care for the horses, participate in cattle roundups at nearby ranches or clinics on farrier work, and design your own custom trail rides. Read about longer trail rides in the Recreation chapter.

Other offerings include a pool, bicycle and four-wheel rentals, and rock climbing with a guide.

It you're looking for a place to both ride and bask in some luxury, there are seventeen cabins here, and they're not rustic. Some have vaulted ceilings, bay windows, hot tubs, and fireplaces. Even your horse can be comfortable; board your equine for an extra charge (feed and hay are not furnished). Alcohol use is limited.

A traditional Western breakfast is served, with simple but hearty food. Guests say the pancakes are "the best in the world," and there are also eggs, sausage, juice, and a cold-cereal and toast bar. Breakfast is served in a giant covered wagon—a perfect beginning to your Western vacation. Other meals can be reserved for groups (ask about picnic lunches or steaks cooked on pitchforks) for an extra charge.

This ranch is "off the beaten path but close to everything," say the owners. The George S. Mickelson Trail goes right through the property (see our Recreation chapter for more on the trail). The ranch is open all year. No credit cards are accepted.

Sweetgrass Inn (formerly Hayloft Bed & Breakfast) $$$-$$$$
9356 Neck Yoke Rd., Rapid City
(605) 343-5351

Sweetgrass Inn specializes in cozy country elegance. The rooms and baths are gorgeous (and large). Peace, quiet, and hospitality reign. The owners pride themselves

Insiders' Tip

Each year at holiday time, the Old-World Christkindlemart ("Christ Child Market" in German) is held at Audrie's Bed and Breakfast. The 1910 Old Powerhouse building, which once generated electricity for the area, is magically transformed into a festive marketplace, with vendors in costume and live musical performances, on the first Saturday and Sunday in December. The cost of admission—a nonperishable food item and $1.00—supports the Black Hills Food Bank and the Cancer Institute of Rapid City. For information call (605) 342-7788.

Morning coffee on the deck in the warm South Dakota sunshine makes a great start to the day.
PHOTO: COURTESY OF SOUTH DAKOTA TOURISM

on their flexibility in accommodating guests' special requests.

Six of the eight rooms are in a separate building near the main house; two rooms are attached to the main house. Four have heated marble whirlpools, and each has a television and VCR hidden away in an armoire. A video library is available for the choosing. The common area has a full-size refrigerator in the kitchen that's also furnished with a microwave and coffeemaker. The hot tub on the deck is for use by all the guests.

Breakfast is full, hearty, and South Dakota country-style, and it is delivered to your room between 8:00 and 10:00 A.M. But don't worry if you have jet lag; the owners are very flexible and will adjust breakfast to your time schedule.

Sweetgrass Inn is open year-round. The owners also run the Dairy Barn right next door (an ice-cream and food business store). Sweetgrass Inn is just off U.S. 16, which has many interesting places to visit. Mount Rushmore is just 12 miles away (see our Attractions chapter).

Willow Springs Cabins $$$$
Bed & Breakfast
11515 Sheridan Lake Rd., Rapid City
(605) 342–3665
www.willowspringscabins.com

Two beautiful cabins and some wonderful breakfasts define the secluded Willow Springs accommodations. The cabins are decorated with family heirlooms and are cozy, comfortable, and very private. The Willows Cabin sleeps four and is open all year. The Frontier Cabin sits on a little hill, sleeps two, and is open from May through October 15 only. Each has a private bath, hot tub, television and VCR, stereo, microwave, coffeemaker, and small refrigerator.

It's an easy drive to Rapid City, Sheridan Lake, and Pactola Reservoir, but you might want to stay right here and bask in the peace and quiet of 140 acres and

adjoining national forest. Walk down to Spring Creek, fish (license required) and swim on the property, ice-skate in the winter, and get to know the friendly resident cats and dog.

Breakfast is served in the dining room of the house or brought to your cabin. The owner calls it "a wholesome and hearty gourmet breakfast." The cabins are stocked with coffee, tea, and popcorn.

Southern Hills

Custer Mansion Bed & Breakfast $$–$$$$
35 Centennial Dr., Custer
(605) 673-3333, (877) 519-4948
www.custermansionbb.com

This gorgeous and fascinating historic home is a charmer. Of Gothic design from the Victorian era (it was built in 1891), it is a tribute to both the success of the rancher/civic leader who built it and the current owners, who lovingly restored it. Listed in the National Register of Historic Places, it has seven gables, two staircases, transoms, stained-glass windows, a butler's pantry, and two rooms and three suites, all quaintly decorated. The mansion is filled with antiques, heirlooms, and lovely old framed prints from the owners' collection.

Breakfast often includes homemade granola (guests say it's the best they've ever had) and rhubarb-strawberry sauce for your pancakes or waffles.

You'll rest well in the gorgeous four-poster king bed in the Evergreen Room. Or you might instead choose to relax in the gabled-wall Shenandoah room, which has a Jacuzzi. The Evening Star family suite has two rooms connected by a tiny charming hallway, and the bathroom features an antique claw-foot tub. You may also choose the Rose of Sharon Room or the Morning Dew Room. Whichever room you choose, you'll enjoy discovering the delightful idiosyncrasies of this historic house. Alcohol use is limited.

Campgrounds and RV Sites

Northern Hills

Central Hills

Southern Hills

Black Hills National Forest

Horse Camps

Thousands of people come to the Black Hills each summer to camp among the pines, and both public and private campground operators are happy to oblige them. Whether you want to pack all your amenities on your back and hike to a primitive tent site, settle down with cable TV in your RV, or bring your horse with you, you'll find plenty of choices that meet your needs. We've listed a number of fine places we would recommend to our camping friends, but please understand that these entries merely scratch the surface. There's an abundance of well-run camping spots, both in and out of town, from one end of the Hills to the other.

Many of the campgrounds in this chapter offer a wide range of creature comforts, but you'll find the owners have also done a commendable job of preserving the natural surroundings that beckon people to the Hills in the first place. And even those with the most campsites have a spacious feel—the great outdoors is all around you. Listen closely and you might even catch the strains of a coyote serenade at dusk.

Privately owned campgrounds often have swimming pools and other recreational opportunities on-site, and many are located near major attractions. But if you'd like to go touring and let someone else do the driving, be sure to ask whether any bus tours stop for passengers where you intend to stay. If you're looking for a public campground with fewer amenities, please see the Bear Butte State Park Campground listing under Northern Hills and look among the Southern Hills listings for state and national parks and recreation areas. You'll find 26 public campgrounds operated by the U.S.D.A. Forest Service (see the National Forest Supervisor listing later in the chapter.) Lastly, we have a separate section for horse camps.

For information about camping in or near the Badlands, please consult that chapter. If you're looking for a cabin to rent, our Accommodations chapter is your best source. Unless we tell you otherwise, the campgrounds listed here have showers, flush toilets, and RV dump stations. Full RV hookups mean water, sewer, and electricity; partial means electricity and water or electricity only. Each listing includes a breakdown of RV and tent sites to help you gauge which campgrounds are most likely to suit your particular camping style. And unless a listing states otherwise, assume your major credit card will be accepted and your pet is welcome on a leash. Naturally, campground owners expect you to observe good pet etiquette by cleaning up after Fido and not leaving him tied to your tent poles while you go off exploring all day.

You'll notice that many campgrounds give opening and closing dates "depending on the weather." Well, that's just the way we operate here, where winters can be long and blustery—or comparatively brief and mild. Please be aware that campgrounds and other accommodations are apt to be packed in early August during the Sturgis Rally & Races (see Annual Events and Festivals). Although it's a good idea to make advance reservations any time you're coming to the Hills, it's especially wise to do so for stays during Rally week.

Whenever you arrive, and wherever you stay, don't be surprised if you find a family reunion or two in progress. Black Hills campgrounds are a popular choice for such activities, and when you think about it, what better way to spend time with those you love?

Northern Hills

Bear Butte State Park Campground
Hwy. 79, Sturgis
(605) 347-5240

If beautiful views and peaceful solitude are your top priorities, you'll appreciate the opportunity to stay here. On clear days you can see Bear Butte reflected in Bear Butte Lake, which is just a short walk from the campground. (You can learn more about Bear Butte and Bear Butte State Park in our Parks and Grasslands chapter.) To the south, the Black Hills form an inviting silhouette on the horizon. You'll find 15 campsites for tents and RVs, but amenities are limited to a pit toilet and a hand pump for water; there are no showers, hookups, or dump stations. Also, because trees don't grow well here, shade is scarce. But there's a picnic shelter for you to use, and, of course, the lake for you to play in (see our Recreation chapter for boating information). East of the main camping area are four fairly well-shaded tent sites with a vault toilet and no water. Overflow camping is available during the Sturgis Rally.

Credit cards and reservations are not accepted but since the campground is not heavily used except during the Sturgis Rally & Races in August, you should have no trouble finding a site on a first-come, first-served basis. There's a self-registration fee of $6.00 per camping unit (such as a tent or RV) but no park entrance fee to use the campground. If you drive into the eastern portion of the park to see the visitor center or use the hiking trails, you'll need a park entrance license (again, refer to our Parks and Grasslands chapter for complete information). If you walk over (a hike in itself), you can get in for free.

The campground is open all year, although the water is shut off during the winter. To get there, go 3 miles east of Sturgis on Highway 34, turn left onto Highway 79, and go about 4 miles. Turn left again onto the dirt road where you see the campground sign and go another mile.

Chris' Campground
701 Christensen Dr., Spearfish
(605) 642-2239, (800) 350-2239
www.blackhills.com/chriscampground

Two-legged kids will delight in the opportunity to bottle-feed the four-legged variety at the petting farm here. Baby animals such as goats, lambs, and calves from local ranches spend the summer at this shady, grassy campground, which has been owned and operated by the Christensen family for 45 years. Feedings are at 8:00 A.M. and 5:00 P.M., and guests are welcome to join in. The rest of the time, a heated pool, rec room, and playground are good places to pass the time.

There are 132 campsites: 45 basic ones for tents or trailers and the rest with full or partial RV hookups. Six camping cabins offer still another option for summer nights. Laundry facilities, paved interior roads, a convenience store, cable TV, volleyball, horseshoes, a basketball court, and lovely mountain views all make your stay that much more enjoyable. Weather permitting, you can visit between mid-April and mid-October. Limited camping is available all winter. Rates for four people range from $15 to $23.

Glencoe Campresort
20555 Glencoe Dr., Sturgis
(605) 347-4712, (800) 272-4712

A magnificent view of Bear Butte greets you as you turn off Highway 34 into Glencoe Campresort. Although serving groups of about 200 or more is the specialty here, the facility also welcomes families and solitary campers. The 1,000 RV sites with

> ## Insiders' Tip
> In 1997 the Forest Service added two wheelchair-accessible campsites at Pactola Lake and one at Sheridan Lake. The sites have raised tent pads and other features that make them user-friendly. See the Black Hills National Forest listing for reservation information.

full hookups are close to the entrance, and then the dirt road winds around to more than 100 cottonwood-shaded, creekside acres for tent camping. Chemical toilets and water faucets are located throughout the grounds.

During the Sturgis Rally & Races each August, campers can buy meals that are prepared in an enclosed kitchen and served in a covered eating area with seating for 320. Geared mainly toward Rally business, the campground nonetheless is open between May 1 and October 1.

Weekly and monthly rates are available; otherwise, plan to pay $8.00 a night for a tent site, $15.00 to park your RV, and, in either case, $3.00 less if you don't use the showers. The campground is 3 miles east of town.

Mountain View Campground
625 Christensen Dr., Spearfish
(605) 642-2170, (800) 365-2170

Trees and grassy areas make this a homey little place to stay in your tent or RV, and the heated pool, game room, and small playground provide good family recreation. There are 80 sites altogether, most with partial or full hookups. Laundry facilities and a convenience store provide more home comforts. Some of the picnic tables even have shelters to keep you out of the rain.

The campground is open from early May until late September, weather permitting. Rates for up to four people range from $15 to $24.

Spearfish City Campground
440 S. Canyon St., Spearfish
(605) 642-1340

Don't be fooled by the name; this quiet, shady campground is on the outskirts of town, alongside Spearfish Creek and D.C. Booth Historic Fish Hatchery (see our Attractions chapter), and little more than a stone's throw from the mouth of incomparable Spearfish Canyon.

Thousands of people descended on the campground in 1989, when the National Horseshoe Pitchers Association held its annual tournament here, but the dust has long since settled. The campground offers about 100 basic sites; there are also 57 RV sites with full hookups and cable TV.

Depending on the weather, you can camp here from early May through mid-October. Prices start at $12 for one person at a basic site and $21 for up to four people using full hookups. Children ages five and younger stay for free. Campers who pay for six consecutive nights get a seventh night's stay for free.

Whistler's Gulch RV Park & Campground
235 Cliff St., Deadwood
(605) 578-2092, (800) 704-7139

Like just about everything in Deadwood, this campground a mile south of historic Main Street is situated on a hill. But the brief climb brings you to 126 immaculately groomed, level campsites and a fabulous view across the gulch. Twenty-six of the sites are reserved for tents, and the rest have full hookups for RVs. You won't find a dump station, but other comforts include a sports court, a heated outdoor pool, arcade games, and a small store. The Deadwood Trolley stops here and for 50 cents takes you downtown to casinos and restaurants (see our Gaming and Casinos chapter). The campground operates May 1 to October 1, weather permitting. Rates for two adults start at $20 for a tent site and $30 for an RV site. If the pool hasn't opened for the season yet, inquire about a discount.

Central Hills

Mount Rushmore KOA at Palmer Gulch Resort
Hwy. 244, Hill City
(605) 574-2525, (800) 562-8503
www.palmergulch.com

If you're looking for a home away from home, this is it. Just about everything your family needs or wants is here, from recreational opportunities to nondenominational Sunday morning worship services. That's because the resort, which started as a guest ranch in the mid-1930s, pays close attention to customer surveys. The state tourism department recognized its efforts recently with the George S. Mickelson Hospitality Award.

The list of services here is impressive. Besides a grocery store, there's the Dakota Store that sells South Dakota–made products and squares cut from huge slabs of fudge. There's an outpost where you can buy tickets for 18-hole minigolf, the water slide (an all-day pass gets the whole family into both), and trail rides; or you can watch a free movie every evening. Two outdoor pools, two hot tubs, two wading pools, two playgrounds, bicycle and paddleboat rentals, and a free trout pond (you do need a fishing license) will probably occupy a good deal of your time. At night, various free family activities are on tap, including hayrides and Native American dancing, and there's free transportation to evening lighting programs at nearby Mount Rushmore and Crazy Horse memorials (see our Attractions chapter).

If all the activity leaves you with hunger pangs, a restaurant serving three meals a day, a lounge with a full bar, an ice-cream parlor, and a sandwich shop come to the rescue. You can even rent a car and fill the gas tank here! And—need we even say so?—there are laundry facilities and cable TV. All this is set against the Black Hills National Forest.

In case you find time to sleep, there are 150 tent sites, 185 partial hookups and 130 full hookups for RVs, 35 full deluxe sites, a group camping area, and 55 camping cabins. There's also an attractive new lodge and a number of furnished cabins, but you'll have to consult the Accommodations chapter about them. The resort, 5 miles west of Mount Rushmore, is open from May 1 until October 1. Prices for campers range from $25.00 to $54.00 a night. Camping cabins start at $46.95. Tent spaces are $25.95.

Mystery Mountain Resort
13752 S. U.S. 16 W., Rapid City
(605) 342–5368, (800) 658–CAMP

Proudly proclaiming itself the official home of the Black Hills Bluegrass Festival, this wooded campground features a natural amphitheater with a stage for small outdoor concerts (see our Annual Events chapter). The Black Hills Country Music Association hosts its yearly show here, too. Most of the time, however, you're more likely to hear birdsong at any of the 140 campsites.

A wire fence at the far end separates the 63 tent sites from the next-door neighbor, Bear Country U.S.A., offering the possibility of a near-wilderness experience. (See the Attractions chapter.)

The resort's 35 full RV hookups are winterized, making this one of a handful of Black Hills campgrounds that are open year-round. (Comfort stations for tenters shut down in mid-October.) There are 20 partial hookups, and 22 cabin-style lodging facilities (see Accommodations).

Besides enjoying the heated outdoor pool, hot tub, playground, and sports courts, you'll want to explore the petrified-wood hiking trail and the gravity-defying mystery house that gives the resort its name. A convenience store and laundry simplify daily chores so you can get out and play. You can even ditch K.P. and buy meals from a newly built kitchen to take back to your campsite. Call ahead, and you can make arrangements to have a rental car waiting for you when you arrive.

Basic rates start at $16.50 for two people and go to $35.00. Children five and younger stay for free.

Rafter J Bar Ranch Campground
U.S. 16-385, Hill City
(605) 574–2527, (888) RAFTERJ
www.rafterj.com

Grassy meadows, mountain views, and spacious campsites are among the first features you notice at this pristine campground. If you like outdoor recreation, you could spend your whole vacation right here, riding horseback, bicycling, and hiking, because the George S. Mickelson Trail borders the property. (See our

Recreation chapter for more about the trail.) A swimming pool, rec room, playground, and hot tub are good places to spend the day, too. In the evening you can watch cable TV in your RV or join fellow campers for a free movie or other family entertainment.

The Ranch Store sells supplies, groceries, and gas for your car (your own or one you've rented at the campground), and there's a laundry for your convenience. There are some 220 campsites, more than half of which have full or partial RV hookups. Some of the tent sites have electricity, too. There are 23 heated camping cabins, 12 with kitchens and bath; the other 11 are sleeping cabins.

The campground, 3 miles south of Hill City, is open from May 1 to October 1. Nightly rates for two people range from $23.95 to $32.95 for a campsite. Cabins are $40.95 or $73.95 a night for two. There's no charge for children seven and younger, but horse and bicycle rentals cost extra.

Spokane Creek Resort
U.S. 16A, Keystone
(605) 666–4609

You're just a mile north of Custer State Park and a short drive south of Mount Rushmore when you camp here. Plus, this campground in the Norbeck Wildlife Preserve is along what many consider to be the most interesting road in the Black Hills—also known as Iron Mountain Road—with rock tunnels and curly "pigtail" bridges.

If that doesn't entice you, perhaps the thought of waking up to the scent of freshly baked cinnamon rolls will. You can buy them, along with breakfast sandwiches and coffee, in the general store each morning; later in the day you can munch on pizza made to order and sub sandwiches prepared on fresh bread. When not eating or exploring, you can swim in the outdoor heated pool or play a variety of sports, including nine-hole minigolf.

The campground has 31 sites for tents and 30 RV sites with full or partial hookups. Two of 17 cabins are for roughing it without plumbing, and the rest have bathrooms and kitchen facilities. (See our

Accommodations chapter for more about the cabins.) A picnic pavilion with electricity and room for 100 can be reserved for family reunions and other events. The cost for two people ranges from $16 to $25. The campground is open from May 15 to September 15.

Southern Hills

American Presidents Cabins & Camp
U.S. Hwy. 16A, Custer
(605) 673–3373
www.presidentsresort.com

Its location a mile east of Custer places this campground within minutes of many of the Black Hills' biggest attractions, including Custer State Park, Crazy Horse Memorial, Jewel Cave, and Mount Rushmore. The place has bragging rights to a new, heated shower house, a spa, and a heated outdoor pool advertised as the Hills' largest. There's also space for basketball, volleyball, horseshoes, minigolf, a playground, and an arcade. A convenience store and laundry simplify life on the road.

You'll find 36 sites with full or partial hookups and 30-plus shaded tent sites. There is no dump station, but the management will let you empty your RV holding tank at a vacant full-hookup site if you need to. Water spigots are plentiful, and picnic shelters are available for family reunions or other gatherings. See the Accommodations chapter for information about the 45 cabins and 15 motel units here.

The campground opens around mid-March if the weather permits, but be forewarned that water might not be available until the first of April. The place shuts down around mid-November, but you probably won't get a shower here after October. Prices for two people range from $21 to $29. Inquire about off-season rates.

Angostura State Recreation Area
Off U.S. 385, Hot Springs
(605) 745–6996, (800) 710–CAMP
www.hotsprings/sd.com (see Attractions)

Angostura Reservoir is the star attraction in this 1,125-acre park, and if you can't

Towering evergreens heighten the back-to-nature feeling of camping in the Black Hills. PHOTO: COURTESY OF SOUTH DAKOTA TOURISM

bear to leave after a day of watersports, you might as well plan to stay at one of 163 campsites spread among four campgrounds. Three of them—Cascade, Hat Creek, and Horsehead—are along the shore; the fourth, Cheyenne, is 150 yards distant and is the only one without electrical hookups. Cascade, close by the marina and with two camping cabins (see the Accommodations chapter) is the shadiest and most popular.

The Breakers Beach Club serves a beachside burgers-and-beer-style menu during the summer, and there's a convenience store with camping and boating supplies. The concessionaire also has four fully furnished, two-bedroom cabins for rent; call (605) 745-6665 for more information.

The campgrounds 10 miles southeast of Hot Springs are open all year, but the comfort stations close when it gets cold in October. You'll have to settle for vault toilets from then until spring, but you can still have electricity for a small fee. Peak-season rates, from mid-May through Labor Day, range from $10 to $13; camp-

ing cabins with heat and air-conditioning rent for $32 a night. The four furnished cabins are $175 a night. When you make your reservation, be sure to ask whether to reach your campground by the north or south entrance.

Beaver Lake Campground
U.S. 16, Custer
(605) 673-2464, (800) 346-4383
www.beaverlakecampground.net

Once the kids find out about the recently upgraded 360-foot water slide at this campground, you might have no other choice than to stay here. But think of the benefits to yourself, too. While the youngsters are happily sliding (and burning off a great deal of energy), you're taking your leisure under a pine tree or beside the heated pool. And the owners make the following promise: If their rest rooms aren't the cleanest you've ever found, your stay is free.

There are approximately 93 campsites here, about 37 of which have full or partial hookups for RVs. A year-round full-service cabin is available also. Your family will have the use of a laundry, small convenience store, arcade, and playground. The campground, 3.5 miles west of Custer, is open from May 1 to October 15. Peak-season (early June to late August) rates start at $16 for four people, with an additional charge for hookups and use of the water slide. Inquire about off-season, monthly, and group rates. Children ages five and younger stay for free. Pets are welcome.

Cold Brook and Cottonwood Springs recreation areas, Hot Springs
(605) 745-5476

If you're looking for solitude and outdoor activities rather than modern amenities, these small recreation areas run by the U.S. Army Corps of Engineers are excellent choices. Somewhat remote, both are situated at reservoirs that are off-limits to noisy, high-speed watercraft. (See Boating in our Recreation chapter.)

Cold Brook, reputed to have the clearest, warmest water in the Black Hills, has a small beach for swimming; Cottonwood doesn't have a beach but offers fine fishing (see our Recreation chapter for more information). Both have hiking opportunities, a wildlife area, and playgrounds.

Neither campground has hookups or showers, but Cottonwood Springs has flush toilets and running water.

Reservations are not accepted: It's first-come, first-served only. Cold Brook has 13 campsites and is open year-round; Cottonwood Springs has 18 sites that are open from mid-May to mid-September or longer if the weather permits. Both cost $5.00 a night, payable through self-registration.

Cold Brook is less than a mile northwest of Hot Springs; follow Evans Street and take the hard left that leads to the project. Cottonwood Springs is west of town off U.S. 18; follow the signs from either direction, then go 2 miles on gravel roads. Credit cards are not accepted.

Custer Mountain Cabins & Campground
U.S. 16A, Custer
(605) 673-5440, (800) 239-5505

If quiet, spacious, shady, and close-to-wildlife are the words you'd use to

describe your ideal campsite, you'd do well to check out this place. You'll be nearly surrounded by U.S.D.A. Forest Service land that invites you to follow wildlife trails on a hike. (There are no marked trails.)

Smack-dab between the city of Custer to the west and Custer State Park to the east—either one is just 1.5 miles away—the campground can accommodate more than 30 tents in a grassy meadow. For RVs there are 21 full-hookup sites plus several more with electricity only and cable TV. Two camping cabins are also available. See the Accommodations chapter to find out about the modern, year-round log cabins. Tents and RVs are welcome between mid-April and late October. Prices are $15 for a tent site and $20 to park your RV. Camping cabins are $40 a night.

Custer State Park
Custer
(605) 255-4515, www.custerstatepark.info
(information); (800) 710-CAMP
www.campsd.com
custerstatepark@state.sd.us (reservations)

Campsites in Custer State Park are in great demand among out-of-staters, and, in fact, the state reservation center starts handling requests for Custer several weeks ahead of those for other parks. You'll find a variety of camping opportunities in the park, all with at least two things in common: showers but no hookups. Yet each of these campgrounds has its own personality.

Center Lake Campground (no flush toilets) is, naturally, near Center Lake and adjacent to the Black Hills Playhouse (see The Arts). Set amid dramatic granite outcroppings, Sylvan Lake's popular namesake campground has a higher elevation that ensures cooler summer temperatures. Blue Bell, the southernmost site, is handy to a stable offering trail rides (see our Recreation chapter) and is a good place to watch for wildlife. All three of these campgrounds offer total shade.

Stockade Lake Campground is shaded on the west side and offers good access to Mount Rushmore and Crazy Horse memorials (described in our Attractions chapter). Centrally located Game Lodge

Custer Campsites

By the time Lt. Col. George Armstrong Custer and his Seventh Cavalry arrived in the Black Hills in 1874, rumors of gold had been trickling out of the area for years. Up to that point the U.S. government, determined to honor the Fort Laramie Treaty of 1868 (which ceded the Hills to the Sioux), had refused to provide military escorts for prospectors eager to invade the forbidden territory in search of riches. Inevitably, however, the War Department at last authorized a Seventh Cavalry expedition to explore the Black Hills. It was to be a reconnaissance mission only, but Custer took miners along to look for gold. (At 23, the vain and daring Custer, who graduated last in his class at West Point, had become the Civil War's youngest general. But the "boy general" was dropped to captain after the war and later made a lieutenant colonel in the Seventh Cavalry, the rank he held on this mission. Nevertheless, you'll often see references to "General Custer" in the Hills.)

One of Custer's party, Horatio Ross, did indeed find specks of gold in French Creek on August 2, and by the end of the year a band of adventurers led by John Gordon had snuck in, intending to stay. Little more than a year later, the Black Hills Gold Rush of 1876 was in full swing. Today you can pull off the highway at Wheels West Campground, 3 miles east of Custer on U.S. 16A, and read a historical marker at the site of Custer's base camp. The expedition stayed here for five days, and its leader named the area Golden Valley. A half-mile farther east, the Gordon Stockade has been re-created.

Another more obscure Custer campsite is 5 miles south of Bear Butte in Meade County. At the intersection of Highway 34 and County Road 12C, County Road 6L heads south. As it narrows you'll find a flagpole and a stone monument with a hand-lettered sign that reads: CAMPSITE, GENERAL CUSTER EXPEDITION, AUGUST 14–15, 1874. ENTIRE COMMAND OF SEVENTH US CAVALRY CONSISTING OF 1,200 MEN AND HORSES, 110 WAGONS AND EQUIPMENT. Custer, on the return trip and two weeks' ride from home, wrote a note to his wife, Elizabeth ("Libbie"), here, saying, "I have the proud satisfaction of knowing that our explorations have exceeded the most sanguine expectations."

Campground (the only one with a dump station) is ideal for large motor homes but also has well-shaded sites along Grace Coolidge Creek. Grace Coolidge Campground, also centrally located, is mostly shaded and close to the park's walk-in fishing area. Legion Lake Campground is in a valley setting across the road from the lake and lodge of the same name, as well as a playground.

It's also close to the Badger Hole (see our Parks and Grasslands chapter for a Close-up on South Dakota Poet Laureate Badger Clark) and the Centennial Trail (see our Recreation chapter).

Sites at Center Lake, Grace Coolidge, and Stockade Lake South are first-come,

first-served; Blue Bell, Game Lodge, Legion Lake, Stockade Lake North, and Sylvan Lake campgrounds are reservation only—but if you show up before noon, you might be able to reserve an unclaimed site on the spot. Game Lodge is open all year with limited facilities and reduced rates during the winter; the others are open from early May until late September, with variations due to weather and maintenance schedules. Except at Center Lake, where the fee is $13, nightly rates are $15 per camping unit (such as a tent or camping trailer) per site.

Group camping is available near two of the developed campgrounds as well. Game Lodge group area has showers and

Campers at Custer State Park should expect to see bison—they are free roaming in the park.

PHOTO: BERT GILDART

flush toilets; Stockade Lake doesn't, but they're within walking distance. The rate is $3.00 per person per night, with a $60.00 per night minimum. Reservations are required.

Hikers might prefer the tranquility of primitive campsites at French Creek Natural Area in the approximate center of the park. Hike in a mile from French Creek Horse Camp on the west end or 2 miles from the Wildlife Loop on the east end. At either end, occupancy is limited to 15 people, but both are open all year on a first-come first-served basis. The fee is $2.00 per person. For more information call (605) 255-4464 or stop at the Peter Norbeck Visitor Center from May to October.

For information about French Creek Horse Camp, see the Horse Camps section below. Information on Custer State Park's cabins and lodges is in our Accommodations chapter. To find out what makes this park such a popular place, read our Parks and Grasslands chapter.

Elk Mountain Campground
U.S. 385 in Wind Cave National Park, Hot Springs
(605) 745-4600, www.nps.gov/wica

Time seemed to stand still when we visited this serene campground on a day in mid-August. Like the rest of the park, it was unspoiled and beautiful, with rolling, grassy hills and a wide prairie sky beckoning us to go for a hike. Indeed, there's a self-guided nature trail that loops around the campground for about a mile.

On summer nights, free ranger-led programs start around sundown in the outdoor amphitheater that has bench seating and a projection booth for slide shows. Check the park's visitor center for the program schedule, because it varies as the days get shorter.

The 75 campsites have no hookups, and there's no dump station or showers. The sole modern comforts—flush toilets and running water—are operational from mid-May until mid-September. The campground in the west central part of the park is open from mid-April until the last Sunday in October. The rate is $10 per night during peak season, half that when the plumbing is shut off. Reservations are not accepted, and payment is by self-registration, but there's always a volunteer host on hand to welcome you and answer questions. During extremely dry conditions, a campfire prohibition will be posted. Credit cards are not accepted.

Flintstones Bedrock City Campground
U.S. 16 W., Custer
(605) 673-4079
(605) 673-4664 (summer only)

You'll especially want to consider staying here if you have little ones who will appreciate the adjacent Flintstones amusement park (see our Kidstuff chapter for more about that). For one thing, your stay allows you unlimited entries to the park once you've paid admission.

In addition to 127 tent and RV sites—52 with full hookups—the 30-acre campground on the edge of town has laundry facilities, a game room, outdoor heated pool, nine holes of miniature golf, plus volleyball, basketball, and horseshoe courts. The campground is open mid-May to Labor Day. Prices range from $16.50 to $21.00 for two people. Six cabins are also available at $38 for two people.

Larive Lake Resort & Campground
1802 Evans St., Hot Springs
(605) 745-3993

Just as the name implies, you'll find a lovely little lake to play in when you stay here. Fishing and swimming are free to guests, and you can rent a paddleboat or canoe for a small charge; or you can bring your own nonmotorized watercraft.

The well-kept grounds with a view of nearby colorful, rocky cliffs offer 20 RV sites with full hookups and 20 or more tent sites, a laundry, game room, playground, cable TV, and camp store. See our Accommodations chapter for information about the eight cabins. The resort is open from May 15 to October 1. Rates range from $12.50 to $21.50; your seventh night in your tent or RV is free.

Insiders' Tip

The state reservation center handles summer reservations for camp-sites, cabins, and picnic shelters in South Dakota state parks and recreation areas from early January until early September. (To make arrangements for the off-season, fall through mid-May, call the individual parks.) In general, your stay is limited to 14 days, and all fees, including a small processing fee for out-of-state residents, must be paid in advance. Call (800) 710-CAMP to make reservations up to 90 days in advance. For general park information, call (605) 773-3391; for information about a particular park, call the park.

Black Hills National Forest

National Forest Supervisor
R.R. 2, Box 200, Custer
(877) 444-6777 (reservations only)
www.reserveusa.com

The South Dakota portion of the Black Hills National Forest has 26 designated campgrounds, from lakeside to rugged. For specific information you need to call or write to the Forest Supervisor's office at the phone number or address above. Ask for the latest copy of the *Black Hills National Forest Recreation Guide*.

Tepee camping is becoming increasingly popular at Black Hills campgrounds. PHOTO: BARBARA TOMOVICK

None of these campgrounds has utilities, but that's probably one reason you wanted to camp in the forest. In most cases, though, you do get the luxury of drinking water. Most have spacious RV sites with lots of trees and bushes for privacy. More than half of the campgrounds are open or partially open all year, but what services do exist are shut down during the winter, and you have to carry out your trash yourself. Be aware that snow can close the roads, blocking your way in or out.

About half operate on a first-come, first-served basis, but others have reservable sites. Your stay is limited to 14 days. In general, fees are charged between Memorial Day and Labor Day weekends only. Rates range from $8.00 to $17.00 a night, except at four remote campgrounds that are maintained with the help of donations, and at the Bear Gulch and Sheridan Lake group areas, where fees start at $40.00 Inquire about specifics. If your horse will be traveling with you, see the Horse Camps listings below. Also see the Hiking and Backpacking section of our Recreation chapter to learn about backcountry camping in the forest.

Horse Camps

Northern Hills

Nemo Guest Ranch
Main St., Nemo
(605) 578–2708
www.nemoranch.com
The atmosphere at this well-kept ranch in Paradise Valley is nothing short of charming, with its Western-style buildings and hitching-post trim. There are plenty of comforts, too, from the Ponderosa Bar and Brandin' Iron Cafe to the turn-of-the-century Nemo Mercantile general store, which also houses a laundry. You can even gas up your truck right here. Take your pick of 13 modern cabins and houses with one to five bedrooms, which rent from $75 to 250 a night; a nearby motel (please see our Accommodations chapter

for complete information about those units); and 14 RV sites with full hookups or unlimited tent sites—but leave your horse in one of the corrals.

The ranch is open year-round. Nightly rates range from $15.00 to $20.00 for a campsite. Horses stay for $5.00 to $10.00 per night. The ranch is 21 miles from the junction of U.S. 385 and Nemo Road, southeast of Deadwood, or 16 miles northwest of Rapid City from the other end of Nemo Road, also called County Road 234.

Central Hills

Mountain Meadow Resort
11321 Gillette Prairie Rd., Hill City
(605) 574–2636
This year-round facility actually caters to many types of sporting, so depending on the season, you can bring your horse, fishing pole, hunting rifle, or even your snowmobile. Snowmobile and ATV rentals are available for use at the resort, too, and a maintenance shop is right there. You'll find more than 66 miles of marked and mapped horse trails as well as more than 340 miles of groomed National Forest snowmobile trails that depart from the resort. Deerfield Lake gleams quietly across the dirt road, offering top-notch

Insiders' Tip

If road grime has you ready to trade your firstborn child for a shower, Beaver Lake Campground west of Custer has a far less drastic solution for you. For a small fee ($4.50), you can use the showers there and be on your way, your family still intact.

Dozens of Black Hills campgrounds temporarily become home away from home for RV travelers.

PHOTO: COURTESY OF SOUTH DAKOTA TOURISM.

trout fishing and no-wake boating for a small fee, payable at the lake.

For lights-out you can either reserve one of four two-bed, heated housekeeping cabins (see our Accommodations chapter) or, mid-May through September, pick a spot for your tent or RV—all 25 sites have electricity, and six have full hookups. There's no dump station, but there is a gas pump as well as a convenience store where you can purchase hunting and fishing licenses, five-day snowmobile permits, groceries, fishing tackle, and worms. From mid-October to March, a small cafe on the premises serves meals.

Camping fees start at $14.00 per night; cabins start at $45. Horses board for $6.00 a day in corrals. You must to be 18 or older to rent a snowmobile or a four-wheeler. Call for rates and reservations.

Southern Hills

Black Hills National Forest
(877) 444-6777
www.reserveusa.com

The National Forest has two public horse camps with sheltered hitching areas, Willow Creek and Iron Creek. Of the two, Willow Creek is the more deluxe: It has drinking water. Neither has showers or utility hookups. Reservations are recommended at both during the summer. Iron Creek, east of Custer, has nine campsites; Willow Creek, on Highway 244 between Hill City and Mount Rushmore, has eight group sites.

Rates are $16 per night at Iron Creek; at Willow Creek, group rates of $18 to $60 apply.

French Creek Horse Camp
CSP No. 4, Custer State Park
(605) 255-4515, (800) 710-2267
www.campsd.com

No more driving 3 miles to Blue Bell Campground to take a shower when you stay here. A new era began in 1998 with the opening of a comfort station housing showers, flush toilets, and sinks with hot and cold running water from a newly drilled well. The familiar vault toilets were left in place, though, to save you a potentially lengthy hike in the

> ## Insiders' Tip
> You can pitch your tent just about anywhere in the Black Hills National Forest (except at highly developed areas such as lakes), but state law and federal regulation allow open fires only in the fire grates in designated campgrounds and picnic areas. Build a fire anywhere else and you could be fined $1,000, jailed for a year, and ordered to pay civil damages.

middle of the night. There are no hookups or dump station.

The campground has 25 reservable sites and five that are available on a first-come, first-served basis. As popular as this place is, it's a good idea to reserve a site well in advance, especially for the summer months. The campground, 3 miles east of Blue Bell Lodge, is open all year. Unlimited corral space is available. The fee is $18 per night per camping unit.

Once here you can ride just about anywhere in Custer State Park except the Sylvan Lake watershed area and the walk-in fishing area that links Grace Coolidge and Center Lake campgrounds. Both areas are posted. Four trails depart from the campground; see our Recreation chapter for more information.

Plenty Star Ranches
U.S. 385, Pringle
(605) 673-3012
www.plentystarranch.com

Owners Jack and Isa Kirk have designed this restful camp for those whose primary purpose in going camping is to commune with nature. A Native American theme prevails here, and a pastoral tepee camp ($45 per night) a short distance from the main area is kept free of cars and other modern trappings that would be out of context.

You can stake out your own tent site (for $15 per night) behind the nineteenth-century ranch house, in a meadow bordered by graceful cottonwood and golden willow trees that grow on the banks of Cougar Creek. The ranch offers cabins, which can accommodate four to six persons each, plus 20 RV sites. The old ranch house can be rented for groups year-round; prices for that start at $100 for a half-day. A washer and dryer are in the heated shower house.

Box stalls and spacious pens are provided for your horse for $10 per day, and you'll find about 4,000 acres of public and private property on which to ride. The owners pride themselves on the horse-camper, hands-on vacations offered to kids. Call Jack or Isa for details. Bicycle rid-

Insiders' Tip
All hay and other feed brought into Custer State Park and Black Hills National Forest campgrounds must be certified weed-free.

ers love to stop at Plenty Star, as the Mickelson Trail runs right along the property. A public breakfast buffet is offered in the summer, beginning in May. The ranch is open from April through November but often has winter campers when the weather is mild. Reservations are taken year-round. Be sure to ask about group rates and packages. The ranch is approximately 9.5 miles south of Custer. Credit cards are not accepted.

Restaurants

Coffee and Sandwich
Shops

American Cuisine

Eclectic Cuisine

Ethnic Cuisine

Sweet Treats

Here in cattle country prime rib reigns supreme, and you'll find any number of steakhouses, restaurants, and cafes that cater to those who relish a simple, hearty slab of beef. Yet you'll also find plenty of creative cookery going on in Black Hills kitchens, and that means lots of diversity, including meatless dishes, on our restaurant menus. No matter what your tastes, we're confident that you'll find something to satisfy your palate as well as your hunger.

We've arranged the restaurants in this chapter in five categories—Coffee and Sandwich Shops, American, Eclectic, and Ethnic cuisines, and Sweet Treats—with geographic subheadings under each. Some serve breakfast, lunch, and dinner, and some serve only one or two meals a day; the individual listings will tell you. The write-ups under Sweet Treats direct you to places you'll want to go for snacks and desserts. Most of our eateries are open seven days a week year-round, and we've noted those that aren't as well as those that extend their hours during the summer. In general, summer means between Memorial Day weekend and Labor Day. We'll mention here that if you plan to dine out on a holiday, it's a good idea to call ahead, because some restaurants close to give their owners and employees those special days off to spend with their families.

We've provided general price information with each listing (note the Price Code key), and unless you see the notation "no credit cards," assume you can pay for your meal with a major card. We've also told you which places are smoke-free or have special areas for nonsmokers so you can decide which ones best suit your needs; if you don't see a smoking prohibition or a nonsmoking section mentioned, that means smoking is allowed throughout the restaurant.

Conversely, if you don't see any mention of alcohol in a write-up, none is served in that particular establishment (but we've informed you which ones serve beer, wine, and cocktails). In addition, we've noted which places provide parking; at others you'll need to park curbside or in a public parking lot (before you head to the restaurant to feed yourself, be sure to check whether there's a meter that needs feeding first).

If you're here on vacation, you'll be relieved to know that we didn't find a single establishment that requires a coat and tie or other formal attire. Some places obviously lend themselves to the dressier outfits in your closet, but it's been our observation that blue jeans fit in just about anywhere. So whether you dress up or down, you're assured a warm welcome.

And one more thing: The listings below, while comprehensive, are not exhaustive. Your wanderings will take you near many fine eateries, including well-known chains not included here because we assume you know them by reputation.

Some places were closed for the season when we did our research, so we didn't get to visit them. But those that appear below come highly recommended by us and other Insiders who patronize them regularly.

With that, we wish you *bon appétit!*

Price Code

Prices are the average cost of dinner (or lunch, for coffee and sandwich shops) for two adults. Drinks, appetizers, dessert, and tip are not included.

$ .... Less than $12
$$ .... $12 to $25
$$$ .... $26 to 40
$$$$ .... $41 and more

Coffee and Sandwich Shops

Although these places specialize in breakfast and lunch, some also serve dinner or at least stay open long enough for a late-afternoon or early-evening meal. Be sure to check the other categories for places that serve early in the day; you'll even find a couple of 24-hour establishments listed under American Cuisine.

Northern Hills

Common Grounds $
111 E. Hudson St., Spearfish; 1301 W. Omaha, Rapid City
(605) 642–9066

This gourmet coffee shop offers a full line of espresso drinks (including icy java slushes) and Italian sodas but also has muffins, bagels, soups, salads, and wrap sandwiches for the vegetarian and carnivore alike. An eclectic mix of furniture and displays of student artwork make this a homey place to relax with a newspaper or good book while you munch and sip, and the rich aroma of bulk coffee you can buy to brew in your own kitchen just adds to the comfortable atmosphere. The cafe serves breakfast and has an all-day deli bar. Hours are 7:00 A.M. to 7:00 P.M. Monday through Saturday, and 8:00 A.M. to 5:00 P.M. Sunday. Smoking is not permitted. No credit cards are accepted.

Central Hills

B&L Bagels $
512 Main St., Rapid City
(605) 399–1777

There's nothing quite like a fresh bagel to start the day or provide a pick-me-up at lunch. Thirty varieties of the bread-with-a-hole are mixed from scratch, then boiled and baked on a stone hearth the old-fashioned way. You'll have around 15 kinds to choose from, and you can order your bagel plain or spread with any of 15 flavors of light (less fat) cream cheese or another topping such as hummus or honey peanut butter. Or order it stuffed with a sandwich filling such as turkey pastrami, roast beef, veggies, or cream cheese and lox. Soups and fat-free pasta salad round out your meal, but if a snack is all you need, try a frosted bagel knot or an energy bar. There's a full espresso bar offering java or tea or a refreshing Italian soda. During the summer, ice cream and smoothies made with fruit and yogurt are available. The shop is open daily for breakfast and lunch. Smoking is prohibited. No credit cards are accepted.

The Beanery "Deli & Bakery" $
201 Main St., Rapid City
(605) 348–6775

The Beanery serves food fast but not fast food. Everything on the menu is made fresh daily, from breads and pies to soups and quiche. The service is cafeteria-style, but the dining area is homey, decked out in cheerful green-and-white checkered tablecloths, quaint wooden crates, retired milk cans, a comely antique cookstove, and a grand old wooden Hoosier cabinet that once did duty in a North Dakota farm kitchen. The Beanery serves lunch Monday through Friday, featuring a daily special (often a pasta dish), a meat and a meatless quiche, soups, salads, and both cold and grilled sandwiches. Thursday is lasagna day. Beverages include premium bottled sodas and fruit juices, and for dessert there's an assortment of pies, cheesecakes, and cookies. The owner told us someone once bought one of the cafe's raspberry peach cream cheese pies, entered it in a contest, and won. Is that cheating or what! But it speaks well for The Beanery, which is smoke-free and located in the basement of the Creamery Mall on the corner of Main and Second streets. No credit cards are accepted.

Black Hills Bagels $
913 Mt. Rushmore Rd., Rapid City
(605) 399–1277

In addition to 37 kinds of bagels, 14 cream cheeses and a variety of bagel sandwiches, you'll find tasty homemade salads here, including Oriental noodle, Italian, and fresh fruit. Or, if you're in the mood for a snack, a homemade cookie, muffin, or cinnamon bagel knot—the low-fat alternative to doughnuts—could be just the thing. The shop is open from 7:00 A.M. to 2:00 P.M. Monday through Saturday and from 8:00 A.M. to 1:00 P.M. Sunday. There is no smoking in the restaurant. Limited parking is available.

Coffee Garden $
360 Main St., Ste. 6, Hill City
(605) 574–9081

Greenery is in season all year, and so are the yummy treats in this delightfully decorated coffee shop. A friend directed us here to sample the hot chocolate, and are we grateful! The conditions turned out to be just right as we ventured forth (unwisely, perhaps) in a heavy, wet spring snowstorm, for we were rewarded with a warming cup of what can only be described as a liquid chocolate bar (it's made with steamed milk, not hot water). Savoring this, we browsed a bit and found bread mixes to bake in a flower pot, pretty tea cups and infusers, dainty coffee spoons, locally roasted coffee beans, and biscotti in unusual flavors such as oatmeal cinnamon current, all for sale. There's also a complete line of espresso beverages and Italian sodas available, of course, as well as muffins, cookies, and locally baked breads and bagels. Organic sandwiches and soup provide more substantial fare. The shop is open daily from 7:15 A.M. to 5:00 P.M. Smokers are welcome on the outdoor deck.

Espresso Blends n Juice Bar $
609 Mt. Rushmore Rd., Rapid City
(605) 399–0912

What could be more refreshing and healthful than freshly prepared fruit or vegetable juice? Your choices range from classic orange and apple to the more unusual cucumber and cabbage; there are more than 30 blends from which to choose. How does pineapple-pear-banana-ginger sound? Or carrot-celery-tomato-cilantro-garlic? You can have a nutritional supplement added to your juice or choose from a menu of juice remedies for a wholesome boost. If espresso is more your speed, you can avail yourself of the coffee bar, where you'll also find Italian sodas and a variety of yummy homemade baked goods. Hours are 6:00 A.M. to 5:00 P.M. Monday through Friday. No credit cards are accepted.

Sixth Street Bakery & Delicatessen $
516 Sixth St., Rapid City
(605) 342–6660

"The Deli" is practically an institution. This down-to-earth cafe has long been a meeting place for those of an artistic or intellectual bent, and you'll note a rotating display of mostly regional artwork on the walls. Feel free to plunk out a tune on the piano, by the way. The meals and bakery items for sale here are all made on the premises from fresh ingredients, and if you can get past the sweet rolls, Danish pastries, turnovers, tarts, croissants, cakes, cookies, and other sinfully rich goodies, you'll find salads, soups, sandwiches (on your choice of tasty homemade bread), quiche, pizza, and calzones. The Deli's wrap sandwiches in herb-garlic tortillas are fast becoming a favorite with the clientele. You can always find vegetarian fare here as well as espresso drinks and Italian sodas. The deli serves breakfast and lunch until early evening but has reduced hours on Sundays. During the summer it stays open for dinner Monday through Saturday. Either before or after you eat, be sure to check the boards in the entryway outside the door for notices about meetings and music events.

American Cuisine

Listed here you'll find restaurants and cafes that specialize in familiar foods such as steak, hamburgers, chicken, fish, and seafood. There's a Southern-style place that serves scrumptious barbecue, a 24-hour truck stop, and a brewpub, too. Some of these places are plain, some are fancy, but each has a definitive place in its community.

Northern Hills

Big Al's Buffalo Steak House $$
681 Main St., Deadwood
(605) 578-1300

This buckaroo-theme restaurant practically shouts "beef" and moos. This eating establishment at the back of the gaming hall serves prime rib as its special daily from 3:00 P.M. until 11 P.M. Open 24 hours, seven days a week, that's a lot of delicious beef served from the brick barbecue pit. You say you'd rather have breakfast today? Try the bacon and sausage to go with the pancakes and omelettes. Or how 'bout the steak, burgers, ribs, or chicken for lunch? And you want a beer or a glass of wine to go with that? Sure thing, partner. But hey, you, in the Stetson hat—No dancin' on the tables with yer spurs on.

Bob's Family Restaurant $$
1039 Main St., Sturgis
(605) 347-2930

A barbecue pit and the world-class pork ribs it produces aren't the only special features of Bob's Family Restaurant. It's also home to one of the nation's largest collections of hot sauces, and the hundreds of bottles neatly lined up around the main dining area's perimeter make a striking display. Except for those enclosed in cabinets as part of the permanent collection, diners can choose any of the sauces to liven up their meals. But forewarned is forearmed—some of these condiments are so hot they promise to deliver a near-death experience! Make sure you read the labels before applying any of the sauces to your food. That goes for breakfast, which is served all day, as well as lunch and dinner. The menu includes such hearty items as assorted skillet breakfasts, hotcakes, omelettes, pork chops, chicken-fried steak, sirloin tips, grilled chicken, and homemade coconut cream and banana cream pies. On Sundays you can treat yourself to brunch.

Regardless of where your booth or table is located, make it a point to view the 1880s photos of Sturgis hanging in the nicely furnished Heritage Room at the back. In the adjoining conference room is a large framed photo of local character Poker Alice, her trademark cigar clenched firmly in her mouth as she deals faro. The photo appeared in the December 3, 1927, edition of the *Saturday Evening Post,* and this print was made from the original negative, then hand-tinted. Also on display in the restaurant are some old bank drafts from early-day Sturgis businesses. The restaurant itself has been a fixture of the town for a good 50 years or more.

Historic Franklin Hotel $$$
700 Main St., Deadwood
(605) 578-1465, (800) 688-1876

The Franklin's 1903 Dining Room serves up a sumptuous menu that includes escargot, crab-stuffed mushrooms, honey-bourbon chicken, seafood fettuccine, and hand-cut, char-broiled steaks—consider the 16-ounce pork porterhouse or a rib eye topped with beer-battered onion rings. While your order is prepared you may want to sip a cocktail from the bar, admire the elaborate pressed-tin ceiling and embossed wallpaper, and mull over the list of famous folks who've stayed in the Franklin's guest rooms and suites (see our Accommodations chapter). After dinner and a dessert of carrot cake or bread pudding perhaps, you can wander around a bit to see Durty Nelly's Irish Pub and Callahan's Sports Bar (see our Nightlife chapter for more information) and check out the rare hand-operated elevator. On summer nights a piano player gives you a reason to linger in the dining room. Although dinner is the highlight here, the Franklin also serves breakfast and lunch (the hours vary in the winter) and a Sunday brunch buffet, and the restaurant caters to both smokers and nonsmokers.

Latchstring Inn Restaurant at Spearfish Canyon Resort $$$
U.S. 14A, Spearfish Canyon
(605) 584-3333

Pan-fried trout is the signature menu item at this beautiful log restaurant overlooking Spearfish Creek, and the management was generous enough to share the recipe with us. You'll find it, along with some fascinating background about this historic eatery, in the Close-up in this chapter.

We make it a point to stop at the Latchstring for a cold drink on the deck after summer bike rides through Spearfish Canyon, but you don't have to work that hard to enjoy a pleasant, leisurely meal in the restaurant's fabulous surroundings. Here it's equally lovely indoors and out because the dining room is decorated with enchanting antiques from the original Latchstring Inn (see the Close-up). Look around and you'll see a stalwart bobsled, a shaggy buffalo hide, dainty dishes, a prim pump organ, and much more. Plaques that accompany many of the displays provide a minitour through local history. In the evening, the electric lights are dimmed to enhance the romantic glow of kerosene lamps and candles. Every window offers a dazzling view of the canyon, and a bird book will help you identity the little creatures that frequent the feeder out back. But we digress.

For breakfast you can order trout, deep fried or pan fried (and with the head removed if you so request), along with eggs and hash browns or eggs and pancakes. Omelettes and other items also are available. For lunch, burgers (including buffalo burgers), sandwiches, and salads provide a hearty midday energy boost. Trout makes an encore appearance on the dinner menu, either pan fried, deep fried, or amandine to suit your preference. Walleye, shrimp, buffalo rib eye, beef steaks, and chicken prepared in a variety of ways are other choices. Beer and wine can accompany your meal, which you'll want to polish off properly with a slice of homebaked pie or a brownie sundae. Don't worry about the calories, because after you eat you can hike to Spearfish Falls or Roughlock Falls. Both are nearby, so ask for directions. And before you leave, ask about the bear on the limestone cliffs across the creek from the dining room. Reservations are recommended for dinner

at the Latchstring, where smokers and nonsmokers are welcome and parking is provided.

Prime Time Sports Grill $$
818 Fifth Ave., Belle Fourche
(605) 892-6666

With menu items such as Field of Dreams Burgers and Sideline Sandwiches, what sports fan wouldn't want to eat here? Prime Time has lots of other advantages for game buffs, too, as you'll see in our Nightlife chapter. But it's also won renown for its Rancher tenderloin tips, a specialty acquired from the once-famous (but now defunct) Rancher Bar and Lounge formerly in the nearby hamlet of St. Onge. Between the *Houston Chronicle* and the *Chicago Tribune*, Prime Time has been dubbed one of the nation's top 10 places to eat and its tenderloin tips called one of the most unique meals in the United States. However, you can also order 16-ounce steaks; steamed, grilled, or breaded fish and seafood; a veggie stir-fry; homemade soup; lemon-pepper chicken; buffalo burgers; salads and other tasty lunch and dinner items; plus root beer floats and ice-cream sundaes. Handcut meats, generous portions, and a full bar are hallmarks of Prime Time, and you'll enjoy the pub's atmosphere (take note of the hand-built oak bar) minus cigarette fumes, thanks to a state-of-the-art smoke-extraction system that lets smokers and nonsmokers share space comfortably. A Sunday breakfast buffet is also offered. There's plenty of seating here, so you won't need reservations unless you're in a party of 15 or more. In any case, it should be easy to find a space in the parking lot.

Sanford's Grub & Pub $$
545 W. Jackson Blvd., Spearfish
(605) 642-3204, (800) 504-6840

We could devote almost a whole chapter to the menu at Sanford's—it's that much fun. (See our Nightlife chapter for a description of the witty decor and more.) You don't even need to be a car buff to appreciate the automotive-repair-shop humor that went into naming the dishes served here (but it helps to know what

Black Hills Trout

Imagine a weary 1876 prospector laying down his tools at the end of another fruitless day, eyeing the sparkling stream that refused to make him wealthy, and reckoning that if he couldn't have a gold pan full of riches he'd just as soon have a frying pan full of fat, fresh trout. Unlike today's vacationer though, that unhappy fortune-seeker would have considered himself doubly unfortunate, because as recently as the Black Hills gold rush (see our History chapter), there were no trout in Black Hills streams. It wasn't until the 1880s that enterprising pioneers brought sloshing wagonloads of trout to this area, and, luckily for anglers ever since, the slippery swimmers took to our habitat like...well, like fish to water.

Anglers have come to the Black Hills in search of rainbows, browns, and brookies for more than a century now, and one of their favorite fishing spots has always been Spearfish Canyon. From the late 1800s until the 1930s, when a flood washed out the tracks, they would ride the Chicago, Burlington & Quincy Railroad to the canyon, fish all day, and take the train back to wherever they were staying. Or they might stay several days at Savoy, a bend in the canyon road between Spearfish and Cheyenne Crossing, where an inn has operated since the early twentieth century. At first it was called Glendoris Lodge, but in 1919 it became the Latchstring Inn, a cluster of rustic cabins and a restaurant that started as a lumber company office in 1892 and was added onto. For decades, cooks at the inn happily fried up trout caught in nearby streams by proud, hungry anglers.

But by 1989 the beloved Latchstring had aged beyond repair, and the owner, Judy Woodworth, sold it to Homestake Mining Co. Homestake razed the old buildings and put up a beautiful log structure that houses the new Latchstring Inn Restau-

Latchstring Inn Restaurant at Spearfish Canyon Resort serves pan-fried trout using a time-honored recipe. PHOTO: JERRY J. BOYER/SPEARFISH CANYON FOUNDATION

rant at Spearfish Canyon Resort (see the write-up in this chapter). In the restaurant are many antiques from the old Latchstring Inn, but another precious relic has been preserved as well: a simple recipe for pan-fried trout that dates back so far that no one, not even Woodworth, knows when it was first used in the Latchstring kitchen. Pan-fried trout is reported to be the most popular item on the menu even today, and the management graciously shared the recipe with us to pass along to you. The measurements are imprecise, but we found that only added to its charm and made us want to spell "recipe" the old fashioned way, "receipt." Here it is:

Latchstring Inn Pan-Fried Trout

Breadcrumbs
Italian seasoning to taste
A dash of paprika
A pinch each of parsley and rosemary
A touch of thyme
A sprinkle of sage
Seasoning salt and black pepper to taste
Flour
Egg
Vegetable oil

Combine breadcrumbs and seasonings. Filet the trout open. Dip in flour, then in beaten egg, then in seasoned crumbs. Pan fry in vegetable oil until the eyes turn white and pop out of the sockets. Serve at once and enjoy—but watch for bones!

(In case you're wondering whether the Latchstring Inn Restaurant serves trout caught from Spearfish Creek, which runs behind the restaurant, the answer is no. The entree on your plate came from a nearby trout farm.)

was popular on TV a couple of decades ago). For instance, a Thermostat is a half-pound burger with jalapeño peppers and mozzarella cheese. Fonz-a-Relli is the name for an Italian-style marinated chicken breast topped with shaved ham and mozzarella. Then there's the Dip Stick, a sliced roast beef sandwich au jus on a sourdough roll. The day we stopped in, 24 new menu items were about to be added to the already mind-boggling number of choices. In addition to burgers and sandwiches, you'll find appetizers (Tune Ups), homemade soups, Cajun food, pasta dishes, salads, steaks, shrimp, chicken, fajitas, meatless items, and rich desserts. And that's just the food—Sanford's has some 110-plus varieties of beer, most bottled but many on tap. (Be sure to ask about joining the Sanford's Hall of Foam.) You can also top off your tank

with wine, wine-based cocktails, and ice-cream drinks. Sanford's has smoking and nonsmoking sections. Getting here is a little confusing, though—turn where you see the Sanford's sign on Jackson Boulevard and look for the corrugated-metal building tucked away in the alley. You'll pass it on your left on your way to the parking lot, which is clearly marked. Sanford's is open from 11:00 A.M. to 10:00 P.M. every day, all year.

Stadium Sports Grill $$
744 Main St., Spearfish
(605) 642-9521

The Stadium serves up just the kind of food you want to accompany your favorite game. (Please see the Sportsbars section of our Nightlife chapter for information about the entertainment here.) Choose shrimp, raw veggies, onion rings, nachos, hot wings, burgers, sandwiches, salads, Indian tacos, steaks, chili, and more from the tabloid-size, newsprint menu, then read the sports pages while you wait for your lunch or dinner. The Stadium has a full-service bar as well as nonalcoholic beverages to go with your food.

Stampmill Restaurant & Saloon $$-$$$
305 W. Main St., Lead
(605) 584-1984

Back in gold-rush days, the local stamp mills kept up a steady pounding, pulverizing ore so the gold could be extracted. This restaurant in the heart of Black Hills gold-mining country pays tribute to the industry that created and has sustained the city of Lead for more than a century (see our History and Area Overview chapters). Fittingly, then, the Stampmill occupies an 1897 sandstone structure that is one of the oldest buildings in town.

Beautifully renovated by a previous owner, it features a brick and wood interior with high ceilings and a gas fireplace to warm those snowy winter nights in the Northern Hills. Breakfast is offered seasonally—call ahead to ask. Lunch items, named for some of the old stamp mills, are mainly burgers and sandwiches on homemade buns. For dinner, steaks cut from lean North Dakota beef plus shrimp and chicken dishes bear the names of former mining claims that became part of Homestake Mining Co.'s Open Cut. A full bar and dessert of the day, generally cheesecake or pie, add the finishing touches to your meal. Be sure to take a look at the old mining photos on the wall while you're waiting to be served. And by the way, the trophies on the wall were bagged by local hunters.

Valley Café $
608 Main St., Spearfish
(605) 642-2423

The Valley Cafe has been a Spearfish fixture since before 1921. The cafe's reputation rests largely on its hot beef sandwiches, chicken-fried steaks, and breakfasts. A breakfast buffet is served daily during the summer and on Satur-

Insiders' Tip

Gotta have chocolate? Go directly to Mostly Chocolates, 1511 Mt. Rushmore Road in Rapid City, (605) 341-2264. In addition to made-on-the-premises truffles and other sweets, you'll find a fine assortment of coffees, teas, and gift items. Be sure to stock up for Sundays, when the shop is closed.

days and Sundays the rest of the year. Lunch and supper buffets are available in summer. The regular menu ranges from old standbys such as omelettes and waffles to the more esoteric liver with bacon, onions, and gravy. Desserts include pies (ask which ones are homemade) and frozen yogurt from the TCBY counter. You can order a beer to go with your meal and choose to sit in either the smoking or nonsmoking section.

Central Hills

Art's Southern Style Smoke House Barbecue $$
609 Main St., Rapid City
(605) 348-5499

A mecca for barbecue devotees, Art's serves up a feast for the senses as well as tantalizing, down-home Southern food. The rich scent of Artis and Marilyn Holmses' homemade barbecue sauce combined with their choice of music—all blues, all the time—will surely satisfy your hunger for atmosphere. ("Blues and barbecue, they kind of go together," Marilyn told us. She ought to know—she and Artis are both from the deep South.) There's a lunch buffet daily that features meats swimming in barbecue sauce, but you can order from the menu too—pulled pork (shredded pork shoulder that's smoked until it falls apart, then smothered with sauce); zesty, Cajun-style red beans and rice; collard greens seasoned with smoked ham hocks; sweet corn-bread muffins; barbecued ribs and chicken; and home-made peach cobbler. You can also order meats in bulk to feed a crowd and a beer or wine cooler to wash down all that tasty sauce. A dinner buffet is offered on Thursdays, Fridays, and Saturdays. After placing your order, take a look at the posters on the walls—they're stunning black-and-white portraits of blues greats including Billie Holiday and a youthful B. B. King at age 16. Art's serves lunch and dinner every day but Sunday. Smoking is not allowed.

Chute Roosters $$
103 Chute Rooster Dr., Hill City
(605) 574-2122

Occupying an old dairy barn, Chute Roosters has plenty of country charm and friendly service. Horseshoe sculpture, a rope twister, a tapestry sidesaddle, and other antiques along the same theme decorate the stone-and-board walls, making this a cross between casual and fancy. That means you'll fit in whether attired in blue jeans or your Sunday best. That even goes for Sunday brunch (summer only), which features a huge buffet in the main dining room. Breakfast and lunch are served in the summers. The nightly dinner offerings consist mostly of steaks, burgers, prime rib, pasta, seafood, and chicken as well as a soup and salad bar. In the homey lounge you'll find a full bar serving cocktails, beer, and wine (see our Nightlife chapter). Smoking is permitted except in the Shebang Room, where a large mirrored back bar is the visual centerpiece. Chute Roosters, on the north end of Hill City, has plenty of parking. It is usually closed after Christmas until mid-February.

Elk Creek Steakhouse & Lounge $$-$$$
I-90 and Elk Creek Rd., Piedmont
(605) 787-6349

Western garb fits right in at this popular restaurant, and you'll see many customers enter the ranch-style building in their best hats and boots. Steaks and seafood are the main menu items, but the kitchen also cooks up such varied dishes as chicken Kiev and liver with onions and bacon. Steak sandwiches are a favorite here, according to the hostess, and are a bit less expensive than a full dinner. Don't overlook the buffalo rib eye and New York steaks, though, for a genuine taste of the Old West. The lounge has a full bar where you can order your beverage of choice. Elk Creek opens nightly for dinner, and reservations are recommended on weekends. The lounge opens at 1:00 P.M. on Sunday and will serve food. Take I-90 exit 46 and you'll be there.

Firehouse Brewing Company $$
610 Main St., Rapid City
(605) 348-1915

South Dakota's first brew pub isn't just about beer, although the 15 varieties made here (only a few available at a time) provide that many reasons to visit the Firehouse. (Please see our Nightlife chapter for more about that.) This is also an excellent place to stop if you're looking for a hearty, appetizing meal in memorable surroundings. As the name and phone number suggest, the restaurant occupies Rapid City's historic 1915 fire station, which is listed in the National Register of Historic Places. It also explains why you're greeted with the lower half of a (mock) firefighter in full regalia ready to slide down a gleaming brass pole in the bar area. Fire-fighting equipment of yore also is suspended near the high ceiling, and garage doors are still in place in the front of the building. There's seating for diners downstairs near the rectangular bar, but nonsmokers will want to climb the stairs to the mezzanine, where the brewing vats are on display behind giant windows.

The menu changes with the season, but the food is always filling and plentiful. Aside from the popular Reuben sandwich and Brewer's Burger, you might find the Fire Extinguisher, an eight-ounce rib eye steak cooked with or without Cajun spices, according to your taste, or the Backdraft, a bean-and-cheese-filled tortilla served with Spanish rice. When you're in the mood for just a beer or cocktail and a snack, you'll find Fire Fightin' Nachos (jalapeños optional) among the tasty appetizers. Or you might find that Gorgonzola ale soup, made with the pub's Wilderness Wheat brew, hits the spot. Be sure to sample the freshly baked beer bread, too, and maybe order a loaf (with 24-hour notice) to take home. And yes, you can buy beer by the half-gallon or gallon and, with 48-hour notice, the keg. The Firehouse is open for lunch and dinner Monday through Saturday. On Sunday, when it is open for dinner only, kids 12 and younger (one per family) eat for free.

The Fireside Inn Restaurant and Lounge $$$
23021 Hisega Rd., Hisega
(605) 342-3900

The inn takes its name from the 8-foot-square stone fireplace in the middle of the dining room, but it's not atmosphere alone that has made The Fireside a hit. The menu begins with a two-page wine list and progresses from there to some 50 or so dinner entrees. Prime rib is the house specialty, but beef, seafood, veal, pork, chicken, and pasta find their way into all manner of elegant dishes. To give you an idea, we'll mention Cajun rib eye, salmon en croute, chicken Wellington with tarragon cream sauce, crab-stuffed chicken, and the stuffed pork tenderloin that won a people's choice award in a statewide pork cookoff in 1997. Two salads are on the menu here; so are two vegetarian pasta dishes, and the kitchen can prepare other meatless entrees upon request. On Wednesday evenings cuts of prime rib are offered for a reduced price. Quality is prized here, which is why all steaks are hand-cut and why the sauté chef prepares sauces individually for each order. The full bar will fill your drink orders, and if you really must have dessert after all that good food, you'll find Chocolate Suicide and other cheesecakes at your disposal.

The Fireside serves dinner daily from 5:00 to 9:00 P.M. in the smoke-free dining room. The inn permits smoking in the lounge and provides parking for its clientele. Reservations are recommended for parties of six or more. The restaurant is 6 miles west of Rapid City on Highway 44.

The Gas Light $$$
13490 Main St., Rockerville
(605) 343-9276

The Gas Light merits a stop even if you're not hungry. Owners and antiques aficionados Dennis Kling and Westly Parker have gone beyond decorating to cast a nostalgic spell throughout their restaurant, soda fountain (see the listing in the Sweet Treats section later in this chapter) and antiques shop (read about that in our Shopping chapter). Every nook and cranny of the building has some delightful touch, be it an advertisement for an elixir of bygone days or a giant poster from an early-day blockbuster film. At Christmas time, Kling and Parker absolutely outdo themselves decorating the restaurant so that between the old-time ornaments and the cheerily burning woodstove, you're tempted to take up residence for the holidays.

You'd eat well, anyway. You could start with a cocktail, beer, or glass of wine at the bar, taking care to admire the century-old back bar from the former Harney Hotel in Rapid City. For an appetizer, you might try saloon-style nachos made with buffalo strips, then choose either a salad (chicken Waldorf for lunch, crab Louis for dinner, perhaps) or something more substantial. The lunch menu includes sandwiches and buffalo burgers, and dinner offers many choices in chicken, pasta, seafood, and steaks. A special list of "old world delights" such as Black Angus bourbon strip and chicken Oscar includes recommendations for the appropriate bottle of fine wine. For dessert order a rich concoction from the soda fountain. Cigarettes are allowed in the dining room, but pipes and cigars are not. The Gas Light is open daily for lunch and dinner as well as Sunday brunch between Memorial Day and Labor Day weekends. During the winter, meals are served Wednesday through Sunday except from late January to mid-April, when the owners take their much-needed vacation. The Gas Light, in the ghost town of Rockerville, is 12 miles south of Rapid City via U.S. 16. Reservations are recommended, and parking is plentiful.

Holy Smoke Restaurant & Lounge $$
U.S. 16A, Keystone
(605) 666-4616

The proprietors vow you won't find a deep-fat fryer or a can opener here, but we'll get to the food in just a minute. First we want to rave about the restaurant itself, which is an authentic log cabin with a Southwestern flair. The dining room features an adobe fireplace, a knotty pine floor and a center post that was cut and peeled right on the property. Mexican furniture and a beehive-shaped stucco-and-lathe fireplace invite you to enjoy a cocktail in the comfortable lounge. And who could resist the opportunity to dine al fresco on the deck on a warm summer evening? Back in the kitchen, hand-cut steaks, barbecued ribs, and homemade jellies and desserts are the Holy Smoke's culinary hallmarks. Chicken dishes and Mexican specialties are available, too. Smoking is allowed everywhere but in the dining room, and reservations are accepted for parties of six or more. The restaurant serves breakfast, lunch, and dinner daily from May 1 through September 30. It is 1.25 miles north of Keystone. Please turn to our Accommodations chapter for information about the Holy Smoke's cabins.

Horse Creek Inn $$$–$$$$
23570 U.S. 385, Rapid City
(605) 574-2908

If the topic were real estate, Horse Creek Inn would meet all three criteria: location, location, location. Not only is this quaint mid-twentieth-century cabin just a short drive from all the fun at Sheridan Lake (see our Recreation chapter), it has a horse pasture out back where you're likely to see deer and coyotes. Formerly known as Old Wheel Inn, the pine-interior restaurant and lounge has retained its rustic ambience and simple furnishings, making it a delightful place to enjoy some fine food. Beef—top sirloin and filets—are the most popular items here, but chicken, seafood, pork chops, and a couple of vegetarian dishes (fettuccine primavera and Oriental stir-fry) are available as well. You'll see them all listed on the hand-drawn and -lettered menus that are framed and propped up on easels in the dining room. Steaks are hand cut and can be ordered with Cajun spices, and you can request a hamburger or appetizer to eat in the lounge, where there's a full-service bar.

During the summer you can take your drink or sandwich out to the deck, although you won't actually be served there. Nightly specials are offered, and the soups, salads, and desserts (such as mud pie and German chocolate cake) are made on the premises. The inn is open daily for lunch and dinner from May through September, for lunch Saturday and Sunday all year, and for dinner Wednesday through Sunday the rest of the year. Reservations are recommended on weekends. Although there is no official nonsmoking area, people who are sensitive to smoke will be accommodated. The inn, with its own parking lot, is one-quarter-mile north of Sheridan Lake Road on U.S. 385, 18 miles west of Rapid City and 7 miles north of Hill City.

Insiders' Tip
If you see Rocky Mountain oysters on a restaurant menu and wonder what they are—well, ask your waitperson. All we'll tell you is that they're not seafood.

Powder House $$
U.S. 16A, Keystone
(605) 666-4646

You'll do more than dine at this well-known eatery—you'll be transported back to the time when a real powder house stored explosives for local mines. Built at the site of the original (the area was called Crossville then), the Powder House dishes up old-time Black Hills atmosphere in a log cabin furnished with pine-board tables and a working fireplace. The menu offers traditional Western fare such as steaks and buffalo stew but appeals to other palates as well. You can get an assortment of chicken and fish entrees, fettuccine primavera topped with feta cheese, or even a veggie burger. Full bar service provides you with the cocktail, beer, or wine of your choice. For dessert, the hostess recommends her personal favorite: Bourbon Street bread pudding accompanied by a cup of freshly ground coffee. The Powder House, which is a mile north of town, is open for breakfast (trout and eggs, anyone?), lunch, and dinner, seven days a week from mid-May until September 30. Reservations are recommended for dinner during the summer. Smoking is not permitted in the dining room. Parking is provided.

Ruby House Restaurant $$
126 Winter St., Keystone
(605) 666-4404

Step through the door and find yourself enveloped in Victorian elegance, Old West style. To your left is the Red Garter Saloon, where you can order drinks from waitresses in period costumes (and we don't mean hoop skirts). To your right, the dining room dazzles with liberal splashes of red and gold amid old photos, fine-art prints, and other antique furnishings (the slightly worn, velvety curtains are from an old movie theater). In the nonsmoking War Eagle Room, a Native American motif prevails with buffalo hides and intricate beadwork. The cuisine is appropriate to the setting, with plenty of hearty meats and sauces. Buffalo steak, elk medallions with huckleberry sauce, pork chops, and smoked prime rib are

among the dinner entree selections, but there's lighter fare as well. The Ruby House serves breakfast, lunch, and dinner between mid-April and mid-October, depending on the weather, and reservations are accepted.

Shooters Restaurant & Sports Bar $$
2424 W. Main St., Rapid City
(605) 348-3348

Warning: Parental permission is required for the hottest of Shooters' famous hot wings. The menu even says so. You're allowed to order spicy chicken wings mild, hot, or thermonuclear on your own, but you need a note from your mother to go all the way to extreme. Not to worry, though, because Shooters has plenty of other menu offerings, from appetizers, soups, and salads to wrap sandwiches, burgers, steaks, ribs, chicken, Southwestern fare, pasta, and stir-fries. You can also choose from a large selection of beers, cocktails, premium wines, and single-malt scotches. Desserts include homemade cheesecake and peanut butter pie. What's more, four satellites bring the wide world of sports to Shooters' 11 TV sets. The clientele includes people of all ages, from 8 to 80, according to the manager, and you can find a table for up to 12 or 15. Shooters accommodates both smokers and nonsmokers and provides ample parking.

Tally's Restaurant $
530 Sixth St., Rapid City
(605) 342-7621

The same family has owned and operated this popular gathering place for more than half a century. Located in the heart of downtown Rapid City, Tally's serves breakfast and lunch to a loyal clientele every day but Sunday, when it's closed. Pancakes made from a secret recipe are a breakfast specialty here, but crepes, huevos rancheros, fluffy omelettes, and breakfast burritos are tempting choices, too. For lunch, hot sandwiches, burgers (including buffalo), prime beef dip, a chicken pita, or brats and 'kraut with homemade potato salad vie for your order. On Friday chicken and dumplings are the main attraction. Soups and pies are homemade, and meats are cut from whole roasts for top quality. You won't find a place to smoke, but you will get a good meal. No credit cards are accepted.

The Windmill Restaurant $$
2803 Deadwood Ave., Rapid City
(605) 342–9456

If you're a fan of truck-stop food, this is your kind of place. And it's open 24 hours a day, ready to get your order from the kitchen to the table in five minutes no matter what time hunger strikes. Breakfast is available around the clock, and the truckers' specials (various meat and egg combinations) come with a choice of toast, biscuits, or cake. You'll also find satisfying hot and cold sandwiches, burgers, fried foods, Indian tacos, John's homemade meat loaf, barbecued ribs, a soup and salad bar, and ice-cream treats on the menu. If you like, try the Friday and Saturday evening buffet or the Saturday and Sunday breakfast buffet. Beer and wine are available, and both smokers and nonsmokers will find a comfortable place to sit. As you can imagine, there's plenty of parking. Take 1–90 exit 55 and you can't miss this place—just look for the big windmill.

Southern Hills

Blue Bell Lodge & Resort $$
Hwy. 87, Custer State Park, Custer
(605) 255–4531

The last guy to criticize the bartender here is still hanging in the resort's Buffalo Wallow Lounge. However, we feel safe saying you won't find much to criticize here at Blue Bell, either in the saloon-style lounge (with a full bar) or the family-style Tatanka Dining Room. Tatanka means "buffalo" in Lakota, so expect to find plenty of menu items based on that wild game, from steak to meat loaf. In fact, the smell of buffalo leather emanating from the cushy lobby furnishings greets you the minute you enter. You'll also find trout, catfish, and other entrees, but no matter what you order, everything comes to the table in big bowls so you can serve

yourself, just like at home. You'll have to refrain from smoking (or we'll tell the bartender).

The Blue Bell complex (see our Accommodations chapter for lodging information) on the west side of Custer State Park takes its name from the Bell Telephone symbol, honoring the phone company executive who built Blue Bell in the 1920s. This is also the departure point for Blue Bell's chuck wagon cookouts, which you can read about in our Attractions chapter. You can park for the restaurant right outside.

Elk Horn Café $$
310 S. Chicago St., Hot Springs
(605) 745–6556

We knew this was not a run-of-the-mill cafe when the glass of water we'd ordered came with a lemon wedge perched on the side and a straw. And although the menu has a traditional selection of sandwiches, burgers, steaks, salads, and fried side orders, there's more homemade food here than you might expect. Popular items include the Dakota steak sandwich, flavored with a special blend of spices. Fried fish is dipped in batter just before cooking, and the chef makes his own pizza dough. Smoked ribs, seafood-stuffed tomatoes, and a fresh-looking salad bar also are among the many lunch and dinner choices, and you may order breakfast any time. You can get a "barley pop" (beer) to go with your meal and a slice of homemade carrot cake for dessert. Smoking is prohibited in the cafe but allowed on the deck when fair-weather outdoor dining is offered. If it's your birthday, ask to join the Birthday Club and get a discount.

Red Rock Café $$–$$$
102 S. Chicago, Hot Springs
(605) 745–4093 (summer only)

Red Rock Café is receiving a reputation as one of the best places to visit in the Black Hills. Not only do owners Evan, Jean, Neal, and Ola Christensen provide a great atmosphere, they also offer fine food and live entertainment. To quote from their menu write-up, the café is "An Unexpected Delight!"

As you might guess, the place takes its name from the red rock cliffs in the area. It is housed in a historic, 100-year-old building and tastefully decorated to reflect its heritage. There is even a gallery, with works by local artists. Offerings include live music during lunch and dinner and an occasional dinner theater. And, can you believe, "Sunday High Tea" is served periodically from noon to 3:00 P.M.!

The menu is extensive, from appetizers (fresh veggies to smoked salmon), soups of the day, spinach salad, Caesar salad, five varieties of sandwiches, burgers and grilled chicken sandwiches, several pasta entrees, and steaks and seafood. A kid's menu is available for the twelve and under group. You can choose from a large beverage menu and the café prides itself on having one of the finest loose tea selections in the Black Hills. Beer, wine, and espresso are also available. If you dare to eat more, desserts include Affagado, cheesecakes, and an assortment of ice cream. Red Rock Café is open Monday through Saturday from 11:00 A.M. to 10:00 P.M. from May until the end of August.

Seven Sisters Steak House $$–$$$
Hwy. 18, Truck-by-Pass, Hot Springs
(605) 745–6666
www.blackhillsbadlands.com/sevensisters

Co-owners Pam Brekke and her mother, Charlene Maxwell, are justifiably proud of and excited by their restaurant. For one thing, it boasts the largest arched windows ever manufactured in the United States. All seats are window seats and overlook the Seven Sisters Mountain range. The lovely cathedral ceiling adds to the ambience of the dining room. A deck lounge seating 50 is open in the warmer weather, and additional dining seating is available downstairs in the lounge, which offers a full-service bar.

The lunch menu includes steaks, grilled chicken, burgers, beef French dip, and buffalo burgers. For dinner choose from a variety of steaks, chicken, pasta, seafood linguini, walleye, salmon, and shrimp. A Sunday brunch is served from 10:00 A.M. to 2:00 P.M. Gaming—such as pool, darts, and South Dakota lottery machines—is available in the lounge. Seven Sisters is open during the summer from Tuesday through Sunday, 11:00 A.M. to 10:00 P.M. and in the winter from Tuesday through Saturday, 11:00 A.M. to 9:00 P.M.

State Game Lodge $$$
U.S. 16 A, Custer State Park, Custer
(605) 255–4541

Welcome to the dining room of American presidents. Both Calvin Coolidge and Dwight Eisenhower took meals in the State Game Lodge's Pheasant Dining Room during their presidencies. In fact, the table in the northwest corner is still referred to as the Eisenhower table, the one where Ike could sit and see all his guests. Just as you'd expect, game is the specialty here, so buffalo, venison, and the South Dakota state bird, pheasant, figure prominently on the menu. You might begin your meal with pheasant sauté or buffalo ribs, then progress to filet of venison sautéed with garlic and topped with mushrooms on wild rice. Or perhaps you'd be interested in marinated, sautéed ringneck pheasant breast topped with plum brandy sauce. If fish is your game, you might prefer a flavorful walleye pike or rainbow trout. Lunch features a deli-style sandwich buffet, buffalo stew, elk burgers, and other items. Chocolate Thunder—fresh brownies layered with vanilla ice cream and hot fudge—is a fitting dessert tribute to the thundering herd of buffalo for which Custer State Park is famous (see our Parks and Grasslands chapter).

The dining room is on the lodge's second level, but downstairs you'll find a lounge with a bar and a welcoming fireplace. Be sure to take note of the lodge's blueprints on the wall as you descend the stairs to the lower-level gift shop. Reservations are recommended for dinner in the smoke-free game lodge, which is open from Mother's Day until early October. Parking is available at the lodge in the northeastern quadrant of the park.

The immensely popular State Game Lodge in Custer State Park offers jeep rides and chuckwagon suppers as well as lodging and dining. PHOTO: COURTESY OF SOUTH DAKOTA TOURISM

Eclectic Cuisine

The restaurants listed here serve an array of dishes that cross many culinary borders. They often have a good selection of vegetarian offerings, and in fact, you'll see that we've even included a vegan eatery. But extraordinary meat dishes are on many of these menus, too. You'll find yourself faced with a number of enticing choices and the prospect of a memorable meal once you decide where to eat.

Northern Hills

The Bay Leaf Café $$
126 W. Hudson St., Spearfish
(605) 642–5462

The menu describes the cafe's rosemary linguine this way: "Oh sigh. Oh heavy sigh." We suspect a few sighs of delight will have escaped your lips even before you see the menu, though, because The Bay Leaf itself is a collection of lovely architectural features. Right off you'll notice the beveled, stained-glass window in the front door and the ceramic tile floor. The regional artists' works you see hanging on the walls will still be there after you've decided what to eat, so take your time perusing the menu. If you're not familiar with some of the items—for instance, babaghanouj, a Mediterranean eggplant dip—you'll find the "Speaking Bay Leaf" glossary at the back of the menu handy.

Entrees run the gamut from trout amandine, elk, and buffalo London broil to tempeh with sautéed vegetables and Cajun-style Bourbon Street pasta plus ever-changing daily specials. Beer and wine are available, and after your meal an espresso drink, Italian soda, or herbal tea goes well with the rich, chocolaty homemade desserts. The food here is completely MSG-free and largely preservative-free as well. And in keeping with the emphasis on health, smoking is not permitted. The Bay Leaf serves lunch and dinner daily during the summer, and because that's an especially busy time of year, it's a good idea to call ahead and ask whether reservations are needed. The cafe is closed on Sunday from early October until Memorial Day weekend.

Jakes Atop the Midnight Star $$$$
677 Main St., Deadwood
(605) 578–3656, (800) 999–6482

You just can't help feeling glamorous when you dine at Jakes. Although you're not likely to rub elbows with the glitterati here (but it's not impossible, either), just knowing this splendid restaurant was created by Hollywood celebrity Kevin Costner and his brother, Dan, lends panache to the evening. Jakes opens each night for dinner on the top floor of the 1879 Phoenix Building, Deadwood's first brick structure—and the only building in town that had a three-story privy out back (demolished in the 1940s). The Deadwood City Council held its first meeting in this space in 1881, but it's doubtful the early-day city leaders had as much fun as you will in this lofty chamber of cherry, mahogany, and double-lead crystal. (The original third floor was torn off several decades ago because of damage from a leaky roof, but the Costners' replacement is architecturally faithful.) With its tall windows and domed skylight, this is an exciting place to be during a summer thunderstorm, but you don't need a taste for thrills to appreciate the amenities. A propensity for stellar cuisine will do you just fine, because there's plenty of that at Jakes.

Begin with a tasty appetizer such as artichoke hearts asiago, garlic and chili smoked shrimp, or tenderloin in cracked mustard. After your salad, let the lemon sorbet intermezzo, served on a lemon leaf, cleanse your palate for full enjoyment of your entree—walleye with macadamia nuts, honey-glazed shrimp, a 16-ounce grilled pork porterhouse steak with brandied pear sauce, steak fillets, or our own favorite, Cajun seafood tortellini. These are just a few of the selections from the menu, which varies a bit every few months. What remains constant is the elegance of the food, including handmade

Diners enjoy the elegant atmosphere at Jakes restaurant on the top floor of the Midnight Star, a three-story Deadwood casino owned by actor Kevin Costner. PHOTO: COURTESY OF DEADWOOD CHAMBER AND VISITORS BUREAU

desserts—when we talked to the chef recently, a macadamia white chocolate cheesecake was in progress in the kitchen. The luxury of two fireplaces, a full bar, and live piano music Tuesday through Saturday are the final exquisite touches. Because this is a popular place, reservations are recommended. Smoking is allowed here but please, no pipes or cigars. Jakes is open daily for dinner.

The Midnight Star has a sports bar, Diamond Lil's, which serves lighter fare, and you'll find it listed in our Nightlife chapter.

Central Hills

Alpine Inn $$
225 Main St., Hill City
(605) 574-2749

For dinner you have your choice of filet mignon or filet mignon—that is, you may order the six-ounce filet or the nine-ounce, depending on the size of your appetite. For such a small menu, this restaurant in the 1886 quarters of the former Harney Peak Hotel has a big reputation and a loyal clientele. Those who want more variety wait for dessert, when there are some 30 selections, including homemade Austrian apple strudel and bread pudding. Or they come here for lunch, which features a good choice of sandwiches served with Schwabian German potato salad. Hearty bratwurst and knackwurst are on the menu but so is more delicate fare such as a turkey croissant Parisienne, a cheese board, and a garden platter. Beer, wine, and Viennese coffee with chocolate and whipped cream are among the beverages served. Reservations are not accepted, but if your party has eight or more people, call ahead and the staff will do its best to make space available for you. Smoking is allowed only in the lounge. The inn is closed on Sunday. When it's nice out you can eat on the veranda (assuming there's a free table!), but if you eat indoors be sure to note the hotel's original wooden banister on the staircase and the sturdy old safe beneath the cash register. Credit cards are not accepted.

> ## Insiders' Tip
>
> You can buy artisanal breads baked fresh daily at Wheat Berries Natural Bakery, 2130 Jackson Boulevard, Rapid City, (605) 342-2232. It's open Monday through Saturday. Stop in just for the smell of it!

Rushmore Supper Club & Lounge $$–$$$
253 Swanzey St., Keystone
(605) 666–4501

This popular restaurant, formerly called the Historical Rushmore Grill & Bar, is a block and a half east of "The Strip" (Winter Street, the town's main drag) in Keystone, but its reputation for authentic, made-from-scratch Mexican food draws hungry crowds in search of the cook's famous fajitas and other specialties served in heaping portions for lunch and dinner. Cajun blackened prime rib is also on the menu, and so are half-pound buffalo and beef burgers, steaks, Cajun chicken sandwiches, and shrimp and taco salads, to name a few of the choices. A So-Sweet Burrito filled with apple and pineapple pie filling, deep fried and garnished with ice cream, three toppings, whipped cream, and a cherry is among dessert choices, although it could pose as a meal in itself. The bar—note the ornate, century-old back bar from a long-ago Custer watering hole—serves highly regarded margaritas frozen, blended, or on the rocks, as well as beer, wine, and other cocktails. After many years of operation, the restaurant moved into larger quarters and added a sports bar in the basement. There's also a covered deck for outdoor dining. During the summer when it's busy, reservations are recommended for parties of seven or more.

GREAT FACES

Aunt Sally

Sarah Campbell called herself "the first white woman that ever saw the Black Hills." But anyone who knew jolly "Aunt Sally" must have chuckled upon hearing that. For Aunt Sally was African-American, and we can assume she meant she was the first non-Native American woman in the Hills.

Aunt Sally arrived here with the gold-seeking expedition led by Lt. Col. George Custer in 1874, which you can read about in our History chapter. The only woman to go along on the trip, she had hired on as a cook for John Smith, a civilian trader who sold food, spirits, and other goods to the soldiers. After engineer Horatio Ross found sparkling flecks of gold in French Creek, a young newspaper reporter who had accompanied the excursion, William Curtis, interviewed the corpulent, well-liked cook for the *Chicago Inter-Ocean*. Curtis affectionately called her "a huge mountain of dusky flesh" and reported that she was more excited than anyone else about finding gold.

After all, Aunt Sally had left her comfortable home in Bismarck, North Dakota, and undertaken the journey for the sole purpose of seeing the Black Hills. Curtis quoted her saying, "I'se heered 'bout dese here hills long 'fore Custer did." Perhaps surprised to find that the Hills were in fact green rather than black, Aunt Sally apparently decided bright yellow was her favorite color and lost no time in filing a mining claim—illegally, we might add. The expedition was soon on its way again, but not before Aunt Sally had decided to return to the Black Hills at the first opportunity.

And return she did, although just when is not known. In time she filed a new claim at Elk Creek in Lawrence County and lived nearby, befriending her pioneer neighbors. They appreciated her cooking and midwifery skills, enjoyed her amusing anecdotes and tall tales, and took her pipe smoking in stride. At some point Aunt Sally reportedly adopted a 10-year-old white orphan boy, whom she had found crying in the street in Deadwood.

Aunt Sally lived to a ripe old age for her day. When she died on April 13, 1888, she was in her mid-70s. With fondness and respect, her friends laid her to rest on Vinegar Hill west of Galena, an old silver-mining district in Lawrence County. Flattering obituaries appeared in two local newspapers, acknowledging her stature in the community. Though gone, Aunt Sally was never to be forgotten, and today the simple wooden marker that first graced her grave is on view in the Adams Museum in Deadwood (see our Attractions chapter).

Tiffany Grille $$$
505 N. Fifth St., Rapid City
(605) 348-4000

This elegant restaurant, lushly decorated with live greenery, is in the spacious atrium lobby of the Rushmore Plaza Holiday Inn. The serving day begins with traditional breakfasts accompanied by a cappuccino cart on weekdays; on Sundays the brunch buffet features a pastry bar and made-to-order omelettes. At midday you can order a fine lunch of a croissant sandwich; a turkey club on a spinach wrapper; a Reuben, chef, or Caesar chicken salad; vegetarian lasagna; or something equally delicious. Dinnertime is when the kitchen pulls out all the stops, however. That's when you can dine on Plaza Portobello, a heady concoction of Portobello mushrooms, grilled sweet red onions, herbs, cheeses, tomatoes, a splash of white wine, and penne pasta. Equally tempting are the rib eye steaks, fillets of beef, Key West chicken breast with a blend of Caribbean spices and pineapple salsa, almond walleye, pork medallions, the herb-crusted orange roughy filet, or roasted-vegetable lasagna. While you're waiting for your order, you might ready your palate with crab-stuffed mushrooms with Mornay sauce. All of the breads are homemade, as are some of the pies you'll see grouped with Chocolate Obsession Cake and other rich offerings on the dessert tray. Tiffany Grille has a full bar, both smoking and nonsmoking areas, and plenty of parking. Groups of 10 or more should make a reservation.

Veggies $
2050 W. Main St. No.7, Rapid City
(605) 348-5019
Besides feeding you, this vegan restaurant's mission is to introduce you to the joys and health benefits of a completely plant-based diet. And because the owners want you to eat that way at home, they offer cooking classes several times a year; please ask for information.

Open for seven years in the same location, success is part of the menu. The food here, served buffet-style, is always tasty and freshly made from an impressive variety of ingredients. The main entree changes daily, but you can always count on finding mock chicken salad sandwiches (made from tofu), veggie wraps, and veggie burgers. Four or more fresh salads with homemade dressings make up the side dishes, and delicious, freshly baked whole wheat bread is included with your meal. Beverages consist of freshly squeezed juices, filtered water, and bottled juice spritzers. Desserts vary but always include vegan ice cream and baked goods. About half the floor space is devoted to Final Harvest, the owners' natural foods store, so you can shop for your own kitchen after enjoying a meal prepared in theirs. Veggies serves lunch and an early dinner Monday through Thursday and only lunch on Friday and Sunday; it's closed on Saturday. As you would expect, smoking is not part of the picture. Parking is available.

Southern Hills

Katz Kafe $
603 N. River St., Hot Springs
(605) 745-6005
The "Katz" in the name is a quirky reference to Queen Victoria's love of feline pets. You won't find any furry, four-legged tabbies here though, just lots of superb food served in a quaint Victorian chamber dressed in mauve, gold, and lace. Three rooms are available for rent upstairs, decorated in turn-of-the-twentieth-century trappings.

Lunch features three or four varieties of homemade soup; an array of imaginative sandwiches, including a veggie combo on your choice of sourdough or dark rye bread; and several salads. Ask about daily specials, too.

Smoking is not allowed anywhere in this restored 1891 building, which is one example of local efforts to preserve Hot Springs' architectural heritage; you can read more about that in the Close-up in our Attractions chapter. After you eat, check out the nifty thrift store, Huckleberry's Cheap Frills, adjacent to the cafe. The cafe is closed on Saturday and Sunday.

Sylvan Lake Resort $$$-$$$$
Hwy. 87, Custer State Park, Custer
(605) 574-2561
The first hotel on Sylvan Lake was built in 1895, just six years after the lake itself.

Insiders' Tip
Although red wine is meant to be served at room temperature, some Black Hills bartenders keep it chilled and even serve it (or any wine) on the rocks. If you're particular, it's a good idea to ask before you order.

Unfortunately, a fire destroyed the popular Victorian-style inn in 1935, but its replacement opened just two years later. Today stone-columned Sylvan Lake Resort hosts Custer State Park's most elegant restaurant, the Lakota Dining Room. Dinner specials the night we stopped in included bacon-wrapped elk tenderloin, sautéed calamari with red chili pasta, and grilled orange roughy with creamed crab. Beef fajitas with guacamole, buffalo steak, grilled Black Hills trout, and South Dakota ring-neck pheasant also were on the menu. On this same late-summer evening diners were relaxing on the stone veranda that overlooks the quiet lake, chatting and sipping cocktails from the bar. The resort, which is in the northwestern-most corner of the park, serves breakfast, lunch, and dinner daily from mid-May until late September. Smoking is prohibited as it is in all state-owned buildings. Parking is provided.

Ethnic Cuisine

Here, we've grouped Asian, German, Italian, and Mexican restaurants to help you satisfy your craving for food from a particular part of the world. Even among those that serve the same kind of cuisine, we found differences in the menus. That means each one has something all its own to offer, so read the listings carefully. Be sure to check the Eclectic listings above as well, because many of those places serve a wide range of ethnic dishes.

Northern Hills

ChinaTown Café $$
649 Main St., Deadwood
(605) 578-7778

Chinese immigrants played an important role in early-day Deadwood, and this restaurant honors their contribution to local history. Your order is prepared individually from fresh ingredients and seasoned to your taste while you sip tea or a beer or wine-based cocktail from the bar. Lunch and dinner feature many standard Chinese favorites, from egg rolls and wonton soup to chop suey, chow mein, fried rice, and sweet-and-sour chicken, shrimp, or pork. However you'll also find plenty of more complex dishes such as Szechwan beef, walnut shrimp, orange-flavored chicken, and two kinds of war ba served on sizzling platters. Daily luncheon specials offer a choice of sweet-and-sour pork or another dish. Although you'll probably be focused on your meal, you'll want to notice the graceful Chinese lanterns and unusual circular seating arrangement here. ChinaTown accommodates nonsmokers as much as possible, so be sure to state your preference. The restaurant is on the second floor of Miss Kitty's gaming hall.

Consuelo's Cantina $$
649 Main St., Deadwood
(605) 578-2828

You'll think you've arrived in sunny Mexico when you step inside Consuelo's. Located on the main floor of Miss Kitty's gaming hall, this brightly decorated, hospitable cafe prides itself on its use of fresh foods. Everything is made from scratch except the tortillas. The lunch and dinner menu ranges from quesadillas and nachos to Tex-Mex plates and fajitas. Fajita a la Barry, topped with wine-butter sauce and pico de gallo—a zingy, fresh-veggie relish—is the most popular dish here, according to the manager, but be sure to ask about the daily specials. Along with the food, beer, and wine-based margaritas, you'll enjoy the turquoise shutters, the windows that look out on painted scenery, the chile pepper ristras, and the pots of flowers—all fake, but all delightful. Adding to the fun are piped-in Spanish renditions of popular songs you'll recognize. Reservations are recommended on weekends and holidays. Consuelo's is closed on Monday during the winter.

Deadwood Social Club $$$
657 Main St., Deadwood
(605) 578–1533, (605) 578–3346

Nestled atop the internationally famous Old Style Saloon No. 10, the Deadwood Social Club offers an astonishing wine selection and outstanding service in addition to excellent food. The kitchen specializes in northern Italian cuisine with selections that feature appetizing chicken, seafood, and meatless dishes, all made from scratch with fresh ingredients. While you peruse the menu, your server will bring you a basket of fragrantly irresistible herb foccacia and, if you wish, a beverage from the full bar. The restaurant, with its high-backed wooden booths and charmingly eclectic ambience, has also established a reputation for heavenly cheesecakes, which are made on the premises. You won't merely eat, you'll bask in your lunch or dinner experience any day but Monday. Reservations are recommended.

Central Hills

B.J.'s Grinder King $
902 Main St., Rapid City
(605) 348–3166

Co-owner Bruce Meister is adamant about the food that comes out of his kitchen, which is why B.J.'s has a reputation for fabulous sandwiches and pizzas. First of all, his grinders are just that—they're grinders, not subs. So expect olive oil rather than mustard or mayo on your sandwich (with an exception or two—ask when you order). And don't look for mozzarella, Swiss, or any other unbecoming cheeses, because only provolone belongs on a grinder. The bread, although not made on the premises, is preservative-free, and Meister's staff uses shredded cabbage instead of lettuce. The filling, however, is up to you, and you can choose from a variety of meats (turkey is the best seller), tuna, or eggplant. Meister's Italian-Portuguese wife and business partner, Joan, makes the meatballs from her father's recipe, using a family-secret blend of spices. For the deep-dish pizzas, Meister stuffs the Italian sausage himself, using very lean meat so you won't find puddles of fat atop your pie. The sauce, too, is homemade, and all meats are fresh, not-packaged pizza toppings. Crowning your pizza is a distinctive white cheddar cheese, or white cheddar with mozzarella on the vegetarian special. Meister's own three-cheese blend provides a base for white pizzas.

B.J.'s advertises New England–style grinders and pizza, but you can take that to mean Greek-style. As Meister explains, once you get out of the Italian neighborhoods back east, you find the pizza shops are run by people of Greek descent. Lucky for us, because that's where the Meisters got their inspiration. Bruce Meister even quizzed us on some New England grinder lore: Where was the first grinder sold to the public in the United States? (We flunked—New London, Connecticut, in 1926.) But there's one more thing about which Meister is adamant: "If I don't like it, you don't find it here," he told us with a hearty laugh. Well, you won't find us complaining.

To our unremitting disappointment, B.J.'s closes on Sunday and from Christmas Eve until February 1 each year. Otherwise it's open for lunch and dinner, and parking is provided. Smoking is not permitted. No credit cards are accepted.

Botticelli Ristorante Italiano $$$
523 Main St., Rapid City
(605) 348–0089

Why pay for plane tickets when you can take a virtual trip to northern Italy by simply walking through the door of this captivating restaurant? From the Old World decor and Italian background music to the authentic cuisine, you'll lose yourself in the ambience. Although good service makes it possible to eat a delicious lunch here (Monday through Saturday only) and still get back to the office on time, we tend to linger and ignore the ticking of the clock. Someday we'll probably come here for lunch and end up staying for dinner, too, which is also served on Sunday from 5:00 to 9:00 P.M. But why not? The extensive menu has so many tempting meat and meatless dishes we'd like to try them all eventually.

Before our meal arrives we indulge in some freshly baked bread, dipping it in aromatic herbed olive oil. We consider this our appetizer, but antipasti, soup, and salads are available as well. For lunch, entree selections include a variety of small pizzas with assorted meats, vegetables, herbs, and cheeses; sandwiches served on focaccia; pasta dishes including ravioli, fettuccine, and lasagna; chicken prepared in various ways; plus steak and fish. The dinner menu exchanges sandwiches for more chicken, veal, and seafood dishes. A fine wine or Italian beer adds a truly continental touch to your meal, which is further improved when polished off with a stout espresso beverage and extravagant tiramisu—lady fingers soaked in rum sauce, topped with mascarpone cream cheese, espresso syrup, and ground chocolate. Mama mia! Botticelli's is nonsmoking, and reservations are gladly accepted.

Great Wall Restaurant $$
315 E. North St., Rapid City
(605) 348–1183

You'll find several varieties of Oriental food here, such as Cantonese Triple Delicacy Pan

Fried Noodles, Mandarin-style sesame beef, Szechwan beef Taiwanese Happy Family, and Shanghai-style minced lobster with pine nuts. Those are a few of the house specialties, and you'll find tried-and-true lunch and dinner favorites on the menu as well, such as egg drop soup, chow mein, broccoli beef, almond chicken, and sweet and sour shrimp. You can also get vegetarian meals here, and there's never any MSG added to your food during cooking. Subdued lighting and a saltwater fish tank create a somewhat mysterious mood in the dining area, which accommodates both smokers and nonsmokers. Beer and wine are available. Reservations are recommended for five or more people. Parking is provided right outside the door.

Hunan $$
1720 Mt. Rushmore Rd., Rapid City
(605) 341–3888

A huge menu is just the beginning at this popular Chinese restaurant. The health-conscious will be pleased to know that the food here is MSG-free, and that special low-fat, sugar-free, and salt-free dishes are available. The regular menu includes everything from egg rolls and wonton soup to a Peking duck so elaborate it must be ordered 24 hours in advance. Although beef, pork, seafood, and vegetarian selections are offered in abundance, chicken—hot and spicy or sweet and sour—seems to be a favorite with guests. Beer and wine can accompany your meal, and cheesecake or litchi nuts (a Chinese fruit) can be your dessert. Please take note of the magnificent photos in the entryway and behind the cash register, which are the work of owner Robert Wong, a native of China. We're sure you'll be impressed, not only by his skill as a photographer but also by the many ribbons, medals, and trophies he has won for his breathtaking images. The prizes are on display in a cabinet in the restaurant. Smoking is prohibited at Hunan. Ample parking is provided. Hunan is open for lunch and dinner.

La Costa $$
603 Omaha St., Rapid City
(605) 388–8780

This south-of-the-border-style restaurant has built its reputation on fajitas and fast service while preparing food the old-fashioned way, from scratch. That means tomatoes and peppers for your complimentary salsa are roasted each morning, and the tamales are encased in real cornhusks. You'll find all your Mexican favorites here, along with seafood, combination plates, and weekday lunch specials. Popular entrees from the menu include fajitas, costenas with char-broiled beef or chicken accompanied by sautéed shrimp and crab, and char-broiled carne asada steak. The sopapillas topped with honey, cinnamon sugar, and whipped cream get rave reviews for dessert. You can order beer, including several Mexican varieties, and wine with your meal. La Costa is open for lunch and dinner seven days a week. And there's always a pre-meal bonus, because in addition to the obligatory homemade chips and salsa, your waitperson will bring refried beans to your table. Seating is set aside for both smokers and nonsmokers, and reservations are recommended for groups of more than 10. Ample parking is provided.

Piesano's Pacchia $–$$
3618 Canyon Lake Dr., Rapid City
(605) 341–6941

Don't be fooled by the amusing play on paisano, the Italian word for friend. Piesano's takes pacchia—Italian for good food and drink—very seriously. Everything is homemade, starting with the cinnamon rolls (with and without pecans) that come out of the oven every morning in time for the 8:00 A.M. coffee crowd. Piesano's attracts a loyal clientele with scrumptious gourmet pizzas—sweet-and-sour cashew chicken is popular, but you can also order chicken Bar-B-Q, healthful vegetable, Happy Hawaiian, and more conventional varieties including primo, with the works. New combinations, such as bratwurst-and-sauerkraut and a breakfast pizza appear from time to time. Pizzas are created on hand-tossed dough made fresh daily, and we're told that the owners are so fussy they follow the wheat crop to make sure they get top-quality flour. Pizzas come in four sizes, including

an 8-inch noon special; other choices include sub sandwiches, salads (with hand-torn lettuce), and special meals such as calzones on Tuesday, lasagna (with meat or meatless) on Wednesday, prime rib subs on Thursday, and Italian chicken breast subs on Friday. And for dessert there's homemade chocolate-marble cheesecake. ("We do take the calories out," we were told. Right—and we're Sophia Loren's hairdressers.) It was no surprise to us to learn that the *Black Hills Restaurant Guide* named Piesano's the best local pizza establishment several years in a row. You can have a bottled or draft beer with your meal, but not a smoke. Featuring homey red-checkered tablecloths, the decor is simple. So is parking—there's space right out front.

Saigon Restaurant $$
221 E. North St., Rapid City
(605) 348–8523

Vietnamese food must build brain cells, because the people who run this popular restaurant have phenomenal memories. It doesn't matter how long ago you ate here, they remember what you ordered, and whether you prefer your glass of water without ice. They recall what Harrison Ford had on his plate when he ate here in 1995, and which vegetarian dish Lindsey Wagner had in 1997. Wagner, TV's bionic woman, could have been speaking for all of the Saigon's loyal clientele when she sent proprietress Mai Goodsell an autographed photo that says, "Mai, Both you and your business are a joy!"

Mai, a native of Vietnam, and her daughter, Rebecca, are the most visible members of the staff, but we suspect the kitchen harbors a team of wizards who whip up magical dishes for lunch and dinner. The menu contains many items you'd expect to find at an Oriental restaurant, but we always skip over them (except for the hot-and-sour soup) in favor of something a bit more unusual, such as tofu lemongrass, a combination of noodles, bean sprouts, herbs, and tofu sprinkled with chopped peanuts and served with fish sauce; or chicken salad Vietnamese-style, with shredded cabbage, carrots, mint, and peanuts. We've even mixed-and-matched menu items here to get just the right combination of ingredients with a preferred sauce. The staff is amazingly flexible, so spicy items come in varying degrees of "heat," and you can request that the cook not use MSG in preparing your order.

When the restaurant moved into a spacious new building recently, the great food and welcoming atmosphere moved in, too. Longtime patrons will recognize the exquisite enamel and mother-of-pearl pieces from the former location amid the new decor, which features oval windows and interesting interior angles. Also new are beer and wine on the menu. There's handy parking in front. The Saigon closes on Sunday and in late January, when the family visits relatives in the old country.

Southern Hills

The Bavarian Inn Restaurant and Lounge $$$
U.S. 16/385 N., Custer
(605) 673-4412

This restaurant's name is your cue to its specialties, which are of the German persuasion. Rouladen, a stuffed, rolled top-round steak, is the most popular item on the menu, according to the staff. Many diners come here for the prime rib au jus, but the restaurant also has a solid reputation for its schnitzel, bratwurst dinner, sweet and sour cabbage, spaetzel and gravy, rib eye steak, and sirloin steak. Fish and seafood, vegetarian lasagna, bratwurst sandwiches, mesquite-flavored steaks, and a burger deluxe satisfy all kinds of appetites, and the bar serves cocktails, beer, and wine to complement the food. A large selection of desserts includes German chocolate cake and, during the summer, homemade apple dumplings. The inn is open only for dinner through the winter, but from late May until Labor Day breakfasts are also served.

The inn offers a nice outdoor deck for candlelight dining (in warmer weather) and also has a 200-seat banquet hall for receptions, weddings, and reunions. Another added attraction is the $2.99 menu for children under age six. Smokers and nonsmokers alike are welcome, parking is provided, and reservations are recommended.

Sweet Treats

Like people everywhere, Black Hills Insiders develop regular cravings for ice cream and other desserts. Luckily, we have industrious purveyors who are more than happy to cater to our collective sweet tooth, and we've directed you to several of them in the listings below.

Central Hills

Fjord's Ice Cream Factory Inc. $
3606 Canyon Lake Dr., Rapid City
(605) 343-6912

If we sampled a few too many of the premium ice creams here—and we admit we did—it was all in the name of research. We did it for you, to make your job easier when you step up to the counter and find yourself faced with about 40 yummy-sounding flavors. (There are more than 100, but not all are available all the time.) Unlike us, you might lose your head when you see the list: banana split cream, chocolate malt ball, cherry nut, pistachio almond, butter brickle, cookie dough, Oreo, both plain vanilla and French vanilla, and on and on. According to the owner, mint chip and chocolate almond are the most popular with customers, but we voted for coffee (really robust, just the way we like it), sour cream raisin (delightfully different), and Black Hills gold (a unique combo of butterscotch ice cream, praline pecans, crushed Butterfingers, and cashews).

Now bear in mind that we didn't try each and every variety—for instance, we were thwarted when it came to Outback strawberry because there was none of the strawberry-marbled kiwi ice cream on hand. Nor did we get so much as a lick of peanut butter M&M, a flavor concocted by an employee. We didn't sample the made-right-there hot fudge, bread pudding, or ice-cream pies, cakes, and other novelties. We can vouch for the plain homemade waffle cones, but not the chocolate ones. We did not order a sundae, shake, or banana split. We resisted the sorbet, sherbet, frozen yogurt, and sugar-free ice cream. And because we had other stops to make, we didn't buy a quart or half-gallon to take home either. In addition, work was underway on a vanilla ice cream promised to knock your socks off, so we haven't tried that—we'll just have to wait until we update this chapter.

However, we can tell you that readers of *Eyes on You* magazine voted Fjord's the state's best ice-cream parlor in 1995, that it's reported the place (small as it is with just seven tables) got an entire chapter in a book called *The Best Ice Cream and Where to Find It,* and that a Keystone branch opened in 1998. Furthermore, we can inform you that you may park right outside the shop, but once inside you may not smoke. Now you know as much as we do. So if you end up eating too much ice cream here, don't blame us. Fjord is closed from December through February. No credit cards are accepted.

The Gas Light $
13490 Main St., Rockerville
(605) 343-9276

First, order an old-fashioned root beer float, chocolate malt (voted the best in South Dakota in 1997 by readers of *Eyes on You* magazine), or other ice-cream extravaganza. Then sit back and take in the decor, from the 1910 back bar with original stained glass to the meticulously displayed collection of antique ice-cream scoops and Coca-Cola memorabilia.

Be sure not to miss the licorice pipes, candy lipstick, wax mustaches, and other anachronistic treats under glass in the turn-of-the-twentieth-century hardware cabinet. You'll want to buy some later, but here comes your order, and you'll be busy for a while, draining a seemingly bottomless glass of thick, creamy milk shake; spooning up mouthful after mouthful of heavenly, gooey sundae; or scooping up the billowing foam from your float after you've plopped in the ball of ice cream perched on the side of the glass. After that you might feel the need to walk, not drive, to Mount Rushmore, some 12 miles away (see our Attractions chapter). Smoking is not allowed in the soda fountain (it wouldn't be in keeping, anyway). You can hitch your horseless carriage right outside. Please see The Gas Light listing in the American Cuisine section for directions and dates of operation.

The Gas Light in Rockerville features an old-time soda fountain with real old-time treats. PHOTO: JOHNNY SUNDBY/DAKOTA SKIES PHOTOGRAPHY

Southern Hills

Old Fashion Ice Cream Parlor $
19 Mt. Rushmore Rd., Custer
(605) 673–4070

Co-owner Arle Reetz says if they ever stop serving her homemade rhubarb pie in this cheery pink-and-purple shop, she and her partner-husband, Terry, will be run out of town. One bite of the flaky crust and not-too-tart, not-too-sweet filling tells you why. It's good a la mode too, but the ice cream is just background music. Proponents of the "life is uncertain, eat dessert first" philosophy, Arle and Terry also serve blueberry and apple pie, ice-cream concoctions, and frozen yogurt (including sugar-free). Afterward, you can have a big cup of homemade soup with a sandwich. In contrast to the eye-popping exterior, the decor inside is simple. When it's nice out, the porch is a pleasant place to eat. The shop opens for lunch and stays open until late in the evening from early May until October 15. Smoking's not allowed, but ample parking is provided.

> ## Insiders' Tip
> You can buy bagels by the dozen at our bagel shops, but be sure to store them properly: in a plastic bag overnight or chilled if you actually have any left for longer than that.

Nightlife

Divvying up the writing chores for the book was easy until we got to this chapter. That's because our idea of a memorable Saturday night is taking time out to curl up with a good book or gaze at the stars (making us quite possibly the cheapest dates around). Not that we're hermits who eschew the social pleasantries; we're simply content to leave the loud music and cigarette smoke to others. So we tend to draw a blank when a bartender asks, "What can I get for you?"

But after rounding up a couple of friends with a certain amount of barroom savvy and heading out to tackle the nightlife scene, we found a lot of pleasant folks relaxing and enjoying each other's company in our local nightspots. And we had fun ourselves. So when someone pointed out, "You should get out more," we had to agree. We think you'll want to get out some, too, while you're here, so please read on to learn about some spots to explore.

We've listed a wide range of establishments here, from the most rudimentary neighborhood bar to the most elegant lounge, along with a few unusually colorful places we hope will never change. You'll also find a section on coffeehouses where you can hear live music and sometimes poetry, a list of sports bars with TVs galore, a couple of country-and-western nightclubs, comedy club listings for a truly lighthearted night out, and a special category for concertlike settings featuring live music and dancing. And we couldn't forget movies, so there's information about our local cinemas in here as well.

This is also our chance to let you know that the drinking age in South Dakota is 21, but anyone who looks younger than 30 should be prepared to show a valid photo ID.

A state law requires businesses that serve wine or hard liquor to also serve food if they're open on Sunday, even if the fare is just hot dogs, snacks, microwave pizza, or sandwiches. The state Department of Revenue calls this Sunday privilege. We call it your guarantee that you can at least find a snack or a meal at a bar or pub on Sunday.

However, we can't guarantee that you'll be able to buy wine or liquor in a package store on Sunday or certain holidays, because those regulations vary from town to town. You'll just have to inquire before attempting to make a purchase. Then again, our source at the revenue department tells us hard liquor can neither be sold nor served anywhere in South Dakota on Memorial Day or Christmas.

Speaking of legal matters, video lottery (see our Gaming and Casinos chapter) was an issue during the 1998 legislative session, and our lawmakers continue to scrutinize this form of state-sanctioned gambling. Unless or until a decision is made to abolish video lottery, you'll find machines in just about any establishment where you can buy a drink. Because they're so prevalent, we've noted those places that *don't* have them.

We've handled closing time the same way—unless otherwise noted, it's 2:00 A.M. You also can assume a business is open seven days a week unless we've mentioned that it's closed on certain days. Most bars and pubs offer discounted drinks during a late-afternoon or early evening weekday happy hour, so we've noted only the exceptions or those that serve food as an accompaniment. And, because so few of our bars and pubs require a cover charge, we tell you those that do.

One more thing: We hope you'll use moderation so you can drive home safely after a night on the town—and return for another.

Ready to party?

Bars, Lounges, and Pubs

We wrote this section happy in the knowledge that we are directing you to what a friend calls local color. We like knowing that at the following establishments you'll experience our unique Black Hills culture and meet some of our interesting residents. A few of these places may be a bit rough around the edges—they're not exactly Planet Hollywood. On the other hand, this isn't California. But all the bars listed here are great places to mingle with Insiders and continue your exploration of what this sometimes untrendy part of the world is all about. If you're a fan of bars as colorful cultural icons, you'll find the following a fascinating addition to your Black Hills adventure.

Northern Hills

B&B Lounge and Back Porch
703 N. Main St., Spearfish
(605) 642–8292, 642–2134

A popular nightspot for dancing and listening to live rock 'n' roll music by local bands, the B&B boasts a clientele whose ages generally range from 21 to 50-something. It has a full bar and also serves snacks and fried foods. When you get tired of dancing, you can play pool, Foosball, and electronic darts.

Biff Malibu's
672 Main St., Deadwood
(605) 578–1919

Finally, a Deadwood nightspot that isn't a casino and doesn't have a speck of Western decor. It's the town's first Internet cafe, with a row of seductive black computers and their wireless mice (the kind without tails) awaiting your surfing pleasure. We won't give away in this chapter the news about the glorious food here (you'll find that in our Restaurants chapter), but the urban, industrial-style decor, exposed ducts, and primary colors make the Old West street outside the windows seem a world away.

The legendary (and nonexistent) Biff is an aging California surfer boy who came to the Black Hills for the Sturgis Rally &

Races (see our Annual Events and Festivals chapter) and never managed to get back home. That's his Volkswagen up there in the rafters. Someday Biff's fame might just rival Wild Bill's.

Biff Malibu's is accessed via its own doorway and stairs to the second floor above Goldberg's casino. It boasts a giant shark (suspended from the ceiling), an 8-foot screen for television or multiplayer electronic games, 14-speaker surround sound, e-mail access, live acoustic music, and comfy chairs but no video lottery. At the nifty bar you can sip specialty coffees, wines, or microbrews.

Biff's is open until midnight Sunday through Wednesday and until 2:00 A.M. other nights. In the winter it's closed on Monday.

Durty Nelly's Irish Pub and
Callahan's Sports Bar
Historic Franklin Hotel, 700 Main St.
Deadwood
(605) 578–2241, (605) 578–7713
(800) 688–1876

The Historic Franklin Hotel just bursts with music and entertainment. First there's Durty Nelly's, with live music by Black Hills and regional bands presented on weekends and special occasions. Nelly's has space for dancing and good bar food. The room next door is the Star of the West casino, the oldest live-gaming room in Deadwood. Upstairs is Callahan's Sports Bar, also with live local bands on the weekends (but no room for dancing) and bar food; it closes at midnight. In the summer, the second floor Veranda has its own bar and is a pleasant place to relax and look down on Deadwood's Main Street. The Veranda closes at 10:00 P.M. The Franklin's restaurant, the 1903 Dining Room, features a piano player who performs all types of music, every night, all summer long. (You can read about the food in the Restaurants chapter.)

Knight's Cellar
604 Main St., Spearfish
(605) 642–4292

We found this terrific place a bit hard to categorize. It's not a bar, not a café—you'll just have to see it for yourself. The owners describe it as a "pre-going-out stop," a place to relax, have a snack, stock up on some goodies, hoist a brew, listen to music, and actually have a conversation (there are no televisions on the premises, and the ubiquitous video lottery machines are absent, too).

Knight's stocks dried fruits, cigars, gourmet groceries, old-fashioned bulk candies, European chocolates, specialty sodas, wine coolers, and 70-some microbrew and import beers that you can mix and match. Select your treats, then sit down and enjoy them to the accompaniment of local artists playing acoustic music every Saturday in the summer and on other days in the winter.

Smoking is not allowed in this unusual family establishment. It's closed on Sunday and is open from 4:00 P.M. to 1:00 A.M. Monday through Saturday.

Moonshine Gulch Saloon
Forest Service Rd. 231, Rochford
No telephone

We hesitate to tell you about Moonshine Gulch. It's a closely guarded local secret. It doesn't advertise and it's so far off the beaten path and deep in the Hills that you'd never find it unless someone told you about it. So, if we give this secret away, you must promise not to tell anyone else, okay?

This is a real saloon—a bit wacky, pretty funky, and gloriously idiosyncratic. The rustic old building has a wooden front porch where you can lounge on a bench and view the tiny town of Rochford, pretending you've gone back in time to its decades-ago mining days. Inside there's simply too much to look at: wildlife trophies, hundreds of hats, antiques, junk everywhere, and stuff covering the walls in a visual extravaganza. Even the bathrooms have quotable quotations on their walls. The food is great—homemade fries, burgers, and sandwiches—and you can have a brew with your meal. You won't find video lottery here, but you will find real locals enjoying real life, deep in the Black Hills. Moonshine Gulch is on the main road through Rochford, a town so small that—if you find it—you can't miss this saloon: It's the main attraction.

Nite Owl Tavern
1111 Main St., Sturgis
(605) 347–9846

A basic, unpretentious bar, the Nite Owl caters to locals of all ages, who were having a good time the night we walked in. Some were playing pool, Foosball, and electronic darts, others were watching the seven television sets and chatting comfortably over their drinks. The establishment is in a long, narrow, high-ceilinged room in an older building, and you'll want to get a close look at the old, attractive bar with its interesting art deco features. In addition to fried foods, snacks, and sandwiches, patrons can also buy dart and pool supplies. The Nite Owl, in the heart of Sturgis, is especially popular and crowded during the August Sturgis Rally & Races (which you can read about in our Annual Events and Festivals chapter).

Sanford's Grub & Pub
545 W. Jackson Blvd., Spearfish
(605) 642–3204, (800) 504–6840

Sanford's decorative theme is "junkyard chic." This charming place is full of antiques, old Coke machines, aging bicycles suspended from the ceiling, and memorabilia from nearby Black Hills

State University. It opens at 11:00 A.M. for lunch and closes at 10:00 P.M., seven days a week.

You'll want to read more about Sanford's menu in our Restaurants chapter, but you'll find yummy foods in jumbo-size portions, half-pound burgers, crawfish, barbecue, pasta, steaks, and seafood—and nightly dinner specials. Choose from among more than 99 beers, including Sanford's very own microbrews, Redline Amber Ale and Oil Can Stout. This pub offers hard liquor, beer, and wine. For recreation, after putting away all that food and drink, you can play pinball or pool, or watch one of the 25 televisions.

Spearfish Billiards
550 E. Colorado Blvd., Spearfish
(605) 642–0324

This upscale poolroom may surprise you. It's not one of those dark and dingy pool halls filled with smoke and unsavory characters. This is a family place where everyone is welcome, from tiny tots to seniors. Although smoking is allowed, the establishment is well ventilated and pleasant.

Patrons can enjoy the jukebox, Foosball, air hockey, the arcade, pinball machines, electronic darts, and 12 pool tables. The snack bar serves hot dogs, pizzas, finger foods, and beer. Spearfish Billiards has a pro shop, too, where pool enthusiasts can buy their own fine Connelly tables and cues. This nightspot opens at 1:00 P.M. every day and closes at 11:00 P.M. Sunday through Thursday; it closes at midnight on Friday and Saturday.

Insiders' Tip
Liquor licenses are issued by the State of South Dakota but approved by the city in which the business is located.

Wrigley Field
Boulder Canyon Rd., Sturgis
(605) 347–4032

On the Saturday night of our visit, this small bar was standing-room only, packed with locals and regulars. The noise and laughter were proof of its popularity, and although we hung out in the adjacent poolroom for a while, seats never did become available.

Though patrons can have a rollicking good time, owner Sherrie Schriver says the establishment will become more restaurant oriented than bar oriented. Schriver, who also serves as cook, offers entrees that include Cajun pastas, spaghetti, beef tips, and a full salad bar.

You can spot Wrigley Field by its cool neon sign, modeled after the one that marks the legendary ballpark in Chicago. But just in case you have trouble finding it, Boulder Canyon Road is also U.S. 14A. Wrigley Field is just west of the main part of Sturgis. The bar is open all week, all year, even holidays.

Central Hills

Brandies
2110 Jackson Blvd., Rapid City
(605) 343–5429

The middle-aged suave set frequents this classy lounge where patrons can cozy up to a welcoming fire in a comfortable leather chair, perhaps to puff on a cigar and nonchalantly swirl the amber liquid in their snifters. You can choose another drink from the wine list, domestic and imported beers, or exotic drinks like chocolate martinis from the full bar. Both the light and the music are kept low here to encourage lofty or intimate conversation, and the ornately carved cherry panels above the gas fireplace branch out into dignified bookcases that display tomes on the law. The high-backed, red-upholstered chairs and bar stools, the faux-marble tables, and the display of golf balls from faraway country clubs only enhance the sense that this is where the elite come to unwind on Friday evening or stop for a drink before catching the late movie on Saturday night.

Carry A. Nation

The most famous and feared leader of the temperance movement, hatchet-wielding Carry Nation, twice visited the Black Hills. Born Carrie Amelia Moore, she married Rev. David Nation and legally changed her name to Carry A. Nation, to better express her iron-willed commitment to ending the use of alcohol as well as its kindred sins, smoking and gambling. Many saloons and gambling halls came under her attack, and she was not averse to using rocks, canes, iron rods, and anything else she could get her hands on to break bottles, destroy furniture, and physically punish the sinners.

Rapid City storyteller Carl Leedy, in his book *Golden Days in the Black Hills,* says that Carry visited Rapid City in 1905 but refrained from breaking any saloon windows. However, he tells that she jerked a pipe away from a smoker and angrily stomped on it, and during her speech to the crowd she addressed more smokers at the back of the auditorium. "You fellows down there by the door," she shouted, "if the Good Lord had intended you to smoke he would have turned your noses up the other way, for a smoke stack."

In 1910 Carry visited Sturgis. Apparently, passionate activism agreed with her. "Carrie [sic] is a pretty spry old lady for her age [she was 64] and moved around like a young girl at the age of 16," the *Sturgis Weekly Record* reported. Four brave male community leaders accompanied her to nearby Fort Meade for a visit, without telling her that two of them—between whom she was seated—were Sturgis saloon keepers. Later, the *Weekly Record* stated, "When informed, she took the joke good naturedly and said it made no difference, that the devil could not be routed until you got next to him."

Brandies serves free hors d'oeuvres every night between 5:00 P.M. and 7:00 P.M.; on Friday you can also feast on 20 shrimp for $1.00. The regular bar menu features meat and cheese trays and shrimp cocktail. Then there's the selection of South American cigars (and a new exhaust system to keep the atmosphere pleasant for the other patrons). The TV sets are tuned to sports channels, but you'll hear nary a whisper from them to disrupt your conversation or your electronic golf game. Brandies is closed on Sundays.

Brass Rail Lounge
624 St. Joseph St., Rapid City
(605) 341–1768

In our ongoing quest for what a friend calls "local color," we discovered the Brass Rail, full of regulars and real people who quite obviously feel comfortable here. It's a fairly quiet bar, a little funky, very down-to-earth, and the sort of place where—if you showed up often enough—everyone would indeed know your name. It's so casual, in fact, that it may close before 2:00 A.M. if business is slow.

The jukebox has a good selection of tunes, and electronic dartboards stand along one wall. You won't find a pool table, live music, happy hour specials, or meals (just hot dogs and snacks). Instead, you will find interesting Rapid City residents, including Red, the friendly bartender who has worked there for years and can tell you a bit about the lounge's history. The sign over the bar that reads Saloon No. 8 refers, for example, to the fact that the Brass Rail holds the eighth liquor license issued in South Dakota after Prohibition, making it one of the oldest bars in Rapid City.

Cheers Lounge and Casino
Ramada Inn, 1721 N. Lacrosse St., Rapid City
(605) 342–2273

This hotel bar is popular with locals, businesspeople, hotel guests, and travelers. It's a relaxed place to hang out, whether you're staying at the hotel or elsewhere. Snack foods are always served at happy hour. Local bands occasionally play here, and there's room to dance, though not a lot. The bar has a pool table, electronic darts, and a dart league, and it serves wines as well as liquor and beer. In the winter Cheers may close earlier than 2:00 A.M.

Chute Roosters
103 Chute Rooster Dr., Hill City
(605) 574–2122

Wondering about the name? A chute rooster is a kind of backseat-driver rodeo cowboy, the kind who perches on the chute and tells the real cowboy how to do his job. We didn't meet any chute roosters here, but we're told cowboy poets sometimes provide entertainment in this charming lounge. Karaoke begins at 8:00 P.M. Tuesday through Saturday. A huge loft above the adjacent restaurant (read about that in our Restaurants chapter) has party facilities. Downstairs the cozy bar has a full array of cocktails and a menu with such items as burgers, rib eye steak, and chili. Dressed up or dressed down, everyone gets a warm welcome here.

Firehouse Brewing Co. and Brew Ha Ha
610 Main St., Rapid City
(605) 348–1915

The Firehouse—which occupies the historic 1915 Rapid City firehouse building—has something for everyone. The restaurant welcomes families with its cuisine (see our Restaurants chapter). Both the rectangular bar and the second-floor mezzanine are comfortable places to relax and watch the crowd. In the summer the big, partially covered patio is a perfect place to eat and listen to the bands that play on its stage. It even has overhead radiant heaters for chilly nights.

The Firehouse brews its own terrific beer on the premises. Several recipes are rotated, and you'll find five to six on tap at any time, ranging from Wilderness Wheat (a light beer served with lemon) to Smokejumper Stout (a dark, coffeelike, and heavy-bodied brew).

Then there's the Brew Ha Ha, which is attracting some of the nation's best comedians. Performances include stand-up comedians as well as variety acts. Sometimes acts include appearances by hypnotists. After performances you can try your talents at Foosball, pool, electronic darts, or the National Trivia Network, an animated, live, interactive game in which players in the bar compete with players in other regions.

Insiders' Tip

South Dakota's legal blood-alcohol limit is 0.10. If a law enforcement officer suspects you're driving under the influence of alcohol, you'll be asked to submit to a breath analysis. If you refuse and are arrested for DWI, your driver's license will be confiscated, and if the officer should smell alcohol on your breath, you may be jailed. As a general rule of thumb, the 0.10 limit is the approximate result of one drink per hour. Please don't drink and drive!

Harley's Lounge
640 E. St. Patrick St., Rapid City
(605) 341–1248

Wanna dance? That's what the 20-something crowd does here on Friday and Saturday night, when a D.J. starts spinning discs at 8:00 P.M. During the week, classic rock attracts an older crowd. Whatever your age, you'll appreciate the decor that gives this place its name: An old time Harley gas pump and Harley Davidson draw you in. A number of display cases with Harley Davidson paraphernalia will grab your attention. The ambience is chrome and black, colors for which the Harley Davidson is so well known. In the main lounge, we counted tables and counters with seating for about 200 plus five pool tables, and then we found a few more tables, four electronic dart machines, and a TV in a smaller room with barn-board paneling. By early evening on Friday, the place was filling up with customers ordering mixed drinks, beer, burgers, and deep-fried appetizers. We have a feeling that the only time Harley's isn't busy is on Sunday, when it's closed.

The Harney Lounge/Garbanzos Grill
24090 U.S. 385 S., Hill City
(605) 574–4417

If the band's not very good, the bartender will entertain you—or so we're told. But since folks come here to dance on Friday and Saturday nights, we think it's safe to assume the music is up to par, be it country, rock, two-step, or something else. Live music begins at 9:00 P.M. on summer weekends and every other weekend the rest of the year. Sunday features cribbage tourneys during the winter. In addition to a full bar, there's a selection of imported beers that adds up to a "virtual candy store," according to that entertaining bartender. You can also get a bite to eat, choosing from a limited Mexican menu, burgers, an assortment of fried foods, and daily specials. In our experience the local clientele here is friendly—and loves to dance. The lounge is a mile south of Hill City.

Paddy O'Neill's Pub & Casino
523 6th St., Rapid City
(605) 342–1210

This classy pub is part of the Alex Johnson Hotel and is named for the hotel's first guest, who registered 70-some years ago. Paddy's clientele includes business-people and hotel guests, but the live music by local bands—presented on Wednesday through Saturday nights—draws a younger, enthusiastic crowd. The pub is small and the music tends to be a bit loud, so don't count on intimate conversation or dancing on live-music nights.

Paddy's patrons can enjoy snacks and dinners (from the adjacent Landmark Restaurant's menu); bar food served during happy hour on Monday, Wednesday, and Friday; yards and half-yards of any tap beer; Guinness Stout on tap and one of the largest selections of imported beers in the area; and small-batch bourbons. You might want to become a member of the Pewter Mug Club—buy one, have a drink, and they'll put your mug on display and your name on a brass plaque. When you come back for another visit, you can quaff from your very own mug.

You'll find the Alex Johnson Hotel in our Accommodations chapter.

Southern Hills

A.J.'s Ore Car Saloon
537 Mt. Rushmore Rd., Custer
(605) 673–3051

A sign above the back bar warns, "No whining." But if the atmosphere is always as pleasant at A.J.'s as it was the evening we were there, we'd see no reason to whine anyway. This small, slightly cramped bar seems like a good place to make friends, and apparently Australians think so, too. According to the owner/bartender, A.J.'s and Crazy Horse Memorial (see our Attractions chapter) are the only two Custer listings in a U.S. travel guide published Down Under. (He got his hearsay information from an Aussie patron who made it a point to stop in a couple of summers ago.)

This is a strictly casual place where 30-somethings sit and shoot the breeze while downing a few beers of the domestic variety. Happy hour, which occurs between 11:00 A.M. and noon on Sundays in addition to weekday evenings, could be a good time to study the shelves full of slow-pitch softball trophies garnered by teams the saloon has sponsored. Having done that, you're ready to turn to the pool table, listen to the stereo, or watch sports on TV. During the summer you can sip a brew or play horseshoes in the beer garden out back. If you're looking for a pool tournament or other games, check with the bartender for the schedule.

Frontier Bar
U.S. 16 W., Custer
(605) 673–8870

The Frontier has a band every Friday at 9:00 P.M., and the music varies from week to week. You might dance to rock, blues, or country depending on the night. Things were pretty quiet when we stopped in on a Saturday evening, though—there was even a little girl playing pool. Adults of all ages were seated at tables and at the bar, where you can order a cocktail or a beer. The Frontier also offers appetizers from fried gizzards to mini tacos, and a burgers-and chicken-strips menu for those wanting a meal. In addition to happy hour on weeknights, it also has happy hour on Saturday from 5:00 until 6:00 P.M. This is a spacious place with a big dance floor and an impressive mounted elk head on the wall.

The Gold Pan Saloon
508 Mt. Rushmore Rd., Custer
(605) 673–8850

The swinging doors and the sawdust on the floor say, "Old West." The antlers, bovine skull, and cattle horns over the bar—not to mention the framed ammunition display—say, "hunters' hangout." Indeed, The Gold Pan Saloon hosts a free wild-game feed each November at which the fare is likely to include such delicacies as moose, and rabbit. The fact that there's also a tequila-thon in November tells you this place has a full bar. The saloon also

offers pool tables and an electronic dart machine. Happy hour is from 4:30 to 6:30 P.M. Monday through Saturday. Though some distance from Sturgis in the Northern Hills, the cordial bartender told us the Gold Pan is a popular stop for visitors to the Sturgis rally & Races in August (see out Annual Events and Festivals chapter).

Still Yogi's Den
625 N. River St., Hot Springs
(605) 745–5949

Karaoke begins at 9:00 P.M. on Friday and Saturday nights, and there are two pool tables and a jukebox for amusement at other times. In addition to beer and drinks from the bar, you can order a gourmet burger made with 14 herbs and spices (known worldwide, it's claimed) or a sandwich made with steak or another filling. There's a separate eating area, and the bartender assured us children are welcome at Yogi's. But this is still a bar, where happy hour goes all day Sunday in addition to late afternoon on weekdays.

Country-and-Western Nightclubs

We were surprised that, in a region devoted to its Western heritage, we found only two C&W nightclubs. However, they're good ones and quite popular.

Central Hills

The Boot
826 Main St., Rapid City
(605) 343–1931

The Boot has a lot to offer the C&W music and dance fan on its big dance floor. You can strut your stuff to the country-and-western bands that regularly play here. If you don't dance, there are 10 pool tables, electronic darts, and Foosball. Pizza is a specialty at The Boot.

Robbinsdale Lounge
803 E. St. Patrick St., Rapid City
(605) 342–7271

Colorfully clad line dancers take a spin during a lesson at The Boot in Rapid City. PHOTO: STEVEN A. PAGE

Robbinsdale Lounge promotes itself as Rapid City's country music showcase and with good reason. Country and country-rock bands perform here Thursday, Friday, and Saturday nights. The music begins at 9:00 P.M., but the lounge's 300 seats start filling up much earlier as patrons settle in with a cocktail or a beer. Two pool tables also help pass the time until the band starts playing. Then the bartender flips a switch and neon cowboy-and-cowgirl couples come to life on the walls around the dance floor, changing from green to purple to yellow and back again. On Wednesday and Friday the bar treats its patrons to free pizza or sub sandwiches during happy hour. Other nights, snacks are served. A more substantial meal of burgers, hot dogs, and the like is available from the cafe in the attached bowling alley, and you can order right at the bar. Customers get to showcase their own vocal chords when karaoke opens at 8:30 P.M. on Sunday, Tuesday, and Wednesday. The lounge opens at 10:00 A.M. Monday through Friday, 9:00 A.M. on Saturday, and 1:00 P.M. on Sunday.

Live Music and Dance

After a day of sightseeing in the Black Hills, what better way to get some rigorous exercise? As you can tell from the previous listings, you should have no trouble finding live music and dance spots here, but in this section we give two establishments that specialize in presentations of live music and provide lots of room for dancing.

In addition we recommend a call to Rapid City's biggest venue, the Rushmore Plaza Civic Center, (605) 394-4115, to see what's scheduled. It hosts concerts, conventions, rodeos, rallies, and more, and it's listed in our chapter on The Arts.

Central Hills

AJ's
Alex Johnson Hotel, 523 6th St.
Rapid City
(605) 342-1210

This banquet room in the hotel's mezzanine sometimes becomes a concert hall

LEGENDS &LORE

Nineteenth-Century Nightlife

On May 15, 1885, the *Black Hills Journal* reported on a meeting of Methodist ministers in Deadwood. Apparently the clergy members were concerned about nightlife in the region, and the discussion centered on which two evils they considered to be the worst—the roller rink or the dance. Some claimed the rink at least took sinners away from the saloons, but the Black Hills Journal said Reverend Bartholomew insisted that "if he had a daughter old enough to go into society, he wouldn't want her associating in the rink with those who, but for the rink, would be in the saloon." Another preacher proclaimed, "The devil invented dancing when he was young. The roller rink was the product of his maturer skill, as a means of bringing the fallen elements into the midst of good society." If these reverend gentlemen came back to experience today's Black Hills nightlife, they wouldn't have to worry much about roller rinks, but we do wonder what they would think of video lottery.

on an occasional and irregular basis and more often during the winter. Regional and national bands play here, and a dance floor and special lighting distinguish this big room that holds about 200 people. We suggest you check the entertainment listings in the Rapid City Journal to learn if anything is scheduled in AJ's, or call the hotel and inquire.

Sports Bars

We were impressed by the popularity of sports bars in the Hills, and we found some very good ones, too. They seem to be in competition over the number of televisions they can pack into their premises, and the benefit for you is that you can watch all your favorite sporting events at once.

Northern Hills

Diamond Lil's Sports Bar
Midnight Star, 677 Main St., Deadwood
(605) 578–1555, (800) 999–6482

Televisions are all over the place here, broadcasting your favorite sports. If you get tired of watching, take a look instead at owner Kevin Costner's movie costumes and photographs on display. Barring that, you can always eat. Here you'll find sand-

wiches, appetizers, steaks, and other hot foods as well as video games, a pool table, and the popular National Trivia Network. Lil's is open every day from 11:00 A.M. to 10:00 P.M.

Prime Time Sports Grill
818 Fifth Ave., Belle Fourche
(605) 892–6666

This establishment gets quite a variety of customers: families, locals, and tourists. The Prime Time opens at 11:00 A.M. for lunch and stays open until midnight, although it closes a bit earlier in the winter. It has no fewer than 16 televisions, a pool table, pinball machines, and a state-of-the-art ventilation system that whisks away cigarette and cigar smoke. Prime Time is a great place to eat, offering burgers, sandwiches, seafood, and salads, but it is best known for the specialty of the house: Rancher Steak Tips, once enthusiastically extolled by none other than the *Chicago Tribune* and the *Houston Chronicle*. There's more about Prime Time in our Restaurants chapter.

The Stadium Sports Grill
744 Main St., Spearfish
(605) 642–9521

Although The Stadium is a sports bar, it's also a family place and offers a full menu of good food served in large portions.

Read about the food in our Restaurants chapter. After 5:00 P.M. it attracts a crowd of businesspeople; the college crowd arrives later. You can play pool, darts, video games, and the jukebox, or watch the 13 televisions, including one large-screen TV. The Stadium also provides interactive fun via the satellite broadcast National Trivia Network, which is free and very popular with the bar's clientele.

Central Hills

Kelly's Sports Lounge
825 Jackson Blvd., Rapid City
(605) 348–1213

Satellite sports are the main event here, complete with on- and off-track horse and dog betting. TV sets are everywhere, but you'll also find four pool tables, Foosball, and electronic darts. There's a full bar here, and the kitchen cooks up burgers, steaks, and chicken strips for a diverse crowd that, we're told, ranges in age from 21 to 101.

Valley Sports Bar & Grill
1865 S. Valley Dr., Rapid City
(605) 343–2528

Eleven televisions, many pool tables, electronic golf and darts, and a separate room for video lottery players make this establishment a favorite of sports bar enthusiasts. Sit at the big, dark-wood bar and have a brew or munch one of the popular half-pound burgers. A full menu is served seven days a week, and on Wednesday you can order fresh prime rib. Live music is presented Friday and Saturday nights.

Waldo's Sports Bar
4225 U.S. 79 N., Black Hawk
(605) 787–9388

At Waldo's you'll find locals and bikers hanging out and enjoying themselves. They'll be playing pinball, air hockey, electronic darts (and the steel-tipped variety), Foosball, pool, or the jukebox. Or they may just be watching TV. This bar is on the site of Black Hawk's old dog-racing track, so there's lots of room. Outside are volleyball

and horseshoe courts and during the Sturgis Rally & Races (see our Annual Events and Festivals chapter), there's camping on the grounds. Waldo's serves standard bar food but offers steak and lemon pepper chicken sandwiches, too. Weekend happy hour is from noon to 2:00 P.M.

Coffeehouses

There's nothing like watching the world go by over the rim of a steaming cup of espresso, latte, or cappuccino. You don't necessarily have to wait until nighttime either. Both coffeehouses listed here open in the early morning.

Northern Hills

Common Grounds
111 E. Hudson St., Spearfish; 1301 W. Omaha Rapid City
(605) 642–9066

A classy, comfortable coffeehouse in a century-old building, Common Grounds entertains a mixed crowd of young people, Black Hills State college students and faculty, retired folks, and visitors. It serves great specialty coffees (including local Dark Canyon Coffee Company's blends) as well as bagels, muffins, sandwiches, soups, cookies and biscotti, and offers a deli bar. Because the food is so good, we've also listed this coffeehouse in our Restaurants chapter. A popular community gathering place, Common Grounds hosts poetry readings, live music performances, and open-mike nights. It's open from 7:00 A.M. to 7:00 P.M. Monday through Saturday and from 8:00 A.M. to 5:00 P.M. on Sunday.

Comedy Clubs

And you thought comedy clubs were the exclusive fare of big cities. Both listed here are great, but one caveat: Performances take place in the hotel lounges, so if you're lounging in the lounge when the performance starts, you'll be asked to purchase a ticket or you'll be expected to exit.

Northern Hills

Nuts Comedy Network
Holiday Inn of the Northern Black Hills
I–90, exit 14, Spearfish
(605) 642–4683

National and regional performers descend on Nuts Comedy Network at 8:00 P.M. on Friday and Saturday nights. During shows you can order from the bar menu then snack and laugh to your heart's content. Tickets are sold at the door, and you might want to come early since shows sometimes sell out. Sunday through Thursday, Nuts doubles as Amelia's Lounge, with nightly specials, Import of the Week night, and good food from a varied menu. Friday is ladies' night and Saturday is men's night when beer is $1.00 for domestic beers, 6:00 to 8:00 P.M.

Central Hills

Filly's Pub at the Radisson Hotel
445 Mt. Rushmore Rd., Rapid City
(605) 348–8300

Filly's features two happy hours: one, 5:00 to 7:00 P.M.; the other, 9:00 to 11:00 P.M. Sandwiched in-between at various times of the evening are free hors d'oeuvres, which can be eaten while you watch NFL on one of their two huge screens. If you tire of football, wait a bit and you'll be offered the chance to participate in karaoke. Conveniently located adjacent to the pub in the Radisson Hotel is their restaurant, which now offers a variety of steaks, which includes their much touted chateaubriand.

Movies

Maybe a nice movie in a comfortably dark theater is more to your liking. We have plenty to choose from, all with fine sound systems, great movie theater popcorn, extra-large sodas, and sticky candies.

Northern Hills

Northern Hills Cinema 4
1830 N. Main St., Spearfish
(605) 642–4212

The six theaters in this cinema show first-run movies, and tickets are $6.75 for adults and $4.75 for children ages 3 to 11. Matinee tickets are $4.75 for adults and $3.50 for kids. The Northern Hills Cinema also hosts a foreign film festival sponsored by the Spearfish Center for the Arts and Humanities; read more about this annual event in our chapter on The Arts.

Central Hills

Elks Theatre
512 Sixth St., Rapid City
(605) 341–4149, (605) 343–7888 (reserved seating)

If you missed that blockbuster the first time it came to town, you're likely to get a second chance at the Elks. You might wait a few weeks, but think of the savings: Seats are just $3.00. When you consider that (at this writing, anyway) this historic theater boasts the biggest screen in South Dakota—a whopping 48 feet wide by 22 feet tall—it's even more of a bargain. And a new eight-channel digital sound system means you won't miss any all-important movie dialogue no matter which of the 605 comfortable seats you choose, even if it's in the balcony.

Your second-run movie choices doubled recently when the more intimate Screening Room opened, featuring a 10-by 20-foot screen and seating for 100. The Screening Room is on the third floor, above the balcony, in what was once the Elks Club's elegant ballroom.

The theater building dates back to the early 1900s, when the Elks hosted live vaudeville shows and, later, motion pictures. In fact, this is one of the oldest movie theaters in the nation. So think of it as carrying on tradition when you catch any of two nightly shows or a Saturday or Sunday matinee. You'll even find some services here that are delightfully reminiscent of the good old days when businesses catered to the public as a matter of course. Thursday is BYOB night—bring your own bag and get three free scoops of popcorn. And, you can request reserved seating for any show by calling up to a week in advance.

Please turn to our chapter on The Arts for information about the annual Friends of the Devereaux Library Film Series at the Elks.

Rushmore 7
350 E. Disk Dr., Rapid City
(605) 341–7021, (605) 341–6960

The seven theaters in this modern cinema boast chairs that rival those in your living room. Comfortably seated, you can see first-run movies, with early matinees (before 6:00 P.M.) costing $4.50 for both children and adults. After 6:00 P.M., tickets for children younger than 12 and seniors 55 and older are $4.50; others pay $7.00.

Southern Hills

Hot Springs Theatre
241 N. River St., Hot Springs
(605) 745–4169

This circa 1912 theater features first-run movies now instead of the vaudeville acts of old. Show time is at 7:00 P.M. Friday, Saturday, and Sunday as well as 2:00 P.M. Sunday; the theater is closed on other days. Ticket prices are $5.00 for adults, $3.00 for children ages 2 through 11, and seniors 60 and older; kids younger than 2 get in free.

Gaming and Casinos

Gaming—also known by the old-fashioned but more straightforward term, gambling—has a long, romantic, and sometimes not-so-illustrious history in these parts.

When placer miners and prospectors began pouring into Deadwood in 1876, other enterprising folks followed right on their heels. Merchants provided supplies, saloon keepers provided liquor and gambling tables, ladies of the evening provided . . . well, you can figure that part out for yourself.

Then there were the professional gamblers, eager to get rich quick at the expense of the boomtown miners, who were also eagerly trying to get rich quick. The lust for riches burned in everyone's veins. Some would pan the streams and chip away at rocks; others would shuffle cards and try to read the inscrutable eyes of the players across the table.

A saloon's downstairs usually had a bar in the front and gambling tables in the back; the ladies of the evening (if they were part of the saloon's services) held court upstairs. Gambling was a way to pass the time, a form of recreation, although when mixed with alcohol it often became a problem. Historians say professional gamblers could make money at the tables if they stayed sober, didn't play against other professionals, understood the game, and knew the odds. Others who weren't quite so clever or disciplined fared less well, often losing everything they had when one unlucky card was turned face-up.

Men sometimes gambled away all their money in one poker game, leaving their families destitute and struggling. It's said that one fed-up wife cured her husband's gambling problem when she stalked into the saloon (it was unheard of that a proper lady would enter such a place), raked all the money on the table into her apron and stalked

Deadwood slot machines have been whirring since low-stakes gaming was legalized there in 1989.

PHOTO: COURTESY OF SOUTH DAKOTA TOURISM

142

back out, followed by her embarrassed husband. The woman certainly remedied her husband's compulsive gambling, if only because no one would ever play cards with him again.

When the founding fathers in the Dakota Territory were trying hard to create a state in 1889, the open gambling going on in the wild town of Deadwood was a source of embarrassment to them. A prohibition against gambling was written into the constitution of the new state of South Dakota, but it continued, although most often in the back rooms of saloons. Even Prohibition barely crimped Deadwood's style.

Slot machines arrived there in the late 1930s. The one-armed bandits, technically prohibited by law, were profitable and popular. In 1947, however, the state attorney general organized a surprise raid on the gambling establishments in Deadwood. All the gambling equipment was seized and, after the trials were over, hauled to the local dump and burned. That event ended open gambling in town for many years, although, true to tradition, it continued in a few back rooms.

Gaming in the Black Hills has always been controversial but also extremely popular, and discussions about how to deal with it have been going on since the gold rush days. On December 4, 1885, in fact, the *Black Hills Journal* reported that an unnamed Rapid City gambler, "about the time Judge Church was trying to have the grand jury indict keepers of gambling houses . . . expressed himself as strongly in favor of prohibiting public gambling in saloons." The man was quoted as saying that "that kind of gambling attracts the worst of characters, and is calculated to take money from poor men. In some cases games are run in which no outsider has a chance to win; such games are run of course by men who would pick a pocket, and in this way gambling with cards gets so bad a name. If gambling were carried on quietly where it did not come into the public eye, it would be better for professional gamblers, and there would be much less odium attached to it. Games conducted in such places would attract only those who felt that they had some money they could afford to risk, and there would be no kicking when they lost."

That gambler didn't get his wish but, right or wrong, the town of Deadwood, the state of South Dakota, and many government programs are better off because of it. By the mid-twentieth century, Deadwood had begun to decay and something had to be done to preserve its glorious gold rush history. Gambling seemed the most obvious solution. South Dakota had legalized gambling in Deadwood in 1988; it was part of the town's history, and, conducted in a controlled, legal manner, it could be downright profitable, too.

On November 1, 1989, at high noon and marked by ceremonial gunshots (quite appropriate, though unlike in the old days, no one was wounded), Deadwood officially—and legally—became a gambling town. Foresighted citizens made sure that much of the future profit was earmarked for historic preservation, and so, thanks to gambling, today Deadwood has been reborn.

Modern Black Hills gaming is highly regulated by the state and conducted by reputable business establishments under strict monitoring. It will always be controversial,

> **Insiders' Tip**
>
> The South Dakota Commission on Gaming requires that all slot machines return at least 80 percent of the money inserted in them in the form of payouts. "Loose" slot machines return an even higher percentage, as an enticement to gamblers. Of course, the trick is to be playing a particular machine when its computer program tells it to follow state regulations and pour out those handfuls of clattering coins.

Lady Luck sometimes smiles on gamblers in Deadwood casinos. PHOTO: COURTESY OF SOUTH DAKOTA TOURISM

but it no longer has that disreputable odium bemoaned by our nineteenth century gambler. Players still approach the games hopefully and—we trust—use only the money they can afford to risk. But we're sure that, just as in the old days, gamblers still kick themselves when they lose.

Some two million enthusiasts now gamble in Deadwood each year, and since 1989 they have wagered more than $4.3 billion (of that, $3.8 billion was won by gamblers). From this staggering amount, many millions have funded grants and low-interest loans to restore historic buildings and landmarks, both public and private.

Gambling funds have been used to improve Deadwood's infrastructure and to repair and renovate the Adams Museum, Days of '76 rodeo grounds, the town's Carnegie Library, Mount Moriah Cemetery, and historic Main Street. Such renovations have in turn increased the wage scale and provided jobs in city and county government as well as in private businesses.

Although modern Deadwood's gaming is somewhat controversial, and some citizens still believe the focus on gaming was an unfortunate choice, no one can argue with the positive changes in the town and the amazing improvements to both its appearance and economic outlook.

Today's Deadwood offers limited-stakes gaming, which means the maximum bet is $100 per blackjack hand, poker bet, or slot machine play.

About 90 gaming establishments—few business names include the word casino— offer live poker, blackjack, Let It Ride, three-card poker, and Rainbow 21 card games, progressive and other slot machines, and video lottery machines. Most have nickel, quarter, and dollar slot machines; you may even find some dime and 50-cent machines. Many businesses also have special events such as slot tournaments and leagues, car giveaways, cash drawings, ladies nights, and happy hours; one (see the Wild West Casino and Entertainment Block below) has an off-track betting parlor, and some offer gaming clubs for frequent visitors. Many have restaurants, bars, adjacent motel or hotel accommodations, or offer travel packages with discounts and incentives.

Deadwood gaming establishments line historic Main Street, but a few are on nearby Sherman Street, too. You'll even find slot machines where you never expected to see them: Shedd Jewelers, the VFW, local hotels and motels, even the Twin City Cleaners. A walk down Main Street is nothing like a walk down the Strip in Las Vegas. Perhaps low stakes also means low-key, because you won't see building-sized neon signs or chorus lines of dancing showgirls, and no football-field-sized casinos or skyscraping hotels. We'd be surprised, in fact, if you heard a police car siren. As you stroll down the sidewalks that line the brick-paved streets and past the buildings restored to their former glory, you'll see gamblers hurrying from door to door, carrying their containers of coins. Some stop to browse in the shops, but most are looking for that slot machine with their name on it, the one that calls seductively, "You're a winner if you put just one more quarter in the slot."

Deadwood still has an old-time, Old West flavor. It revels in its rich history and has mined its past to create a modern-day gold rush. Enter a casino and you'll hear the metallic clinking and clanking of coins pouring out of slot machines. Twinkling lights and neon light up the interiors of beautifully decorated businesses, music plays over the loudspeakers, the smell of good food is in the air, and both players and employees are relaxed and friendly. Many casinos boast gorgeous wood trim, elegant bars, and enticing light and color, and their pleasant ambience is enhanced by the lively electronic music of gaming devices. Although we can't list all the Deadwood casinos here, read further for a few we think you'll want to visit.

Deadwood businesses sponsor a special event nearly every month (you'll find them listed in our Annual Events and Festivals chapter) and many gaming establishments participate with their own parties or special offers.

South Dakota's state-operated video lottery—the machines that offer poker, keno, blackjack, and other electronic games—can be found in both casinos and other types of businesses in most Black Hills towns. Video lottery is highly controversial and has been the focus of repeal efforts in the state legislature, but the state has come to depend on the revenues from thousands of video lottery machines.

Video lottery is purported to be one of the most addictive forms of gambling. A study published in the *South Dakota Medical Journal* reported that players who don't have problems with other types of gambling, and who don't display tendencies toward gambling addictions, tend to have problems with video lottery. During the 17-month study period, 143 patients out of 146 struggled with an addiction to these electronic games.

For this and other reasons, including government dependence on the revenue, some state legislators believe it was a mistake to institute video lottery, which was legalized in 1989. Replacing that revenue (which includes a 50 percent take on losses, plus licensing fees and gaming taxes) will be difficult, however, especially since the most likely replacement would be a sales or income tax, an alternative that is unpopular with voters. Video lottery also generates income for the business owners and communities offering it, and they are understandably less than enthusiastic about losing that source of revenue.

The future of South Dakota video lottery thus remains uncertain, but, at this writing, you can still play the machines, which you'll find in restaurants, bars, hotel and motel lounges, and convenience stores in addition to casinos and gaming establishments.

For fans of lottos—the kind played with paper tickets instead of electronic machines—the state offers several options. Among others, there's a Cash for Life game and a Wild Card game. One of the most popular is the South Dakota Powerball game; its large jackpots come from a pool of bets placed in several states. Several kinds of instant "scratch" tickets are available, too. You'll find them for sale at most convenience stores.

The few bingo parlors in the Hills are run by private organizations; they are listed in the Yellow Pages under "Bingo Games."

Although the Black Hills definitely isn't Las Vegas, fans of gaming will find a great variety of lotteries, games, machines, and events (albeit low-stake and mild-mannered) from which to choose. Gaming is part of both the tourism and local entertainment scenes in the Black Hills and generates income for many. But we hope you'll use a light hand for this form of entertainment and have fun while betting responsibly. If gaming becomes a problem, you'll find the Gamblers Anonymous hotline listed in an Insiders' Tip in this chapter.

Bullock Hotel
633 Main St., Deadwood
(605) 578-1745, (800) 336-1876

The historic Bullock has been beautifully redecorated to exceed its original elegance, and we've written about the charming features of the hotel in our Accommodations chapter. The first floor casino has huge windows, gorgeous chandeliers, and a wide staircase that, from the bottom, seems to go up forever. It's decorated with lovely wainscoting and wallpaper, and wicker and Victorian furniture. You can eat in Bully's Restaurant, have a drink in the bar, visit the small gift shop on the first floor, and play the many slot machines.

First Gold Hotel & Gaming
270 Main St., Deadwood
(605) 578-9777, (800) 274-1876

Need to get away from Main Street for a while? First Gold is a bit removed, out where it's quieter on Lower Main Street on the eastern edge of town. A lucky-winner's car giveaway is often in progress inside this big building, and you can stay in the adjacent rooms and dine in the Horseshoe Restaurant on the premises.

Four Aces
531 Main St., Deadwood
(605) 578-2323

The Four Aces boasts lovely floral carpeting, cherry-stained woodwork, swanky

Games of poker and blackjack are among the amusements found in Deadwood. PHOTO: COURTESY OF SOUTH DAKOTA TOURISM

chandeliers recessed into the high ceilings, and elegantly tall windows. It has a big, beautiful bar and its own restaurant. Here you can play blackjack, three-card poker, and many slot and video lottery machines.

Gold Dust Gaming and Entertainment Complex
688 Main St., Deadwood
(605) 578–2100, (800) 456–0533

The Gold Dust is a classy place. The floral patterned carpet is an eye-catching bright red. The walls are rose and glass, and the trim is polished brass. Small, cozy lounges are scattered throughout the complex, or you can have your drink on the upstairs balcony. If you're hungry after cranking a slot machine or studying a hand of cards, have a bite in the buffet restaurant. There's even a liquor store on the premises.

Midnight Star
677 Main St., Deadwood
(605) 578–1555, (800) 999–6482

As much as we tried to resist using the word "swanky" here to describe the Midnight Star, we couldn't do it. It is indeed swanky. The award-winning restaurant, Jakes, is described in our Restaurants chapter and the sophisticated sports bar, Diamond Lil's, is in our Nightlife chapter. The Midnight Star's casino has one of the most beautiful wood-paneled bars we've seen, plus a wonderful chandelier that hangs elegantly above the crowd. Co-owner Kevin Costner's movie memorabilia, costumes, and posters decorate the walls. Upstairs on the balcony level are a small bar and poker and blackjack tables. To the back of the balcony are stairs and an elevator that will whisk you up to Diamond Lil's and Jakes.

> ### Insiders' Tip
> Gamblers must be age 21 or older to wager in South Dakota's casinos and at least 18 years old to bet on simulcast and live horse racing.

Mineral Palace Hotel & Gaming
601 Main St., Deadwood
(605) 578-2036, (800) 847-2522

Hotel rooms make this gaming business a perfect place to spend some time; you'll find more about them in our Accommodations chapter. The Mineral Palace has multiple gaming rooms you can stroll through, with a gift shop, liquor store, both small and large bars, a cafe, and even an old buggy suspended from the ceiling.

Silverado Gaming Establishment
& Restaurant
709 Main St., Deadwood
(605) 578-3670, (800) 584-7005

A car or two (often Cadillacs) are nearly always up for grabs by lucky winners at the Silverado, which is appropriate because it occupies a building that was formerly an automobile showroom. This is a big, wide-open space with beautiful decor, a restaurant, and plenty of gaming action, both at table and at machines.

Casinos line Deadwood's historic Main Street, offering endless chances to strike it rich. PHOTO: COURTESY OF SOUTH DAKOTA TOURISM

Tin Lizzie Gaming & Garden Cafe
555 Main St., Deadwood
(605) 578–1715, (800) 643–4490

The Tin Lizzie caters to the senior crowd, and that's part of its charm. Each time we visited something special was going on: free food, an event, specials, a holiday celebration, Senior Appreciation Days. The building is small and charming, and it's packed with plants, old cars, old-time pictures, and mirrors over a geometric-patterned carpet. There's the Garden Cafe that serves meals, a snack bar with quickly made foods, and a small stage for occasional live entertainment.

Wild West Casino
and Entertainment Block
622 Main St., Deadwood
(605) 578–1100

You can tell when you reach for the six-guns that double as door handles that you've come to the Wild West. The carpet has a cowboy pattern, Western art hangs on the walls, the ceiling is embossed tin, the lounge area has a slate fireplace, and the chandeliers are made of rawhide (really!). The casino sits on the site where Wild Bill Hickok was shot and killed. When we visited on St. Patrick's Day, we were treated to a performance by the local Scottish bagpipe band. Afterward they wet their whistles at the downstairs bar, where green tap beer could be had for a quarter. The year's other holidays are equally intriguing events.

> ## Insiders' Tip
> If you should find yourself in need of the services of Gamblers Anonymous or Gam-Anon while you're in the Black Hills, call its hotline at (888) 781–4357 for a referral to a local chapter or meeting.

Shopping

For the folks who live in sparsely populated western South Dakota and northeastern Wyoming, the Black Hills probably look like shopping mecca. It's true that our stores and businesses do a good job of meeting our material needs and many of our wants, and there's a lot of support for local commerce. At the same time, however, there's a limit to what a low-density area such as ours can support, and many Insiders head south to Denver or east to Minneapolis and the Mall of America when they can't get what they want here. So you won't find giant department stores with mind-boggling arrays of goods or streets lined with rows of specialty boutiques here. You will find gift shops galore and stores selling items you can probably buy just about anywhere; with a few noteworthy exceptions, those places aren't listed here because you won't have any trouble locating them.

Instead, we're going to direct you to the more unexpected shopping opportunities and those businesses that offer something that truly says "Black Hills." We've even included a full-page Close-up on that quintessential local product, Black Hills Gold jewelry, and a list of some other indigenous goods we want you to know about. If you're looking for original works of art, please see the gallery listings in The Arts chapter. Whatever your interests, keep in mind that most area businesses, even those that are open seven days a week, close on major holidays such as Thanksgiving and Christmas.

The Mall

When Black Hills Insiders talk about "the mall," it's a safe bet that they're referring to Rapid City's Rushmore Mall (www.rushmoremall.com), the area's largest fully enclosed shopping center. Anchor stores at the mall include three national giants: Sears, JC Penney, and Target. There are lots of specialty stores here, too, including a large assortment of casual-clothing stores that cater to a youthful clientele. Among them are The Buckle (purveyor of trendy Dr. Martens clunky shoes), Pacific Waves, Maurice's, and Vanity.

The Pro Image stocks sport jerseys, jackets, caps, and team banners. Athletics North, Foot Locker, Lady Foot Locker, and Kids Foot Locker carry athletic shoes and a few clothing items; Famous Footwear, Tradehome, Payless Shoe Source, and Payless Kids all specialize in a wide variety of fashionable shoes. Men will find suits and sweaters at Halberstadt's, and Victoria's Secret lingerie boutique caters to women. Both genders can find good-looking casual wear at American Eagle Outfitters, and the entire family can find stylish clothes at Herberger's department store or the latest sportswear from Eddie Bauer.

Western Outlet and RCC Western Store carry extensive inventories of boots, jeans, shirts, and dresses for all sizes. Top off your new outfit with a jacket, attaché case, or purse from Wilsons the Leather Experts. Gold, gems, watches, and other fine accessories can be found at Riddle's Jewelry, Kay Jewelers, and Zales Jewelers.

To maintain that healthy glow that complements your jewelry, visit General Nutrition Center for nutritional supplements and Bath and Body Works for skin care. Then reward the kids for their

Say "the mall" and everyone knows you mean Rushmore Mall in Rapid City, the Black Hills' largest fully enclosed shopping center. PHOTO: BARBARA TOMOVICK

patience with a trip to Sam Goody's or Musicland for CDs, Suncoast Motion Picture Company for videos, or K-B Toys for—guess what? With your children happy, you're free to browse for bestsellers, cookbooks, foreign dictionaries, and travel guides in Waldenbooks.

Now it's time for refreshments (this would be a good time to drop off that roll of film for one-hour processing at Ritz Camera, too) before heading for Someone's in the Kitchen, a gourmet cookware shop, and Scheels All Sports, which has clothing and equipment for just about any sport you can think of: fishing, camping, hunting, tennis, baseball, football, basketball, soccer, hockey, pool, darts, snow and waterskiing, snowshoeing, golf, kayaking, canoeing, mountain biking, in-line skating—have we left anything out? You'll also find athletic and good-looking casual shoes here. Rushmore Mall is open seven days a week at 2200 North Maple Avenue in Rapid City. For more information call (605) 348-3378.

Separate from the mall but just across the parking lot is Toys R Us, at 400 E. Disk Drive, (605) 399-9410. The name is self-

explanatory, and since it's a chain we assume you know it's a wonderland of toys. For the uninitiated we add that you can get baby furniture and supplies here, too. You'll find additional shopping in the hearts of our downtown centers and in small shopping areas on the outskirts of them. There are too many of the latter to list here, but we would like to mention Heritage Plaza on Colorado Boulevard off I-90, exit 14, in Spearfish. This complex is anchored by Kmart and includes Corral West Ranchwear, Payless Shoe Source, Maurice's, Gallery 21, and Andrew's Hallmark. Keep reading to find out about some of our outstanding independently owned stores.

Antiques

If you like to browse among old things, you'll have ample opportunity at any number of places that hang out an ANTIQUES shingle. Many offer a jumble of items in their raw, just dug-out-of-the-barn condition, but other dealers are discriminating about their inventory and

Black Hills Gold and Silver

A few specks of shining gold were all it took to touch off a wild stampede to the Black Hills in 1876 (see our History chapter). The rush didn't last long—such phenomena seldom do—but a style of world-famous jewelry that dates back to those turbulent days ensures that they will not soon be forgotten. Accounts vary about the origin of the yellow, green, and pink jewelry that is the signature of Black Hills Gold. Legend says the original grape-and-leaf pattern appeared to a French jeweler in a starvation-induced vision at the height of the gold rush; another variation says that early prospectors found grapes where they discovered gold. Yet another version has the motif originating in the California gold fields of 1849 and making its way east through other gold camps. We do know that Deadwood merchant S. T. Butler was making Black Hills Gold jewelry here in 1878, but whether he created the design, or perhaps borrowed it from the ancient Romans, is unclear.

What matters most is that the design endures today, and that Black Hills Gold is still being made by hand right here. Variations on the original pattern are still the most popular, but local manufacturers are coming up with new ones all the time. They still use the "lost wax" method, in which each piece is cast in a plaster mold made from a wax pattern. The wax is burned out and replaced by molten gold. The colored accents—leaves, grape clusters, and whatever else—are spot-welded on, then "wriggled" to give them a frosted look, and finally engraved for intricate details. The different colors are made by alloying gold with copper, silver, and other metals in varying proportions; some outfits still make their own alloys.

Although new designs are always in the works, the original tricolor grape-and-leaf pattern is still the most popular for Black Hills Gold Jewelry. PHOTO: COURTESY OF STAMPER BLACK HILLS GOLD JEWELRY MANUF. INC

You can see artisans handcrafting 10-, 12-, and 14-karat Black Hills Gold jewelry at several places around Rapid City. Mt. Rushmore Black Hills Gold, 2707 Mt. Rushmore Road, (605) 343–7099, offers tours six times a day, Monday through Friday, during the summer and by request the rest of the year; call ahead to make arrangements. At Stamper Black Hills Gold Jewelry Manufacturing Inc., 4 miles south of Rapid City on U.S. 16, (605) 342–0751, and at Landstrom Original Black Hills Gold Creations, 405 Canal Street, (605) 343–0157, (800) 843–0009, you can watch through windows and see a video.

But does the gold in Black Hills Gold actually come from the Black Hills? Until recently, we could say an assured "yes" because Homestake Gold Mine in Lead (see our History and Area Overview chapters) used to sell gold directly to local manufacturers. But those we spoke with said they now buy gold from out-of-state middlemen, so the answer today is "probably," or even "possibly."

However, silver is a by-product of local gold extraction, and a Spearfish man, Jim Langer, has used Homestake silver to create a whole other industry. When he retired as head saw technician for the Homestake sawmill in 1974 he created Langers Original Black Hills Silver, a jewelry line distinguished by a leaf-and-acorn motif signifying life and longevity. The leaf-and-acorn logo stamped inside each piece is your guarantee that it was made from native silver. You can drop by Langers Black Hills Silver Inc., 638 Main Street, Spearfish, (605) 642-2383, (800) 526–4377, to see all six of his jewelry lines and take a tour of the fascinating gem and mineral museum. Tours of the production floor are by special arrangement.

You'll find many brands of Black Hills Gold and Black Hills Silver rings, bracelets, brooches, pendants, earrings, watchbands, belt buckles, money clips, and other items offered for sale in jewelry and gift stores across the country and in Europe and Asia. The tricolor gold in particular has become such a classic that it has been imitated by other manufacturers who know a good thing when they see one. However, only jewelry made right here in the Black Hills can legally carry the name "Black Hills Gold." Be sure to check before making your purchase.

Black Hills Gold artists create numerous designs. PHOTO: COURTESY OF STAMPER BLACK HILLS GOLD JEWELRY MANUF. INC

take pains to display their wares to best advantage. If you're like us, you enjoy poking around looking for hidden treasure as much as you appreciate an elegant presentation.

Central Hills

Antiques & Art
21424 Clover Pl., Piedmont
(605) 347–5016
There's a reason many of the Western and Plains Indian items in this bursting-at-the-seams shop look like museum pieces: They once were. Owners James and Peg Aplan spurn reproduction and modern artifacts, often buying museum collections in their quest for authentic Old West treasures and collectible guns. They even sell rare and out-of-print books on Western Americana. There's hardly room to turn around in here, but each time you do you discover something delightful: remarkable photographs, eye-catching beadwork, stunning military uniforms, star-shaped sheriff's badges, well-worn

stirrups, creaky saddles, fierce-looking branding irons, sturdy stone tools, an extraordinary Crow woman's dress decorated with elk teeth, exquisite dolls, and much more. Look up and you're likely to be startled by a mounted longhorn steer's head sporting three hats. The store is open daily, so you can return as often as you like. To get there, take 1–90 to exit 40.

The Gas Light
13490 Main St., Rockerville
(605) 343–9276
Dennis Kling and Westly Parker don't just know antiques, they know how to make you want to buy them. The partners have a knack for selecting old items and collectibles that range from charming to quirky, and they're equally skilled in the art of display. Collectors of any age will find something here to delight them whether it's a silly postcard, a set of elegant china, a kerosene lantern, or an archaic tool or kitchen implement. We didn't know whether to laugh or cry when we found the *How to Keep Him (After You've*

Caught Him) Cookbook from 1968. The shop is part of The Gas Light steakhouse and old-fashioned soda fountain—talk about nostalgia—but you'll have to turn to our Restaurants chapter to find out about them. The entire complex is open daily between Memorial Day and Labor Day weekends and closed Monday and Tuesday during the winter (it's closed altogether from late January until mid-April). To get there, go 12 miles south of Rapid City on U.S. 16 and follow the signs to The Gas Light.

St. Joe Antiques & Gift Mall
615A St. Joseph St., Rapid City
(605) 341–1073
We're betting that the blue jingle bobs on those fancy silver spurs made a pretty sound on the dance floor—and that the cowboy who kicked up his heels in 'em must've been quite a dude. That wasn't the only display to arouse our sense of romance about the past, however. Old photos, leather valises, and a subtly shaded Mexican serape woven from fine woolen yarn had us ready to hit the dusty trail. But instead we stayed and perused both fascinating floors of this store where we found arrowheads, a matching pair of hand-painted leather parfleches, genuine ruby glass, hand-stitched quilts, antique tools, dishes for every possible table setting, an autographed photo of Roy Rogers and Trigger, and a peculiar Cuban alligator purse with a broken strap and a baby alligator's head for a clasp. We can't wait to go back and see all the stuff we missed, but it won't be on a Sunday when the shop is closed.

Talking Leaves
23849 U.S. 385, Hill City
(605) 574–9090
This tidy little shop has just the right mix of old and old-timey items begging to go home with you. In fact, past and present blend so well it's sometimes hard to tell which is which. Whether it's vintage dishes sweetly displayed in an antique cupboard or a collection of brand-new but unusual candles that catches your eye, it would be hard to leave empty-handed. It even smells

good in here, and the owners keep the CD player stocked with soothing music by local artists. We succumbed to the album of original acoustic tunes that was playing when we entered but managed to walk out—regretfully—without a vividly painted Japanese lusterware tea set and a fine old wooden airplane propeller. The shop, and a separate shed where you'll find more primitive antique furniture and other decorative items, are open daily May through December; call ahead January through April. You'll find them approximately 3 miles northeast of Hill City.

Southern Hills

Pioneer Trading Co.
143 S. Chicago St., Hot Springs
(605) 745–5252
Cowboy and Native American items lend this shop an Old West theme. Guns, poker chips, and saddles share space with beaded moccasins, arrowheads, and ceremonial pipes, to name just a few of the fascinating, nicely displayed artifacts found here. A couple of old "one-armed bandits" (slot machines) were begging to have their reels spun, but the written warning DO NOT PLAY prevented us from attempting anything so frivolous. The shop is closed on Sunday.

Shaman Gallery
108 N. Chicago St., Hot Springs
(605) 745–6602
Owner Linda Heath and her husband, manager Adam Heath, are justifiably proud of the Shaman Gallery, located on one floor of a historic sandstone building next to the Post Office and the Red Rock Café. The room has a 14-foot-high ceiling and stretches from 26 to 60 feet, boasting an inventory of well over one million dollars. One transplanted California artisan called their displays "better than anything he had ever seen in California." Here you can find Native American artifacts, works by well-known Native American painters, a large collection of Western art, works by New York artists, Illustration art from the 1940s and 1950s, as well as offerings by local artists and potters, just to mention a

sampling. In a small building out back, Adam does framing, as well as his own writing and editing.

Shaman Gallery is open each day in the summer from 10:00 A.M. to 9:00 P.M. and on Thursday through Monday from 10:00 A.M. to 6:00 P.M. in the winter.

Bookstores

If you love books—and we hope you're enjoying this one—you know how much they enrich your life. When you visit our bookstores, be sure to look over the titles of local and regional interest, especially those by our local authors.

Central Hills

Everybody's Bookstore
3321 W. Main St., Rapid City
(605) 341-3224

Bargain-hunting bookworms can have a heyday in this used-book store, which has "previously read" books, mostly in paperback editions, in just about any category you can name: arts and crafts, how-to, religion, history, romance, biography, and travel and literature, just to name a few. You'll even find foreign language books—we've seen texts in French, German, Span-

ish, and Norwegian. If you're looking for an out-of-print title and it's not on the shelves, the staff will conduct a search (ask about fees). The only new items regularly in stock are books of regional, Native American, and Western interest, plus maps, including topographic maps and globes. If you don't want to pay for your purchases, you might be able to trade for some of your old books. The store is closed on Sunday.

Prince & Pauper Village
902 Mt. Rushmore Rd., Rapid City
(605) 342-7964, (800) 354-0988
www.info@princeandpauperbooks.com

When we had day jobs, lunch hours were never long enough for a stop in this mesmerizing shop. We invariably got lost in the stacks and were late getting back to work. The independently owned business is justly proud of its extensive collections of children's books, literary classics, and titles of local interest, including books by local authors. But the emphasis on customer service is unmistakable, too. If you're looking for a special book, or one that's out of print, or if you want a list of available books on a given subject, just ask for help. (There's a fee for some services, so be sure to inquire.) In stock you'll find a wide range from a complete set of Hardy Boys mysteries to the latest bestsellers. There are also sections on Native American fiction and Sioux history, racks of exceptionally lovely greeting cards, and baby books to melt your heart. The shop, which also hosts book signings for local and nationally known authors, is closed on Sunday except during December.

The Storyteller
520 Sixth St., Rapid City
(605) 348-7242

Comic books rule at this storehouse of fantasy. Look for entertaining books, games, and other items with a sci-fi or comic-related focus plus nonsport trading cards and collections of old and new comic-book series. The owner told us his clientele is mostly between the ages of 14 and 25, but also includes college professors and doctors—he just laughed when

> ## Insiders' Tip
> Looking for a slinky little number covered in sequins or accented with spangles? See the scintillating selection of party dresses at Kathleen's, 622 Main Street in Spearfish, (605) 642-3843. This ladies' boutique also carries dressed-up casual clothes and fashionable sportswear.

we teasingly asked him to name names. You can shop at The Storyteller seven days a week all year.

Clothing

We're proud to say that the hatters who make custom headgear around here aren't the mad variety. In fact, we found them to be pretty personable and justifiably proud of what they do. They're just a few of the fine crafts and businesspeople who outfit our working (and urban) cowboys.

Central Hills

Star of the West Hat Company
2255 N. Haines Ave., Rapid City
(605) 343-7345

After just three years of full-time hat making, Tod Christensen was proud to know that spectators at a recent National Finals Rodeo would get a look at his handiwork on the heads of three contestants. Christensen makes custom hats with varying percentages of beaver fur and trimmings as plain or fancy as you like—and in just about any color, too. Recently his stock included a dainty bone-colored bonnet shaped with a women's dress crease and adorned with a cascading ivory veil trimmed with ribbons and roses. He'd made it to go with an outfit worn by his wife, Phyllis, who's a singer, but he told us customers do come in with orders for wedding attire. He also offers a variety of reconditioning services for hats that have been in service for a while. The average wait for a beautiful custom hat of your own is two weeks. The shop is closed on Sunday.

Vintage Cowboy
360 Main St. No.1, Old World Plaza, Hill City
(605) 574-4655

Imagine the Old West the way it really was: fellers wearing britches hitched with suspenders instead of belts and ladies dressed in skirts even while riding horses or mending fences. Some of the duds you'll find in this fascinating shop were made from turn-of-the-twentieth-century patterns

Insiders' Tip

Don't let a broken guitar string ruin your plans for a fireside serenade. Haggerty's Musicworks at 2520 W. Main Street, (605) 348-6737, and 514 St. Joseph Street, (605) 348-4801, in Rapid City has replacement strings and just about everything else "instrumental" to an evening's entertainment.

preserved in the Smithsonian Institution; a few are authentic in design but have modern touches for practicality. (Some ladies' things have zippers, but men's pants don't, because zippers weren't used until 1913, and you won't find women's pants here at all, because they were unheard of.) Look for tapestry vests, Gibson Girl blouses, broomstick and riding skirts, shirts, frock coats, spurs and other accessories, and even replica revolvers (firing and nonfiring). Be sure to sashay over to the tape and CD counter for a selection of contemporary and classic—we're talkin' Gene Autry and Roy Rogers—Western tunes to go with your new outfit. (Ever wonder whether the folks from a hundred years ago would've had as much fun pretending to be us as we do playing them?) The store is open daily all year, but closes on Sunday in winter.

Southern Hills

Stockman Boot and Saddlery Co.
106 S. Chicago St., Hot Springs
(605) 745-6771

You won't give even brand-name cowboy boots a second glance once you've seen the custom-made footwear. Imagine boots that fit perfectly not by coincidence but because they were made that way. Add to that the pleasure of picking out leathers and deciding on colors and patterns (your brand or initials, even) for a pair that is uniquely yours. Personally, we're dreaming of inlaid leather roses and yards of fancy stitching . . . and we'll be placing our order as soon as we produce that *New York Times* bestseller. When we visited the store, the sales clerk showed us rolls of various leathers such as kangaroo (in gold and silver, no less), buffalo, horse, elephant, bull, and calf (including azure and jade). Then, because we were having so much fun, she dug out all her favorite scraps—shark, snake, lizard, and ostrich foot—and showed us the pair of knee-high burgundy beauties trimmed with hearts that she's making for herself. "Wouldn't it be a waste not to tuck your pants in?" she asked with a delighted laugh. We could only sigh. Even if we'd ordered our own boots on the spot, we'd have had to wait a year or more for them to be finished. Besides filling custom orders, the staff does repairs on about 1,000 pairs of well-worn boots each year. Stockman Boot and Saddlery Co. is fun by boot and saddle-maker Jim Bultsma and is closed on Sunday.

Leather and Wool

The territorial battles between early-day Western cattle interests and sheep ranchers are legendary, but those days are over. Now you can choose to wear leather or wool without being accused of taking sides. Be sure to check our Saddles 'n' Stuff and Clothing sections for other apparel outlets.

Northern Hills

Trevino's Leathers
U.S. 385, Deadwood
(605) 578-1271

Outside, it's a charming log cabin. Inside, it's black-leather heaven. Rhea (pronounced like Ray) Trevino has been stitching leather for a quarter-century, and for most of that time he's had a steady clientele for his custom elk-hide chaps and vests. His rustic shop 6 miles south of Deadwood caters to motorcyclists with a yen for all kinds of leather garments, and the racks here are hung with ready-made jackets, vests (both fringed and plain), belts, caps, and gloves. Wallets, handmade leather purses, and select jewelry items (yep, those rattles

Insiders' Tip

Sure, you can buy a perfect Christmas tree, but think of the fun (and warming exercise) you get tramping around the woods looking for a tree unlike any other. You can cut your own Christmas tree in the Black Hills National Forest by obtaining an $8.00 permit from any Forest Service office (see our Recreation chapter for a list of locations). You can cut up to five trees as long as you have a permit for each one. Choose from pine, spruce, or juniper— just be sure to use that saw carefully, and don't get your vehicle stuck in the woods!

GREAT FACES

Phoebe Apperson Hearst

Great wealth and personal popularity never went to Phoebe Apperson Hearst's head. Even as a much-courted Missouri belle, the lively brunette was known for her kindheartedness and generosity, traits she continued to cultivate after becoming the wife of George Hearst—she was 19 and he 41 when they married in 1862. George would later become a founder of Homestake Mining Co. (see our History chapter) and a U.S. senator from California. The couple, who lived in San Francisco, occasionally visited the Black Hills City of Lead, where the Homestake Gold Mine is located.

Although they never made the rough-and-ready mining camp their home (George found the Black Hills a bit crude for his refined tastes), Phoebe's philanthropic efforts there earned her the admiration and affection of its citizens. In 1896 Phoebe gave Lead a public library for Christmas, and it bears her name to this day. She also came to the aid of the Lead Women's Club when financial problems threatened to shut down its free kindergarten. Her support for education spread far beyond Lead, however, as she helped found the PTA (originally The National Congress of Mothers) in 1897. That same year she became the first woman regent of the University of California, a post she held until her death in 1919.

In return for her many gifts to Lead, the citizenry and business community commissioned a Boston silversmith to create a large, ornately decorated and engraved "loving cup" in Phoebe's honor. No doubt the gesture pleased her, and perhaps the trophy did as well. Phoebe's love of fine things showed in her patronage of the arts and in the elegant clothes and jewels in which she posed for her portraits. The fact that she had Homestake stock issued in her own name (albeit misspelled "Phebe") hints that she was as astute in the acquisition of money as she was lavish in her dispensation of it.

Less well-loved than his mother was George and Phoebe's only child, publishing tycoon and "yellow journalist" William Randolph Hearst, believed to be the model for Orson Welles's film *Citizen Kane*. William Randolph's ostentatious California home, Hearst Castle, is the setting for Murder at San Simeon, a book blending fact and fiction written by his granddaughter, Patty Hearst. The heiress made headlines of her own when she was kidnapped by the Symbionese Liberation Army in 1974 and transformed into the terrorist Tania. After her 1975 arrest and subsequent conviction for bank robbery, Patty married a prison guard, Bernard Shaw, and is reported to be living happily (and quietly) ever after.

---

were once attached to real live snakes) help round out the inventory. It's worth stopping here even if you're not in the market for some new leathers because Trevino has some nice Native American artifacts displayed in glass cases. The shop is open seven days a week all year. At Trevino's it's always leather weather.

The Wool 'n' Shop
325 Roundup St., Belle Fourche
(605) 892–2578

This retail outlet is a sideline for Mid-State Wool Growers, which buys local producers' wool and sells it to mills all over the country. Some of it ends up back in this shop as clothing. You'll find businesslike as well as casual garments, plus sweaters, blankets, slippers, socks, shearling mittens, and more. For the spinner, the shop sells wool tops neatly combed and packaged. The store is closed on Sundays all year and on Saturdays too during July and August.

Native American and Other Ethnic Items

Long revered by various Native American tribes, the Black Hills became a richly diverse melting pot with the gold rush of 1876. To read more about the many cultures that mingled here, please turn to our History chapter. To enjoy the artistic expression of some of those cultures, as well as others from around the world, visit the shops listed below and find wonderful handmade decorative items, clothing, and even foods.

Northern Hills

La Pagoda
647 Main St., (in Miss Kitty's), Deadwood
(605) 578–1348
Shankar Arts
29 Deadwood St., Deadwood
(605) 578–3808

La Pagoda and Shankar Arts are owned by Phil Breland and his Moroccan-born wife, Georgette Ohayon. Shankar Arts was their first store, and now they've added La Pagoda for more room to display their beautiful handmade items (and so that at least one store is open when they travel abroad during February, March, and April to replenish their incredible inventory). They've been traveling to the far side of the globe for 20 years, bringing back exquisite silver and gemstone jewelry, woolen jackets, brass Buddhas, hand-knotted tribal carpets, crystals, antique ritual pieces, and other fascinating items. Their buying trips take them to North Africa, India, Thailand, Tibet, Indonesia, Nepal, and the Middle East where they search out markets, fairs, and festivals for new folk crafts. Every piece reflects the culture from which it came, and Breland and Ohayon can tell you its story. You can buy unset gemstones here, order custom work, or have your gold and silver jewelry repaired.

Shankar Arts is open daily from early May through January, when it closes for three months. But don't despair, you will be able to visit La Pagoda, which is open daily from May 1 until Christmas, then on Thursday through Monday during the winter.

Central Hills

Global Market
617 Main St., Rapid City
(605) 343–4051
617 Main St., Spearfish
(605) 642–9014

It's said that if you remember the '60s, you weren't there. Well, if you were there, or think you might have been, or only wish you had been, Global Market will transport you back to those days of head shops and clothes from the India Imports of Rhode Island catalog. This is the place to find imported hand-batiked clothing, garments woven from flax and other natural fibers, incense, candles, silver-filigree jewelry, South American wool sweaters, bongo and conga drums (made in New Jersey), kilim rugs, carved masks, handmade soap, baskets, books, tapes, CDs, and more.

Just think: If you shop here and you're a kid, your parents (if they're over 40) will approve of your good taste; if you're a

Insiders' Tip

If you've always dreamed of owning handmade, custom-fitted golf clubs, you'll want to consult with Mark Speirs of Deadwood. Speirs has been crafting beautiful woods, irons, and putters (and doing club repairs) for 15 years at Spiro's Golf Club Shop, which is in his home. Call (605) 578–1179 for directions and to make sure he's available.

LEGENDS &LORE

Cornish Pasties

First, some clarification. We're talking here about an ethnic food called a "pasty," which rhymes with "nasty" but is really very pleasant to eat. This has nothing to do with the pasties (pronounced with a long a, as in "hasty") worn by exotic dancers. But we'll get to that in a minute. A pasty in this context is a turnover filled with heavy foods like meat and potatoes. The resourceful wives of tin miners in Cornwall, England, concocted pasties long ago as a sustaining meal to tuck into their hard-working husbands' lunch pails.

According to Bonnie King, who has made more than one million pasties at King's Grocery in Lead, the first such handheld pies had a barley crust and were filled with fish. Today's "traditional" pasty consists of a pastry crust with a steak, potato, and onion filling. When Cornish miners and their families immigrated to the Black Hills gold fields (see our History chapter), they brought their pasty recipes with them. That was fortunate for women like Bessie Richards, who lost her husband to silicosis and supported her 14 children by baking and selling pasties.

Local descendants of immigrant miners say they're not sure whether the Cornish folk imported their custom of leaving a bit of pasty crust at the mine to keep the tommyknockers from making mischief. Held to be the spirits of Jews captured by the ancient Romans and forced to work in the English tin mines, the existence of tommyknockers explained knocking noises heard in the mines.

You might never get to hear a tommyknocker, but you can experience the time-honored taste of a pasty at King's Grocery at 622 E. Main Street in Lead. (It's closed on Sundays; call 605–584–2318 if you need directions.) Bonnie, who learned to make pasties from a daughter of early-day immigrants, offers four varieties: traditional, pizza (with a yeast crust), breakfast, and sausage 'n' sauerkraut. Lots of first-time customers mispronounce the name, but Bonnie and her husband, Wayne, will never forget the time a woman stepped up to the meat counter, asked for the other kind of "pasties" and left in a huff. "I was going to ask her what size," Wayne recalled with a grin.

parent, your kids will think you're totally cool. My, how times have changed.

By the way, that's not a typo in the listing—the identical street numbers for the two stores were a cosmic coincidence. (We're convinced the owner has good karma.) Even if you don't notice some subtle differences in the merchandise, you can tell the shops apart because the one in Rapid City has an espresso bar in the back. Both are open daily.

House of Scandinavia
13774 U.S.16, Rapid City
(605) 348–3858

If you're of Scandinavian descent, you've probably been teased about lutefisk, the odoriferous Limburger of fish dishes. Well, here's a place where you can bask unabashedly in your ethnic heritage. For 40 years this red-and-white chalet 9 miles south of Rapid City has stocked quintessential Northern European goods, from Norwegian sweaters (to die for) to lefse mix. Along with Sweden and Norway, Denmark, Finland, Iceland, Holland, and Germany are represented here in such items as brightly painted Delecarlian horses, needlepoint kits, delicate pewter jewelry, pretty table linens, glassware, china, funny troll dolls, kitchen utensils, food items, clogs, toys, glass Christmas ornaments, and blue delftware. The shop is open daily from May through October;

in November and December, when co-owner Jean Watkins (she's of Swedish parentage) serves hot cider and glogg and homemade lefse, it's open Friday through Sunday and by appointment. It's closed from the weekend before Christmas until May 1.

The Indians
141 Winter St., Keystone
(605) 666–4864, (866) 845–3426
www.theindianskeystone.com
Items on the shelves here represent the work of artisans from many tribes, and the store's Indian Arts and Crafts Association membership certificate (it's a charter member) is your guarantee of authentic Native American craftsmanship. There are works by local artists and crafters and an array of Southwestern silver-and-turquoise jewelry, baskets, sand paintings, kachina dolls, and genuine Navajo rugs. Beadwork, quillwork, pottery, dance sticks, drums, moccasins, denim clothing, toys, and a great selection of books also keep you browsing. The store is open seven days a week year-round.

Prairie Edge Trading Co. & Galleries
606 Main St., Rapid City
(605) 342–3086, (800) 541–2388
www.prairieedge.com

If you're captivated by Native American crafts and culture and you love fine handmade items, go straight to Prairie Edge. You'll know you're someplace special the instant you step into the spacious showrooms gleaming with polished-wood floors and fixtures. It's a good idea to set aside plenty of time for your visit, not only because there are three floors' worth of wonderful merchandise to look at, but also because the serene beauty of the displays makes you want to linger over them to examine each exquisite piece.

When you enter, locally made star quilts and colorful Pendleton blankets catch your eye, and cases of jewelry, beadwork, and intricate quillwork beckon. You might even feel inspired to buy supplies for your own creations in the Sioux Trading Post portion of the store. The toy assortment, with games, marbles, puzzles, and many breeds of fuzzy stuffed animals, will delight you. You're sure to be dazzled by the Italian Glass Bead Library, where jars upon jars hold beads in all kinds of colors and almost as many sizes—intriguingly, they're from a Venetian supplier that provided beads to nineteenth-century fur traders and only recently went out of business.

Most enchanting of all, perhaps, is the Plains Indian Gallery, where you'll see

Insiders' Tip
You'll notice lots of South Dakota-made items on the shelves in our stores and gift shops. Here are some that are made in the Black Hills: The Country Caterer jellies, bread mix, and more, Belle Fourche; Dakota Delights and Homespun Naturals vegetable soaps, Custer; Dakota Gold Mustard, Spearfish; Dark Canyon Coffee, Rapid City; Daystar Candles, Custer; eggspressions! hand-decorated goose and other eggshells, Rapid City; Heart of the Earth bath products, Fruitdale; Jewelry by Waldron, including the Circle of Nations and Water-Song lines and EarthCharms ornaments, Rapid City; and Prairie Gold Coffee Co., Rapid City.

magnificent reproductions of traditional clothing and artifacts, including beaded cradle boards, fringed and beaded leather dresses, ceremonial garments embroidered with porcupine quills, decorative vessels, dolls, and more. From here, climb the wide staircase to browse among the fascinating books on Native American subjects, crafts, and the West, as well as a selection of tapes and CDs by Native American musicians. Finally, visit the third-floor art gallery to see works by acclaimed regional and national artists, sculptors, photographers, and craftspeople. If once is not enough, you can return seven days a week to see it all again at this 125-year-old building.

Sioux Pottery
1441 E. St. Joseph St., Rapid City
(605) 341–3657, (800) 657–4366
www.siouxpottery.com

This isn't just a place to buy beautiful, hand-decorated pottery in muted rainbow colors. You're also invited on a self-guided tour through the plant to ask questions and watch the craftspeople and artists at work. It's an interesting process. Clay slip, a liquid mixture of Black Hills red and Kentucky white clays and water, is poured into molds. After the edges harden, the excess slip is poured out, leaving a perfectly formed vase or other vessel. Once dry the pieces are unmolded, trimmed, sanded, painted, hand decorated, glazed, and fired. The artists use traditional geometric designs and their own imaginations in their etching and painting, which makes each piece unique. You can buy one piece or several, as well as other Native American-crafted items in the gift shop. Sioux Pottery is open daily June through August and weekdays the rest of the year.

Natural Foods

If it tastes good it's bad for you, right? Wrong. Stock up on food from the stores listed here and you'll have everything you need for a yummy, nutritious feast. All four of these stores are closed on Sunday.

Northern Hills

Good Earth Natural Foods
138 E. Hudson St., Spearfish
(605) 642–7639

The displays here are so attractive and welcoming you feel good even before you buy any of the healthful merchandise. Along with a good selection of grains are books, nutritional supplements, bulk herbs, grooming supplies, biodegradable cleaning products, frozen and canned foods, lots of bottled and canned beverages, and many other items. Our most recent visit turned up some locally produced honey, too.

Central Hills

Main Street Market
512 Main St., Rapid City
(605) 341–9099

The shelves in Main Street Market are well stocked with nutritional supplements, herbs, personal-care products, books, pasta, tea, soups, condiments, and lots of other tasty, tempting goods for wholesome meals and nutritious snacks. Add the personal service and attention on which the owners pride themselves, and you will come away with a warm feeling as well as a filled market basket. The market is open Monday through Saturday, all year.

Staple & Spice Market
601 Mt. Rushmore Rd., Rapid City
(605) 343–3900

Since 1921 this tried-and-true market has been able to boast the largest selection of bulk herbs and spices in South Dakota. But that's not why it was named the state's 1994 Small Business of the Year. Upgrades in customer satisfaction, customer count, and appearance, all at the hands of current owner Carol Veldhuizen, earned the well-deserved award. The current confines are bursting with nutritional supplements, homeopathic remedies, personal-care products, teas, and staples for wholesome eating. Special items include free-range

The huge selection of bulk herbs and spices at Staple & Spice Market in Rapid City takes up the better part of one wall and makes an intriguing display. PHOTO: STEVEN A. PAGE

buffalo, chicken, turkey, and beef, whole-bean coffee, organic fruits and vegetables, and bulk honey. If the item you want isn't in stock, it's been our experience that the staff will bend over backwards to try to get it for you.

Southern Hills

Earth Goods Natural Foods
738 Jennings Ave., Hot Springs
(605) 745-7715

Owner/herbologist Jackie Gericke recently doubled the size of the store and increased its inventory of nutritional supplements, herbs, and other items. Even before the expansion, however, we found a generous variety of bulk dried fruits, nuts, flours, seeds, grains, and beans, plus frozen entrees and desserts, essential oils, juices, teas, and the usual items you'd expect to find in a natural-foods store. It's all offered in a comfortable, friendly atmosphere.

Photo Supplies and Service

We've wondered how many professional photographers per square mile live in the Black Hills—we're betting it's quite a few. So it's rather baffling that we don't have a large camera store to serve them. If your photo needs are limited to basic cameras, print film, and quickie processing, you won't have any trouble finding what you're looking for, but fortunately we also have a few places that offer specialized services and higher-end equipment. Here is one that we recommend.

Southern Hills

Camera Corner and Carroll Photo Studio
819 Mt. Rushmore Rd., Custer
(605) 673-4856

This shop, about 3 miles west of Custer State Park, offers an array of services, including one-hour 35mm color-print processing (ask about extra charges), black-and-white printing, enlargements, contact sheets, color copying, and basic camera repair. A limited selection of cameras, tripods, and other equipment is available as are Polaroid, slide, and 120 roll film. The shop also houses a studio specializing in family and group reunion portraits. It's open Monday through Saturday and by appointment on Sunday.

Rock Shops

The subject of Black Hills rocks covers a wide spectrum that includes precious metals, gemstones, and fossils. To learn more about this mineral diversity, please see our Natural World chapter.

Northern Hills

Gallery of Stone
8228 Elk Creek Rd., Piedmont
(605) 787-4560

Black Hills petrified wood isn't the world's most colorful, but according to the folks who run this shop, it rates high for tree integrity—meaning features such as growth rings of the once-living tree are readily discernible. Also featuring a good selection of fossils and gifts, the shop is part of the Petrified Forest of the Black Hills complex, which is described in our Attractions chapter. It's open daily May through mid-October. To get there, take 1-90 to exit 46.

Central Hills

Dakota Stone Co.
23863 Palmer Gulch Rd., Hill City
(605) 574-2760

Stones for your fireplace, patio, rock garden, or rock veneer—they're all here, along with local alabaster for the sculptor in you. Not surprisingly, beautiful rose quartz, the South Dakota state mineral, is this store's biggest seller, and you'll find many lovely specimens from which to choose (the owners have their own quarry). Browse among

the outdoor bins, where you'll see everything from milky selenite to jet-black obsidian, then do the same in the gift shop, where you'll find speckled leopard-skin rock, tumbled and polished stones, books, carvings, jewelry, and geodes—hollow rocks you can break open with a hammer to see the pretty crystals inside. (Watch your fingers!) The store, 3 miles north of Hill City on U.S. 385, is open daily June through August but is closed on weekends the rest of the year.

Southern Hills

Scott's Rock Shop and Free Museum
1020 Mt. Rushmore Rd., Custer
(605) 673-4859

Out front you'll find rocks sold by the pound for carving, landscaping, and whatever other uses you can come up with. Inside you'll see polished stones, semiprecious gems, colorful bismuth crystals from Germany, fossils, jewelry, carvings, and...fishing tackle. The museum contains rocks and minerals from around the world. Scott's is open daily from April through October with reduced hours in November and December; it's closed from January until mid-March.

Saddles 'n' Stuff

Even if the only horse you've ever ridden was on a carousel, you understand the animal's appeal. Around here folks rely on horses for the three R's: ranching, recreation, and rodeoing.

Northern Hills

Croft's Saddlery
U.S. 385, Deadwood
(605) 578-3228

If you saw the Tom Selleck movie *Quigley Down Under*, you saw one of Jerry and Duffy Croft's saddles. Make that two—in movie work, matching pairs of everything are required for the actors and their stunt doubles. Croft's meticulously handcrafted saddles appeal to working cowboys as well

Knowledgeable staff at area sporting-goods stores help customers get outfitted for some of the Black Hills' exciting outdoor recreational opportunities. PHOTO: STEVEN A. PAGE

as to the world of filmmaking, since the saddles combine an authentic antique look with modern comfort. The Crofts, a husband-wife team, pride themselves on using top-quality materials and not cutting corners. Then again, corners are a Croft signature—look for the classy spot braiding in them. The Crofts do most of their business by phone, taking measurements for both horse and rider that way. A custom saddle order takes six to eight months to fill, but other items such as chaps and bridles can be completed in two to three weeks. Croft's is open Monday through Friday.

J&S Saddle & Tack
2221 Junction Ave., Sturgis
(605) 347-4667

It's hard to think of anything the equestrian needs that can't be found here. There's a whole room full of new and used saddles plus saddle blankets, bridles, and other tack for the horse to wear. For the rider, the shop also has boots, chaps,

decorative leather belts, and gift items such as pretty key rings. Of course, you don't have to own a horse to shop here; if you just like the Western look, that's a good enough reason. The store is open every day but Sunday.

Central Hills

Bader Saddles
317 Main St., Rapid City
(605) 342-5791

Everything you need to outfit your horse in style is here: saddles (new and used), saddle blankets, tack, and rodeo equipment such as bronc saddles and bareback riggings. But the truly discerning horse will want his or her own custom-made saddle, fashioned by the expert hands of store owner Boyce Bader. At this writing a custom order was taking 19 months to fill—but both you and your horse know it'll be worth the wait. Boot and shoe repair is also available. Stop in any day but Sunday for more details.

Southern Hills

Stockman Boot and Saddlery Co.
106 S. Chicago St., Hot Springs
(605) 745–6771

Jim Bultsma specializes in custom-made saddles but also does repairs and just about any other kind of leather work you might call for. His shop (see the listing under Clothing, above), stocks ready-made saddles and tack, too. Operations are in full swing Monday through Saturday.

Sporting Goods

If you've seen our Recreation chapter, you understand why we have so many sporting-goods stores. Several of them have their main store in Rapid City with a branch store in the Northern Hills, so check the addresses in the listings carefully if you're looking for supplies and equipment in our northern towns.

Central Hills

Adventure Sport
900 Jackson Blvd., Rapid City
(605) 341–6707
215 E. Jackson Blvd., Spearfish
(605) 642–5557

One feature we appreciate about this pair of shops is the friendly, knowledgeable service. Staff members, who are active sports folks to begin with, are also well trained and can help you find the most suitable backpack, tent, skis, or other equipment for your needs and capabilities. We also just plain like their stuff, which includes top-name outerwear and equipment for alpine and cross-county skiing, snowboarding, snowshoeing, climbing, camping, and other activities (the Spearfish shop also sells swimwear) plus essentials such as ski waxes, goggles, multiuse automobile racks, freeze-dried meals, stuff sacks, boot laces, tent repair tape, biodegradable camp soap, and much more. Certified technicians are on hand to give your snowboard and skis tune-ups and mount your bindings, too.

The shop in Rapid City is open seven days a week; the store in Spearfish is open Monday through Saturday, and Sunday between Thanksgiving and Christmas.

Dakota Angler & Outfitter
513 Seventh St., Rapid City
(605) 341–2450

When you think about it, an entire store devoted to fly-fishing makes sense in the Black Hills. Just ask any local fly fisher (and there are plenty of women among them). Need a float boat? No problem. Looking for fly-tying supplies? There's a whole wall full. In addition to all the practical items like rods, reels, books, magazines, and maps, there are items to keep you in the spirit even when you can't be streamside: jewelry, watches, artwork, T-shirts, dishes, and even wild rice to serve alongside your catch. For information about Dakota Angler's guide service and lessons, please see the listing in the Fishing section of our Recreation chapter. The store, which is an authorized Orvis dealer, is closed on Sunday all year and on Monday during January and February.

Golf Etc.
627 Main St., Rapid City
(605) 342–2886

Your custom clubs will be ready in two days, or you can buy ready-made ones off the shelf. Golf balls, bags, shoes, hand-carts, scoring accessories, club-head covers, and a variety of gifts for the golf lover in your life are also available, and club repairs are handled promptly on a walk-in basis. If you need to warm up before heading for the golf course, you can go into the Shaft Lab which analyzes your swing and recommends proper flex. Golf Etc. is closed on Sunday.

Granite Sports
301 Main St., Hill City
(605) 574–2121

Granite Sports' mission statement includes a commitment to stocking the largest selection of climbing equipment in the area. But owner (and climber) Susan Scheirbeck also shows great taste in her assortment of camping gear, backpacks (both human and canine), hiking boots, brand-name outerwear, technical clothing, casual duds (for kids, too), and rugged sweaters. The shop is the Patagonia dealer for the area. We always find something new and fun here that we don't see in other stores. The shop is open daily from May through October and closed Tuesday and Wednesday the rest of the year.

Peak Sports
1002 Jackson Blvd., Rapid City
(605) 341-5445

This shop specializes in downhill skis, snowblades, snowboards, and everything you need to be attired for playing in the snow. Personal attention is yours when you need the proper fit in a boot or a custom insole, and certified personnel are on hand to keep your skis or board in topflight condition. The store does not carry rentals. Peaks Sports is open daily between Labor Day and early spring and is closed the rest of the year.

The Runner's Shop
615 Mt. Rushmore Rd., Rapid City
(605) 348-7866

Lots of stores sell athletic shoes, but how many have this kind of selection, or offer the kind of knowledgeable service you find here? At last count it carried 90 styles of running shoes in stock and at least that number in other types of footwear for hiking, walking, and other activities. The staff has more than 45 years of combined experience fitting runners—and they're runners themselves, which helps—and specializes in modifying shoes for optimal comfort and performance to avoid problems. If it's too late for that, they'll work with you on problem resolution. (We'll spare you our testimonial concerning shin splints.) You can pamper more than your feet here, though, because the shop carries the latest high-tech running wear plus accessories and books, shoe-care products, and even free maps to help you find the best trails. You can also get information about competitive and fun runs here. The store is closed on Sunday.

Terry Peak Ski & Sport
32 Fantail Gulch, Lead
(605) 584-3644

Terry Peak is a retail and rental store for your winter sports needs, so it's a great place to visit if you find yourself exploring the Black Hills in winter, but unprepared for fun in the snow. Skis, snowboards, snowblades, boots, pants, goggles, and personal attention to your needs are all found at Terry Peak. The store is open daily between Labor Day and early spring and is closed the remainder of the year.

Two Wheeler Dealer Cycle and Fitness
100 E. Blvd. N., Rapid City
(605) 343-0524
215 E. Jackson Blvd., Spearfish
(605) 642-7545

So you want to get in shape. Now all you have to do is decide whether to buy a bicycle, treadmill, elipticals, glider, strider, weight machine, or some other type of fitness equipment to help you get the job done. The decision will be much easier after you visit with the folks here, who carry all of the above and more. In bikes alone they stock mountain, road, BMX, fitness, and cruiser models. If you're our age, you remember cruiser bikes with one speed and brakes you activate by pushing backward on the pedals. People are buying "new old bikes," the owner told us, and you can rent bikes here also. The clothing and accessories you need for your active lifestyle are here, too, along with a full-service repair and maintenance shop. You can drop in any day of the week in Rapid City, and Monday through Saturday in Spearfish.

Wide Ride Inc.
210 Cottonwood Dr., Box Elder
(605) 923-3955

Not to be smug or anything, but we'd like to point out that two top names in snowboarding, Wide Ride and Phile 13, are based right in our backyard in the tiny community of Box Elder east of Rapid City. If you're into snowboards, you'll be impressed by the 360-degree cap construction, tip-to-tail wood core, and full-wrap steel edge of these boards that are sold worldwide but also right at the factory. The production facility and retail outlet are open year-round, but hours vary, so call ahead. Guided tours are available on a limited basis by appointment To get there, take 1–90 east from Rapid City, get off at exit 63, and turn east onto the four-lane service road. Follow this road until it narrows to two lanes and turn right onto Cottonwood Drive.

This 'n' That

This fun place gets its own category since it doesn't fit neatly into any of the others. It's located in the Central Hills.

Mistletoe Ranch
23835 U.S. 385, Hill City
(605) 574–4197

Who said you can't have Christmas every day of the year? You can if you visit Mistletoe Ranch, where there are always more than 30 artificial trees decorated in different themes plus high-quality gifts, ornaments, and collectibles galore. The selection changes all the time, but we saw handcrafted Saint Nicholases dressed in brocade and suitable for the most reverent occasion as well as delightfully chubby fleece Santas and reindeer that made us giggle. Of course we fell in love with the irresistible porcelain dolls and the quaint miniature villages with their charming inhabitants. The red plaid carpet, Christmas music, and sweet scents here could turn the grumpiest Scrooge into a right jolly old elf anytime of the

Insiders' Tip
The Black Hills Farmers' Market sets up booths two to three times a week in Rapid City from early July through the end of October. It doesn't have a permanent home, though, so to find out when and where to buy those farm-fresh fruits and veggies, contact the Rapid City Area Chamber of Commerce, 444 Mt. Rushmore Road, (605) 343-1744.

year—he'd probably even want to play the antique pump organ (it really works). Believe it or not, co-owner Joan Davis said she never gets tired of Christmas, not since she stopped hearing carols in her sleep. The store, 3 miles northeast of Hill City, is open daily, and refreshments are served during open-house events each Friday through Sunday in November and December. We passed up the cookies but got a special treat anyway—we watched through the window as a flock of wild turkeys strutted out of the woods and into the side yard.

Attractions

Northern Hills
Central Hills
Southern Hills

We'll let you in on a little Insiders' secret: There's enough to see and do in the Black Hills of South Dakota to keep you busy for months. Still, if you're in the Hills for a two-week visit (and you really work at it), you just might make a good dent in this list of attractions. Otherwise . . . well, you'll just have to come back for another try.

One marvelous feature of the Hills is its great diversity of attractions. We've included the highlights, the places you'd be sorry to miss, the places your South Dakota friends would take you, the places we recommend to our own friends and relatives. This chapter highlights family-style attractions and those of interest to adults. For fun things that are primarily for children, please see our Kidstuff chapter. Other chapters—Daytrips and Weekend Getaways, Recreation, The Badlands and Nearby—provide their own information on things to do and see. For easier planning, we've cross-referenced entries, and tell you where to look for other write-ups.

Our glorious Black Hills summers are the high point of our year, and most visitors come here in June, July, August, and September. Many attractions open a week or two before (or on) Memorial Day weekend and close for the winter on (or a couple of weeks after) Labor Day. Many shorten their hours and days of operation in the early and late part of the season, too. If you're visiting during these times, please call ahead. We also want to point out that many attractions are family owned and operated. They tend to be a bit casual about their operating seasons (due in part to our rather unpredictable winters). Many attractions may plan to close in November, but if the snows begin in October, they'll close early. Some may open in early May, only to find that spring rains are keeping visitors away. They may close again until later in the month or shorten their

The four faces of famous Mount Rushmore are the main attraction in the Black Hills. PHOTO: COURTESY OF NATIONAL PARK SERVICE

GREAT FACES

Calamity Jane

Calamity Jane, one of Deadwood's most famous citizens, passed away in 1903 in debt to the Goldberg Grocery for the sum of $7.00. Calamity is buried at Mount Moriah Cemetery. In recent years the grocery changed ownership and is now a casino and soda fountain (albeit in the original building), but the ledger book with Calamity's still-outstanding balance can be seen at the Adams Memorial Museum.

hours. These South Dakotans have learned to adjust to their weather, so it always pays to call ahead before driving to an attraction.

Not only can seasons affect times of operation but they might also affect prices, as can age makeup and group size. Many establishments have a sliding scale of rates for seniors and children. Seniors, it seems—and young children in general—either get in free or are awarded price breaks in deference to maturity or lack thereof. So, too, with groups. Rates for large groups may be less than for small groups. Rates may also be less in the winter months if, in fact, the establishment is even open. Again, because things can change so rapidly, if the tour is one you really want to make, call again.

Many places listed in this chapter have the additional benefit of being educational. You'll be entertained while you learn about geology, the history of the Wild West, the culture of old Dakota Territory, and the critters and folks who inhabit the present-day Black Hills. By the time you've worked your way through this chapter, you'll feel like an Insider.

Name your attraction. Choose your fun. Indulge your interests. Visit as many as you can. Whichever you choose from in this chapter, you'll have a great time experiencing the delightful blend of entertainment and education that makes Black Hills attractions some of the best and brightest you'll find anywhere.

Northern Hills

Adams Memorial Museum
54 Sherman St., Deadwood
(605) 578-1714

William Emery (usually known as W. E.) Adams came to the Black Hills in 1877 as a miner and eventually became one of Deadwood's most influential and prosperous citizens. The city approached him in the 1920s about funding a museum. It was the perfect time. People were taking a keen interest in history, and many early Deadwood pioneers were still alive. Thus, the museum has many objects and collections that came straight from the collectors, their history and authenticity intact.

You can view displays on Wild Bill Hickok, Calamity Jane, Potato Creek Johnny, the Chinese workers and business owners who came here for the gold rush, the ladies of the night, the gamblers and miners, the first locomotive in the Black Hills, and much more.

This delightful and well-maintained museum, which takes up three floors in a lovely historic building, is open during the summer (May 1 through September 30) from 9:00 A.M. to 6:00 P.M. Monday through Saturday and 9:00 A.M. to 5:00 P.M. on Sunday. Winter hours (October 1 through April 30) are 10:00 A.M. to 4:00 P.M. Tuesday through Saturday and noon to 4:00 P.M. on Sunday. The museum is closed on Thanksgiving Day, Christmas Day, and New Year's Day. Admission (by the stipulation of Mr. Adams himself) is free, but donations are appreciated. A tour of the house is $4.00 for adults.

Black Hills Mining Museum
323 W. Main St., Lead
(605) 584–1605

This museum is a trip through the industry that created and still supports the city of Lead: mining. You'll find plenty of historic photographs and exhibits on mining culture and local history. The museum also offers a video program, guided five-minute tours of a simulated underground mine, and gold panning demonstrations. Plan to try your hand at panning your own gold, too.

All displays and tours are available from mid-May through September 30, seven days a week, from 9:00 A.M. to 5:00 P.M. Admission prices are $4.50 for adults, $4.00 for seniors, and $3.50 for students (age six through college). Kids age five and younger get in free, and the family rate is $15.00. Gold panning is $4.50. From October 1 through early May, the museum is open from 9:00 A.M. to 4:00 P.M. Tuesday through Friday for self-guided tours and video programs. During these months, admission is $2.25 for adults and $1.50 for kids. Groups should call ahead to book special tours.

Black Hills National Cemetery and VFW Memorial Chapel
I–90, exit 34, Sturgis
(605) 347–3830

Row upon row of gleaming white headstones framed against green grass and blue sky are an impressive sight. This is a place of tranquility, where more than 14,000 veterans and their family members lie at rest. The cemetery opened in 1948; veterans from World War I and every war and conflict since are buried here.

If you're looking for the grave of a relative, stop at the Administration Building by the front gate, pick up a map, and use the locator book in the foyer to find the location. While you're in the foyer, note the human-interest stories jotted in the comments column in the guest book. On the day we visited, we found poignant and personal notes of farewell and closure there. Perhaps the atmosphere of peace and the open landscape encourage visitors to leave heartfelt messages like "Miss you,

Dad" and "I'm showing my mom and dad pictures of their grandkids."

The cemetery is open all year and accessible 24 hours a day. The Administration Building is open from 8:30 A.M. until 4:30 P.M. Monday through Friday, but the foyer is always unlocked.

The tiny Veterans of Foreign Wars Memorial Chapel is not part of the National Cemetery, but visitors use it as a place of contemplation before or after their visit. Take the cemetery road (which goes under the interstate) the short distance to the grounds. The chapel is usually unlocked, although it is closed in the winter and sometimes locked after occurrences of vandalism.

The Black Hills Passion Play
I–90, exit 12, Spearfish
(605) 642–2646
(800) 457–0160 (reservations)

The passion play's history dates back to 1242. Josef Meier brought this production to the United States from Germany in 1932, and it has been performed in Spearfish since 1938. The last days of Jesus Christ are reenacted by professional actors and more than 150 volunteer actors in a two-and-one-quarter-hour performance. The amphitheater seats 6,000 and has the largest outdoor stage in the nation. A covered section seats 1,000, but do be prepared for an evening spent outdoors: Bring a jacket and bug spray, just in case you need them.

The play is performed during June, July, and August only, on Sunday, Tuesday, and Thursday at 8:00 P.M. From exit 12 (Jackson Boulevard), follow the signs to St. Joe Street and the amphitheater. Ticket prices are $10 to $18, depending on seat location.

Buckskin Johnny Spaulding Cabin
800 Block of State St., Belle Fourche
No phone

If you admire the pioneers for their courage, independence, and toughness, you should see this cabin to understand how strong they really were. It's difficult to imagine braving a South Dakota winter in this vulnerable home. Built in 1876, the tiny, reconstructed cabin sheltered pioneer and adventurer Buckskin Johnny and his sister's family, the first white settlers in the area. It is now a minimuseum and an eye-opening glimpse into the primitive lives of the early settlers.

Be sure to read the story on the plaque on the cabin's outside wall (or ask a volunteer) of how Johnny and his childhood sweetheart, Nettie, were separated in their youth. They were finally reunited after a 53-year separation and were married from 1927 until 1932, when Johnny died.

The cabin is open only from May 15 to September 15. Hours of operation vary with peak months. There is no telephone, but you will find further information at the Tri-State Memorial Museum (see later entry), which operates the cabin. Admission is free; donations are appreciated.

CB&Q Engine House
Sherman St. Parking Lot, Deadwood
(605) 578-2082

The railroad changed Deadwood from just another muddy mining camp into a town with real transportation, linked to the rest of the Black Hills. The railroad changed Deadwood's future and culture, too, and this interpretive center is the place to learn how that happened. The displays are especially rich in railroading legend and fact. The building is the actual 1930 engine house where huge steam-driven Mallet locomotives were serviced and readied for their trips. The engine house is in the parking lot next to the old depot (now First Western-Bank). It is not staffed and there is no phone.

It is open mid-May to mid-September, and hours are from 8:00 A.M. to 8:00 P.M. (they do vary). For information or to check on hours, call Deadwood's Department of Planning, Zoning, and Historic Preservation at the number above during business hours. There is no charge for admission.

Days of '76 Historic Museum
17 Crescent Dr., Deadwood
(605) 578-2872

This museum is a terrific, free attraction. It's pleasantly stuffed with interesting artifacts that are more casually collected and displayed than the Adams Memorial Museum's (see earlier listing). The bricks on the floor are the original bricks from the streets of old Deadwood, and there are plenty of Old West artifacts, photos, and letters here to keep you browsing for an hour.

The horse-drawn vehicle collection is extensive and delightful. You'll see real buggies, buckboards, carriages, covered wagons, three hearses, and the original Cheyenne-to-Deadwood Stage, which navigated wild Western terrain for 11 years.

The museum is open approximately late April to early October, from approximately 8:00 A.M. to 8:00 P.M. You'll find it off U.S. 85-14A on Crescent Drive. Donations are accepted.

Insiders' Tip

Belle Fourche claims the designation of Geographical Center of the U.S. (it's the only town of size near the official spot). In 1959, after Alaska and Hawaii became states, the U.S. Coast and Geodetic Survey moved the center from Kansas to a point about 20 miles north of Belle Fourche. The site is on inaccessible, rattlesnake-infested land, but you can read the official plaque at the Center of the Nation Information Center, 415 Fifth Avenue, Belle Fourche.

GREAT PLACES

Historic Houses

The historic houses of Lead and Deadwood appear to perch—some quite precariously—on the rocky hillsides on which the towns are built. Some houses have been beautifully renovated and others allowed to decay. Most streets are quite narrow, some are one-way deadends, and you don't want to attempt them in the winter.

Both Lead and Deadwood sprang up during the gold rush days, although Lead was a camp built for the employees of the Homestake Mine. Today the mine spreads out beneath much of the town, and Lead home owners own just the surface rights to their properties. The Homestake mine owns the rights to everything underneath—dirt, minerals, and maybe gold.

D.C. Booth Historic Fish Hatchery,
National Fish Culture
Hall of Fame and Museum
and Historic Booth Home
423 Hatchery Circle, Spearfish
(605) 642–7730

You don't have to be a fishing enthusiast to enjoy this attraction. If you are, though, you'll find the historic hatchery and museum a delight. Trout hatchlings were once raised here to stock Western streams. You'll learn about the hatchery process and how it evolved as technology and knowledge improved. The fish car, an early 1900s railroad car that was equipped to transport fish all over the country on their way to new trout streams, is open for viewing.

If you're less than enthusiastic about fishing, you'll still enjoy strolling the grounds, feeding the always-hungry ducks and fish, and touring the Booth home. The house was built in 1905 and is listed in the National Register of Historic Places. Furnished in period antiques and Booth family memorabilia, it is a delightful example of the attention to design and detail obvious in the gracious homes of that era. Be sure to visit the underwater viewing window near the entrance to the grounds, where the resident rainbow trout and brown trout swim by, as curious about you as you are about them. It's a chance for a rare fish-eye view as well as a humorous glimpse from below of paddling duck feet.

The hatchery, museum, and home are open from mid-May through mid-September, seven days a week, from 10:00 A.M. to 5:00 P.M. There is no admission charge, but donations are accepted. The hatchery and grounds are next door to the Spearfish City Park and are open from dawn until dusk.

High Plains Heritage Center Museum
Heritage Dr., Spearfish
(605) 642–WEST

The center's impressive building sits alone atop a high hill, where it is whipped by wild plains winds and overlooks the green hills beyond. If you're lucky you might get to watch a high plains thunderstorm blow in from far away—complete with roiling black clouds and jagged lightning. The setting is perfect for a museum dedicated to high plains life, which is greatly affected by the landscape and the weather.

Inside the center you'll see many forms of western art and artifacts, including old buggies and wagons; saddles and spurs; a barbed-wire collection (old barbed wire is an art form itself); re-creations of shops from the past; wood carvings; original art and photographs; and plenty more. A 17-foot-high sculpture of legendary trail boss Tennessee Vaughn astride his rearing horse is especially impressive.

Outdoors, get a close-up look at grazing longhorn steers and buffalo, a one-room schoolhouse, a log cabin, and a sod

Belle Fourche sculptor Jim Maher created Generation for the D.C. Booth Historic Fish Hatchery grounds in Spearfish, using his father and daughter as models. PHOTO: KIMBERLY METZ

dugout. Kids will love the petting farm in the summer months.

The museum is open year-round seven days a week. Hours from Memorial Day through Labor Day are 9:00 A.M. to 8:00 P.M.; hours for the rest of the year are 9:00 A.M. to 5:00 P.M. Admission prices are $4.00 for adults and $1.00 for students 6 to 16. To get there, take I-90 to exit 14 S. and go to Heritage Drive, 1 mile south.

Homestake Gold Mine Surface
Tours and Visitor Center
160 W. Main St., Lead
(605) 584-3110

The Homestake Gold Mine was the oldest continuously operating underground gold mine in the world until 2001. Financial considerations, however, forced closure and today, the former mine retains only its visitor center and gift shop, which features Black Hills gold. Hours of opera-

tion will be flexible, but generally the store will be open during the summertime operation between 8:00 A.M. and 5:00 P.M. on weekends. The visitor center will be free.

Mount Moriah Cemetery (Boot Hill)
Lincoln St., Deadwood
No telephone

No dedicated Deadwood visitor leaves without paying respects to those who lie at Boot Hill. Calamity Jane's and Wild Bill Hickok's graves are the main attractions, though lesser-known—but no less interesting—folks are also buried here. Pick up a walking-tour guide at the ticket booth. It will furnish the human-interest stories lacking on traditionally succinct tombstones. Take note of the nearly empty Chinese section (most bodies were eventually returned to China), the Jewish section (where many stones are inscribed in Hebrew), and the three Potter's Fields.

The Homestake Lode proved to be the most important gold discovery in the Black Hills. This old photo shows early-day miners working underground in the Homestake Gold Mine in Lead. PHOTO: COURTESY OF BLACK HILLS MINING MUSEUM

Spearfish Canyon is especially beautiful under a blanket of new snow. PHOTO: COURTESY OF SOUTH DAKOTA TOURISM

Among the colorful characters buried here are madam Dora Dufran, who is buried with her parrot, Fred, and Blanche Colman, the first woman member of the South Dakota Bar, who, nonetheless, was self-taught. Mount Moriah is built on a hill, and the paths are steep and lined with gravel; they may be difficult for some to negotiate. Bus and trolley tours are available, but they don't cover the entire cemetery. See our Getting Here, Getting Around chapter for transportation options.

The cemetery is open all year, but the ticket booth is open from May to Labor Day from 7:00 A.M. to 8:00 P.M., then from 9:00 A.M. to 5:00 P.M. for the rest of September, and intermittently until winter sets in. Admission is $1.00 for adults and 50 cents for children older than 12.

Old Fort Meade Museum
and Old Post Cemetery
U.S. 34, Ft. Meade
(605) 347–9822

Stepping into the museum is like stepping back in time. From 1878 until 1944 the soldiers of the Fort Meade Army Post helped to guard the Black Hills from conflicts triggered by Custer's discovery of gold in 1874 and the gold rush that began two years later. (See our History chapter for more information.) Today Fort Meade includes the Veterans Administration Medical Center and the Veterans Affairs complex.

The museum chronicles historic events and changes with displays chockfull of artifacts, clippings, photographs, and stories. Fort Meade was the home of Custer's Seventh Cavalry (after Little Big Horn and the death of Custer) and the Buffalo Soldiers of the 25th Infantry, Dakota Territory. It was also one of two South Dakota prison camps during World War II, housing soldiers from Gen. Rommel's African Corps.

To get to the museum building, enter the grounds at the Fort Meade complex entrance and follow the blue signs. It is open daily from May 15 through September 15. From Memorial Day weekend through Labor Day weekend, hours are 8:00 A.M. to 6:00 P.M. Hours are 9:00 A.M. to 5:00 P.M. from May 15 until Memorial Day weekend and from Labor Day weekend until September 15. Admission prices are $3.00 for adults and children 12 and older.

The Old Post Cemetery is on a hill south of the museum, accessed by a gravel road. It's best to ask for directions at the museum before attempting to find it on your own. Soldiers, their relatives, and civilians were buried in the cemetery from 1878 until about 1948, when the Black Hills National Cemetery opened. In the tradition of the time, headstones have very little detail (some even lack dates), and the number of children buried there may shock you. Those who are fascinated by historic cemeteries will find this one interesting. Others will enjoy the tranquility of the spot and the added bonus of beautiful Bear Butte in the distance. It's open all year, 24 hours a day. There is no fee for admission.

Spearfish Canyon Scenic Byway
U.S. 14A

One of the glories of South Dakota is the amazing diversity of scenery: mountains, prairie, badlands, forest, high plains. But nothing quite compares to Spearfish Canyon. The canyon—six times older than the Grand Canyon—is so spectacular, in fact, that it is a National Scenic Byway, a designation that acknowledges its famous beauty. Highway 14A is a 19-mile winding paved road that ends at Cheyenne Crossing and U.S. 85 at its south end and at the Spearfish city limits at its north end.

The byway is often a bit crowded, especially in summer and also in fall, when the aspens burst into autumn color framed by deep green spruce and pine. The highway follows Spearfish Creek through towering limestone cliffs and thick forests as it spills over and out into spectacular Bridal Veil Falls and Roughlock Falls. The shoulders of the highway are wide enough for bicycles (the grade is a comfortable 3 percent), and there are picnic areas and pullovers so you can safely stop and take photographs.

Allow enough time to hike into the woods or an adjoining canyon. The creek is also known for its trout. You can find plenty of listings for nearby places to dine

LEGENDS & LORE

Col. Carlton's Patriotic Legacy

In 1892 Fort Meade post commander Col. Caleb Carlton and his wife discussed their idea that the United States needed a national "air." Mrs. Carlton suggested the well-known "Star Spangled Banner" written by Francis Scott Key. Col. Carlton commanded the melody be played at the fort's retreats, parades, and concerts. He took the opportunity to explain this new custom to the governors of South Dakota and Pennsylvania and interest spread. Soon Secretary of War Daniel Lamont ordered that the composition be played each evening at every U.S. Army post.

Col. Carlton initiated the practice of standing and removing hats while the music played. The heart-stirring song and the respectful acts of patriotism accompanying its performances were so popular that in 1931 Congress declared the "Star Spangled Banner" our national anthem.

---

or spend the night in our Restaurants and Accommodations chapters. Be sure to allot enough time for a relaxed drive through the idyllic canyon. Your only concern should be the other drivers, who are gazing around in awe as much as you are.

Sturgis Motorcycle Museum & Hall of Fame
Junction & Main (The Old Post Office across
the street from the Armory), Sturgis
(605) 347–2001
www.sturgismotorcyclemuseum.org

When does a motorcycle sound like a vegetable? When it's a Harley-Davidson! It's said that idling Harleys, with their deep-throated, staccato rumble, sound like "potato, potato, potato." (Listen, they really do.) Plan on visiting the Sturgis Rally held early each August, so you can hear lots of that sound. (See the Annual Events and Festivals chapter for details on the Sturgis Rally & Races.) And while there, you'll want to see the new Sturgis Motorcycle Museum & Hall of Fame. Be aware, however, that the location has changed and so has the name.

According to Director Mark Smith, the change came about when the national organization decided to move its museum to Ammamosa, Iowa. "Everyone associates motorcycles with Sturgis," said Smith. "In fact, the Sturgis Rally is almost as traditional as motherhood and apple pie. And we deserve a museum. Everyone knows that, and that's why we decided to create our own museum right here in Sturgis."

Like the old museum, this one also has vintage Harleys and lots more. You'll be intrigued by 100 or so historic motorcycles, including Indians, Royal Enfields, BSAs, Triumphs, Nortons, and others, plus cycling memorabilia and the photos and stories of Hall of Fame members.

In general, those inducted into the Motorcycle Hall of Fame are drawn from those cyclists who support the rally and have in some way made a substantial contribution to the sport of riding. Names in the list include Senator Ben Nighthorse Campbell and South Dakota Governor William Janklow, as well as many writers and editors associated with cycling publications.

Like the old museum, the new one will be open all year from 9:00 A.M. to 9:00 P.M. Monday through Saturday and 11:00 A.M. to 4:00 P.M. on Sunday after Labor Day and until Memorial Day and from 9:00 A.M. to 6:00 P.M. Sunday from Memorial Day through Labor Day. During Rally week (for seven mid-August days or so), hours are 9:00 A.M. to 9:00 P.M. Admission is $3.00 for adults; children 12 and younger get in free.

Tri-State Memorial Museum
831 State St., Belle Fourche
(605) 892–3705

This often-overlooked tribute to local Western history is staffed by friendly senior citizens and stuffed with an amazing array of artifacts, all nicely displayed. You'll enjoy the wonderful, whimsical collection of 4,000 old salt and pepper shakers, a button collection that includes a dress covered in buttons, a doll collection with a rare wax doll that mustn't get too warm, a tender display of handsome wedding dresses donated by local ladies, and much more.

Be sure to see the family histories told in photos and clippings on the panel displays. They're a fascinating look into juxtaposed past and present, with pictures of homesteading pioneer great-great-grandmothers next to recent snapshots of the school-age great-great-grandchildren they never got to meet.

From May 15 through June 1, and September 1 through September 15, hours are 2:00 to 8:00 P.M., Monday through Friday. From June 1 through August 31, hours are 8:00 A.M. to 8:00 P.M. Monday through Saturday and 2:00 to 8:00 P.M. on Sunday. The free museum closes after September 15 each year.

Central Hills

The abundant attractions in the Central Hills are listed alphabetically as usual—with one exception. Since this area is dotted with caverns and caves, we've culled a few of our favorites and placed them at the end of this section under that heading. Also see the Jewel Cave and Wind Cave entries in the Southern Hills listings.

Bear Country U.S.A.
U.S. 16, Rapid City
(605) 343–2290
www.bearcountryusa.com

It's not every day you have to brake for a big, burly bruin or a gaggle of geese, but at Bear Country you can count on it. Here it seems natural for the animals to roam about while the people are confined to their cars with the windows up. Besides bears you'll see elk, reindeer, mountain goats, bighorn sheep, wolves, bison, mountain lions, wild turkeys, and other species as you drive through the 200-acre park on paved roads. The day we visited, a black bear lumbered across the road in front of our car, sat down in the grass, and reached back to scratch itself on the hip with a hefty-looking forepaw.

After your drive you'll be able to get out and walk through the Wildlife Center for a (relatively) close look at bear cubs and other small animals. If you have little ones of your own in tow, a visit to the barnyard animals in the petting area is a must. The youngest visitors can also take a few turns around the pony pen. You'll find more critters, though not live ones, in the Bear's Den gift shop and gallery, where quality collectibles, clothing, and other items are for sale. There's also a snack bar and picnic area for hungry folks and brownbaggers.

Bear Country, 8 miles south of Rapid City, is open from early May to late October, weather permitting. During peak season, mid-June to mid-August, hours are 8:00 A.M. to 7:30 P.M. daily; the rest of the time it's roughly 8:00 A.M. to 5:00 P.M., but it would be wise to call ahead. Plan to spend at least an hour and a half once you get there. Admission is $9.50 for adults and $5.50 for children ages 6 to 15. A carload of visitors tops out at $35.00. Pony rides are $1.00.

Berlin Wall Exhibit
Memorial Park, Eighth St., Rapid City

Take a break from your busy activities and visit this quiet, thoughtful tribute to freedom. Take Mount Rushmore Road north from Omaha Street (there it becomes Eighth Street) and park in the Rushmore Plaza Civic Center parking lot. Walk over to the grim concrete wall sections, with the rounded tops that make them nearly impossible to climb over. These are replicas of the wall (the originals contain asbestos and cannot be imported to the United States), but the wicked-looking steel tank traps in front of them are authentic. Read the story of the Berlin Wall—how it came about, its harsh history, and how it ended—on the displays.

Rapid City's sister city is Apolda, Germany, whose mayor attended the exhibit's opening in 1996. This free exhibit is accessible 24 hours a day, year-round. After your visit continue your walk through Memorial Park and explore the fantastic Rapid City park system. Read about it in our Recreation chapter.

Big Thunder Gold Mine
604 Blair St., Keystone
(605) 666–4847, (800) 314–3917

Learn about the history of Black Hills gold mining, explore an 1800s underground mine, and try panning streamside for your own specks of gleaming treasure. Guided tours begin with a 10-minute film, and each hard-hatted visitor is rewarded with a free sample of gold ore at the end of the 68-foot tunnel. If your best panning efforts fail to yield anything, you can purchase a small vial of pure, 24-carat gold leaf in the gift shop that also carries souvenirs, books, rocks, and that great pretender, fool's gold.

The mine is open May through September. Hours are 8:00 A.M. to 8:00 P.M. from Memorial Day through Labor Day and 9:00 A.M. to 5:00 P.M. the rest of the season. Tours cost $6.95 for adults and $3.95 for children ages 6 to 12; those 5 and younger get in free. For $3.50 more you can go gold panning too. If you want to pan for gold and skip the tour, you'll pay $5.50 per pan.

Black Hills Central Railroad/The 1880 Train
222 Railroad Ave., Hill City
(605) 574–2222

It's the late nineteenth century and the train has brought you safely to the depot at the end of a rugged journey through the mountains. At least you might find yourself believing that after your 20-mile round-trip on The 1880 Train—except that you'll have taken lots of pictures with your modern-day camera. Vintage railroad cars pulled by a steam locomotive chug along the original Chicago, Burlington & Quincy route that served the mining district around Hill City and Keystone more than a century ago. Before or after your ride you can dine at the Highliner snack shop, where seating is available on the deck or in a railcar decorated with railroad memorabilia. In the gift shop you'll find train-related videos, books, and other items.

The 1880 Train in Hill City takes you on an excursion into yesteryear. PHOTO: COURTESY OF SOUTH DAKOTA TOURISM

After Memorial Day and before Labor Day, the train pulls out from Hill City at 7:15 A.M., 9:45 A.M., 1:15 P.M., and 4:00 P.M. Monday through Friday. From Keystone, the train pulls out at 8:30 A.M., 11:00 A.M., and 2:30 P.M. Before Memorial Day and after Labor Day, the schedule is limited. Reservations are recommended because space for the two-hour rides is limited. A restricted timetable is in effect from mid-May to mid-June and after Labor Day until early October; call for information. You also need to call if you want to board at the Keystone junction or to find out about special evening rides during July and August. Tickets cost $18 for adults and $10 for youths.

Borglum Historical Center
(Rushmore-Borglum Story)
342 Winter St., Keystone
(605) 666–4448
www.rushmoreborglum.com

Get acquainted with Mount Rushmore sculptor Gutzon Borglum before visiting the mountain he carved. A self-guided, narrated tour provides background about the artist's personal and professional history as well as the significance of the masterpiece that immortalized him. Texts of the tour are available in English, French, Spanish, German, Japanese, and Mandarin Chinese. (Please see the Mount Rushmore listing later in this chapter for more on Borglum.)

The tour, begun in 1978, includes a 25-minute newsreel compiled from old photos, news clips, and broadcasts, narrated by Lowell Thomas. The gallery displays more of Borglum's work. The large museum/gift shop features a wide array of artwork, books, and videos; more sculpture is displayed outside.

Located in Keystone, 3 miles north of Mount Rushmore, the Center is open daily May through the first week of October. The hours are 8:00 A.M. to 7:00 P.M. June through August. Call for hours in May, September, and October. Admission is $7.00 for adults, $6.50 for seniors, $3.25 for ages 7 to 17, and free for those younger than 7. There's a special family rate of $20.00 and a discount rate during Sturgis Rally & Races week each August.

Chapel in the Hills (Stav Kirke Chapel)
3788 Chapel La., Rapid City
(605) 342–8281

Known in English as Chapel in the Hills, and in Norwegian as Stav Kirke, the little wooden church in the pines is a 1969 replica of the twelfth-century Borgund Church in Laerdal, Norway. The ornately carved, unique structure takes its name, which means stave church, from the 12 staves around which it is built. The staves represent the 12 Apostles, the foundation of the Christian church. With its wooded backdrop and broad, well-kept lawn, the chapel and its grounds impart a sense of peace and well-being. It's no wonder couples from a wide area choose to be married here.

Visitors can sit on wooden benches in the chapel and listen to a continuous tape to learn more about the building's many intricate features, including the dragon heads that adorn the roof. There's also a late-nineteenth-century log cabin built by Norwegian immigrant Edward Nielsen that has been turned into a museum cozily furnished with authentic Scandinavian antiques. The reception center/gift shop, housed in a grass-roofed stabbur imported from Norway, continues the Scandinavian motif with carvings, handcrafts, and books. In addition to its spiritual and architectural significance, Chapel in the Hills reminds visitors of the many northern Europeans who immigrated to South Dakota, imbuing the state with their steadfast, vivid heritage.

Chapel in the Hills is open from 8:00 A.M. until dusk daily, from May 1 through September 30. A half-hour nondenominational vespers service begins at 8:00 P.M. each evening from mid-June through late August. Weddings may be scheduled from mid-March until mid-November. Admission is free, but donations to support the nonprofit operation are appreciated. To get there, take Highway 44 to Chapel Lane in Rapid City and follow the signs to the Stav Kirke.

Cleghorn Springs State Fish Hatchery
Hwy. 44, Rapid City
(605) 394–2399 (summer only)
(605) 394–2391

No sense trying to worm your way out of it—even if you've never been caught by the lure of fishing, you're likely to get hooked on the hatchery. Besides ponds full of trout for stocking South Dakota waters, there's an Aquatic Center where you can learn about watersheds, fish, and fishing. There are nature programs, too, and pellets are available if you want to feed the fish.

Hours are 9:00 A.M. to 4:30 P.M. daily from Memorial Day to the end of August, and you can call for information about summer programs. Programs and admission are free.

Cosmos Mystery Area
U.S. 16, Rapid City
(605) 343–9802, (605) 343–7278

If you want to stand up straight at Cosmos, just lean forward, especially if you're standing on the wall. To learn more about this baffling place, see our Kidstuff chapter.

The Journey Museum
222 New York St., Rapid City
(605) 394–6923
www.journeymuseum.org

Housed in a spectacular building, this museum is a techno-wonder. Your own journey through it starts with a dramatic movie about the geologic and cultural history of the Black Hills. Then continue with a self-guided tour that's both educational and entertaining, thanks to hand-held sound sticks that allow you to walk, stop, and listen at your own pace. The sound sticks explain the exhibits in Lakota or English (other languages will be available in the future).

The Journey was designed as an interactive excursion through time, beginning with the earth-shattering birth of the Hills and moving through detailed accounts of the Native American way of life, the arrival of white explorers, the gold rush, pioneer days, paleontology and archaeology, ranching and farming, and much more.

Here's a secret: When you reach the tepee, sit on the bench in front of it, hold the sound stick to your ear, and wait for the moon to come up over the tepee. You'll be treated to a holographic visit with Nellie Two Bulls, Lakota elder. Other exhibits also "materialize" if you wait for them. The museum was designed to provide a contemplative experience; it's not to be hurried through—take your time and enjoy.

We recommend you make The Journey one of your early stops: It will enhance your understanding of the rich culture of the Black Hills. The gift shop, stocked with Native-made crafts, is above average. The Journey houses two galleries, the Sioux Indian Museum Gallery, and another displaying original South Dakota and Midwestern artists.

The museum is open daily year-round. From Memorial Day to Labor Day, hours are 9:00 A.M. to 5:00 P.M. In winter, it's open from 10:00 A.M. to 5:00 P.M. Monday through Saturday and from 1:00 to 5:00 P.M. on Sunday. Admission prices are $6.00 for adults and $4.00 for students ages 11 to 17. Call the museum for group student rates.

Motion Unlimited Museum and Antique Car Lot
Hwy. 79, Rapid City
(605) 348–7373
www.motionoldcars.com

You don't have to spend half your life under the hood of a car to appreciate the automobiles, motorcycles, and other memorabilia on display here. Even the toys in glass cases look like they've been lovingly restored. The car collection spans several decades and changes over time, but you might find among the more unusual exhibits a 1926 Model-T paddy wagon with bars on the rear windows (more fun for today's spectator than yesterday's passenger, no doubt), an airplane car, a 1925 Studebaker motor home, and a 1932 Ford dragster.

We were bowled over by the motorcycle room where we discovered such gems as a red-upholstered 1960 Harley-Davidson ServiCar swanky enough to take Cinderella to the ball and a tiny, turquoise

Wyss kid's cycle—ISN'T IT CUTE? the sign read. (Yup.)

What you see is all the more impressive when you learn that owners Bill and Peggy Napoli have done much of the restoration work themselves. They have a parking lot full of "project" cars waiting for the right owner to purchase and fix up. How about an Edsel?

The museum, 2 miles south of Rapid City, is open from 9:00 A.M. to 6:00 P.M. Monday through Friday and 9:00 A.M. to 4:00 P.M. Saturday, April through September. Admission is $4.00 for adults, and free to those 12 and younger. There's no charge to look around the car lot, which is mostly open all year. Call ahead for winter hours.

Mount Rushmore National Memorial
Hwy. 244, Keystone
(605) 574-2523

Egypt has the pyramids; England has Stonehenge. But ancient artisans were not the last to create world-class stone monuments, for a modern-day example is found in the Black Hills at Mount Rushmore. One of the nation's most recognizable landmarks, the towering busts of four U.S. presidents—George Washington, Thomas Jefferson, Abraham Lincoln, and Theodore Roosevelt—stand in tribute to the American ideals of freedom and progress. But the carving by American sculptor Gutzon Borglum can't help inspiring awe as an impressive feat of engineering and an extraordinary work of art as well.

Insiders' Tip

Visitors like to photograph Mount Rushmore through the tunnels on Iron Mountain Road, and that requires tricking your camera. The darkness of the stone is a high contrast to the light on the tunnel's other end. Your camera's meter will read the darker stone, overexpose the shot, and, when your photos are developed, the great faces will be washed out. The trick is to ignore your camera's meter reading. "Stop down," or close down, the lens aperture to let in less light. (For those of us who always forget the aperture rule, the higher the number, the smaller the aperture, because it's a reciprocal.) You'll need to use F8, F11, F16, and maybe F22, and you should also match (or approximate) the shutter speed to the film speed. Another method to photograph Mount Rushmore from the nearby tunnels is to move to the mouth of the tunnel, point the camera directly at the faces and set your exposure by the meter reading you get. Then move back and photograph, ignoring the metering changes your camera wants you to make. Don't forget, too, that Mount Rushmore's southeastern exposure makes morning the best time to take pictures of the faces.

George Washington's was the first presidential face to appear on Mount Rushmore and was dedicated with great fanfare on July 4, 1930.

PHOTO: STEVEN A. PAGE

Flamboyant, patriotic, and hugely talented, Borglum, the son of Danish immigrants, believed a great nation deserved public art as big as all outdoors. So when he was invited to Georgia in the 1920s to create a Confederate soldiers' memorial, he envisioned giant likenesses of Dixie leaders carved onto the granite face of Stone Mountain. With the work under way, a bitter quarrel with his sponsors over artistic freedom, funding, and other differences led to Borglum's dismissal—and an invitation to start over in South Dakota.

Borglum was 60 years old in 1927 when he started work on Mount Rush-more, hiring nearly 400 workers to drill, blast, and chisel rock off the mountainside. They were almost done when the sculptor died on March 6, 1941, leaving his son, Lincoln, to oversee the job's completion within a few months. In the years since, assorted promoters have lobbied to add other faces, but the younger Borglum said Mount Rushmore should remain true to his father's vision, and the National Park Service, which administers the memorial, is committed to keeping it as is. Besides, it would take an act of Congress to change the mountain—and Park Service officials say there's no more carvable rock.

Newsweek columnist George F. Will has called Mount Rushmore "an agreeable example of American excess," and indeed, more than 2.5 million people from around the world visit the Shrine of Democracy each year. Before viewing the 60-foot-tall faces, you'll want to stop in the information center to learn about the monument and the 1,240-acre park's other features and free activities. For starters, you can see original tools, models, and other relics in the Sculptor's Studio, and the wheelchair-accessible Presidential Trail will take you to the talus slope along the base of the mountain. The park service offers a variety of guided walks and talks daily throughout the summer, and those in the 5- to 12-year-old crowd even have their own activities that make learning about Mount Rushmore fun. Parents can help their youngsters earn a certificate through the Junior Ranger Program or have them take part in a 30-minute ranger-led program. (Turn to our Kidstuff chapter for more details.)

(For other Mount Rushmore-related attractions, see the Borglum Historical Center, Rushmore Aerial Tramway, and Rushmore Helicopters listings in this chapter.)

In 1998 a new interpretive center/ museum complex opened with 5,000 square feet of exhibit space and two theaters for viewing an informational video. It's just one of numerous recent improvements that include the pergola, or grand entryway, the Information Center and rest room complex, the amphitheater, a new Avenue of Flags, a spacious gift shop, and

GREAT PLACES

Rapid City's Place in Aviation History

Think pioneer aviation and you're likely to think of Kitty Hawk, North Carolina, where the Wright brothers made a short hop in the world's first airplane in 1903. But a spot near Rapid City in the Black Hills earned a place in aviation history in 1935, when two army officers, Orvil Anderson and Albert Stevens, set an altitude record in a helium balloon launched from the Stratosphere bowl. The balloon, Explorer II, ascended 72,395 feet, enabling its crew to collect new data on Earth's upper atmosphere. Today the gondola that carried the men and equipment is in the National Air and Space Museum in Washington, D.C.

The Stratobowl, as it has come to be called, is a flat, circular field sheltered by rocky cliffs. Its unique characteristics have attracted numerous other balloonists, including millionaire adventurer Steve Fossett, who launched an unsuccessful around-the-world flight from the bowl on January 8, 1996. The bowl itself is privately owned and not open to the public, but you can look down into it from the rim. (You'll have to hike in about three quarters of a mile.) In addition to the view, there's a plaque commemorating the 1935 launch, which was sponsored by the National Geographic Society and the U.S. Army Air Corps.

To get to the Stratobowl rim, look for the gate and cattle guard off U.S. 16 about 10 miles southwest of Rapid City. Pull in and park at the gate; if you find yourself at the Black Hills National Forest overlook, you've gone too far. The rim is on U.S. Forest Service land, so all agency rules and laws apply.

---

a new food-service facility with two snack bars and a cafeteria.

Most of these additions are the product of a nearly $24 million fund-raising campaign by the Mount Rushmore National Memorial Society, an organization Borglum himself formed in 1930. Contributions poured in from dozens of South Dakota communities, all 50 states, and about 20 foreign countries. Private donors have included descendants of New York attorney Charles Rushmore, who was visiting the Hills on behalf of mining interests when the mountain was named for him, partly in jest, in 1885. The successful campaign will permit the completion of Borglum's final dream of a Hall of Records, a stone chamber behind the faces for storing documents about the making of Mount Rushmore.

No doubt the artist would approve of the sophisticated monitoring and maintenance procedures now in place to preserve his masterpiece as well. Each fall, for instance, hairline cracks in the granite faces are painstakingly sealed by hand with silicone caulk.

One of the best ways to share Borglum's vision is to attend the evening lighting ceremony that begins with a talk and a film at 9:00 P.M. in the amphitheater each summer evening. Lights illuminate the faces at 9:30 P.M. (Everything begins an hour earlier between Labor Day and mid-September.) Weather-related cancellations are rare, but call ahead if in doubt. Even during the off-season, the faces are bathed in light for an hour or two each evening, beginning shortly after dusk. It's a tradition that at least some local people take seriously—a temporary federal government shutdown in 1996 left Mount Rushmore in the dark, so Keystone rancher Art Oakes dug into his own pocket and took up a collection to pay the light bill.

Mount Rushmore is open 24 hours a day all year except Christmas Day. The Information Center is open from 8:00 A.M.

Hot Springs' Sandstone Buildings

When late-nineteenth-century white settlers discovered natural warm waters in the southern Black Hills, a health resort was the inevitable result. (See our History chapter for more information.) But enterprising developers of the day were quick to also capitalize on a second treasure trove to promote Hot Springs as a premier destination. It seemed that local sandstone quarries held the perfect material to build an illustrious city, for the giant, rosy blocks that were cut and hauled to construction sites were not only enduring but also beautiful.

Present-day Hot Springs boasts 32 sandstone buildings from the late 1800s and early 1900s. They are what you notice when you arrive in town and what you remember after you've gone. Fred T. Evans, whose name resounds throughout Hot Springs today, must have had that in mind when he set about building the Minnekahta Block in 1891 and the Evans Hotel a year later. Both structures are included on a walking tour of historic buildings; you can pick up a color brochure and go on your own or make an appointment for a guided tour by calling the Hot Springs Chamber of Commerce at (605) 745–4140.

Your tour will take you to the sprawling, tile-roofed 1907 Veterans Administration Medical Center and the world's smallest Union Depot, built in 1891; to the 1889 State Veterans Home, the first major stone building; and to the 1932 post office, the last local building to be built from local stone.

As you walk around town, look for details such as the carved face and purple accent blocks on the Petty building on Albany and Chicago streets, and the multiple

The 1907 Veterans Administration Medical Center, featuring a red-tile roof, is one of Hot Springs' most impressive sandstone buildings. PHOTO: BARBARA TOMOVICK

styles of tooling on City Hall. Before it got serious about preservation, the town lost some of its old beauties, and even now public opinion is divided on whether to try to save others. The 1913 Carnegie Library building, for example, was condemned and vacated in 1995 because of cracking, and at least some preservationists are unhappy about plans to raze all but the facade and build new.

Since 1976 the city-appointed Hot Springs Historic Preservation Commission has headed up efforts to save what remains of the town's grand architectural legacy. Things got under way in 1977 when the National Trust for Historic Preservation named Hot Springs one of three pilot sites nationwide for a Main Street USA restoration project funded with matching grants. The commission has since strengthened its own ability to obtain grants for additional projects by gaining certified local government status in 1994. It's also begun stockpiling sandstone blocks from fallen buildings to use in restoration work. In addition, the local Save Our Sandstone Foundation Inc. raises money and provides labor to acquire and restore buildings. The two groups acted together to save the Evans Hotel after it was gutted by fire in 1979; it now houses 84 low-income apartments for the elderly.

The city's historic district is listed in the National Register of Historic Places, making tax credits and other advantages available for preservation work. But the high cost of restoration means that saving all the buildings, some of which are privately owned, would take many years and millions of dollars.

Nonetheless, although the trains that used to puff into town four times a day have vanished along with the red carpets and bands that greeted passengers, it's nice to think that if Fred Evans arrived today he'd be able to recognize the little city he so energetically endorsed. He'd find tourists relaxing at his old Plunge Bath (now Evans Plunge), and he'd surely note with satisfaction that sandstone from his quarry still graces the streets of Hot Springs.

to 10:00 P.M. during the summer and from 8:00 A.M. to 5:00 P.M. for the winter. The season for special activities is May 15 to September 30.

You can park for free if you don't mind climbing 60 or more steps from the parking lot. Otherwise, parking in the new tri-level ramp just outside the grand entryway costs $8.00 per passenger vehicle for as many visits as you care to make in a single calendar year. (Buses pay $25.00 every time they enter.) The parking fees were established in 1997 to pay off an $18 million loan to the Mount Rushmore Society for the parking ramp and related roadways. So although admission to the actual park grounds is free, your Golden Eagle, Golden Age, or Golden Access pass won't be honored at the parking ramp.

Museum of Geology
501 E. St. Joseph St., Rapid City
(605) 394-2467
(800) 544-8162 ext. 2467 (weekdays)
www.hpcnet.org/sdsmt/geologymuseum

Even if you're not a scientist, it's easy to spend hours among the exhibits in this working museum on the campus of South Dakota School of Mines and Technology. The Badlands (see our chapter called The Badlands and Nearby) and Black Hills provide a ready supply of fossils and minerals, respectively, but you'll also see fascinating, colorful rocks from around the world on display here. There are even meteorites, models of famous diamonds, gold nuggets (we figured the 2,168-ounce "Welcome Nugget" from Australia would take care of our bills, plus a few vacations), and a case full of South Dakota minerals. Dinosaur skeletons (including a dino leg bone you can touch), polished agates, fossilized fish, and a slice of faulted sandstone (you can see where it buckled) are other eye-catching exhibits. And here's your chance for a close-up look at boxwork, popcorn, and frostwork, which are some of the mineral formations in Wind Cave National Park (see our Parks and Grasslands chapter). There's a small selection of books and minerals for sale here, too.

The museum is open year-round, with summer hours from 8:00 A.M. to 6:00 P.M. Monday through Saturday and noon to 6:00 P.M. on Sunday. Winter hours are slightly shorter; you can call for information. Admission is free, and donations are gratefully accepted.

The museum, where students and others do research, offers several two-week paleontology digs each summer. Each one costs about $450, and you have to take your own tent and sleeping bag. Call or write for information about getting college credit, which costs more.

Petrified Forest of the Black Hills
1–90, exit 46, Piedmont
(605) 787-4560

The Petrified Forest's motto is "Stop here first, then you'll understand and enjoy the Black Hills even more," and that just might be a good idea. Start your self-guided tour with the informative video made by the geologist owner, Jerry Teachout. The prehistoric formation of the Hills is explained clearly, and the video will greatly enhance your knowledge and appreciation of the area. Next, visit the museum, where you'll see displays on geologic history and collections of rocks and minerals. Then head outside to walk the property and check out the petrified logs unearthed there. These once-wooden logs are so ancient that they predate the Hills themselves. In fact, they were already petrified when the slow geologic uplift that created the Black Hills exposed them, and that began 62 to 65 million years ago. Stop by the excellent rock shop at the end of your tour. (See the listing in our Shopping chapter.)

The Petrified Forest is open from May 1 through October 15. Hours are 8:00 A.M. to 7:00 P.M. seven days a week and 9:00 A.M. to 5:00 P.M. after Labor Day. Admission is $6.00 for adults, $3.50 for ages 6 to 12, and $4.50 for ages 13 to 18 and for seniors 55 and older. Kids five and younger get in free. Group discounts are also available.

Reptile Gardens
U.S. 16, Rapid City
(605) 342–5873, (800) 335–0275

Everyone from lizard lover to flower fancier will be enchanted by the displays and plantings at Reptile Gardens. This award-winning attraction—the pink building capped by the Sky Dome 6 miles south of Rapid City—claims the world's largest reptile collection as well as the largest variety of venomous species on exhibit anywhere. But if creepy, crawly creatures make you cringe, you can soothe your nerves with an extravagant indoor orchid display or the more than 40,000 bedding plants in the outdoor gardens. There's more here than meets the eye, however.

Reptile Gardens also offers educational 20-minute shows featuring alligators, snakes, birds and trained animals. The shows promote conservation and understanding of the important role animals play in our world. The U.S. Fish and Wildlife Service's Raptor Rehabilitation Center, based at Reptile Gardens but closed to the public, treats injured birds of prey in an effort to return them to the wild.

Millions have toured Reptile Gardens since it opened in 1937 after a local man, the late Earl Brockelsby, found that visitors enjoyed meeting the pet rattlesnake he kept under his hat. Along with your self-guided tour, you can have a light meal or snack in the Green Parrot Cafe and shop for jungle- and rainforest-related items, New Guinea tribal art, and other treasures in the gift shop.

The complex is open from April 1 to October 31. Hours are 8:00 A.M. to 7:00 P.M. from Memorial Day through Labor Day and 9:00 A.M. to 4:00 P.M. the rest of the season. During the summer, shows run throughout the day, with the last one starting at 7:00 P.M. Prices are $10.00 for adults, $6.00 for youths ages 6 to 12, free for children 5 and younger, and $9.50 for seniors 62 and older.

Rushmore Aerial Tramway
U.S. 16A, Keystone
(605) 666-4478

Trams depart about every five minutes for a short ride to an observation deck where you can look out over a scenic valley to Mount Rushmore, about a mile and a half away. Trails lead to other overlooks, and you can pack a picnic and stay as long as you like before returning to the gift shop to browse for souvenirs.

The tramway runs from 9:00 A.M. to 6:00 P.M. or later, weather permitting, from late May through mid- to late-September. Rides are $8.00 for those 13 and older, $4.00 for ages 6 to 12, and free for children 5 and younger. Call for group rates.

Rushmore-Borglum Story

You'll often see Borglum Historical Center referred to as the Rushmore-Borglum Story. This is a highly recommended preview to your visit to Mount Rushmore, but we've already written it up—turn to the Borglum Historical Center listing in this chapter.

South Dakota Air and Space Museum
Ellsworth Air Force Base, I-90, exit 66
(605) 385-5188

If you're a military or aviation history buff, or if you just love airplanes, you'll enjoy this museum. Outside displays include more than 27 planes and helicopters, including General Eisenhower's personal transport, a Mitchell B-25 bomber. Inside, explore the history of the base, tour a mock-up of a Minuteman launch control center, and see military memorabilia.

The South Dakota Aviation Hall of Fame is housed here, too, with tributes to pioneer aviators that are especially interesting. Read about Nellie Willhite, who—despite deafness—became South Dakota's first licensed female pilot (see the Close-up in our Getting Here, Getting Around chapter); Clyde Ice, barnstormer, wing walker, and aerobat; and aviatrix Violet Cowden, who made her first parachute jump on her 74th birthday.

Hours are 8:30 A.M. to 6:00 P.M. from mid-May to mid-September and 8:30 A.M. to 4:30 P.M. the rest of the year. Admission to the museum is free. A narrated bus tour of the base is $4.50 for those older than 12 and $2.50 for ages 12 and younger. The tours, available from mid-May to mid-September only, last about an hour and include a descent into a real Minuteman II missile silo. The museum is near the base's main gate; watch for signs and lots of parked planes.

Stav Kirke Chapel

Stav Kirke is the Norwegian name for the stave church at Chapel in the Hills. The names are used interchangeably, but we've listed it under the one most often used by Insiders, Chapel in the Hills. Please turn back to that listing to read about this unique and beautiful place.

Supper Music Shows

If you like beef with a little lively music on the side, you'll want to catch one of the area's nightly dinner shows. Starting times and prices vary for the attractions listed below. Ticket prices are in the $12-to-$25 range for adults; inquire about prices when you call for reservations. Cowboy boots and a Stetson are not required—but if you're not sure what to wear, ask about that, too.

Couples travel from all over to exchange wedding vows at tranquil Chapel in the Hills, also called Stav Kirke, in Rapid City. The reproduction Norwegian church is open to visitors all summer. PHOTO: COURTESY OF SOUTH DAKOTA TOURISM

For a cowboy-style chuck wagon supper of beef 'n' beans with all the trimmings, your choices include Circle B Ranch on U.S. 385, (605) 348-7358, north of Rapid City, where you'll find a Western town, minigolf, trail rides, gold panning, and other activities.

Or perhaps you'd like to visit Fort Hays, (605) 394-9653, a movie set from *Dances With Wolves,* on U.S. 16 south of Rapid City with continuous free showings of the four-hour version of the film.

The owners offer a 99-cent cowboy breakfast from 6:30 A.M. to 11:00 A.M. and a chuck wagon supper beginning at 6:30 P.M. For about $54.00 you can join a day-long tour starting at 9:00 A.M. that takes you to Mount Rushmore, Custer State Park, and the Crazy Horse Memorial. Upon your return to Fort Hays, you'll be treated to supper and a show. Fort Hays is open daily from May 12 to October 1.

Flying T Cowboy Supper and Show, (605) 342-1905, also on U.S. 16 south of Rapid City, has provided Western tradition since 1979 with a variety music and comedy show.

Trout Haven
U.S. 385, Rapid City
(605) 341-4440

Here you can catch a trout (all fishing gear furnished), have it cleaned and fried up fresh, and you won't even get your hands dirty. It's a family place, but you can read all about it in the Kidstuff chapter.

Caverns and Caves

Caves lace the limestone beneath the central Black Hills. Exploration is difficult, so no one knows for sure about their depth, whether they are connected, or what natural wonders the unexplored regions may conceal. You can, however, tour the previously explored nether regions of each cave listed below. Stalactites, stalagmites, popcorn and frost crystals, cave flowers, and flowstone are just some of the fascinating geological formations you'll see.

The caverns have easy and safe walking trails, although the nature of caves makes them inaccessible to wheelchair-users. Remember that cave temperatures are in the range of 45 to 50 degrees, and they can sometimes be damp—take a jacket and wear your walking shoes (preferably with sturdy rubber soles).

The following caves are privately owned and operated, and many have gift and rock shops, snack bars, hiking trails, and picnic areas. Some are open only during the summer, approximately Memorial Day to Labor Day. In planning your trip to the caverns, remember that the last tours of the day often leave some time before the official closing hour. It's always a good idea to call ahead.

You'll find the Southern Hills' Jewel Cave in a separate write-up in that section. Wind Cave is included in our Parks and Grasslands chapter.

Beautiful Rushmore Cave
13622 Hwy. 40, Keystone
(605) 255–4467

During its season, this cave is open seven days a week. From May 1 through Memorial Day, hours are 9:00 A.M. to 5:00 P.M. After Memorial Day and through Labor Day, hours are 8:00 A.M. to 8:00 P.M. After Labor Day until its closing on October 31, hours are 9:00 A.M. to 5:00 P.M. Admission prices are $7.50 for adults (14 and older) and $4.50 for ages 7 to 13. Discounts are available for AARP members and active military personnel.

Black Hills Caverns
2600 Cavern Rd., Hwy. 44 W., Rapid City
(605) 343–0542, (800) 837–9358
www.blackhillscaverns.com

Guided tours start every 20 minutes in summer. Hours are 8:00 A.M. to 8:00 P.M. seven days a week, from mid-June through Labor Day. From May 1 to mid-June and from Labor Day until October 15, hours are 8:30 A.M. to 5:30 P.M., seven days a week. Prices range from $7.00 to $8.00 for adults

and from $4.00 to $5.00 for children 6 to 12, depending on your choice of two tours.

Crystal Cave Park
Hwy. 44 W., Rapid City
(605) 342–8008

Summer hours are 8:00 A.M. to 8:00 P.M., seven days a week. After Labor Day, hours are 9:00 A.M. to 5:00 P.M. on weekends only, but call ahead for fall and winter hours. Adult admission is $6.75 and for children it's $4.00.

Sitting Bull Crystal Caverns
U.S. 16 S., Rapid City
(605) 342–2777,
www.sittingbullcrystalcave.com

This cave is open approximately May 1 through September, seven days a week from 7:00 A.M. to 8:00 P.M. and on weekends only in October from 8:00 A.M. to 5:00 P.M. Admission is $4.00 for kids ages 6 to 12 and $7.50 for anyone 13 and over.

Stage Barn Crystal Cave
1–90, Exit 46, Piedmont
(605) 787–4505

Open from Memorial Day through Labor Day, this cave's hours are 8:00 A.M. to 7:00 P.M. Open seven days a week, the cave is in beautiful, natural Stage Barn Canyon; all the flora and fauna native to South Dakota is found in this canyon. The excellent interpretive guides are prepared to lead you on the one-hour tour as you arrive; usually there is no waiting time. Admission is $7.00 for visitors 14 and older, $4.50 for kids 8 to 13.

Wonderland Cave Natural Park
Vanocker Canyon Rd., Nemo
(605) 578–1728

This cave is accessible from U.S. 385 from Deadwood or via I-90, exit 32. Hours are 8:00 A.M. to 4:00 P.M., seven days a week, from May 1 through November 1 (or until the first snowfall, sometimes as early as October). Admission prices are $12.00 for those 14 and older and $8.00 for ages 6 to 13.

LEGENDS &LORE

Wild Bill Hickok's Last Hand

When the legendary Wild Bill Hickok was shot in Deadwood by the infamous Jack McCall (the first and last time Bill ever sat at cards with his back to the door), he reportedly was holding black aces and eights, known ever after as the "dead man's hand." Deadwood's Adams Memorial Museum displays what are purported to be the actual cards.

Southern Hills

1881 Custer County Courthouse Museum & Book Store
411 Mt. Rushmore Rd., Custer
(605) 673-2443

The exhibits here provide a good overview of early life in the Custer area. Old photographs play a prominent role in telling the story, but you'll also see George Armstrong Custer's dress epaulets and antelope rifle. Rocks and minerals, native bird and animal specimens, authentic costumes, Native American artifacts, and exhibits depicting mining, lumbering, farming, and community life round out the displays. Don't miss the chilling stone jail in the basement, the courtroom on the second floor, or the buildings out back—where Custer County's only legal hanging took place. Bookstore attendants are ready to answer your questions as you browse among the reading matter.

The museum, which is staffed by volunteers, is open from June 1 to August 31, from 9:00 A.M. to 9:00 P.M. Monday through Saturday and from 1 to 9:00 P.M. on Sunday. Admission is free, but donations are "more than appreciated," in the words of one staffer.

Black Hills Institute of Geological Research
217 Main St., Hill City
(605) 574-4289
(605) 574-3919 (for tour info.)
www.bhigr.com

What this small, unassuming museum lacks in size it more than makes up for in outstanding fossil exhibits. You'll be just as impressed by the displays of smaller creatures as you are by gargantuan Stan, the mounted Tyrannosaurus rex skeleton. There are rocks, minerals, meteorites, and fossilized plants, too. Some of the specimens are on loan, but others belong to the Black Hills Institute of Geological Research, which has a lab in the basement (closed to the public) and a reputation for quality work. Even the gift shop, Everything Prehistoric, is a wonder world of ancient lifeforms, with drawers full of specimens for sale. You'll also want to linger over the fossils, minerals, cast items, books, and toys.

From May through September the museum is open from 8:30 A.M. to 6:30 P.M. Monday through Saturday and from 10:00 A.M. to 5:00 P.M. on Sunday; the rest of the time, hours are 10:00 A.M. to 5:00 P.M. Tuesday through Saturday. Admission is free, but donations are welcome. Student tours are free by reservation. Guided tours of the paleontology lab are available by appointment for a fee.

Black Hills Playhouse
Hwy. 87, Custer State Park
(605) 255-4141, (605) 255-4551

This rustic playhouse, fashioned from an abandoned 1934 Civilian Conservation Corps camp, has offered professional summer theater since 1946. Quality performances in a novel setting have made it a popular attraction for locals and tourists alike. For information about shows, see our Arts chapter.

Black Hills Wild Horse Sanctuary
Rocky Ford Rd., Hot Springs
(605) 745-5955, (800) 252-6652
www.wildmustangs.com

The drive to Black Hills Wild Horse Sanctuary is worth every dusty mile (the last 5.5 are on gravel roads), for the preserve is a place of tranquility and wild beauty. Two-hour bus tours through the 11,000-acre sanctuary stop for unforgettable views of the Cheyenne River, an intact set from the TV movie *Crazy Horse*, ancient petroglyphs, sacred caves, and, of course, free-roaming horses. Along the way you'll learn about the area's natural and human history, and whether you're a novice or an expert equestrian, you'll have plenty of opportunity to talk horses with your fellow passengers.

Author, rancher, and conservationist Dayton O. Hyde established the sanctuary in 1988 as a haven for unadoptable wild horses. The grounds support 350 mares and their foals; stud colts are sold to help support the nonprofit operation. Registered Cheyenne River paints also are for sale. If you're interested in helping out with work around the place, call for information about the volunteer program. You can also inquire about sponsorships.

Tours leave at 10:00 A.M., 1:00 P.M., and 3:00 P.M., May 1 through September 30, and cost $20.00 for adults, $18.50 for seniors 55 and older, and $12.50 for children 12 and younger. Call for information about group rates or to make special arrangements for off-season tours. During the summer you can catch a horse-drawn wagon for a riverside chuck wagon cookout at 5:00 P.M. Tuesday, Thursday, and Saturday, but you must reserve your spot a day ahead. The steak dinner with fixings costs $35.00 for adults, $32.50 for seniors and $25.00 for children ages 12 and younger. The sanctuary is 14 miles west of Hot Springs; to find it, follow Highway 71 south and turn right after the Cheyenne River Bridge.

Blue Bell Lodge & Resort Hayride & Chuck Wagon Cookout
Hwy. 87 S., Custer State Park
(605) 255-4531

An hour-long hayride with live, sing-along folk music winds through the park to Parker Canyon for a chuck wagon dinner and continued entertainment. The hay wagon is pulled by a vehicle, not by horses, but you get a complimentary cowboy hat and bandanna to take home plus your choice of steak or hamburger for supper. Plan to spend two and a half to three hours relaxing and enjoying the park's splendid scenery when you sign up here.

The lodge recommends making your reservations by 2:00 P.M., but walk-ins are welcome until 5:00 P.M. if there's space left. Rides depart at 5:30 P.M., but guests are asked to arrive by 5:00 P.M. The cost is $30 for adults and $27 for children.

Crazy Horse Memorial
U.S. 16 and 385, Custer
(605) 673-4681
www.crazyhorse.org

Seven years after work ceased on Mount Rushmore (see the listing earlier in this chapter), a fifth granite face started to emerge from another Black Hills mountaintop. This still-unfinished carving-in-the-round of Lakota Sioux leader Crazy Horse will pay homage not to U.S. presidents but to the legacy of those who preceded them. The monument and the museum complex below it are dedicated to Native Americans of all tribes. Because no known portraits of Crazy Horse exist, sculptor Korczak Ziolkowski created one from oral reports of those who had known the chief, intending that the monument stand as a symbol of the leader's spirit rather than an exact likeness.

The project was initiated by another Lakota chief, Henry Standing Bear, who wrote to the Connecticut artist after reading that Ziolkowski's marble bust of Polish pianist-composer-statesman Ignacy Paderewski had taken top honors at the 1939 New York World's Fair. Standing Bear's now-famous invitation read, in part, "My fellow chiefs and I would like the white man to know the red man has great heroes, too." The first blast at Crazy Horse removed 10 tons of rock on June 3, 1948. Hampered by South Dakota weather and dependent entirely on private funding (at Ziolkowski's insistence), it took 50 years to complete the sculpture's nine-story-tall face. When the last bit of rock is carved away at some unknown time in the future, the head alone will be big enough to hold

When it is finished, the spectacular "carving in the round" at Crazy Horse Memorial will be the largest in the world at 563 feet high by 641 feet long. Here, the granite mountain carving forms a backdrop for a 1/34th -scale model by sculptor Korczak Ziolkowski. PHOTO: ROBB DEWALL

all four faces on Mount Rushmore. Then, Crazy Horse, who was killed at Fort Robinson, Nebraska, in 1877, will sit astride his horse for all time, his left hand pointing proudly toward home: the place where his people lived and lie buried.

Ziolkowski himself is buried near the mountain carving. Since his death in 1982, his wife, Ruth, and many of their 10 children have continued his work. Knowing from the start that he would not live long enough to complete the 563-foot-tall memorial—taller than the Washington Monument—the self-taught sculptor drew up a detailed master plan to guide his successors.

A visit to Crazy Horse begins on the Avenue of the Chiefs, which takes you to the visitor complex where there's a model of Crazy Horse's face carved from a native pine tree, a slide show, photos depicting the work on the mountain, and many examples of Ziolkowski's Fighting Stallions sculpture. Continue to the Native American Educational and Cultural Center to see beadwork and prehistoric tools and to watch a documentary video. In the Indian Museum of North America, tribes from every corner of the nation are reverently represented in collections of artifacts and costumes. The sculptor's studio-home showcases more of his work. In years to come, Ziolkowski's master plan calls for a new museum, a university and medical training center for Native Americans, and other additions.

The visitor complex, where you can also buy Indian-made and South Dakota products, is open all year, with summer hours from 7:00 A.M. to dark and off-season hours from 8:00 A.M. until dark. The Laughing Water Restaurant is open from early May to late October. Admission is $9.00 or $20.00 per carload. Children six and younger, Native Americans, active military personnel with I.D., and Girl Scouts and Boy Scouts in uniform get in free.

Evans Plunge
1145 N. River St., Hot Springs
(605) 745–5165
www.evansplunge.com

Evans Plunge

Although no longer a destination point for the weak and ailing, Hot Springs still draws tens of thousands of visitors each year with its famous Evans Plunge. The original 1890 Plunge Bath came into the hands of builder Fred Evans (see the Close-up in our Attractions chapter) after the springs that feed it had traded hands several times—at one point, for a $35 horse. But legend says that long before white men claimed and bartered the renowned healing waters among themselves, Indian tribes fought each other for its exclusive use. The Sioux are said to have triumphed over the Cheyenne in a clash on Battle Mountain north of present-day Hot Springs. When white settlers took over the land, they readily added their own stories of near-miraculous cures to those handed down by the natives.

You'll find not only the world's largest natural warm-water indoor swimming pool but also a host of other recreational facilities for the entire family, including water slides, a sauna, steam room, and fitness center. Evans Plunge is open all year; for more information, turn to our Recreation chapter.

Fall River County Historical Museum
N. Chicago St., Hot Springs
(605) 745-5147

If taking a step back in time is one of your pleasures, this museum will delight you. The musty scent of yesterday greets you as you open the door and tread the well-worn wooden stairs of this three-story former schoolhouse. The 1893 sandstone structure, whose halls rang with the sound of youthful voices until 1961, houses extensive collections of everything imaginable, all smartly arranged in clusters and groupings. You'll find a room devoted to kitchen implements, for instance, and another filled with musical instruments and related items. There's a dentist's office well equipped enough to make you wince, and a Victorian parlor that makes you want to set a spell over tea and polite conversation.

The museum is open from 9:00 A.M. to 5:00 P.M. Monday through Saturday from June 1 until September 30. The free, volunteer-run museum relies on donations.

Jewel Cave National Monument
U.S. 16, Custer
(605) 673–2288, (800) 967–2283
www.nps.gov/jeca

The narrow, winding road to Jewel Cave primes travelers for a voyage into the mysterious depths of the earth. Rich in history and natural wonders, if not in actual gems, this cave 13 miles west of Custer was discovered by prospectors Frank and Albert Michaud and Charles Bush in 1900. Mistaking a sparkling layer of calcium carbonate (also called calcite crystal) for diamonds, the men staked a mining claim but failed either to extract anything of value or to mine tourists by turning the cave into an attraction. Yet Jewel Cave's vast chambers hold a treasury of stalactites, stalagmites, and other marvels, and in 1908 President Theodore Roosevelt declared it a national monument.

Continued exploration has established Jewel as the second-longest cave in the United States, at 121.21 miles (outdone only by Kentucky's 350-mile Mammoth Cave, the world's longest). Half-mile guided tours that depart from the visitor center last 80 minutes and incorporate 723 stairs—the equivalent of 40 flights, but it's mostly downhill. Sturdy, rubber-soled shoes and a light jacket are de rigueur.

Tours leave every 15 to 30 minutes beginning at 8:30 A.M. The cost is $8.00 for

A spelunker explores Jewel Cave, one of a number of caves in the Black Hills. PHOTO: COURTESY OF SOUTH DAKOTA TOURISM

adults, $4.00 for ages 6 to 16, and free for those younger than 6. Tickets are sold on a first-come, first-served basis, so your best bet is to arrive during the morning. Candlelit historic tours begin daily on a varied schedule, mid-June to mid-August, at the cave's natural entrance in Hell Canyon, a mile west of the visitor center. Prices are the same as for the regular tours, but children younger than six are not permitted on these tours, which last 105 minutes and cover a half-mile. Call ahead for the tour schedule. The last tour is at 6:00 P.M.

Reservations are required for the half-mile, four-hour spelunking tours in the cave's undeveloped areas, where groups of five begin their adventure at 12:30 P.M. daily from mid-June to mid-August. Hard hats and headlamps are complimentary, but you're required to bring ankle-height, lace-up, lug-sole boots, gloves, and soft knee pads. Be prepared to crawl through a concrete-block tunnel to qualify for this tour, which is off-limits to anyone age 16 or younger. Those age 16 or 17 must have their parent's or guardian's written con-

sent. The cost for the spelunking tour is $27.00 per person.

It's okay to take your camera but not your tripod on any of the tours. Touching any part of the cave's interior is prohibited, since skin oils and general wear and tear will damage the fragile formations. Anyone who's been recently hospitalized or who has respiratory or circulatory problems is advised to consult a park ranger before embarking on any cave tour. Jewel Cave is open all year except Thanksgiving, Christmas, and New Year's Day. The visitor center's summer hours, from mid-June to mid-August, are 8:00 A.M. to 7:30 P.M.; off-season hours vary; call for information.

Mammoth Site of Hot Springs
1800 U.S. 18 Bypass, Hot Springs
(605) 745–6017

If you think an elephant is big, wait until you meet Sinbad the mammoth. The full-size replica of a Columbian mammoth skeleton greets you at the Mammoth Site, where scientists have unearthed the fossilized remains of ancient creatures that became trapped in a sinkhole and died. The find was discovered accidentally in 1974, when the ground was being excavated for housing construction. Since then, the site has provided research data about animals and the environment from thousands of years ago. It is the only in-situ mammoth fossil display in the United States; that is, the only one in which the bones are left lying where they were found. This may be the only place you'll ever see honest-to-gosh mammoth hair on display, too.

You can take a guided tour or walk through the exhibits yourself with a guidebook from the ticket counter. (The text is available in English, French, German, Dutch, Italian, and Japanese.) In the gift shop area, children will find a hands-on paleontological dig. The shop itself features a big selection of books for all ages in addition to other items.

Mammoth Site is open daily; during the peak season, mid-May to late August, hours are from 8:00 A.M. to 8:00 P.M., with the last tour at 7:15 P.M. Hours vary the rest of the year, so call ahead. Rates are $6.48 for ages 13 to 59, $6.21 for those 60 and older, $4.59 for children 6 to 12, and free for children ages 5 and younger.

Mountain Music Show
U.S. 16, Custer
(605) 673-2405, (605) 673-4318
(888) 886-7094

C'mon down to the Mountain Music Show, back by popular demand for more than 20 years. The Pee Wee Dennis family's hillbilly style of entertainment dishes up two hours of country and bluegrass music and cornball humor in an indoor theater next to Flintstones Bedrock City. (See our Kidstuff chapter.) Sunday is country-gospel night. The show normally goes on each evening from Memorial Day weekend to Labor Day weekend, but the season may vary; call ahead to confirm. Curtain time is 8:00 P.M.

Tickets are $7.25 for adults, $3.75 for student ages 7 to 17, and free for ages 6 and younger. Reservations are recommended. A free bus gets you there from any Custer motel or campground.

National Museum of Woodcarving
U.S. 16 W., Custer
(605) 673-4404

Ignore the old saw, "Don't take any wooden nickels," when you get to the National Museum of Woodcarving: You're going to need three of them to take full advantage of the displays. The museum, 2 miles west of town, features the work of Dr. Harley Niblack, a Denver chiropractor who gave up his practice at age 42 to devote his time to wood carving and animation. His talent in that area made him one of Disneyland's earliest animators, and some of his work has been displayed by the Smithsonian Institution.

When you buy your ticket, you'll get enough wooden nickels to set three of the carvings in motion. But before entering the exhibit area, you'll want to watch videos in the Wooden Nickel Theater about the collection and about wood carving. The self-guided tour ends with a

Complimentary cowboy hats and bandannas certify that you've been to a real chuckwagon supper in Custer State Park. PHOTO: COURTESY OF SOUTH DAKOTA TOURISM

look at work by some of the nation's other top wood-carvers and a stop in the gallery where you can buy quality carvings. An adjacent gift shop sells snacks and souvenirs.

The museum is open from May 1 until late October. Hours vary throughout the season, so call ahead. Ticket prices are $6.25 for adults and $4.25 for children ages 6 to 14.

The Original Singing Cowboys
Heritage Village, 1 Village Ave.
Crazy Horse (Custer)
(605) 673–4761, (888) HAVEFUN
www.heritage-village.com

You might call this group the South Dakota version of the Sons of the Pioneers. And indeed, one of the members of this traditional Western-style band, Jim Lovell, won the Old West Trail Foundation Award for the Preservation of Western Music in 1980, an honor also bestowed on the aforementioned Sons. Lovell and fellow Cowboys Buddy Meredith, Kenny Hamm, Dale

Noe, and Walt Copeland sing enduring songs about enduring values, and their arrangements are so true, you just might get the urge to stretch out in a bedroll under the stars. That's especially so if you've had a filling meal from the buffet table on the main floor at Heritage Village before heading downstairs for the show in the Show Barn Theater.

Performances are at 8:00 P.M. nightly from early May through Labor Day, and on weekends until mid-October. Prices for the show only are $7.25 for adults and $3.25 for youths. Tickets for the supper and show range from $16.00 for adults to $3.70 for children ages 3 to 6; call for a complete breakdown. The buffet starts at 4:30 P.M. Reservations are recommended.

Peter Norbeck Scenic Byway

This 66-mile loop, named for the late nature-loving South Dakota governor and U.S. Senator Peter Norbeck, takes in some of the most rugged scenery in the Black Hills. The National Scenic Byway

Looping "pigtail" bridges are a distinctive feature of Iron Mountain Road (U.S. 16A), which is part of the Peter Norbeck Scenic Byway. PHOTO: COURTESY OF SOUTH DAKOTA TOURISM

will take you into the Norbeck Wildlife Preserve, the Black Hills National Forest, and Custer State Park when you travel the Needles Highway (Highway 87), Iron Mountain Road (U.S. 16A), Horse Thief Lake Road (Highway 244), and Sylvan Lake Road (Highway 89). Norbeck laid out portions of the route himself on foot and horseback.

Along the way you'll encounter switchbacks, looping "pigtail" bridges, narrow 1930s tunnels that open onto breathtaking views (look for Mount Rushmore and the Needles Eye, an aptly named granite spire) and Sylvan Lake, so be sure to have your camera ready. There are historic sites, too, such as the spot along U.S. 16A that served as a base camp for Lt. Col. George Custer's 1874 expedition to the Black Hills, when reports of gold set off a human stampede to the area.

The Needles Highway is in the Custer State Park fee area, so you'll need to buy a park entrance license if you go that way. You'll also need a license if you plan to tour or stop in the park. See our Parks and Grasslands chapters for information about park features and license fees. Parts of Iron Mountain Road and the Needles Highway are closed during the winter.

Wind Cave
U.S. 385, Wind Cave National Park
(605) 745-4600

One of about half a dozen caves in the world to harbor honeycomb-like boxwork formations, Wind Cave offers four informative guided tours ranging from an hour to 90 minutes. Reservations are recommended for special candlelight and spelunking tours. See our Parks and Grasslands chapter for prices and more information.

Kidstuff

Northern Hills
Central Hills
Southern Hills

A young friend visiting with her family from Minnesota last summer greeted us by saying, "It's so nice here." We knew what she meant: beautiful scenery, peace and quiet, room to roam. We can't help wondering whether she'll someday join the ranks of those who have moved here as college students, workers, or retirees because they fell in love with the Black Hills as children.

Taking advantage of the area's natural bounty is only part of the picture, however. There's no shortage of human-created activities to keep the younger generation entertained day after day. Better still, mom and dad are apt to have just as much fun as the kids, playing games, taking rides, exploring, seeing the sights, and maybe even experiencing something new and amazing.

Be sure to check other chapters, including Attractions, Recreation, Parks and Grasslands, The Badlands and Nearby, and Daytrips and Weekend Getaways for more great stuff to do with kids.

Northern Hills

Broken Boot Gold Mine
Hwy. 14A, Deadwood
(605) 578-9997

So you think you might strike it rich here? It could happen, but, more likely, you'll get rich quick in historical knowledge. The Broken Boot is a real gold mine, abandoned and closed for about 50 years, then reopened in 1954 for tours. When modern-day engineers explored the mine, they found a miner's boot that had been abandoned inside, half a century before; hence the name.

Today you can follow a tour guide 840 feet back and deep into the hillside. You'll learn about the way early miners looked for gold and about the history of the Black Hills gold rush.

Mining is hard work, but this tour isn't, and you should have enough energy left over for gold panning. The Broken Boot will provide the pans and other supplies, show you how to look for gold in the panning troughs, and let you keep the shiny stuff if you find some.

The mine is at the intersection of Upper Main Street and Highway 14A, at the south end of Deadwood. It is open from mid-May through mid-September, from 8:30 A.M. to 5:30 P.M., seven days a week. Tours leave every 30 minutes during those hours. The mine is not wheelchair accessible.

Admission prices are $6.25 for adults, $3.20 for seniors, $4.25 for teens ages 13 to 17, and $1.00 for kids ages 7 to 12. Admission is free for children 6 and younger. The charge for gold panning is $4.75 for all ages.

Ghosts of Deadwood Gulch Wax Museum
12 Lee St., Deadwood
(605) 578-3583

You couldn't be in Deadwood during the rip-roaring days of the Wild West and the Gold Rush of '76, but you can see it come to life at the wax museum. More than 70 people are represented here; some you'll recognize and some you've not yet heard of. Each life-size figure wears an authentic costume in an authentic setting. And you'll hear their stories on your guided tour.

The wax museum is open from Memorial Day through Labor Day. From Memorial Day weekend through late August, catch the tour from 9:00 A.M. to 6:00 P.M.; through September 15, tours are conducted from 9:00 A.M. to 5:00 P.M.

Admission prices are $5.00 for adults and $1.00 for kids ages 3 to 12. Children 2 and younger get in free.

You'll find the wax museum in the Old Town Hall building, 1 block off Main Street. The Trial of Jack McCall takes place in the same building (look a couple of listings down).

Gulches of Fun Family Fun Park
U.S. 85 S., Deadwood
(605) 578-3386

If (for some reason) you'd want to stay in one spot for your entire Black Hills vacation, Deadwood Gulch Resort (across the road) is a great place to hole up. There's enough to keep you busy for a week, but you'll have to see our Campgrounds and RV Sites chapter for that information. We're going to concentrate here on Gulches of Fun. Hey kids, you can keep your parents entertained at the resort while you play for hours.

Ride the bumper boats and go-carts, play through the 18-hole miniature golf course, test your skill in the batting cages, play every arcade game, and fill up at the snack bar. For little kids, there are kiddie go-carts and rides. This place does birthday parties (with pizza), too.

Gulches of Fun is open from Memorial Day through Labor Day, but may be open earlier and later in the season if weather permits.

Each activity at the park requires one or more tickets, which are $4.00 each. However, all-day wristbands are available for between $15.00 and $25.00, and are more cost-effective. Gulches of Fun is on Deadwood's south side, on the way to Lead.

Spearfish City Park
Canyon St., Spearfish

The playground here isn't just another collection of swings and slides. Local kids worked with an architect to design it, and it was built by local volunteers, including kids, in 1996. You'll find an area with a sandbox and smaller equipment just for tots as well as swings, slides, monkey bars, a tire swing, and other fun equipment for older children. A wooden fence encloses the entire playground. When you're played out, soak your feet in Spearfish Creek, which runs along the west side of the park. City Park is on the south end of town.

Trial of Jack McCall
12 Lee St., Deadwood
(605) 578-3583

It happened in Saloon No. 10 on Deadwood's Main Street. It wasn't wild Bill Hickok's habit to sit at the poker table with his back to the door. He was already a famous gunfighter, and he had to be careful. No one will ever know why he chose to sit facing away from the door that day but, sure enough, during the card game, a drifter called Jack McCall sneaked in with his gun and ... Wild Bill's days were over.

The story of the trial is as interesting as the crime, but we don't want to give it

Insiders' Tip

Kids younger than 21 are welcome in Deadwood gaming halls if they come with their parent or guardian. But according to state law, they are not allowed to touch or play the gaming machines or handle money used for gambling, and they must stay 3 feet behind any player. The halls enforce these rules, and some do not admit children after certain evening hours. However, several gaming establishments also have arcades for children.

GREAT FACES

Laura Ingalls Wilder

Laura Ingalls Wilder gently drew the curtain on her *Little House* books in DeSmet, the "little town on the prairie" in eastern South Dakota. But several characters from her enduring tales of pioneer childhood went west and left their imprint on the Black Hills.

Laura's younger sister Carrie pursued a newspaper career that took her to Keystone in 1911. There she married a widower with two children, David Swanzey (who played a part in naming Mount Rushmore), and lived there until her death on June 2, 1946. Mary, the blind sister of the stories, died at Carrie's house on October 17, 1928; both sisters are buried with Ma and Pa in DeSmet.

Laura's Uncle Henry and Aunt Polly, from the Big Woods of Wisconsin, also came to the Black Hills and are buried with their daughter, Ruby, in Harney Cemetery east of Keystone.

Laura herself traveled to Keystone with her husband, Almanzo, to visit Carrie and see the sights.

But long before any of that, when Laura, Mary, and Carrie were still little girls on the banks of Plum Creek and before sister Grace was even born, their Uncle Tom Quiner, Ma's brother, ventured to the Hills in search of gold with the Gordon Party. (See our History chapter for more.) Years later, Uncle Tom visited Laura and her family in DeSmet and told them about his adventure; much later still, when Laura was in her 70s, she recalled Uncle Tom's story and wrote it down in *These Happy Golden Years*.

away. These performances reenact the trial of Jack McCall, charged with the murder of Wild Bill Hickok. Will he go free? Find out at 8:00 P.M. every night (except Sunday) in the restored Old Town Hall. Performances run from Memorial Day through late August.

Call for admission prices and reservations. The Town Hall is 1 block off Main Street. The Ghosts of Deadwood Gulch Wax Museum is housed in the same building (see that listing earlier in this chapter).

Central Hills

Bear Country U.S.A.
13820 S. U.S. 16, Rapid City
(605) 343-2290

Lions and reindeer and bears, oh my! Look who's looking at you, kid, as you drive through this wildlife park. Here, you're in a "cage" and the animals get to wander around. For more about Bear Country, turn to our Attractions chapter.

Black Hills Maze & Amusements
6400 S. U.S. 16, Rapid City
(605) 343-5439
www.blackhillsmaze.com

If you like puzzles you'll love this bi-level, ever-changing maze with more than a mile of mind-boggling paths. Time yourself to see how quickly you can find your way out of the fortresslike network of towers, bridges, stairs, and sharp corners. There's also Bankshot Basketball and Water Wars with water balloons, a climbing wall, a zipline, paintball, and giant slingshots. Worn out yet? Take a break at the snack bar and pick up a South Dakota souvenir at the gift shop.

The maze, 3 miles south of Rapid City, is open from 8:30 A.M. to 10:00 P.M. daily from Memorial Day through Labor Day, except on Flashlight Fridays, when it's open an hour later and the lights go out. During September and October it's open Friday through Sunday on a varying schedule, so call ahead for times.

Prices are $6.00 for adults, and free for seniors and kids five and younger. Call for group prices.

Cosmos Mystery Area
U.S. 16, Rapid City
(605) 343–9802, (605) 343–7278

You'll be confounded by the Cosmos, where balls roll uphill, people get shorter, and the laws of physics are unenforceable. What's more, your guide on a half-hour tour will do everything possible to confuse you. Don't expect to get an explanation for the odd things that occur here; according to the staff, even scientists can't agree on what causes folks to feel off-balance at the Cosmos. It's been a tourist attraction since 1952, when two college boys discovered the area known as "the strangest location in the Black Hills."

The Cosmos is open from 7:00 A.M. to dusk daily, June 1 to Labor Day; and from 10:00 A.M. to 4:00 P.M. Monday through Friday during April, May, September, and October. Admission is $7.00 for anyone age 12 or older; children 11 and younger get in free with their parents.

Cosmos is 18 miles south of Rapid City; look for signs pointing to the turnoff.

Dinosaur Park
Skyline Dr., Rapid City
(605) 343–8687

It's not every kid who gets to slide down the face of a dinosaur. That's because most towns don't have a special park full of the green monsters. These seven life-size beasts are gentle, though, and they've stood patiently on a hill overlooking Rapid City for about 60 years, ever since the Works Progress Administration built them out of steel and concrete in tribute to some prehistoric Black Hills residents. You'll see the brontosaurus poking his head above the treetops from some distance away; at night he continues his watch in the soft glow of the park lights.

Dinosaur Park, which is owned by the city, is listed in the National Register of Historic Places. It's open from 6:00 A.M. to 10:00 P.M. year-round, and admission is free. A gift shop and snack bar are open from 8:00 A.M. to 8:00 P.M. daily, June through August, and 9:00 A.M. to 5:00 P.M. in May, September, and October. It's closed from November through April.

Moonrise seems to bring the inhabitants of Dinosaur Park to life. PHOTO: STEVEN A. PAGE

GREAT FACES

The South Dakota Triceratops

The South Dakota state fossil is the Triceratops, one of the last dinosaurs to live in North America. The word *triceratops* means "three-horned face." This 30-foot-long, 12-ton dino had a head more than 6 feet long, protected by those three fierce horns. His neck was topped by a bony plate and beaked snout. A heavy, pointed tail made him well armed against his predator, the much larger Tyrannosaurus rex.

The South Dakota Triceratops's skull was discovered in Harding County in 1927 and is on display at the Museum of Geology, but his concrete likeness can be seen at Dinosaur Park. Both are in Rapid City.

From Quincy Street in Rapid City, follow the signs west to Dinosaur Park. It's seven-tenths of a narrow, twisting mile up Skyline Drive.

Flags and Wheels
405 12th St., Rapid City
(605) 341–2186
www.flagsoffun.com

If you want to go fast, get excited, and let off some steam, this is the place. For older kids there are sprint cars (to drive these you must be 14 or older), a slick track for thrills, bumper boats, bumper cars, and go-carts. You'll also find miniature golf and batting cages. For the younger set there are bumper cars and boats and kiddie rides. And after all the excitement, you can refresh yourself at the snack bar.

Flags of Fun is open all year. Summer-season hours are noon to 10:00 P.M., seven days a week. Prices range from 50 cents to $14. Call for off-season hours.

Gigglebees
937 E. North St., Rapid City
(605) 399–1494

The name of this pizza arcade says it all. There's enough to do to keep you giggling for hours. Check out the kiddie rides, video games, skeeball, pinball, and the play space. The restaurant—specializing in kid food—will help you keep up your energy for play. Gigglebees hosts birthday parties, too, with cakes, game tokens, even hats.

Open year-round, Gigglebees' hours are 11:00 A.M. to 10:00 P.M. Monday through Thursday, 11:00 A.M. to 11:00 P.M. Friday, and 10:30 A.M. to 11:00 P.M. on Saturday.

There is no admission fee, but all games and rides require one or more tokens that cost 25 cents each. Token specials are often available, too.

Insiders' Tip

Looking for a great deal? The American Lung Association of South Dakota offers the Children's Fun Pass that gives youngsters ages 6 to 12 free or reduced rates on admission, games, and food at more than 40 Black Hills area attractions (and others across South Dakota). The pass costs $15 but is valued at more than $150. Call the Lung Association at (800) 873–5864 for more information.

Mount Rushmore National Memorial
Hwy. 244, Keystone
(605) 574–2523

Youngsters ages 5 to 12 can do much more than tag along with mom and dad when the family visits Mount Rushmore. Kids who participate in the park's learn-and-earn Junior Ranger Program pick up a booklet at the Information Center and fill it out as they gather information about the monument by watching a video, taking a tour, or doing other activities. When they're done an hour or so later, a park ranger will sign their book, entitling them to a certificate. Those who wish to may also buy a patch for a small charge to sew on their hat or coat.

The park's children's program offers age-appropriate talks on a variety of topics related to Mount Rushmore. Talks are offered once each afternoon and last about 30 minutes; call ahead for the schedule or check at the Information Center when you arrive.

Take U.S. 16 south from Rapid City or U.S. 16A south from Keystone and follow

Insiders' Tip

South Dakota law prohibits fireworks of any kind, including firecrackers, in the Black Hills Forest Fire Protection District, except within the incorporated boundaries of municipalities. The district encompasses pretty much all of the Hills from Spearfish to Edgemont and Rapid City to the Wyoming border. Call the local fire department or law enforcement agency to find out what's permitted and where.

the signs to Highway 244 and Mount Rushmore. For more information about the memorial, see our Attractions chapter.

The Ranch Amusement Park
6303 S. U.S. 16, Rapid City
(605) 342–3321

This place has enough stuff to keep just about anyone busy for hours. Where to begin? You could start at the go-carts with about a mile of track, then move on to the bumper boats or a bounce on the trampoline, and dry off with a round of miniature golf before heading for the video arcade. No matter which order you take them in, at some point you're likely to wind up tuckered out at the snack bar.

The Ranch is open from 10:00 A.M. to 10:00 P.M., from the end of April to Labor Day. Days and hours vary during April, May, and September, so call ahead. It's a good idea to call when the weather's iffy, even during the height of summer.

Prices for each attraction range from $2.00 to $5.00 and a "family fun pack" of 30 is $50.00. On bargain day Wacky Wednesday, each attraction is half-price. Call for group rates.

Reptile Gardens
U.S. 16, Rapid City
(605) 342–5873

Like rattlesnakes? How about tropical flowers? Either way, you'll find what you're looking for at Reptile Gardens. Plus, you'll get to know more about alligators, birds, and other animals. See our Attractions chapter for a more complete description of one of the Black Hills' most popular stops.

Rockin Robin Fizz Kids
E. St. Joe & E. St. Paul (behind Blockbuster)
Rapid City
(605) 342–1818

A terrific resource for both kids and parents, Rockin Robin Fizz Kids Mini Mall houses several businesses. Of most interest to you kids, however, is Fizz Kids itself. It's a three-dimensional play scape with slides, ladders, swings, ramps, and tubes. There's an admission fee for the play scape: $4.95 for kids to age 17 (two enter

river ride, a short ramp, and a kiddie slide. You'll also find volleyball, basketball, and horseshoe courts. If constant motion isn't your mode of operation, you can soak in the 30-foot hot spa, take shelter in the shaded picnic area, mosey along the 19-hole minigolf course, sneak over to the snack bar, or browse among the beach accessories in the gift shop.

The park, which is 3 miles south of Rapid City, is open early June to the end of August, from 10:00 A.M. to 7:00 P.M., depending on the weather. Call ahead if it's questionable.

Prices range from $8.00 to $15.00. Coin-operated lockers and hot showers are available, as are swimsuit, life-preserver, and towel rentals. There's even a fenced area to keep your dog safe while you play.

Storybook Island
1301 Sheridan Lake Rd., Rapid City
(605) 342–6357

Looking around for something to do? Storybook Island is fun for you. Nursery rhymes are the theme here, where tykes and grown-ups enter the world of characters from some of the best-known children's stories. Cinderella and her pumpkin coach are here, along with Dorothy and Toto, the Crooked Man, and many others. The Storybook Island Theatre Troupe performs all season; call for the schedule.

The park is open from 9:00 A.M. to 8:00 P.M. daily from Memorial Day weekend through Labor Day. It reopens on weekends from the day after Thanksgiving through Christmas, when miles and miles of lights deck the trees and displays, and special events are planned. Call for more details.

The Rapid City and Rushmore Rotary clubs support Storybook Island, so admission is free. However, donations are always welcome.

Trout Haven
U.S. 385, Rapid City
(605) 341–4440

This place is quite a catch. It's your chance to hook a trout, and you won't have to stand in the middle of a stream and get cold water in your waders to do it.

for the price of one on weekdays, and on Wednesday admission for kids is $2.00); parents enter free. There's also a food court, a snackbar that serves pizza and subs, and an arcade, which are all free. Fizz Kids also throws parties and provides a "sitting service," for parents who need a break.

The Imagination Station educational gift shop and science lab is also in the Mini Mall, along with the nonprofit Science Linkages in Education and a day-care and preschool called For the Children. More kid-related businesses are being added, and the Mini Mall is right across the street from the Rushmore Mall (see our Shopping Chapter).

Rushmore Waterslide Park
1715 U.S. 16 Bypass (Catron Blvd.), Rapid City
(605) 348–8962
www.rushmorewaterslides.com

In the mood for some liquid refreshment? Make a splash at the water slides, where you can take your pick of the superspeedy Bonzai or something slightly more sedate. In addition to the two steep slides, there are four 400-foot descents, an inner-tube

Her pumpkin coach stands ready to whisk Cinderella to the ball at Storybook Island. PHOTO: STEVEN A. PAGE

It's also your chance to tell a big fish story.

Trout Haven furnishes poles and bait, encouragement and advice. When you've got that big one, they'll clean it and either fry it up in the restaurant or pack it in ice. If you and your family are traveling for a while, they'll even keep your filleted and frozen fish until you return.

Trout Haven is open from approximately Memorial Day to late September, but call ahead to be sure. Hours are 8:00 A.M. to 6:00 P.M. seven days a week during the summer.

Your big catch will cost you 50 cents an inch, or $4.95 for a meal that supplements your fish with french fries, Texas toast, and coleslaw. Breakfast is also served (and if you've never tried fresh trout for breakfast, you're in for a treat). Other items are available on the restaurant's menu if you don't like fish.

Trout Haven is 19 miles west of Rapid City, 20 minutes south of Deadwood on U.S 385. There are plenty of signs on the highway to guide you.

Southern Hills

Evans Plunge
1145 N. River St., Hot Springs
(605) 745-5165

Take your pick of the water slides before taking the plunge into a swimming pool heated with naturally warm water. For information about other things to do at Evans Plunge, see our Recreation chapter.

Flintstones Bedrock City
U.S. 16 W., Custer
(605) 673-4079
www.flintstonesbedrockcity.com

Fred, Wilma, and the gang are ready to welcome kids of all ages to Bedrock City. Enter the Stone Age and see the faces of Mount Rockmore, ride the Flintmobile and the Iron Horse train, and zip down the Slideasaurus. Then get your strength back with a Brontoburger or Dino Dog at the Drive-In, and check out the licensed Flintstones items in the gift shop.

Bedrock City, at the west end of town, is open from mid-May through Labor Day. From early June to mid-August, hours are 9:00 A.M. to 8:00 P.M.; call for times the rest of the season.

Admission costs $5.50 for everyone age 6 or older; those 5 and younger get in for free. Call for group rates for 10 or more people.

For information about the park's campground, see our Campgrounds and RV Sites chapter.

Four Mile Old West Town
U.S. 16, Custer
(605) 673-3905
www.fourmilesd.com

A talking outhouse with a sense of humor? That's just the beginning of your self-guided trek through the Old West at its most rustic. More than 50 wooden shacks house artifacts from days gone by, and there are plenty of witticisms sprinkled in with the history lesson—for instance, the proprietress of the seamstress shop is Mrs. Hattie Coates. But only the worthy may enter through the front door. A sign outside admonishes, TINHORNS, GAMBLERS AND LAYABOUTS, USE THE BACK DOOR. There is even a rebuilt stockade.

Stagecoaches used to stop here to water their horses at Four Mile Spring, and the town of Moss City was located here more than a century ago.

The owners are proud to offer lots of "hands-on" activities for the kids.

The present-day tourist complex 4 miles west of Custer is open from 8:00 A.M. to 7:00 P.M. Monday through Saturday and 10:00 A.M. to 7:00 P.M. on Sunday, May through September, and by appointment or chance during the winter. Admission is $5.00 for anyone older than 10; anyone younger gets in free with an adult.

Mammoth Site of Hot Springs
U.S. 18 Bypass, Hot Springs
(605) 745-6017

How is an elephant's ear like an air conditioner? Find out at Mammoth Site, where you can touch an elephant's ear, see the giant (and sometimes tiny) bones of ancient animals that died here, and "dig" for fossils. To find out more, see our Attractions chapter.

Annual Events and Festivals

Folks of the Black Hills sure know how to have a good time. With winters as long and cold and snowy as ours, we've learned that summers are not to be wasted. Every fine moment of glorious good weather must be treasured. We know how to "make hay while the sun shines."

This make-every-moment-count attitude is reflected in the array of events and festivals in spring, summer, and fall. There's so much to do every weekend, in fact, that you'll have to plan ahead and be carefully organized to find time to sample it all.

Deadwood, for example, has more special events than any other town in the Hills. There's always something cookin' there, and the town really knows how to throw a party—usually rolling the shindigs right out onto the streets and including everybody around.

Because some events change dates from year to year, only approximate dates are listed here, so call ahead or check the local papers or visitor guides for firm dates. And please note that the information here is not meant to be exhaustive—many events change from year to year, new events are added and those decreasing in popularity sometimes fall by the wayside.

You'll notice a minimum of events in January, February, March, and April. Blame it on our South Dakota winters and wet springs, which usually make getting out and about a bit difficult and undesirable (we tend to stay in, snuggle up, and make our own entertainment at home or go play in the snow). If you're visiting during those months, you'll still find plenty to do, but a variety of festivals and events won't be part of that. You're on your own at that time of year, but—trust us—difficult weather has its own rewards. Check the Recreation chapter for cool winter sports like snowmobiling and cross-country and downhill skiing. Don't worry, you won't be bored.

These festivals and events are your chance to get in on some local celebrations and festivities. You'll get a taste of our culture and favorite entertainments, and understand what makes the Black Hills a special place to live. Have fun!

January

Black Hills Moonwalks
Various locations throughout the Hills
(605) 343-1567

Moonwalks take place one day each month, year-round (usually the Friday or Saturday nearest the full moon), and each is held at a different park or recreation area. They are sponsored by the Black Hills National Forest and the Black Hills Parks and Forests Association and conducted by people who can tell you a lot about each place. Programs vary. During past moonwalks Native American stories were told at Bear Mountain Lookout near Hill City, "Listen to the Coyotes Howl" was held at Badlands National Park, and Black Hills weather was discussed at Pactola Dam.

The moonwalks begin in the evenings (between 7:00 and 9:00 P.M.) and are usually 1- to 3-mile round-trips that last two to three hours. There is no charge, but you may have to purchase an entrance license to some of the parks and recreation areas. Bring your binoculars, something to drink, sturdy shoes, and layers of clothing (it can be chilly at night).

Check with the Pactola/Harney Ranger District office (at the number above, or visit 800 Soo San Drive, Rapid City) or see local newspaper listings for details and directions.

Northern Hills

Dakota Rush Snowmobile Rally
Various locations throughout the Hills
and Deadwood
(605) 578–1876, (800) 999–1876

It's like a motorcycle rally, except that it's for snow machines. Dakota Rush brings snowmobile enthusiasts from many states to the white-gold-covered Black Hills. They tour our miles of prime trails and backcountry, sightsee, win prizes, participate in games and rodeos (the snowmobile kind), try their hand at the snow sculpture contests, and enjoy vintage snow machines, social events, and vendors displaying winter wares. It takes place in mid-January and is based in Deadwood, although some of the events occur elsewhere in the Hills.

Chinese New Year Celebration
Miss Kitty's Casino
647 Main St., Deadwood
(605) 578–1811, (800) 668–8189

Since Chinese New Year is a lunar holiday, it's hard to pin down the exact date of this celebration, which takes place in late January or early February.

Deadwood history has quite a fascinating chapter on the Chinese immigrants and businesspeople who joined in the glory days of the gold rush. The city celebrates that culture on Chinese New Year with lion dancers, a parade, fireworks, firecrackers (which drive away evil spirits that threaten the coming year), and a display of photographs and artifacts from the Adams Memorial Museum.

Central Hills

Black Hills Stock Show and Rodeo
Rushmore Plaza Civic Center
444 Mt. Rushmore Rd., Rapid City
(605) 394–4115

Begun more than 44 years ago, the Black Hills Stock Show and Rodeo is the third largest stock show in the country. This annually anticipated event is a place for ranchers to show, buy, and sell cattle and horses, and a great community get-together.

If you've never been to a stock show, you'll find that they're highly educational and a great way to learn about the trials, tribulations, and rewards of the South Dakota ranching life. You may even learn to tell the difference between one breed of cow and another. There are plenty of other things to look at, too: art, clothing, gifts, and food.

The show is held in late January or early February and runs for about 10 days. Admission to the stock show is free, but tickets must be purchased for the rodeo and a few other events.

Insiders' Tip

According to the *Guinness Book of World Records,* on January 22, 1943, the temperature in Spearfish rose an amazing 49 degrees in just two minutes. This event was recorded by a thermometer disc that marked the 7:30 A.M. temperature at minus four degrees; at 7:32 A.M., a temperature of 45 degrees was recorded. This astounding change was the result of a chinook wind, and the sudden change from frigid to mild cracked glass windows around town.

Governor's Ride
Snowmobiling Event
Various locations throughout the Hills
(605) 642–7103

This weekend event is sometimes attended by South Dakota's governor (if he can get away from his office). If you plan to attend, call ahead to make your reservations.

The South Dakota Snowmobile Association sponsors the event, and it knows all about snow! Its various clubs vie for hosting honors, so locations vary. Everyone, including nonmembers, is welcome.

The event itself is free, but meals (breakfast, lunch on the trail, and the awards banquet) range from $5.00 to $15.00. Riders and their snowmobiles meet at a central location, then take off for a short (1.5-hour) or long (3-hour) ride and a get-together afterward.

Northern Hills

Hot Chocolate Days
Various locations in Spearfish
(605) 642–2626

Warm up winter at this community event, held during mid-February in charming downtown Spearfish. The special winter art show is held at the Matthews Opera House (614½ Main Street), and there's also a children's carnival, a chili cook-off, shopping promotions, and an ice-skating evening (with lots of hot chocolate).

Mardi Gras Celebration
Main St., Deadwood
(605) 578–1876, (800) 999–1876

It's the Mardi Gras of the West, with costumes, a night parade, and all the trappings (well, most of them) of New Orleans. But this one also has gaming and the charming amenities and atmosphere of Deadwood, South Dakota—something New Orleans can't claim.

Our Mardi Gras takes place in late February or early March and it's an outrageous party you won't soon forget, done up in Deadwood style.

Central Hills

Black Hills Community
Theatre Season
713 Seventh St., Dahl Fine Art Center
Rapid City
(605) 394–1786, (605) 394–6091

The community theater presents five quality performances—a good mix of drama, comedy, and music—throughout the year, with the first scheduled for February. Performances are professionally staged by dedicated local actors in the theater at "The Dahl." Ticket prices vary and season tickets are available, so call ahead to check prices and reserve seats.

The Black Hills Community Theatre also conducts classes and workshops and presents plays for children. You can read all about it in The Arts chapter.

Northern Hills

Campfire Series
Heritage Drive, High Plains Heritage Center
Spearfish
(605) 642–9378
www.members.mato.com/hpmuseum

If you want to hear and be part of a "real deal," catch one (or more) of the four-series Campfire shows held at the Heritage Center theater. One show per month is held in March, April, September, and October. The dates may be tentative, so call ahead to find out the schedule.

The idea behind this informal presentation around a fire is for area descendants, artists, writers, craftspeople, and storytellers to have the opportunity to relay their unique stories of the High Plains and to display their crafts.

Afterwards, the audience is invited to ask questions and perhaps also reminisce, as well as to view the articles from the show. The Chuckwagon Hour (finger food) begins at 6:00 P.M. and the show starts at 7:00 P.M. Admission is $5.00.

dors. You'll find the newest craft and gift trends here, as well as old favorites. Admission is free, although vendors pay for their booth space.

April

Easter Egg Hunts and Festivities

Many Black Hills towns celebrate Easter and the pending arrival of spring weather with Easter egg hunts and other activities. Most are small community celebrations and, thus, aren't planned as organized annual events, but we mention them here because they're fun, especially for children. Check local papers and visitor publications for current information.

Northern Hills

Historic Matthews Opera House
614½ Main St., Spearfish
(605) 642-7973

The delightful community theater performances are presented in the restored opera house. Please read about them, and the beautiful venue, in The Arts chapter, and call the above number for information.

St. Patrick's Day Celebration
Downtown Deadwood
(605) 578-1876, (800) 999-1876

Show your colors (as long as they're green) at St. Paddy's parade and celebration in Deadwood. There are usually Irish bands, green beer, and special events taking place in the casinos and restaurants on Main Street.

Central Hills

Country Fair Arts and Crafts Shows
Various locations in Rapid City
(605) 342-3694, (605) 343-8783

Six shows are held each year, beginning in late March (with others held in July, early October, mid- and late November and December). Most are at the Rushmore Plaza Civic Center, but the mid-July show takes place outdoors in pretty Canyon Lake Park.

Crafters come from all over the country, and local and regional artisans participate. This is the largest indoor craft show in the area, and it's been a popular annual event for more than 20 years.

Sometimes there is informal musical entertainment, and homemade baked goods and candy are available from ven-

May

Spring Open House and
Free Fishing Weekend
Various locations throughout the Hills
(605) 773-3534
www.state.sd.us/gsp

This is a very special event held at all 38 South Dakota state parks and recreation areas. It's a sort of "visitor appreciation weekend," a way of inviting visitors back to the parks in the spring.

This event is held the weekend before Memorial Day, and from Saturday morning through Sunday evening, there is no charge for park entrance and fishing licenses are not required. Each park and recreation area offers entertainment, naturalist programs for kids, fishing tournaments, and presentations.

LEGENDS & LORE

Elvis

Elvis Presley performed one of his final concerts at Rapid City's Rushmore Plaza Civic Center on June 21, 1977, less than two months before his death on August 16 at the age of 42. And, no, he hasn't been seen in Rapid City since.

For more information call the South Dakota Parks and Recreation Department in Pierre at the above number.

Northern Hills

Cowboy Music and Poetry
Heritage Dr., High Plains Heritage
Center, Spearfish
(605) 642-9378
www.members.mato.com/hpmuseum

It's not Shakespeare, but then again this ain't jolly old England, pardner! If you've never listened to cowboy poetry and music, you're in for a surprise. It's a genre all its own, and it's darned good stuff.

From Memorial Day through Labor Day on Wednesdays, starting at 7:00 P.M., the Heritage Center opens the doors of its theater to fans of the Robert and Rooster Roundup (featuring the Cowboy and The Sheepherder). If you know your Western history, you know that's gonna be some kind of roundup!

Admission is $5.00 and includes entrance to the museum, so plan to arrive early and tour the exhibits, then settle in at the theater for the Roundup.

Read about the High Plains Heritage Center in our Attractions chapter.

The Quick Draw
Heritage Dr., High Plains Heritage
Center, Spearfish
(605) 642-9378
www.members.mato.com/hpmuseum

It's not what you think—that is, if you're envisioning two hard-bitten gunslingers shooting it out on Main Street. This is a much more refined (but no less exciting) event involving artists. It's held on Memorial Day Monday and starts at noon with a champagne reception, when the participating artists are available for chat and questions.

At 1:00 P.M., the quick draw begins (there may be a gunshot to mark the start; we don't know). The artists go to work—drawing, sculpting, painting, using whatever medium they choose—for just one hour. The public gets to watch as the works progress. At 2:00 P.M., work stops and the auction begins. This is your chance to purchase a freshly created work of art and meet the artist, too.

Don't forget to tour the Heritage Center while you're there. Read about it in our Attractions chapter.

June

Northern Hills

Black Hills Folk Festival
Black Hills State University Campus
Spearfish
(605) 341-5714

A university-sponsored event, the festival encourages participation in all phases of music-making, with an emphasis on folk music. It spans two weeks in mid-June, with two all-day, weeklong classes/workshops, one of which is always in songwriting.

Two evening open-stage events are planned for a Friday and Saturday night; local and area artists are encouraged to share their music.

The Big Performance takes place in the middle of the festival and is held on campus and at other city locations. Nationally known artists Michael Smith, Anne Hills, Claudia Schmidt, and Brooks Williams have performed there.

Center of the Nation All Car Rally
Off Eighth St., Herrmann Park, Belle Fourche
(605) 892-2676, (888) 345-JULY
www.bellefourche.org
Collectible cars and trucks from across the nation show up here to show off. Owners can participate in the poker run, show and shine competition, barbecue, and a dance.

Most types of collectible cars and trucks are welcome, but call ahead to learn if there are restrictions.

There's a registration fee for vehicle owners, but spectators and those who just want to ooh-and-aah don't have to pay. The All Car Rally is held the second weekend of June on Friday, Saturday, and Sunday.

Sturgis Cavalry Days
Various locations in Sturgis and at Ft. Meade
(605) 347-2556
Honoring the history of the West, and Sturgis's part in it, this mid-June event takes place at different locations and offers some interesting western-style activities. Past ones have included an arts festival, horse and carriage rides, living history and cavalry reenactments, a buffalo feed, a trial of Lt. Col. George Custer by real-life modern-day lawyers, a military ball, and a trader rendezvous. And it's all free.

Charlie Utter Days
Downtown Deadwood
(605) 578-1876, (800) 999-1876
This late-June celebration is named for Charlie Utter, who was a friend of Wild Bill Hickok. It's a history-oriented event with free concerts (one past performer was Glen Campbell), an ice-cream social, clog dancing demonstrations, and bed races. As with most events in Deadwood, this one takes place on Main Street.

Central Hills

Music in the Park
Memorial Park, Rapid City
(605) 343-5176

Free outdoor concerts are presented each summer at the Memorial Park band shell, and indoor winter concerts are held at coffeehouses or the Dahl Fine Arts Center. Please read about Music in the Park in The Arts chapter.

Family Cruiser Night
Various locations in Rapid City
(605) 394-4133
On one hand, this is a chance for proud car owners to parade down Mount Rushmore Road, then display their shiny vehicles at the Rushmore Plaza Civic Center parking lot or downtown. It's also a chance to participate in the long-standing pastime of cruising. But it's really an evening for families—an opportunity for parents to cruise with their kids and to spend time together. Spectators have great fun, too, watching the streams of beautifully restored, well-cared-for and customized cars, from classic '57 Chevys and antique Model A's to snazzy low-riders with fuzzy dice dangling from their rearview mirrors.

The event starts and ends at the civic center, next to Memorial Park, and is sponsored by the Rapid City Police Department. There's usually music downtown or at the band shell, plus public-safety displays, and demonstrations by the department's drug dogs. Food and T-shirt sales benefit the DARE program.

Family Cruiser Night is held on a Friday evening in mid-June, but it is sometimes canceled because of rain, so call ahead.

West Boulevard Summer Festival
Mt. Rushmore Rd., Wilson Park, Rapid City
(605) 342-6497
A very popular community arts and crafts festival, this one is held in pretty Wilson Park, just a block from historic West Boulevard, in mid-June.

You'll enjoy shopping for creative arts and crafts, listening to the musical performances, and munching on a great variety of ethnic food. Then stroll over to West Boulevard and take a look at the beautiful historic houses.

Vendors pay a fee for their booth space, but browsers are admitted free.

Black Hills Bluegrass Festival
U.S. 16, Mystery Mountain Resort, Rapid City
(605) 394–4101

It's a weekend of toe-tapping, feel-good bluegrass and acoustic music. For more than 20 years, the festival has taken place on the last full weekend in June, starting Friday night and ending Sunday morning with a gospel show.

Prices for a single show are $10; a ticket for all day Saturday is $18; a weekend ticket is $25. Discounts are available for advance purchases and children under 12 are admitted free.

This is a warm and homey event, with concerts by nationally known entertainers, workshops, informal jam sessions, food, and plenty of music. The organizers describe it as a big family reunion because so many people come back year after year.

Southern Hills

Black Hills Playhouse
Custer State Park, Custer
(605) 255–4141, (605) 255–4551
www.blackhillsplayhouse.com

A visit to the playhouse is a perfect chance to tour beautiful Custer State Park and catch a great stage performance, too. The summer season runs from June through August each year and you'll need a South Dakota state park sticker to access the park. You'll find detailed information about the playhouse in The Arts chapter.

Crazy Horse Volksmarch
Crazy Horse Memorial, U.S. 16-385, Custer
(605) 673–4681
www.crazyhorse.org

Just once each year, participants are allowed to walk right up to the huge carved face of Crazy Horse and view the work-in-progress close up. (You can read about Crazy Horse Memorial in our Attractions chapter.)

In recent years, between 10,000 and 14,000 hardy folks have made this 6.2-mile trek.

The Crazy Horse Volksmarch, which is the largest volksmarch in the country, is held on Saturday and Sunday during the first full weekend of June, and costs just $2.00 per person.

To receive official credit for your volksmarch, you must pay $2.00; to receive the "Volksmarch Crazy Horse" medal, you must pay $7.00.

July

Most Black Hills towns and cities hold their own Fourth of July celebrations, patriotic community events that may include such family-style entertainment as parades, picnics, barbecues, street dances, craft fairs, special events for children, and, of course, fireworks after dark. Check local papers and visitor publications for details.

Northern Hills

Black Hills Roundup
Roundup St., Roundup Grounds
Belle Fourche
(605) 892–2643, (888) 345–JULY
www.bellefourche.org

The first roundup, in 1918, was a Red Cross benefit. This longstanding and entertaining event still takes place over five days around the Fourth of July and there's a lot to see and do. You can enjoy carnival rides, a free barbecue, roundup and horsemanship performances, fireworks, a 10K run, a parade, and the Miss Rodeo South Dakota Pageant.

The Roundup itself is a Professional Rodeo Cowboys Association (PRCA) event, with traditional rodeo competition and entertainment. Brothers Marvin and Mark Garrett, Belle Fourche's world champion riders, usually attend and compete as well.

Ticket prices for the rodeo range from $8.00 to $14.00 for adults, depending on seating selection, with discounts for children. Most other Roundup events are free.

The Roundup Grounds are 1.5 blocks west off U.S. 85 (Fifth Street).

GREAT PLACES

The 1997 America's Holiday Tree

The Black Hills had the great honor of providing "America's Holiday Tree" to decorate the west lawn of the Capitol Building in Washington, D.C., for Christmas 1997. It's not the first time the state has been so honored. In 1955 and 1970, trees from South Dakota served as the "President's Tree" that decorated the White House.

Also known as "The 1997 People's Tree," the 65-foot white spruce was a gift from the people of South Dakota to the people of America, in commemoration of the 100th anniversary of the Black Hills National Forest. Several trees were nominated for the honor and the Capitol Landscape Architect arrived from Washington to select the winner. The 90-year-old tree was cut in Spearfish Canyon in the Northern Hills and, along with 50 smaller Black Hills trees and thousands of ornaments (handmade by South Dakota children and adults), made a circuitous, ceremony-filled trip to Washington. A special convoy wound its way through South Dakota (stopping at major towns so proud residents could view the tree) before proceeding though nine other states to reach its destination.

America's Holiday Tree was illuminated during a special ceremony. The smaller trees decorated agency offices in the Capitol Complex. Funds for the trees' trip east were raised through donations, sponsorships, and the sale of keepsakes and prints from Hill City artist Jon Crane's watercolor of the People's Tree as it stood in the forest.

Family Creek Fair
D.C. Booth Historic Fish Hatchery
423 Hatchery Circle, Spearfish
(605) 642–7730

The fair is held on Father's Day on the lovely grounds of the hatchery. It's designed as a family event, a day when dads, moms, kids, and their extended families can be together in a beautiful setting and have some fun.

Besides children's activities, there's brunch in Mrs. Ruby Booth's garden at the historic house. Parents can watch the demonstrations on fishing and wildlife, and everyone will enjoy feeding the trout and ducks and touring the hatchery museum. It's all free, except for the brunch (advance reservations are required). Read more about the D.C. Booth Fish Hatchery in our Attractions chapter.

Festival in the Park
Spearfish City Park, Spearfish
(605) 642–2311

The Festival in the Park, held on a mid-July Saturday and Sunday is a huge, popular event with more than 200 vendors. This juried art show is held in a lovely setting: Spearfish's city park on the banks of Spearfish Creek.

Arts and crafts of every variety, having passed the jury's discriminating eye, are presented in booths for the public's pleasure and purchase. In addition, there's a wonderful variety of food, jazz bands, dancing, music, and children's events and performances. These entertainments run all day long, so you can rest and snack, then walk around and look some more.

The vendors pay a fee to display their work, but the festival is free to everyone else.

Black Hills Corvette Classic
Various locations in Spearfish
(605) 334–1621
www.spearfish.sd.us

Twenty-eight years ago, the Sioux Falls Corvette Club (which consisted of seven couples and their cars) took a vacation together in the Black Hills. The event took on a life of its own and hundreds of people and their Corvettes have been having fun together ever since.

In recent years, some 1,500 people and 870 cars from 38 states have attended. The

Classic takes place on the third full weekend of July (Thursday through Sunday). On Thursday, the group caravans from Sioux Falls to Spearfish and everyone is welcome to tag along (not just club members, and not just Corvette owners). On the way home Sunday morning, everyone takes a detour to Mount Rushmore.

The main event is "Vette Street USA," when all those cars park on Main Street for a giant car show. Music, food, and merriment abound, plus competitions, touring and side trips, autocross, drag races, and a fish fry.

The registration fee is $100 per couple or $60 for one person, and participants must register by July 1. The fee includes entrance to all the parties. If you just want to wander and browse through all that gleaming, curvy steel (no drooling on the cars!), there's no charge.

A cowboy takes a wild ride at the Days of '76 Rodeo in Deadwood. PHOTO: COURTESY OF SOUTH DAKOTA TOURISM

Days of '76
Various locations in Deadwood
(605) 578–1876, (800) 999–1876
www.deadwood.org

This event began more than 80 years ago. It's a great Old West–style celebration that takes place in late July, over five days.

The traditional parade is 3 miles long and mostly horse-powered. The Professional Rodeo Cowboys Association (PRCA) rodeo events attract enthusiastic crowds and sometimes the Budweiser Clydesdales show up. Even President Coolidge attended the Days of '76 in 1927. It's a real (and real entertaining) tradition around Deadwood.

National Impala Association's
International Convention
Various locations in Spearfish
(605) 642–5864

You don't have to be an Impala owner to appreciate those roomy old beauties; in fact, any full-sized Chevrolet made from 1958 to 1969 is welcome.

Members of the National Impala Association, and others who want to participate, can register for $25 (there are extra charges for meals and some events). But there's no charge for just being in Spearfish during the convention and watching all those shiny cars cruise down Main Street and around the Hills.

Going on each year for more than 22 years, the convention is held over six days in late July and is headquartered at the Holiday Inn of the Northern Black Hills, though many of the events take place at other locations. There are two show-and-shine competitions, tours of the Hills, a car-part swap meet, breakfasts, a 1950s and 1960s dance, a picnic, an evening excursion to Deadwood, a poker run, and an awards banquet.

Central Hills

Black Hills Heritage Festival
Off Mt. Rushmore Rd., Memorial Park
Rapid City
(605) 341–5714

It's the largest festival in western South Dakota, now in its 17th year. The Heritage Festival celebrates the arts (literary, visual, performing, and all the rest), as well as the Black Hills' ethnic and cultural heritage.

Held in Rapid City's Memorial Park, the festival takes place over the Fourth of July weekend (Thursday through Sunday) and admission is free. National and regional touring artists perform and there are fireworks, arts and crafts displays and demonstrations, an international food bazaar, a children's area and carnival, strolling performers, and a talent contest.

Gem and Mineral Show
444 Mt. Rushmore Rd., Rushmore Plaza Civic Center, Rapid City
(605) 394-4115

This is a great show for rock hounds, gem and mineral fans, and folks shopping for interesting gifts and treasures. Vendors come from all over the country to sell, buy, swap, and exhibit their collections. You can find jewelry, rough rock, fossils, and specimens here, and enjoy demonstrations, educational programs, and the silent auction.

It's sponsored by the Western Dakota Gem and Mineral Society and held on the third weekend in July. Admission is $2.00.

Black Hills Jazz and Blues Festival
Off Mt. Rushmore Rd., Memorial Park, Civic Center Grounds, Rapid City
(605) 787-6619

This is a very special event for jazz and blues lovers. Each year on the last Saturday in July, five nationally and regionally known performers make Memorial Park come alive with the sound of their music. It starts at noon and lasts until 10:30 P.M., and it's a great family day spent in a beautiful setting, with music all around.

Food is available; bring lawn chairs and blankets for seating. Wristbands, which cost $10, enable you to come and go as you like, skipping one performance and reentering the grounds for another. Discounts are available for children, too (please inquire).

August

Northern Hills

Ruby's Garden Party
D.C. Booth Historic Fish Hatchery
423 Hatchery Circle, Spearfish
(605) 642-7730

The elegantly beautiful D.C. Booth home and gardens on the fish hatchery grounds are the setting for Ruby's Garden Party. Mrs. Ruby Booth, a charming hostess, loved to entertain; this party is named in her honor and is patterned after her gracious style and evokes the charm of the early 1900s.

This lovely, dressy affair is held in mid-August in the garden behind the home and includes a champagne dinner with musical accompaniment. Advance registration is required. The cost is $50 per person, with proceeds helping the D.C. Booth Society to maintain the historic home and grounds.

Sturgis Rally & Races
Various locations around the Hills, Sturgis
(605) 347-9190
www.sturgismotorcyclerally.com

It's the Black Hills' biggest party, and a crazy one it is. The "Rally" (sometimes simply known as "Sturgis") is virtually indescribable, but we'll try.

The Sturgis Rally & Races are into their 62nd year; that's a lot of years of biking and partying in staunchly individualistic biker style. The little town of Sturgis, South Dakota, (normal population about 7,000), swells to a temporary population of about 275,000 to 475,000 each year during the event. How this happens is a sort of motorcycling miracle. (For more about the history and idiosyncrasies of the Rally, see the Close-up in this chapter.)

The Rally officially runs from Monday through Sunday in mid-August, but bikers begin to descend on the Hills about a week early, and some stay for days after the rally ends. For about two weeks each

Traditional rodeo competition and entertainment are the main events at the five-day Black Hills Roundup in Belle Fourche. PHOTO: COURTESY OF SOUTH DAKOTA TOURISM

summer, the Black Hills vibrate constantly to the thunderous music only hundreds of thousands of motorcycles can make. After you're here for a couple of days, you can even sleep right through it.

So many events of vast and amazing variety are held during Rally week that it's impossible to describe them all, but here's a sampling. Official events include motorcycle auctions and displays, demonstration rides, parties, motorcycle jumps and hill climbs, races and ride-ins, guided tours of the Hills, exhibits, and poker runs. Four blocks of Main Street are closed to all vehicles except bikes, and you haven't seen anything until you've viewed thousands of shiny motorcycles parked perpendicular to the curbs, and in a double row down the middle, stretching as far as the eye can see.

Almost every downtown storefront is occupied by someone selling nearly every type of food you can imagine, or T-shirts, leather clothing, bandannas, cigars, motorcycle parts and accessories, and souvenirs.

Other Black Hills towns throw their own parties for bikers, and Rapid City's Rushmore Plaza Civic Center hosts the free Harley-Davidson show, with vendors,

seminars, competitions, and demonstrations, plus a major concert (past performers have included ZZ Top, Willie Nelson, Lynyrd Skynyrd, and Def Leppard). You must purchase tickets to the concert.

Call the number or browse the Web site listed in the heading for information and schedules, to register, and for help in finding accommodations (which you should book months in advance). You aren't required to officially register (and there's no charge for doing so), but you can stop at Rally Headquarters in the Armory building on Main Street to enter your name in the guest book and put a pin in both the U.S. and world maps to mark where you're from. The number of pins in those maps may surprise you. And even if you're not a biker, you'll enjoy the people-watching opportunities.

Black Hills Steam and Gas Threshing Bee
Hereford Rd., Sturgis
(605) 787–4647, (800) 626–8013
www.spearfish.sd.us

Elders remember the farming equipment you'll see at this show: early steam- and

Blacksmithing demonstrations draw curious onlookers at the annual Black Hills Steam and Gas Threshing Bee near Sturgis. PHOTO: KIMBERLY METZ

The Sturgis Rally & Races

Every year in mid-August, tens of thousands of black-leather-clad folks ride their roaring steeds into Sturgis, South Dakota. They take over the town, park in every available parking space, fill the restaurants, crowd the sidewalks, and stay up half the night partying. The air is filled with the thundering sound of their iron horses and normal conversation is downright impossible.

Why don't the good citizens of Sturgis do something about this intrusion, you ask? Don't they resent this yearly invasion of their peace and quiet, of their quaint little town? Heck, no! They invited these invaders, and they even gave the event a name: Sturgis Rally & Races.

It all started in 1938 when J.C. "Pappy" Hoel (who owned the local motorcycle shop) and his friends organized a race. Nineteen people showed up and it was so much fun that they formed the Jackpine Gypsies Motorcycle Club and started an annual tour of the Hills. Events and activities were added each year; attendance grew, and the whole thing just snowballed.

The Rally really picked up in the 1980s. An estimated 30,000 people attended in 1981; 63,000 attended in 1987, and 170,000 were there in 1996. The 50th Rally saw a whopping 400,000 attendees. And the 60th, a landmark event commemorated in the year 2000, played host to 500,000 people! (The mathematical discrepancy is due to the two years during World War II when the Rally was canceled.)

There's probably no other sport that brings out individuality, freedom, and wildness like motorcycling, and there's a wannabe biker in most of us. (Even South Dakota's governor rides.)

Nearly everyone attending the Rally takes the opportunity to show off in some way. You'll see incredibly creative custom bikes and paint jobs, wild headgear, bikers with parrots, bikers with snakes, bikers with dogs in sidecars, Christian bikers and unregenerate ones, tattoos that cover more square inches of skin than clothing, piercing on every conceivable body part, and raunchy T-shirts. Everyone's just having fun and being his or her eccentric self. It's all pretty wacky, but we recommend you experience the Rally at least once, just so you can say you did.

Although "biker" might sound a bit scary—conjuring up visions of burly, mean, criminal types—most bikers aren't like that at all. They just love motorcycling and expressing themselves under the guise of biker culture. Some of that self-expression,

The Sturgis festivities go on into the night.
PHOTO: COURTESY OF SOUTH DAKOTA TOURISM

however, can get a bit raunchy and rowdy. Whatever you hear about the Rally being a "family event," don't believe it. Rally-goers are adults and they engage in adult behavior. This being basically an outdoor event, you'll see things on the streets (occasional nudity, lots of bare skin) that may astound you and that you may not want your kids to witness.

However, don't be too fooled by the hard-core demeanor, the mean-looking bikes, and all that black leather. Although earlier rallies attracted "real" bikers, recent ones have increased in popularity so much that they attract enthusiasts who "play biker" for the week, shipping their motorcycles into town and getting scruffy just for the Rally. Under that short, ragged beard, dirty bandanna, and T-shirt may beat the heart of a big-city lawyer, doctor, or stockbroker. Witness ads in the *Rapid City Journal* inviting physicians attending the Rally to "stay and explore practice opportunities in the Black Hills."

Longtime bikers growl that the Rally has changed over the years. It's true. Nowadays, you can't tell the "real" bikers from the wannabes. But it's fun to try.

gas-powered machinery that (in those days) made work easier. At least it was easier than doing it by hand and with horses.

The Threshing Bee will mark its 34th year in 2002. That's an indication of how popular it is, and how the old equipment still strikes a chord in the heart. More than 200 pieces of antique equipment are exhibited.

The Threshing Bee takes place on Friday, Saturday, and Sunday of the third weekend in August, on the grounds owned by the Western Dakota Antique Club, one-half mile east of the Sturgis Airport, off Highway 34. Admission is $3.00 per day for anyone 13 and older.

The Threshing Bee will transport you back to a simpler, but more strenuous, time. It may even be a chance for elders to share their stories and heritage with those who are younger. You'll see antique tractors, threshing machines, saw mills, steam engines, miniature engines, blacksmithing, a one-room schoolhouse, and more. There are plenty of demonstrations, threshing, and hay binding in the field next door, an auction, a barbecue, tractor races, and a daily parade. Music is provided by the Grimm Reapers (would anyone else be more appropriate?).

Kool Deadwood Nites
Various locations in Deadwood
(605) 578–1876, (800) 999–1876
www.deadwood.org

It's the finest kind of retro concert 'cause you get to pretend you're back in the '50s and '60s again. It's held on Friday, Saturday, and Sunday in late August.

You can dance at the sock hop and win prizes for your skill. Classic cars are displayed, and prizes are awarded for beauty.

The "prom," complete with authentic music, is on Saturday night, and everyone is encouraged to dress up in style. (You can even rent a tux in town.) In the past, music has been provided by Bill Haley's Comets, Chubby Checker, Jan and Dean, and Johnny Rivers, and equally great performances are expected in 2002.

You won't believe it, but all these events are free. Is Deadwood a Kool town, or what?

Black Hills Airport Fly-In
Black Hills Airport, Spearfish
(605) 642–0277

Pilots and aviation buffs alike love this annual event, which takes place on a Saturday in late August.

Seventy-some planes have been displayed, including vintage war birds as well as experimental planes, ultralights, and helicopters. Pilots can fly their planes in, and spectators can take rides and enjoy the displays. Demonstrations and food are offered, too. You can watch the South Dakota Aviation Hall of Fame induction ceremony, a very special event.

The fly-in is free to everyone, pilots and spectators alike.

Central Hills

Ellsworth Air Force Base
Open House
Ellsworth Air Force Base
(605) 385–4414

"There's always a plane in the air during this exciting open house," say the organizers, and if you like planes, you'll get your fill of them here. You can watch aerial demonstrations, fly-bys, and parachute jumps, and see both vintage and modern combat aircraft. The Golden Knights Army parachute team has appeared, and attendees have been treated to aerobatic stunts, air rescue demonstrations, and pyrotechnics as well.

Central States Fair & Rodeo
Central States Fairgrounds, Rapid City
(605) 355–3861
www.centralstatesfair.com

This is a free traditional fair, with those familiar events that make country fairs so much fun. You can browse 4-H and agricultural exhibits, sit in on classes and demonstrations on cooking and crafts, walk through the livestock barns, pet an exotic critter at the petting zoo, ride the carnival rides, catch a horse show or parade, and stuff yourself with cotton candy and caramel apples. Or sit back in the grandstand and be entertained by some nationally famous musical talent (past performers include The Turtles and Deana Carter). If you'd rather sit on the edge of your seat, try the Professional Rodeo Cowboys Association rodeo instead.

So many things go on at this eight-day fair that you'll have trouble finding time to enjoy them all, so check the local newspapers and sort out each day's events. The 57th annual Central States Fair takes place in mid- to late August.

September

Northern Hills

Deadwood Jam
Downtown Deadwood
(605) 578–1102, (800) 999–1876
www.deadwood.org

The "Jam" is a long-standing musical event, and if you're a music fan you won't want to miss it. It's held in mid-September each year, outdoors. Ticket prices are $18 in advance and $20 at the gate.

John Mayall and the Blues Breakers, Chris Duarte, John McEuen, Suzy Bogguss, and Tonic have performed in the past. It's a big street party, really, and you're invited.

Harvest Fest
Various locations in Spearfish
(605) 642–2626
www.spearfish.sd.us

Two blocks of Main Street will be blocked off for the eighth annual Harvest Fest in 2002. Enjoy crafts, kids' entertainment, apple pie-baking contests, music, displays, puppet shows, the Tour de Fish Bicycle Race, a quilt show, and more, all free.

An additional and related event is the "Taste of Spearfish," a chance to sample food prepared by area caterers and restaurants. Admission is $1.00, and participants can buy tickets for food that costs from one to eight tickets per taste.

The Taste of Spearfish is held in the Pavilion in the Spearfish City Park. Both events take place in late September.

Central Hills

Annual Dakota Polka Festival
2900 Canyon Lake Dr., Canyon Lake
Viking Hall, Rapid City
(605) 787-5584

Admit it: You've always wanted to polka. This is your chance. This festival takes place on a September weekend, and 2002 marks the 13th annual event. All kinds of dance steps are performed, not just polka. Live bands provide the music and the Friday and Saturday night dancing goes on until 11:00 P.M. (Just because it's held at a senior center, you thought it would end at 8:00 P.M.?)

Enthusiasts—some of whom have been dancing most of their lives—swear that dancing keeps them young. If you don't polka, you can observe, or ask one of the friendly enthusiasts to teach you on the 5,400-square-foot-floor.

Food and RV parking are available at the center. A two-day pass is $15.00 per person, a Friday-night pass is $6.00 per person, and a Saturday night pass is $10.00 per person. Smoking and alcohol are not permitted.

Come on, party with these fun people—if you can keep up.

Black Hills Community Theatre
Dahl Fine Arts Center,
713 Seventh St., Rapid City
(605) 394-1787, (605) 394-1786 (box office)

The annual performance season, which begins in September (and ends in May) is a great chance to watch our fine local talent in professionally staged plays. Please read about this outstanding community theater in The Arts chapter.

West River History Conference
1101 Madill St., Keystone Community
Center, Keystone
(605) 666-4630,
(605) 666-4494 (summer number)

Black Hills and Great Plains history buffs will adore this conference, and if you're new to the area or just visiting, you'll learn things that will enhance your visit.

The mid-September conference is packed full of history- and heritage-related workshops and presentations, some over breakfast, dinner, or a banquet. It's open to the public and the registration fee is just $15 for the entire three-day conference. There is an additional charge for meals.

More than 50 papers are presented on fascinating local topics that range from Black and Native American history and Wild Bill Hickok to early aviation and Mount Rushmore.

Call to request a schedule and to register. The conference is sponsored by the Keystone Historical Society.

Southern Hills

Crazy Horse Night Blast
Crazy Horse Memorial, Custer
(605) 673-4681
www.crazyhorse.org

This ceremonial blast on the mountain takes place each year in early June and on September 6. (You can learn about the Crazy Horse Memorial in our Attractions chapter.) The latter date commemorates both Crazy Horse's untimely death in 1877 and the late sculptor Korczak Ziolkowski's birthday.

The blast takes place after dark for spectacular effect, and it's free with your entrance fee. An open house, during which you can tour the visitor complex and exhibits, is held on Labor Day weekend.

Fall Color Heralds Bison Roundup

In the Black Hills, fall is a time when bighorn sheep bang heads and when artists assemble to display their goods. It's a time of immense bird migrations; a time when many American Indians indigenous to the area seek out the lonely land of their ancestors. But perhaps most significant for Black Hills visitors is the fact that autumn is also a time when managers at Custer State Park reduce bison numbers to be compatible with the land's carrying capacity. The time is right, for the blood of the bison has cooled following the intensity of their summer ardor. Now, as the Black Hills begin to turn gold, bison plod along like patriarchs of old, at least that is until the roundup begins. Then, their blood is anything but cool.

Game Lodge campground is conveniently located for the roundup, which the park holds the first Monday after the last weekend in September (after Art in the Park), as one of their fall interpretive programs. Set against the plains that thread throughout the hills and the ponderosa pine, the fall prairie provides a splendid backdrop for the roundup. The herd thuds over hills, finally charging through the coulees and ravines, urged on by riders. Once the bison are in motion, the direction is easy to sustain, for as managers say, "A moving herd is easier to contain than a stationary one."

After the herd is contained in a huge holding area, biologists begin the process of reduction. Bison are herded into various chutes according to age and sex. Culled

Bison charge during fall roundup at Custer State Park. PHOTO: BERT GILDART

animals are then auctioned off to the highest bidders. After the roundup, the much-reduced herd of about 400 is returned to roam the park, where it joins those that eluded the riders. The two-day event is one of the most dramatic in the Black Hills, and it's made even more spectacular as it coincides with a time when the Black Hills turn gold.

Badger Clark Hometown Cowboy Poetry Gathering
The Mueller Center, 801 S. Sixth St.
Hot Springs
(605) 745-3446
www.hotsprings/sd.com

Locally and regionally famous cowboy poets tell their tales and play their music in this late September event. It's designed to pay tribute to both Badger Clark, South Dakota's "Poet Lariat," and the popular art of cowboy poetry. In addition to the performances, there are also symposiums, displays of Western gear, jam sessions, open sessions where amateur poets can give tale-telling a try, and more cowboy boots in the audience than you can shake a stick at.

October

Northern Hills

Oktoberfest Celebration
Downtown Deadwood
(605) 578-1876, (800) 999-1876
www.deadwood.org

This is a German-style celebration, presented Deadwood-style. It takes place on a Friday, Saturday, and Sunday in early October.

You can enjoy German and other music, clog dancing, a microbrew expo, a German cookoff and food tasting, accordion music, a lederhosen contest, and a home-brewers beer contest. Nationally known musicians perform in concert, too; past performers include the Bellamy Brothers, Three Dog Night, the Myron Floren Orchestra, and the Grass Roots.

It all takes place on Deadwood's Main Street, though most downtown casinos, restaurants, and hotels also have something special to offer. The entertainment and events are free.

Enjoy some hearty German-style entertainment and take home a specially designed beer mug. You might want to check out the Frozen Chicken Bowling Contest, too.

Deadweird
Downtown Deadwood
(605) 578-1876, (800) 999-1876
www.deadwood.org

Don't miss out on this spooky event, because it happens only once each year—on Halloween night. It's a citywide bash, with trick-or-treating for the kids and a costume contest (for big kids older than 21) that rewards winners with a great prize: cold, hard cash.

Since Deadwood is haunted by such illustrious ghosts as Calamity Jane, Seth Bullock, and Wild Bill Hickok, this event is perfectly appropriate. You and your spirits are invited to attend.

Central Hills

Black Hills Chamber Music Society
First Congregational Church
1200 Clark St., Rapid City
(605) 718-5666
www.rapidcityweb.com

The society's five-performance series begins in October (and runs through April) and always boasts outstanding performances. We've included some examples and more information in The Arts chapter.

Mount Rushmore
International Marathon
Various locations, Rapid City
(605) 348-7866 (information on routes)
www.rapidcitycvb.com

The annual marathon takes place on a Sunday in early October. The route winds through the scenic Black Hills and ends

Powwows are spectacular events and a rich opportunity to learn about Native American culture and tradition. To participants, powwows are a spiritual experience, a celebration of culture, a chance to dance together and to renew old friendships and make new ones. The steady drumbeats accompanying the dancers represent the heartbeat of the people, a powerful emotional experience.

The Pow Wow and Art Expo take place in mid-October and last for three days. Call the number given above for exact dates.

Traditional and contemporary art is on display and for sale, and in past years there have been storytellers, flute players, dance and drumming performances, educational activities for children, and a Native American fashion show. Pre-powwow programs are held at The Journey Museum (see the Attractions chapter) several days prior to the event. There is a charge for one- and three-day passes.

Be sure to watch the Grand Entry, an event that is repeated on all three days of the powwow. Observers, who are expected to respectfully stand during the entry, are treated to a stunning visual and auditory display of finery, drums, dancing, and passionate musical voices. The participants enter the arena in a line, singing and dancing as they go, accompanied by drumbeats and preceded by the sacred eagle staff and tribal and U.S. flags. Hundreds of dancers fill the arena in a sacred circle, winding round and round, until the floor is a whirl of movement, color, and sound. It's a spectacular sight, especially from the Civic Center's seats high above the arena.

in Rapid City, and for the entry fee ($35) you can compete and enjoy the scenery at the same time.

A marathon relay is run in conjunction with the marathon itself, a 5-mile noncompetitive run/walk is held the day before, and a pasta buffet at Mount Rushmore is on the schedule, too.

Rapid City Concert Association
Rushmore Plaza Civic Center Theater
444 Mt. Rushmore Rd., Rapid City
(605) 394-4101, www.rapidcitycvb.com

The annual six-concert series begins in October (and ends in April) and presents fun and exciting musical performances. You can read more about them in our chapter on The Arts.

Black Hills Pow Wow and Art Expo
444 Mt. Rushmore Rd.,
Rushmore Plaza
Civic Center, Rapid City
(605) 343-5718
www.rapidcitycvb.com

Ski For Light Ski Swap
444 Mt. Rushmore Rd., Rushmore Plaza
Civic Center, Rapid City
(605) 341-3626
www.rapidcitycvb.com

The Black Hills Regional Ski For Light organization holds its annual fund-raiser in late October or early November. It's an equipment consignment swap, where 20 percent of the sale price goes to the nonprofit organization to fund programs that help the visually impaired ski, camp, canoe, and enjoy the outdoors.

This is your chance to pick up some great used equipment at a fair price and help support the Ski For Light programs, too. There is no entrance fee to shop at the swap.

For information on outdoor and recreational programs for the visually impaired (including a January ski event at Deer Mountain, near Lead, which draws participants from all over the country), call Ski For Light at the number above.

Southern Hills

Annual Buffalo Roundup and Arts Festival
Custer State Park, Custer
(605) 255-4515

Organizers have called this event "Feel the Thunder." You can't quite understand why until you've seen, heard, and felt 1,500 buffalo running across the plains, herded by cowboys, cowgirls, and park rangers (riding pickups and horses) into corrals. It's really something to experience.

The roundup, in existence for more than 36 years, is held on a Monday in late September or early October in the corral area south of the State Game Lodge on Wildlife Loop Road. You can watch the critters being branded and vaccinated (but you need to arrive between 6:30 and 7:30 A.M. and stay until the "all clear" signal is given). Read about the roundup in our Parks and Grasslands chapter. The buffalo not returned to the park for the winter are sold at auction in November (that write-up follows).

Plenty of less dramatic (but equally interesting) events take place during roundup weekend, on the Saturday and Sunday before the roundup itself. The arts festival is staged near the State Game Lodge and you'll find great collectibles and gifts in the booths.

There's also terrific entertainment: Native American dancers, cowboy poets, cloggers, fast-draw competitions, and Western music. You can enter the Buffalo Wallow Chili Cookoff, or just sample the entries, and enjoy a pancake feed and chuck wagon cookout, too. It's all free, except for the food.

For convenience, you can stay at the Custer State Park campgrounds (see the

A young boy dances at the Black Hills Pow Wow.
PHOTO: STEVEN A. PAGE

Campgrounds and RV sites chapter) or resorts (see the Accommodations chapter).

Native American Day Observances
U.S. 16/385, Crazy Horse Memorial, Custer
(605) 673-4681
www.crzyhorse.org

A special program and events are held each October at Crazy Horse Memorial to commemorate the struggles, triumphs, heritage, and legacies of Native Americans.

You can enjoy lectures and demonstrations, drumming, singing, dancing, and storytelling. Tour the Indian Museum of North America and the Native American Cultural Center; both are housed on the grounds.

A special day blast is planned on the mountain (see more about the sculpture in our Attractions chapter), and there's a buffalo stew feed at noon. It's all free with your admission to the memorial.

November

In November, holiday home tours, craft shows, "festival of lights" parades, and Christmas tree decorating festivals are popular. Check a local newspaper for details.

Central Hills

Black Hills Symphony Orchestra
Rushmore Plaza Civic Center Theater
444 Mt. Rushmore Rd., Rapid City
(605) 348–HORN (season tickets)
(605) 394–4111 (individual performance tickets)

Six fine concerts are presented by our very own symphony orchestra each season. Please read about these great events in The Arts chapter.

Southern Hills

Buffalo Auction
Custer State Park, Custer
(605) 255–4515, (605) 255–4814

Read about the Annual Buffalo Roundup and Arts Festival that takes place in Custer State Park in October's listing (Southern Hills) or in our Parks and Grasslands chapter. The surplus animals culled from the herd along with the park's surplus burros are sold at this mid-November auction, which helps support the park's operations.

It's an interesting event to watch, even if you're not inclined to take a buffalo or burro home.

December

Northern Hills

Adams Family Victorian Christmas
Open House
Adams Memorial Museum
54 Sherman St., Deadwood
(605) 578–1714

The charming, historic Adams Museum is the perfect setting for a Christmas celebration. It's also a chance to learn about the devoted (albeit tragic) Adams family of Deadwood, who funded the museum and for whom it is named. You can read more about the museum in our Attractions chapter.

Enjoy Christmas readings, a masquerade, dramatic musical presentations, and special exhibits (the events change from year to year). It's free and takes place on the first Saturday in December.

Christmas Stroll
Downtown Spearfish
(605) 642–2626

This lovely community event takes place on a Sunday afternoon in early December, on Spearfish's charming Main Street. With a little luck, you can bask in the sunshine of a Black Hills winter day, or at least listen to music and carolers, shop for crafts, enjoy the food, and take a horse-drawn sleigh ride. The fun is free, although there is a charge for food.

Insiders' Tip

Need accommodations for your trip to the Sturgis Rally in August? Check these chapters in this book: Bed and Breakfast Inns and Ranches, Campgrounds and RV Sites, and Accommodations. Or call Sturgis Rally & Events, Inc. at (605) 347-9190 or the Sturgis Chamber of Commerce at (605) 347-2556 and request accommodation information.

Elaborate costumes add to the excitement during powwow dances. PHOTO: JON FROST

Festival of Trees
Historic Matthews Opera House
614 Main St., Spearfish
(605) 642–2626

Beautifully decorated Christmas trees are on display for about four days in early December; you can view them without charge. It's also your chance to tour the restored opera house, which is used as a performing arts center.

The festival is sponsored by the businesswomen's community service organization, Zonta. At the end of the display period, the trees are auctioned at a gala event, and proceeds go to charity. You can take home a decorated tree and help out those less fortunate at the same time.

Hatchery Holidays
D.C. Booth Historic Fish Hatchery
423 Hatchery Circle, Spearfish
(605) 642–7730

The hatchery grounds and D.C. Booth historic home are lovely places, and the perfect backdrop for a Christmas, event.

The house is decorated in the finery of a long-ago Victorian Christmas, and the many trees on the grounds are draped in finery of their own. You can take a horse-drawn wagon ride and tours of the house and museum and enjoy the special displays and events. It's all free and a charming way to spend a holiday Sunday in early December.

Southern Hills

Christmas in the Hills
Various locations in Hot Springs
(605) 745–4140

The folks in Hot Springs—who work hard together to present this event—are rightfully proud of this old-fashioned festival, which goes back more than 24 years. Traditions include a children's procession and living nativity, an arts and crafts fair, music, art shows, community dinners and chili suppers, a tour of local homes, and appearances by Mrs. Santa Claus. It takes place during the first weekend of December and attracts visitors from surrounding states as well as residents and folks coming home for Christmas.

The Arts

You might assume that a trip to the Black Hills means leaving the world of the fine arts behind. And you may be right, but only in some respects; it's true that we don't have a world-class ballet company or an internationally famous art museum. But in other respects, you'd be mistaken, and that just might surprise you.

Artists have always been influenced by their environments. The gentle Black Hills and the rugged Badlands have compelled artists with their natural powers, both physical and spiritual. The landscape, the people, the weather, animals, and seasons have been catalysts for the creation of many fine works of art. But it's the feeling of this area that has the strongest influence—the accessibility, the beauty, the welcoming openness strike chords in artists' hearts. Thus, there's no shortage of creativity being expressed here, whether it is danced, sung, painted, photographed, written, or sculpted.

You'll find art on display and for sale at many events (see our Annual Events and Festivals chapter). Especially worthy of note are the Black Hills Pow Wow and Indian Art Exposition, the Black Hills Heritage Festival, even the Black Hills Stock Show and Rodeo, all in Rapid City, and the Festival in the Park and High Plains Heritage Center's Quick Draw in Spearfish.

The rich traditions of this area also have an influence. Western themes and traditional Native American art predominate, although some visual artists choose other themes or abstract forms and a growing number of Native American artists are exploring contemporary paths. Literary arts run the gamut from cowboy poetry and stories of Western life to work that transcends the sense of place that defines the Black Hills.

Proof of our passion for art are the organizations that abound, although visitors may see only their achievements. These groups raise money, support artists, and fund exhibits and events. Rapid City has the Allied Arts Fund Drive, (605) 394-4106; Rapid City Arts Council, (605) 394-4101; Alliance for Arts Education, (605) 394-4106; Black Hills Artist Support Network, (605) 394-4101; and Dakota Artist Guild, (605) 394-4108.

Further evidence of our enthusiasm is "Many Voices: The Rapid City Cultural Plan," an ambitious 2-year planning document that proposes to bring more art activities to more citizens and encourage their involvement. A *Rapid City Journal* editorial on October's designation as National Arts and Humanities Month, stated that "if the past and present are any indication, the future here for culture and the arts is promising; Rapid City has demonstrated a passionate, ongoing commitment."

As have the state government and nearly every town in the Hills. The South Dakota Arts Council, (605) 773-3131, is part of the state's Department of Education and Cultural Affairs. Among other projects, it funds residencies and grants to help local artists share their work with schoolchildren, who experience poetry, Lakota dance and flute music, stories, photography, mural painting, rodeo clowns, puppets, classical guitar, and more through the program.

The Sturgis Area Arts Council sponsors theater performances, Art for Lunch Bunch discussions, book signings, a juried art show, and the Community Sculpture Garden. The Spearfish Center for the Arts and Humanities, (605) 642-7973, helped restore the town's Historic Matthews Opera House, now a performing arts center, and sponsors art shows and an annual foreign film series.

The Historic Deadwood-Lead Arts Council, (605) 584-1461, sponsors exhibitions in the under-renovation Historic Homestake Opera House, which will one day also be a performance space. South Dakotans for the Arts, (605) 578-1783, based in Deadwood, is an arts advocacy, service, and education organization that sponsors the U.S. West Artists in Rural Schools program, the five-state Art Beyond Boundaries Conference, and much more.

Hill City prides itself on a growing reputation as an art community. The Hill City Area Arts Council, (605) 574-5507 or (605) 673-3365, supports exhibits and demonstrations, including June's Heart of the Hills Art Show. A cultural center is in the works, too, which will include a theater and performance space. The Hot Springs Area Arts Council, (605) 745-4225, manages the Main Street Arts and Crafts Festival (more than 20 years old) and children's programs and scholarships. Southern Hills Arts and Humanities, (605) 745-6473, promotes all types of arts activities, including a summer music series.

We encourage you to learn about the arts in the Black Hills in this chapter—then watch, listen, read, tap your toes, browse, participate, enjoy, and maybe even take some of it home.

Dance

Central Hills

Black Hills Dance Theatre
4939 Spring Tree Court, Rapid City
(605) 342-1564

This dance theater is managed by an all-volunteer board, a sure sign of community commitment. It sponsors two professional dance performances each year, one in the spring and another in the fall, with master classes and school activities coinciding. In recent years, the North Carolina Dance Theater, a contemporary ballet company, has performed, as has Kim

Robards's modern dance company from Denver, and Spectrum, a jazz company from Seattle.

The theater performs the *Nutcracker* ballet biennially, bringing in a professional performer to complement local talent, and also offers weeklong summer dance workshops for both children and adults.

Ticket prices vary for each performance, but range between $7.00 and $20.00.

Film

Northern Hills

The Foreign Film Festival
Northern Hills Cinema, 1830 N. Main St.
Spearfish
(605) 642-7973

The Spearfish Center for the Arts and Humanities sponsors this tribute to films from other nations. Four are shown on alternate weekends in September and October, and each is run twice, on Sunday afternoon and Monday evening. Those planning the event choose a variety of film subjects, but usually include one in English and three in other languages, with English subtitles.

Central Hills

Friends of the Devereaux Library
Film Series
Elks Theatre, 512 Sixth St., Rapid City
(605) 394–1262

The Friends of the Devereaux Library, at South Dakota School of Mines and Technology, sponsor this annual film series, a fundraiser for the library.

Ten foreign and domestic classic films are presented, one each Sunday evening from mid-January through mid-March. A recent season included such classics as *The Philadelphia Story*, *The Graduate*, *West Side Story*, and *Deliverance*. The cozy, historic theater has a great, old-fashioned balcony and a huge screen. You can purchase season tickets for about $30.

Galleries and Exhibit Spaces

We've included here the galleries that carry original art (for display, for sale, or both), although many also offer prints, custom framing, art supplies, and gifts. All are great places to see what's being created in artists' studios around South Dakota, or to purchase a work of art. Some galleries close for the winter or shorten their operating hours, so you may want to call ahead.

Northern Hills

Ruddell Gallery of Art
Black Hills State University
Student Union Bldg., Spearfish
(605) 642–6852

A small gallery tucked away on the second level of the building, the Ruddell is a pleasant space with some fine exhibitions. Recent shows included a bronze sculpture invitational, an alumni show, the work of South Dakota art teachers, and selections from Red Cloud Heritage Center's vast collection (see our Daytrips and Weekend Getaways chapter). An especially intriguing show was *Elders in Their Faith*, Mark McGinnis's portraits and interviews with older people who are deeply rooted in their religions. On the other end of the spectrum was the hilarious *Bad Taste Show*, in which students displayed their favorite kitsch art.

Termesphere Gallery
Christensen Dr., Spearfish
(605) 642–4805
www.termesphere.com

Dick Termes has become internationally known for his six-point perspective spherical paintings, known as Termespheres. When you step across the threshold of his geodesic-dome gallery, you enter a magical room filled with so many colorful spheres and mobiles twirling from the ceiling that you'll be browsing in awe for an hour. If you're lucky, Termes himself may explain his complicated techniques for making these unique works of art.

One-of-a-kind originals, reproductions, and limited editions are on display and for sale.

In addition to spheres, you'll see cubes, tetrahedrons, polyhedrons, icosahedrons, and dodecahedrons (if you flunked geometry, ask for an explanation). Each gives

Loretto in the Round is an intriguing spherical study of the interior of the Loretto Chapel in Santa Fe, New Mexico. It's one of the many Termespheres created by Spearfish artist Dick Termes using six-point perspective. PHOTO: COURTESY OF DICK TERMES

you the sense of standing in the very center of the environment that is the subject of each piece, yet—at the same time—you are viewing it from the outside.

Often compared to M. C. Escher, Termes attended the Escher Centennial Congress in Rome in the summer of 1998, held in honor of Escher's 100th birthday. Termes was one of just three artists, and the only American, invited to speak.

You'll want to call ahead for directions. The gallery is on Christensen Drive, in the countryside south of Spearfish.

Wet Edge Gallery & Studio
309 W. Main St., Lead
(605) 584-2719

Sidestep the typical Black Hills Wild West experience and enter this classy consignment gallery—it's like walking into another world. Beautifully decorated, peaceful, and full of great art, the Wet Edge has the work of about 50 professional South Dakota artists, as well as books and music. You'll see the stark and wonderful graphite drawings of D. George Prisbe from Lead, who portrays our landscape in unusual ways. James Van Nuys of Rapid City is well represented with linocuts, engravings, monoprints, bronzes, watercolors, and oils. You'll also see Grete Bodogaard's colorful tapestries, T. R. Chytka's bronze sculptures, Michael Hill's raku pottery, and Loy Allen's representational glass pieces. We suggest calling ahead for times open.

Central Hills

Apex Gallery
South Dakota School of Mines and Technology
501 E. St. Joseph St., Rapid City
(605) 394-2481, (605) 394-4127

The fact that "Tech" encourages art studies (there's not yet a formal art program) impresses us; that outside-the-lines thinking shows in the quality of exhibitions at this gallery. There's more about Tech in our Education chapter.

Students have displayed their work in the Apex Gallery in a show called *Drawing and Perception*. Erik Maakestad's sculptures and Camille Riner's color relief monoprints (with handmade paper and handcrafted frames that are integral to each piece) have been shown too, as have the drawings and monotypes of Larry Schuh, and the brutally frank work of Garry Kaulitz, in recognition of Domestic Violence Awareness Month.

Exhibits change monthly and are usually launched with an opening reception. Even though you'll have to park in the main lot and walk a bit to reach the gallery, it's well worth a visit.

Black Hills Glass Blowers
901 Old Hill City Rd., Keystone
(605) 666–4542

This is the working studio of glass artists Gail Damin and Pete Hopkins. You can watch them create their glass art but, they stress, only when they're working, which is not all the time. It's best to call ahead if you want to see a glass artist in action, or in the winter months to make sure the studio is open. Gail and Pete do both lamp (or flame) working and offhand (or traditional) glassblowing. They make figurines, such as unicorns and dragons, and colorful art glass, including vases and bowls.

Changing Exhibition Gallery
The Journey Museum, 222 New York St.
Rapid City
(605) 394–6923

We've written about The Journey Museum in our Attractions chapter, but the adjacent Changing Exhibition Gallery is separate from the museum and has its own exhibitions. In fact, visitors can tour the gallery without paying the museum's fee. Each exhibit is launched with a reception, often held in the evenings, when guests can wander the museum (again, without charge).

Exhibitions are accompanied by educational programs for children and gallery talks by experts. Recent shows included *Native Sons*, combining the work of two famous South Dakota artists, Harvey Dunn and Oscar Howe; *The Rodeo Road*, cowboy art and artifacts; a display of work with petroglyphic and pictographic themes; the Russian icons of Father Peter Wilke; and *Fine Art and Bikes*, in conjunction with the August Sturgis Rally & Races (see our Annual Events and Festivals chapter).

Dahl Fine Arts Center and Dakota Art Gallery
713 Seventh St., Rapid City
(605) 394–4101, (605) 394–4108

Plan to spend some time at "The Dahl." The Ruth Brennan Gallery has 8 to 10 exhibitions every year, each with an opening reception. Themes vary widely, from Mexican folk art and impressionistic oils to photography and Black Hills landscapes. The gallery focuses on education—and this includes regional, national, and international work, and traveling exhibits.

The center also has a 170-seat theater and offices and serves as the hub for several arts organizations in Rapid City.

Adjoining the Ruth Brennan Gallery is the Dakota Art Gallery, operated by the Dakota Artists Guild, which displays juried work by members and others. One artist is featured each month, and works on continuing display include jewelry, paintings, pottery, glasswork, and much more. The guild has classes for children that include drawing, pottery, 3-D and sidewalk art, paper bag puppets, and papier-mâché; their work is exhibited in the gallery.

The *Cyclorama* mural by Bernard Thomas is in a room adjacent to the Central Gallery. It is a representation of 200 years of American history, from an economic perspective (it was commissioned by the Dahl's founder, a banker). Ask a staff member to turn on the taped narrative and lighting system to accompany your look at the mural.

Dakota Rose Art Gallery
816 South St., Rapid City
(605) 399–3954

The gallery features the work of award-winning watercolorist Sarah Rogers, a Wyoming resident known for vivid wildlife and floral renderings. You'll also find original work and limited-edition prints by other regional and nationally known artists, thousands of frame and mat samples for custom framing, and handcrafted gift items. The gallery, always beautifully decorated, is in a renovated 1907 English Renaissance house that is practically a work of art in its own right.

Jon Crane Watercolors
336 Main St., Hill City
(605) 574-4440

"Art That Takes You Home," this gallery's motto, perfectly describes the work of nationally known watercolorist Jon Crane. His subjects are often the rural landscapes of isolated farms and aging homesteads, lovely forests and trout streams, and heartwarming scenes that remind the viewer of home. Even the titles are often nostalgic: *Home for Hot Chocolate, A Great Day to Be a Kid, Heartland Legacy,* and *Almost Christmas* are among the many works you'll see here.

The pleasantly decorated gallery carries original work, framed and unframed open-edition miniature prints, and limited-edition prints and note cards. Custom framing is offered as well.

Crane was commissioned to paint the 1997 America's Holiday Tree as it stood in the Black Hills National Forest and later graced the Capitol Building lawn in Washington, D.C., during the Christmas season. Crane donated the reproduction rights to the painting to help raise funds for the project. Read more about the Holiday Tree in our Annual Events chapter.

The MDU Gallery
703 Kansas City St., Rapid City
(605) 394-4101

Our local natural gas company, Montana-Dakota Utilities, generously donated space for this gallery in its building, just down the street from the Dahl Fine Arts Center. It serves as the Dahl's satellite gallery and is often used to display the work of students. Each exhibition is arranged and installed by the Dahl's staff.

The Perfect Hanging Gallery
520 Kansas City St., Rapid City
(605) 348-7761

Insiders' Tip
The *Rapid City Journal* publishes an Arts Calendar each Sunday in its "Life & Style" section. It's a one-stop source to learn about upcoming events you won't want to miss.

The Perfect Hanging is a display space for both prints and original art, including that of P. Buckly Moss, Gene Stocks, and Ellie Weakley. It's also a custom framing shop that specializes in conservation and museum-quality mounting and framing. It stocks 600 mats, 2,500 frame samples, and 12 types of glass.

Prairie Edge Trading Company & Galleries
606 Main St., Rapid City
(605) 342-3086

Prairie Edge is a local landmark. It's a great place to shop (more about that in our Shopping chapter), and the restored building's stunning architecture alone is worth a visit. The second-floor fine art gallery is yet another gem in the Prairie Edge crown. Here, basking in the light from the huge old windows, you may see the amazing photographs of Robert Wong of Rapid City and Rod Planck of Wisconsin, or the work of local artists Cat Deuter, Paul Goble, Loy Allen, and James Van Nuys. Changing exhibits feature the art of many artists, but the astounding cast paper art of Allen and Patty Eckman is on permanent exhibit, so be sure to have a look.

Rimrock Art & Frame Company
1108 Jackson Blvd., Rapid City
(605) 342-7263

The oldest frame shop in Rapid City, Rimrock Art & Frame is also an artists' gallery that displays original work and prints of regional artists, including the oils of Jan

Wiedmeier, the original lithographs of Russell Chatham, sculptures by Jim Erickson, and the fantasy art of John Backlund. Jon Crane's prints (both current and secondary market editions) are also here, as is the work of Kay Williams and Ron Holyfield, longtime summer artists-in-residence at Custer State Park.

The owners, Mike and Debbie McLane, are fine artists themselves: Mike, a certified professional framer, produces great watercolors, and Debbie is a talented photographer. They also offer custom framing and their own line of South Dakota-made hardwood mouldings.

Sioux Indian Museum Gallery
The Journey Museum
222 New York St., Rapid City
(605) 394-2381

This small gallery is devoted to Native American art. It is inside the Journey Museum, near the gift shop, and your Journey ticket will admit you at no additional charge. The gallery has shown delightful and colorful contemporary Sioux quilts from the Journey's permanent collection; the paintings and three-dimensional art of Jim Yellowhawk of Rapid City; the acrylics and oils of Del Iron Cloud, also of Rapid City; and the sculpture of Alfred Belgarde of North Dakota.

SnowCreek Gallery
360 Main St., Hill City
(605) 574-2553

Located in Hill City's Old World Plaza, artist Deborah Carroll Weber's warm and welcoming shop carries her limited-edition prints and her original watercolors of scenes and symbols of times past.

Warriors Work Studio and Gallery
310 Main St., Hill City
(605) 574-4954

The smell of leather greets you as you open the door to this gallery. Artist Randy Berger creates deerskin-wrapped frames, each individually designed, hand-cut, and handcrafted according to his IDT ("I Don't Tell") method. Each is an original work of art, although some are limited editions of just two to seven.

The gallery carries the work of several artists, including Jim Yellowhawk, Ryan Burr, Frank Howell, Peggy Detmer, Kirby Sattler, Doug Fast Horse, and James Oberle. You'll find pencil and pen-and-ink drawings, original lithographs, serigraphs, and much more. But, as Berger puts it, "You never know what I'm coming up with here," and there's always something new and interesting to see.

Berger's unique frames sometimes have a symbolic message or tell a story related to the picture inside. He knows most of the artists and creates his frames as an extension of the spirit of their work. Some frames are inlaid with colorful beads or other decorative or symbolic items. Each takes from two days to more than a week to complete. Berger laughingly told us his favorite tool for detailed

Insiders' Tip

The Black Hills Symphony League supports not only the symphony orchestra, but also the Black Hills Chamber Music Society, the Music in the Schools program, and the Young Artists' competition. It also awards music lesson scholarships to children. This worthy organization sponsors a Homes for the Holidays fund-raiser tour each year in early November; tickets can be purchased at the Dahl Fine Arts Center, (605) 394-4101.

leatherwork is his pocket knife's bottle opener, a humble apparatus that helps create his exquisitely beautiful art.

Southern Hills

Cabin Fever
444 Mt. Rushmore Rd., Custer
(605) 673-2525
This downtown Custer gallery is a pleasant space that displays art all the way up to the high ceiling. You'll see Brenda Bruckner's pencil drawings of horses and the ranching life, silver handcrafted jewelry, photographs and pottery, as well as gifts and prints. Take note of the antler carvings by Custer resident Tony Ramer, a nationally known artist whose work graces the White House. Also represented are works by Tim Cox and Merle Locke, both local artists. Cabin Fever carries tack, blouses, and leather and suede jackets among other offerings.

Libraries

Many libraries offer special programs and events, including book signings, readings, and discussions. The staff members can tell you what's scheduled when you call. Most carry the works of local writers (at the Rapid City Public Library, for example, these books are labeled "South Dakota Author" on the spine).

Libraries are great places to learn more about the Black Hills. The Rapid City Public Library has a large South Dakota Collection (about 2,000 books about the state, not necessarily by local authors). Although some of these books can be read only at the library (where they're kept under lock and key), many of the titles are also in the circulating collection. Be sure to ask, since these books are a rich source of information.

Northern Hills

Belle Fourche Public Library
905 Fifth St., Belle Fourche
605) 892-4407

Insiders' Tip

Even the Rapid City Regional Airport has art exhibits. The works of selected artists are displayed in glass cases in the terminal; artists are selected by the Dahl Fine Arts Center staff. The airport also has a Termesphere, a six-point perspective acrylic sphere created by artist Dick Termes of Spearfish.

Deadwood Public Library
435 Williams St., Deadwood
(605) 578-2821

Grace Balloch Memorial Library
625 Fifth St., Spearfish
(605) 642-1330

Phoebe Apperson Hearst Free Library
315 W. Main St., Lead
(605) 584-2013

Sturgis Public Library
1040 Second St., Sturgis
(605) 347-2624

Central Hills

Hill City Public Library
324 Main St., Hill City
(605) 574-4529

Rapid City Public Library
610 Quincy St., Rapid City
(605) 394-4171

Southern Hills

Custer County Library
447 Crook St., Custer
(605) 673-8178

Edgemont City Library
412 Second St., Edgemont
(605) 662–7712

Hot Springs Public Library
1543 Baltimore St., Hot Springs
(605) 745–3151

Literary Arts

If you're a fan of reading, you'll be happy to know that a fair number of book signings take place here. In Rapid City, they often are held at Prairie Edge Trading Company and Galleries and Prince & Pauper Village (both discussed in our Shopping chapter). In smaller towns, you might find signings at bookstores (most of which have sections dedicated to local authors), art galleries, libraries, or community centers. Check the local newspapers for announcements; book signings are great opportunities to meet local authors.

Insiders' Tip

The Northern Plains Watercolor Society sponsors an annual juried exhibition of watercolors each fall. The show includes the work of its members and is open to watercolorists from other states. The exhibition is usually held in November at Prarie Edge Art Gallery, Sixth and Main Streets, Rapid City. For information go to www.prarieedge.com.

Black Hills Writers Group
(605) 341–3224

Founded in 1956 by local author Laura Bower Van Nuys, this group meets at the Rapid City Public Library, 610 Quincy Street, on the fourth Tuesday of each month (except December). Members plan events, read their work, critique, and conduct impromptu writing assignments. The group sponsors the fine Black Hills Writers Conference in the fall of odd-numbered years, and the Laura Bower Van Nuys Writing Contest in even-numbered years.

The contest, which receives entries from writers all over the United States and from other countries, is named for the author of *The Family Band*, a history of Van Nuys's family that was made into the Disney movie *The One and Only Genuine, Original Family Band*. For information on the contest, which accepts fiction and nonfiction entries, has an April 15 deadline, and is judged by professional writers, call (605) 341–3224 to request guidelines.

Music

Central Hills

Black Hills Chamber Music Society
(605) 718–5666

The society celebrates its 35th year in 2002. Its series runs from October to April and most performances are held at the First Congregational Church, 1200 Clark Street. The Dakota String Quartet has performed, as well as the Black Hills Chamber Orchestra, Nebraska Brass, the Rawlins Piano Trio, and the Dakota Woodwind Quintet. The Chamber Music Society also has outreach programs for children and seniors, including performances in schools, local nursing homes, and rehabilitation centers.

Ticket prices range from $30.00 to $35.00 for season tickets and $5.00 to $10.00 for individual performances.

Black Hills Symphony Orchestra
(605) 348–HORN (season tickets)
(605) 394–4111 (individual performances)

Rapid City may be a small city, but it has a symphony with big-city quality that's 60-plus years old. Conductor Jack Knowles celebrates his 32nd season in 2002. Six concerts are scheduled each season, and all take place at the Rushmore Plaza Civic Center. Concerts have included *Halloween II-The Concert, New Year's Eve with the Symphony, A Night in Old Spain, Passport to Scandinavia,* and *Symphonasaurus,* a concert especially for children.

Ticket prices for adults range from $5.00 to $20.00 for individual performances; season tickets are available.

Cathedral Concerts
520 Cathedral Dr., Rapid City
(605) 342-0507

The Cathedral of Our Lady of Perpetual Help boasts the largest pipe organ in a five-state region, a 62-rank Casavant. The American Guild of Organists held its 100th anniversary concert here and presents an annual concert, too.

The Fifth and Broadway Dessert Theater, featuring Broadway tunes, is presented each June in the cathedral. Each year the South Dakota School of Mines and Technology choir presents two free concerts in early December.

Dakota Choral Union
(605) 394-4111 (tickets)

The Dakota Choral Union is composed of more than 100 vocalists from the South Dakota School of Mines and Technology and the Black Hills community. It includes several choral ensembles and is the official chorus provider to the Black Hills Symphony Orchestra. Recent concerts included *Kantorei Khristmas, Venetian Splendor,* and *In Praise of Music.* Performances are held at varying locations around the Black Hills, including the Rushmore Plaza Civic Center.

Ticket prices for adults are $12 for individual concerts and $40 for season tickets. Five concerts are presented each season.

Music in the Park
(605) 348-6295
www.panachepages.com

Backroom Productions presents six to seven free Music in the Park concerts each summer, on Thursday evenings at the Memorial Park band shell. There's always a great variety of music scheduled: jazz, country, rock, big band, bluegrass, a cappella vocals, Irish folk, classical, and Native American music and dance. Call the Rushmore Plaza Civic Center at (605) 394-4115 for more information.

Rapid City Children's Chorus
(605) 394-2564, (605) 341-5304

Children in grades three through nine audition to join the Children's Chorus, which has been performing since 1986. Most concerts feature classical choral music, but some include ethnic, jazz, and gospel, too. The chorus presents winter and spring concerts at Dakota Middle School, 615 Columbus Street, and travels around the country to perform as well. Tickets are $5.00 for adults and $12.00 for families.

Rapid City Concert Association Series
713 Seventh St., Rapid City
(605) 394-4101

The volunteer Rapid City Concert Association plans and schedules five concerts each year, presenting national touring artists who perform at the Rushmore Plaza Civic Center. In recent years Ray Charles, Si Zentner and His Orchestra, the Boston Brass, and Hotlanta have per-

Rapid City student artists painted this striking mural in tribute to Native American culture and to beautify this North Rapid City neighborhood. PHOTO: KIMBERLY METZ

formed. The series runs from October through April. Ticket prices range from $25 to $110. Call for more information.

Southern Hills

Hot Springs Area
Concert Association
801 S. Sixth St., Net Springs
(605) 745–4140

Three concerts are presented each season, and admission is by membership only (that is, only season tickets are sold). Ticket prices range from $10 to $60. Tickets include reciprocity to concerts in Newcastle, Wyoming, and Scottsbluff, Nebraska, and an additional charge will admit you to Belle Fourche and Rapid City concerts, too.

Recent performers have been The Malins (vocals), Hotlanta (Dixieland), and Double Stop (stringed instruments and vocals). Instrumental groups have been featured too, as well as dancing, a cappella vocals, and Latin American music.

Concerts in the Park Series
(605) 745–6473

Southern Hills Arts and Humanities sponsors this annual series of 10 concerts, which runs from mid-June through mid-August. The concerts take place in Hot Springs, in Centennial Park on North Garden Street and begin at 7:00 P.M. on Tuesday evenings. Performers have included The Grain Exchange (contemporary folk music), Hill City Slickers (bluegrass and country swing), Syd Phelps and the River Street Five (Dixieland), and Straight No-Chaser (jazz and swing). All concerts are free, but donations are appreciated.

Public Art

You may want to make some side trips to see our public art while you're visiting Black Hills towns. In addition, two fine works of art grace the lobby of the Radisson Hotel at 445 Mount Rushmore Road, Rapid City. Both are mosaics; one a landscape of the Black Hills and the other a depiction of Mount Rushmore. These are not public art (they're owned by the hotel) but are worth a visit because of their outstanding quality.

GREAT FACES

Ambrose Bierce

Ambrose Bierce was never happy. And after trying his hand at gold mining in the Black Hills, he was more miserable than ever.

Born in 1842 into a large, pious family, Bierce was a gloomy, withdrawn child. As a young man he distinguished himself during the Civil War but questioned the Union cause for which he fought. Later he became a renowned journalist but was contemptuous of the press. Even his wife, Mollie, and their three children didn't please him.

Settling in San Francisco after the war, "Bitter Bierce" became famous for his scathing "Town Crier" and "Prattle" newspaper columns. But at age 38, perhaps suffering from a midlife crisis (or trying to run away from himself), and hoping to quit journalism for good, Bierce resigned from his job and left home to become general agent for the Black Hills Placer Mining Company in Rockerville, in Dakota Territory. One of his assignments was to complete a 17-mile wooden flume to carry water from Spring Creek to Rockerville. That was in 1880, but today you can hike along the Flume Trail and see remnants of his work (please see our Recreation chapter for more information). To protect the company's assets, Bierce hired a famous gunslinger named Boone May, and listed him on the payroll as "Boone May, Murderer."

The mine proved unsuccessful though, and Bierce returned to San Francisco within a few months, broke, depressed, and jobless. He soon was offered editorship of the *Wasp*, a satirical journal, and revived his "Prattle" column. Readers noticed he was even more bitter than ever, hurling savage verbal attacks at seemingly every person and institution in sight. He later became chief editorial columnist for the *San Francisco Examiner* under William Randolph Hearst, and then Washington correspondent for Hearst newspapers. He wrote for *Cosmopolitan* and put together a collection of his works.

Bierce never "mined" his experiences in the Black Hills for his writing, though, and biographers speculate that he simply couldn't bear to admit failure, even though it wasn't his fault. His most enduring work is a short story, *An Occurrence at Owl Creek Bridge,* that influenced many later writers, including Stephen Crane and Ernest Hemingway.

In 1913, when he was 71 years old, Ambrose Bierce disappeared. Many people think he went to Mexico and died in Pancho Villa's revolution. But some think he took his own life in the Grand Canyon. In any case, he got his last, bitter wish—that no one would ever find his bones.

Northern Hills

Bust of Wild Bill Hickok, Korczak Ziolkowski, Custer. Granite sculpture. Sherman Street Park, Deadwood

Generation, Jim Maher, Belle Fourche. Bronze sculpture. D.C. Booth Historic Fish Hatchery, 423 Hatchery Circle, Spearfish

Gold, Tony Chytka, Spearfish. Entrance to Days of '76 rodeo grounds, Crescent Dr., Deadwood

Kinship, Dale Lamphere, Sturgis. Bronze sculpture. Community Sculpture Garden, 1401 Lazelle St., Sturgis

Lasting Legacy, Tony Chytka, Spearfish. Bronze sculpture. Centennial Park, U.S. 85 and National St., Belle Fourche

Peace Memorial, Dale Lamphere, Sturgis. Bronze and granite sculpture. Visitor Center, 415 Fifth Ave., Belle Fourche

Spherefish, Dick Termes, Spearfish. Termesphere. Spearfish City Hall, 625 Fifth St., Spearfish

Wild Bill Hickok, James Borglum and Monique Ziolkowski, Custer. Bronze sculpture. Four Aces Casino, 531 Main St., Deadwood

Central Hills

Bluestem Woman, Dale Lamphere, Sturgis. Metal and found objects sculpture. Rapid City Public Library, 610 Quincy St., Rapid City

Cyclorama, Bernard Preston Thomas, Florida. Oil on canvas. Dahl Fine Arts Center, 713 Seventh St., Rapid City

Endless Horizon, Dick Termes, Spearfish. Termesphere. Rushmore Plaza Civic Center, 444 Mt. Rushmore Rd., Rapid City

He Is, They Are, Glenna Goodacre, New Mexico. Bronze sculpture. Prairie Edge Trading Company and Galleries, 606 Main St., Rapid City

Iron Eagle, Vic Runnels, Aberdeen. Metal and wood sculpture. Central High School, 433 Mt. Rushmore Rd., Rapid City

Legacy, Dale Lamphere, Sturgis. Bronze/concrete sculpture. Memorial Park, Omaha and Sixth Sts., Rapid City

Mitakuye Oyasin (All My Relatives), Richard UnderBaggage, Rapid City, and Dale Lamphere, Sturgis. Bronze sculpture. Southwest corner of Sixth and Main St., Rapid City

Monolith, Fiorenzo Berardozzi, Rapid City. Western Dakota Technical Institute, 800 Mickelson Dr., Rapid City

Pinocchio, John Eng, Hill City. Wood sculpture. Rapid City Public Library, 610 Quincy St., Rapid City

Rapid Trout, Martin Wanserski, Vermillion. Concrete sculpture. Founders Park, Omaha St. near 12th St., Rapid City

St. Thomas More Mural, Fr. Peter Wilke and Julia Poage, Rapid City. Porcelain tile mural. St. Thomas More High School, 300 Fairmont Blvd., Rapid City

Martin Wanserski's concrete Rapid Trout *closes in on the bait in Founders Park, Rapid City.*
PHOTO: KIMBERLY METZ

Spirit of Healing, Dale Lamphere, Sturgis. Bronze sculpture. Rapid City Regional Hospital, 353 Fairmont Blvd., Rapid City

The Ingalls Family, Harvey Hultquist, Minneapolis. Wood carving. Rapid City Public Library, 610 Quincy St., Rapid City

Toth, Andrew Leicester, Minneapolis. Timber, concrete, and steel sculpture on a hill above South Dakota School of Mines and Technology, 501 E. St. Joseph St., Rapid City

Untitled, student artists under the direction of artist Vic Runnels. Painted mural. At the railroad overpass, East Blvd. near New York Street, Rapid City

Vigilance, Peggy Detmer, Rapid City. Bronze sculpture. Memorial Park, Rapid City

Theater

Northern Hills

The Black Hills Passion Play
1–90, exit 12, Spearfish
(605) 642–2646
(800) 457–0160 (reservations)
Please read about the 63-year-old Passion Play in our Attractions chapter. It is performed during June, July, and August in a 6,000-seat outdoor amphitheater. Recent ticket prices ranged from $12 to $18.

Historic Matthews Opera House
614 Main St., Spearfish
(605) 642–7973
A working performing arts center, the renovated opera house (where operas are not performed) was built in that wonderful turn-of-the-century Western style that walks the line between ornate and practical. Summer community theater productions, events, and exhibits are held here; it is also the home of the Spearfish Center for the Arts and Humanities.

Community theater performances run during March, May, August, October, and December for one weekend each month. Past plays have included *Steel Magnolias, The Vaudevillians,* and *The Boys Next Door.*

Ticket prices are $10.00 for adults and $5.00 for children. You can sometimes purchase tickets at the door, but it's best to call ahead and reserve them.

From June through September, Monday through Saturday, you can tour the opera house. When plays are scheduled, you can visit until the plays begin at 7:30 P.M. Call ahead to ask about visiting during the remainder of the year. Staff members are available to answer questions during your visit, and there is no admission charge.

Central Hills

Black Hills Community Theatre
713 Seventh St., Rapid City
(605) 394–1787, (605) 394–1786 (box office)
This community theater was established in 1968. Its five-performance series runs from September to May; each play runs two to three weeks, with both matinee and evening presentations. Professionally staged performances are presented by dedicated local actors, and most take place in the Dahl Fine Arts Center's theater, but larger productions and musicals may be held at the Rushmore Plaza Civic Center. Past performances included *To Kill a Mockingbird, Moon Over Buffalo, Quitters, The Imaginary Invalid,* and a January dinner theater fund-raiser.

Season ticket prices range from $35 to $54. Tickets for single performances go on sale at the Dahl's box office a few days before each performance begins.

Black Hills Community Theatre presents plays for both children and adults and offers theater workshops and classes. A children's troupe gives four performances each year.

Southern Hills

Black Hills Playhouse
Custer State Park, Custer
(605) 394–7797, (605) 255–4141, seasonal (tickets)
(800) GOT–MINE (season tickets)
www.blackhillsplayhouse.com
The playhouse is inside Custer State Park, which provides a beautiful setting for this

Native American dance is performed at the Black Hills Pow Wow. PHOTO: STEVEN A. PAGE

professional theater. Summer season begins in June and continues through August. Each play runs two to three weeks and has matinee and evening performances. Past performances have included *I Hate Hamlet, Brigadoon, Crimes of the Heart, Steel Magnolias,* and *Cat on a Hot Tin Roof.*

Ticket prices range from $13 to $20. Discounts are available for groups of 20 or more.

You must purchase a park entrance license, since you'll be accessing the park to reach the playhouse (for license fees, see our Custer State Park listing in the Parks and Grasslands chapter). Take advantage of the opportunity: Come early, and visit the park before having dinner and enjoying the play.

When you make your ticket reservations (at least 48 hours in advance), you can request a dinner reservation at one of the park's resort restaurants (see our Restaurants chapter). Then just pick up your theater tickets when you arrive for dinner.

Venues

You'll find several venues mentioned in this chapter: the Dahl Fine Arts Center's intimate theater, the Historic Matthews Opera House's restored stage, the band shell at Rapid City's Memorial Park, and various churches, schools, and community centers where the acoustics and size lend themselves to performances. But the largest and most versatile venue in the Black Hills is the Rushmore Plaza Civic Center, listed below.

Central Hills

Rushmore Plaza Civic Center
444 Mt. Rushmore Rd., Rapid City
(605) 394-4115

The civic center is the major venue in the Black Hills and accommodates an amazing variety of events. It has hosted ice shows, The Black Hills Stock Show and Rodeo on the last weekend in January, monster truck rallies, ballet and Broadway performances, theater troupes, concerts, powwows, art and antique shows, and conventions. Its grand-opening con-

Insiders' Tip

Black Hills Community Theatre is justifiably proud of Friends of the Theatre, its volunteer action group that claims some 350 local volunteers. These enthusiastic people help with everything from fund-raising and ticket sales to ushering and painting sets. The Friends can be reached through the Theatre's office at (605) 394-1787.

cert in 1976 was one of Elvis's final performances. The staff has become quite adept at hauling in and spreading thousands of tons of dirt for rodeos and such, then hauling it all back out (with backhoes and bulldozers) and cleaning up again.

The center boasts 150,000 square feet of exhibit space, a 10,000-seat arena, the 1,779-seat Fine Arts Theater, two large halls (La Croix and Rushmore), 27 meeting rooms, and 3,000 free parking spaces. It's set on nine acres adjacent to Rapid City's Memorial Park and is less than 100 steps away from the Rushmore Plaza Holiday Inn.

Among the many events here is the Broadway Play series, which recently included touring productions of *Damn Yankees, Bye Bye Birdie, Les Miserables,* and *West Side Story.* Ticket prices for those performances range from $25 to $60; season tickets are available.

Les Miz is the largest production ever staged in the theater and required that the backstage area be gutted and rebuilt. Although Rapid City and its surrounding area is the smallest market the touring company ever played, the civic center's theater was the only one in a five-state area large enough to accommodate it.

Parks and Grasslands

Northern Hills
Central Hills
Southern Hills

South Dakota has a wealth of parks, grasslands, recreation areas, and reservoirs, each a recreational and environmental treasure.

The granddaddy of them all is the 1.2-million-acre Black Hills National Forest, which encompasses most of the towns mentioned in this book. Its eastern border is west of Rapid City, and it runs, in places, past the Wyoming state line. Angostura Reservoir ends its southern border, and the northern border is just outside Spearfish.

Within the Black Hills region, you'll find Angostura Recreation Area near Hot Springs, Pactola Dam and Reservoir near Johnson Siding and Silver City, and Jewel Cave National Monument near Custer. Every park has an amazing array of recreational opportunities: horseback riding, snowmobiling, hiking, mountain biking, fishing, swimming, picnicking, boating, camping, and more. For information about these activities, see our Recreation and Campgrounds and RV Sites chapters.

In this chapter we'll tell you all about four wonderful places: Custer State Park, Wind Cave National Park, Bear Butte State Park and Buffalo Gap National Grassland. The recreation, camping, and accommodations available at each are listed in those specific chapters. Here we'll tell you about the history, the beauty, the animals . . . the reasons you'll want to experience these parks and grasslands, and the reasons you'll remember them long after you leave. We'll also tell you the fees and hours you can enjoy them.

Northern Hills

Bear Butte State Park
Off Hwy. 79, north of Sturgis
(605) 347-5240

As you drive into the area around Sturgis, you'll see Bear Butte rising blue-gray in the distance. It's impressive and intriguing from afar, but not until you're up close do you recognize its awesome proportions and mystical magic. Looking like a huge sleeping bear, it stands all alone on the flat surrounding plains aloof and majestic, yet somehow gentle and comforting, too.

This is *Mato Paha*, Lakota for "bear mountain." The Cheyenne call it *Noavosse* ("good mountain"). For centuries it has been a place of worship, a powerful site from which to contact the holy, and a Native American landmark. Cheyenne legend tells

that the prophet Sweet Medicine received four sacred arrows here and four commandments for his people to live by.

It appears that Bear Butte has always been sacred. Artifacts 10,000 years old and an ancient ceremonial site have been unearthed here. Today Native Americans still climb the mountain to pray and fast, leaving medicine bundles, tobacco offerings, and prayer ribbons as the physical manifestations of their prayers. Please respect this holy site and don't disturb the privacy of worshipers or the offerings, including rocks placed in the forks of branches, which are the traditional markers of someone's visit.

The mountain will offer you some incredible views, both out over the plains and toward the Black Hills. Take all the scenic photographs you like, but do not photograph the ceremonial items, offer-

GREAT FACES

Peter Norbeck

The name of Peter Norbeck is one you encounter often as you travel around the Black Hills and Badlands. That's because Norbeck—art lover, conservationist, South Dakota governor, and U.S. senator—did so much for the area. Therefore it seems only fitting that an overlook, a wildlife preserve, a visitor center, and a scenic byway, all in or close to Custer State Park, as well as a pass through Badlands National Park are among the places named in his honor.

Norbeck loved the outdoors and played a major role in the establishment of both parks. His efforts to set aside a game preserve and map out a scenic route through rugged, virgin Black Hills terrain also bore fruit. And he answered the call when South Dakota's state historian, Doane Robinson, sought his help in promoting and funding the carving of Mount Rushmore National Memorial.

His influence extended well beyond the borders of his home state, however, when he left his mark on the creation of Wyoming's Grand Teton National Park and passage of the federal Migratory Bird Conservation Act.

Born to Norwegian immigrant parents on a Clay County homestead in southeastern South Dakota on August 27, 1870, Norbeck learned early the value of hard work. Unwilling to become a farmer himself, however, he accumulated a modest fortune with a well-drilling business and Wyoming oil interests. His prominence in the private domain helped propel him to positions of leadership in public life.

Nicknamed "the benevolent buffalo," the 225-pound Norbeck's honesty and can-do enthusiasm inspired confidence and loyalty in his supporters. Yet he had a stormy relationship with Mount Rushmore sculptor Gutzon Borglum, whom Norbeck deemed a poor businessman.

The two were still at odds when Norbeck, suffering from cancer, died at his home in Redfield on December 20, 1936. Fifteen years later, a decade after Borglum's own passing, they made a sort of posthumous peace when the sculptor's bronze bust of his most ardent backer, Norbeck, was placed in the state capitol building in Pierre.

ings, or worshippers. The signs at the trailhead ask that you walk quietly and reverently and speak in low tones. Use the same respect you would feel when touring a cathedral where the worship service is in progress, for that is what Bear Butte is.

The first white men to see the mountain, and the Black Hills, were the Verendrye brothers, François and Louis-Joseph, French explorers who climbed Bear Butte in 1743. They called it *Montagne des Gens des Cheveaux*, the "Mountain of the Horse People," because the inhabitants there (unlike some tribes of that era) had horses.

In 1855 Dr. Ferdinand Hayden, a geologist, climbed Bear Butte and discovered, 600 feet up, a previously unknown, delicate little flower, *Anemone patens*, the

pasqueflower, a lavender beauty that blooms in the very early spring. You may find it sprouting up through melting snow. It later was designated South Dakota's state flower. For more on this flower, see our Natural World chapter.

The Teton Sioux held a great council at Bear Butte in the summer of 1857. Men from Custer's 1874 expedition climbed it while the troops camped nearby, resting for the last leg of their trip back to Fort Lincoln. In 1880 Rev. George Pelton traveled through the area on his way to Deadwood and reported in his journal that it took "nearly three hours" to get around the mountain with horse and wagon.

A pioneer's landmark because it could be seen at such great distances, Bear Butte eventually overlooked three gold-rush roads, a stage line, and Fort Meade, the military post of the Seventh Cavalry.

Bear Butte State Park was created in 1961, and the mountain was named a Registered Natural Landmark in 1965. It was entered into the National Register of Historic Places in 1973, under the National Preservation Act, because of its spiritual significance to Native Americans and its importance as a landmark to early pioneers.

Geologically speaking, the mountain (which is not really a butte) is a laccolith, a cone-shaped pocket of molten lava that expanded and bulged upward through the overlying surface rock, which slowly eroded away. Basically, it's a volcano that didn't erupt. From a distance Bear Butte looks almost touchable and soft. Rising more than 4,400 feet above sea level, more than 1,200 feet above the surrounding plains, it is mostly bare rock, but some trees and vegetation are scattered on its sides.

History books cite eyewitness accounts of fires on Bear Butte in the 1800s and claim that it was once more heavily forested than in recent decades. Until recently ponderosa pine was the most predominant species at the higher elevations, and elm, cottonwood, hawthorn, juniper, chokecherry, and native grasses dominated the middle and lower regions.

In August 1996 an out-of-control ceremonial fire burned much of Bear Butte in a spectacular blaze that lasted two days. Between 80 and 90 percent of the ponderosa pines died, and it will be years before they reestablish themselves. Ceremonial fires are permitted for Native American ceremonies only (inquire at the visitor center). Campfires are not allowed.

Today Bear Butte's environment is making a comeback. For nearly a year the National Hiking Trail that climbs the summit was closed for repairs and to protect the mountain from erosion caused by the lack of vegetation and tree canopy. In 1997 the summit trail reopened with new wooden steps and erosion edging, the lumber for which was airlifted to the top by National Guard helicopters. The mile-long Ceremonial Trail reopened in 1998. The trails are rocky and switchback often,

Insiders' Tip

If you'd like to support educational programs and research in Black Hills forests and parks, you can join the Black Hills Parks and Forests Association, which publishes and sells books and educational materials and funds research and intern programs. Membership, at a cost of $5.00 to $25.00, includes a semiannual newsletter and a 15 percent discount on books, maps, and posters at their sales outlets (including Custer State Park, Wind Cave, and Jewel Cave) and most National Park bookstores. Call (605) 745-7020 for information.

but are only moderately difficult The north end of the Centennial Trail starts at the summit of Bear Butte. Read more about the Centennial Trail in our Recreation chapter.

The state park is open year-round. At the visitor center (open 9:00 A.M. to 5:00 P.M., seven days a week, from May to early September only), you can learn about the geologic and cultural history of Bear Butte and the park. The center contains a museum and presents educational videos. The current entrance fee is $2.00 per person per day. There is no charge for children 11 and younger. A Custer State Park entrance license or annual state park pass will admit you without charge.

Bear Butte State Park is, like Buffalo Gap National Grassland, a low-key entertain-yourself park. Organized activities are few, but summer programs for groups can be arranged with the staff naturalist, who will give presentations on history and natural history and conduct hiking tours. Special programs need to be arranged in advance.

No concessions are available in the park, but the town of Sturgis is just 5 miles away.

You can also watch the park's buffalo herd, fish (by state permit—see our Recreation chapter), swim in the lake, camp in the campground (see our Campgrounds and RV Sites chapter), and hike. Try photographing the mountain at different times of day, when it changes color and texture in the light of sunrise and sunset, thunderstorm and snow.

You can sit at its base and stare at it, mesmerized by its powerful beauty. Or

Black Hills travelers encounter some rather unusual traffic signs in public parks.

you can climb it and look out over the plains and hills, imagining Custer and his men marching by, or the Verendrye brothers climbing up beside you, or wise Sitting Bull waiting patiently for the mountain to speak.

But, always, Bear Butte is the main attraction at the park, a dynamic, living, natural monument. You'll feel that, too, when you visit. It has always been here and will always stand, long after those of us who climb it are gone.

Central Hills

Buffalo Gap National Grassland
South of Wall and South of Hot Springs
(605) 279–2125 Visitor Center via the Forest
Service

Don't be deceived. If you think you know about grass—that it's boring stuff—you'll miss out on a little-known secret of the plains: Grasslands are magical and mysterious, richly alive, a precious natural resource, and an exercise in the appreciation of the subtle.

Modern life is often about speed and special effects, high color and haste. The grasslands, though indifferent to your presence, force you to slow down and look carefully. Their mysteries are not revealed to those in a hurry.

Be sure to stop at the National Grasslands Visitor Center on Main Street in Wall (there's no admission charge). Outside, there's a black-footed ferret in his pen. He's endangered, and a project is underway to reintroduce his species to Buffalo Gap and Badlands National Park (see the Close-up in our Natural World chapter). On the day we visited, the resident ferret was sleeping and dreaming, thrashing his legs and squinting just as a dog or cat does. (Perhaps he was dreaming of chasing prairie dogs, his favorite meal, all over the plains.) The ferret and the fascinating exhibits and videos inside the center will help prepare you for your grasslands experience.

When the Great Plains, in the heart of the United States, were first explored in the 1800s, the early explorers called it "The Great American Desert." They considered it a wasteland. But as the United States grew and civilization in the East pushed westward, there was a clamor for more room. All that vast emptiness in the middle of the country was available, so the government passed the Homestead Act of 1862. The cry of "Free Land!" soon went up and adventurous folks were on the move, westward to the Great Plains.

The migration continued until the early 1920s. Until then, prairie farmers and ranchers had been relatively successful. There was enough rain, and the market for wheat and cattle was strong. Unfortunately, no one at that time understood that the Great Plains are much more fragile than they appear. By the mid-1920s the plains had been overgrazed and over-cultivated and were ripe for the disaster that soon struck. The combination of the Depression, drought, and high winds of the 1930s added to the land's burden. It is estimated that, during those Dust Bowl years, 2.5 million homesteaders gave up in despair and abandoned their ranches and farms.

In 1934 the federal government's Resettlement Administration began to purchase both never-owned and abandoned acreage, eventually amassing more than 10 million acres and relocating thousands of failed homesteaders. In 1937 the Soil Conservation Service began to "rehabilitate" the wind-eroded land. Using Civilian Conservation Corps and Works Progress Administration labor, shelter belts and stock ponds were created and new grass was seeded.

In 1954 the management of the grasslands was transferred to the Forest Service, and in 1960 nearly four million acres were designated National Grasslands. The 20 National Grasslands throughout the United States serve as multiple-use public land. Ranchers graze their livestock there, by permit, and have built stock tanks on the land at their own expense; the stock tanks water both livestock and wildlife. Hunting and fishing are also allowed (state laws apply).

Buffalo Gap National Grassland covers more than 591,000 acres of prairie and badlands, and there is no admission charge to enjoy it. On a detailed map (which you're encouraged to pick up at the National Grasslands Visitor Center), you'll see it is not a "solid" mass of land; its blocks of acreage are mixed with private and state-owned property. The eastern half of the grassland, for example, is near Badlands National Park, and the western half is south of the Black Hills. Buffalo Gap is one of three South Dakota National Grasslands; the others are Fort Pierre and Grand River, which you can read about in our Daytrips and Weekend Getaways chapter.

It's important to get information and a map at the visitor center before entering the grassland. Camping here is primitive, with no designated campgrounds or concessions. There are no established hiking

Insiders' Tip

Never feed a wild animal, even those that seem tame, like the occasional pretty deer that comes right up to your car. Human food is simply not good for animals. Sometimes park officials are forced to kill wild animals that have sickened after eating human food. Wild animals that are hand-fed also lose their natural fear and are then at greater risk of being struck by a vehicle or abused by a less-than-kindhearted person. Feeding wild animals can also be dangerous to people. The animal may suddenly bite, kick, scratch, or attack.

Insiders' Tip

Some state parks use prescribed burns to mimic the work of wild prairie fires: the destruction of vegetation and subsequent rejuvenation of the land. These burns help restore the natural balance between grasslands and pine forests. While traveling through a park, you may come across fire trucks and personnel monitoring the blazes, smoke, and wind direction. No need to worry, and it's fine to watch and learn from what you see. You might even get to ask questions of the people stationed near the road to direct traffic. If there's danger the road will be closed, but do drive slowly and use caution.

trails and only one bike trail, but you can trek cross-country or follow a road or animal path.

Grassland regulations are quite different from those for a national forest: You can pick wildflowers and hunt for rocks, and it's illegal to remove or disturb only the vertebrate fossils. You can dig for agate southwest of Kadoka and east of the old town of Conata, too; the exact sites are on the map.

If you drive in (four-wheel drive or high-clearance vehicles are recommended), stay on the roads and close all gates behind you (watch for splinters; some of the gates are primitive). Don't disturb the cattle, who will think you've brought their dinner but probably won't bother you. Don't cross private land without prior permission, and do be aware that it's hard to identify that land without a map.

Since grasslands only offer basic, entertain-yourself recreation, you'll need to pack everything in with you and pack it back out. Take plenty of water, and watch your campfire; this is semiarid, windy country. The folks at the visitor center ask that you use common sense about fires, and they'll tell you if fire danger is high while you are there.

The grasslands are home to many wildlife species. You might see pronghorn antelope, deer, meadowlarks, sharp-tailed grouse, hawks and eagles, badgers and weasels, fox, and prairie dogs. Watch out for prairie rattlers, too. For advice on handling encounters, see our Natural World chapter.

Remember that you're miles from anywhere and possibly from anybody. If your vehicle becomes stuck in wet clay after a rain or you get into trouble, help is a long way off. Use common sense and lots of caution.

The best approach to the grasslands is to drive into one of the vast Buffalo Gap areas and park your car. Get out and look around. This is your exercise in subtlety. Take close looks at everything. This country will not shout at you or perform for your benefit; it's up to you to pay attention. If you're used to smaller, closer landscapes, all that treeless vastness may unnerve you at first. South Dakota novelist Dan O'Brien, in his book *In the Center of the Nation,* wrote, "When you feel that everybody is watching you but no one cares, you're on the prairie."

You're not likely to see other people or vehicles, an exhilarating experience in itself. The wind may be ferocious, the sky an extraordinarily blue bowl above you, but the silence is the best of all. Listen— you won't hear a freeway, siren, or radio, only the sound the wind makes as it rushes past. The grass ripples like the ocean, prairie surf without roar or spray but comparable in majesty and beauty.

And if, in the rush of the wind, you think for a moment that you hear voices, it's only that awesome wind singing through a barbed wire fence...or maybe it's the ghosts of the old homesteaders, talking of the prairie that conquered them.

Don't underestimate the grasslands the way those early settlers did. This is not empty land. You just have to appreciate the subtlety. Watch closely, walk quietly, and listen carefully in order to see its incredible beauty.

Southern Hills

Custer State Park
Hwy. 87 S. or N., Hwy. 36 W., or
U.S. 16-16A E.
(605) 255-4464 (Peter Norbeck Visitor Center)
(605) 255-4515 (general information)
(800) 658-3530

In the Black Hills the words Custer State Park are often said in an awe-tinged voice, accompanied by a faraway look in the eye. The co-authors of this book even had a bit of a good-natured spat over who would get to write about it. It's that kind of place, a destination in itself. You could spend your entire vacation wandering over its 73,000 acres and never see or do the same thing twice. You can access the park from the north or south via Highway 87, from Hermosa by taking Highway 36 West, or from Custer by driving east on U.S. 16-16A.

The landscape will strike you first. It's a beautiful mixture of dark-green pine-covered hills, light-filtered, woods and rolling, grassy prairie. In the distance, hills appear to blend together, some capped by a lonely tree or two and others by a blanket of dark pine. The roads twist and turn, down through sun-dappled forests, then up again to the top of grassy foothills where you'll need to stop and catch your breath at the view before you.

Custer State Park was the idea of Peter Norbeck, a popular U.S. senator and the governor of South Dakota from 1916 to

This bison bull is part of the herd that is the main attraction at Custer State Park. PHOTO: DICK KETTLEWELL

1920. Originally from eastern South Dakota, Norbeck visited the Black Hills in 1905 and conceived the idea of establishing a wild game park in Custer County. Legislation was passed in 1913.

A practical man, Norbeck planned that timber production and resource management would help keep the park self-sustaining. Today camping fees, revenue from buffalo sales, entrance fees, concession revenue, and timber sales generate the multiple-use revenue that maintains the park and its facilities. Custer State Park is self-funded on a day-to-day operational basis, although major deferred maintenance projects are sometimes funded by tax dollars.

If you'd like to stay in the park, you have your choice of four resorts: the State Game Lodge (where President Calvin Coolidge stayed during his 1927 summer vacation), Legion Lake Resort, Blue Bell Lodge, and Sylvan Lake Resort. Both Legion Lake and Sylvan Lake resorts rent boats, kayaks, and hydrobikes, and you

"Buffalo Are Dangerous. Do Not Approach."

You'll see this and similar signs in Custer State Park and Wind Cave National Park. But the animals we call "buffalo" are not buffalo. That species includes African cape buffalo and water buffalo, which are not native to North America. The big, shaggy creatures of the West are North American bison, but most people just call them buffalo. Their Lakota name is *tatanka*.

These big creatures may look docile, but they are not livestock, nor are they domesticated. Bison are wild, can run at 35 MPH or faster and turn on a dime and are equipped with sharp horns, which they use to make their point when they feel threatened. People have been gored and attacked when they got too close or harassed bison. Cows with calves are especially prickly tempered.

Males (standing 5 to 6 feet high at the shoulder and weighing 2,000 pounds) keep to themselves or live in bachelor groups, while cows and calves stay in a herd. The rut (breeding season) begins in July and lasts through September. Bulls fight for females, and you may hear their roars or witness fierce battles. The bison are quite temperamental at this important season, so don't leave your car to get a better look. Don't approach the buffalo!

can reserve a mountain bike at Legion Lake. Each resort in the park has dining facilities and a store or gift shop where you can purchase food or a special souvenir. Please read about these resorts in our Accommodations chapter.

There are also seven modern campgrounds, two primitive and two group campsites, and the French Creek horse camp, which has corral space. You can read about these facilities in our Campgrounds and RV Sites chapter.

At Custer State Park you can cross-country ski, fish, hike, and climb the rocks. Scale Mount Coolidge to its 6,023-foot peak and get a look at the Badlands 90 miles away. Or travel back in history at the re-created Gordon Stockade, where, in the summer, you can watch daily activities as they were carried out in 1874 by gold-seeking pioneers. Both Mount Coolidge and the Gordon Stockade are on the west side of the park. We recommend you pick up maps and brochures at the visitor centers or the park entrances, which will make everything easy to find.

When you're ready for a break from your own activities, there's plenty of daily organized entertainment in the park (summers only, though). You can enjoy educational programs, slides and films, guided nature and historic walks, informal lectures, and fishing demonstrations. Some great programs for kids are offered, too, including a Junior Naturalist Program that teaches children about nature. Call the Norbeck Visitor Center for more information about these programs.

At Blue Bell stables you can sign up for trail rides or overnight pack trips (see our Recreation chapter) or go on the Old-Fashioned Hay Ride and Chuck Wagon Cookout (with cowboy fixins). If motorized transportation is more your speed, try the Buffalo Safari Jeep Tour and Chuck Wagon Cookout Adventure, which start at the State Game Lodge. These activities are daily summer happenings. Each attraction and resort area is well marked with highway signs and easy to find on park maps. Some activities require advance reservations; call the general information number to inquire about hours and fees.

The State Game Lodge has a rotating Artist-in-Residence program for wildlife and Western artists. In the gallery off the lobby, you can watch artists create,

A costumed host greets visitors at the Gordon Stockade in Custer State Park. The stockade is a replica of one built by illegal gold seekers in 1874. PHOTO: STEVEN A. PAGE

Coolidge General Store

The Coolidge General Store at Custer State Park has a most amazing ceiling. It was built to resemble the hull of a ship (turned upside down, above you), and it's beautifully constructed of native ponderosa pine. It is said to have 11,000 angle cuts (the cuts made in the boards to make them all fit perfectly together). Virtually every board meets the adjoining board or beam at an angle, in a stunning display of fancy craftsmanship. If you try to count all those angles, however, you'll get a crick in your neck for your efforts. The ceiling was crafted in 1927 by shipbuilders from Minnesota, who built the general store and other buildings to accommodate President Coolidge and his entourage during their summer vacation at Custer State Park.

browse through their displayed work, and take home an original work of art.

Theater lovers will want to take in a summer theater performance at the Black Hills Playhouse (more information on this treasure can be found in our Arts chapter). Poetry buffs will enjoy a pilgrimage to the Badger Hole, the carefully preserved cabin that was the home of Badger Clark, South Dakota's first poet laureate. It's open in the summer from 10:00 A.M. to 5:00 P.M. Monday through Friday and from 1:00 to 4:00 P.M. Saturday and Sunday. Admission is free with your park entrance license.

You can take a scenic drive along the Needles Highway (14 miles), which wanders through the Needles formations, granite spires that point to the sky. The Needles Highway is closed in the winter (approximately November 1 to April 1, depending on the weather).

Shipbuilders crafted the ceiling in Custer State Park's Coolidge General Store to look like an upside-down ship's hull. PHOTO: STEVEN A. PAGE

Insiders' Tip

Three scenic roads within Custer State Park have tunnels that are great fun to drive through unless you're steering a big RV, camping trailer, or bus! Few of the tunnels have a bypass, so your overlarge vehicle will have to turn around, which may not be an easy task. These roads, and their pull-offs, are narrow. Plan ahead! Iron Mountain Road (U.S. 16-A North) has three tunnels, each 12 feet 6 inches high and 13 feet 6 inches wide. The tunnel near Sylvan Lake on the Needles Highway (Highway 87/89) is 10 feet 8 inches high and 10 feet wide. There are two other tunnels on the Needles Highway (Highway 87 North). One is 11 feet 5 inches high and only 8 feet 7 inches wide and the other is 12 feet high and just 9 feet wide.

Or try Iron Mountain Road, which winds between the intersection of U.S. 16A and Highway 36 and Mount Rushmore. Along that route you'll see the marvelous pigtail bridges, artistically engineered creations designed by Governor Norbeck that ingeniously switchback up steep hills. The 70-mile Peter Norbeck Scenic Byway is another great drive; there's more information about it in our Attractions chapter.

A drive on the Wildlife Loop is a must. Its 18 miles go directly through the areas most often frequented by the park's wildlife. Try it in the early mornings and evenings when you're likely to spot white-tailed and mule deer, pronghorn antelope, mountain goats, bighorn sheep, wild turkeys, and prairie dogs. You're less likely to see the elk and coyotes, but you might get lucky. You'll also see many birds, including—quite possibly—hawks and golden eagles as well as small mammals such as squirrels, chipmunks, and skunks. You might even see a snake or two.

These roads were designed as scenic drives. Take your time, enjoy the scenery, and don't travel too fast. As Governor Norbeck himself said about the scenic byway, "You're not supposed to drive here at 60 miles an hour. To do the scenery half justice, people should drive 20 or under. To do it full justice, they should get out and walk."

While driving on the Wildlife Loop and Iron Mountain Road, you'll eventually be slowed by a wily burro (or two, or several). Do be careful and watch out for them. Attempted escape is not recommended, sometimes not even possible. These guys will simply stand in front of your vehicle and solicit handouts. They'll even lick your windshield in retaliation if you refuse. Or they'll poke their big heads in your window and stay there a while, keeping you effectively trapped...and possibly drooled upon. The burros are not indigenous; they are the descendants of those brought to the park in 1927 to take visitors to Harney Peak. The park management discourages feeding of the critters. Roll up your windows and enjoy watching them until they become bored and let you pass.

The 1,400- to 1,500-head buffalo herd is the park's main attraction. You may find the animals standing in the road, too, or

Bison roam freely in Custer State Park. PHOTO: COURTESY OF SOUTH DAKOTA TOURISM

Badger Clark, Poet Laureate

South Dakota once had a Poet Lariat.

In reality, Badger Clark was named the first Poet Laureate in 1939, but many people—including the poet—preferred the humorous cowboy title of honor, a tribute to his Western heritage, a larger-than-life designation for a colorful, larger-than-life man.

Charles Badger Clark was born in Iowa in 1883. His family moved to the Dakota territory when he was three months old. Just months shy of being born a Dakotan, he nevertheless is considered a native son and our own beloved poet.

When Clark was 15, his mother died. Several years later, his frontier-minister father married a strong woman with an interest in writing, a woman Clark loved and admired enough to call "Mother Anna." She would push him along the paths of poetry, prodding him to write, to submit his work to publications, and to publish books.

As a boy, Clark spent vacations at his uncle's Wyoming ranch and developed a taste for the wide-open, romantic West and cowboy life. In 1903, having given up on college and not knowing what he wanted for his future, he accompanied a party hoping to colonize Cuba. The expedition was a failure, but Clark stayed on, seeking adventure. After Cuba he came home, joined a Badlands surveying party, tried (and failed at) business, and got a taste of the writing life at the Lead newspaper.

Then near-tragedy struck: Clark was diagnosed with tuberculosis. On his doctor's advice, he moved to Arizona and found an ideal job on a Tombstone ranch, tending cattle and enjoying time to write and think. The dry air and rest sent his tuberculosis into remission. And when he mailed his stepmother a poem and she sent it on to a magazine that published it, a surprised new poet was born. Later he wrote one of his most famous poems, "The Cowboy's Prayer," in which he captured the souls of the men of the West:

Oh Lord, I've never lived where churches grow.
I love creation better as it stood
That day You finished it so long ago ...
I know that others find You in the light
That's sifted down through tinted window panes,
And yet I seem to feel You near tonight
In this dim, quiet starlight on the plains.

Clark, a bachelor, spent years in Hot Springs, then moved to a cabin he built in Custer State Park. Although a friendly, popular man, he craved the solitude and independence only a rustic cabin in the woods could provide. In the 30 years he lived there, he wrote and read,

Badger Clark, South Dakota's Poet Laureate. PHOTO: COURTESY OF BADGER CLARK MEMORIAL SOCIETY

answered fan mail, fed pancakes to the deer, received intrigued visitors, and gave poetry readings.

His two cabins still stand. The first he lived in while building the larger home, which is just as he left it in September 1957 when he went to his nephew's Rapid City home three weeks before dying of lung cancer. His fans still visit the Badger Hole, the property and the cabins. There you can delight in his fine library—the comfortable spot where he wrote late into the night—and his kitchen, still stocked with staples and utensils.

As any legendary character does, Clark always wore a trademark outfit: high riding boots and breeches, and an officer's coat and hat. His boots still stand in his bedroom, and his jackets hang on their pegs, seemingly awaiting their owner's return.

You can walk the Badger Clark Historic Trail, which winds up the hill behind the cabin and down again. Carry a brochure (available at the cabin) with some of his many poems, and stop at the markers and read a verse that commemorates that spot. When you reach this one, pay closer attention. It's called "I Must Come Back":

No, when the waning heartbeat fails
I ask no heaven but leave to wend,
Unseen but seeing, my old trails,
With deathless years to comprehend . . .

Badger Clark is buried in Hot Springs but his spirit lingers in Custer State Park. You can almost feel his presence there.

grazing alongside. In the spring the pretty little red calves are born. They are shy, and their mothers are protective, but (from your car) you can get some good pictures. In October the herd is rounded up, corralled, vaccinated, and sorted during the Buffalo Roundup (more about this in our Annual Events chapter). Of these, about 950 are returned to the park to winter (that's the amount the range can support), and the rest are auctioned in November. The sale provides income for the park and helps control the herd population.

Custer State Park is open year-round, and you must purchase an entrance license to enjoy it. An annual license is $20.00 and a second license for another of your vehicles is $10.00. You can also purchase a daily license, for $3.00 per person (six and older) or $5.00 per vehicle. An additional benefit is that your entrance license allows you to enter any state park or state recreation area during the term of the license.

Custer State Park has a way of enchanting visitors. The animals, the landscape,

and the history will all work their way into your heart. Don't be surprised if you keep thinking about the place, even after you've returned home. Perhaps it's nature's way of encouraging you to come back.

Wind Cave National Park
Hwy. 87 S. or U.S. 385 E. or N.
(605) 745–4600 (visitor center)

This park has as much to offer below ground as above. Adjacent to Custer State Park (directly south), it is a wildlife park as well, set on 28,000 acres. It has similar rolling prairie hills and pine-forest vistas, and it also boasts pronghorns, a buffalo herd, prairie dogs, deer, elk, coyotes, and more.

But this park has one feature Custer State Park lacks: Wind Cave, one of the most complex caves in the world. Its explored maze today totals about 101 miles, all within 1 square mile of land area. But there's more down there; scientists estimate that only 5 percent of the cave has been explored. An early adventurer,

Wind Cave Lint

No one would accuse Wind Cave of being dirty, but it does have a lint problem. Every visitor impacts the cave in the same way: by leaving behind microscopic skin cells, some hair, some clothing fibers... It all adds up to lint! And with 100,000 visitors each year, lint is a big problem.

How do you clean a cave? Wind Cave National Park organizes lint cleaning camps, where volunteers carefully brush and vacuum sections of the cave and its trails, then remove bag after bag of lint. Wind Cave National Park management strives for a balance between public enjoyment of the cave and protecting it from the impact of all those intrigued visitors.

Alvin McDonald, wrote in 1891, "Have given up the idea of finding the end of Wind Cave." Fortunately, explorers who came after Alvin didn't give up, and the cave is still being explored and mapped.

Wind Cave became the nation's seventh national park in 1903. It was also the first cave to become a national park and is the world's sixth longest cave. More than 100,000 people tour the cave each year.

Wind Cave's natural opening is a (barely) adult-sized hole in the ground. It was discovered in 1881 by two hunters, one of whom was Tom Bingham. When Tom bent down for a look, the wind escaping from the hole blew his hat off his head. Tom excitedly went to tell his friends and brought them back to the opening. When he leaned down to show them, the wind sucked his hat inside.

Today we know that Wind Cave is a breathing cave; that is, the wind escaping or entering the cave is controlled by the atmospheric pressure outside. When the pressure rises, air is drawn inside the cave; when the atmospheric pressure lowers, the air blows out. You can stand outside the natural entrance today and experience the same phenomenon.

Wind Cave has beautiful and delicate subterranean formations such as flowstone, frostwork, popcorn, and helictites, but it is best known for a rare formation called boxwork. The cave has more boxwork than any other in the world. Millions of years ago, when the area was covered by ocean, limestone formations were created below the waters. Later the ocean receded and, over millions of years, other waters seeped in and out, the limestone slowly dissolved, and passageways began to form. About 62 million to 65 million years ago, the slow geologic uplift that formed the Black Hills also caused the limestone to shift and crack and more passages were opened.

Acid-laden water filled the cracks in the underground limestone. As the limestone dissolved in the slowly seeping water, hardened calcite boxwork formations were left behind. They are delicate and fragile, thin honeycombs clinging to the walls and ceilings of the cave.

Although early explorers and owners used the cave for commercial tours and blasted caverns and paved walkways, today it is very carefully protected. Its vital signs (humidity, temperature, and water quality) are constantly monitored to spot environmental problems early.

This living, breathing cave is constantly changing, but the temperature inside is always around 53 degrees. Wear a jacket and sturdy, rubber-soled walking shoes, and remember that some of the ceilings are low and some paths are wet. It's fine to take flash photographs and video shots, but tripods are prohibited. It's also forbidden to touch the cave walls; disturb the formations in any way; or smoke, eat, chew gum, or leave litter behind. There are no rest rooms underground either, so plan ahead.

Wind Cave and the visitor center are open year-round (the center does close on Thanksgiving and Christmas), but tour

Wind Cave contains more formations of rare, delicate boxwork than any other cave in the world. PHOTO:
COURTESY OF SOUTH DAKOTA TOURISM

hours vary by season. You can take your choice of different walking tours that, during the summer season, leave every 20 minutes or so. Each is led by a well-informed park ranger. The tours are quite popular, and in the summer you may have to wait. Try the morning tours, which aren't as crowded.

Children younger than six can participate free of charge in the first three tours listed. Golden Age discounts apply for each tour (you must show your Golden Age Passport).

The Natural Entrance Tour lasts 75 minutes. You will navigate 300 stairs, most of which go down, and exit the cave by elevator. Prices range from $4.00 for children 6 to 16 to $8.00 for adults 17 and older.

The Garden of Eden Tour lasts one hour and is the least strenuous (you will navigate only 150 stairs and enter and leave by elevator). Prices are $3.00 to $6.00. It is the only tour offered in winter.

The Fairgrounds Tour lasts 90 minutes and navigates 450 stairs. You'll enter and exit by elevator. Prices are $4.00 to $8.00.

The Candlelight Tour is conducted entirely by candlelight in an unlighted part of the cave. It's the longest tour: It lasts two hours and covers a mile of strenuous trails. You must make reservations (sometimes a month in advance), and children must be eight or older to participate. Prices are $4.50 to $9.00

The Caving Tour is for the most adventurous types. It's a three- to four-hour tour with a beginning course in spelunking on trails the other tours don't cover. You'll be crawling quite a lot, so wear old clothes, long pants and sleeves, sturdy shoes, and gloves. The park will provide the hard hats and lights. Only those 16 and older may participate, and reservations are required. The cost is $20.

You can make reservations for tours here by contacting Wind Cave National Park at (605) 745–4600.

There are also summer-only activities held outside the cave. Discovery programs are held three times each day (ask at the visitor center), a two-hour prairie hike takes place once a day, and evening campfire programs are presented at Elk Moun-

Antelope are common throughout the Black Hills. PHOTO: BERT GILDART

tain Campground. You can stay at the campground or in the backcountry (inquire at the visitor center for permits), hike cross-country or on the trails, and bicycle on the roads (off-road biking is not allowed). You can also ride horseback.

Whether your preference is for the above-ground or below-ground sights and scenery, you'll thoroughly enjoy Wind Cave National Park, a South Dakota natural treasure.

The Badlands and Nearby

With its stony face and jutting spine, your first glimpse of Badlands National Park might well prompt comparison to a giant, mythological beast or bring to mind a bleak lunar surface. Indeed, the parched soil and eroded, barren peaks of the Badlands give many visitors the impression of a place overlooked by evolution and long ago forsaken.

Yet this eerie world unto itself is very much alive. Get acquainted with it, and you might be surprised to find yourself warming to those thirsty slopes and windy plains that, like patient teachers, show us how to look beyond the surface. All they ask is that we take time to notice and to marvel at their splendor.

Badlands National Park is a place for meandering and making frequent stops, whether you are in your car or on foot. The scene changes, it seems, minute by minute. Yet the more time you spend in the Badlands, the more familiar, and precious, its features become.

Those who have lived here all their lives will tell you there's no place like home—the Badlands are in their blood, and they wouldn't live anywhere else. "I love it here," one steadfast resident told us, smiling and hugging herself. "Especially when the moon comes up; that's my favorite time."

We who live close by, near enough to make frequent visits, understand. Yet we also know that a single evening spent watching the buttes and spires turn from ivory to gold is enough to make you want to linger here. And when the sun comes up again, the memory makes you want to step outside, first thing, to see the sentinels of the Badlands glowing almost white against a brilliant blue sky.

There is much to observe and experience here, and we urge you to do both with care and deliberation. Hike along a dry wash, and listen as curled leaves of parched mud crackle beneath your boots. On the compacted hardpan, look back and notice how you leave almost no trace at all. Watch closely as a long-tailed magpie takes flight, white wing patches flashing like outspread, gloved fingers against coal-black wings. Feel the wind brush your face like ghosts bearing ancient dreams.

A long thread of life weaves through the Badlands, both in its rich fossil beds and in stories handed down. We hope you'll take time to learn and think about the living things, human and otherwise, that have found this to be a good land.

Then, when you are irresistibly drawn back, you'll find its jagged peaks and rippling grasslands as welcoming as the weathered face of a dear friend.

History

The Lakota Sioux called it *mako sica*, "land that is bad." Eighteenth-century French fur traders who traveled the area spoke of *les mauvaises terres à traverser*, "the bad lands to cross."

Not until the mid-nineteenth century did scientists become convinced that this eerie place, with its rugged cliffs, baked soil, and ferocious weather, was in fact a storehouse brimming with fascinating information about the ancient past.

Majestic cliffs are representative of the Badlands' landscape. PHOTO: BERT GILDART

By studying the striated rock formations of the Badlands, researchers have learned that the area was covered by a warm inland sea millions of years ago. Then, as the Black Hills laboriously rose skyward, the sea drained away, and the seabed oxidized. Eons passed, and layers of silt, sand, clay, and volcanic ash were deposited. Today these mineralized layers are seen as varicolored bands sweeping across the craggy landscape.

Through millennia the land underwent many transformations, from dense forest to vast plain to grassland. The climate changed as well, from subtropical to cool and dry. Four-legged creatures roamed and grazed where invertebrates had lived submerged in the sea, and over time the four-leggeds' bones joined those of the sea-dwellers, settling into the earth to turn to stone. The Badlands are now an extensive source of fossils; local rocks from the Oligocene epoch, roughly 25 million to 35 million years ago, contain some of the world's best-known specimens. A fairly recent discovery, known as

the "Big Pig Dig," yielded the remains of an archeotherium, or ancient wild boar, and other animals from the Eocene period some 55 million years ago. You can see Big Pig Dig bones at the Museum of Geology on the campus of South Dakota School of Mines and Technology in Rapid City. (Please see our Attractions chapter for more information on the museum.)

Eventually, water and wind gouged out cliffs and canyons in the soft sediment, and the climate ripened into extremes of hot and cold. More than 10,000 years ago—recently, in geologic terms—humans appeared in the Badlands, hunting mammoths. (You can see bones and hair from these ancient creatures at Mammoth Site of Hot Springs, which is listed in our Attractions chapter.) Indian tribes followed—first the Arikara and later the Lakota Sioux—then white trappers, traders, fossil collectors, ranchers, and homesteaders. Some of their stories are recorded in books such as *Reflections of the Badlands,* by Philip S. Hall. You can browse for books in the park's two visitor centers, which are listed under Attractions in this chapter.

In the 1920s, South Dakota U.S. Senator Peter Norbeck and Ben Millard, an early Badlands homesteader and founder of the Cedar Pass Lodge (see the listing below, under Accommodations), joined forces to create a national park in the Badlands, an effort actually begun by the South Dakota Legislature in 1909. President Franklin Roosevelt issued a proclamation establishing Badlands National Monument in 1939, three years after Norbeck's death. In 1976 the monument expanded to include the Stronghold (South) and Palmer Creek units, both on Pine Ridge Indian Reservation land that had been used as a gunnery range during World War II. In 1978 the monument achieved national-park status through an act of Congress; today Badlands National Park contains 244,000 acres.

Climate

Badlands weather is a lot like the landscape: often harsh and subject to rapid change. Most of the park's million-plus annual visitors arrive during the summer, when the thermometer can easily register three digits. But just as easily, blazing sunshine can give way to a downpour that turns hiking trails and back roads into a gummy mess. Lightning, high winds, hailstorms, flash floods, and, rarely, tornadoes, are other warm-weather hazards for

Insiders' Tip

Of all the hazards you might encounter in Badlands National Park, lightning looms largest. Stay off ridges and away from lone trees to avoid being struck during a storm.

which it is wise to be prepared. The climate is semiarid (annual rainfall is about 15.5 inches) and, combined with prairie winds, dehydration is a very real concern in hot weather, especially if you're out hiking or otherwise working up a sweat. Carry plenty of drinking water with you, because opportunities to wet your whistle are few—essentially at facilities in the Cedar Pass area and at the White River Visitor Center (which is open only during the summer). Sunscreen and suitable clothing are essential.

During the winter, ice storms and blizzards can strike with little warning. Bitter cold and howling winds are to be expected, but so are mild, sunny days and picturesque snowfalls.

That said, spring, when the baby animals are born and the land greens up, and fall, when the weather is generally more moderate, are lovely times to visit the Badlands.

The Natural World

The towering, 60-mile-long Badlands Wall dominates the Badlands moonscape with a series of eroded ridges and valleys running from the northeast to the southwest. Other, smaller rock formations (and we use the term "rock" somewhat loosely here—much of what you see is essentially dried mud) have inspired comparisons to everything from castles and ancient ruins to oversized ribs and toadstools.

So it might surprise you to know that wide-open, mixed-grass prairies, not barren rocks, make up most of the Badlands. Some 170,000 acres nourish more than 50 species of grass (about 70 percent are native) and numerous varieties of wildflowers that flourish from early spring until the first hard freeze. Yellow plains prickly pear, pale green yucca, golden prairie coneflower, and white snow-on-the-mountain are just a few of the varieties of flowers to be seen. Theodore Van Bruggen's *Wildflowers, Grasses & Other Plants of the Northern Plains and Black Hills* is a color-coded guide to local plants that you might find useful; also, a brochure titled *Badlands Nature Guide* is handy for identifying fauna as well as flora. Both publications can be purchased at the park.

A program of prescribed burns has been instituted in recent years to promote a balanced ecosystem in much the same way as wildfires of the past did, by recycling nutrients into the soil and promoting the natural succession of plant species.

Trees and shrubs are scarce in the Badlands, growing for the most part near creek drainages. Most notable are the aromatic Rocky Mountain junipers that give Cedar Pass its name. You can get a close look at these trees and enjoy their cooling shade on the Cliff Shelf Trail (see the listing below under Recreation). Cliff Shelf is a slump, a place where surface runoff collects as it drains underground, thus providing sufficient water to nourish a sizable stand of trees.

Other forms of life also find sustenance in Badlands National Park, which is a key player in efforts to save the black-footed ferret from extinction. These black-masked members of the weasel family prey on prairie dogs and live in their holes, and ferrets bred in captivity have been reintroduced to the wild here. You're not likely to see ferrets in the park, though, because the nocturnal little burrowers spend almost all their time underground. In the event of a sighting, however, please watch from a respectful distance—binoculars or a telephoto camera lens will give you a close-up look—so as not to disturb these endangered creatures. (For more on these creatures, see the Close-up in our Natural World chapter.) Prairie dogs, on the other hand, are commonly seen—try Roberts Prairie Dog Town on Sage Creek Rim Road in the western portion of the park.

Bighorn sheep, wiped out in 1925, have been restored to the park along with bison, which were once hunted to near-extinction. But wolves, elk, and bears no longer roam here. (Whether bears actually inhabited the Badlands is in dispute, although stories of early-day encounters persist.) You might see antelope, deer, rabbits, coyotes, foxes, badgers, grouse, and many other animals as you explore the park, but please remember that they are wild and potentially dangerous. Keep

The purple coneflower was once used for medicinal purposes by Native Americans. PHOTO: JANE GILDART

A Black Hills fawn is partially camouflaged by the terrain. PHOTO: BERT GILDART

your distance no matter how placid they seem—the rule of thumb is, if an animal responds to your presence, you're too close. We also caution you to be on the lookout for poisonous prairie rattlesnakes, especially around prairie dog holes, rocky areas, grass, and brush.

And remember, the only things you're allowed to take home from the park are your memories. Removing or harming the plants, animals, minerals, fossils, and other features is a federal offense, and it spoils the park for others. If you do come upon fossils, notify a park ranger so the specimens can be handled professionally.

Getting Here, Getting Around

There are several entrances to Badlands National Park. Most travelers arrive in the North Unit via I-90; if you're approaching from the east, take exit 131 and follow Highway 240 (Badlands Loop Road) for about 3 miles to the park's Northeast

Entrance and another 5 miles to Ben Reifel Visitor Center (see the write-up under Attractions later in this chapter). From the west, take exit 110 at Wall and head straight south on Highway 240 for 8 miles to the Pinnacles Entrance. Badlands Loop Road links these two entrances.

Once you've arrived, you can pick up a free official map and ask for information and directions at the visitor center. Roads and attractions in the North Unit are well marked with signs to help you find your way. One caution, though: Unpaved roads can be slippery from winter ice or summer rain, so use extra care under those conditions.

From the north or south, Bureau of Indian Affairs (BIA) Road 27 takes you to the White River Visitor Center in the southeast corner of the Stronghold (South) Unit, which is on the Pine Ridge Indian Reservation. The Stronghold and nearby Palmer Creek units, although part of the park, are isolated, undeveloped, and not well suited to tourism. Grazing and subsistence hunting (with a permit) are allowed here, and there is only one

Photographers gather at sunset on summer evenings on lofty vantages to watch as the craggy badlands undergo a colorful transformation. PHOTO: BERT GILDART

official road, unpaved at that; Sheep Mountain Road (off County Road 589) narrows and turns from gravel to dirt, winding around until it dead-ends after 7 miles at a sheer drop on top of Sheep Mountain Table. There's the added complexity of private land that can't be crossed without permission—check on local access at visitor centers before you try to enter. And there's always the possibility of stumbling upon unexploded ordnance (UXO) from the gunnery-range days; information about what to do in that event is available at visitor centers.

For a less complicated backcountry experience, consider Badlands (Sage Creek) Wilderness Area in the North Unit. (Please see the Recreation section in this chapter for more information.)

North of the park, Wall Municipal Airport, at an altitude of 2,810 feet, has a hard-surface runway rated up to 12,500 pounds for single- and twin-engine planes. Services here are minimal; fuel is available on an emergency basis only, and there are no car rentals or taxis. However, motels, restaurants, and tourist attractions, including world-famous Wall Drug (see the Close-up in this chapter) are within easy walking distance (nine blocks or fewer). For airport information, call (605) 279-2666.

Badlands National Park is open all year, and a $20.00 annual pass allows you unlimited visits. Seven-day passes cost $10.00 per noncommercial vehicle ($5.00 for Oglala Sioux tribal members). Single-person entry (on motorcycle, bicycle, or foot) is $5.00. Admission is free on National Parks Day, August 25.

Attractions

Strictly speaking, the Badlands are one big attraction all in themselves. But we've gone ahead and listed the primary tourist draws, which are located along Badlands Loop Road in the North Unit of the park and within a few miles of its northern boundary. Be sure to check out the Wall Drug Close-up in this chapter, too.

Badlands National Park

Badlands Loop Road
Hwy. 240, Badlands National Park

Badlands Loop Road is the most heavily traveled road in the park, doubtless because it takes you to the most popular hiking trails and overlooks. Points of interest along the road are well marked, and all are worth stopping for. The wheelchair-accessible Fossil Exhibit Trail, for instance, is a short, circular boardwalk along which you'll find "fossils under glass"—replicas of fossils found in the area and displayed in boxes with domed, heavy plastic lids. The Journey to Wounded Knee Overlook tells a poignant tale of a doomed people and a dying leader trapped between two worlds. (You'll find more information about the 1890 Wounded Knee Massacre in our Daytrips and Weekend Getaways chapter.) At the Seabed Jungle Overlook you'll see low, ancient hills that oxidized and turned yellow after the inland sea receded. There are others you also won't want to miss, so plan to take your time.

Ben Reifel Visitor Center
Hwy 240, Interior
(605) 433-5361

A stop at the visitor center 5 miles from the park's Northeast Entrance will make your journey through the Badlands more meaningful. By studying the geologic displays, you'll be able to recognize a variety of natural features throughout the park and understand how they came to be formed. Cultural displays will help you appreciate the area's human history. In the "You Can Touch" room, you'll become acquainted with the park's flora and fauna. A table there with fossil riddles and puzzles grabs the attention of kids, and so does a cow backbone you can try to assemble. Every half-hour during tourist season and by request during the winter, you can view an 18-minute video on the natural and cultural history of the area; it's shown in audio and closed-caption versions simultaneously. Afterward, you might want to browse among the gift shop's selection of books, videos, posters, and puzzles. Services at the center include information, rest rooms, water, a public pay phone, and brochures in German and French.

The center is named for the late Oglala Lakota leader Benjamin Reifel, known to his tribe as Wiyaka Wanjila, or Lone Feather. Reifel was superintendent of the Pine Ridge Indian Reservation, a U.S. congressman, and the U.S. Commissioner of Indian Affairs.

The center is open year-round; summer hours are 7:00 A.M. to 8:00 P.M. daily, with reduced hours at other times.

Naturalist Programs
(605) 433–5361

Free educational programs are available each day during the summer, including evening talks that begin at dusk at the Cedar Pass Campground amphitheater. Times and topics (such as Badlands natural or human history, fossils, geology, and animals) are posted on park bulletin boards at Ben Reifel Visitor Center, Cedar Pass Lodge, and park campgrounds. Additional programs offered recently were the twice daily Evolving Prairie Talk and Fossil Talk; check bulletin boards for information. The park newsletter, *The Prairie Preamble* (you'll get a copy when you pay your entrance fee), also lists regularly scheduled programs; you can ask at the visitor center about additional, special programs.

White River Visitor Center
Junction of BIA Rd. 27 and BIA Rd. 2
Badlands National Park
(605) 455–2878

The center, located on the Pine Ridge Indian Reservation but operated by the National Park Service, features displays on Lakota Sioux history and culture. There's also a video you won't want to miss, The Great Plains Experience, which originally aired on public TV. The items for sale in the bookstore here are also available at Ben Reifel Visitor Center, so you get two chances to make up your mind about what to add to your (or some-

one else's) home library. Information, maps, rest rooms, and water are available here too. The center is open from late May through August, from 10:00 A.M. to 4:00 P.M. daily.

Nearby

National Grasslands Visitor Center
708 Main St., Wall
(605) 279–2125

How about a game of Grassland Jeopardy? That's just one of many things to do and see at this enchanting visitor center. Learn about Great Plains history and the dustbowl years that inspired the formation of national grasslands. Or stroke animal pelts and decide which one feels the nicest. And by all means, follow the painted footprints to see a black-footed ferret in his cage—you can read all about him and the center's other wonders in our Parks and Grasslands chapter.

The White River Visitor Center displays of Native American war paint and headdress. PHOTO: BERT GILDART

Prairie Homestead
Hwy. 240, Interior
(605) 433–5400

You'll experience something rare at this original 1909 sod dugout: an authentic sense of life on a prairie homestead, with all of its hardships and rewards. It's not hard to imagine the covered wagon coming to a stop at this spot, to picture Ed and Alice Brown, and their son, Charles, newly arrived from Nebraska, scanning the landscape and saying, "Yes, here. This is home."

The family dug a hole into a low hillside, plowed bricks from the hard soil and built themselves a sod house with a kitchen and a bedroom. Later, they dug a root cellar, built a chicken coop and barn, and moved a wooden claim shack into place beside the "soddie" —then they had a proper parlor where they could relax and entertain their neighbors.

Ed Brown died in 1920, but Alice stayed on the homestead with Charles until 1934, when she moved to California. The sod house was last occupied by bachelor George Carr until 1949 and then, abandoned, it started to decay. But in 1962 present owner Keith Crew (who has never lived more than 2 miles from the site) and his late wife, Dorothy, started restoration work on the place. Today you can tour the grounds and authentically furnished buildings at your own pace while prairie dogs scamper and scold, chickens roam and peck in the sweet-smelling grass, and the calls of songbirds drift on the air like voices from the past. Take it all in, and you'll understand why the Browns and thousands like them were willing to sacrifice creature comforts to build a life on the Great Plains.

Prairie Homestead was entered into the National Register of Historic Places in 1974, and numerous prestigious publications have carried articles about it—many of them are posted on the wall outside the gift shop. The shop itself has an excellent assortment of books about prairie life, featuring collections of Laura Ingalls Wilder, Willa Cather, and Mari Sandoz, as well as numerous other titles of interest to children and adults.

The homestead, which is 2 miles south of I-90 exit 131, is open for tours during daylight hours between mid-April

The sparsely furnished sod hut at Prairie Homestead gives visitors a look at pioneer life in the Badlands.
PHOTO: BARBARA TOMOVICK

and mid-October. Admission prices are $4.00 for adults, and $3.25 for seniors 62 and older and youths ages 11 to 17. Children 10 and younger get in free.

Wild West Historical Wax Museum
601 Main St., Wall
(605) 279–2915

Begin your tour under the strict warning, "Positively no profanity or dancing." From Sitting Bull and the Sundance Kid to John Wayne and the James Gang, the displays here tell the ripsnortin' version of Western history. You'll meet famous outlaws such as Billy the Kid as well as some whose names might be less familiar, like Clay Allison. But there are "good guys" in this hall of fame too, including "Little Sure Shot" Annie Oakley, courageous Sacagawea, and a trusty Pony Express rider. Signs and taped narratives give lots of details about each one (although historians might take issue with a couple of pieces of information). In addition to more than 50 wax figures, you can see displays of barbed wire, antique cavalry swords, silver dollars, old photos, and more. There's also a gift shop with jewelry, souvenirs, books, and CDs.

The museum is open from early May until mid-October or later. Summer hours are 8:00 A.M. to 8:00 P.M. Admission (which also gets you a coupon for post-tour free popcorn) is $4.50 for adults ages 16 to 61, $4.00 for seniors 62 and older, $2.50 for youths 6 to 15, and free for kids 5 and younger. Inquire about discounts for groups of 10 or more.

Kidstuff

Badlands National Park

Junior Ranger Program
Badlands National Park
(605) 433–5361

Summer programs for kids ages 5 to 8 and 9 to 12 allow youngsters to learn about the fascinating Badlands in entertaining ways.

By picking up a Junior Ranger booklet at Ben Reifel Visitor Center, kids are on their way to adventure. Once they complete the book, which usually takes a couple of hours, and have it signed by a park ranger, they receive a free certificate and badge. Booklets cost $1.50.

Ask at the visitor center about other summer kids' programs. Discovery hikes, games, and other activities are offered on certain days.

Nearby

Wall Drug
510 Main St., Wall
(605) 279–2175

You're not afraid of a little dinosaur, are you? Well, how about a big one? For a roarin' good time, visit the (mechanical) T. rex in the Back Yard at Wall Drug—he speaks his mind about every 15 minutes. Less intimidating are the 6-foot rabbit, Singing Sam the Gorilla Man, and a hitch of singing reindeer. A tepee from the movie *Dances with Wolves* and a video arcade offer hands-on fun. The Back Yard closes for the winter, but there's lots more stuff inside. Read all about Wall Drug, where admission is free, in the Close-up in this chapter.

Accommodations

With all the fascinating things to see and do in and around Badlands National Park, we're sure you're going to need a place to stay for a night or two, or even longer. To give you a head start, we scouted around and located a number of good motels—several of them are listed below. Please refer to the following price code key for price information, and feel free to use your major credit card.

Price Code

Prices are for double occupancy during the peak season—generally, June, July, and August. Inquire about off-season rates and senior discounts.

$	Less than $50
$$	$51 to $75
$$$	$76 to $100

Naturalist Teri Chapman discusses fossils common to Badlands. PHOTO: BERT GILDART

Badlands National Park

Cedar Pass Lodge $-$$
Cedar St., Interior (in Badlands National Park)
(605) 433-5460

Awake to the twitter of birds, and step out the door of your cabin for a fabulous view of the Badlands first thing in the morning. The furnishings are basic—no phone, TV, or cooking facilities—but comfortable, especially considering how little time you'll be spending indoors. The real fun is outside in the park. The lodge, which is operated by the Oglala Sioux Tribe under contract with the National Park Service, has 24 air-conditioned cabins with one to two bedrooms that afford relative privacy, and grassy areas in which to sit and ponder nature's mysteries. There's also a cottage with full kitchen that sleeps up to 10 people. You'll find a restaurant (see the listing later in this chapter), pay phones, and a gift shop with Native American–made items. The lodge is open from approximately April 1 until October 31 and is easy to find, just 5 miles from the park's Northeast Entrance off I-90 exit 131. There's a $5.00 charge if your pet stays with you.

Nearby

Ann's Motel $$
114 Fourth Ave., Wall
(605) 279-2501

Twelve clean, cozy units and more than the usual amenities make this a home-away-from-home kind of place. Whether you choose two double beds or one queen-size, you get a small refrigerator, microwave, coffeepot, phone, and remote cable TV in your room. Add a tub-shower combo and you've got all the basics and then some. Pets are allowed, but you can't leave them alone in your room.

Badlands Budget Host Motel $
Hwy. 377, Interior
(605) 433-5335, (800) 388-4643
(800) BUD-HOST

The 21 units here are simply appointed but adequate and reasonably roomy, and you can choose either two double beds or two queen-size. If a hot soak is on your list of must-dos, ask for a room with a tub-shower combination; some have a shower only. You won't have a phone in your room, but you will have a coffeepot (which is probably more important when you're on vacation anyway), and there is a pay phone you can use. There's also a laundry at your disposal and a restaurant that serves simple, all-you-can-eat breakfasts and suppers. The motel shares the grounds with Badlands Interior Campground, which is listed in the Campground section of this chapter.

Open from May 1 to September 31, the motel is near the Interior Entrance to Badlands National Park, on the southeast end of the park and the north end of Interior.

Best Western Plains Motel $$-$$$
712 Glenn St., Wall
(605) 279-2145, (800) 528-1234

You'll get the royal treatment at this sparkling-clean place, where the beds come in either king- or queen-size. Best of all, you can choose family accommodations with two beds in a separate room for the kids. All 74 rooms have a tub-shower combination, coffeepot, phone, and TV with movie channel. There's also a heated outdoor swimming pool and a game room. The lobby has free coffee and a gift shop with clothing and Western gifts. Pets are allowed, and plenty of nonsmoking rooms are available.

Super 8 Motel $$
711 Glenn St., Wall
(605) 279-2688, (800) 800-8000

This attractive, 29-room motel has a couple of outstanding features: a wheelchair-accessible room and extra-long double beds. (You can get a queen-size bed if you prefer.) In addition, nonsmokers will appreciate the availability of smoke-free rooms. Other comforts include free local calls, cable TV with Showtime, tub-shower combinations, and free coffee in the lobby during the morning and evening. Babies have the use of a free crib and are welcome, but pets are not.

Dramatic cliffs form the backdrop for guest cabins at Cedar Pass Lodge. PHOTO: BARBARA TOMOVICK

Campgrounds

Badlands National Park has two campgrounds with minimal amenities, plus backcountry camping opportunities for the strong of heart and back (please see the Recreation section later in the chapter). Regardless of your camping preferences, it's important to keep in mind that campfires are not allowed anywhere in the park. If you plan to cook, bring along a camp stove or, if you're staying in a campground, a small charcoal grill. The same arid conditions that make fire such a hazard also make drinking water essential, and unless you stay at Cedar Pass Campground, which has potable water, make sure you take a good supply with you.

Group camping is available in Cedar Pass Campground for $2.50 per person, with a minimum fee of $25 per night. Groups must have a designated leader and make advance reservations by writing to Group Camping, Badlands National Park, P.O. Box 6, Interior, South Dakota 57750, faxing (605) 433-5404, or calling (605) 433-5235 or (605) 433-5361. Otherwise, campsites are available on a first-come, first-served basis; for information, call (605) 433-5361.

Private campgrounds are available outside the park, and you'll find two shady ones listed here. Both are just a short distance away.

Badlands National Park

Cedar Pass Campground
Hwy. 377, Interior
(605) 433-5361

About 100 sites are available for tents and RVs. You won't find hookups here, but the rest rooms have flush toilets and electricity. When winter comes, however, the rest rooms (and the RV dump station) are closed, but if you're a diehard camper, you'll gladly make do with pit toilets. Running water is available year-round from a spigot near the group loop area (which is the only section of the campground open during the winter). On hot days you'll welcome the relative shade of the covered picnic tables.

Stays are limited to 14 days and cost $10.00 per night during the summer, $8.00 during the off-season, which usually runs from some time in October (depending on the weather) until May.

The campground is a short distance south of Ben Reifel Visitor Center and is well marked.

Sage Creek Primitive Campground
Sage Creek Rim Rd.
(605) 433-5361

There's no charge for your stay of up of to 14 days here. Presently, there are unlimited sites to pitch a tent or park an RV, but the only comforts are picnic tables and two pit toilets. You'll have to bring your own water, although park officials are considering providing water here in the future. (If they do, there will be a fee.) The campground, which is 10 miles west of the park's Pinnacles Entrance, offers a semi-wilderness experience without the hazards of more remote places, plus it's a good starting point for treks into Badlands Wilderness Area, listed later.

There are two areas with tie-offs for horse camping here as well. Ask at the visitor centers for information and a brochure explaining horse regulations.

Nearby

Badlands Interior Campground
Hwy. 377, Interior
(605) 433–5335, (800) 388–4643

This modest little campground is surrounded by great views of the Badlands in all directions, and a generous sprinkling of trees and grass provides a nice contrast to the stark moonscape. Some 60 sites for tents and RVs, a swimming pool, playground, laundry, rest rooms with showers, small convenience store, an arcade, and a restaurant serving basic breakfasts and suppers for a small charge take care of your basic needs when you're not out roaming. Full and partial hookups and a dump station are available. There are also two air-conditioned camping cabins and a 21-unit motel, which is described in the Accommodations listed earlier.

The basic rate for two people is $11.50, with an additional charge for hookups. Cabins are $29.95 with air-conditioning. The campground is open from May 1 until September 31 and is on the north end of Interior, a short drive from the park's Interior Entrance.

Badlands/White River KOA
Hwy. 44, Interior
(605) 433–5337, (800) 562–3897

With more than 700 shade trees, this is a cooling, restful place to come home to after a day spent exploring under a searing Badlands sun. Situated on the south bank of the White River, the campground has 56 grassy tent sites (six with water and electricity), 81 RV sites (38 with full hookups, 43 with water and electricity) and eight camping cabins. A swimming pool, playground, nine-hole minigolf course, and game room provide recreation, but you might find yourself perfectly content to simply lap up the peace and quiet at this "oasis in the Badlands," as it calls itself. Showers, laundry facilities, and a dump station are provided, and a convenience store sells groceries, supplies, and souvenirs. A modestly priced pancake breakfast is available.

The campground is open from April 15 to October 15. Rates for two adults start at $18 per night for a tent site and $23 for an RV site; hookups are extra. A night in a cabin costs $34. Campers ages five and younger stay for free.

The campground is 4 miles southeast of Interior.

Recreation

Many who visit Badlands National Park are what we call "windshield" tourists, folks who like to view the scenery from the comfort of their vehicles but who never really get out and explore. We think they're missing out on the best part, so we've compiled what we think are some pretty enticing recreational opportunities in the listings below.

This section deals only with the park because, Wall Drug notwithstanding (see the Close-up in this chapter), that's the main attraction in this part of the country. Here we give information on hiking, backpacking, and horseback riding. If you bring your bicycles, you'll be required to stay on the paved and unpaved roads; they're not allowed in the park's backcountry or on hiking trails. Climbing in the park is limited to scrambling, since the soft, crumbly soil that makes up Badlands cliffs won't support standard climbing gear.

And now, a few generalizations. By all means, take a compass and a topographic map (available for $8.95 at park visitor centers) when you venture away from populated areas. Be prepared for sudden changes in the weather, guard against sunburn, and stay off ridges during lightning storms. Avoid slick, muddy trails—the gumbo will bog you down and make you think you're wearing lead boots.

And yes, we've said this before, but we'll say it again: When you're out exploring, take water, water, water—at least a gallon per person per day. You can't drink the chalky-looking, sediment-laden stuff in the Badlands backcountry, nor can you filter it without clogging your expensive filtering apparatus.

Last but not least, if you carry it in, carry it out.

Hikers heat up quickly in the Badlands, where high temperatures and dry air make a good supply of drinking water a must on the trail. PHOTO: BARBARA TOMOVICK

Stronghold Table

In a last, desperate attempt to make their world right again, Lakota Sioux ghost dancers gathered at Stronghold Table, a remote mesa in what is now the Stronghold (South) Unit of Badlands National Park, to hold ceremonies in late 1890. The ghost dance belonged to a religion preached by Paiute prophet Wovoka, who promised that the Messiah would restore the old ways. Purifying themselves and eschewing violence, adherents danced in a circle, appealing to their deceased relatives and praying for a miracle to drive out the White invaders and bring back the buffalo.

Whites, viewing the ghost dance as a threat to their own safety and objectives, and hearing reports that ghost dancers wore special shirts to protect them from bullets, were suspicious and tried to repress the ceremonies. Efforts to prevent ghost dancing led to the death of Chief Sitting Bull, who was killed December 15, 1890, by Native American police sent to keep him from joining the ghost dancers on Stronghold Table. Two weeks later, on December 29, the Wounded Knee Massacre took place when the Seventh Cavalry intercepted Chief Big Foot's band, believed to be en route to Stronghold Table but in fact bound for Pine Ridge to meet with Chief Red Cloud in a quest for peace. You can read more about Wounded Knee in our Daytrips and Weekend Getaways chapter.

Hiking and Backpacking

Badlands National Park Hiking Trails

A number of mostly short, mostly easy trails are accessible from Badlands Loop Road in the park's North Unit—this well-traveled route and the wheelchair-accessible Fossil Exhibit Trail are covered in the Attractions section of this chapter.

Other popular trails include the half-mile Cliff Shelf Nature Trail, which meanders along a dirt track interspersed with wooden boardwalks and stairs and takes you through a cool, fragrant bower of Rocky Mountain junipers. At the end of the 600-yard-long Door Trail, it's not too hard to block out traffic noise and imagine the vast, bleak silence that greeted early denizens and explorers in the Badlands. Both of these trails, which are north of the Ben Reifel Visitor Center, have self-guiding brochures available.

To the west of the visitor center is Saddle Pass Trail. A mere two-tenths of a mile long, it's still a demanding climb from the base of the Badlands Wall, and you'll want to be in good condition before you attempt it. Make sure you carry your water bottle and camera in a pack, because the trail is covered with a layer of loose, crumbly soil and you're going to need to use your hands when the scrambling gets tough, especially on the way down. But your effort will be rewarded by a terrific view when you reach the top. You might even want to keep going by picking up the Castle Trail (you can go east or west) or the Medicine Root Loop, which heads east for 2 miles and leads you back to the Castle Trail. The Castle Trail itself links the Badlands Loop Road (from the Door Trail parking lot) and the Fossil Exhibit Trail (see the Attractions section above) and can be done as a 5-mile, end-to-end excursion through badlands and prairie or taken in sections. Free maps available in the park will help you decide.

Badlands (Sage Creek) Wilderness Area

If you've ever longed to experience the prairie the way its early inhabitants did, here is a place to realize that dream. Few visitors venture into this panoramic paradise, making it an ideal place to escape civilization—a plus when you're seeking

Hundreds of miles of trails, such as Notch Trail, course through the Badlands. PHOTO: BERT GILDART

Insiders' Tip

Although Badlands National Park is in South Dakota, other "badlands" are to be found in other states, including North Dakota. The South Dakota badlands are sometimes referred to as the Big Badlands or the White River Badlands to distinguish them from the others.

solitude, a potential hazard if you run into trouble. At 64,144 acres, this is the nation's largest prairie wilderness, a home on the range to bison, pronghorn antelope, eagles, and other wild creatures. Although mixed-grass prairie dominates, you'll also find barren badlands formations to explore.

Vehicles are not allowed here, and the only trails are those of the bison. (You can leave your car at Sage Creek Primitive Campground.) You don't need a permit to hike or camp in this territory, but park officials recommend checking in with a ranger at Ben Reifel Visitor Center and signing a backcountry register before you head into the trackless wilds. Registers can be found at Conata Picnic Area off Badlands Loop Road, Rodeo Point Overlook off Sage Creek Rim Road (ask for directions), and Sage Creek Campground. Camping is prohibited within a half-mile of any road or trail, and your campsite must not be visible from a road. Also, be sure to stay clear of bison trails when making camp, since the giant creatures are not likely to make a detour—after all, they were here first.

And make this your mantra: "No open fires." They are absolutely forbidden in Badlands National Park.

Horseback Riding

Horses are allowed throughout the park except on marked trails and roads or in developed areas. No permit is needed, but at this writing new rules were being drafted for backcountry horse use; check at park visitor centers for current regulations and a map. Horses usually don't like Badlands water any better than do humans (for whom it's not safe), so it's wise to pack at least five gallons of drinking water for your horse each day, along with your own gallon. You can park your horse trailer at an overlook or parking area if you just want to ride around the Badlands for the day; if you're staying overnight, you'll find Sage Creek Primitive Campground equipped for horse camping. Please see the Campgrounds section above as well as the Horse Camps section of our Campgrounds and RV Sites chapter for information about camping with your equine. Also check under Trail Rides and Pack Trips in our Recreation chapter to find out about commercial expeditions into the Badlands. Backcountry camping and grazing are allowed (remember, no campfires), but check with park rangers for the latest regulations. They can also tell you where to buy certified weed-free hay, the only kind allowed in the park.

Restaurants

It would be hard to visit the Badlands and not work up an appetite, but you don't need to worry about that. There are plenty of places serving good food throughout the area. Keep reading for some Insider recommendations. Most meals are moderately priced, but check the following price code key for more information. Unless otherwise noted, major credit cards are accepted.

Price Code

Prices are for two dinners not including appetizers, drinks, dessert, tax, or tip.

$ .... less than $15
$$ .... $15 to $30

Badlands National Park

Cedar Pass Restaurant $$
1 Cedar St., Interior (in Badlands National Park)
(605) 433–5460

The first thing you're likely to notice when you enter the dining room are the huge windows along two walls. Since it's seat-yourself, you can pick the booth or table with the view you want. The house specialty is Indian tacos (made with meat for dinner or scrambled eggs for breakfast), but trout and grilled halibut sound equally irresistible after a day of vigorous exploring. Sandwiches, burgers, steaks, chops, and ribs also are among the choices. You can have bottled beer or a glass of wine with your meal, but not a smoke.

The restaurant serves breakfast, lunch, and dinner daily from around April 1 until October 31. It's on Highway 240, 5 miles from the park's Northeast Entrance.

Nearby

A&M Café $
Hwy. 44, Interior
(605) 433–5340

The most popular menu item is reported to be chicken-fried steak, but we suspect that the best reason to eat here is the homemade cinnamon rolls, dinner breads, and pies: apple, rhubarb, mixed berry, cherry, and pecan. Sandwiches, steaks, halibut, liver and onions, Indian tacos, and homemade soups also appear on the menu, and the staff will fix your order to go. Smoking is allowed at all the booths and tables in this small, county-style cafe, which does not serve alcohol.

You can order breakfast, lunch, and dinner seven days a week all year. If you're 62 or older, you're entitled to a 10 percent discount.

Cactus Cafe and Lounge $$
519 Main St., Wall
(605) 279–2561

Steaks and Mexican entrees such as Butch's Barnbuster—a large burrito

Insiders' Tip
Badlands rock formations make a perfect reflective surface for sunlight, and it's a good idea to wear sunscreen while touring the park, even during the winter.

smothered in green-chili gravy—are the specialties at this cafe, which has been run by three generations of the Beach family for the past 40 years. (It's been in existence even longer than that, though.) Other choices include daily specials and a soup, salad, and fruit bar (although it's not available during the winter). There's ordinary fare such as chicken strips, sandwiches, fish, and pasta, but you'll also find veggie burgers and, among the appetizers, breaded gizzards. Carrot cake and homemade pies appear on the dessert list. The decor is simple but dressed up a bit with brick arches and hanging planters. In the lounge, which has a full bar (plus a pool table and other diversions), there's a mural depicting scenes of early prairie life, including the building of the railroads. The cafe serves breakfast, lunch, and dinner daily all year. Smoking is allowed throughout.

Cuny Table Café $
BIA Rd. 2, Buffalo Gap
(605) 455–2957

The year sisters Freda Yaeger and Nellie Cuny opened their cafe—they don't recall whether it was 1980 or 1981—a San Francisco tour bus got stranded nearby. The two good-natured women let the travelers use their cooking facilities and dip into their tractor diesel fuel supply. Ever since, the tiny cafe with seating for 20—maybe—has been a stop on the tour company's cross-country summer treks. Other buses stop here, too, yet the remote eatery on a

Wall Drug

They're everywhere, they're everywhere—signs to Wall Drug, that is.

You'll see them for miles along I–90 long before you get to the town of Wall in western South Dakota. ALL ROADS LEAD TO WALL DRUG. SHOOTIN' GALLERY, WALL DRUG. WALL DRUG OR BUST. And the most famous of all, the one that got things started: FREE ICE WATER.

It was a sweltering summer day in 1936 when Dorothy Hustead told her husband, Ted, that hot and thirsty travelers on the nearby highway would stop at their store, a pharmacy and soda fountain, if they knew they could get a free drink of ice water there. To spread the word, Dorothy said, they should post a series of signs along the road. Tourists have been flocking to Wall Drug ever since, and the business now takes up the greater part of a city block, forming the heart of Wall (population about 900)—and still giving away ice water 361 days a year. (It's closed on Thanksgiving, Christmas, New Year's Day, and Easter.)

Wall Drug (officially, Wall Drug Store, Inc.) is still a Hustead family business, too. Now it's in the capable hands of Ted and Dorothy's grandsons, Teddy and Rick—the third generation. But what's the big attraction?

Here's a short list of what you'll find on the shelves of present-day Wall Drug: cowboy hats, jelly beans, pottery, camping supplies, leather chaps, fine-art prints, moccasins, rubber snakes, Christmas ornaments, binoculars, fudge, reproduction pistols, corncob jelly, sculpture, copperware, jackknives, cameras, film, Levis, birch-bark items, books, roping saddles, turquoise jewelry, videos, stick horses, cowboy boots,

Miles of highway signs lead travelers to Wall Drug. PHOTO: COURTESY OF WALL DRUG STORE

popcorn, tapes and CDs, lariats, Black Hills Gold jewelry, figurines, spurs. And, yes, there's a real pharmacy where you can buy a toothbrush and get a prescription filled.

But that's not all. You can take a few minutes for spiritual renewal at the Travelers Chapel and admire its antique stained-glass windows. At the information table you'll be greeted by the word "hello" written in more than 60 languages. The life-size, animated Cowboy Orchestra will entertain you, and you can entertain yourself for hours in the Back Yard looking at old regional photos, Hustead family photos, and photos of people holding WALL DRUG signs in every corner of the globe—seriously!

If you're hungry you can chow down in the Western Art Gallery Cafe, which features original paintings, buffalo burgers, and homemade pie. At the cafeteria you can find a hot meal and ladle yourself up a cup of free ice water from a big stainless steel bucket. And at the soda fountain you can order scoops of homemade ice cream or a can of beer, or both.

For some folks, no visit to Wall Drug is complete without a five-cent cup of coffee and a huge homemade donut. These cake donuts with just a hint of lemon (and, if you want, chocolate or maple frosting) are so locally famous, that an unwritten policy in the *Rapid City Journal* newsroom dictates that any reporter, photographer, or editor on assignment in the Wall area has to bring back a batch for the staff.

(Wall, by the way, was named for the Badlands Wall, which you can read about under The Natural World in this chapter.)

Wall is 50 miles east of Rapid City along I–90 and 8 miles north of the Pinnacles Entrance to Badlands National Park on Highway 240 (the Badlands Loop Road). But approach from any direction, and we guarantee you won't have any trouble finding Wall Drug—all signs point that way. Once there, be sure to stop by the drug counter or the checkout stand in the souvenir department and ask for, you guessed it, a free WALL DRUG sign.

dirt road on the Pine Ridge Indian Reservation doesn't advertise and doesn't need to. Word of mouth alone brings in the crowds, and you can see by the guest book that they come from all over the world.

The Indian tacos served here are legendary, and they're probably not quite like any you've had anywhere else. The hot sauce—served on the side, because Freda and Nellie aren't taking any chances—is made from fresh jalapeño peppers and whatever other veggies are on hand. (Once, when they had too much zucchini around the place—well, figure it out.) "It's different every time. You never know; it's a surprise," Freda told us, chuckling.

There's nothing highfalutin' about this place, which prides itself on its down-to-earth, nofrills food like burgers and ham and eggs. Our request for decaf elicited a perturbed look from the cook, who replied (after a noticeable silence),

"We have iced tea and lemonade." We wondered later whether we'd been the first customers ever to ask.

The atmosphere, too, puts the term "casual" to the test. The cooking area is along one wall of the dining room, and, according to Freda, when the single round table, the counter with handmade chairs, and the two wooden booths fill up, the overflow crowd is likely to wander outside and find a picnic spot under the prairie sky.

The cafe serves breakfast, lunch, and dinner from early May until late September or early October. Smoking is tolerated but not encouraged. And because the cafe is on the Pine Ridge Indian Reservation, where alcohol sales are prohibited, none is served.

Just behind the brown metal building that houses the cafe is the little Singing Horse Trading Post, where you can buy beads and craft supplies as well as Native American–made items. That's sweetgrass you smell when you open the door.

You'll find all this, and a warm welcome, 8 miles west of White River Visitor Center (see the listing above) on BIA Road 2, a wide, well-maintained but dusty gravel road. Look for the sign on BIA Road 27 that says, FOOD 8, HEAD WEST, and when you see a roadside sign advertising, CAFE. HOME-COOKING. CAMPGROUND. RV HOOKUP. HIKING. FUN., you've arrived. No credit cards are accepted.

Elkton House Restaurant $–$$
203 South Blvd., Wall
(605) 279-2152

Low-fat and low-calorie items distinguish this eatery. You'll have to ask for them, but nonfat sour cream, zero-cholesterol margarine, low-fat salad dressing, and steamed seafood and chicken are available. The rest of the menu is a mix of typical cafe-style food such as steak, sandwiches, and grilled fish along with more distinctive dishes including buffalo burgers. There's a soup and salad bar, too. The atmosphere is comfortable, and non-smokers will be happy about the section set aside just for them. Bottled beer is available.

Elkton House serves breakfast, lunch, and dinner daily, year-round.

Wall Drug $
510 Main St., Wall
(605) 279-2175

This legendary attraction—known for free ice water and nickel coffee—has cafeteria service and a cafe with seating for more than 500. The fare is simple—burger baskets, soup and sandwiches, and the like—but wine is available. Breakfast, lunch, and dinner are served daily all year; during the summer a sub shop and restaurant serving low-fat food are open in the Back Yard. Although the food services here do a brisk business, there's far more to Wall Drug than you can imagine. Please see the Close-up in this chapter to learn more.

Recreation

This chapter answers the question, What do you do for fun in the Black Hills? As you'll see, recreational opportunities are abundant here; in fact, if we gave you all the details, it would take longer to read this chapter than to hike the 111-mile Centennial Trail. The trail was a present to ourselves when we celebrated South Dakota's 100th birthday in 1989, and it recently earned National Recreation Trail status.

So we'll tell you about the Centennial and some of our other multiuse trails (including two other National Recreation Trails, Flume and Lost Cabin) as well as a great many other places we wouldn't want you to miss. (The numbers in parentheses in the trail listings below correspond to the trail numbers in Forest Service literature.) But we'll also turn you loose to explore on your own with the help of maps and handbooks, which are readily available at stores, at U.S.D.A. Forest Service offices, and at other spots around the Hills. A book we've found helpful is *Exploring the Black Hills & Badlands,* by Hiram Rogers. It has trail information for mountain biking, hiking, and cross-country skiing, a.k.a. riding, striding, and gliding. You should also check out Falcon-Guide's *Hiking South Dakota's Black Hills Country,* by Bert and Jane Gildart. Please also peruse our chapters on Parks and Grasslands and The Badlands and Nearby for information about other hiking trails.

If staying on dry land isn't your idea of a good time, turn to the Boating and Fishing sections in this chapter for a preview of our recreational waters. We have more than a dozen lakes, all of them man-made, and more than 300 miles of streams at your disposal. As much as possible, we've tried to let you know about licensing and other regulations so you can get a head start on meeting those requirements and have more time to play.

With additional sections on ballooning, climbing, golf, horseback riding (including commercial trail rides), hunting, Jeep tours, skiing, swimming, and even skydiving, you might conclude (correctly) that this chapter is heavily weighted toward outdoor activities. But we haven't forgotten those who like their sports under a roof. Look for the sections on bowling, roller-skating, and organized sports and other recreation possibilities. And be sure to check our Spectator Sports chapter to find out where to see others competing in the games you love to watch.

We've provided information about where and how to get rental equipment for many of the activities listed here. Some rentals have to be reserved ahead of time, and we've told you about them. Even when it's not necessary, though, we think it's a good idea to call in advance so you have a better chance of getting what you need. Be sure to check our Shopping chapter if you've arrived minus some vital piece of gear or clothing.

Perhaps the most complex information in this chapter has to do with our multiuse trails, so we've consolidated some of the special rules and exceptions here. Before you turn to the sections on cycling, hiking and backpacking, and horseback riding, please take a moment to read the next few paragraphs.

Balloning
Boating
Bowling
Climbing
Cross-Country Skiing
Cycling
Fishing
Golf
Hiking and Backpacking
Horseback Riding
Hunting
Jeep Tours
Organized Sports and Other Recreation
Roller-Skating
Skiing and Snowboarding
Skydiving
Snowmobiling
Swimming

If camping is part of your plan, remember that campfires are allowed only in the grates in designated campgrounds, and violating this regulation can cause you—and potentially others—a great deal of trouble. The possible penalties are explained in an Insiders' Tip in our Campgrounds and RV Sites chapter. And, as the name implies, there's extensive camping information in that chapter.

Some of our trails will take you through wildlife areas, and we remind you to use caution in the presence of wild animals, no matter how docile they appear. Bison may look cumbersome, but they can gallop faster than you can, even when you're on two wheels.

We'd like you to note that the Black Elk Wilderness, 9,824 acres in the heart of the Norbeck Wildlife Preserve, is off limits to all but those on foot or horseback. No mechanized equipment is allowed here, not even a chain saw, because modern-day disruptions are out of place in the wilderness.

If you're out in the wilds during the summer, be prepared for afternoon thunderstorms, which sometimes unleash some pretty hefty hailstones (ask any local auto insurance agent). When winter's here, storms and blizzards in the higher hills can dump an average of 150 inches of snow a year, so pack with that in mind.

Just so you know, the elevation along our trails varies from approximately 4,200 feet to about 7,200 feet; maps and brochures will give you the specifications for individual trails. If a trail is closed for natural-resource management, please respect that and move on to a different one—there are plenty of paths to go around. Remember that trail etiquette gives horses the right of way.

And please, tread lightly. Don't litter. Leave your mark by leaving no trace. Then, when you return, we'll say, "Welcome back."

The wind sets your course when you take a balloon ride over the Black Hills. PHOTO: COURTESY OF SOUTH DAKOTA TOURISM

Ballooning

What could be prettier than sunrise over the Black Hills? And what finer way to experience it than at a leisurely pace in a hot-air balloon? Most people choose this activity during the summer, but winter is a good time, too—you even have the advantage of beating the windchill factor as you travel at the same speed as the breeze. Whatever time of year you go ballooning, dress in light layers (more when it's cold) so you can make adjustments. And plan to be up before dawn—around here, balloons fly mostly during the calm of early morning.

Central Hills

Dakota Balloon
3758 Jolly La., Rapid City
(605) 393–8808

A balloon ride is just the thing to sweep you off your feet for a special occasion. David Hendrickson, a licensed commercial balloon pilot, instructor, and designated FAA examiner, specializes in what he calls "personal rides" for anniversaries, birthdays, marriage proposals, and other significant events. You might kiss the treetops, dip low in the wicker basket for a "splash and dash" into a pond, or rise to 10,000 feet on your hour-long flight over Rapid City and the foothills. Depending on the wind direction, you might head for the Hills or soar over the prairie or Ellsworth Air Force Base. Upon landing you'll toast each other with champagne and receive a certificate as a memento.

Rides are available during early mornings and evenings year-round, weather permitting, and you can even arrange a "night flight," a glorious predawn excursion that lifts off in the dark and is guided back to Earth with the first rays of the sun. The price is $175 per person; call for night-flight prices. All rides include transportation back to the launch site. Weather conditions and other factors dictate the number of passengers, with a maximum of four.

Southern Hills

Black Hills Balloons
U.S. 16 W., Custer
(605) 673–2520, (800) 568–5320

Gain a new perspective as you leave Earth and drift at altitudes of 7,500 feet (2,100 feet above the ground) or more, for an hour or longer. Seen from aloft, pine-clad peaks, buffalo herds, elk, deer, Mount Rushmore, or Crazy Horse Memorial will leave an indelible impression. Any way the wind blows, your hot-air balloon ride will be an unforgettable experience—and since no two flights are identical, the owners guarantee that yours will be unique. When you touch down you'll mark the occasion with champagne, croissants, muffins, and cheeses, and your free-spirited daring will earn you a flight certificate. Plan on three hours to accommodate launch preparations, flight time, and the return van ride. Flights with experienced, licensed balloon pilots are available daily (weather permitting) between early May and the end of September and during the rest of the year by special arrangement. Five balloons with leather and wicker gondolas are available to carry two to 12 passengers, but reservations are needed for all flights.

The fare is $165 per child and $210 per adult. Black Hills Balloons is just outside the Custer city limits across from Pizza Hut.

Boating

For a region with no natural lakes, we have an astonishing number of places to launch boats. Most popular are motorized pleasure boats and personal watercraft, but you'll also see sailboats, catamarans, fishing boats, paddleboats, canoes, kayaks, and rowboats on our waters.

Power boaters, water-skiers, sailers, and riders of personal watercraft are drawn to our largest lakes, all of which are accessible from U.S. 385: Pactola Reservoir west of Rapid City, Sheridan Lake southwest of Rapid City, and Angostura Reservoir southeast of Hot Springs. All

A variety of human-powered boats is available for rent at Sylvan Lake in Custer State Park.
PHOTO: STEVEN A. PAGE

three have marinas where you can rent boats and buy supplies (see below).

Many of our smaller lakes are set aside for no-wake boating (less than 5 MPH) to heighten the enjoyment of trollers, canoeists, and others seeking a slower-paced, more contemplative experience. Among them is popular Deerfield Lake, which is off Pennington County Road 17 northwest of Hill City.

Additional restrictions apply at still other locations. For example, motors with more than 25 horsepower are not allowed in Bear Butte Lake, located off Highway 79 northeast of Sturgis. Electric motors only are allowed at Cold Brook and Cotton-wood Springs reservoirs, which are off U.S. 385 and U.S. 18, respectively, west of Hot Springs. Motors are prohibited alto-gether on Sylvan, Legion, and Center lakes in Custer State Park. And boating is not allowed at all in zoned swimming areas.

This list is not exhaustive; for more information call the Forest Supervisor's Office at (605) 673-2251 or the state Game, Fish & Parks Department at (605) 394-2391. The department's annual South Dakota Fishing Handbook also contains information about boating regulations.

The Cheyenne River offers limited canoeing, although the water level is often too low during the summer and fall. There are no designated access points, but the lower end of Angostura Reservoir is a convenient launch site.

Any boat more than 12 feet long and all motorboats must be registered either in South Dakota or your home state. An out-of-state license allows you to enjoy our lakes for 60 days. If you dock here, you need a South Dakota license, which is available from any county treasurer's office or the licensing office of the state Division of Motor Vehicles, 118 West Capitol Avenue, Pierre, South Dakota 57501. Boats can be licensed for one to three years, and license fees range from $11 to $81.

Life jackets are mandatory, as are proper lights between sunset and sunrise. The following locations rent boats to the public.

A catamaran catches the wind on Angostura Reservoir. PHOTO: BARBARA TOMOVICK

Central Hills

Pactola Pines Marina
23060 Custer Gulch Rd., Rapid City
(605) 343–4283

Pontoon boats can be rented for two hours or a full day. Rates depend on the size of the boat and day of the week; generally they range from $60 to $160. Fishing boats with six-horsepower motors are also available for rent, either hourly or daily; the rates range from $25 to $55. Life jackets and instruction are included. A snack bar at the marina serves chicken, ice cream, and beverages.

The marina also rents its 200-plus boat slips, mostly by the season, but overnights can sometimes be accommodated with advance notice. Prices vary, so please call for that information.

The marina is on Pactola Reservoir's south shore. To get there, turn right off U.S. 385 at the Black Hills National Forest Visitor Center.

Sheridan Lake Marina
16451 Sheridan Lake Rd., Rapid City
(605) 574–2169

A variety of boats and recreational equipment can be rented here. Canoes that accommodate three to four people rent for $8.00 for the first hour, $5.00 an hour thereafter. Fourteen-foot, four-passenger aluminum fishing boats with outboard motors cost $20.00 for two hours, with reduced rates for additional time. Pontoons that can hold 8 to 10 people start at $60.00 for two hours. All rentals include fuel, life jackets, and other mandatory safety equipment. Please call for age limits to rent various boats. The marina offers ice fishing in the winter.

About 4 of the approximately 70 boat slips are available for short-term rental at $10.00 a night; other prices vary, so call. The marina store with boat and equipment rentals is at the North Recreation Area, which is accessible from Sheridan Lake Road or U.S. 385. The marina is closed in March and October.

Southern Hills

Common Cents Marina
Off U.S. 385 at Angostura
Reservoir, Hot Springs
(605) 745–6665

A 16-foot fishing boat and pontoons in two sizes can be rented here. Boat rental costs $100 per day. An 18-foot pontoon rents for $150 per day, while a 20-footer goes for $200. Life jackets and safety equipment are included, but you pay for your own gas. The minimum age for all rentals is 21.

Boat slips are available by the day, week, month, or season. Daily rates are $10; call for other rates. The marina is at the north end of the reservoir.

Custer State Park Custer
(605) 255–4772, (800) 658–3530

Paddleboats, rowboats, and one-person kayaks can be rented at Sylvan Lake and Legion Lake resorts. Aquacycles and hydrobikes are also for rent. Call for prices.

Bowling

Bowling is a serious sport for many Black Hills residents, as evidenced by the heavy use local leagues make of our bowling alleys. Most of the bowling opportunities are in the Northern and Central Hills, and we've listed some, though not all of them, below.

Northern Hills

Bedrock Lanes
145 Glendale Dr., Lead
(605) 584–9013

There's a strong emphasis on youth league bowling here, but the 12 lanes of tenpins are open to everyone. Hours are noon to "closing" in winter and 6:00 P.M. to "closing" in summer seven days a week, and reservations usually are not needed. An arcade room, a pro shop selling equipment, a snack bar, a bar serving beer and wine coolers, and even party facilities add to the amenities. You can bowl for $2.00 per game and rent shoes for $1.00 Lessons from a certified coach are available.

Key City Lanes
910 First St., Sturgis
(605) 347-2741

Key City Lanes caters to many crowds, with Rockin' Bowl for teens on Friday nights (9:00 P.M. to midnight), Scotch Doubles on Saturday nights (9:00 P.M. until around 1:00 A.M.), and plenty of league play every evening from 6:30 until 8:30 or 9:00 P.M. It's a good idea to call and ask how many of the 12 lanes are open at any given time. In addition to tenpins, you'll find video games, pool, and Foosball, plus a full-service restaurant and lounge and a pro shop selling equipment.

Key City opens at 9:00 A.M. on weekdays and 11:00 A.M. on weekends. Closing time is "whenever," meaning 10:00 P.M. or later, depending on the demand for play. Games cost $1.75; Rockin' Bowl is $8.00 for three hours and Scotch Doubles are $5.00. Shoes rent for 50 cents a pair.

Lucky Strike Lanes
1740 Ryan Rd., Spearfish
(605) 642-7367

No frills, just six lanes of tenpins are what you'll find here. You don't need a reservation, but since Lucky Strike hosts plenty of local league competition, we're told it's a good idea to call ahead and make sure there's space available when you want to play. Hours vary, but generally Lucky Strike is open from noon to 10:00 P.M. daily. Rates vary, too, but during the times of heaviest play (after 6:00 P.M. and on weekends) games cost $2.00 and shoes cost 50 cents. Senior and student rates are available.

Central Hills

Meadowood Lanes
3809 Sturgis Rd., Rapid City
(605) 343-5985

There's enough enthusiastic clientele to keep this bowling alley open 365 days a year. With 36 lanes of tenpins and computerized scoring, the place is busy all the time. During the winter, leagues play every night, so it can be difficult to find a spot between 6:00 and 9:00 P.M. (except on Saturdays). You'll want to call ahead to find out how many lanes are open during those hours. There are frequent tournaments for every age group too, and you can call or stop in to check the schedule. This could be the perfect place to host a birthday party (most people bring their own cake and dishes) or other gathering, because there's more to do here than bowl. There's a lounge with a full bar, a full-service restaurant, pool tables, video games, and video lottery machines. For the serious bowler, the pro shop sells the accessories you need for your game, and there's an expert on hand to answer questions and make sure you get the right equipment.

Meadowood Lanes is open from 8:00 A.M. until midnight every day except Thanksgiving, Christmas, and New Year's Day, when it's open from 2:00 P.M. to midnight. Prices range from $1.90 to $2.70. Shoes may be rented for $1.50. Inquire about reduced rates for parties, and summer rates.

Climbing

You'll find world-class rock climbing among our granite peaks and limestone outcroppings, and listed below are the areas most highly recommended by local climbers. The most frequented spots have their own guidebooks, and we've mentioned some of them in their respective listings. And we've listed some of the most popular climbs along with their difficulty ratings, which are in parentheses. If you need books, maps, gear, or information, don't hesitate to stop in at our local climbing shops, which are listed here. We also tell you where you can find lessons and guide services.

Please be aware that helicopter tours operate in the Hills during the summer (see our Attractions chapter), and that climbers say the noise sometimes interferes with their communication. This is particularly true in the Cathedral Spires area of the Needles.

A growing number of rock climbers looking to expand their abilities are turning to ice climbing these days. Opportunities are limited here, but Spearfish Canyon (Bridal Veil Falls in particular) in the Northern Hills offers short, grade 1 climbs that are close to the road. The back side of Harney Peak, in the Black Elk Wilderness, develops 130-foot floes, but the area is hard to reach and you have to snowshoe in when the snow is deep. Also, there are no comprehensive guidebooks to tell you where to ice climb, so the best way to get information is to contact the local climbing shops.

Northern Hills

Spearfish Canyon
U.S. 14A, Spearfish

As if we needed any more reasons to brag about Spearfish Canyon, its limestone palisades are becoming increasingly popular with climbers. These routes are primarily bolted sport climbs, requiring little in the way of your own hardware. No maps or guidebooks are available for this area, so you'll have to contact one of the shops listed below for information.

Central Hills

Falling Rock
Hwy. 44, Rapid City

Another bolted sport climbing area on a limestone ridge, Falling Rock is 3.1 miles west of Rapid City. Turn left (if you're coming from town) off Highway 44 onto Falling Rock Road, a dirt road where you'll find two parking areas a short distance apart, both on your left. Trails leading from the first parking area will take you to the top of the limestone cliff, and those leading from the second one go to the cliff base. Again, contact our local climbing shops for information about routes.

Mount Rushmore Climbing Area
Hwy. 244, Keystone

Over the past couple of decades, the area northwest of the four famous faces has become increasingly popular among climbers. The routes along the granite here tend to be bolted, so you won't have to pack much hardware; you can learn more about them in the Mount Rushmore National Memorial Climber's Guide by Vernon Phinney, which is widely available. You can park along the highway in any of several pull-offs between Horse Thief Lake (on Highway 244) and the monument. Recommended classic routes include Waves (5.6), Stardancer (5.8), Baba Cool (5.9), and Mr. Critical (5.11).

Southern Hills

The Needles
Hwy. 87, Custer State Park

Climbers popularized the granite spires along the Needles Highway (Highway 87) in the 1940s and 1950s, and this well-known area still offers traditional climb-

Rock climbers come to the Black Hills for sport, traditional, and wilderness climbing adventures.

PHOTO: COURTESY OF SOUTH DAKOTA TOURISM

ing as well as bolted routes. On many of them you'll have to pack various forms of hardware and place your own gear for protection. The Needles area is recommended for somewhat more experienced climbers with good route-finding skills. Many of the newer routes are not included in Paul Piana's comprehensive *Touch the Sky*, which was published in 1983; other titles include *Recommended Climbing Routes in the Needles of Custer State Park*, by John Page; and *Black Hills Needles, Selected Free Climbs* by Dingus McGee and The Last Pioneer Woman; and *# 07 Devils Tower, Needles*, by John Harlin, published by Falcon Publishing.

Please note that this area is within the boundaries of Custer State Park, and you'll need a park entrance license if you drive in. Parking is available along the highway from Sylvan Lake to the spires. Classic routes include Riddle (5.7), Tricouni Nail (5.8), and Nantucket Sleighride (5.10). If you want a mountaineering wilderness experience, read up on the many spectacular outcroppings in the Norbeck Wildlife Preserve.

Wyoming

Devils Tower National Monument
U.S. 24, Devils Tower, WY
(307) 467-5283, (800) 354-6316

You'll find a wealth of information about Devils Tower in our Daytrips and Weekend Getaways chapter, but we've included it here because it's one of North America's premier crack-climbing areas. *Devils Tower Monument National Climbing Book,* by Guilmette, Carrier, and Gardiner, lists more than 200 routes. Among the most popular are Durrance (5.7), Soler (5.7), Walt Bailey Memorial (5.9), and Matador (5.11). Climbers are asked to refrain from climbing here in June, especially during the weekends before and after the summer solstice, out of respect for Native American religious observances.

Lessons, Equipment, and Guide Services

Northern and Central Hills

Adventure Sport
900 Jackson Blvd., Rapid City
(605) 341-6707
215 E. Jackson Blvd., Spearfish
(605) 642-5557

Climbing classes and guided climbs for all skill levels are available with experienced, certified (first aid and CPR) guides through these stores, who can take you to Devils Tower, the Mount Rushmore area, and the Needles. Call for information about the Black Hills Climbing Coalition. Group rates are available. It's best to call ahead for reservations. The shops also sell equipment, clothing, maps and guidebooks, and they rent out climbing shoes.

Granite Sports
301 Main St., Hill City
(605) 574–2121

The helpful staff here is made up of experienced climbers. The shop is an excellent source for climbing gear and Patagonia clothing, maps, guidebooks, and lots of local climbing information. For lessons, guide service, and shoe rentals, you can simply step around the corner to the climbing school.

Sylvan Rocks Climbing School & Guide Service
81 Elm St., Hill City
(605) 574–2425
www.sylvanrocks.com

Started in 1989 by expert climber and Black Hills native Susan Scheirbeck, Sylvan Rocks offers courses from entry level through advanced. The school is accredited by the American Mountain Guides Association, which has reviewed and approved its safety programs and operation procedures. Classes are available daily from May through October, weather permitting; you can sign up for a couple of hours or one to three days of instruction, and courses can include a climb to the summit of Devils Tower (see the listing above). Rates vary and include all the gear you need to learn the ropes. Ask about group rates for six or more people. Reservations are strongly recommended.

Guide service, including guiding at the Tower, is available for climbers with solid technical skills who want to make optimal use of their climbing time. Climbing shoes can be rented.

Cross-Country Skiing

Forgive us if we brag a little bit about our cross-country skiing. Our moderate altitudes and temperatures, combined with plenty of dry, powdery snow, provide just the right conditions for a satisfying, invigorating workout in a beautiful alpine setting. And although you're likely to meet kindred spirits on the trails, you'll never feel crowded. If you're feeling brave, you can strike out on your own and break trail in the Black Hills National Forest. All the trails listed below are in the Northern Hills, where the snow is deepest and most dependable.

Big Hill
Spearfish Ranger District,
2014 Main St., Spearfish
(605) 642–4622
(800) 445–3474 (conditions)

Beginners and experts alike will find something to match their skills on 16 miles of mostly groomed trails that wind through groves of aspen, pine, and spruce 8 miles south of Spearfish. The area is on Forest Service land but is maintained for skiing through an agreement with the Northern Hills Cross-Country Ski Club, which pays for the grooming. The donation box at the trailhead is for that purpose. The popular Loop A.1 is recommended for beginners; other trails are more challenging. The demanding Loops C and D cover a lot of ground and appeal mostly to accomplished skiers. C has the best overlooks, with views of dazzling Spearfish Canyon; a casual tour with time out for stops can easily take three hours. Maps are available at Forest Service ranger stations and at the trailhead.

To get to Big Hill, take Jackson Boulevard in Spearfish west, turn north onto Jonas Boulevard, and then turn west onto

Oliver Street. Pass Pope & Talbot sawmill, turn south onto Forest Service Road 134, and go about 8 miles to the trailhead.

Deer Mountain Ski Area
U.S. 85, Lead
(605) 584-3230
(888) 265-2197 (conditions)

About 10 miles (15 kilometers) of gently sloping, groomed trails wind through the woods, beginning near the base of the downhill slopes. You can ski from 9:00 A.M. until dark. You can also rent skis, poles, and boots at the ski lodge. Deer Mountain is open from approximately late November until about the end of March. It's closed Monday and Tuesday except during the Christmas season.

Eagle Cliff
Spearfish Ranger District, 2014 Main St.
Spearfish
(605) 642-4622
(800) 445-3474 (conditions)

Approximately 23 miles of marked, ungroomed trails southwest of Cheyenne Crossing offer some of the finest skiing in the Hills. (Cheyenne Crossing is at the junction of U.S. 85 and U.S. 14A on the south end of Spearfish Canyon.) The closest trail, Dead Ox, is about 4 miles from the Crossing, with the nearest official trailhead (Bratwurst) and parking area another 3 miles down the road. Trail names such as Bratwurst, Wipeout, and What the Hell are descriptive and amusing and serve as a lasting legacy to the volunteers who forged and named them (including, dear readers, one of the authors of this book) in the 1970s and 1980s. Most of these trails are easy to moderately difficult, but steep canyons and twisting turns test your mettle. If you're lucky enough to have two cars, you can park each in a different lot and enjoy a nice long trek without having to retrace a single glide of your skis. But the trails interconnect and loop around so that you can sally forth with plenty of options and still wind up back at your starting point if you're limited to one vehicle.

Cross-country skiers find ideal conditions in the Black Hills. PHOTO: COURTESY OF SOUTH DAKOTA TOURISM

Sunny Meadow and Bratwurst are good trails for beginners and the single-vehicled. Eagle Cliff is a fairly easy trail, as well; Roller Coaster, Deep Snow, and Wipeout are more demanding. Dead Ox, the most popular trail in the system, gets twisty and steep, and Lily Park can be downright scary.

The Forest Service has made Eagle Cliff an official ski area (although it doesn't sanction trails that are on private property), making it easier to maintain the trails and keep roadside parking areas plowed. Maps are available at Forest Service ranger stations, the Cheyenne Crossing Store, and the Bratwurst trailhead.

Rentals

Northern and Central Hills

Adventure Sport
900 Jackson Blvd., Rapid City
(605) 341–6707

215 E. Jackson Blvd., Spearfish
(605) 642–5557

The shops rent cross-country skis and snowshoes for the day or for the weekend. Season rates are available, too; call for information.

Cycling

Many of our communities have recreational paths that are ideal for riding a bicycle, whether for fun or transportation. They're easy to spot, because they're almost always in use by cyclists, joggers, and walkers. If you're a mountain biker with a yen for the backcountry, just keep reading: We've listed some Insider favorites. Don't bypass our back roads and cross-country ski trails (see the cross-country skiing entries), which offer excellent riding, too.

Centennial Trail (No. 89)

If you've read the introduction to this chapter, you already know something about this trail. Here we'll add that bikes are allowed along most of it except the portions in the Black Elk Wilderness and Wind Cave National Park. Alternate routes are available around the Black Elk Wilderness that add just a few miles to your trip—a trail map will help you choose your path. Plans for an official bypass never reached fruition, but at this writing the Forest Service has a grant to study the concept anew.

The trail ends (or begins) in Wind Cave park, so avoiding the 6-mile stretch there is simply a matter of ending or beginning your trek at the park boundary. The trail itself winds through grasslands and mountain peaks between Bear Butte

Cycling is popular in the Black Hills and most trails permit multiple forms of usage. PHOTO: BERT GILDART

State Park in the north and Wind Cave park in the south. (You can read about these two great parks in our Parks and Grasslands chapter.) Along the way you'll see lakes, streams, grasslands, dramatic rock outcroppings, and wildlife. There are more than two dozen well-marked trailheads and access points, some with night parking for extended trips. For complete information, consult the *Centennial Trail User's Guide,* which is widely available wherever you find brochures in the area.

Its length and accessibility make the Centennial Trail ideal for any style of trip—it's really just a matter of deciding where you want to start and where you want to end up. One section we recommend is the 10-mile stretch between Pactola Reservoir and Sheridan Lake. Start at the Rapid Creek Trailhead at Pactola. From Highway 44 west of Rapid City go 2.1 miles south on U.S. 385, turn left onto gravel Pactola Basin Road, then go one-half mile to a four-way intersection, turn left, and park at the trailhead. Drop a second vehicle at Dakota Point Trailhead by taking U.S. 385; go east 1.6 miles on Sheridan Lake Road southwest of Rapid City, turn right onto gravel Dakota Point Road (Forest Service Road 434), and go another 0.3 of a mile to the trailhead, which will be on your left. Needless to say, you can do this in reverse if you want to.

Custer State Park
Custer
(605) 255-4515

The park has a variety of trails that are moderately difficult to difficult. The shortest is through the 3-mile Grace Coolidge Walk-in Fishing Area, which runs between Center Lake and Grace Coolidge Campground, with a trailhead at either end. Three other trailheads—Iron Creek, Badger Hole, and French Creek—provide access to the 22 miles of Centennial Trail that thread through the park. The most difficult section, from Badger Hole to French Creek, is also the shortest at 4.2 miles. Less strenuous are the 7.3 miles between Iron Creek and Badger Hole, and the 10.3 miles from French

Creek to the Wind Cave National Park border. Big Tree Robbers Roost Draw Trail makes a 10.5-mile loop that begins and ends at French Creek Trailhead. Maps are available at Custer State Park visitor centers, but you can also ride on any trail or logging road in the park that isn't posted as closed.

See listings below under Bike Tours and Rentals for information about where to find bicycles.

Deerfield Lake Loop Trail (No. 40L)

This fairly easy 10-mile trail circles Deerfield Lake, which is not only scenic but gives you the added advantage of a place to take a cooling dip after, or even during, your ride. Also, three campgrounds are a short distance from the trail—Dutchman, Whitetail, and Custer Trails—where you can refill your water bottle en route during the summer. Access points with free parking are Gold Run and Hilltop trailheads on the south side of the lake off F.S. 17 (also called Deerfield Road, which runs northwest from Hill City), and North Shore Trailhead on the northwest side (follow FS 17 to FS 461 and turn south). You can access the trail from Custer Trails Campground, too, but during the summer you'll pay a user or camping fee to leave your car there. The trail offers varied scenery from pine forest on the south side of the lake to an open meadow, known as Reynolds Prairie, on the north.

George S. Mickelson Trail (No.104)
www.mickelsontrail.com

Named for the South Dakota governor who championed it and then met an untimely death in a 1993 plane crash, the Mickelson Trail is an abandoned railroad bed that has undergone a rails-to-trails transformation through the joint efforts of government agencies and local volunteers. Completed in the fall of 1998, the 10-foot-wide trail offers 114 miles of scenic beauty and gentle grades for nonmotorized recreation between Deadwood and Edgemont. Restored tunnels and existing trestles along the Rochford-to-Mystic stretch speak to its railroading past.

Linda Sandness, who in her capacity as a Coordinator for Visitor Services for South Dakota's Parks and Recreation Service, says that although she's traveled the trail's length and enjoyed it all, she nevertheless has a favorite section. Sandness says she's partial to the 18-mile section between Dumont and Mystic. She says she likes it because "It's all downhill, making it very nice for a family outing." Of course, that leaves one person having to ride back uphill to retrieve the car, but, generally, that doesn't take much more than an hour.

But Sandness says the area offers more than just an easy ride. She says the trail parallels a creek and as you ride, you can hear the brook and all kinds of birds. Sandness also enjoys the stretch for its rich and exciting interpretation of local history. Ms. Sandness played an integral role in creating interpretative materials, which may, in part, help explain her preference. Bottom line: She has a right to be proud, for the bike trail passes by old towns, such as Standoff and Montana Miner that are no longer in existence. Explaining the role they played in South Dakota's rich history has been a major department thrust. The work required several years of planning and creation, but beginning in the year 2002, interpretive information will be posted at strategic sites along the trail. As well, most trailhead locations now include shelters with water and interpretive information.

This trail relies on small user fees to help with its upkeep. Those 12 and older are required to buy a daily ($2.00) or annual ($10.00) trail pass. Fees are payable at self-registration boxes and some businesses along the trail. No fee is required within city limits. Check out the Web site for great information and registration for the annual fall trail ride.

Bike Tours and Rentals

Northern Hills

Latchstring Village All Season Sports Center
U.S. 14A, Spearfish Canyon
(605) 584-2207, (800) 439-8544

Mountain bikes can be rented here for a half or full day, including helmets. Trails depart from the premises of Spearfish Canyon Resort.

Central Hills

Two Wheeler Dealer Cycle & Fitness
100 East Blvd. N., Rapid City
(605) 343-0524

Here you can rent mountain bikes, kiddie carts, tandems, and car racks. Helmets are included with bike rentals; call for daily or extended rates.

Southern Hills

Custer State Park
Custer
(605) 255-4515

You can rent mountain bikes for use in the park at Legion Lake Lodge, (605) 255-4521, during the summer. Rentals range from $8.00 to $35.00, and prices include a helmet. Reservations are recommended.

Trailside Bikes
35 Sixth St., Custer
(605) 673-5526, (888) 673-2453
www.trailsidebikes.com

Suspension mountain bikes rent for $25 a day and solid-frame bikes for $22; half-day rentals are $22 and $18, respectively. All prices include a helmet and bike lock. Trailside Bikes also offers customized backcountry tours with optional support-and-gear wagon, food, camping gear, pickup, and delivery. A new feature is weeklong tours with the Mickelson Trail as the backbone for daily side trips. Tour prices vary. The shop is open from mid-May to mid-October. Bike sales and service also are available.

Fishing

Around here, angling is a year-round activity, and we seem to have enough lakes and streams to satisfy all enthusiasts, whether they prefer to fish while standing on shore, sitting in a boat, crouched over a hole in the ice, tucked into a float tube, or slogging up to their wader tops in midstream.

Fishing is a favorite pastime of Black Hills visitors and residents alike. PHOTO: STEVEN A. PAGE

Lake and in Spearfish Creek up north. And you'll find bass swimming in Pactola Reservoir west of Rapid City.

Needless to say, these are just a few of our excellent fishing holes. For a complete rundown, pick up a free copy of the Game, Fish & Parks Department's *South Dakota Guide to Public Fishing Waters,* which is available through license agents.

And speaking of licenses, you'll need one unless you're fishing at an attraction or campground where it's not required—you'll find those places listed in their respective chapters in this book. Licenses are available at sporting goods stores, convenience stores, and other businesses as well as at some county treasurers' offices. And don't forget about entrance fees at our state parks and user fees at some of our lakes.

Daily and possession limits for trout have gotten stricter since a survey of local anglers showed they want to catch bigger fish. (Raising bigger fish in our hatcheries means raising fewer of them.) Thus, the daily trout limit is five, with just one of those being 14 inches or longer. You're allowed to have not more than 10 trout in your possession—and that includes the ones back home in your freezer or packed in ice at your campsite—at any one time.

Limits are higher for other species, and you'll find all that information, along with regulations for organic bait, catch-and-release areas, and so forth, in the yearly *South Dakota Fishing Handbook* issued by Game, Fish & Parks. Make sure you get the current copy, which comes out around the first of the year.

Wheelchair-accessible fishing is available at Pactola Reservoir and at Strawberry Lake, which is off U.S. 385 south of Deadwood.

Guide Service

Central Hills

Dakota Angler & Outfitter
516 Seventh St., Rapid City
(605) 341–2450, (888) 319–3474
www.flyfishsd.com

Everything here is geared toward fly-fishing. The shop offers guided half- and full-day trips as well as fishing and fly-tying les-

Although trout aren't native to this area (having arrived by wagon in the 1880s), we think it's safe to say they're the main attraction for Black Hills anglers, along with walleye and largemouth bass. Most of our trout—brookies, browns, rainbows, and a brook-lake cross called splake found in Deerfield Lake—are spawned in our fish hatcheries. Nevertheless, some native reproduction is taking place, particularly among brook trout.

Walleye fishers tend to gravitate toward the warm waters of Angostura Reservoir near Hot Springs. Sheridan Lake southwest of Rapid City is a good place to cast for perch and northern pike. Colorful rainbow trout bite in Custer State Park's Sylvan

As many an angler knows, Black Hills trout streams were made for fly-fishing. PHOTO: COURTESY OF SOUTH DAKOTA TOURISM

sons. Trips start at $185 to $275 and include transportation and lunch or a snack. Reservations are required. The cost for lessons varies, so call for information. The shop also sells equipment, clothing, gifts, and even artwork. You can rent a fly rod, reel and waders.

Golf

You don't have to live in Florida or Arizona to be a golf nut, as many Black Hills Insiders can attest. Some love the game so much you can find them on the golf course in the middle of winter if it's free of snow. Most of our communities have well-managed public or private nine-hole courses, and some can offer you 18 holes as well. We've listed a few Insider favorites here, but local city parks departments (see the gray box at the end of this chapter) can help you locate others.

All the courses listed here have golf shops as well as motorized carts, pull-carts, and clubs that you can rent. All have grass greens, and most have a spikeless policy, so ask about footwear when you call to reserve a tee time. It's also wise to call ahead and make sure the course you want to play won't be closed for a special event just when you're ready for a round of golf.

In the listings, yardages are for white tees, and weekdays are Monday through Friday. Please be aware that although we tend to be pretty casual around here, appropriate golf attire is required on the course.

Northern Hills

Spearfish Canyon Country Club
Intersection of U.S. 14 and 14A, Spearfish (605) 642-7156

The only 18-hole golf course in the northern Black Hills has a lot to recommend it, not the least of which is the historical integrity of its original nine holes (the front nine, or nos. 1 through 9). You can play them today the same way golfers did in pre-heavy-equipment 1922, when the natural lay of the land dictated the design of greens and fairways. The views here are still beautiful, too, and at the eighth hole (par 3), which is situated on a ridge looking into the mouth of Spearfish Canyon, you're required to aim the ball through a narrow lane of tall pine trees. Tee times are requested for the par 71, semiprivate course. You'll find bentgrass greens and a wide variety of elevation changes, plus an outdoor driving range, a Professional Golf Association pro and teaching pro on staff, and a full-service bar and restaurant.

The course is open all year, weather permitting, and play is allowed from dawn 'til dark whenever the weather permits. Weekday greens fees are $38 for 18 holes, $19 for nine. Weekend and holiday fees are $43 and $22, respectively. Cart rentals are $12 for 18 holes, $7 for nine holes.

Tomahawk Lake Country Club
U.S. 385 S., Deadwood
(605) 578–9979, (605) 578–2080

You'll play on a true mountain course here, where five tee boxes are elevated to compensate for the rolling terrain. Two creeks run through the picturesque nine-hole course, making your game more challenging in spite of wide fairways. There are two par 5 holes for men and one for women, with a total par 36 for the 3,300-yard course. A practice range, full bar, and restaurant take care of your needs off the course. Open play means there's no need to reserve a tee time, but you do have to abide by the rules governing ladies' day, which begins at 2:00 P.M. on Wednesday, and men's day, which starts at noon on Thursday.

The course opens as early as possible in the spring but for sure by May 1. It closes October 31. Hours are 7:00 A.M. until dark. Greens fees are $15 for nine holes and $22 for 18. Carts are $12 for nine holes, $20 for 18.

Tomahawk is 8 miles south of Deadwood.

Central Hills

Hart Ranch Golf Course
23759 Arena Dr., Rapid City
(605) 341–5703

Bring your A game, not your B game, advises resident PGA pro Craig Hatch. This challenging 18-hole course is for veteran golfers who can play around Spring Creek where it winds through the 6,285-yard, par 72 course. The peaceful valley setting could inspire you to walk as you play your round. Lessons and a complete practice facility are available, and there's also a snack shop. Alcohol is not served and is not allowed on this well-manicured course. Tee times can be requested up to seven days in advance.

The course is open daily from the last Saturday in April through October 31, weather permitting. Starting time varies with the season, but from late May until early September, the course opens at 7:00 A.M. Monday through Friday and 6:30 A.M. on weekends. At all times, it closes at dark. Greens fees are $34 for 18 holes and $18 for nine holes. Cart rentals are $23 per person and $14 per person, respectively.

To reach Hart Ranch Golf Course, take U.S. 16 8 miles south of Rapid City, turn left onto Neck Yoke Road across from Reptile Gardens, and left again at Spring Creek Road, then go 1.5 miles to the entrance.

Meadowbrook Municipal Golf Course
3625 Jackson Blvd., Rapid City
(605) 394–4191 (advance reservations)
(605) 394–4192 (same-day reservations)

Rated South Dakota's No. 3 golf course by *Golf Digest* in 1997, this city-operated, scenic course rates high with golfers who like a challenging game. Open daylight to dark whenever the weather permits, the 6,520-yard, par 72 course has 18 holes with bentgrass greens. A driving range, PGA pro, and lessons are at your disposal, and beer and snacks are available.

Weekday greens fees for nonresidents are $14.50 for nine holes, $25 for 18. Weekend and holiday nonresident fees are $16.75 for nine holes and $28 for 18. Rapid City area residents, juniors 18 and younger, and seniors 62 and older enjoy lower rates; please call for information. Cart rentals are $10 for nine holes, $18 for 18.

Southern Hills

Rocky Knolls Golf Course
U.S. 16 W., Custer
(605) 673–4481

Curious deer and marmots might be watching while you tee off at this tree-lined, nine-hole course, which borders West Dam and French Creek. Following the contour of the land, the 5,938-yard, par 36 course features rock outcroppings, bentgrass greens, and outstanding views of the Black Hills. Off the course, you'll find a grill, a full bar, and a putting green. Tee times are by reservation.

Rocky Knolls is open from May 1 to October 15; most of that time the hours are 7:00 A.M. to dusk. The course is closed to outside play every Tuesday afternoon beginning at 1:00 P.M. Greens fees are $13 for nine holes and $22 for 18 holes. Carts are $10 for each nine holes.

Southern Hills Municipal Golf Course
W. U.S. 18, Hot Springs
(605) 745–6400

This exceptionally lovely nine-hole course has won national recognition for its playability, turf conditions, aesthetics, and other advantages. *Golf Digest* rated it one of 50 four-star courses for the 1996–97 season, and several years earlier the National Golf Foundation named it one of the Midwest's top 32 courses—and it was the only facility in western South Dakota to win that distinction. The fairways here wind among abundant ponderosa pine trees, and most tee boxes are set on cliffs where you're required to shoot over canyons to the bentgrass greens. Most golfers play 18 holes, making the 5,700-yard course par 70. Riding is recommended because of the steepness, but walkers are welcome. Lessons and a driving range are available, and snacks and beer are served. Reservations are recommended but not required for tee times.

The well-groomed course is open from early March to October 31, weather permitting; summer hours are 7:00 A.M. to 7:00 P.M. Greens fees are $13 for nine holes, $22 for 18 holes Cart rentals are $13 for nine holes, $22 for 18.

The golf course is about one-half mile west of town.

Hiking and Backpacking

Trails in the Black Hills National Forest range from easy (see the George S. Mickelson Trail listing under Cycling) to steep (Crow Peak and Harney Peak, below). That means everyone from small children to veteran trekkers can ramble at his or her own pace. Needless to say, there are scores of scenic hiking opportunities not covered in this chapter; we have no doubt, however, that you'll find at least some of them in your wanderings, including those in our state and national parks.

Regardless of the length of your hike, make sure you take a good supply of drinking water, because in all likelihood you won't find any on the trail. And if you need water bottles or other equipment, stop by any of our sporting goods stores—you'll find several listed in our Shopping chapter.

Of special interest are four wheelchair-accessible trails. In the Northern Hills the mile-long Roughlock Trail begins at the parking lot at Spearfish

Canyon Lodge (see our Accommodations chapter) and goes to Roughlock Falls; take U.S. 14A through the canyon to the resort and turn onto F.S. 222. In the Central Hills are Veterans Point Trail (No. 56—please see the Close-up in this chapter), at the north end of Pactola Dam at Pactola Reservoir, the trail at Norbeck Overlook on U.S. 16A south of Keystone, and the Presidential Trail at Mount Rushmore.

Centennial Trail (No. 89)

We've covered much of the general information about the Centennial Trail in our Cycling section above, so we'll just add a few details about hiking and backpacking here. We'll also remind you about the prohibition on open fires that's addressed in the introduction to this chapter. Be aware that collecting natural objects in Wind Cave National Park is prohibited.

The entire 111 miles of the Centennial Trail are open to hiking, and if you've brought your tent along, you can set it up either in a designated campground or in the wilderness. (Most campgrounds charge a fee; please see our Campgrounds and RV Parks chapter.) If you want to camp in Wind Cave National Park's backcountry zone in the northwest section of the park, you need a free permit that's available at the park's visitor center or at either end of the Wind Cave portion of the trail. You must stay 100 feet from the trail or any water source and out of sight of the road while camping. If you camp in Custer State Park, you must stay in one of the campgrounds. (See our Campgrounds and RV Parks chapter for information about reserving campsites in the park.)

Many of the trailheads have long-term parking space, but if you plan to leave your car overnight or longer in Fort Meade National Recreation Area, Bear Butte State Park, or Wind Cave National Park, please notify a ranger.

Northern Hills

Crow Peak Trails (No. 64)

This hike is rated difficult, but you'll be glad you made the effort once you reach the summit of this historic landmark. Crow Peak takes its name from the Sioux Paha Karitukateyapi, "the hill where the Crows were killed" in a long-ago battle. After gaining 1,600 feet of elevation (to 5,800 feet) in a little more than 3 miles, you'll have a 360-degree view of South Dakota (including Bear Butte, which you can read about in our Parks and Grasslands chapter) as well as parts of Montana and Wyoming. There's also the half-mile Beaver Ridge Spur Trail for a side trip about halfway up the mountain. To reach the trailhead, which is southwest of Spearfish, take Utah Boulevard west out of town to Higgins Gulch Road (F.S. 214), turn south, and go 4 miles. Please note that this trail isn't intended or maintained for mountain bikes.

Central Hills

Flume Trail (No. 50)

This National Recreation Trail is reserved for hikers and with good reason: Along it

National Forest Trails

To build or to maintain—that is the question foresters face each year when presented with their limited trail budgets.

The Black Hills National Forest trail system consists of some 360 miles of track for hiking, horseback riding, bicycling, and cross-country skiing The heavy use those trails get shows how important they are. But in recent years, tighter purse strings in Washington, D.C., have meant tough choices about whether to build new trails to keep up with demand or maintain those we already have. Frequently, the choice is painfully obvious.

"When things start to deteriorate, they accelerate. You've got water coming down a trail and you've got to take care of it," said Rusty Wilder, a civil engineer at the Forest Supervisor's office in Custer.

The U.S.D.A. Forest Service gets some very welcome help from volunteers who clear downed trees, clean drainage structures, work on trail surface maintenance, repair and replace trail markers and signs, and perform heavy tasks such as bridge repairs. There's even an Adopt-a-Trail program that allows a volunteer group or individual to assume official responsibility for maintenance of a trail, or portion of a trail, under specific guidelines.

First, of course, trails have to be planned for and built, and both processes are more complex than you might expect.

The first step is to identify a need and the type of prospective users looking for new trails. Foresters survey potential sites—often old roads—by walking the area and examining aerial photos and topographic maps to ensure that a new trail will meet

A hiker in the Black Hills. PHOTO: BERT GILDART

specifications for grade and varied terrain. Then a decision is made about whether to do the work themselves or hire a contractor.

Wolfgang Schmidt of Nemo is one contractor who has worked for the Forest Service. In one instance, Schmidt said, he used a shovel and hand tools to build a trail in an area where heavy equipment couldn't be used.

"For me, to build one just by hand was quite a challenge. I really enjoyed that," said Schmidt, an affable man with a charming German accent. "I like the hard work and being outside in nature. It's been a wonderful experience for me."

Loren Poppert, a recreation forester in the Custer/Elk Mountain Ranger District, also finds satisfaction in the hard labor of trail building. He helped cut trees, move rocks, dig out trail tread on a side slope, and build retaining walls for the recently completed Hell Canyon Trail. Especially gratifying, he said, is the positive feedback, "hearing the comments about how nice of a trail it is and the number of people who love to hike it."

Doing things the old-fashioned way extends to hauling materials on pack mules into the Black Elk Wilderness, where federal regulations prohibit the use of mechanized equipment of any kind. Most years, local officials import a 10-mule pack string from Colorado for the beast-of-burden duties. In 1997, the most recent year when the sturdy Forest Service animals were used here, they hauled a whopping 28,000 pounds of gravel into Black Elk.

Most trail work is not so romantic, however. Without the help of present-day dirt-moving equipment, many of the trails we enjoy would not be so readily accessible.

But the human spirit can be just as powerful as any big machine. Thanks to a cooperative effort between the Forest Service and the Rapid City chapter of Disabled American Veterans (DAV), a paved trail at the north end of Pactola Reservoir allows people with disabilities to enjoy the outdoors in new ways. The DAV raised money to help with initial construction of the Veterans Point Trail, where anglers can now fish from wooden piers and future improvements are planned.

So the next time you set booted foot, waxed ski, or nubby tire on a Black Hills recreational trail, we know you won't take it for granted. In fact, we're certain you'll appreciate the hard work that's gone into making it available for you to enjoy.

are fragile historic artifacts and tunnels from 1880s gold mines that relied on the Rockerville Flume to carry water from Spring Creek to their operations. Read the trailside signs to learn more about that, and see our History chapter for information about the Black Hills gold rush.

Trailheads are located at the east end of Sheridan Lake, which is off U.S. 385 southwest of Rapid City; at Coon Hollow, off County Road 233 about one-fourth mile west of the intersection with U.S. 16 in Rockerville (which is south of Rapid City); and at points in between. A trail map will help you locate them.

The Upper Spring Creek Trailhead is closest to the two tunnels; it's about a mile west of the Spring Creek picnic area on Sheridan Lake Road southwest of Rapid City. You can leave the 11-mile-long trail for the 3-mile Spring Creek Loop at the north end or to ascend the trail to 5,331-foot Boulder Hill, whose summit provides awesome views of the Black Hills, Badlands, and prairies. The 1.5-mile stretch along the southeast shore of Sheridan Lake from the Calumet Trailhead is flat and doable for young children. You'll have to pay the $2.00 daily fee to park at Sheridan Lake Southside Campground where the trailhead is, but we think you'll agree that's a bargain for a memorable hike with your little ones. Turn east off U.S. 385 at the lake onto Calumet Road and follow the signs for the campground.

Harney Peak (Multiple trails)

To the Lakota of the Black Hills, Harney Peak was a mythical mountain. Black Elk, a prominent medicine man among the Oglala people, considered Harney Peak the center of the world. For him it was a place for vision quests and spiritual rejuvenation. In addition to the mountain's spiritual embodiments, Harney Peak is a significant mountain because it is the highest peak east of the main chain of the Rocky Mountains.

Harney Peak was named after General William S. Harney, the commanding officer of Lieutenant G. K. Warren, who mapped the peak during a military expedition to the Black Hills in 1857. Valentine McGillycuddy also climbed the peak in the nineteenth century, completing the ascent in 1875 at the age of 26. McGillycuddy mapped the peak and also photographed it. Later he served as an agent on the Pine Ridge Reservation and as the first president of the South Dakota School of Mines. When he died in 1940, his remains were cremated and placed at the base of a fire tower that had been con-structed on Harney Peak. A bronze plaque is cemented in the base of the stairway to the tower containing an inscription that reads, in part, *Wasicu Wakan*. In Lakota, the words mean "holy white man."

The stone fire tower was constructed in 1938 and 1939 by the Civilian Conservation Corps (CCC). The CCC also constructed stone steps leading to the tower, steps that hikers still ascend today. The peak's importance for detecting fires had long been recognized. From 1911, the tower had made the life of a fire lookout here a little less extreme. In 1967, more modern techniques of spotting fires took over, and today, the tower stands in mute testimony to the lonely life spotters led on the peak.

You'll find moderate or challenging hikes to the top of the Hills' tallest peak, depending on where you start. The easier—and more popular—hikes begin at Sylvan Lake in Custer State Park; the round-trip is about 7 miles. On the north side, Willow Creek/Harney Peak Trail (No. 9 North) ascends from just outside Willow Creek Horse Camp (off Highway 244, 3

At 7,242 feet, Harney Peak is the highest point between the Spanish Pyrenees and the Rocky Mountains. PHOTO: COURTESY OF SOUTH DAKOTA TOURISM

From Harney Peak Lookout you can gaze over four states as well as the Black Elk Wilderness Area.

PHOTO: BERT GILDART

GREAT FACES

Black Elk

Most people think of John G. Neihardt's classic book when they hear the name of Black Elk. First published in 1932 and still in print, *Black Elk Speaks: Being the Life Story of a Holy Man of the Oglala Sioux* recounted Black Elk's visions so powerfully and affected readers so profoundly that it has been credited with planting the seed not only for the 1960s cultural revolution but for the ongoing revival of Native American cultural and spiritual life.

Born in 1863, Black Elk participated in the Ghost Dance movement and rescued an infant from the carnage at Wounded Knee (see our Daytrips and Weekend Getaways chapters for information about the Wounded Knee Massacre). He also toured with Buffalo Bill's Wild West Show. In later life, he converted to Catholicism but also used the Red Road/Black Road (good actions/evil actions) approach in his tribal ministry. In the wrenching conclusion to Black Elk Speaks, he climbed Harney Peak with Neihardt and cried, "O make my people live!" Now, thousands of people each year visit Harney Peak in the protected Black Elk Wilderness, and Black Elk's people are finding renewed strength and identity in the old ways.

miles east of U.S. 16) and is considerably more strenuous, somewhat longer (about 11 miles round trip) and less populous. Either way, your reward for reaching the 7,242-foot summit is a spectacular, 60-mile view from the stone lookout tower that once was used to watch for fires and is now listed in the National Register of Historic Places.

From the lookout tower, hikers have distant panoramic views of South Dakota, Nebraska, Wyoming, and Montana, as well as close-up vantage points of the granite formations and cliffs of the Black Elk Wilderness. One caveat: Sylvan Lake/Harney Peak Trail (No. 9 South), gets extremely heavy use during the summer, and the Forest Service is asking hikers to use alternate routes to the summit whenever possible. The most likely choices for hikers are No. 9 North and Cathedral Spires Trail (No. 4), which departs from Sylvan Lake and heads east, then picks up No. 9 South near the summit.

Southern Hills

Hell Canyon Trail (No. 32)

This 5.5-mile loop starts out steep, but after a half-mile the going is easy along fairly level grades. The trail winds along

the base of the limestone plateau for about 2 miles, and the last 2 miles take you along the canyon floor, which is especially pretty in the fall when hardwood trees in riparian areas there show their colors. Note the ruins of a Civilian Conservation Corps camp along the bottom of the trail. The trailhead is about 1 mile west of the entrance to Jewel Cave National Monument and 11 miles west of Custer on U.S. 16.

Horseback Riding

Horses are practically synonymous with the West, and they continue to occupy an important place in our local culture and economy. The trails listed below are a tip of the hat to our equine tradition. Please also see our Campgrounds and RV Parks chapter for more horseback-riding opportunities. And, of course, you're free to ride almost anywhere in the Black Hills National Forest. Just be sure to avoid private land or get permission before you cross it.

Centennial Trail (No. 89)

To avoid being redundant, we'll ask you to see our Cycling and Hiking and Backpacking sections for basic information about this trail. But to be thorough, we'll tell you that horses are not allowed on the Wind Cave National Park section (although a free horse-riding permit from the park's visitor center allows you to ride alongside the trail or anywhere else in the park). Please be aware that horses aren't allowed in the eastern portion of Bear Butte State Park, where the Centennial Trail begins (or ends, if you're coming from the south).

Central Hills

Norbeck Wildlife Preserve and Black Elk Wilderness

The Forest Service's two horse camps, Willow Creek on Highway 244 between Hill City and Mount Rushmore and Iron Creek off U.S. 16A east of Custer, are the starting points for a dozen pathways in the 50-mile Harney Range Trail System in this protected area. All of these forested trails provide lots of opportunities to see wildlife, but we'd also like to call your attention to some other interesting features. The rugged Grizzly Bear Creek Trail (No. 7) will take you to beaver ponds and old-growth vegetation; Lost Cabin Trail,

one of three National Recreation trails in the national forest, passes near two old mining sites. This area has the highest concentration of trails in the Hills; any comprehensive trail map can help you sort them out. You can also contact the Forest Service for information about the trails and about riding as well as horse camping in the backcountry.

Southern Hills

Custer State Park
Custer
(605) 255-4515

A favorite riding place with abundant wildlife, the park gives almost free rein to equestrians. Horses aren't allowed in the Sylvan Lake watershed area or the walk-in fishing area that links Grace Coolidge and Center Lake campgrounds (both areas are posted), but otherwise, you're free to ride to your heart's content through this fabulous park. If you want to follow marked trails, you have options for both long and short rides. The park's Trail No. 6, Blue Bell Lodge & Store (distinct from Trail No. 6 in the National Forest system), takes 45 minutes from French Creek Horse

Riding the range is still a family tradition in the Black Hills. PHOTO: JON FROST

The Black Hills National Forest Visitor Center at Pactola Reservoir features outstanding natural history and cultural exhibits and offers educational programs between Memorial Day and Labor Day weekends. Plus, the center is in a scenic spot overlooking the lake.

Camp (listed in our Campgrounds and RV Parks chapter) to the lodge. Park Trail No. 1, French Creek, is a seven-hour loop that departs from the horse camp and joins up with the Centennial Trail on the return trip. Maps and detailed information about these and other trails are available at the park or by calling (605) 255-4464 or (605) 255-4515.

Trail Rides and Pack Trips

Summer trail rides are plentiful, and you'll find a number of roadside corrals offering one- to two-hour rides. Those we've listed are a bit more off the beaten path or offer unusual opportunities. Some of them require reservations.

Central Hills

Gunsel Horse Adventures
Box 1575, Rapid City
(605) 343-7608
www.gunselhorseadventures.com

Take a real Old West-style pack trip of four to 10 days (or longer), camping along the way. No modern amenities are found along the trail, just plenty of fabulous scenery and folksy song and poetry entertainment at night. Trip choices include riding the length of the Centennial Trail, Fort Meade, the Badlands, or a ride to Deadwood's historic Main Street.

Trips are available from mid-April through September or October, weather permitting. Prices are $190 per person, per day (with a four-person minimum); this price includes everything but personal gear.

Bob Lantis, proprietor of Gunsel, is one of the oldest (since 1968) outfitters in Yellowstone National Park. He is also the Trail Boss at the annual fall bison roundup at Custer State Park. For hearty souls, Bob offers a bison roundup trip or a cattle roundup for $800 a person, as well as a spring turkey hunt for the same price. Call, write, or use the above Web site for more information and directions to the place.

High Country Guest Ranch
12172 Deerfield Rd., Hill City
(605) 574-9003
www.highcountryranch.com

Ride for one to three hours, sheltered in seclusion in the Black Hills National Forest. Even the shortest ride treats you to a view of Harney Peak, and the longest takes you to an abandoned gold mine. This is a small operation offering intimate rides for fewer than 10 people at a time, and reservations are required. Riders must be at least six years old to go on the trail, but little people can take a pony ride around the ranch as long as their parents accompany them on foot. You can ride from mid-May to mid-September here. The cost is $15 to $40 per person, depending on the length of your ride. A one-hour ride with breakfast in the ranch's covered wagon costs $18.50. To get here, look for the little covered wagon 4 miles west of town. The guest ranch has 17 cabins for rent.

Southern Hills
Blue Bell Stables
Hwy. 87 S., Custer State Park
(605) 255-4571

There are many fine ways to view the natural wonders of Custer State Park, but sitting astride a horse has to be one of the best. On a one- or two-hour guided trail ride departing from the stables at Blue Bell Lodge & Resort, you can expect to come upon wildlife and learn about the park itself from your guide. The rides are extremely popular, and reservations are recommended; they're required for half-day, full-day, and overnight pack trips. There are no age restrictions, but children must be able to sit in the saddle by themselves and reach the stirrups.

Rides are available daily from 8:00 A.M. until 4:30 P.M., mid-May until mid-September. Fees start at $15.00 for adults and $12.50 for children 11 and younger; ask about the special rate for groups of 10 or more. Other rides range from $60 to $150 per person.

Hunting

Autumn deer and spring turkeys are the most sought-after game that beckon hunters to the Black Hills, where abundant public land is open to their sport. A number of other animal and bird species have their seasons, too; some, such as elk and bighorn sheep, are severely restricted and/or off-limits to out-of-staters. Custer State Park holds an annual bison hunt that's open to all hunters—we've provided information about that below.

Licenses for big game are issued through a state-run lottery system. Applications are available at many hardware, sporting goods, and convenience stores; county treasurers' offices; and the state Game, Fish & Parks Department's Wildlife Division regional office, 3305 West South Street, Rapid City, South Dakota, (605) 394-2391. Or contact the department's main office at 523 East Capitol Avenue, Pierre, South Dakota, (605) 773-3485.

The seasons and prices for deer and turkey are long and varied. For details contact: www.sdgfp.info or the phone numbers above.

The list of licenses, prices, and other details for hunting grouse, rabbits, and other animals is also long and complex, so we'll let you inquire on your own for the information you need. We'll also be brief about predators and furbearers: Nonresidents are not allowed to trap at all in South Dakota and are not allowed to take mink, beavers, bobcats, and certain other species by any other means either; those privileges are reserved for state residents.

With a mishmash of public and private land, you need to know where you are and who owns what before you begin. Make sure you have permission before you enter private property. Atlases and maps are available from Game, Fish & Parks and from the U.S.D.A. Forest Service R.R. 2, Box 200, Custer, South Dakota 57730, (605) 673-2251. Game, Fish & Parks also issues an annual hunting handbook with all the latest regulations, including restrictions in state parks—be sure to get the current copy (which comes out around Labor Day) when you buy your license or pick up your application. Knowing the rules is your responsibility.

And one more thing: We'd like to call attention to the fact that uncased .22 caliber rimfire firearms are prohibited at all times in our state parks and recreation areas and on the George S. Mickelson Trail. Further, firearms and bows may not be discharged on or across the Mickelson Trail right of way.

The Custer State Park bison hunt, which runs from November into January, helps the park cull old breeding bulls out of its herd. Up to 10 licenses costing $4,000 each are issued by lottery for three-day guided hunts. Hunters get individual park guides and do their scouting in a pickup truck. In all cases, old 45-70 buffalo cartridge black powder guns (as well as modern rifles) are allowed, but bows

Insiders' Tip
Dogs are welcome on national forest hiking trails, but they must be on a leash or under voice control by their human friends at all times.

and muzzle loaders are not. For an application or more information, call the park at (605) 255–4515.

Jeep Tours

We've listed Custer State Park's enormously popular rides here.

Southern Hills

Buffalo Safari Jeep Rides
Wildlife Loop Road, Custer State Park
(605) 255–4541
www.custerresort.com

Feel the wind in your hair as you head out in an open-air Jeep in search of wildlife and scenic splendor. Guided trips of one and one-half to two hours take you through rolling hills and into the park's backcountry while your driver tells you about the park and its denizens. To prolong the experience, you can join a chuck wagon cookout (see the Blue Bell Lodge & Resort Hayride & Chuck Wagon Cookout listing in our Attractions chapter) with live folk music before returning in the evening.

Rides are available from 8:00 A.M. to 6:00 P.M. daily, from Mother's Day until the weekend before the roundup in late September. Prices range from $17.50 to $20.50 per person with a minimum of $50.00 per jeep. Group rates for 10 or more are available. Reservations are recommended.

The cookout ride departs at 4:30 P.M. and returns by 8:30 P.M. The price is $40 for those older than 12 and $37 for children. Reservations are required by 2:00 P.M.

Organized Sports and Other Recreation

Black Hills communities do a good job of providing organized sports for youths and adults, often thanks to the work of volunteers. Activities may include team sports such as baseball, softball, basketball, soccer, and volleyball. If you enjoy individual sports such as racquetball, swimming, tennis, running, and walking, you're likely to find free and low-cost indoor and outdoor facilities wherever you are. To help you get involved and find what you need, we've compiled the addresses and phone numbers of information and recreation centers for most of our communities; you'll find them in the gray box at the end of this chapter. More esoteric pursuits such as martial arts, yoga, and aerobics also are available at certain public and private facilities, and you can inquire about them as well.

Roller-Skating

Like everywhere else in the nation, in-line skating is a popular form of recreation that practically doubles as a mode of transportation here. Before you buckle on your skates, though, be sure to check with the local city hall or police station to find out whether there are any areas in your town that are off-limits to skating—in Rapid City, for instance, a local ordinance bans skating downtown, but there are no signs to that effect. Below you'll find a listing for an indoor rink that adds another dimension to your skating opportunities.

Central Hills

Rapid Skate
2302 E. St. Andrew St., Rapid City
(605) 342–8944

A popular place for skating parties, Rapid Skate has a special party room and a snack bar in addition to a skating rink. Summer hours vary, so call for information. Winter hours also vary, but Rapid Skate is usually open Wednesday, Friday, Saturday, and Sunday. Hours on other days change weekly. Rates include skates; speed skates and in-line skates are extra. Lessons, including artistic dance skating, are available. Call for rates and times.

Skiing and Snowboarding

All right, we're not Colorado, but the Black Hills have some darned good downhill. Our two ski areas have very different

A snowboarder takes to the air at Terry Peak, one of two downhill ski areas in the Black Hills. PHOTO: COURTESY OF SOUTH DAKOTA TOURISM

personalities, which is an excellent reason to try them both.

Northern Hills

Deer Mountain Ski Area
1000 Mountain Rd., Lead
(605) 584-3230
(888) 265-2197 (conditions)
www.skideermountain.com

Natural snow, night skiing, and groomed cross-country trails (which we've covered in the Cross-Country Skiing section of this chapter) are the hallmarks of Deer Mountain. At an elevation of approximately 6,800 feet, with a 750-foot vertical drop, you'll find downhill slopes for all skill levels—Meadow and Snow Bowl for beginners, Racers' Cliff or the Chute for hotdoggers. A 3,000-foot triple chairlift and two other lifts serve the trails, which get plenty of use between 4:00 and 9:00 P.M. Friday and Saturday, when the area is lighted for night skiing. Deer Mountain has doubled the size of its recreation area, adding a 2,200-foot double chairlift and

about 10 new intermediate and Black Diamond trails on what's called the West Ridge side of the ski hill, which has a vertical drop of 850 feet. Snowboarders have their own territory in the regulation-size half-pipe and a terrain park with table tops and jumps. Even tubers have a trail all to themselves.

When it's time to come in from the cold, patrons head for the cafeteria and full-service bar in the lodge. Lessons from certified instructors, equipment rentals, and a ski shop round out the amenities.

Lift ticket prices range from $18 to $25. Call for information about season passes and group rates. A half-day of tubing costs $10, with tube rental included.

Ski rentals were $15.00 (day) and $10.00 (night) for adults, and $9.00 and $8.00, respectively, for kids. Snowboards were $22.50 day or night. Poles (for skis) and boots are included.

Deer Mountain is closed on Monday and Tuesday except from about mid-December to early January, when the lifts run seven days a week. Hours are 9:00 A.M.

The Black Hills' two downhill ski areas have slopes for skiers of all skill levels. PHOTO: COURTESY OF SOUTH DAKOTA TOURISM

to 4:00 P.M. Wednesday, Thursday, and Sunday, and 9 A.M. to 9 P.M. on Friday and Saturday.

To get there, go 3 miles west of Lead on U.S. 85-14A and watch for the well-marked turnoff to the ski area.

Terry Peak Ski Area
Nevada Gulch, Lead
(605) 584–2165
(800) 456–0524 (conditions)
www.terrypeak.com

Our largest and tallest ski area (7,076 feet, with 1,052 feet of vertical drop), Terry Peak also sets itself apart with its hi-tech, computerized snow-making machinery. Five chairlifts, including a high-speed detachable quad chair, serve more than 20 miles of slopes for all skill levels. Stewart Slope and River Run offer beginners a gentle start (and a beautiful, modern lodge when they reach the bottom), while Ben Hur and Holy Terror give advanced skiers a run for their money. Snowboarders will find a terrain park on the Snowstorm trail. Stewart

Lodge has a cafeteria, lounge, ski shop, and rentals. Nevada Gulch Base Lodge has a cafeteria, ski shop, and the adjacent Dark Horse Saloon. If you are new to skiing or if you are a novice skier, lessons are available through the certified ski school.

All-area day passes cost $32 for adults ages 13 to 69, $25 for juniors 6 to 12, and are free for children 5 and younger and seniors 70 and older. Reduced rates are available for limited access and for half-days. Call for information about that and season passes as well as group rates.

Complete ski sets (skis, boots, and poles) rent for $18 for adults and $13 for juniors. Snowboards with boots are $20, and snowblades are $15.

Traditionally, Terry Peak opens the day after Thanksgiving, assuming there's enough snow, and operates on weekends until mid-December, when it's open seven days a week. Hours are 9:00 A.M. to 4:00 P.M.

To reach the ski area, turn off U.S. 85-14A at the Terry Peak billboard just west of Lead.

Rentals

In addition to the rental information that we provide below, also see the previous Deer Mountain and Terry Peak listings.

Northern and Central Hills

Terry Peak Ski & Sport
32 Fantail Gulch, Lead
(605) 584-3644
www.rentmyskis.com

Prices for daily ski, snowblade, and snowboard rentals were being firmed up as this chapter was being prepared, but we were told adult rental packages would start at $18 for skis, and $22 for snowboards. Call for prices for children's rentals. Seasonal rates also are available.

The Lead store is a quarter-mile west of town on U.S. 85-14A, just before the turnoff to Terry Peak Ski Area.

Skydiving

Northern Hills

Black Hills Air Sports
Black Hills Airport/Clyde Ice Field, Spearfish
(800) 794-JUMP

Skydiving just might be the closest you'll ever come to sprouting wings. The sensation is more like floating in midair than falling, and even first-time jumpers almost universally report a feeling of accomplishment and exhilaration when they return to Earth. The certified instructors and jump masters at Black Hills Air Sports will teach you all you need to know for a tandem jump, in which you jump with your instructor, hitched to a parachute built for two, or a static-line jump, in which a 15-foot line attached to the plane opens your chute automatically. They also offer skydiving for experienced jumpers who want to free fall and deploy their own chutes. A licensed pilot will take you and your instructor—and a cameraman, if you've ordered a video and/or still photos—10,000 feet up for a tandem or 3,500 feet for a static-line jump.

Skydiving is available on three weekends each month, year round when the weather permits. Prices range from $235 for first-time jumpers needing instruction; for others, it's $195. Video and photos are extra. Reservations are required and when you call, be prepared to state your weight—there's a 220-pound limit.

Snowmobiling

Black Hills snowmobiling consistently ranks high among people who know and love the sport, and not only because of our roughly 300 miles of well-marked, groomed trails and superb snow. It also has something to do with our million-plus acres of national forest where pine woods and wide-open meadows give sledders ample opportunity to abandon the trail and explore hidden places. Restrictions are few, just so you avoid logging areas, plowed roads, private land, cross-country ski trails, and wildlife winter ranges. Ski trails and winter range are defined on the South Dakota *Snowmobile Trails Map*, which is available at no charge at trailside businesses and other locations around the Hills, by calling the state Tourism Department at (800) 732-5682, or logging on to www.travelsd.com. Call (800) 445-3474 for current conditions.

Snowmobiles must be licensed (a valid out-of-state license is acceptable); if yours isn't, you can purchase a five-day license for $10 at trailside businesses and other locations. A state license costs $20 for two years and is available at county treasurers' offices.

You can legally snowmobile in the national forest whenever there's enough snow, but the agreements on which the trail map is based (and which make it valid) are in effect only between December 1 and March 30. Trail grooming doesn't begin until December 15.

The Northern Hills and the Deerfield area in the Central Hills tend to get more snow and colder temperatures than elsewhere, and those are two places we recommend; the O'Neill Pass area along U.S. 85 near the Wyoming border is especially consistent in the quality of its snow. The trail system, however, rambles through the western portion of the Hills from Spearfish practically to Custer, a stretch of almost 80 miles. And when the Needles Highway in Custer State Park is snow-covered, it becomes a paradise of switch-backs, tunnels, and spectacular scenery for snowmobilers.

Parking is provided along the state trail system, and the map will show you where the lots are. Some trailside businesses also have space for your road vehicle, but it probably doesn't hurt to ask permission before you take to the trails.

Rentals

Here we've listed rental outlets that are close to popular trails and areas that get heavy snow. But you'll find rentals at other places, too, and several are listed on the snowmobile trail map mentioned previously.

Northern Hills

Latchstring Village All Season Sports Center
U.S. 14A, Spearfish Canyon
(605) 584–2207, (800) 439–8544
www.spfcanyon.com

Single-seat sleds rent for $85 for a half-day, $120 for a full day. Double-seaters are $105 and $145, respectively. Snow-suits, gloves, and boots are extra. Packages are available for guests of Spearfish Canyon Resort, where the sports center is located. Call early to reserve a machine—they're mighty popular.

Mountain Meadow Resort
11321 Gillette Prairie Rd., Hill City
(605) 574–2636

Single sleds recently rented for $115 per day and doubles for $135. Half-day rates were $60 for up to two hours and $10 an hour thereafter for a single-seater. Prices include a helmet for each rider. You can read about the accommodations here under Horse Camps in our Campgrounds and RV Sites chapter.

Snow Adventures Lodge
U.S. 85 S., Lead
(605) 584–1466, (605) 578–1294
(800) 662–SLED

Double and single sleds are available for full and half-days. Weekday (Monday through Thursday) rates are $79 single, $89 double for a full day, or $60 and $70, respectively, for a half-day. Weekend and holiday rates are $110 single, $125 double but no half-days. Prices include a helmet and oil for your sled. Full clothing setups (suit, boots, and gloves) are $15.00 for a full day, $9.75 for half; each piece also rents separately for $5.00 all day, $3.25 for half.

Guests of Deadwood Gulch Resort in Deadwood and Golden Hills Resort & Convention Center–Best Western in Lead receive a discount. And if there's enough snow, you can begin your ride from your hotel. Snow Adventures Lodge itself is 18 miles southwest of Lead.

Trailshead Lodge
U.S. 85 S., Lead
(605) 584–3464

Insiders' Tip

Forest Service ranger district offices are open Monday through Friday year-round and are excellent places to get maps, brochures, information, and directions. They also sell Christmas tree- and firewood-cutting permits. Hours vary, depending on which station you visit, but check outdoor racks for maps and brochures if the doors are locked.

Single sleds recently rented for $99 a day Monday through Thursday and $120 Friday through Sunday. Doubles were $115 and $135, respectively. Half-day rates started at $87. Prices include a helmet and the first tank of gas and oil. A full set of outerwear rented for $15, with varied prices for individual pieces. The lodge is 21 miles southwest of Lead.

Swimming

Many of our communities have public indoor swimming pools in their community or recreation centers or YMCAs; please see the gray box at the end of this chapter for information about them. Here we've listed some outdoor pools (plus famous Evans Plunge, which is indoors), but don't forget about our lakes and reservoirs, some of which are mentioned in the Boating and Fishing sections above. If you're staying in one of our campgrounds (see the Campgrounds and RV Sites chapter), chances are you'll have access to a pool there.

Central Hills

Parkview Pool
4221 Parkview Dr., Rapid City
(605) 394–1892

Brand-new in 1997, Parkview Pool has a water slide, sandbox, waterworks fountain, and snack bar that appeal to kids; a picnic area and the sloping, walk-in entry appeal to their elders. Daily rates recently were $4.00 for swimmers 18 and older, $3.00 for those ages 2 to 17, and free for those younger than 2.

The city has three other public outdoor swimming pools that are older and more basic but that have wading pools for kiddies ages 1 to 6. They are Horace Mann Pool, 818 Anamosa Street, (605) 394–1891; Roosevelt Pool, 301 East St. Louis Street, (605) 394–1893; and Sioux Park Pool, 1000 Sheridan Lake Road, (605) 394–1894. Rates are $3.00 for adults, and $2.00 for those 17 and younger.

Insiders' Tip
If you know about poaching or other wildlife law violations, you can make an anonymous report by calling the South Dakota Turn In Poachers (TIPs) hot line at (800) 592–5522.

All pools are heated, have full-time lifeguards, and offer lockers and showers. They generally open Memorial Day weekend and close, one by one, between mid-August and Labor Day. Hours are 1:00 to 8:00 P.M.

Southern Hills

Evans Plunge
1145 N. River St., Hot Springs
(605) 745–5165
www.evansplunge.com

The warm mineral waters that made Hot Springs a turn-of-the-twentieth-century health resort still feed the swimming pools at Evans Plunge. Inside, a long, twisting water slide and a short, zippy one will dump you into the 87-degree water in the 200-by-50-foot pool, touted as the "world's largest natural warm-water indoor swimming pool." Outside, you can speed slide into a smaller pool when the summer sun warms the water even more. Added attractions include giant tubes for your paddling or floating pleasure, Tarzan rings for the strong of bicep, water basketball and volleyball, a 3-foot kiddie pool with tyke-size slide, spas, a steam room and sauna, weight and exercise rooms, a snack bar, and a gift shop.

The Plunge is open from 5:30 A.M. to 9:00 P.M. during the summer and from 8:00 A.M. to 9:00 P.M. in the spring, fall, and winter. Daily rates are $8.00 for ages 13 and older, $6.00 for children 3 through

Recreation Resources

Recreation Centers

Here is a list of places to call for information about organized sports and other recreational opportunities in Black Hills communities Also listed are public recreation centers with swimming pools, fitness equipment, and other facilities you can use for a daily fee. In some cases, the recreation center is also the place to call for information.

Northern Hills

Belle Fourche Area Community Center
1111 National St., Belle Fourche (605) 892–2467

Deadwood Recreation Center
105 Sherman St., Deadwood (605) 578–3729

Northern Hills YMCA
845 Miners Ave., Lead (605) 584–1113

Spearfish Parks, Recreation and Forestry (Public Works Department)
625 Fifth St., Spearfish (605) 642–1333

Sturgis Community Center
1401 Lazelle St., Sturgis (605) 347–6513

Young Sports & Fitness Center
1200 University St., Spearfish (605) 642–6098

Central Hills

Hill City City Hall
324 Main St., Hill City (605) 574–2300

Hill City Youth Center
111 McGregor St., Hill City (605) 574–2010

Rapid City Recreation Department
2915 Canyon Lake Dr., Rapid City (605) 394–4167

Rapid City YMCA
815 Kansas City St., Rapid City (605) 342–8538

Southern Hills

Custer City Pool
Crook and Third Streets, Custer (605) 673–3935 (summer)

Custer YMCA
644 Crook St., Custer (605) 673–3154 (school year)

Hot Springs City Hall
303 N. River St., Hot Springs (605) 745–3135

Forest Service Ranger Stations

Here is a list of U.S.D.A. Forest Service Ranger Stations where you can get information about the Black Hills National Forest. For general information, contact the Forest Supervisor's Headquarters at R.R. 2, Box 200, Custer, South Dakota 57730, or call (605) 673–2251.

Northern Hills

Spearfish/Nemo Ranger District
2014 N. Main St., Spearfish (605) 642–4622
Highway 14A, Deadwood (605) 578–2744

Central Hills

Pactola/Harney Ranger District
803 Soo San Dr., Rapid City (605) 343–1567
23939 U.S. 385, Hill City (605) 574–2534

Southern Hills

Custer/Elk Mountain Ranger Districts
330 Mt. Rushmore Rd., Custer (605) 673–4853

12, and free for those 2 and younger. Use of the spa and fitness center costs $2.50 extra, or $7.50 if you don't swim. Inquire about group discounts and membership rates. Forgot your suit and towel? You can rent those here, along with life jackets and lockers. For your safety, lifeguards are on duty; children younger than 13 are not allowed in the weight room and exercise area.

Spectator Sports

Baseball
Basketball
Cross Country
Football
Rodeo
Soccer
Track and Field
Volleyball

Whatever our differences, most Black Hills Insiders share a common trait: We spend time on sports, either participating, watching, or both. If you've read our Recreation chapter, you already know about our numerous outlets for vigorous physical activity. In this chapter you'll find out about some opportunities to watch and cheer from the sidelines. If you're a basketball fan, you'll jump at the chance to watch a home game by our professional team, the Black Hills Gold. Starting in 2000, professional arena football came to Rapid City in the form of the Black Hills Machine, a first-year expansion team.

We also take considerable pride and interest in our college athletes and their achievements in football, basketball, volleyball, cross country, track and field, soccer, and rodeo. As members of the National Intercollegiate Rodeo Association's Great Plains Region, our men's and women's college rodeo teams enter some pretty arduous competition, both at home and away. We've also seen some outstanding performances by students in the National Association of Intercollegiate Athletics (NAIA). Black Hills State University and South Dakota School of Mines and Technology are Division 2 members of the NAIA's South Dakota–Iowa Conference. National American University, where the intercollegiate athletics program is still in its infancy, is an independent member of the NAIA Great Plains Region.

To make it as simple as possible for you to find out about your favorite game, we've arranged this chapter by sport, in alphabetical order, and have mixed the professional in with college and amateur action.

In addition, Rapid City saw the dawn of a new era in American Legion baseball with the signing of a unique agreement in early 1998. At that time the state American Legion approved a request to allow two Rapid City programs to be open to players from the entire community–normally, communities with more than one program are divided geographically. Newly chartered Rapid City Post 320 began recruiting players after the agreement became final, offering a less intensive schedule than that demanded of players in the decades-old Rapid City Post 22 program.

Posts in other towns—Spearfish and Sturgis in the Northern Hills and Custer in the Southern Hills—also sponsor teams; because organizers and contact phone numbers may change from one season to the next, it's best to check local newspapers for information about those game and tournament schedules.

You'll need to call or check the sports pages for information about college game schedules, too. We've provided phone numbers, and it shouldn't be hard to find a newspaper on your own.

'Nuff said? All right, we'll be quiet and let you watch the game.

Insiders' Tip

Most Black Hills Insiders share a common trait: We spend time on sports, either participating, watching, or both.

Baseball

National American University
321 Kansas City St., Rapid City
(605) 394-4999

A men's baseball team formed in 1999 and began competing in 2000. Games are held between mid-February and late May at McKeague Field, across from Fitzgerald Stadium. The stadium is at the corner of Canyon Lake Drive and Sheridan Lake Road next to Storybook Island (see our Kidstuff chapter). Admission is $2.00 per game, but the schedule varies, so please call for information.

Basketball

Black Hills State University
1200 University Station, Spearfish
(605) 642-6882

The BHSU men's and women's basketball season runs from November until March. Yellow Jackets home games are at the Donald E. Young Sports and Fitness Center on campus. Tickets are sold on-site; prices are $6.00 for adults and $3.00 for students of all ages.

The women's team finished second in Division II national championship competition in 1997, the second of three straight years the team had qualified.

South Dakota School of Mines and Technology
501 E. St. Joseph St., Rapid City
(605) 394-2601

The men's and women's basketball season begins in early November and continues until mid-March. Home games are in Goodell Gymnasium (called the New Gym) on the Tech campus. Women's games generally begin at 5:30 P.M. and men's at 7:30 P.M. Tickets are available at the gym; prices are $5.00 for adults, $2.00 for youths 10 to 18, and free for those 9 and younger. In 1998 the Lady Hardrockers made their fourth appearance at the national championship tournament, reaching the final four. The men's team played in national competition for the second time in 1997.

Cross Country

Black Hills State University
1200 University Station, Spearfish
(605) 642-6882

Men's and women's cross-country running events take place from September to November at Spearfish Canyon Country Club, (605) 642-7156, at the intersection of U.S. 14 and 14A. Admission is free.

South Dakota School of Mines and Technology
501 E. St. Joseph St., Rapid City
(605) 394-2601

Men's and women's cross-country events generally take place on Saturday during the fall. Each year a meet featuring regional teams is held in conjunction with the school's homecoming events. The meet is open to the public at no charge, but since the location varies you'll need to call for information.

Football

Black Hills State University
1200 University Station, Spearfish
(605) 642-6882

Football season for the BHSU Yellow Jackets runs from early September until the first week of November. Home games are played at 1:30 P.M. on Saturday at Lyle Hare Field on the university campus. Ticket prices are $6.00 for adults and $3.00 for students of all ages. Tickets are sold at the stadium at game time.

Insiders' Tip

Rapid City hosts a boys' high school basketball tournament each year in March, alternating between Class A and Class AA.

Action-packed rodeo events help preserve Western tradition in the Black Hills. PHOTO: COURTESY OF SOUTH DAKOTA TOURISM

South Dakota School of Mines and Technology
501 E. St. Joseph St., Rapid City
(605) 394-2601

The Hardrockers' season begins around the first part of September and goes until early November. Home games are usually at 1:00 P.M. or 1:30 P.M. on Saturdays at O'Harra Field on the Tech campus. Tickets are available at the stadium, and prices

are $5.00 for adults, $2.00 for ages 10 to 18, and free for anyone 9 or younger.

Rodeo

Teams from two local institutions—National American University and Western Dakota Technical Institute—take part in regional rodeo competition, with two events held in the Black Hills each year.

The Maverick Stampede, hosted by National American University, takes place on a weekend in late April or early May at Hart Ranch Arena (see the listing below for directions). Ticket prices are $5.00 for adults and $3.00 for children 12 and younger. For more information call (605) 394-4916.

Hart Ranch Arena
23759 Arena Dr., Rapid City
(605) 737-0271

Amateur rodeo takes place Tuesday and Thursday evenings during the summer in the big indoor arena. Starting times, prices, and other details can differ from year to

> ### Insiders' Tip
> If watching sports on TV with fellow fans is one of your pastimes, you can visit any of our sports lounges. Flip to the Sports Bars section of our Nightlife chapter to find out where they are.

GREAT FACES

Mattie Goff Newcombe

From the time she was a teenager, Mattie Goff Newcombe had a reputation. She was known as the fastest trick rider on the fastest horse in rodeo.

Even when she was a little girl, Mattie knew she was born to ride. When she sat astride a horse for the first time, she was just three years old. Luckily, growing up on her family's Meade County ranch gave her plenty of opportunity to break wild horses and become a skillful rider, and at 14 she entered her first rodeo. Back then, in 1921, not many women competed in rodeo, and Mattie helped pave the way for other talented riders of her gender.

Weighing only 100 pounds, Mattie was an agile woman who wore a wide-brimmed hat atop her smiling face and fancy boots on her tiny feet (we've talked to her boot maker). She quickly earned fame for performing exciting stunts with names like "the slick saddle liberty stand," "spin the horn," "under the neck," "under the belly" and, most dangerous of all, "the suicide drag." She loved to square dance on horseback in a quadrille made up of four couples. And no one could beat her at relay racing–she was that fast and that good at leaping from horse to horse without touching the ground.

Mattie was fearless to boot. The only time she felt a little nervous was just before she performed for President Calvin Coolidge in 1927. But once she got on her horse, her jitters faded. She later reported, with some disappointment, that Silent Cal had talked to her and wasn't silent after all.

She never intended to retire, but then Mattie married Maynard Newcombe in 1927 and discovered, as she often said, "You can't run a ranch and rodeo, too." So she came home to South Dakota and a life of hard work but no regrets. She stayed active, and 60 years after she entered her last rodeo she could still fit into her trick-riding costume.

In 1961 Mattie became a charter member of the National Cowboy Hall of Fame, and for more than 30 years after that she continued to accumulate honors. In 1989 she was inducted into the South Dakota Hall of Fame, and three years later Mattie was named South Dakota Rodeo Personality of the Past by the Casey Tibbs Foundation. (You can read about Tibbs, himself a rodeo legend, in an Insiders' Tip in our Annual Events and Festivals chapter.) Local sculptor T. R. (Tony) Chytka cast a small bronze statue of Mattie that's on display in First Western Bank in Sturgis, where she settled after her husband died. A life-size version will go in the Casey Tibbs South Dakota Rodeo Center now under construction in Fort Pierre, in central South Dakota. In 1994 Mattie became a Cowgirl Honoree in the National Cowgirl Museum and Hall of Fame.

While this book was being written Mattie was in frail health and not up to having visitors. But she was sweet and generous on the phone when we called. The only thing she wouldn't discuss was her age. "I don't think about that," she said. And why should she? After all, when she turned 91 a couple of weeks later, she still had her reputation.

year, so you'll need to call for information. But we can tell you that events in past years have included typical rodeo sports such as bareback, saddle-bronc and bull riding, barrel racing, and team roping. Between events a clown's antics might provide entertainment, and there may be special activities for kids, including foot races and mutton bustin', in which sheep rather than horses serve as the trusty mounts.

Hart Ranch is 8 miles south of Rapid City. Turn east off U.S. 16 across from Reptile Gardens, then turn left onto Spring Creek Road, and go 3 miles to Arena Drive.

Soccer

National American University
321 Kansas City St., Rapid City
(605) 394-4825

Men and women play soccer at Omaha Field, at the corner of Mountain View and Omaha streets in Rapid City. Home games for the Mavericks are on weekends.

The men's soccer team was the Great Plains Sectional champion in 1997; the same year one team member made third-team All-American, and two others earned honorable mention All-American. One member of the women's team also made honorable mention All-American in 1997, the team's first year of competition. Admission is $3.00.

Track and Field

Black Hills State University
1200 University Station, Spearfish
(605) 642-6882

The men's and women's indoor season is in January and February, with Yellow Jackets events at the Donald E. Young Sports and Fitness Center on the BHSU campus. Outdoor events take place from late March through May at Lyle Hare Field on the campus. There is no cost to attend.

South Dakota School of Mines and Technology
501 E. St. Joseph St., Rapid City
(605) 394-2601

Men and women hold indoor track competition during January and February. Outdoor events for the Hardrockers are generally on Saturday from late March through late April at O'Harra Field on campus, with one regional meet each year open to the public at no charge, usually at 11:00 A.M. on the first Saturday of April.

Volleyball

Black Hills State University
1200 University Station, Spearfish
(605) 642-6882

South Dakota–Iowa Conference champions in 1997, the women's Yellow Jacket team plays from August through November, with home games in the Donald E. Young Sports and Fitness Center on campus. Admission is free.

National American University
321 Kansas City St., Rapid City
(605) 394-4825

Women's competition takes place between August and November, with home games played at the university gym. Most Mavericks games are in the evening. Admission is $3.00

South Dakota School of Mines and Technology
501 E. St. Joseph St., Rapid City
(605) 394-2601

Women's volleyball competition takes place from early September through mid-November. The Lady Hardrockers' home games are in Goodell Gymnasium (the New Gym) on the school campus, but you'll need to call for the schedule. Tickets are sold at the door and cost $5.00 for adults and $2.00 for ages 10 to 18. Admission is free for those age 9 and younger.

Daytrips and Weekend Getaways

We're a bit biased toward our beloved Black Hills, but we readily admit that there are some delightful destinations all around us, too. In this chapter we'll direct you toward some of those and tell you what you might expect to see and enjoy when you arrive.

These daytrips and weekend getaways are within three to four hours' drive of the Black Hills, so you can drive to these destinations and back with time left over to explore, or choose to stay overnight or for a weekend.

We haven't given you accommodation or restaurant information in this chapter, but you should have no trouble finding such amenities in larger towns. Do remember that you'll be traveling through some of the nation's largest states, and traversing some very rural country, with many miles between towns.

We encourage you to call ahead to check hours and admission prices. Although these western states have great fall and winter recreation opportunities, many attractions close for the winter and their phones go unanswered. In those cases, call the state tourism offices (or use the Web sites) for information—we've included those numbers so you can call for visitor packets and maps, too. Before heading out on your adventures, get a map for each state you'll be visiting. We've only hit the high spots near the Black Hills in this chapter, so a map will help you find other interesting destinations in between and beyond.

Northward, you'll find North Dakota, our sister state and one of the most misunderstood states (it's quite beautiful, even though the winters can be . . . well, challenging). To the west is beautiful, expansive Wyoming, to the northwest is the big sky country of Montana, and to the south are the rolling prairie and sandhills of Nebraska.

We've included more of South Dakota in this chapter, too. North, east, and southeast of the Black Hills lie very different worlds: prairie flatlands, the Pine Ridge Indian Reservation, the state capital, the broad Missouri River, and numerous pioneer-turned-tourist towns along I-90.

We've just scratched the surface of what these adjoining states—and our own—have to offer you. Use this as an introduction to each area, and have a good time as you explore the rest of the Wild West that surrounds the beautiful Black Hills.

North of the Black Hills

Northwestern South Dakota

The **Sioux Ranger District**, (605) 797-4432, maintains Camp Crook and two national monuments called Capital Rock and Castles in Harding County, west of Buffalo, off Highway 20. These are mixed-use and mixed-landscape areas, with buttes, grasslands, and pine forests, where you can hike, hunt, watch wildlife, and camp (limited facilities only) at no charge, year-round. It's best to get a map because

GREAT PLACES

A Bogus Banner

North Dakota and South Dakota were admitted to the Union at the same time, as the 39th and 40th states. When President Benjamin Harrison signed the statehood act on November 2, 1889, he intentionally shuffled the papers so neither state could claim admittance before the other. The Fort Meade Museum, near Sturgis, South Dakota, displays an old flag with 39 stars, but it's a bogus banner, for the United States never had only 39 states, having gone directly from 38 to 40, thanks to North and South Dakota.

the district's land units are not always contiguous or easy to find.

Grand River National Grassland, (605) 374-3592, southwest of Lemmon, South Dakota, off Highway 75, is on 197,000 acres on the North Dakota and South Dakota border. It's a primitive place without developed facilities (except fishing ponds) and, like most grasslands, is broken up into blocks of federal, state, and private land. Do call ahead for a map. It's open year-round, and there are no entrance fees. The Shadehill Reservoir Recreation Area is within the grassland, off Highway 73 near the town of Shadehill.

For more information on northwestern South Dakota, call the South Dakota Department of Tourism at (605) 773-3301 or (800) SDAKOTA, or, better yet, log on to South Dakota's Web site, www.travelsd.com.

North Dakota

The 19th-largest state, North Dakota is a huge expanse of prairie, farm, and ranch land that is quietly and understatedly beautiful. The state is rich in history and historical sites; Teddy Roosevelt, Sitting Bull, Custer, Lewis and Clark, and Sacagawea all left their mark there. Roosevelt said, "My experience when I lived and worked in North Dakota with my fellow ranchmen, on what was then the frontier, was the most important educational asset of my life." Outsiders often snicker when they hear the words "North Dakota," but that just makes it obvious they've never been there. The state is still relatively undiscovered, and that fact alone makes it a special place.

U.S. 85 from Buffalo, South Dakota, will take you into North Dakota. From there, U.S. 12 will lead you east to **Cedar River National Grassland,** (605) 374-3592, east of Lemmon, South Dakota, an entertain-yourself recreation area. There are no facilities or established trails, but you can camp and hike without charge. It's open year-round and is on the border of the two states. Reportedly, men with Custer's 1874 expedition carved a "US 7" into a hillside at Cedar River, and you can still see it there today. When you call for a map, ask for the location.

Backtracking west and north, you'll come to **Theodore Roosevelt National Park,** one of the best reasons to visit North Dakota. The only national park named for a person, it encompasses the spectacular Badlands, where Roosevelt rode and hunted in 1883. Teddy called the area "the romance of my life" and went on to work to preserve such beautiful places as national parks and monuments. The South Unit, (701) 623-4466 (on Mountain Time), is near Medora and I-94 cuts through it. The North Unit, (701) 842-2333 (70 miles away and on Central Time), is near Watford City, off U.S. 85. The Little Missouri River flows through both, and the North Unit is said to be more rugged and heavily forested. Views at both are glorious, and you can mountain bike, hike, ride horses, camp, or take a scenic drive and watch buffalo, wild horses, deer, and prairie dogs.

The **Little Missouri National Grassland,** (701) 225-5151, has one million acres that surround Theodore Roosevelt National Park. It's open year-round, and there are no entrance fees. It's primitive, although there are some established camping sites and hiking trails. It's a great (and great big) place to view wildlife, birds, and butterflies, or to fish and hunt and just get away from it all. Call ahead for a map.

Historic **Medora,** (800) 633–6721, (701) 623–4444, near the south entrance to the South Unit of Theodore Roosevelt National Park, is a 3-block-long restored Old West town. To get there, take I-94 to exit 27 (westbound) or exit 24 (eastbound). Walk on the boardwalks along gaslighted streets, visit the museums and galleries, and have a meal of beef or buffalo. Tour the 28-room Chateau de Mores, the historic 1880s home once owned by the Marquis de Mores, a local rancher, and his wife, Medora. Other attractions include the Doll House (antique dolls and toys), the Rough Rider Time Machine (a free multimedia presentation), and the Museum of the Badlands. Medora attractions operate from about Memorial Day through Labor Day.

The Medora Musical (call phone numbers for Medora above) is performed outdoors in the 2,750-seat Burning Hills Amphitheater on a bluff outside town (there's no official address, but there are plenty of signs). It has a nifty reversible outdoor escalator. The rollicking musical is a boot-stomping salute to Teddy Roosevelt and the American spirit. It is held nightly at 8:30 p.m. from early June through early September; ticket prices are $17.50 for adults, $10.00 for students (grades 1 through 12), and free for preschoolers and those younger. We recommend you order tickets in advance.

The interstate will take you east to Dickinson and the **Dakota Dinosaur Museum,** (701) 225–DINO, 200 Museum Drive, exit 61 off I-94. Here you can look at more than 12,000 fossils, rocks, minerals, shells, and re-created dinosaurs. The museum has educational activities for kids, including a once daily Dino Dig (Memorial Day through Labor Day, kindergarten through sixth grade students only). The museum is closed November to April; however, groups of 20 or more can make advance arrangements to visit during that time. From April until

Memorial Day and after Labor Day, hours are 9:00 A.M. to 3:00 P.M., Thursday through Saturday, and noon to 3:00 P.M. on Sunday. From Memorial Day through Labor Day, hours are 9:00 A.M. to 6:00 P.M., seven days a week. Admission prices are $5.00 for adults, $3.00 for children, and $5.00 for the Dino Dig. While you're there, visit the other museums on the grounds. The Joachim Regional Museum (local artifacts and displays) is open year-round. The Pioneer Machinery Museum and Prairie Outpost Park operate from Memorial Day through Labor Day.

Request a visitor packet from the North Dakota Tourism Office by calling (800) 453–5663, or log on to the Web site at www.ndtourism.com

Northwest of the Black Hills

Montana

The landscape of the fourth-largest state is striking and gorgeous, and it makes a great backdrop for the places you'll visit there. Best of all, Montana—despite its size—has fewer than a million residents, which means you can find lots of elbow room. Eastern Montana, the flatter and less well-known part of the state—revels in its history, and you'll find many museums there. Montana, the Treasure State, truly is filled with treasures.

Cross into Montana from Belle Fourche, South Dakota, on U.S. 212. The first town you'll come to is Alzada, in ranching country. Enjoy the scenery until

Insiders' Tip

The Anatosaurus, or duck-billed dinosaur, is the Montana state fossil, and the mighty ponderosa pine is the state tree.

you come to Broadus, where you can visit the free **Powder River Historical Museum,** (406) 436-2977, on the town square, and see the old county jail, a chuck wagon, artifacts, antique cars, and a collection of 200,000 seashells. The **Powder River Wagon Train and Cattle Drive** is an annual August event in Broadus, and you can participate on horseback or by wagon. Call (406) 436-2404 or (800) 492-8835 to sign up.

Continue on U.S. 212 and you'll come to Ashland and Lame Deer, on the Northern Cheyenne Reservation. Custer's last camp before his troops began the Battle of Little Bighorn was in the area. The free **Cheyenne Indian Museum** is in Ashland, (406) 784-2746, on the St. Labre Indian School campus. There's no street address—Ashland is a small town—but you can't miss it. It's open year-round. In the winter, hours are 8:00 A.M. to 4:30 P.M., Monday through Friday; from Memorial Day through Labor Day, hours are 8:00 A.M. to 5:30 P.M., seven days a week. The **Ashland Pow Wow** is held each year on Labor Day weekend, and the **Northern Cheyenne Pow Wow** is on the Fourth of July weekend. For information about the powwows, call the tribal offices at (406) 477-6284.

Head north on Montana Highway 39 to Colstrip, the energy capital of Montana. At the visitor center, (406) 748-5046, corner of Main Street and Homestead Boule-

vard, you can take a free tour of the open-pit mine, Monday through Friday (reservations required). The **Schoolhouse History and Art Center,** (406) 748-4822, corner of Woodrose and Pine, has an exhibit of historic photographs, revolving art shows featuring the work of local artists, and a museum store. It's open from noon to 4:00 P.M., Tuesday through Friday, year-round except in January, when the center is closed.

Next on Montana Highway 39 is Forsyth, on the Yellowstone River's banks. Be sure to see the free **Pioneer Museum,** (406) 356-7547, 1300 Main Street, and the neoclassical **Rosebud County Courthouse,** (406) 356-7318, 1200 Main Street, listed on the National Register of Historic Places.

I-94 will take you back east to Miles City, home of the annual **Jaycee Bucking Horse Sale,** (406) 232-2890, held downtown on the third weekend in May. You can watch as the horses run down Main Street, and there's a parade, good Western home cooking at the steak fry and pancake breakfast, and more fun events. The annual **Western Art Roundup,** (406) 232-2890, is held in conjunction with the Bucking Horse Sale. At nearby **Pirogue Island State Park,** (406) 232-0900, Kinsey Highway, you can hunt for agates. Don't miss the free **Custer County Art Center,** (406) 232-0635, Water Plant Road, which features work by local and regional artists. The **Range Riders Museum,** (406) 232-6146, just west of town and across the Tongue River on Montana Highway 10, displays the town's original Main Street, a heritage center, and exhibits devoted to local history. There is an admission charge; please call ahead for hours.

From Miles City head north to Terry, also on the Yellowstone River. The **Lady Cameron Museum,** (406) 635-4040, Logan Street, has an exhibit of wonderful photographs taken by a British woman pioneer who arrived there in the late 1800s. The **Prairie County Museum,** also (406) 635-4040, next door to the Lady Cameron, is another museum filled with historic artifacts and worth a visit. Both are open only from Memorial Day through Labor Day and accept donations in lieu of paid admissions.

Farther north is Glendive, home of the free **Frontier Gateway Museum,** (406) 635–4040, Belle Prairie Road, a collection of Plains Indian, ranch, and farm artifacts that's open only in the summer. You'll also want to visit **Makoshika State Park,** (406) 365–6256, Snyder Avenue, where erosion has created some spectacular rock formations on 8,800 acres that also contain fossils, including the amazing Triceratops, whose skull is on display in the visitor center (open year-round). A Montana state park license is required to enter the park; the license is $4.00 daily per car or $20.00 annually and admits you to any state park in Montana. A complement to the strange natural wonders of Makoshika is Buzzard Days, an annual spring celebration dedicated to the return of the turkey vultures to the park. Call for the exact date; it varies each year. You can take a bird-watching tour, participate in the 10K run, and enjoy breakfasts and barbecues. The park's entrance fee is waived during the celebration.

As the interstate turns east, you'll come to Wibaux, named for cattleman Pierre Wibaux, who owned the Roubaix Mine and the 777 Ranch in South Dakota's Black Hills. The town is also the home of St. Peter's Catholic Church, downtown, built in 1885, which has an unusual lava rock facade and beautiful stained glass. You can't tour the church, and there's no telephone, but you can take a look at the outside of the structure. At the free **Pierre Wibaux Museum Complex,** (406) 795–9969 or (406) 795–2381, Orgain Street, you'll learn about eastern Montana through the exhibits and by touring Wibaux's 1892 home and offices as well as the other historic buildings in the complex, which is open only in the summer. The Wibaux County Fair is held in late August.

Driving south, you'll come to **Medicine Rocks State Park,** (406) 232–0900, off Montana Highway 7, 10 miles north of Ekalaka, where it is said Native American hunting parties found magical spirits. The sandstone rocks there do indeed have strange and mystical forms. Ekalaka has

an almost-complete Anatosaurus (duck-billed dino) skeleton that awaits you in the downtown **Carter County Museum,** (406) 775–6686.

A bit farther south are the Chalk Buttes and Custer National Forest, but Montana Highway 7 is unpaved after it leaves Ekalaka, so you may want to turn back to town and choose another route to your desired destination.

For a Montana travel packet, call Travel Montana's Custer Country offices at (406) 665–1671 or (800) 346–1876, ext. 6. You can also call Travel Montana's Helena office at (406) 444–2654 or (800) VISITMT, or log on to the fill Montana Web site at: www.visitmt.com.

South of the Black Hills

Nebraska

Nebraska, like North Dakota, is an "undiscovered" state, often believed to be just an uninteresting flat expanse of rangeland. Although parts of the state are indeed flat and plain, western Nebraska—known as the Panhandle—will probably surprise you. This is a varied landscape of rocky geological wonders, grasslands, rolling hills, and the fabled, mysterious sandhills. The western counties of Box Butte, Sioux, and Dawes hold a wealth of sightseeing adventures, especially for the traveler interested in history and natural wonders.

U.S. 385 from Hot Springs, South Dakota, will take you to the town of Chadron. The **Chadron State College** Administration Building's second floor,

> ### Insiders' Tip
> Nebraska, the Cornhusker State, became a state in 1887. Arbor Day originated in Nebraska, the 16th-largest state.

(308) 432-5276, Main Street, has local author Mari Sandoz memorabilia and archives as well as a Sandhills library.

Chadron State Park, (308) 432-5167, 8 miles south of Chadron off U.S. 385, is set in the spectacular Pine Ridge cliffs and buttes of the Nebraska National Forest. You can camp, hike, swim, cross-county ski, and trail ride, and planned activities such as cookouts and demonstrations are offered in the summer. Cabins are available from mid-April through mid-November. A Nebraska state park entrance license is $2.50 daily per car or $14.00 for the season. The northern section of the park closes in the winter.

The fascinating **Museum of the Fur Trade,** (308) 432-3843, east of Chadron on U.S. 20, will give you insight into how the trade helped develop western Nebraska. It is open only from Memorial Day through Labor Day, 8:00 A.M. to 5:00 P.M. Fur Trade Days are held in Chadron on the second weekend of July each year.

The 22,000-acre **Fort Robinson State Historical Park,** (308) 665-2900, U.S. 20 near Crawford, is both the site of the 1874 fort where Crazy Horse was murdered and a recreation area. It's open year-round for hiking, cross-country skiing, and mountain biking. The **Fort Robinson Museum,** (308) 665-2919, and the **Trailside Museum,** (308) 665-2929, are also on the grounds and are open Memorial Day through Labor Day. Cabins and the lodge are open mid-April through mid-November. You

Insiders' Tip

Just beyond the Black Hills lie prairie flatlands, the Pine Ridge Indian Reservation, the state capital, the broad Missouri River, and numerous pioneer-turned-tourist towns. Neighboring states beckon with attractions, too.

must purchase a state park entrance license to enjoy this or any other Nebraska state park. The annual **Western Art Show** is held at the fort over the 4th of July weekend.

This is also the region of the Nebraska Badlands, with some spooky natural scenery. Visit strange **Toadstool Park,** (402) 471-0641, Toadstool Road, off secondary state highway Nebraska 2, a National Geologic Site that has hiking trails and picnic facilities.

The **Agate Fossil Beds,** (308) 668-2211, are about 20 miles south of Harrison on Nebraska Highway 29. At this National Monument, you'll see fossil beds 19 million years old and paleontology exhibits in the visitor center. The free center is open year-round, 8:30 A.M. to 5:30 P.M. daily.

As you journey south on U.S. 385, you will cross the Niobrara River, ranked among the top-10 canoeing rivers in the country. Then turn east (at Alliance) on Nebraska Highway 2, and you will come to the Sandhills, once called the Great American Desert. Wildlife refuges and tiny lakes are scattered over this area; to learn more about them, call the Nebraska Game and Parks Commission at (402) 471-0641.

Check out the town of Alliance, the Coal Capital of Nebraska and a railroad town since the late 1800s. The town's Central Park encompasses the Sunken Gardens, Sallows Conservatory and Arboretum, and the Central Park Fountain, a WPA project listed on the National Register of Historic Places. The free **Knight Museum,** (308) 762-2384, 908 Yellowstone Avenue, has cavalry and Native American artifacts and is open May 1 through Labor Day weekend.

Somewhat less elegant, but equally fascinating, is Alliance's **Carhenge,** (308) 762-4954 or (308) 762-1520, 2.5 miles north of Alliance on U.S. 385, which replicates England's Stonehenge using old cars instead of stone. The hilarious display was created in 1987 using Stone Age construction methods: lots of people pushing and pulling, and probably muttering and groaning. Although the state Department of Roads insisted it was a junkyard and tried to have it removed, it is still maintained by the Friends of Carhenge, which accepts donations for its upkeep (admission is free). Sculptures on the grounds are also made of car parts. Some 80,000 people visit this pseudomystical shrine to used transportation each year.

South of Alliance, near Bridgeport, are **Courthouse Rock, Jailhouse Rock,** and **Chimney Rock National Historic Site,** (308) 586-2581, impressive geologic formations that were milestones for pioneers traveling the Oregon and Mormon Trails. **Scottsbluff National Monument,** near Gering, (309) 436-4340, is another great landmark, with a fine visitor center. To the pioneers, these formations were signs that they had made it through the vast prairie and were about to embark on the difficult trails through the mountains. History buffs will want to tour the **North Platte Valley Museum** in Gering (308) 436-5411, where Nebraska pioneer history is lovingly preserved.

The Nebraska Division of Tourism can give you more information about the state on their Web site at www.visitnebraska.org.

Southeast of the Black Hills

South Central South Dakota

South and east of the Black Hills lies the Pine Ridge Indian Reservation, with several sites you'll want to visit. Follow U.S. 18 from Hot Springs east across the reservation. Pine Ridge is home to the Oglala Lakota people, many species of wildlife, and some beautiful, expansive landscape. The Oglala tribe is one of the seven that make up the Great Lakota (Sioux) Nation. Famous leaders Crazy Horse, Red Cloud, and American Horse were Oglala Lakota.

The annual Oglala Nation Pow-Wow and Rodeo is held in August. You can take scenic drives across the reservation, too, watching for spectacular geological formations with romantic names such as Yellow Bear Canyon, Slim Buttes, and Wolf Table. Some bus and van tour companies offer sightseeing tours of the reservation; these are listed in our Getting Here, Getting Around chapter. For information about Pine Ridge scenic drives, events, and tourism, call the Oglala Sioux Tribe's Office of Tourism at (605) 867-5301.

If you'd like to try your money-winning luck, your first stop as you enter the reservation could be the **Prairie Wind Casino,** (605) 867-6300, (800) 705-WIND, off U.S. 18, near the town of Oglala. The casino is open 24 hours a day.

Four miles west of the town of Pine Ridge is the **Red Cloud Indian School,** (605) 867-1105, off U.S. 18, founded in 1887 when Chief Red Cloud asked the Jesuits to teach his people. The **Holy Rosary Church,** completed in 1898, was the first brick church west of the Missouri River. It burned on Good Friday 1996, a sad event. But—a testament to the strength and faith of parishioners—a ground-breaking ceremony for a new building took place on Good Friday 1997, and the new church was ready for services on Easter Sunday 1998.

In the original building on the Red Cloud campus (built in 1888), you can tour the **Heritage Center,** (605) 867-5491, which was also rebuilt after the fire. The center houses a rich Native American art collection, with paintings, traditional artifacts, sculptures, beadwork and quill-work, and a gift shop. The Red Cloud Indian Art Show is sponsored annually by the school, from the first Sunday in June through the third Sunday in August. It's the largest juried show of its kind for Native American art in the country and is attended by collectors from all over the world. Other pieces remain on permanent display at the Heritage Center.

Ask at the administrative offices (adjacent to the Heritage Center) for a tour of the cemetery atop the hill, where the grave of the venerable Red Cloud is located. The great chief, who died in 1910, possessed admirable foresight about the education of the children of his people. Many others are buried in the historic cemetery, both Native American and white, including nuns and priests who served at the school.

Next you'll come to the town of Pine Ridge, headquarters of Oglala tribal government. And at the intersection of Bureau of Indian Affairs (BIA) Route 27 and U.S. 18, where a sign points to the town of Wounded Knee, you'll see a ceme-

The annual Oglala Nation Pow Wow and Rodeo takes place each August on the Pine Ridge Indian Reservation. PHOTO: COURTESY OF SOUTH DAKOTA TOURISM

Oglala Lakota Chief Red Cloud's final resting place is in the cemetery at Red Cloud Indian School on the Pine Ridge Indian Reservation. PHOTO: BARBARA TOMOVICK

tery and church on the hill. Look for a cement block and iron arch at the entrance—it is not otherwise marked. This is the site of the 1890 Wounded Knee Massacre. You can look around without charge, but please don't disturb the offerings you see on the graves. The cemetery is open year-round all day long; if you need information, call the Oglala Tribe's Office of Tourism at (605) 867-5301. A large sign across the highway tells the story; note where the word "Battle" has been corrected to read "Massacre."

East of the Black Hills

West Central South Dakota

As you head east on I-90, you'll pass some interesting and quaint farming towns. The Badlands and Wall area east of the Black Hills are in their own chapter in this book (see The Badlands and Nearby).

Stop at Murdo, where the line that separates the Mountain Standard Time and Central Standard Time zones is just to the west of the town limits—don't forget to reset your watch! Murdo is the home of the **Pioneer Auto Show and Antique Town,** (605) 669-2691, I-90, exit 192, with the country's largest private collection of vehicles. Elvis Presley's motorcycle is there, as are 250 other classics. There are also collections of minerals, antique tractors, old china and crystal, antique clothing, organs and music boxes, and antique toys. The exhibits are housed in 39 buildings on 10 acres that also include a restored town. You can lunch at the food court and shop for gifts and antiques, too. The Pioneer Auto Show is open year-round. From May 1 through October 1, hours are 7:00 A.M. to 8:00 P.M. During the winter, hours are 8:30 A.M. to 6:00 P.M. Call ahead because these hours may change with weather conditions. Admission is $7.00 for adults and $3.50 for children.

To take a side trip to South Dakota's capital, Pierre (pronounced "Peer"), turn off I-90 at exit 212; Pierre is about 35 miles farther north on U.S. 83, and you'll

LEGENDS &LORE

The Massacre at Wounded Knee

The Wounded Knee Massacre site, on a windswept hill sloping down to a valley and ravines, is a powerful place that marks a shameful incident. Here, in 1890, 14 years after their comrades and commander Lt. Col. George Custer were wiped out at Little Big Horn, and still nursing a grudge, the Seventh Cavalry opened fire on men, women, children, and elderly Lakota of Chief Big Foot's band, including the chief himself, who was dying of pneumonia.

Although the massacre started when an accidental rifle shot panicked the soldiers, eyewitness accounts say the cavalry then methodically hunted down the fleeing people. Bodies—including those of mothers with babies and small children—were found as far as 3 miles away, and many had been shot at close range. Although the military immediately began an investigation, charges against officers were soon dropped, and several soldiers received the Congressional Medal of Honor for their part in the massacre.

It's estimated that 100 to 300 Lakota died that day, or later, from their wounds. Many were found by their kin, taken to camps to die, and buried elsewhere. Of the cavalrymen, 25 died then and 39 were wounded, some of whom died later. Eyewitnesses and researchers' accounts conflict. Some believe the Lakota were unarmed; others believe that despite being disarmed, a few warriors had hidden guns. Some historians think that many soldiers were killed by their comrades' panicky cross fire. Whatever the historical truth, that night, four days after Christmas, a number of survivors were taken to the nearby Episcopal mission where, it is said, a festive holiday banner still hung. Ironically, it read: "Peace on earth, good will to men."

On the night of the massacre, a blizzard hit, with raging winds and minus-40-degree temperatures. By the time the storm passed and a burial detail arrived, three days had gone by. A 60-foot-long trench was dug at the top of the hill, and frozen Lakota bodies were laid in it, after first being stripped of clothing and possessions, which were sold as artifacts. This grave is now fenced and marked by a monument at the Wounded Knee Cemetery, which is still in use.

Near the mass grave is the burial site of Lost Bird, who, just four months old, miraculously survived frigid temperatures for three days before being discovered beneath her mother's body. Her tragic story is told in *Lost Bird of Wounded Knee* by Renee Sansom Flood. Lost Bird died in 1920 at age 29 in California. In 1991 her remains were returned to Wounded Kneed and reburied with her own people.

pass through the Fort Pierre National Grassland on your way. The elegant **State Capitol** building, (605) 773-3765, in the Capitol Complex between Fourth Street and Capitol Avenue, is worth a visit. Built in 1910 with a South Dakota granite foundation and solid copper dome, the building has been restored to its early-1900s glory. Free tours are conducted from 8:00 A.M. to 5:00 P.M., Monday through Friday, and must be scheduled in advance at the visitor information center in the Capitol building.

While you're at the complex, visit Capitol Lake where, in the fall, hundreds of migrating Canada geese use the lake as a stopover. You'll also want to see the Fighting Stallions Memorial created by Crazy Horse Memorial's sculptor, Korczak Ziolkowski, in memory of the eight victims of the 1993 plane crash that claimed the life of South Dakota's governor, George S. Mickelson.

Pierre celebrates its visiting Canada geese with the annual Goosefest in late September. Recently the festivities included a wine tasting, arts and crafts displays, concerts, and the Honker 5K and 10K runs. Call the Pierre Area Chamber of Commerce, (605) 224-7361 or (800) 962-2034, for information about the annual event.

The **Museum of the South Dakota State Historical Society** and the **Cultural Heritage Center,** (605) 775-3458, are also on the Capitol Complex grounds, north of the Capitol building. You'll find exhibits on cultural, pioneer, and Native American history, the State Archives (which the public can use for genealogical research), an observation gallery with views of the Capitol grounds and Pierre, and a gift shop that carries South Dakota–made products. Admission for those 19 and older is $3.00; those 18 and younger are admitted free. Hours are 9:00 A.M. to 4:30 P.M., Monday through Friday, and 1:00 P.M. to 4:30 P.M., Saturday and Sunday (it's closed for Thanksgiving, Christmas, and New Year's Day).

Kids will enjoy the **South Dakota Discovery Center and Aquarium,** (605) 224-8295, 805 West Sioux, Pierre. It's the state's only year-round science and technology center, with 60 hands-on activities, planetarium shows, and several aquariums with fish from the local aquatic environment (no dolphins or performing seals). After Labor Day until Memorial Day, it's open 1:00 to 5:00 P.M., Sunday through Friday, and 10:00 A.M. to 5:00 P.M. on Saturday. From Memorial Day through Labor Day, it's open from 10:00 A.M. to 5:00 P.M. Monday through Saturday, and 1:00 to 5:00 P.M. on Sunday. Admission is $3.00 for those 13 and older, $1.75 for children 3 to 12, and free for kids younger than 3.

At Fort Pierre (across the river from the Capital) visit the 60,000-acre **Triple U Buffalo Ranch,** (605) 567-3624, 2631 Tatanka Road. You can take a motorized tour of the ranch and see the herd of about 4,000 bison and the site where the movie *Dances with Wolves* was filmed. The cost is $21.00 for one to four adults or $5.00 each for five or more adults. For children 6 to 12, the cost is $3.00, and those younger than 6 take the tour without charge. Reservations in advance are required.

The 231-mile-long **Lake Oahe** reservoir, which dams the great Missouri River, stretches from Pierre to Bismarck, North Dakota, and is the fourth largest in the nation. One of the state's greatest recreational treasures, Lake Oahe has more than 2,200 miles of shoreline (nearly twice that of California), seven dams (three in North Dakota) and 900 square miles of water. It's a great place to fish for walleye, salmon, bass, and trout; or to sail, ski, and windsurf. The Pierre Area Chamber of Commerce, (605) 224-7361 or (800) 962-2034, has more information.

Hunkpapa Sioux Chief Sitting Bull left his mark over a wide area. He was born in South Dakota, helped defeat Custer's Seventh Cavalry in Montana, and was buried in North Dakota and reburied in South Dakota, ending a dispute over who should have his bones. PHOTO: COURTESY OF SOUTH DAKOTA TOURISM

A monument honors the Lakota people who died during the Wounded Knee Massacre and marks the mass grave where they are buried. The bits of brightly colored cloth tied to the fence are among offerings left by Native American visitors.

PHOTO: SOUTH DAKOTA TOURISM

Lake Sharp is another great fishing and recreation waterway, south of Lake Oahe, off South Dakota Highway 47 on the way to Chamberlain. If you're there in the summer, you can also visit nearby Lower Brule and Crow Creek Indian Reservations and watch the annual powwows. Or try your luck at the tribes' casinos; the Crow Creek tribe operates the Lode Star, (605) 245-6000, and the Lower Brule tribe operates the Golden Buffalo, (605) 473-5577. For information about visiting the reservations, call the Crow Creek Sioux Tribal Office at (605) 245-2221 or the Lower Brule Sioux Tribe Office at (605) 473-5399.

Back on I-90, continue to Chamberlain (about 2 miles from exit 263), home of the **Akta Lakota Museum and Cultural Center,** (605) 734-3452 or (800) 798-3452 (there's no address, but you'll see it as you drive through Chamberlain). On the grounds of St. Joseph's Indian School, the museum has been amassing a rich collection of Lakota art and artifacts since the school was founded in 1927. Admission is free, but donations are appreciated. Both a gift shop and a gallery of original art are part of the museum. From May 1 through September 30, hours are 8:00 A.M. to 6:00 P.M., Monday through

Friday. From Memorial Day to Labor Day, Saturday (8:00 A.M. to 6:00 P.M.) and Sunday (1:00 to 5:00 P.M.) hours are added. From October 1 through April 30, hours are 8:30 A.M. to 4:30 P.M., Monday through Friday only.

West of the Black Hills

Wyoming

Our neighbor to the west is Wyoming. You'll be surprised how the landscape changes in the northeastern part of this state, after you cross the South Dakota border. It quickly becomes more rugged, steeper, rockier, and more heavily forested—a landscape that is quite Western-looking, if you will.

Try the tiny town of Aladdin first. Take South Dakota Highway 34 from Belle Fourche, South Dakota, which becomes Wyoming Highway 24. Just east of town, you'll come to the free Aladdin Historic Interpretive Park, site of the coal mine that sustained the town. Only about 15 people live in Aladdin now, and its main attraction is the big old **Aladdin General Store** and post office, (307) 896-2226, right off the highway. It was built in 1896 and still operates both as a supplier to area ranchers and as a tourist draw. The funky store has groceries, gifts, and crafts, and there's a great antiques shop and boutique in the deteriorating, but charming, upstairs. The store is open every day, although hours are shortened a bit in the winter. The Hard Buck Cafe next door is a fun place to eat for adventurous visitors who aren't afraid of a casual cleaning philosophy. Ask about the homemade pies.

Then journey on to Hulett, (307) 467-5430, where Devils Tower National Monument will appear on the horizon as you approach. You'll be passing through the Bear Lodge district of the Black Hills National Forest and the Bear Lodge Mountains. Hulett is a Western logging town with interesting buildings and shops, and the town hosts a rodeo on the second weekend in June.

In 2002 **Devils Tower,** (800) 354-6316, 9 miles from Hulett on Wyoming

Black Hills' Time Zones

Until the 1880s, the United States had no time zones. Each town simply operated on its own "local time," which for farmers was nature's time, clocked by the sun's movement. As railroads became the most popular means of travel and transportation, "railroad time" was instituted to make timetables simpler. But, eventually, there were 100 different railroad times, and it became quite confusing. Travelers found themselves arriving at a station before they'd left the previous station—according to the timetable, that is.

In 1883 the railroads in the United States and Canada established four time zones to alleviate the problem. On November 18, the newly coordinated times were telegraphed to cities all over the country, and everyone—even farmers—adjusted his or her schedule to the newfangled way. It is said that a Mr. Sears, agent at the Minneapolis and St. Louis railroad station in Minnesota, made a tidy sum selling pocket watches to people who had never needed them before. And it wasn't long before he moved to Chicago and started a new business called Sears, Roebuck and Company.

The time zone system was so successful that Congress made it official in 1918. The dividing line between the Central and Mountain Standard Time zones runs through the Great Plains, but the railroads chose its exact route. Thus, the line meanders and jogs, apparently for the convenience of the railroads and their scheduled stops. You'll find some towns, even the mighty Missouri River, divided by the line and—theoretically, anyway, neighbors on Central Time living next door to folks on Mountain Time.

Highway 24, celebrates the 96th anniversary of its designation as a National Monument (so declared by President Theodore Roosevelt, the great conservationist. It was also the first National Monument in the United States). The spectacular tower is 865 feet high, 1,000 feet in diameter at the bottom, and rises 1,267 feet above the Belle Fourche River valley below. The 1.3-mile Tower Trail meanders around the base and past huge granite columns that have fallen from the tower. The 3-mile **Red Beds Trail** circles the tower and explores the nearby forest and river valley. When you see this ancient, eroded volcano core, you'll agree that the makers of the movie *Close Encounters of the Third Kind* rightly chose the tower to portray a mystical icon people couldn't resist. It's quite magical in real life, too.

Devils Tower National Monument is open year-round, 24 hours a day. You can stay at the campground there from April through October. The visitor center is open daily 8:00 A.M. to 8:00 P.M. May through October only, and has a museum and natural history exhibits. Daily programs and demonstrations on geology, wildlife, history, climbing, and more are conducted by staff in the summer. The park entrance fee is $10 per vehicle. You can find refreshments at the **Devils Tower Trading Post,** (307) 467–5295, at the entrance to the monument. For more on Devils Tower, see the Close-up in this chapter.

Drive on down U.S. 14 to Sundance (where the Sundance Kid got his name) and visit the free **Crook County Museum and Art Gallery,** (307) 283–3666, in the courthouse basement at 309 Cleveland. Kids love the exhibits about the Kid, who was tried for horse stealing in town. The museum has the original court records, even the "Wanted" posters, plus Western artifacts and an exhibit devoted to the nearby Vore Buffalo Jump. Each month a local artist exhibits work at the museum, too. It's open year-round, Monday through Friday, 8:00 A.M. to 8:00 P.M. in

Devils Tower National Monument

There is no word for "devil" in the Lakota language. How, then, did Devils Tower get its name?

The massive landmark was christened by Col. Richard Dodge in 1875. Dodge and his Army troops accompanied the Jenney-Newton expedition, a scientific team ostensibly studying the Black Hills region (although they were also looking for gold). The expedition was in violation of the Fort Laramie Treaty of 1868, which had ceded the Hills to the Plains tribes.

Dodge wrote that when he asked Native American scouts about the Black Hills, they responded with what he called "studied silence." Perhaps they hoped the intruders would give up in disappointment and go away. If so, it didn't work. The scouts did say that the enormous tower's name was "bad god's tower," and again, this may have been an attempt to frighten the explorers, whose curiosity was then only more intensely piqued. Dodge decided the proper translation of the tower's name was "Devils Tower."

For centuries, native people have had great respect for the mystical tower. It was the site of the ancient Sun Dance and is still a place of great power that plays a consecrated part in seasonal rites. The Lakota call it *mato tipi la paha,* "the hill of the bear's lodge." Other tribes revere the tower, too, and have their own names for it.

The Devils Tower reflects in Belle Fourche River. PHOTO: COURTESY OF NATIONAL PARK SERVICE

Several tribes share a legend about its origin: It is said that seven little girls, playing outside their camp, were chased by a huge bear. Frightened, they jumped atop a rock and prayed for help. Hearing their pleas, the rock began to rise, higher and higher above the bear. The angry bear clawed at the rock as it rose, straining to reach its prey until the rock was so high that it had to give up. The little girls were pushed upward into the sky where they became a group of seven stars, *wicincala sakowin,* the constellation Pleiades. The bear's claw marks are still there on the tower's sides, a legendary reminder, perhaps, of nature's power to aid respectful believers.

Those less interested in mystical nature and ancient legend offer a scientific explanation: Some 60 million years ago, molten volcanic magma forced its way upward through rock layers but did not break the surface, instead cooling and hardening below. This cooling process caused the volcanic rock to fracture into the huge columns on the tower's sides. Over millions of succeeding years, the softer rock above and around the core eroded away, and the tower rose higher as the rock around it disappeared. The sides of Devils Tower are nearly vertical, all the way to the slightly sloped top, which is about the size of a football field and covered in grasses, sagebrush, and cactus. Small animals—chipmunks, wood rats, snakes—live on the top, having apparently climbed there.

Since 1893 people have climbed the tower, too. That year, two entrepreneurs were first (it's not known if Native Americans climbed the tower), and many thousands followed. In recent years climbers began to interfere with Native American religious observances still held at the age-old place of worship, creating controversy. In 1995 the National Park Service proposed a plan to curtail climbing during June's traditional summer solstice observances. Several climbing guides then secured a federal injunction, claiming violation of laws separating church and state. The National Park Service instead instituted a voluntary restraint policy. In June 1995, 193 people climbed the tower (down from nearly 1,300 in June 1994), but since then the number of climbers has risen again. The controversy has yet to be completely resolved.

Devils Tower National Monument offers many opportunities, recreational and spiritual, for Americans both native and newcomer. The tower itself, however, is above it all. It is simply there, a place of power and wonder, reverence and beauty.

the summer and 8:00 A.M. to 5:00 P.M. in the winter.

A visit to the Vore Buffalo Jump is a must. Exit I-90 at Beulah and drive 2.5 miles west on the frontage road. Pull off the road at the sign, walk down the trail, and read the interpretive display there. Over a period of 300 years (beginning in the 1500s), Native American hunters drove 20,000 stampeding bison into a natural sinkhole to their deaths. There the animals were butchered (nearly every part was used) and their bones were left in the hole to slowly compress and be filled in with earth. The Vore site is one of the largest and best-preserved sites of its kind in the world.

The layers of bones (along with tools that were left behind) are some 20 feet deep and can be counted and studied, much like tree rings, to learn about ancient weather and ecological conditions. In the summer you can look over the shoulders of University of Wyoming archaeologists and students as they work. For information about excavation schedules, call (307) 766-5136, (307) 766-2208, or (307) 283-1192. The Vore Buffalo Jump Foundation and the university are raising funds to construct a visitor center, so donations are appreciated.

Continue to Moorcroft, where the Old Texas Trail crosses the Belle Fourche River, and Pine Haven. Nearby **Keyhole State Park and Reservoir,** (307) 756-3596, 353 McKean Road, has mountain biking, camping in primitive sites and the backcountry, boating and swimming, fishing, and cross-country skiing.

West on 1-90 is Gillette, Energy Capital of the Nation, and the **Rockpile Museum,** (307) 682-5723, U.S. 14-16, open all year. Gillette, founded in 1891 and originally a ranching town, is now the largest coal-producing city in the country. You can take a tour of one of the 16 mines in the area (summers only). Reserve your place by calling (307) 686-0040.

Backtrack east via the interstate to U.S. 16 and the towns of Newcastle and Upton. Newcastle is the home of the free **Anna Miller Museum,** (307) 746-4188, Delaware Washington Park, off U.S. 16, which has local artifacts, fossils, dinosaur bones, dolls, an original stone cavalry barn, treasures from nearby Cambria ghost town, a re-created country store, and old pioneer buildings. The museum is open year-round, Monday through Friday, 9:00 A.M. to 5:00 P.M. Saturday hours (9:00 A.M. to noon) are added in the summer, but the museum is always closed on

Insiders' Tip

While traveling around South Dakota and its adjoining states, you may change time zones. Wyoming and Montana are on Mountain Standard Time, but the line between the Central Standard and Mountain Standard time zones runs through North Dakota, South Dakota, and Nebraska—and the dividing line takes a wild westward swing in northern North Dakota. Time zone lines are marked on most maps and on telephone directory maps, too.

Sunday. The annual Sagebrush Festival is held in late June in Newcastle; it features cowboy poetry, arts and crafts, and parades.

The Wyoming Division of Tourism, (307) 777-7777 or (800) 225-5996, can provide more information and send you a visitor packet. Or, log on to the tourism Web site at www.wyomingtourism.org.

Real Estate

Real Estate in the Black Hills

Real Estate Publications

Real Estate Agencies

You've fallen in love with the Black Hills and decided this is where you want to live, if not right away then as soon as possible. Maybe these are some of your reasons: gorgeous mountain scenery, abundant recreation opportunities practically—or maybe literally—in your backyard, clean air, peace and quiet, and friendly people (and not too many of them).

Whether you're ready to start house hunting or merely want to begin your research, you've turned to the right page. In this chapter we'll give you a preview of the Black Hills real estate scene and direct you to some additional resources where you can get more detailed information. (For a broader look at the area, please see our Area Overview chapter.)

"Everybody wants acreage with Forest Service around it, facing south, with a stream, five minutes from a stoplight," one real estate agent told us. He has a point—the chance to live in a comparatively unspoiled environment is what induces most people to move here or, if they've grown up here, to stay. Yet the Hills are compact enough that no one need feel isolated. You might say it's possible to have your cake and eat it, too—or to have both solitude and conveniences.

Depending on where you live now, you might think our finer homes are overpriced or an incredible bargain. We believe the area has something for everyone, and we encourage you to keep looking until you find what you want in your price range.

In the meantime you might want to rent a house or apartment; believe us, you're not alone. Many (not all) communities report a shortage of rental property, even if, as in Rapid City, there are hundreds of options from which to choose. Newspaper classified ads are an excellent resource for rental listings. You can find information in our real estate publications, too, or you can consult a real estate agency—we've included details about who handles rentals in our individual agency write-ups at the end of this chapter. Sometimes you stumble onto the perfect place through word of mouth, so ask around. And don't hesitate to check the laundromat bulletin board while you're washing your clothes—you never know what might turn up, and we've found persistence always gets results.

This chapter is not by any means meant to be an exhaustive list of places to live. There are small cities and neighborhoods near those mentioned here where you could easily find the home of your dreams, and there are far too many subdivisions for us to list them all. Your best bet is to shop around for a real estate agent with whom you're comfortable, and then use his or her expertise to guide you as you begin shopping for a home. The agency profiles later in the chapter should give you a head start on your search.

Happy hunting!

Real Estate in the Black Hills

Northern Hills

People who want the hospitality and safety of small-town life but don't wish to be isolated from urban comforts find the northern Black Hills provide a number of pleasing variations on that theme. The tranquil towns of Belle Fourche, Spearfish, Lead, Deadwood, and Sturgis all have their own personalities, yet all are reasonably close to the population hub of Rapid City. Some working folks even choose to live in the Northern Hills and commute up to an hour or more to their Rapid City jobs.

Crow Peak trail ascends to lofty areas, which serve to provide stunning views of Spearfish and Bear Butte. PHOTO: BERT GILDART

Belle Fourche

A growth spurt in Belle Fourche several years ago has slowed to a steadier pace, but the town continues to attract home owners looking for the last of the wide open spaces, as one real estate agent so aptly put it. Many of those moving to the Belle Fourche area have pulled up stakes from metropolitan regions; others work in the surrounding towns but choose to own a home here, where prices tend to be lower.

Belle Fourche has responded to growth with the new in-town Ridgefield subdivision, where homes on the approximately 21 lots will be wood-frame. A bit farther out and already established are the Sonoma Estates and Grandview subdivisions. Jewell Estates and rugged Redwater Ranchettes accommodate both wood-frame and mobile homes. At SRK Ranchettes east of town, lots of anywhere from 10 to 30 acres with water, electricity, and phone service— and in some cases, views of the Black Hills— are available for building a new home. Historic homes and fixer-uppers can be found closer to downtown. Home prices range from $25,000 to around $157,000 in Belle Fourche, with the average at $61,000. Rentals, primarily multifamily houses, are plentiful.

Spearfish

In Spearfish, growth and prices have leveled off after a period of robust construction and brisk property sales. A high percentage of homes in this picturesque college town (see the Black Hills State University write-up in our Education chapter) have been built in the past 10 years, and many were custom-built for their owners. Accordingly, prices have nearly doubled in the last decade; the average price of a home in Spearfish today is around $110,000, but you can easily find something for $200,000 or more. Nice homes have made developments such as the Jorgensen, Evans, and Mountain Plains subdivisions quite popular. Mountain Plains, above Spearfish City Park, features large lots with wood-exterior houses that are among the most expensive in town—around $170,000 to $300,000— even though city services aren't provided. Properties in the newer Sandstone Hills subdivision on the southern slope of Lookout Mountain do have city services, and houses being built here run in the $350,000 to $400,000 range. Mountain Shadows Estates is the newest, most modern mobile-home park, with about 300 well-groomed lots designed primarily for larger homes.

The university guarantees there will always be an abundance of mid-priced rentals in Spearfish, and in fact, a number of townhouses and apartment complexes have been built for just that purpose.

Lead and Deadwood

The twin cities of Lead and Deadwood have always been attractive to recreation lovers who want a vacation cabin near our ski areas and snowmobile trails (see our Recreation chapter), thus ensuring a continuing market for country properties here. But home buyers are also interested in owning a house in town, and in Lead especially it's a buyer's market; we saw homes listed for $39,900 and less. Subdivisions offer the best of both worlds, making the new Hearst development in Lead and well-established 76 Ranch Estates near Deadwood extremely popular. There, wood-exterior houses and large lots lend a rural feel; Hearst's paved roads and city utilities make it convenient to live up high enough to have a breathtaking view. Expect to pay $100,000 to $300,000 for an upscale house in Hearst or about $25,000 to $45,000 for a lot. The rental market here has been soft of late, with apartments of all kinds ready for occupancy.

Sturgis

Situated along I-90 between Spearfish and Rapid City, Sturgis is both smaller and slower-paced than either. That helps keep prices down, making it possible to find a nice home at a reasonable cost in a convenient location—as escapees from more crowded parts of the West are discovering. Many who choose Sturgis want to live in the country or on the outskirts of town, but new subdivisions called Pine Acres, Hurley, and Vernon Heights Estates

also are filling up quickly. The average price of a house in Sturgis is $70,000, but one agent we spoke with said more mid-priced housing is needed here. Three new apartment buildings help make up the rental market in Sturgis, where few houses are rented.

Central Hills

With the entire Black Hills to choose from, people pick Rapid City for its economic and cultural advantages. Nevertheless, folks relocating here want to feel as if they live in the country; trees and privacy are tops on the list of what they say they want in a home. As construction heads south, new housing developments offer just that type of setting, whether in town or miles away.

Rapid City

Extensive growth is taking place in the area of Rapid City Regional Hospital and the increasing number of medical facilities clustered around it. St. Thomas More High School, a private Catholic institution (see our Education chapter), has a beautiful new building here across from the hospital. And subdivisions such as Terracita are making it an increasingly

> ## Insiders' Tip
>
> New in town? If you've moved to the Rapid City area in the last few months, New Neighbors Welcome Service will send a representative to greet you and supply you with literature, maps, and merchandise certificates to help you get acquainted with your new community. Call (605) 341-5737.

Sandstone Ridge in Rapid City has new, upscale apartments overlooking the golf course at Arrowhead Country Club. PHOTO: STEVEN A. PAGE

residential area, with newer homes listed for around $200,000 and appreciating. Several miles to the southwest, along U.S. 16 outside the city limits, are housing developments such as Copper Oaks, Enchanted Hills, and the exclusive Hart Ranch. The area around Neck Yoke Road off U.S. 16 near Rockerville is noted for its secluded homes.

The Sheridan Lake Road area southwest of town is also the site of new, upscale housing developments such as Countryside (where all the streets are named for bird species) and Countryside South. Homes in Countryside South, which run in the $175,000 to $250,000 range, realize an exceptionally high appreciation rate. Chateaux Ridge and Autumn Hills subdivisions are along Sheridan Lake Road inside the city limits. Lots average around $25,000 to $35,000.

Nemo Road (County Road 234) and Rimrock Highway (Highway 44), which link Rapid City and U.S. 385 to the northwest and west, respectively, are the sites of smaller developments as well as gated Cinnamon Ridge on Rimrock Highway. This scenic road follows the route of the old Crouch Line, a rail line with so many twists and turns that it made a dozen complete circles on every trip between Rapid City and Mystic, crossing more than 100 bridges each way (see our History chapter for more on the arrival of the rails).

Closer to downtown, New Robbinsdale in the southeastern part of the city is attracting home owners who like the newer housing and new Parkview swimming pool there (see our Recreation chapter). Existing homes are in the $125,000 to $150,000 range (with the exception of those in the Rapid City Defense Housing subdivision for Ellsworth Air Force Base personnel, which are less). Several new apartment complexes have been built in New Robbinsdale in recent years. In Old Robbinsdale, folks on a budget can find quaint post–World War II houses and fixer-uppers in the $60,000 range or even as low as $45,000. One resident we know points out that although the houses all looked about the same when they were built in the 1950s, each has since become an individual through decades of remodeling and landscaping—or, in some cases, neglect.

West Rapid City is considered desirable both for its lovely city parks, including Sioux and Canyon Lake parks, and its newer neighborhoods. Stevens High School occupies an expansive site in West Rapid. Prestigious developments in Pinedale Heights, Chapel Valley, and the older section of Carriage Hills have been established for some time and are filled up, but new million-dollar, mansionlike homes are taking hold in the uppermost reaches of Carriage Hills. Lots there carry price tags of around $70,000.

In the historic district around West Boulevard, buyers can find older but well-maintained, higher-end homes in the $400,000 range. The boulevard, one of downtown Rapid City's loveliest features, is popular with fitness-conscious residents who can be seen jogging or power-walking down the tree-lined median just about any time of the day.

The northwestern and northeastern parts of town are well developed, and the area beyond is flat, windy, and less desirable for development. North Rapid includes some subsidized-housing neighborhoods and is becoming increasingly commercial. Rushmore Mall (see our Shopping chapter) is out that way, and I-90 runs through the area.

Rapid Valley to the east offers attractive, affordable homes that are closest to Rapid City Regional Airport (see our Getting Here, Getting Around chapter). Rapid Valley also boasts a Blue Ribbon elementary school, which you can read about in our Education chapter.

The average price of a single-family home in the Rapid City area is $98,000. In a recent year, the highest-priced home went for $700,000, and more than $129 million worth of residential property traded hands. Houses have been appreciating at the rate of about 3 percent per year, a figure attributed at least in part to easy access to the interior of the Black Hills and to Mount Rushmore National Memorial (see our Attractions chapter).

Apartments and rental houses are plentiful in Rapid City, but so are people who want to occupy them. Rentals come in all types, so whether you're looking for a place over a store downtown, a furnished room, an apartment in someone's house, a duplex or multifamily house, a luxury space in an apartment, a townhouse complex beside a golf course, or a furnished or unfurnished house, you're sure to find listings. But expect lots of competition, too. The property management division of a real estate agency can sometimes be your best bet if you're in the market for something new and upscale such as the Sandstone Ridge apartments that overlook Arrowhead Country Club.

North of Rapid City, homes and businesses are going up in the Black Hawk area, where property taxes are lower and building codes and zoning laws are less restrictive. Home owners not concerned with conformity in their neighborhoods or a certain proximity to commercial development may find their heart's desire here.

Hill City

At one point in the mid-1990s, disillusioned exiles from populous places discovered tiny Hill City and dubbed it a cool place to live. But the influx of newcomers to this town of fewer than 1,000 people was short-lived, largely because 85 percent

Insiders' Tip

Before buying country property be sure to inquire about the availability of water. Insiders recommend asking adjacent landowners and checking with a local well driller to find out whether you'd be able to drill a productive well on your piece of paradise and how deep it would have to be.

of the land around Hill City is controlled by the U.S. Forest Service. That leaves little room for private development, and one real estate agent we spoke with views Hill City as an up-and-coming bedroom community for Rapid City, a place where families can find small-town atmosphere and lower housing costs. It will take time, however, because growth here is slow, and development takes place on demand rather than on speculation. In general, Hill City home shoppers are looking to spend $60,000 to $120,000.

Top of the Hills subdivision in the city limits is helping to fill a need for subsidized housing for those on a modest income; an adjacent but yet-unnamed development offers buildable lots with utilities and maintained roads in the $18,000 range for middle-income home buyers. Matkins Addition No. 4, beside Major Lake and also inside the city, offers improved lots as part of a four-acre parcel to be developed in phases. Few existing homes are for sale, and even fixer-uppers are scarce. Desirable out-of-town lots can run around $5,000 to $10,000 an acre but with potentially high costs for improve-

ments because of rocky soil. That's something for prospective buyers to inquire about. However, we've seen beautiful country homes in the Hill City area listed for $130,000 and $230,000, making the good life affordable to a variety of buyers.

Southern Hills

About 90 percent of Custer County comprises public lands. But Custer State Park, Wind Cave National Park (see our Parks and Grasslands chapter for information about both), Jewel Cave National Monument (see our Attractions chapter), and the Black Hills National Forest (see our Recreation chapter) also make this area a special place where people want to buy a plot of land, build a nice house, and settle in to enjoy the wilderness. Trouble is, those places are pricey (by Black Hills standards, anyway), starting at around $150,000, and buildable land is becoming scarce. Finding water can be a tricky business, too, especially to the south and west. So although Custer was the state's fastest growing county a decade or so ago, the pace has slowed since then.

Even on a leafless winter day, trees form a graceful arch over the West Boulevard median in Rapid City. This lovely neighborhood is in a historic district. PHOTO: STEVEN A. PAGE

Custer

New subdivisions are appearing in Custer, such as Weaver subdivision, which accepts double-wide mobile homes on a foundation as well as frame houses. Lots at Crystal Pines go for $37,500 to $47,500, depending on proximity to Rocky Knolls Golf Course (see our Recreation chapter). Two-acre lots in Beaver Lake subdivision are advertised at $25,000, and a five-acre lot in Grey Rocks Estates at $50,000. A typical newer home on five acres runs anywhere from $125,000 to $200,000, and a fixer-upper in town runs around $30,000 to $50,000. But mid-priced homes are in short supply in Custer. So are rentals, which makes it hard for college kids who work in the parks, restaurants, and gift shops to find summer lodging.

Hot Springs

The demand for farms and ranches is high around Hot Springs, especially from out-of-staters who want thousands of pristine acres on which to roam in privacy. Then again, many who are looking in this area want a lot in a subdivision so they can build a house. The 12-acre Hot Brook Overlook 5 miles north of town, Water's Edge on Angostura Reservoir, and Battle Mountain Ranch on U.S. 385 next to Wind Cave National Park (see our Parks and Grasslands chapter) are among subdivisions where lots of several acres may be found. Lone Elk Ranch is a development west of town; to the south are Mountain High subdivision and Country Club Estates, where we saw a new four-bedroom house on 10 acres for $165,000. In town, houses average in the $60,000 to $70,000 range. Rentals tend to be small and quite scarce.

Real Estate Publications

Each area of the Hills has its own publication available for free from real estate agencies and, in some cases, selected newspapers, information centers, and businesses.

The monthly *Home Journal* comes out in a Saturday edition of the *Rapid City Jour-*

Insiders' Tip

Need a plumber? A builder? A siding expert? The Black Hills Home Builders Association can provide you with a list of members to do the job, or just about any other home-building task. Stop in at 3121 West Chicago Street, Rapid City, or call (605) 348-7850.

nal around the middle of the month. The *Home Journal* contains listings for the entire Black Hills—turn it one way and you can leaf through the *Rapid City* pages; flip it over and turn it upside-down to get listings for the rest of the Hills.

Black Hills Real Estate Review is published 10 times a year and contains information about Northern Hills properties.

In Rapid City, look for *Rapid City Homefinder*, which is also available by mail for a subscription fee; write to *Rapid City Homefinder*, P.O. Box 9217, Rapid City, South Dakota 57709, or call (605) 343-7684.

Southern Black Hills Real Estate Review is published 10 times a year and includes listings for Hill City as well as Custer and Hot Springs.

Real Estate Agencies

You'll recognize some of our agencies as big-name franchises with solid reputations in real estate sales. But don't overlook our smaller, independent agencies. Many of them were started in recent years by agents who have been in the local real estate business for a long time and know the area intimately. You'll find additional agencies listed in the Yellow Pages, or you can contact our local boards of Realtors, which are listed below.

Hills-wide

Century 21
607 State St., Belle Fourche
(605) 892–2021
50 Cliff St., Deadwood
(605) 578–1417
123 E. Jackson Blvd., Spearfish
(605) 642–4607
942 14th St., Sturgis
(605) 347–4567
2210 Jackson Blvd., Rapid City
(605) 343–6800, (800) 888–1474
503 Mt. Rushmore Rd., Custer
(605) 673–2433
646 Jennings Ave., Hot Springs
(605) 745–5141

One of the world's largest residential real estate franchises has seven independent offices in the Black Hills. In addition to national name recognition, the franchise offers buyers and sellers a large coverage area. Although the offices operate separately, they do make referrals to each other whether for a house, commercial property, or country acreage. For rental information call individual offices.

The Real Estate Center
376 Main St., Deadwood
(605) 578–3030
140 W. Jackson Blvd., Spearfish
(605) 642–2525
1921 Lazelle St., Sturgis
(605) 347–9300, (800) 510–9301
8 W. Mt. Rushmore Rd., Custer
(605) 673–2629

These four independent offices are part of a limited partnership that started as a single office in Spearfish in 1992. Other agents liked founder Rich Harr's concept and, one by one, asked to be part of it. The partnership specializes in helping people relocate to the Black Hills, and all offices work together, making referrals between them. Combined, they cover the entire area through regional multiple listing services.

Northern Hills

Dakota Gold Realty
719 W. Main St., Lead
(605) 584–2662, (888) 313–GOLD

A small independent company with four agents, Dakota Gold Realty handles seasonal rentals at Terry Peak and Deer Mountain ski areas (see our Recreation chapter), where several privately owned cabins are available. The agency also manages regular rentals as well as sales of residential, commercial, and recreational country properties in the northern Black Hills. People interested in moving to the area can call for a relocation packet.

Johnson Joy Real Estate
1230 North Ave., Ste. 5, Spearfish
(605) 642–5723

This 30-year-old agency deals in homes, ranches, land, and recreational properties in Spearfish and western Wyoming. Ten knowledgeable agents can also help you learn about this beautiful area and send you a packet of information if you're thinking of relocating here.

Johnson Real Estate
722 14th St., Sturgis
(605) 347–0141, (888) 297–1334

An all-purpose, independent agency, Johnson Real Estate has been handling residential and commercial listings in the northern Black Hills, Piedmont, and Black Hawk for about five years. The four agents here handle numerous referrals from other agencies as well as their own walk-in clients.

Insiders' Tip

Realtor is a trademark name for a member of the National Association of Realtors. GRI stands for Graduate Realtor Institute, and CRS stands for Certified Residential Specialist; both mean the agent has taken advanced courses through a Realtor organization.

Abundant year-round sunshine makes elaborate decks a popular feature of Black Hills homes. PHOTO: STEVEN A. PAGE

Real Estate 2000
506½ State St., Belle Fourche
(605) 892-2000

Three agents handle a diverse mix of properties, from rural land, farms, and ranches to traditional residential listings. The company has covered northwest South Dakota and northeast Wyoming since the early 1990s.

Central Hills

Central Hills Real Estate, Inc.
441 Main St., Hill City
(605) 574-6000, (800) 682-9149

This small, independent agency sold between $4 million and $5 million worth of real estate in 1997, its second year in business. Four agents handle commercial and residential listings primarily in Hill City, Custer, and Rapid City. The company also sells real estate at auction.

Coldwell Banker Lewis-Kirkeby Hall Real Estate, Inc.
2700 W. Main St., Rapid City
(605) 343-2700, (888) 343-2700

One of the nation's largest franchises, Coldwall Banker has been established in Rapid City since 1963. Approximately 40 agents handle residential, commercial, business, land, farm, and ranch sales in Rapid City and the Black Hills. A separate property management department can help in your search for any type of rental, and relocation kits are available for prospective newcomers.

Hallmark Realtors Inc.
821½ Columbus St., Rapid City
(605) 343-4545, (800) 343-8301

Three agents sell business, commercial, and residential properties of all kinds in Rapid City and the surrounding Black Hills. The independent agency, which has been in operation since 1985, also provides information packets to clients who are interested in relocating to the area.

Heartland Real Estate Better Homes and Gardens
902 Mt. Rushmore Rd., Rapid City
(605) 343-1600, (800) 998-6128

This local office of a well-known franchise has been specializing in residential listings since 1990. Nine agents focus primarily on Rapid City but sometimes handle sales in other communities as well. They can also help you find a rental house. Their relocation packet has information about the Black Hills and Rapid City areas and includes a mover's guide to help you get organized, plus details about specific homes if you have something special in mind.

Matkins Realty
114 Main St., Hill City
(605) 574-2628

Three agents deal in all types of real estate in Hill City and the surrounding area, including Keystone and Custer. The office, which opened in 1983, can help you locate a rental house or apartment, too. Relocation information is available.

Prudential Kahler Realtors
2020 W. Omaha St., Rapid City
(605) 343-7500, (800) 658-5550

After 35 years as an independent company, Kahler joined the Prudential franchise. The 25 agents here specialize in residential and commercial sales throughout the Black Hills area. The property management division handles all types of rentals, from houses and apartments to offices, warehouses, and strip malls. The relocation division sends information packets upon request.

Raben Real Estate
302 Main St., Rapid City
(605) 342-7272, (800) 888-1619 (relocation information)

Relocation is a major part of Raben Real Estate's business. Folks with serious inquiries receive a two-hour video tour of the Black Hills, from the backcountry to attractions and shopping; a book on many aspects of life here; several smaller publications; and even customized information for those with specific requests. About 20 agents handle primarily residential listings in this company, which opened in 1972. They can also provide you with a list of available apartments.

RE/MAX Realtors
1240 Jackson Blvd., Rapid City
(605) 341-4300, (800) 341-4305

The Real Estate Maximum concept that originated in Denver in the mid-1970s has made RE/MAX an internationally successful franchise. Under the formula, each agent is an independent producer committed to providing top-quality service, and the 23 agents in the Rapid City office are no exception. The office deals in residential and commercial properties in Rapid City and within a 50- to 60-mile radius. Relocation packets are available upon request.

Rossum & Neal, Realtors
2400 W. Main St., Rapid City
(605) 342-9112, (800) 888-1430

The motto at this independent agency is, "Our reputation is your guarantee." About 18 agents sell homes, commercial properties, and land in Rapid City and the immediate area. Whether you're moving in or moving away, Rossum & Neal can make the relocation process easier, either by providing an information packet with a free video about the Black Hills or by helping you find an agency in your future hometown. Local rentals of all kinds are handled here as well.

Southern Hills

Black Hills Land Co.
428 Mt. Rushmore Rd., Custer
(605) 673-3167

Broker/owner Patrick D. Krantz has more than 10 years of experience in selling land, which is his specialty. He started his own company, where he's the sole agent, in 1996 to handle sales of farms, ranches, recreational properties, and acreages for building a custom home (occasionally, he'll list one with a house already on it). Krantz's coverage area in western South Dakota and eastern Wyoming includes the entire Black Hills.

Wyatt's Real Estate
309 N. River St., Hot Springs
(605) 745-3140

Boards of Realtors

Local boards of Realtors primarily serve the agencies in their territory, but they can also provide home buyers with a list of member firms and handle ethical complaints against real estate agents. Some also offer mediation service for a fee when buyers and sellers get into a dispute, or provide statistical data about property sales. Here's a list of our local boards:

- Northwestern South Dakota Board of Realtors, Inc., 121 West Hudson Street, Spearfish (605) 642–0200

- Black Hills Board of Realtors, 1836 West Kansas City Street, Rapid City (605) 341–2580

- Southern Black Hills Board of Realtors has no permanent headquarters because officers rotate, so you need to get in touch with a member agency for contact information. When this book was written, all of the Hill City, Custer, and Hot Springs agencies listed here were members, with the exception of Matkins Realty in Hill City.

Wyatt's recently celebrated 25 years of selling real estate. You'll find specialists in ranches and appraisals among the three agents at this independent company, which also deals in residential, commercial, and undeveloped properties within about a 20-mile radius of Hot Springs. Requests for relocation information are handled individually.

Education

Public Schools

Private Schools

Montessori Schools

Head Start Programs

Colleges and
Technical Schools

As South Dakotans, we take a lot of teasing about being backward. Admittedly, some of us were just discovering espresso about the time Seattlites had had their fill of heavy-duty joe and switched to soup. But it didn't take a caffeine craze from the West Coast to get us wired. We did that all on our own through a state program called Wiring the Schools, an initiative aimed at getting every school in South Dakota connected to the Internet. So although we might be a bit behind the times when it comes to the latest fad, we're anything but backward in the field of technology.

That's because we're as serious as anyone about educating our young people and preparing them to make their way in life. For instance, we provide school-to-work opportunities so students can experience the career world firsthand while earning credit toward graduation. For our gifted students, we have academic enrichment programs to let them stretch their abilities to the fullest. And although we know there's always room for improvement, we see our efforts paying off in test scores that are slightly to significantly higher than the national average, particularly in math and thinking skills. Approximately 85 percent of our high school students stay in school and graduate (our dropout rate is less than 3 percent a year); of those, 43 percent go on to our state four-year colleges, 18 percent go to colleges in other states, and 20 percent attend other postsecondary institutions. Another 5 percent enter the military.

We face some difficult issues, nonetheless. One of our shortcomings is in teacher pay: South Dakota has been 50th or 51st in the nation (counting the District of Columbia) for more years than we care to recall. Another point of contention is the way we fund our public schools. Roughly half of school funding comes from property taxes, a system that has produced several citizen-initiated ballot measures aimed at shifting more, or all, of the burden elsewhere. So far, however, the state legislature has failed to come up with a satisfactory school-funding alternative, in part because the thought of a state income tax is anathema to most South Dakotans. Currently, the state's funding formula provides 50 percent of school funds, paying districts approximately $3,605 per student.

Still, we've been able to move ahead on other issues. With the advent of open enrollment in 1998, our parents and students entered an arena of brand-new choices and challenges. Under open enrollment, most students can attend any public school in the state without paying tuition, subject to limitations aimed at maintaining reasonable attendance levels. The idea is to help students find schools best suited to their needs.

Not everyone in South Dakota is concerned with open enrollment, of course. In a recent school year, 2,724 of our students were receiving alternative instruction, with 1,938 of them in home schools taught mostly by dedicated mothers. Alternatively schooled students must achieve proficiency in English and take math and reading/language arts as well as nationally standardized achievement tests, the same as their peers in public school. But it's up to individual districts to decide what course work they'll accept for credit toward graduation for students who want a diploma from an accredited public high school. For more information about alternative schooling, call your local school district.

Districts throughout the Hills contract with Black Hills Special Services Cooperative for special and alternative- education services, various forms of therapy, and a full range of other benefits for special-needs students. In addition, the co-op's Technology

Learning to use a computer is an important task for today's students. PHOTO: STEVEN A. PAGE

and Innovations in Education (TIE) office is involved in a sophisticated technology project in schools across South Dakota. The co-op has been a national leader in rural education services since the 1970s.

Learning doesn't end at adulthood though, and older learners find intellectual stimulation in community education programs. In most cases the local school district is the place to call for information about that as well as about General Educational Development (GED) preparation and testing; in Rapid City, however, contact the Career Learning Center, 730 East Watertown Street, (605) 394-5120.

Below you'll find thumbnail sketches of many of our school districts, private schools, and colleges. We couldn't squeeze all of their accolades into this chapter, but we're certain that administrators and teachers at each one would be happy to fill in the blanks. Naturally, the best way to get acquainted with a school is to pay a call, or several, and observe it for yourself. We encourage you to do so, but the profiles here will serve as an introduction.

Public Schools

Northern Hills

Belle Fourche School District
1113 National St., Belle Fourche
(605) 892-3355

Redbook magazine and its staff of educational experts named the Belle Fourche elementary school system the best in South Dakota in 1995, and its superintendent said strong parental involvement in the schools was a big reason. More than 1,400 students attend school in the Belle Fourche district, where the focus is on a child-centered curriculum that strives to meet each student's individual needs, especially in math and science. Spanish is offered in elementary school, and there's an eclectic approach to English that incorporates both whole language and phonics.

Advanced-placement classes in biology and calculus (plans are in place to add English) allow high school students to earn college credit early. Vocational studies are another strength, as the district has articulation agreements with Western Dakota Technical Institute (WDTI). Students studying the building trades here can transfer their credits to WDTI without cost if they enroll there after graduation. Class projects have included building homes for people in the community from start to finish. Computer-aided drafting is a popular class.

District residents are serious about educating their youth, as evidenced by several community/school partnerships, such as the Community Council for Education and the School Improvement Council, which looks at curriculum changes before they go to the school board. Both are made up of professional educators and community members.

Belle Fourche teachers have won four national Presidential Science and Math Awards; honors among students include state football and girls' basketball championships; and the district has even produced a Rhodes scholar.

The district has one elementary school spread out among several buildings, a new middle school, and one high school. High school students who don't do well in a traditional classroom setting may be referred to Education Connection, an alternative school in Spearfish. Read more about it in the Spearfish School District listing later in this chapter.

Lead-Deadwood School District
320 S. Main St., Lead
(605) 584-1301

This district in the heart of Black Hills gold-mining country is still proud of the fact that Lead High School won a prestigious National Bellamy Award for overall excellence and teaching of Americanism in 1970. But the school hasn't rested on its laurels in the decades since then. In recent years LHS physics and chemistry students have excelled in regional competition with their peers, and the school band was chosen to represent South Dakota at the 150th anniversary of the laying of the Washington Monument cornerstone in Washington, D.C., in 1998. Student athletes have brought recognition to Lead-Deadwood by winning state championships for the girls' cross-country team in 1997 and 1996, when they won a combined championship with the boys' team, which went on to become the 1998 Class A champ.

The district's approximately 1,000 students are divided among one elementary school, one middle school, and the high school in Lead.

Meade School District
1230 Douglas St., Sturgis
(605) 347-2523

At 3,200 square miles, this is the state's largest geographic school district. Primarily encompassing Sturgis, Piedmont, Black Hawk, and rural Meade County (South Dakota's largest county), it also includes Whitewood, in Lawrence County. The Meade district is further distinguished by its rural schools, most of which are reached via miles and miles of gravel roads—the most remote one is some 90 miles from school administrative offices in Sturgis. One principal oversees and visits them all. Students who attend these one- and two-room schools on the prairie benefit from a close-knit, family-style atmosphere and lots of individual attention from teachers, but those advantages can also make adjusting to a larger school difficult. The rural schools carry students through eighth grade in the same curriculum as their peers in town; after that it's on to high school in Sturgis or somewhere closer to home. Some rural families move into town during the week so their high schoolers can get to school more easily, or students might board with town families for the school year.

In addition to the rural schools, the Meade elementary system includes five attendance centers in Sturgis that are broken down into various grade levels, one building each in Piedmont and Stagebarn plus one school in Whitewood. Some children in Black Hawk attend the Piedmont-Stagebarn schools, but others go to Black Hawk Elementary School, which is in the Rapid City Area School District. All Meade students, except those in the rural schools, are assigned to Williams Middle School in Sturgis. From there they go to Sturgis Brown High School. Black Hawk children attend middle and high school in either Sturgis or Rapid City.

Sturgis Brown High School is noted for its excellent wrestling and girls' basketball teams—probably no one was surprised when the school won the 1999 Greater Dakota Conference wrestling championship—as well as its strong vocational and School to Work programs. Brown was one of two high schools in the nation to receive the Army's Planning for Life Award in 1997. The USA Today Community Solutions for Education Award and other honors have also gone to the district. An applied-academics curriculum helps Meade students find practical applications for their classroom studies, and a law-related education program helps them stay out of trouble—or see the error of their ways if they stray. An alternative academy associated with Brown High School serves students with a variety of needs, from work-related scheduling problems to struggles in the classroom.

Despite its large coverage area, the Meade district has a modest enrollment of about 3,000 students.

Spearfish School District
525 E. Illinois St., Spearfish
(605) 642–1201

As the home of Black Hills State University (see later listing), Spearfish is able to offer its public school students dual enrollment, enabling high school juniors and seniors to take certain classes at the university level and earn college credit.

Spearfish's progressive attitude won recognition in 1996 when the district was chosen to participate in a nationwide, five-year, federally funded "best practices" study being conducted by a Colorado research institution, McREL (Midcontinent Regional Educational Laboratory). Chosen for its inclusion of special-needs students in the classroom, Spearfish will be able to share its successful programs with schools around the country as a result. It was one of three districts named in South Dakota, along with Custer (see the Southern Hills public school listings) and Dell Rapids in the eastern part of the state.

Spearfish has dedicated a good share of its resources to making sure its students acquire current technology skills. In addition to its academic advantages, Spearfish is justly proud of its athletic teams—the high school football team won the state AA championship in 1997, and Spearfish boys won state and conference

> ## Insiders' Tip
> It took only 70 minutes for the Belle Fourche School District to auction off 50 homes that the U.S. Air Force vacated and gave to the district in 1997. The auction raised $2.1 million for school renovation and construction.

Willard Water

It heals burns, grows gargantuan squash, helps you sleep, relieves pain, and keeps your pets healthy. Those are some of the claims made by folks who swear by Willard Water, a mysterious fluid discovered in the 1960s and patented by John Willard, a chemistry professor at South Dakota School of Mines and Technology in Rapid City.

Doc Willard, as he was called, developed "catalyst altered water" as a solvent but found it had health properties when he used it to soothe a burn on his arm. Once on the market it naturally attracted considerable curiosity, and in 1980 veteran TV reporter Harry Reasoner interviewed Doc Willard and a number of Willard Water devotees on *60 Minutes*. The testimonials claimed all sorts of benefits and no bad effects. Independent lab tests and a Congressional investigation found it to be harmless. But no one could explain why Willard Water worked. As Doc himself said, "I see it but I still don't believe it."

One hypothesis holds that by altering the molecular structure of ordinary water, Willard Water boosts the assimilation of nutrients and hastens the elimination of toxins. It's also said to be a powerful antioxidant that helps the body rid itself of damaging free radicals. Users who drink it mixed with filtered water say they can't taste it, but they can tell a difference in the way they feel. And they say they feel better.

Doc Willard passed away in 1991, but Willard Water is still manufactured in Rapid City by his heirs and associates and distributed on a limited basis. There are imitations and diluted forms on the market, too, and representatives of Nutrition Coalition, a Moorhead, Minnesota, marketer, say the only way to know whether you're getting the real thing is ... if you get results. If you're curious about Willard Water, call Nutrition Coalition at (800) 447–4793 for more information.

---

championships in track in 1999. It's also proud of its music programs: Some 200 students participate in band alone.

Recent enrollment was around 2,120. Currently, kindergarten through grade five are distributed among three elementary schools. The single middle school and one high school are in adjoining buildings. The Education Connection academy is available for students who need an alternative to a traditional classroom but still want to earn a diploma from Spearfish High School. At Education Connection, students who have been referred by their school district tackle a full, accredited curriculum through independent study, block courses that focus on one subject area, and self-paced computer course work. Students who are at risk of dropping out or are behind on credits find help through a combination of group work and individual tutoring,

and they must also complete a careers course and be involved in job-related activities.

Central Hills

Douglas School District
400 Patriot Dr., Box Elder
(605) 923–1431

Named for the family that founded it in 1891, the Douglas School District started as a one-room school and expanded to meet the needs of military families who arrived when Rapid City Army Air Base—now Ellsworth Air Force Base—was built in 1942 (see our History and Area Overview chapters for more information on the air base). Today, Douglas educates more than 2,400 students a year from Ellsworth, the town of Box Elder, the surrounding rural area, and part of Rapid Valley.

There are three elementary schools, each containing just two grades. Students attend Douglas Middle School for grades six through eight, then move on to Douglas High School, which in 1971 became first in the state to have an ROTC program. The program has ranked in the nation's top echelon in recent years, consistently winning an Honor Unit or Meritorious Unit rating from the Air Force.

The school has an outstanding family and consumer sciences classroom with a progressive home economics and life-skills curriculum that's a hit with both male and female students. In the building and trades classes, students are building houses that are for sale to the public. The School to Work program has been implemented at all levels, from kindergarten through 12th grade, to help students "learn a living." (On-the-job training doesn't begin until the later grades.) Educators, parents, and other community members work together to improve education through the Douglas Community Partnership Council and the Curriculum Coordinating Committee.

Hill City School District
421 Main St., Hill City
(605) 574-3030

When First Western Bank officials learned that Hill City would take part in the Wiring the Schools program (see the introduction to this chapter), they offered the district a $100,000 grant for hardware to help get the job done. The bank, based in Huron, South Dakota, has a branch here.

This small district of about 600 students was the second in South Dakota to get connected to the Internet and establish a school computer network through the state wiring program. The focus here is on academics, as evidenced by accelerated offerings in high school math, but there's lots of participation in extracurricular activities, too. The high school is strong in football, boys' and girls' basketball, chorus, band, and art, including graphic arts. Enhancement and remedial courses via the Internet are available.

The district serves students from Hill City, Keystone, Silver City, Rochford, and the surrounding rural area. Despite its relatively small student population, the school complex has been recently enlarged with an addition to the middle school and a new high school.

Rapid City Area School District
300 Sixth St., Rapid City
(605) 394-4037 (elementary)
(605) 394-5147 (secondary)

Approximately 13,300 students attend classes in South Dakota's second-largest school district, which includes 16 elementary schools (including one for children with disabilities), five middle schools, two high schools, four alternative academies that allow at-risk students to work at their own pace toward a diploma, and a technical school (see the Western Dakota Technical Institute listing below).

The district is committed to giving its youths a solid academic foundation from the very beginning of their educational career. In 1997 the school board approved a restructuring plan that lowered student-teacher ratios in the earliest grades as a means of increasing literacy from the start. It's too soon to measure results, but outstanding primary programs have already garnered honors for the district. Rapid Valley Elementary School won a national Blue Ribbon Award in 1997 from the U.S. Department of Education, one of 262 schools to be recognized for excellence. The school combines multi-age

Insiders' Tip
Most South Dakotans who take General Educational Development (GED) tests are between the ages of 20 and 24 and have completed 10th grade. The minimum age to take the tests is 16.

Multi-age classrooms like this one helped earn a national Blue Ribbon Award for Rapid Valley Elementary School in the Rapid City School District. PHOTO: STEVEN A. PAGE

classrooms, looping, and traditional self-contained classes with progressive teaching techniques and a welcoming, "community of learners" atmosphere that makes children want to go to school—really! (We know; we've talked to them.) Rapid Valley has also won national recognition for its home page on the Internet.

On the secondary level, Central and Stevens high schools consistently excel in track and cross country, and the two schools garnered a collection of championships in gymnastics and boys' and girls' golf. The music program as well is recognized among educators nationwide for the technical expertise shown by students.

Overall, the district prides itself on doing a good job teaching basic skills and on the success of its science students in local and national competition. Noteworthy, too, is an active, successful exchange program with educators from Rapid City's Japanese sister city, Imaichi.

Southern Hills

Custer School District
147 N. Fifth St., Custer
(605) 673-3154

Technology programs and boys' basketball have made Custer a standout school district. Presently, it is the only district in South Dakota to operate on a four-day week. When the schedule changed in 1995, closing school on Fridays and adding almost an hour a day Monday through Thursday was supposed to save the district money. In fact, savings were realized in transportation but little else, yet district voters overwhelmingly chose to continue the four-day week. According to the school superintendent, both rural and town residents like having their children home an extra day each week, and teachers like the longer class periods. In addition, co-curricular activities on Fridays no longer interrupt instructional time.

Custer's technological innovations made it one of three in South Dakota to be chosen for a "best practices study" by a Denver research institution in 1996 (see the earlier Spearfish School District write-up for more information). Custer schools use computer technology across the curriculum at all levels, from kindergarten through 12th grade. A few students even use the Internet to take classes that earn them high school and college credit. Advanced placement classes are offered in calculus, with plans to add chemistry.

In the athletics arena, the names of Coach Larry Luitjens and the Custer High School boys' basketball team are practically synonymous with the title "state championship." Together, they've won four this decade. Recent academic honors have included placing in the Odyssey of the Mind world finals and a Sallie Mae national teaching award for a teacher at the rural school in Spring Creek.

The Custer district has three rural schools that teach kindergarten through eighth grade, including a new one in Fairburn. It's one of only a few two-room rural schoolhouses built in the last 50 years in South Dakota. An eight-room school in Hermosa also goes through eighth grade. In the city of Custer are one elementary, one middle, and one high school. A program for at-risk students is in place.

The school district embraces Custer State Park and Wind Cave National Park within its boundaries, and one superintendent likes to say his district has 1,100 kids, 1,300 buffalo, and 1,500 square miles. (Close enough—the actual area is 1,148 square miles.)

Hot Springs School District
1609 University Ave., Hot Springs
(605) 745-4145

Maybe it's the Southern Hills' gorgeous scenery and pleasant climate that produce top athletes at Hot Springs High School. In 1997 the school's girls' track team was voted best athletic team in South Dakota by the state's sports writers, and in 1998, the girls' cross-country team won the state Class A championship.

But students here also focus on academics and technology skills. Hot Springs High School is one of 26 in the nation participating in a program that has students writing their own CD-ROMs. Students are also active in a foreign-exchange program and in a mentorship program with the Hot Springs Veterans Administration Medical Center (see our Healthcare chapter).

Approximately 930 students attend elementary, middle, and high school in Hot Springs and a rural school in Oral that goes through grade eight. A program for at-risk students helps keep struggling scholars on track to graduation.

Private Schools

With the exception of our Montessori schools, private schools in the Black Hills generally are religious institutions. Many of them are affiliated with a specific church and can be located through the churches.

Insiders' Tip

If you know someone who needs help learning to read, have him or her call the South Dakota Literacy Council in Pierre at (800) 423-6665, or inquire at the local library. In Rapid City the number to call is (605) 394-4171; as soon as the recorded greeting starts, the caller should dial 255 and leave a message after the beep. Messages are retrieved daily.

GREAT FACES

Billy Mills and Randy Lewis

Billy Mills and Randy Lewis didn't have to take up mining to find gold. They used their talents and worked hard to win gold medals in Olympic competition—20 years apart. So far, they're the only South Dakotans ever to do so.

Billy, an Oglala Lakota from the Pine Ridge Indian Reservation, became the only American in Olympic history to win the 10,000-meter running race. A virtual unknown, he stunned the crowd at the 1964 Tokyo games when, with a mighty burst of speed, he shot ahead of the front-runners and crossed the finish line in a record 28 minutes, 24.4 seconds, beating a world champion. The spectacular win caused such a sensation that it halted his victory lap. Winning the gold made Billy a national hero, but it didn't make him conceited. Instead, he became a role model for Native American youth.

Billy had been orphaned at age 12 and sent to an Indian school in Kansas. Later, at the University of Kansas, he'd competed in track and field, then joined the Marines after graduating in 1962. In 1965, when he was already an Olympic champion, he won the U.S. national championship in the 6-mile run and set another world record. Billy retired from track and field due to injuries in 1968, but he was later inducted into the National Track and Field Hall of Fame and the U.S. Olympic Hall of Fame. A movie, *Running Brave,* was even made about him.

All the while Billy never forgot his roots or the folks back home struggling with deprivation. After 23 years in the insurance business, he sold his company to become a full-time motivational and inspirational speaker. He formed the Billy Mills Speakers Bureau in Fair Oaks, California, and became national spokesperson for Running Strong for American Indian Youth. In the latter capacity he visited the Loneman School on the Pine Ridge reservation in 1997 to hand out awards in a student poster contest. Billy also wrote a book, *Wokini: A Lakota Journey to Happiness and Self-Understanding,* published in 1991.

While Billy was making history, Randy Lewis was a little boy growing up in Rapid City. He was still quite young, just 10 years old, when he started wrestling. He was a natural at it, and Olympic gold soon became his goal. He worked hard at his studies too, keeping up his grades at Stevens High School even as he won three state wrestling championships. He even set a national record with 45 consecutive pins. The year he graduated, 1977, he won a junior world championship and two national championships. While studying business at the University of Iowa, Randy won two National Collegiate Athletic Association (NCAA) championships and others besides. In 1980 he qualified as the youngest member of the U.S. Olympic wrestling team, but his hopes were dashed when President Jimmy Carter decided the United States would boycott the games. Randy got his chance four years later in Los Angeles, though, and in 1984 he won the gold medal in the 136½-pound weight class.

In his wrestling career Randy was victorious over eight other world or Olympic champions and scored wins over dozens of other top wrestlers. For about eight years he was rated among the world's top three wrestlers, and he won numerous championships. But possessing excellence didn't go to his head, and, like Billy, Randy wanted to pass on something of value to the next generation. Even before he became an Olympic star, he had developed a series of summer wrestling camps for elementary and high school athletes, and after graduating from college in 1982 he coached his alma mater's postgraduate Hawkeye Wrestling Team for 13 years. His days on the mat ended after that, and at this writing Randy was living in Arizona, running a business. He was inducted into the National Wrestling Hall of Fame in 1998.

Check the Yellow Pages or inquire at the local school district for information. Here we've listed several of our private schools, including one that principally serves Native American students.

Central Hills

Rapid City Christian High School
1212 E. Fairmont Blvd., Rapid City
(605) 341–3377

Approximately 145 students in grades 7 through 12 attend this interdenominational Christian school, which opened in 1981. Accredited by the state and the Association of Christian Schools International, the school combines religious instruction with a traditional approach to basic learning. Students are required to enroll in a Bible class every semester and attend chapel once a week, and they must be committed to learning through a Christian world view. A full activities schedule also keeps them busy in football (the team competes in two conferences), basketball, volleyball, track, drama, and more.

The school occupies space in the Bible Fellowship Church building but is not affiliated with the church. The school's long-range plan calls for a building of its own.

Sioux Chapel & Christian Academy
415 MacArthur St., Rapid City
(605) 341–0652

Operated by Wesleyan Native American Ministries, Sioux Chapel & Christian Academy teaches nearly 50 students in grades kindergarten through 12. About 80 percent of the student body is Native American, but enrollment is open to all. And despite the school's affiliation with the Wesleyan church and its Christian emphasis, non-Christians are welcome. The unaccredited school uses the School of Tomorrow curriculum for an individualized approach to self-motivated learning. Classrooms are arranged by age, with more than one grade level per room. Student athletes compete in the Christian Athletic Conference in flag football, boys' basketball, and girls' volleyball.

St. Elizabeth Seton School
431 Oakland St., Rapid City
(605) 348–1477
St. Thomas More High School
300 Fairmont Blvd., Rapid City
(605) 343–8484

These two fast-growing, accredited Catholic schools comprise a single school system under the auspices of the Saint Elizabeth Seton Central Catholic School Corp. Recently, enrollment at St. Elizabeth Seton was 520 students in preschool through grade eight, with a waiting list in every grade. St. Thomas More had 257 scholars in grades 9 through 12. About 90 percent of the students came from Rapid City, and about one-fourth were non-Catholics.

Both schools strive to deepen understanding of the meaning and importance of the Catholic faith, and in addition to receiving religious instruction, students participate in regular prayer services and retreats. Eighth-graders take on a community service program, and seniors must complete a 30-hour Christian service project to graduate. Academic performance is boosted by strong discipline and a heavy homework load, backed by vigorous parental involvement and commitment to the schools' vision.

St. Elizabeth Seton School opened in 1961, replacing the Cathedral school that had been established in 1916. St. Thomas More High School began humbly, taking up temporary quarters at National American University in 1991 after the closure of St. Martin's Academy, a coed high school started by Benedictine nuns more than a century ago.

Commitment to St. Thomas More was such that enough money was donated to permit groundbreaking for a beautiful new building in 1994. The high school with a chapel in its center opened the next year, and a middle-school wing is being planned.

St. Thomas More offers an accelerated college preparatory program with advanced placement courses, traditional college prep, and general studies for those who plan to go on to junior college or vocational school. For students needing extra help, tutoring is provided. In general, however, all students take the same level of course work. As a member of the South Dakota High School Activities Association, St. Thomas More competes with other local schools in football, basketball, wrestling, golf, debate, and many other activities.

Southern Hills

Bethesda Lutheran School
1537 Baltimore Ave., Hot Springs
(605) 745–6676

Between 40 and 50 youngsters attend this grade school, which is a ministry of Bethesda Lutheran Church and is accredited through National Lutheran Schools. Located in the church complex, the school teaches a standard curriculum like that found in public schools, with the addition of a literature-based reading program and Lutheran doctrine. Pupils receive religious instruction four days a week and attend chapel one day a week. Kindergartners attend class for half a day, sharing a room with first graders. Second and third grades also are combined, as are

fourth, fifth, and sixth. The school, which opened in 1980, is affiliated with the Missouri Synod but is open to all students.

Montessori Schools

Maria Montessori was the first woman in Italy to receive a medical degree. Her work as a doctor led to her belief that children learn best at their own pace, a philosophy that has been the cornerstone of Montessori education since she opened her first school in 1907. The classroom materials she designed then are still in use today.

Children's House Montessori
3520 W. Main St., Rapid City
(605) 341–0824
www.chkids@rushmore.com

Bringing the outdoors in is one area of focus at this school for children from age three through grade five. Raising butterflies, tending a butterfly garden, growing pumpkins, and building a compost heap on the one-and-a-half-acre wooded campus are just a few of the activities that are

Co-curricular activities, including competitive sports such as wrestling, are an important part of education at Black Hills schools. PHOTO: BARBARA TOMOVICK

integrated into the classroom. Studies include individual and group learning in a variety of subjects. Children also participate in a cultural exchange by visiting and writing to their peers in the Montessori school at Red Cloud Indian School on the Pine Ridge Indian Reservation (see our Daytrips and Weekend Getaways chapter). A multigenerational exchange takes place when parents and grandparents volunteer their time for reading, gardening assistance, and other activities.

Preschool and kindergarten are offered on a part-time basis, with limited extended care before school and at lunchtime. Teachers are required to obtain Montessori certification. But after a snowfall, even they can turn into kids again when everybody goes sledding.

Children's House is closed during the summer.

Life Tree Montessori School
St. Martins Dr., Rapid City
(605) 343–1541

Life Tree Montessori School offers part-time and full-time programs for children from age 18 months through sixth grade. Tykes up to age 3 enroll in the toddler program; from 3 to 6 they're in prepri-mary, which includes kindergarten; and 6- to 12-year-old students receive elementary instruction. Extended care is available before and after school for students who attend Life Tree. All activities take place in open, sunny classrooms under the nurturing tutelage of Montessori-certified teachers. Parental involvement is evident, too, in the wooden play equipment that was built by a parent for the big outdoor playground.

Head Start Programs

Just as the name implies, these publicly funded programs give preschoolers a solid foundation before they enter kinder-garten. Call the programs for income guidelines. For private preschool pro-grams, check the Yellow Pages and see our Childcare chapter for information about locating a day-care center with preschool.

Dakota Transitional Head Start
612 Crazy Horse St., Rapid City
919 Main St., Ste. 201, Rapid City, SD 57701
(mailing address)
(605) 341–3163

This center-based program serves 75 Native American children ages three to five and their families who move to the Rapid City area from an Indian reservation. Because the transition may involve several moves back and forth, enrollment is open at all times. Four classroom sessions are offered Monday through Thursday for the youngsters, and their parents can find assistance with their own educational and social needs, including obtaining a GED, planning for career development, and finding work and housing.

Dakota Transitional is under the auspices of Rural America Initiatives, 919 Main Street, Rapid City, (605) 341–3339, an organization that offers a variety of education-related services to Native American youth.

Youth and Family Services
1920 Plaza Blvd., Rapid City
(605) 342–4195, (800) YFS–9832

This comprehensive agency offers a wide range of services (see our Childcare chapter), including home-based and center-based Head Start programs for educational enrichment, starting at age four, with strong parental involvement. A center-based Early Head Start program promotes healthy relationships between parents and children from birth to age three. YFS also administers home-based Head Start programs in Butte, Custer, Fall River, Lawrence, and Meade Counties. For information about those programs, call (800) 568–0202.

Colleges and Technical Schools

The Black Hills are a favorite location for students who love the area's recreational opportunities, but they also come here for a quality education. Many of them are non-traditional and international students who find the courses they need at our postsecondary schools. Rapid City is the higher-education hub, but Spearfish boasts a four-year liberal arts college in an exceptional setting. For information about attending intercollegiate sports events, please turn to our Spectator Sports chapter.

Northern Hills

Black Hills State University
1200 University Station, Spearfish
(605) 842–6262, (605) 642–6343

This small, accredited four-year liberal arts and teachers' college is situated on a pristine 123-acre campus on the west side of Spearfish. Aside from its desirable setting and academic programs, it prides itself on an outstanding athletic facility, the Donald E. Young Sports and Fitness Center. The $10.5 million center opened in 1990, the result of a cooperative funding effort by the school, the city, the state, and private sources, including alumni. It serves the entire community with two swimming pools, a wide range of other athletic facilities, and classroom and meeting space (see our Spectator Sports chapter for more information).

BHSU, one of six state-run colleges in South Dakota, was founded in 1883 as a teachers' training institution called Spearfish Normal School. Many old-timers still call it that, even though for many years it was Black Hills State College before getting the university designation. Although still primarily a school for aspiring teachers, it draws more business majors than any other South Dakota school.

Today BHSU has three colleges: Arts and Sciences, Business and Technology, and Education. Major courses of study for a bachelor of arts or bachelor of science degree include, but are by no means limited to, such diverse fields as accounting, American Indian studies, art, biology, business administration, chemistry, communication arts, mass communication, environmental physical science, history, human resource management, English, Spanish, outdoor education, political science, psychology, speech, theater, vocal music, tourism and hospitality management, human services, education, and more.

The school also has two-year pre-professional programs in agriculture, dentistry, forestry, law, nursing, medicine, and other subjects. Associate degrees are offered in administrative assistance, drafting technology, general studies, and tourism and hospitality management.

Masters programs are offered in education and tourism.

The school's athletes are known as the Yellow Jackets, and its colors are green and gold. Football, men's and women's basketball, and volleyball are high-profile competitive sports at BHSU. The football field, Lyle Hare Stadium, seats 3,200 and hosts high school as well as college football games.

Of the approximately 2,743 students who attend the Spearfish campus, about 650 live in campus housing and the rest live off campus, mostly in Spearfish. Extension courses are offered at Ellsworth Air Force Base (with about 930 students), Crazy Horse Memorial, the Pine Ridge Indian Reservation, and other locations.

Central Hills

South Dakota School of Mines and Technology
501 E. St. Joseph St., Rapid City
(605) 394–2554, (800) 544–8162

Started as the Dakota School of Mines in 1885, Tech, as it's called today, has been known for its science and engineering programs for the last half-century or more.

Four colleges—Materials Science and Engineering, Earth Systems, Interdisciplinary Studies, and Systems Engineering—provide courses of study toward nine undergraduate degrees in engineering and five in science. There are master's programs in 10 disciplines and three doctoral programs in science and engineering.

The Institute of Atmospheric Sciences, established in 1959, is located on campus, and students are encouraged to take part in research there. The institute collaborates with the National Weather Service, which has a station nearby, through a student internship program and by helping develop models for more accurate weather prediction. A fiber-optic cable connected to Weather Service computers affords the institute instant access to data so scientists can watch storms as they develop; that information is then used in research and teaching.

The institute also works with the EROS (Earth Resources Observation Systems) Data Center in Sioux Falls, the world's largest storehouse of earth science information, to interpret and use data to delve into problems such as pollution, climate change, and weather phenomena. The institute has done major weather-modification field research for several federal agencies and has developed studies for air quality and air pollution. Also, scientists there use the world's only armor-plated, instrumented airplane capable of penetrating hailstorms in their studies of thunderstorm development. Currently, institute staffers are looking into the ways human activity affects Earth's atmosphere, a science called biogeochemistry.

The Museum of Geology on the Tech campus welcomes visitors who want to ogle dinosaur skeletons, meteorites, minerals, and other fascinating objects from the natural world. Read about the museum in our Attractions chapter.

About 2,200 students attend Tech, 500 of them housed in campus dorms. Under the watchful eye of their mascot, Grubby the miner, the blue-and-yellow Hardrockers compete in football, basketball, volleyball, track and field, and cross-country. O'Harra Stadium, with its playing field and all-weather running track, is surrounded on three sides by terraces where some 300 cars can park while their occupants watch college and high school sports.

South Dakota State University College of Nursing
1011 11th St., Rapid City
(605) 394-5390

Nursing students need not attend the main South Dakota State University campus in Brookings to obtain a bachelor of science or master of science degree in nursing. This Rapid City department offers all the courses needed. Through a consortium agreement, students take support courses such as biology, anatomy,

A student researches an assignment in the Learning Resource Center at National American University in Rapid City, one of several colleges in the Black Hills. PHOTO: JOHNNY SUNDBY/DAKOTA SKIES PHOTOGRAPHY

and microbiology at South Dakota School of Mines and Technology in Rapid City. They may elect to take other classes through Black Hills State University, either on the Spearfish campus or at the Ellsworth Air Force Base branch. The remaining classes are offered at the nursing school's main building downtown. The R.N. Upward Mobility Program allows registered nurses with associate degrees to earn a four-year degree in three semesters.

With a bachelor's degree in nursing and a year of work experience, students may enter the graduate program to study for a master's degree in any of several tracks: family nurse practitioner, educator, administrator, or clinical nurse specialist.

Presently, 200 students are pursuing degrees here. All are on their own for housing and meals, since the school does not have student housing or a cafeteria.

South Dakota State University
West River Graduate Center
501 E. St. Joseph St., Rapid City
(605) 394–6823

This SDSU extension offers master's programs in education administration, curriculum and instruction, and counseling. All classes are held in the evening on the South Dakota School of Mines and Technology campus; student housing and meals are not provided. Recent enrollment was approximately 130 students in all three programs; enrollment is limited for the counseling program, based on factors that vary from semester to semester.

The University of South Dakota
1011 11th St., Rapid City
(605) 394–5396 (nursing)
(605) 394–6720 (business)

The University of South Dakota Department of Nursing offers a two-year associate program in registered nursing that is identical to that on the main USD campus in Vermillion, in southeastern South Dakota. Through a consortium agreement, students take academic classes at South Dakota School of Mines and Technology and/or Black Hills State University and take their nursing courses in a mock hospital with a lab and computer lab at the USD facility. About 80 students are enrolled.

The USD graduate extension offers a master's program in business administration with a health-service option and master of science programs in administrative studies with three options: human resources, health services, and interdisciplinary studies. At this writing 88 students were studying for an advanced degree. All classes are offered at night. Students live and dine off campus.

The USD School of Medicine, which is located on the main campus in Vermillion, has a West River campus at 3625 Fifth Street, Suite 200, in Rapid City, (605) 394–5105, where third- and fourth-year medical students can complete a portion of their studies.

Western Dakota Technical Institute
800 Mickelson Dr., Rapid City
(605) 394–4034

One of four state-created technical schools in South Dakota, Western Dakota Technical Institute provides training for jobs in the fields of medicine, engineering, science, law, agriculture, mechanics, and more. Students can choose among more than 20 programs that lead to an associate of applied science degree or a diploma. Courses of study at the accredited school include accounting, agriculture, business management, automotive technology, business management and marketing, cabinetmaking, collision-repair technology, computer-aided drafting (architectural and mechanical), industrial electronics, law-enforcement technology, medical transcription, paralegal/legal assistance, pharmacy technician, phlebotomy/patient care technician, practical nursing, welding, and others. A ranch management program is offered on a 496-acre working ranch in Sturgis.

The approximately 1,000 students who go to school here also have the use of on-site childcare and a retail clothing store where they can get outfitted for a job interview or internship for a reasonable price. Students can buy meals on campus; however, they must find their own housing.

Childcare

Parents in South Dakota know just how important it is to leave their children in capable hands when they go off to work each day. In fact, South Dakota has the nation's highest percentage of working moms with preschoolers. As of the 1990 census, 71 percent of our mothers with preschoolers were employed, compared to 60 percent nationally. And about 82 percent of all South Dakota women with school-age children were in the workforce, versus 75 percent nationwide.

With our rural economy and generally low wages, that's not surprising. It goes without saying that there's an enormous demand for quality childcare, an issue that's becoming an increasingly high priority for state officials and communities alike. The governor has even appointed a state coordinator of childcare services to help us do a better job of watching over our kids. There's widespread agreement that more infant and toddler care is needed here, and the state is doing its best to create more slots with a new reimbursement rate structure and more accessible training for childcare providers.

In the Black Hills especially, both providers and parents have an outstanding number of training opportunities available. In addition, numerous agencies provide services or referrals for special-needs children. You'll find some of both listed in the following information, evidence of our commitment to our most precious resource—our children.

We're also getting innovative when it comes to looking after children when they're not in school. In Rapid City, for instance, the YMCA and the school district joined forces to create the Kidstop and Morning Kidstop programs to provide before- and after-school supervision and activities in many of the elementary schools. You can learn more about their approach by calling the YMCA at (605) 342-8538.

On the issue of kids who are too sick to go to day care, Rapid City Regional Hospital has taken the lead with its Tendercare program for employees' children. And we're taking steps to meet the needs of parents who work at night and on weekends as some day-care centers begin experimenting with expanded hours. As day care becomes an ever more permanent fixture in our lives, we're reaching out with a growing array of public and private childcare options, from licensed day-care centers and home-based facilities to preschools and after-school programs. Even some of our schools now have day-care programs for students who are raising children.

With so many choices, be sure to shop around. By using the resources listed in this chapter, we're confident you'll find the right place for your child to spend the time he or she can't spend with you.

Locating Childcare

If you're new to the area, or to the demands of finding childcare, the Black Hills Parent Resource Network, (605) 348-WARM or (800) 219-6247, is an excellent place to begin your search. Information specialists at the agency, which operates under the auspices of the Black Hills Special Services Foundation, keep an up-to-date list of state-licensed and state-registered childcare providers. What's more, the network's database has specific information about which providers have openings and for what ages. If you're looking for a provider close to home, or close to work, the network can help you narrow your search that much further. There's no charge for this service.

You can also get a list of local licensed and registered day-care providers from any state Department of Social Services. You

With its high percentage of working moms, ensuring quality childcare is an important issue for South Dakota. PHOTO: STEVEN A. PAGE

can find the phone number in the government pages in the front of the phone book, or call the DSS Office of Child Care Services in Rapid City at (605) 355-3545 and ask for a list. Childcare Seekers Directory of Rapid City publishes a free bimonthly list of licensed and registered providers that's available in some Black Hills supermarkets and other stores. You can also call the directory service at (605) 342-5052. The information is free; however, these sources don't have the in-depth details about openings that the network has.

The Parent Resource Network, which originated in 1994, may even be able to help you get in touch with people such as college students who are willing to babysit part-time in your home. There are no direct referrals; instead, an intermediary will convey your needs to prospective baby-sitters who can then contact you. This is a very informal process that does not require potential baby-sitters to undergo background checks or meet other qualifications. If you choose to explore this option, consider meeting your babysitter for a get-acquainted visit before you actually hire him or her to watch your youngster.

If you want full-time, in-home care for your child, the network can tell you about nanny agencies beyond the Black Hills region.

The information specialists can also fill you in on parent support organizations and send you brochures to help you make the best possible decision about childcare. And if you have questions about parenting or need help deciding when your child is ready to get along without a sitter, the network is glad to provide that kind of information as well. Again, there's no charge.

What to Ask

One of the most important steps in choosing a caregiver is often overlooked, according to network information: visiting the home or center you are considering before you enroll your youngster. While there,

observe how the staff members interact with the children, look over the facility to ensure that it's clean and spacious enough for the number of children who stay there, and inspect the outdoor play area.

Questions you should ask include: How long has the provider been in business? What are her or his ideas about discipline and learning? What kinds of age-appropriate activities are offered? What kinds of meals and snacks are served? How many children attend each day, and what are their ages?

You'll also need to know whether there's a policy that requires you to have backup care if your regular provider gets sick or has an emergency, and whether the day care closes for staff vacation time.

It's a good idea to ask for parent references and to find out whether parents are welcome to drop in unannounced—if not, you might want to look elsewhere.

Insiders' Tip

The Rapid City Area Chamber of Commerce and the city of Rapid City recognize registered family home day-care providers who go above and beyond the call of duty. Those who show proof of 20 hours of training a year receive a certificate signed by the mayor and the chamber president and are placed on the Blue Ribbon Provider Recognition List. To request a copy of the list, call the chamber at (605) 343-1744.

Training and Other Support

Whether or not you work outside the home, the time you spend with your child is precious. Here is a partial—and we do mean partial—list of services and training opportunities that can help enrich the hours you have together. These agencies serve the entire Black Hills. For information about Head Start programs and preschools, please turn to our Education chapter.

Early Childhood Connections
809 South St., Ste. 304, Rapid City
(605) 342–6464

Monthly educational sessions offered to childcare providers and parents for a small fee cover topics such as health and nutrition, positive guidance, and much more. Pediatric CPR and first-aid training and American Red Cross certification are available, as is nationally approved Child Development Associate instruction. The agency also performs free vision, hearing, and developmental screening for children ages three to five at day-care centers and preschools. It provides free technical assistance for providers in areas such as bookkeeping, staffing, and management. Other aids include a resource library.

Parents as Teachers
525 E. Illinois St., Spearfish
(605) 642–9088
730 E. Watertown St., Rapid City
(605) 348–WARM, (800) 219–6247
215 N. 3rd St., Custer
(605) 673–2660

Program staffers make free home visits to families with children up through age five, providing information about growth and development as well as age-appropriate activities for parents and children to do together. Other services include developmental screenings, group meetings for parents, referrals to other services, and toy-lending programs.

Single Points of Contact

Northern Hills Interagency Network
2885 Dickson Dr., Sturgis
(605) 347–6260, (800) 219–6247

Pennington County Interagency Network
1719 W. Main St., Rapid City
(605) 394–6089

Youth and Family Support Network
1039 Montgomery St., Custer
(605) 673–5600, (888) 673–2660

These agencies provide screening for developmental delays, help set up evaluations, and assist parents in locating and coordinating medical, educational, social-services, and mental-health resources for their special-needs children from birth to age three. They're also an information resource for families with children of any age.

Youth & Family Services
1920 Plaza Blvd., Rapid City
(605) 342–4195, (800) YFS–9832

Youth & Family Services is a comprehensive agency whose services include the YFS Counseling Center, with a 24-hour crisis line, (605) 342–4303, for children and families. Free training in drug-abuse and violence prevention is available to school districts, individuals, and community groups through the Western Prevention Resource Center. Please turn to our Healthcare chapter for information about other mental-health and emergency resources.

Regulation

The state of South Dakota keeps a vigilant eye on those who tend and nurture our children by setting strict standards and making regular inspections to enforce them.

State law requires licensing for any day-care center that serves 21 or more children, as well as for group family day-care centers that serve 13 to 20 children. Providers who care for up to 12 children in

A pint-sized cowgirl finds a prime vantage point for a parade in Deadwood. PHOTO: JOHNNY SUNDBY/
DAKOTA SKIES PHOTOGRAPHY

their homes must register with the state if they or their clients receive public funds. In other cases, family home day-care registration is voluntary, but providers who don't register also don't get listed with the Black Hills Parent Resource Network or notified of certain training opportunities.

From a parent's point of view, registration may offer added reassurance since it extends system-wide screening for reports of child abuse and neglect to anyone age 10 or older who lives in the provider's home.

All licensed and registered providers must meet in-service training requirements that range from 6 to 20 hours a year, comply with nutrition standards, and keep up-to-date immunization records on the children in their care. Additionally, licensed day-care center directors are required to have a combination of education and experience in the early childhood field. Everyone who works in a regulated childcare facility has to maintain current certification in CPR and first aid.

There are limits to the number of children who can be supervised by one adult. For infants and toddlers, it's 5 children to 1 adult; for children ages 3 to 6, it's 10 to 1; and for school-age youngsters, it's 15 to 1.

Insiders' Tip

Rockin Robin Fizz Kids, 120 Knollwood Drive in Rapid City, (605) 342–1818, has a Parents' Timeout program that provides two hours of supervised play for your child—and freedom for you—for a fee. For more information, see the Rockin Robin Fizz Kids listing in our Kidstuff chapter.

State fire, health, and safety codes offer further protection for kids in day care, as do local city ordinances that may require criminal background checks, business permits, fenced yards, building code inspections, or other areas of compliance. Call city hall to find out what's required in your community.

Healthcare

We hope you won't need the information in this chapter, especially the emergency services. But whether you're visiting, planning a move, or just passing through, you'll want to have this information handy.

On the other hand, reading about available health-care services is a great way to learn about a community, so we've included not only hospitals and medical centers, but also some information on the (unfortunately few) wellness-oriented businesses such as spas and fitness centers and alternative practitioners.

You'll also find a list of veterinarians, just in case you need that information for your furry traveling companion (again, we hope not). And we've included some local support organizations that can be called upon, should you need them.

Stay well!

Hospitals

Northern Hills

Fort Meade VA Medical Center
113 Comanche Rd., Fort Meade
(605) 347–2511, (800) 743–1070
Fort Meade VA Center is part of the Department of Veterans Affairs (VA) Black Hills Health Care System that provides primary and secondary medical and surgical care along with domiciliary, extended nursing home care, and tertiary psychiatric inpatient care services for veterans residing in South Dakota and portions of Nebraska, Wyoming, North Dakota, and Montana. Other specialty programs include addictive disorders, post-traumatic stress, and compensated work therapy. VA Black Hills features medical centers at Fort Meade and Hot Springs along with many community-based outpatient clinics, including Rapid City. It is ranked among the nation's top five VA healthcare facilities for patient satisfaction.

Fort Meade VA Center, 2 miles east of Sturgis, has been a VA facility since the birth of the VA in the 1940s, but there's been a hospital at the 120-year-old fort since its founding (there's more about the fort in our History chapter). Today it features inpatient and outpatient care, an inpatient psychiatric unit, and a rehabilitation-focused nursing-home care unit.

Lookout Memorial Hospital
1440 N. Main St., Spearfish
(605) 642–2617
A primary-care facility with 31 beds, Lookout Memorial was named one of the top 100 hospitals in the nation and one of the top 38 rural care facilities. It has an adjacent family medical center, an emergency room, home healthcare (for in-home visits), rehabilitation services, and an award-winning cardiopulmonary rehabilitation program.

Lookout belongs to the Black Hills Regional System of Care.

Northern Hills General Hospital
61 Charles St., Deadwood
(605) 578–2313
A $1.8 million project gave the hospital a new lobby, an entrance and parking for the disabled, renovated rehabilitation facilities, and expanded services. The primary-care hospital has been in existence since 1897.

Services include an emergency room, cardiac care, obstetrics, cardiac and pulmonary rehabilitation, home health, respiratory and physical therapy, and medical equipment. The facility has 18 beds.

Sturgis Community Health Care Center
949 Harmon St., Sturgis
(605) 347-2536

This 32-bed primary-care facility has an adjacent family medical center, emergency room, a medical equipment component, a home health program, and rehabilitation services for the elderly and the disabled. The hospital also has an 84-bed long-term care facility and offers wellness and education programs.

Central Hills

Black Hills Surgery Center
216 Anamaria Dr., Rapid City
(605) 388-9440

Rapid City's smaller licensed hospital was built by doctors. It is a specialty hospital where many surgical procedures can be performed, including neurosurgery and dental, pediatric, gynecological, and other operations. This 25-bed center does not accept heart attack victims or patients requiring intensive care, as it does not have an emergency room or intensive care facilities. It specializes instead in most routine (and some advanced) surgical procedures, both inpatient and outpatient.

Rapid City Indian Hospital (Sioux San)
3200 Canyon Lake Dr., Rapid City
(605) 355-2500

This Indian Health Service primary-care hospital is one of just three such facilities in the nation not located on a reservation. It was founded in the early 1950s as a tuberculosis sanitarium. Operated by the federal government, the 32-bed hospital treats only Native American patients.

Services and facilities include an emergency room, community health nursing (home care), specialty clinics such as dentistry and optometry, walk-in clinics, and the only mental health inpatient unit in the Indian Health Service. There are no facilities for surgery or obstetrics, which are handled at Rapid City Regional Hospital.

Rapid City Regional Hospital
353 Fairmont Blvd., Rapid City
(605) 341-1000

Rapid City Regional Hospital was created in 1973. It is a 417-bed regional medical center providing services in more than 40 medical specialties. The hospital complex encompasses the Cancer Care Institute, Black Hills Rehabilitation Hospital, the Heart Care Center, Same-Day Surgery Center, and other components. Emergency services include a 24-hour emergency department and regional LifeFlight, a 24-hour emergency air-and ground-transport service.

The not-for-profit Rapid City Regional Hospital System of Care, operated by a board of trustees, has affiliation agreements with several area hospitals and healthcare providers, including Custer Community Hospital, Northern Hills General Hospital in Deadwood, the Massa Berry Clinic in Sturgis, and others.

Southern Hills

Custer Community Hospital
1039 Montgomery St., Custer
(605) 673-2229

> ## Insiders' Tip
>
> There are plenty of specialist physicians in Rapid City and, in recent years, many new medical offices have sprung up near Rapid City Regional Hospital, creating a sort of "medical neighborhood." New offices have become quite concentrated in the area bordered by U.S. 16, Cathedral Drive, and South Fifth Street. Specialists are listed, by their specialties in the Yellow Pages under "Physicians."

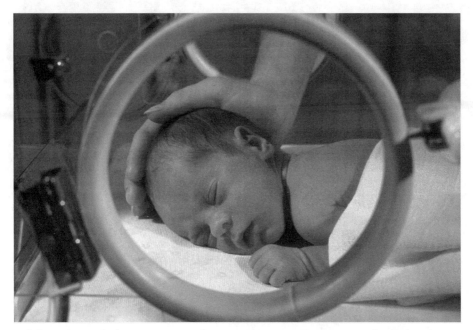

A baby receives tender loving attention in the Neonatal Intensive Care Unit, one of a number of specialty centers at Rapid City Regional Hospital. PHOTO: MARK WANEK, COURTESY OF RAPID CITY REGIONAL HOSPITAL

Custer's hospital is a 16-bed primary-care facility with an emergency room and an adjacent urgent care and family practice facility. It also has a home-health program.

Hot Springs VA Medical Center
500 N. 5th St., Hot Springs
(605) 745–2000, (800) 764–5370

The Hot Springs VA Medical Center—like the VA Medical Center in Fort Meade—is part of the Department of Veterans Affairs (VA) Black Hills Health Care system that provides primary and secondary medical and surgical care along with domiciliary, extended nursing home care, and tertiary psychiatric inpatient care services for veterans residing in South Dakota, and portions of Nebraska, Wyoming, North Dakota and Montana. The Hot Springs facility was founded in 1907 as the Battle Mountain Sanitarium. Today it features inpatient and outpatient medical care and a variety of residential-based programs in its Domiciliary.

Information and Services

American Cancer Society, South Dakota Division Inc.
353 Fairmont Blvd., Rapid City
(605) 342–7740, (800) 529–0024

Above and beyond raising money for research, the local office of the American Cancer Society provides educational materials and programs to heighten cancer awareness, and it has a number of volunteer services for patients. In the Reach to Recovery program, for instance, volunteers who have survived breast cancer help current patients understand what to expect and how to care for themselves during treatment. Additional volunteer services include transportation to treatment centers and assistance with appearance, such as help with skin care from trained cosmetologists. Pamphlets that explain different cancers and treatments also are available from the office, which is located in the Cancer Care Institute at

Medical Centers and Day Clinics

Some of these clinics are open early and late for minor emergencies, sudden illnesses, routine physicals, or when your regular doctor isn't available. Many take walk-in patients; some require appointments. For major emergencies please go to a hospital emergency room instead.

Northern Hills

Belle Fourche Health Care Center
2200 13th Ave. (605) 892-3331

Black Hills Medical Center
71 Charles St., Deadwood (605) 578-2364

Black Hills Medical Center
1320 North Ave., Spearfish 605) 642-5648

Massa Berry Clinic
890 Lazelle St., Sturgis 605) 347-3616

Queen City Medical Center
1420 N. Tenth St., Spearfish (605) 642-8414

Sturgis Family Medical Center
949 Harmon St., Sturgis (605) 347-4520

Sturgis Medical Center
1010 Ball Park Rd., Sturgis (605) 347-3684

Central Hills

Black Hills Pediatrics and Neonatology
2905 Fifth St., Rapid City (605) 341-7337

Family Practice Residency Center
502 E. Monroe St., Rapid City (605) 342-2060

HealthSouth Medical Clinic
2201 Jackson Blvd., Rapid City (605) 348-4645

Hill City Medical Clinic
114 E. Main St., Hill City (605) 574-4470

Piedmont Medical Center
8018 Stage Stop Rd., Piedmont (605) 787-6714

Rapid City Medical Center
2820 Mt. Rushmore Rd., Rapid City (605) 342-3280

Rapid City VA Health Clinic
2823 W. Main St., Bldg. 550, Rapid City (605) 399-6655
(accepts veterans only)

RapidCare Medical Center
408 Knollwood Dr., Rapid City (605) 341-6600

Southern Hills

Custer Clinic
1039 Montgomery St., Custer (605) 673-3417

Edgemont Medical Clinic
908 H St., Edgemont (605) 662-7250

Rapid City Regional Hospital. The office serves the entire Black Hills area.

Black Hills Healthcare Network
930 10th St., Spearfish
(605) 644-4000

With a focus on comprehensive rural healthcare, the network, a division of Lutheran Health Systems, provides an array of services and housing options for seniors from one end of the Black Hills to the other, and even beyond. Costs are adjusted depending on clients' ability to pay, and all services are open to people of any income level.

The network also has home healthcare and home medical equipment available to help people continue to live in their own homes. A hospice program provides at-home care and comfort for terminally ill people and their families, regardless of a patient's ability to pay.

The network also has a number of visiting physicians who bring specialized services such as audiology and optometry to network facilities in Belle Fourche, Spearfish, Sturgis, and Hot Springs.

Here's a look at what's available in various communities through the network.

Belle Fourche Health Care Center, 2200 Thirteenth Avenue, (605) 892-3331, includes a long-term care unit, adult day care, assisted living, senior apartments, and a visiting-physician clinic.

In Spearfish, David M. Dorsett Health Care Facility, 1020 Tenth Street, (605) 642-2716, includes long-term care with an Alzheimer's unit, congregate housing, assisted living, adult day care, senior apartments, and a visiting-physician clinic

with dentistry. Lookout Memorial Hospital is in a separate location but is part of the network.

Sturgis Community Health Care Center, 949 Harmon Street, (605) 347-2536, includes a long-term care facility with an Alzheimer's unit, senior apartments (with more under construction), a visiting physician clinic, and a hospital.

Western South Dakota Chapter of the Alzheimer's Association
1719 W. Main St., Ste. 203, Rapid City
(605) 394-5766

The local Alzheimer's Association chapter has a wealth of information for caregivers of Alzheimer's patients. Telephone counseling can help guide the caregiver in new or difficult situations, and there's a library with informative videos, books, and audiotapes. Free brochures also are available on numerous aspects of coping with Alzheimer's. The Alzheimer's and Related Dementia Care Group meets twice a month at the office, from 1:30 to 3:30 P.M. on the second Tuesday of the month and from 6:00 to 8:00 P.M. on the third Tuesday of the month.

Massage and Alternative Treatments

A great many therapeutic massage practitioners have located in the Black Hills. Some offer additional services, such as acupuncture, reflexology, steam and sauna baths, herbal wraps, facials, yoga classes, and more. You may want to ask about the different types of massage therapy offered—such as Swedish, Esalen, sports, and deep tissue techniques—as well as about the practitioner's certification. To find a massage practitioner, we suggest you check the Yellow Pages under "Massage."

Of course, some alternative treatments are provided by practitioners specializing exclusively in their chosen fields. We offer one listing below.

Herbs
1320-B Mt. Rushmore Rd., Rapid City
(605) 342-7543

Halina Hladysz is an herbalist and certified iridologist who offers health and fitness consultations and iris photography and analysis. In the field of iridology, the iris is a sort of mirror of the changes taking place in the body; it is analyzed to determine the cause of illness. The Herbs store carries vitamins and minerals, homeopathic remedies, flower essences, essential oils, books, and, of course, herbs.

Natural Foods

You'll find a list of natural foods stores in our Shopping chapter, under the Natural Foods section.

Spas and Fitness Centers

Most spas and fitness centers require memberships in order to use their facilities, but they also offer day or temporary passes for visitors. In addition, the charge is often lower if you are visiting the spa with a current member.

Central Hills

Spa 80 for Women and Pace Fitness
512 Main St., Rapid City
(605) 342-8080

This fitness center is for women only. It offers aerobics, step aerobics, body toning, stair climbers, treadmills, weight machines and free weights, a circuit training program called Pace, a whirlpool, and a sauna. Tanning beds and a nursery are available, too, but there's an extra charge for those services. The spa also has a certified personal trainer on staff. It offers nutrition classes and fun classes in stationary biking and spinning, which will really help you work up a sweat.

The Weight Room
615 St. Joseph St., Rapid City
(605) 348-5070

This center specializes in the heavy stuff: weight lifting, free weights, Hammer-Strength equipment, and bodybuilding. Personal trainers are on staff and vitamins and protein supplements are for sale.

YMCA
815 Kansas City St., Rapid City
(605) 342-8538
www.rcymca.org

The YMCA was recently renovated, adding a new gym, drop-in childcare center, and the Randy Travis Wellness Center in honor of the singer who performed a benefit concert to raise money for the new facilities. The wellness center has free weights, cardiovascular machines, Nautilus weight lifting machines, and more, including an indoor track, racquetball courts, and three gyms. Fitness trainers are available for fitness testing, health appraisals, consultations, and exercise prescriptions (in collaboration with Rapid City Regional Hospital). Massage therapy is available by appointment.

Three indoor pools get a lot of use. One is a training pool (4-foot maximum depth) where water aerobics and other water workouts are held; the others are 25-meter pools for general use.

A variety of classes is offered at the YMCA, including aerobics and Jazzercise. Call to ask what's scheduled.

Southern Hills

Springs Bath House
501 N. River St., Hot Springs
(605) 745-4424

This bath house has brought the day spa concept back to Hot Springs, where such facilities were once common.

Springs Bath House offers therapeutic massage, juice and oxygen bars, reflexology, cleansing steam therapy, and many different kinds of healing baths, including aromatherapy, mud, milk, herbal, and mustard (good for when you have a cold).

The famous Hot Springs water has a high mineral content and is used in the handmade soaps, lotions, shampoos, conditioners, bubble baths, and face creams carried in the gift shop, where you can also purchase gift baskets.

Wellness Centers

Central Hills

**Black Hills Health & Education Center
19 Battle Creek Rd., Hermosa
(605) 255–4101**

A true wellness facility, the center uses education to improve the lives and health of its participants. It's open year-round, except it is sometimes closed in December, and programs run from five to 20 days. Participants stay at the center and learn new ways of improving their health.

They hike; work out; attend lectures on medicine, nutrition, cooking, and stress; and enjoy massages and hydrotherapy monitored by two staff physicians. Meals are vegan (no meat, eggs, or animal products), as the staff are members of the Seventh-day Adventist Church. The center, however, is nondenominational and nonprofit.

Veterinarians

Most area veterinarians work with small and large domesticated animals and livestock. Most can care for horses, either off-site or in their facilities, but we recommend you call ahead and ask.

Northern Hills

**Belle Fourche Veterinary Clinic
406 Summit St., Belle Fourche
(605) 892–2618**

**Johnson & Jones Veterinary Service
713 Anna St., Sturgis
(605) 347–3606**

Metzger Animal Clinic
729 7th St., Spearfish
(605) 642–3422

Spearfish Animal Hospital
710 Colorado Blvd., Spearfish
(605) 642–5771

Sturgis Veterinary Hospital
S. Junction St. and Vanocker Canyon Rd.,
Sturgis
(605) 347–4436

Tri-State Veterinary Clinic
Hwy. 212 W., Belle Fourche
(605) 892–2844

Central Hills

Animal Clinic
1655 E. 27th St. (Valley Dr.), Rapid City
(605) 342–1368

Black Hills Animal Hospital
2909 U.S. 79 S., Rapid City
(605) 343–6066

Canyon Lake Veterinary Hospital
4230 Canyon Lake Dr., Rapid City
(605) 348–6510

Dakota Hills Veterinary Clinic
1571 U.S. 44 E., Rapid City
(605) 342–7498

Green Meadows Veterinary Clinic
3400 Elk Vale Rd., Rapid City
(605) 348–3727

Meiners Animal Clinic
220 Krebs Dr., Rapid City
(605) 343–5089

Mountain View Animal Hospital
1112 Jackson Blvd., Rapid City
(605) 343–8050

Noah's Ark Animal Hospital
1315 Mt. Rushmore Rd., Rapid City
(605) 343–3225

Southern Hills

Fall River Veterinary Clinic
Fall River Rd., Hot Springs
(605) 745–3786
U.S. 385 S., Custer
(605) 673–4018

Insiders' Tip

Rapid City Regional Hospital has a special benefit for its patients' families: discount rates at the Best Western Town & Country Inn, 2505 Mount Rushmore Road, just 2 blocks from the hospital. Family members must request a Hospital Visitor Card at the hospital's information desk (in the lobby) and present the card at the motel, where they will receive a discounted rate on a room. The hospital also has "accommodation rooms" on its ninth floor, which are rented for a minimal charge. Inquire at the information desk.

Support Organizations
and Other Information Numbers

AIDS Hotline	(605) 394–8061
	(800) 342–2437
Al-Anon	(605) 342–9808
Alcohol/Drug Helpline	(605) 394–6128
Alcoholics Anonymous	(605) 394–9214
Black Hills Parent Resource Network	(605) 348–9276
Church Response	(605) 342–5360
Crisis Hotline	(605) 342–4303
Gamblers Anonymous	(888) 781–4357
Gay and Lesbian Coalition	(605) 391–8080
Narcotics Anonymous	(605) 394–8008
Poison Control	(800) 764–7661
Working Against Violence	(605) 341–4808
	(women's shelter crisis line)
	(605) 341–2046
	(sexual assault crisis line)

Retirement

Information and Services

Working and Volunteering

Senior Centers

Retiree Housing

For a certain number of Black Hills residents, retirement means winters on the sunny golf courses of Arizona. For others, it can mean moving here to live full-time in the family vacation cabin. Some build a dream home and settle down after years of moving around in the military or another line of work. Still others see retirement as a time to start a new career—one man we know prefers to be called a "pension recipient" rather than a "retiree."

Whatever your lifestyle, retirement brings change, and we hope it's the welcome kind that frees you to pursue the activities you've been waiting to find time for. In this chapter we'll direct you to some of the opportunities and challenges reserved just for folks in their golden years. We'll also tell you about a couple of retirement communities where you can live in comfort and privacy with others who share your interests. And we'll provide information about some of the many services that are available to you.

For a comprehensive look at housing and medical care, please turn to our Real Estate and Healthcare chapters.

Information and Services

We were amazed and heartened at the wealth of information and support available to seniors as well as the wide-ranging networks that can help you find what you need. This section will help you take the first step in making contact.

Hills-Wide

Dakota Plains Legal Services
528 Kansas City St., Ste. 1, Rapid City
(605) 342–7171
(800) 742–8602 (SD residents)

Dakota Plains Legal Services provides free legal help to U.S. citizens age 60 or older

regardless of income as well as to income-qualified younger people. Areas of assistance include Social Security, Medicaid and Medicare, elder abuse, spousal abuse, powers of attorney and living wills, housing and homelessness issues, employment, and more. The agency covers the entire Black Hills and beyond. Call for an appointment.

M.E.A.LS Program
303 N. Maple Ave., Rapid City
(605) 394–6002

Seniors can enjoy a hot noon meal five days a week at sites throughout the Black Hills, and volunteers deliver meals to those who are homebound because of a mental or physical disability. Participants must be 60 or older, but their spouses younger than 60 are also welcome. Operating under the auspices of Western South Dakota Senior Services, the agency also provides information about home healthcare agencies in Rapid City and makes referrals to the state Department of Social Services. Payment is by donation; those younger than 60 paid a flat fee of $4.75. Call to reserve a place at the table, or sign up at one of the meal sites.

> ### Insiders' Tip
>
> About 270 seniors who have celebrated their 100th birthday belong to the South Dakota Health Care Association's Century Club.

Several senior centers participate in the program, including Belle Fourche Senior Center, Custer Senior Citizens Center, Hill City Senior Citizens Center, Springs Senior Citizens Center, Keystone Senior Citizens Center, Canyon Lake Senior Citizens Center, and Minneluzahan Senior Citizens Center. See the Senior Centers section of this chapter for their addresses and phone numbers.

In addition, some apartment buildings in Rapid City are in the program.

Call the main number above for other serving sites, brochures, menus, and service.

SHIINE Program
2628 W. Main St., Rapid City
(605) 342–3494, (800) 822–8804

SHIINE stands for Senior Health Information and Insurance Education. Trained volunteers in almost every county in the state help seniors sort out the complexities of health insurance, including Medicare, private long-term or supplemental insurance, and other benefits. One-on-one meetings can be arranged when questions are too involved to be handled by phone. All services are free of charge.

Central Hills

American Association of Retired Persons
AARP Connections, 2200 N. Maple St.
(Rushmore Mall), Rapid City
(605) 394–7798

The American Association of Retired Persons is practically a one-stop shopping information outlet for people age 50 and older. Not only does the advocacy organization have its own education and assistance programs—for instance, a safe-driving course and help at tax time—but volunteers keep a truly astounding list of resource people and organizations that can answer your questions and direct you to service providers. So whether you want to find out if there's a local adult soccer team, get help with a legal or medical problem, obtain a list of nursing facilities, or get information on just about any topic, the AARP can tell you where to turn.

The office is open and staffed by volunteers from 10:00 A.M. to 3:00 P.M. Monday through Friday. Two chapters hold regular meetings, so ask about joining.

Financial Services Exchange
2040 W. Main St., Ste. 310, Rapid City
(605) 348–4573

Using dedicated computer software, an independent financial consultant can help you decide how much money you'll need for retirement and how to invest for it. You'll get help analyzing your current savings situation and understanding different kinds of Individual Retirement Accounts and pension plans. Setting aside funds for your children's college education, learning to manage your portfolio, and estate planning can be addressed as well. Charges for services vary.

Pennington County Council on Aging
Rapid City
(605) 348–0403, (605) 574–2273

The council advocates for seniors and puts them in touch with some of the services and benefits available to them in Pennington County, such as transportation. A board of directors oversees the council, which is funded through a county appropriation and membership dues of $5.00 a year. Membership is open to people of any age; meetings are at 1:30 P.M. the second Friday of the month at Minneluzahan Senior Citizens Center, 315 North Fourth Street, (605) 394–1887.

Widowed Persons Service
(605) 341–3255, (605) 394–7798

Volunteers who have experienced profound loss through widowhood themselves provide one-on-one support and understanding for the newly widowed. Meetings are arranged individually with an outreach volunteer who treats your situation with the strictest confidentiality. Literature also is available to help the bereaved cope with the changes faced after losing a spouse. Support groups for younger as well as senior survivors meet to help sustain members over the long term. Please call for information about meeting times and places, as they vary. Begun in 1994, the organization is cosponsored by the AARP (see the listing above).

Working and Volunteering

Forget the rocking chair. Today's energetic, involved seniors are apt to be looking for work and volunteer opportunities. Here we've listed a few agencies that can help in the search for both. If you're interested in volunteering, also consider checking with hospitals, libraries, schools, community sports programs, national organizations, and the U.S.D.A. Forest Service. And don't forget about the valuable contribution to be made by serving on a civic committee or board.

Hills-Wide

Retired & Senior Volunteer Program (RSVP)
333 Sixth St., Rapid City
(605) 394–2507
430 Oriole Dr., Spearfish
(605) 642–5198
919 Second St., Sturgis
(605) 347–5048

> ## Insiders' Tip
> Under South Dakota law, door-to-door salespeople must advise you of your right to cancel purchases of $25 or more made in your home and provide you with a cancellation form. You have three days in which to mail the form, preferably by certified mail, if you want to return the merchandise for a refund.

This national organization has put the skills of seniors age 55 and older to use on worthy community projects for a quarter of a century. Local chapters provide services to nonprofit agencies that ask for help with anything from collating bulk mailings to tutoring in schools to pushing the juice cart at the local hospital. The organization tries to match individual skills and training to specific tasks, be it helping other seniors fill out their tax returns, working in a literacy program, guiding children safely across the street as a crossing guard, or joining a chorus to entertain nursing home residents. In Spearfish, RSVP and other community volunteers gather each spring to replenish RSVP Memorial Garden on North Main Street with an eye-catching array of colorful flowers.

Work Experience (Hills-wide)
2500 Minnekahta Ave., Hot Springs
(605) 745–5101
Northern Hills
(605) 347–9362
111 New York St., Rapid City
(605) 394–1745

It's been 30 years since former first lady Lady Bird Johnson urged us all to plant a tree, a bush, or a shrub to beautify our highways. But the Green Thumb program implemented by the Johnson administration in 1966 has branched out to include more people doing more jobs.

Seniors 55 and older who are eligible to work in the United States can get help finding employment through Work Experience, the nation's largest organization of its kind. You'll find Work Experience representatives serving the entire Black Hills; in the Northern Hills, however, there's not a permanent office, and you'll need to call ahead.

An offshoot of Work Experience, Experience Work Staffing Service, 1719 West Main Street, Rapid City, (605) 394–5755, is a temp agency for mature workers of all ages and income levels. Skills assessment and testing are done here at no charge.

Central Hills

Community Development Dept.
300 Sixth St., Rapid City
(605) 394-4181

If serving on a city committee, task force, or commission is up your alley, contact the mayor's office at (605) 394-4110.

Senior Centers

Nearly every community in the Black Hills has a senior center where you can engage in fun activities, make friends, and find out about local services such as transportation. We've listed a number of senior centers here, but check phone book listings or contact the local chamber of commerce for others. There is no residency requirement for the centers listed below, so you can join any or all of them, regardless of where you live. Most of these sites serve meals, and you'll find information about that under the Information and Services section above. Blood-pressure checks and other wellness clinics often are provided, too, as well as assistance with income tax preparation.

Northern Hills

Belle Fourche Senior Citizens Center
828 Kingsbury St., Belle Fourche
(605) 892-6285

The lively seniors here take part in line dancing, cards and other games, pool, holiday dances, and a greeting card recycling program. When we called, plans were in the works for organized sewing and crafts and monthly dinners.

Members must be at least 45 years old (voting privileges come at age 55) and pay an annual fee of $7.00.

Meade County Senior Citizen Center
919 Second St., Sturgis
(605) 347-5877

The center serves about 5,000 breakfasts during the annual Sturgis Rally & Races (see our Annual Events and Festivals chapter) each August. It also provides "Meals on Wheels" weekly to senior citizens and shut-ins. The rest of the year, members get together for card games, dances, choral performances, crafts, and sewing for the center's semi-annual craft fairs. Special activities include potlucks and fund-raising meals, dances, exercise classes, and a thrift shop. Annual dues are $10 for membership at age 55 or older.

Spearfish Senior Service Center
1306 loth St., Spearfish
(605) 642-2827

Seniors here enjoy pool, card games, bingo, chorus and band, exercise classes, and dances. Other activities include monthly breakfasts, potluck luncheons, and fund-raisers (all on different days). Achieving age 50 and paying annual dues of $10 are the only membership requirements.

Twin City Senior Citizen Center
609 W. Main St., Lead
(605) 584-1261

Bingo, card games, and aerobics are available to members age 50 and older who pay their yearly $10 dues. Monthly

GREAT FACES

Comanche and Tipperary

Two of the most famous Black Hills retirees were horses. Comanche was a steady, faithful Seventh Cavalry steed. Tipperary, Comanche's temperamental opposite, was an outlaw bronc that was never tamed.

When troopers reached the battlefield at Little Big Horn—site of the "last stand" of Lt. Col. George A. Custer's Seventh Cavalry—two days after the 1876 battle, they found only one participant still alive: the seriously injured Comanche. He had been ridden into the battle by Capt. Myles Keogh, the commander of I Company.

The stoic horse eventually recovered and spent the rest of his life as the pet of the Seventh. By regimental order, he was retired, never to be ridden or worked again. He participated only in ceremonies, draped in mourning and led by a trooper. During the Seventh Cavalry's nine years at Fort Meade, Comanche lived a life of ease, had the run of the grounds and reportedly developed a taste for treats and beer, panhandled from his fond fellow soldiers.

In 1888 the Seventh was sent to Fort Riley, Kansas, where Comanche died in 1891 at the age of 31 (or 28, depending on the source). His battle-scarred body was stuffed, mounted, and caparisoned, and it is still on display at the University of Kansas Natural History Museum in Lawrence.

Tipperary was born in 1905 near Camp Crook, north of the Black Hills. A range horse, he gave little indication of his ability to buck off the best until 1915, when Ed Marty tried to break him. The wild ride lasted only seconds. The cowboy gingerly picked himself up from the mud and broke into the popular refrain, "it's a long way to Tipperary," and the horse had his name.

The outlaw bronc loved cowboy-busting and constantly learned new tricks to outwit them. He could rear straight up, twist, jump, sunfish, and buck, anything to get a man off his back. Although he was mounted about 100 times, only eight men were not thrown from him.

Tipperary was retired in 1926. But he made his final appearance at the 1931 Black Hills Roundup in Belle Fourche (see our Annual Events chapter), where he had thrown so many riders. He stood there, head down, feeble, tired . . . until the band struck up "Tipperary." Then the old bronc raised his head and, keeping time to the music as he had done in his younger days, strutted proudly before the cheering crowd one last time.

Tipperary died during a 1932 blizzard on the rangeland of his birth. A monument to the great horse still stands in Buffalo, South Dakota.

potlucks and fund-raisers are on the agenda, and efforts are being directed at arranging regular Sunday social activities.

Central Hills

Canyon Lake Senior Citizens Center
2900 Canyon Lake Dr., Rapid City
(605) 394–1798

Seniors age 60 and older find a wealth of activities and services here, including aerobics, bingo, cribbage, bridge, a discussion group, ceramics, dances, Ping-Pong, pool, shuffleboard, line dancing, exercise classes, and limited computer training. There's a rug loom for weavers, a library for book lovers, and a garden where you can rent space for your summer flowers and veggies. Those with a flair for the performing arts will want to take part in community presentations by the Joyful Guys and Gals singing group and the center's drama group. Special activities include cross-country ski trips, golf lessons, hikes, and more. Yearly dues are $10, and there's a small fee for certain activities.

Hill City Senior Citizens Center
303 Walnut Ave., Hill City
(605) 574–2988

Recent remodeling added new windows, an office, and an entryway for greater comfort at the center, where members participate in a greeting card recycling program, pool, the Merry Music Makers singing group, and birthday potlucks. New ideas are welcome, a spokesperson told us, as are members of any age. Only those 60 and older can vote, though. Dues are $5.00.

Keystone Senior Citizens Center
517 First St., Keystone
(605) 666–4808

The center is used mostly for community functions, we're told, but seniors congregate here to share meals (especially at holiday times), celebrate birthdays, and talk—sometimes heatedly, when the subject is politics, our informant said. Dues are $5.00 a year for members 55 and older.

Minneluzahan Senior Citizens Center
315 N. Fourth St., Rapid City
(605) 394–1887

There's no excuse for idleness when exercise classes, dances, bingo, cards, table

tennis, crochet classes, pool, shuffleboard, volleyball, and so much else is available here. The musically inclined will find a place in the Rambling Larks singing group or the Merry Music Makers "kitchen band." Potlucks for members and suppers that are open to the public provide additional social opportunities, and a monthly bus trip to Deadwood provides a change of scenery. Members make good use of "retired" items through a greeting card recycling program and a thrift room where used clothing and household items are sold. Those 55 and older pay $5.00 a year to belong.

Southern Hills

Custer Senior Citizens Center
538 Mt. Rushmore Rd., Custer
(605) 673–2708

You don't even need to be a senior citizen to enjoy the benefits of membership at this active center. Associate members of any age pay $5.00 a year to belong; those 60 and older pay $12.00 and get voting privileges. Line dancing, exercise classes, bingo, greeting card recycling, ceramics, movies, a Stitches 'n' Sew group, pool, and card games are some of the fun activities found here. The center has a support group for widowed people, as well as programs for greeting new area residents and visiting or staying in touch by phone with those who are alone or isolated. The local ministerial association's food pantry is located in the center, and the Coalition on Aging holds its meetings here.

Springs Senior Citizens Center
206 S. Chicago Ave., Hot Springs
(605) 745–6123

Bridge, cribbage, and pinochle are just some of the card games members enjoy playing here. Pool, exercise classes, and, occasionally, a dance offer additional opportunities for fun and well-being. Bingo players find their game of choice at the regularly scheduled potlucks, and fund-raisers, greeting card recycling, and a small rummage area for nonclothing items help support the center. Seniors 55 and older pay $7.50 a year or $50.00 for lifetime membership.

Insiders' Tip

The Social Security Administration has an office at 605 Main Street, Suite 201, in Rapid City. Call (605) 342-1819 between 9:00 A.M. and 4:00 P.M. Monday through Friday, or call (800) 772-1213 for automated service.

Retiree Housing

When it's time to move into a smaller home, many seniors want to retain their independence while finding comfort, convenience, and companionship among their own age group in a retirement community. We expect to see more such housing opportunities in our region in coming years, but meanwhile here are a few currently available.

Northern Hills

Juniper Court
1121 10th St., Spearfish
(605) 642–4744

Each of the 14 apartments here is at ground level and has a walk-out patio and a small plot for a flower garden. Seniors 62 and older can rent a one- or two-bedroom apartment but must bring their own appliances—a plus if you swear by your kitchen range or washing machine and don't want to use another! But because retirement means less time spent on chores, there's a community room for socializing. Juniper Court is part of the Black Hills Healthcare Network, which you'll find listed in our Healthcare chapter.

Central Hills

Primrose
224 E. Minnesota St., Rapid City
(605) 342–6699

New in 1997, Primrose has 48 one- and two-bedroom apartments for seniors 60 and older, 16 of which are for those who require residential care or assisted living. Each has a fully equipped kitchen and, depending on whether it's on the first or second floor, a patio or a balcony. In the common area are a library, cozy fireplace, exercise room, entertainment center, and multipurpose room. During the summer, residents can have a garden spot on the grounds.

Westhills Village Retirement Community
255 Texas St., Rapid City
(605) 342–0255

You don't have to be retired to move into one of the 202 lovely private apartments at Westhills village, a life-care community that compares itself to a first-class hotel with five sizes and floor plans from which to choose (all with fully equipped kitchens). If you're 62 years old and capable of living on your own, you're eligible. You'll want to get your application in early; you can expect to be on the waiting list for at least a year, so plan ahead.

Established in 1994, nonprofit Westhills Village offers a full spectrum of options for moderate-income seniors. In addition to the apartments already mentioned, 31 private suites at adjacent Westhills South offer assisted living with staffers on hand around the clock. For those needing the highest level of care and supervision, Westhills Village Health Care Facility is a state-licensed, Medicare-approved skilled nursing facility with 44 beds in private and semiprivate rooms. Registered nurses are on staff 24 hours a

Insiders' Tip

If you're too busy or otherwise unable to run your own errands in Rapid City, you can pay someone else to do the job for you. For an hourly rate of $8.00 to $12.00, Needful Things Errand Service Inc. will dispatch a driver to help you or to give you a ride. Drivers are available from 9:00 A.M. to 3:00 P.M. Monday, Tuesday, Thursday, and Friday. Call (605) 341-6308, or leave a message on the voice pager at (605) 394-1471.

Westhills Village Retirement Community in Rapid City offers private apartments, assisted-care living, and a licensed healthcare facility. PHOTO: STEVEN A. PAGE

day. The Home Health Agency of Westhills Village provides in-home care in Rapid City and the surrounding area.

The monthly service fees for Westhills Village apartments include a daily meal, utilities, and many services such as limited housekeeping and scheduled transportation. Woodworkers, gardeners, and crafters find ample space for their pastimes in the common area, and the beautifully manicured grounds feature gardens and walking paths.

Media

Newspapers
Magazines
Radio
Television
Film

Visitors to the Black Hills will find plenty to listen to, watch, and read—on the radio and television and in print publications, that is. You'll find a diversity of music, a smattering of homegrown magazines, plenty of newspapers, and a wide variety of television programming.

Just for fun, we've also included some information about our film industry. After your visit here you may catch some big—or small—screen films or advertisements in which the landscapes look very familiar.

While you're here you can easily keep in touch, through a variety of media, with what's going on in the rest of the world or what's going on in the Black Hills.

Newspapers

If you're interested in learning about daily life in Black Hills towns, local newspapers are your best source. The largest, the *Rapid City Journal,* offers state, national, and international coverage, as well as general coverage of smaller towns. However, there are many small papers that provide thorough and personal coverage of their own hometowns, from community news and local government information to features and the quaint community and small-town neighbor news that defines the distinct personality of each area.

Northern Hills

Dailies

Black Hills Pioneer
315 Seaton Circle, Spearfish
(605) 642–2761

A daily tabloid (Monday through Saturday), the *Black Hills Pioneer* is distributed in the Northern Hills and focuses on the news and events in Lead, Lawrence County, and Spearfish. It's one of the larger papers, with a circulation of 5,000, and it includes an advertising supplement, the *Weekly Prospector,* on Tuesday.

Insiders' Tip

It isn't easy to find *The New York Times* in the Black Hills. It's easier to find the Sunday *Denver Post* (Denver is the nearest large metropolitan area) or *USA Today*—in vending boxes and some retail stores and hotels. You can find the *Times* in some convenience stores and in scattered bookstores, grocery stores, and hotels. Or call its local distributor, Rushmore News, at (605) 342–2617 and ask where you can find it. Be aware, however, that these businesses carry only the *Times'* Sunday edition. You won't find daily editions on sale anywhere in the Hills, but you can read the daily *Times* at the Rapid City Library, which receives its copies by mail, three days late.

Weeklies

Belle Fourche Bee/Belle Fourche Post
1004 Fifth St., Belle Fourche
(605) 892–2528

The *Bee*, a 108-year-old weekly, comes out on Saturday. Its sister paper, the *Post*, comes out on Wednesday. Both serve the Northern Hills, with a focus on Belle Fourche and surrounding areas.

Together, their circulation totals 2,000, and both papers have won South Dakota Newspaper Association and state American Advertising Federation awards.

Black Hills Press/Meade County Times-Tribune
1238 Main St., Sturgis
(605) 347–2503

The *Black Hills Press* is issued each Saturday and the *Times-Tribune* each Wednesday. Both have a circulation of 2,700 and serve the Northern Hills, focusing on the Sturgis and Meade County area.

Lawrence County Centennial
68 Sherman St., Deadwood
(605) 578–3305

This semiweekly (Wednesday and Saturday), which has a circulation of 2,100, covers the Northern Hills and is distributed throughout the Spearfish, Deadwood, and Lead areas.

Tri-State Livestock News
1022 Main St., Sturgis
(605) 347–2585

It has served the Midwest's agricultural industry for four decades, and if you're a farmer or rancher, you'll find its reports and news very helpful from your business point-of-view. If you're not an agriculturist, it's a great way to learn what the real "cowboy life" is like. The *Tri-State Livestock News* is published weekly on Saturday.

Central Hills

Dailies

Rapid City Journal
507 Main St., Rapid City
(605) 394–8300, (800) 843–2300

The *Journal* is the largest newspaper in the Hills, with a circulation of 35,000 and bureaus in Spearfish and Pierre. It focuses on the entire Hills area and also covers eastern Wyoming, northern Nebraska, and the rest of South Dakota. It provides national and international news and features as well. A daily morning paper founded in 1878 as the *Black Hills Journal*, the *Rapid City Journal* is sold in vending boxes and stores in all Hills towns.

Wednesday editions include advertising supplements (the majority of which are grocery store ads) and the *Rapid City Advertiser* (the *Northern Hills Advertiser* goes to towns north of Rapid City). Sunday editions include *Parade* magazine and the most extensive help-wanted ads of the week. Friday editions have weekend entertainment information, and Saturday editions offer religious articles and church service listings.

Weeklies

Indian Country Today
1920 Lombardy Dr., Rapid City
(605) 341–0011

Although there are other Native American newspapers published by organizations, *Indian Country Today* is one of the few independently owned papers in the nation focused solely on Native American issues. It was founded in 1981 as *Lakota Times* to serve the Pine Ridge Reservation in south-central South Dakota. Its popularity steadily expanded the coverage and distribution areas, so it was renamed and relocated to Rapid City.

Indian Country Today is an Indian-owned paper distributed nationwide and in 17 foreign countries and is read by more than 100,000 people. It's published weekly on Wednesday and focuses on news, political issues, and the culture, events, and people of "Indian Country," wherever in the world that may be.

Locally, you can find *Indian Country Today* in many stores and in coin-operated vending boxes.

Pennington County Courant
212 Fourth Ave., Wall
(605) 279-2565

The *Courant* circulates 1,100 copies throughout eastern Pennington County. It's an award-winning broadsheet that was founded in 1906 and is a window to the happenings in Wall, the Badlands, and surrounding area.

Pennington County Prevailer News
114 Main St., Hill City
(605) 574-2538

The Prevailer is published on Wednesdays; its 1,800 copies are distributed throughout both the Central and Southern Hills. The Western Trader is its weekly shopper supplement.

Southern Hills

Weeklies
Custer County Chronicle
602 Mt. Rushmore Rd., Custer
(605) 673-2217

The *Chronicle* calls itself "your hometown newspaper" and is one of the oldest newspapers in the Hills. In fact, it celebrated its 120th anniversary in 1999.

Distributed in the Southern Hills on Wednesday, the *Chronicle* has won South Dakota Newspaper Association awards for excellence and best feature story.

Hot Springs Star
107 N. Chicago Ave., Hot Springs
(605) 745-4170

The Star was founded in 1885, is published on Tuesday, and serves the Southern Hills. It focuses on the people and events in and around Hot Springs and also publishes a shopper, the *Hot Springs Star Extra.*

Magazines
An interesting array of locally published magazines can be found in the Black Hills. Some are published "East River," far from the Hills, but they're popular and available here (some by subscription only, though) and contain information you may find helpful while visiting. Each is a resource to learn more about an aspect of the Hills, from business and culture to hobbies and attractions.

Dakota Outdoors
333 E. Dakota St., Pierre
(605) 224-7301

This Midwestern sportsperson's magazine offers information on outdoor recreation in the Dakotas, with a focus on hunting and fishing. In the Black Hills area it's available by subscription only for $10 per year. (It's on newsstands east of the Missouri River.) *Dakota Outdoors* is published monthly, and two stand-alone issues are included with subscriptions: the *Fishing Guide* in January and the *Hunting Guide* in August.

Deadwood Magazine
4851 Cliff Dr., Rapid City
(605) 343-2950

This entertaining little bimonthly has a nice blend of western South Dakota history and entertainment, with current events, attraction information, and occasional fiction, most focused on Deadwood and the Northern Hills.

It's distributed free in visitor centers, area stores, and selected hotels and travel agencies as well as on newsstands and in racks. You can also subscribe ($15 per year) by calling the number above.

Panache Magazine
(605) 399-0859

Panache is a hip little publication you'll find for free at trendy coffeehouses and restaurants. The newsletter-style magazine is devoted to the Black Hills–area arts and entertainment scene from the perspective of the younger crowd; features, profiles, and columns are angled accordingly. However, anyone looking for arts-related entertainment will find the "Around the Scene" events calendar informative. Panache is published biweekly.

Rapid City Homefinder
2218 Jackson Blvd., Rapid City
(605) 343-7684
This monthly real estate guide is available free in racks around town or by mail.

Rapid City Home Journal/
Black Hills Home Journal
507 Main St, Rapid City
(605) 394-8300, (800) 843-2300
This is a two-in-one monthly real estate publication (produced by the *Rapid City Journal*) with listings arranged by real estate agency. One half contains Rapid City listings; flip it over to check out listings for the Black Hills.

South Dakota Conservation Digest
523 E. Capitol Ave., Pierre
(605) 773-3485
This magazine started out in 1934 as mimeographed sheets produced by the state's Department of Game, Fish & Parks. Today the bimonthly has a circulation of 16,000 and is still devoted to outdoor recreation, wildlife, and conservation. Its articles are about hunting, fishing, camping, wildlife, parks, and issues relating to all these. The November/December issue contains a calendar of events for the following year. You can't buy *South Dakota Conservation Digest* on newsstands, but you can subscribe for just $5.00 per year.

South Dakota Hall of Fame Magazine
100 W. Lawler St., Chamberlain
(605) 734-4216, (800) 697-3130
This magazine provides a wealth of information about our South Dakota heritage. The nonprofit Hall of Fame began in 1974 to recognize those "who have contributed to the development and heritage of South Dakota." Since then, hundreds of note-

worthy people, living and deceased, have become hall-of-famers commemorated in this quarterly magazine.

Fifteen people are inducted each year, in 15 categories, including historical, agriculture, Indian heritage, religion, professional cowboy, and "unsung heroes and good hearts." The Hall of Fame sells books and displays a photo collection, and its magazine files are open to the public. The historically valuable archives are computerized, and a database is available for public use.

You won't find this magazine on newsstands, but it's available at Wall Drug (see our Badlands and Nearby chapter) or can be browsed at most South Dakota libraries. Both subscriptions and single copies are available at the number above.

South Dakota Magazine
410 E. Third St., Yankton
(605) 665-6655, (800) 456-5117
South Dakota Magazine was founded in 1985 and has been highly successful, now reaching 100,000 readers with bimonthly issues.

It celebrates the heritage of South Dakota with a rich mix of articles about interesting characters, small towns, historical events, fascinating wildlife, and local lifestyles. It's a well-loved magazine, produced by people who obviously care deeply about their state. The extensive monthly collection of letters to the editors saying "thanks for the memories" and enthusing "I remember that!" attests to its popularity. *South Dakota Magazine* is available on newsstands around the state or by subscription.

Radio

This being the wild West, you'll find several country music stations (both contemporary and classic styles), but the airwaves also carry choices for fans of talk radio, rock, oldies, alternative, and Christian.

We haven't listed these radio stations by our usual Northern, Central, and Southern Hills categories. Instead, these are listed by format, so you can easily find the type of music you prefer.

Many stations are powerful enough to span more than one of our usual geographical designations, but the Hills themselves may interfere occasionally with your reception of less-powerful stations, especially as you drive.

If you're a fan of public broadcasting, try South Dakota Public Radio, which started in 1922. It broadcasts from nine radio stations and 10 translators, 24 hours each day, seven days each week. While you're visiting the Black Hills, you won't have to miss *All Things Considered, Morning Edition, Car Talk, A Prairie Home Companion,* or your other favorite Public Broadcasting System radio programs.

Alternative

KTEQ 91.3 FM

Christian

KLMP 97.9 FM (inspirational and talk)
KSLT 106.3/107.3 FM (adult contemporary Christian)

Country

KBHB 810 AM (traditional country)
KIMM 1150AM (classic country)
KIQK Kick 104.1 FM (contemporary country)
KOUT Kat Country 98.7 FM (contemporary country)
KZZI KZ Country 95.9 FM (mainstream country)

Oldies

KKLS Kool 92 AM (good-time oldies, '50s, '60s, '70s)
KTOQ 1340 AM (nostalgia)

Public Radio

South Dakota Public Radio:
KBHE 89.3 FM, Rapid City
Translators: 88.1 FM, Belle Fourche and Hot Springs; 91.1 FM, Spearfish; 91.9 FM, Lead; 88.5 FM, Pringle

A KELO-TV reporter conducts an interview for a newscast that will be seen across the state.

PHOTO: BARBARA TOMOVICK

GREAT FACES

South Dakota Public Television

South Dakota Public Television celebrated its official 32nd anniversary in 1999. Although educational television station KUSD-TV first went on the air in 1961, the South Dakota State Legislature secured a federal grant (with matching funds from the state) in 1967 to increase the station's power, create more transmitters, and form a board of directors. The board was given the task of creating a network of stations across this huge state so that every single school could access instructional television programming for classroom use. Today, there are nine television/radio transmitters in place, with coverage areas that blanket the entire state.

Public television in South Dakota provides national programming and news from the Public Broadcasting System; South Dakota–oriented programs such as *Arts Advocate Report, Buffalo Nation Journal,* and legislative reports from the state capital; and programs for children and teens. In addition to instructional television programs broadcast to schools, it offers adult continuing education telecourses, overnight educational programs that teachers or day-care providers can tape and use later, and live videoconferences for professionals via the Rural Development Telecommunications Network.

More than 20,000 people are Friends of South Dakota Public Broadcasting, supporting quality cultural and educational programming with both their financial contributions and their time and energy as volunteers. To become a Friend, call (800) 333–0789.

Rock

KDDX The X 101.1/103.1 FM (album-oriented rock)
KFXS The Fox 100.3 FM (classic rock)
KKMK Magic 93.9 FM (adult contemporary)
KRCS Hot 93.1 FM (top 40 contemporary hits)
KSQY K-Sky 92.1/95.1 FM (adult-oriented rock)

Talk

KILl 90.1 FM (88.3 FM in Rapid City) (Native American traditional, community, and public radio)
KOTA 1380 AM (news/talk)

Television

Although cable or satellite service isn't necessary to receive network stations (it does improve reception, however), many consumers here do subscribe.

There are several Black Hills companies to choose from, including Black Hills Fibercom, (605) 348–1701; Primestar, (605) 343–0755; Rapid Choice, (605) 343–3806; WANTV, (605) 348–6255; and TCI Cablevision, (605) 343–3402.

Local Television Stations and Their Network Affiliates

There are five local stations. We've listed them below, with their network affiliates and their local channel numbers. Please note that the channel numbers will be different if you're watching a television with cable or satellite service, as these use different channel numbers.

KBHE Channel 9, South Dakota Public Broadcasting (PBS)
(605) 394–2551, (605) 677–5861

(800) 456-0766 (administration)
(800) 568-6922 (network production)

KELO Channel 15 (CBS)
(605) 341-1500, (800) 888-KELO

KEVN/KIVV Channel 7 (Fox)
(605) 394-7777

KNBN Channel 27, Rapid City; Channel
    31, Lead/Deadwood (NBC)
(605) 355-0024

KOTA Channel 3 (ABC)
(605) 342-2000

Film

South Dakota Film Office
711 E. Wells Ave., Pierre
(605) 773-3301, (800) 952-3625

The beauty of the Black Hills and Badlands has enticed many a filmmaker to bring camera and crew to South Dakota. Thus, the state's Department of Tourism created a film office to promote South Dakota to the film- and video-producing industries, and to assist and support filmmakers when they arrive.

The popularity of Kevin Costner's *Dances with Wolves* brought the state's visual attributes to the attention of many. A state with open spaces and gorgeously varied vistas; herds of buffalo, horses, and cattle; eager extras; Old West-style towns and buildings; skilled horse riders; and Mount Rushmore is a real find in the film industry.

Insiders' Tip

Channel 2 is the local government access channel. You can view it only if you subscribe to TCI Cablevision, (605) 343-3402. It's a good way to stay informed about Rapid City government, because Channel 2 broadcasts city council meetings, board of education meetings, and other informative public service programs.

The $100 million science fiction feature *Starship Troopers* was filmed here, as were the Hitchcock thriller *North by Northwest* and Turner made-for-cable movies *Lakota Woman* and *Crazy Horse*. You'll also spot South Dakota scenery in *Thunderheart* and portions of *Wyatt Earp, Twister,* and the Emmy Award–winning documentary *Lewis and Clark: Journey of the Corps of Discovery*.

South Dakota, the Black Hills, and the Badlands are also popular with producers of commercials and still photographers seeking scenery for advertising, magazine, and fine art photographs.

Worship and Spirituality

Many Black Hills residents are firmly rooted in faith, as are their contemporaries in other regions of our country's heartland. In a place where many claim pioneers as their very recent ancestors, it's not surprising that the faith of those forebears still plays an essential role in modern life. Also, in a part of the world where so many depend on nature and weather for their livelihood (farmers, ranchers, and loggers come to mind), faith and religion keep people going when those two always-unpredictable elements sometimes disappoint.

The mix of religions in the Black Hills is typical of religious representation in the heartland. That is, you won't find many of the so-called alternative or New Age religions common in cities such as Boulder, Colorado; Santa Fe, New Mexico; or San Francisco. What you will find is a healthy traditional religious foundation—a solid bedrock of spirituality, if you will—that is rooted in everyday life.

Ancient forms of spirituality were permeating the lives of the native people when the Black Hills were "discovered" by newcomers seeking gold. Other religions (also ancient, but new to this area) came along with the pioneers. Each of these developed, changed, and grew right along with the burgeoning Black Hills population.

The majority of religions here are traditional: mainstream and nonaffiliated Protestant, Catholic, and Jewish. Most have a solid base in the community and devoted members who are committed to their faiths. They also have interesting histories that reflect the immense changes that began here in 1876 with the gold rush.

Protestants and Catholics

For example, the first Episcopal service conducted by an ordained priest was in 1878. It was held in Rapid City, when the town was still so new and tiny that it had only one street. A story tells that Rev. Edward Ashley was in town to attend court as a witness. The courtroom was above the saloon, so the enterprising priest asked if he could hold a church service in that room the following Sunday. He put up notices around town, but on Sunday morning Rev. Ashley and the saloon's janitor were the only worshippers present at the appointed time. After waiting 20 minutes, the good reverend was ready to give up when a large group of noisy folk came pounding up the stairs and into the courtroom, singing "Hold The Fort For I Am Coming," and the service began.

The first Episcopal service conducted by a resident, however, was the funeral of Preacher Henry Weston Smith in 1876. Deadwood Sheriff Seth Bullock borrowed a Book of Common Prayer in order to conduct the burial service for Smith, who was, interestingly enough, a Methodist clergyman. Preacher Smith had heard the call to minister to the people of Deadwood and had held services on an itinerant basis for just a few months before he was murdered by someone whose identity remains a mystery. The devout minister was the Hills' only clergyman at that time and its first religious martyr. Sheriff Bullock wrote that the funeral "was the most serious business that ever happened in the Hills, a lot of wicked, illiterate miners burying a minister, a man of God."

Both gold rush and pioneer towns attracted clerics and missionaries who

An Indian Prayer

O Great Spirit, Whose voice I hear in the winds,
and whose breath gives life to all the world, hear
me!

I am small and weak.
I need your strength and wisdom.

Let me walk in beauty, and make my eyes
ever behold the red and purple sunset.

Make my hands respect the things you have made
and my ears sharp to hear your voice.

Make me wise so that I may understand the things
you have taught my people.

Let me learn the lessons you have hidden
in every leaf and rock.

I seek strength, not to be greater than my brother,
but to fight my greatest enemy—myself.

Make me always ready to come to you with
clean hands and straight eyes.

So when life fades, as the fading sunset,
my spirit may come to you without shame.

*Reprinted with the kind permission of Red Cloud Indian School,
Pine Ridge, South Dakota*

intended to save the souls of the residents and build up a bedrock faith. Many of the new pioneers had left more "civilized" eastern towns and discovered—some with glee, some with shock—that the recently sprung-up Black Hills towns had a shortage of law enforcement, schools, and churches, as well as peaceful and civilized behavior.

The devout men of the cloth were respected and appreciated by most, but they still contended with the rough-and-tumble life of the frontier, with all its lawless, sometimes downright wacky, behavior. In 1882, for example, the *Black Hills Journal* carried this story: "Rev. Ira Wakefield, well known here, was surprised, while riding along the road near Custer recently, by the report of a pistol shot, followed by another and another, and hearing the bullets

whistling, in what he imagined to be close proximity to his head, he pulled up, and was immediately joined by a man coming from the rear, who said he had merely wanted the reverend gentleman's company on the road, and took that method of bringing him to, until he could overtake him."

Another godly man was approached by an inebriated fellow who requested money to purchase some lunch. Afraid that if he simply handed over the donation it might be used to purchase whiskey, the good samaritan bought a·nourishing lunch of cheese and crackers for the fellow, only to discover that the beggar, immediately afterward, "staked the lunch against a drink in a game of seven-up."

As men who had come to the Hills to look for gold began to send for their waiting families, as women and children began to move into the towns, and as merchants set up shops, more and more religious organizations formed. These had little effect on the hard-drinking, rowdy types who made the gambling halls, saloons, and brothels so successful, especially in Deadwood. But perhaps those "unchurched" folks actually managed to encourage the growing number of congregations as counterpoints to the seamier side of life in these small towns.

Religious congregations often met in any space available until they could build their own house of worship, and the citizens of smaller, less-populated towns usually had to conduct their own services, or wait until a circuit-riding minister or priest made his rounds. As their numbers grew and they raised funds, however, these groups built their own buildings.

The first religious organization in the Hills was Deadwood's First Congregational Church, founded in 1876. Its members met in two different hotels, then a carpenter's shop (a nice bit of symbolism, we think), before building a fine structure in 1877.

The first Catholic priest in Deadwood, Rev. John Lonergan, arrived in 1877 and conducted the first Mass in another carpenter's shop. He and his parishioners built their church that year. Another priest preceded Father Lonergan to the Black Hills, however. Father Pierre DeSmet, a Jesuit pioneer missionary, visited the Native American tribes of the area in 1848.

Father B. Mackin established Catholic parishes in Lead and Central City in 1878 but also covered much of the Black Hills in his circuit-riding ministry. This busy man brought the Holy Cross Sisters to Deadwood to establish a hospital in 1878. The first Mass in the Southern Hills was in 1887 at St. Anthony of Padua Catholic Church. The historic building no longer exists, but the parish still functions in Hot Springs. The first church in Rapid City was a Catholic church, constructed in 1882 at a cost of just $345. Although the building is gone, it boasted the first church bell in town.

Just two years after Preacher Smith's untimely death, another Methodist minister, Rev. James Williams, organized a congregation in Deadwood in 1878, but it was not until March of 1883 that the church was completed. A mere two months later the building was destroyed in a flood, and the Episcopal congregation generously offered the basement of its own church until the Methodists could complete a new structure in 1885.

The Jewish Faith

Jewish people came to the Black Hills from other sections of the United States and from Europe, arriving during the gold rush to set up shops that provided goods and services to miners and pioneers. The impressive tombstones—beautifully inscribed in Hebrew—of some of those early Jewish merchants and their families can be seen at Deadwood's Mount Moriah Cemetery in the Hebrew Hill section.

Soon after Rapid City was founded in 1876, Jewish services began there. They

Insiders' Tip

There are several religious bookstores in the Black Hills. In Rapid City, you'll find Bible & Book Store at 618 Main Street, (605) 343-3720, (800) 888-1639; Gospel Garden Book Store at 610 Seventh Street, (605) 348-6313, (800) 843-8080; and Mustard Seed Catholic Book Store at 523 Seventh Street, (605) 348-5228, (800) 456-1893. A Peace of the Black Hills is in Hill City at 312 Main Street, (605) 574-4226.

were first held in local homes; it wasn't until the 1960s that they were moved to the chapel at Ellsworth Air Force Base. Worshippers built their own Rapid City building, the Synagogue of the Hills, in 1996. The synagogue's Torah is the original scroll used by Deadwood's early Jewish population. It came from Konigsberg, Germany, in 1888, along with Freda Lowensberg who traveled here to join her sweetheart, settler Benjamin Blumenthal.

Native American Spirituality

Spirituality pervades the daily lives of many Native Americans and is usually not seen as separate from other aspects of life. Religious ceremonies such as sun dances and sweat lodges are not usually open to non-Indians, whose participation in such rites often evokes controversy. A few area Christian churches have predominantly Native American congregations, but these tend to be low-key and are not listed as such in the Yellow Pages. If you are interested, you will need to call the denomination of your choice and ask if such a church is in the area.

Visitors may not realize that powwows are also sacred ceremonies, ancient worship services celebrated with dancing (the Dakota, Lakota, and Nakota word for powwow means "dance"), singing, drumming, and much symbolism. Powwows, however, unlike some other ceremonies, are open to visitors, and there's one held nearly every weekend in the summer at reservations or in Black Hills towns. Call the South Dakota Department of Tourism, (605) 773-3301, for information on annual powwows. You'll find a write-up on the best-known event, the Black Hills Pow Wow, in our Annual Events and Festivals chapter.

Powwows are important in the spiritual lives of Native Americans. Organizers ask that visitors conduct themselves with respect, wear modest clothing, speak quietly, and always ask for permission before taking pictures. Photography may, in fact, be prohibited at powwows, and some elders may not want to be photographed.

Historic Houses of Worship

Of the many houses of worship built in the Black Hills, many original buildings no

Bear Butte is a holy place where Native Americans have gone to worship for centuries. PHOTO: COURTESY OF SOUTH DAKOTA TOURISM

The steeple of a pioneer church points heavenward. PHOTO: COURTESY OF DAILY CAMERA

Lakota Creation Story

The Lakota people have a beautiful creation story. They believe they came from their First World into another life, the Second World or Root Nation. They then evolved into the Third World and lived at *Wahutopa Oyate,* the Four-Legged Nation, where their bodies and spirits were their beloved buffalo. The people came up to the earth's surface through the "breathing cave"—Wind Cave, in the southern Black Hills. They lived there with all their many relatives, those who lived in the water, walked on the land, and flew through the air, all part of Creation.

longer exist, having been lost to time, weather, or "progress." One of the remaining, and the oldest continuously used, is St. John's Episcopal Church at 405 Williams Street in Deadwood. It was completed in 1881, and the congregation still uses its 554-pipe organ that was built in 1904.

Rapid City's Emmanuel Episcopal Church, 717 Quincy Street, still stands as well. It was completed in 1887 and is listed on the National Register of Historic Places. When its elegantly cut sandstone blocks were cleaned by sandblasting in 1976, it was discovered they had been cemented with good old Black Hills mud, a common technique in those days.

The modern era saw the construction, in 1963, of The Cathedral of Our Lady of Perpetual Help, 520 Cathedral Drive, in Rapid City. It's a richly symbolic building and the largest church structure in the Hills. Anyone may view the architectural features and stained-glass work by requesting a tour at the rectory office.

Religion Today

Whatever religion or denomination you're looking for, a quick glance through the Yellow Pages will help you locate it. You'll have no trouble finding a Baptist church, or a Methodist, Wesleyan, Lutheran, or Catholic congregation. You will, however, have fewer choices if you're looking for an Assembly of God, Jehovah's Witnesses, Church of God, Reformed, Church of Christ, Episcopal, or Presbyterian church.

Jewish, Unity, Salvation Army, Pentecostal, Christian Science, Nazarene, Mormon, Quaker, Eckankar, Unitarian Universalist, Christian & Missionary Alliance, and Seventh-day Adventist faiths are represented by just one congregation each. There are several interdenominational, nondenominational, and community churches in the region as well.

Whatever religion or faith you claim, whether you're visiting for just a single worship service or looking for a new spiritual home, you'll most likely be welcomed wholeheartedly by any Black Hills congregation. These strong and devoted people know that their historically strong faith becomes even more unshakable when it's shared.

Insiders' Tip

Some local denominations have church camps or conference and retreat centers, a way to combine a pleasant vacation in the Black Hills with spiritual refreshment and personal enrichment. Inquire at the church of your choice to learn if such facilities are available.

Index

About the Authors

Barbara Tomovick

Barbara Tomovick grew up in New England, but a part of her always yearned to go west. So in 1981 she set out for the Arizona mountains, stopping along the way for a few days of hiking and camping in the Black Hills. Continuing on, she decided she preferred pine forests to desert and turned around. She never intended to stay permanently in the Hills, but with the exception of a year spent working in eastern South Dakota, she never quite got around to leaving. There were too many intriguing places to explore, and too many captivating stories to write.

Convinced even as a child that she was born with ink in her veins, Barbara found her calling in journalism and earned a degree in mass communications. Ever since, she has worked as a writer and editor. In 1986 she founded the *Rapid City Journal's* Northern Hills Bureau and spent the next five and a half years covering issues and events in a three-county area. That led to another pioneering news job on the far side of the state establishing the Vermillion Bureau of the Sioux Falls *Argus Leader* in 1994. Barbara spent a memorable year there interviewing such prominent figures as Gore Vidal, Charles Kuralt, Ossie Davis, and Simon Ortiz; getting to know the denizens and customs of the nations heartland; developing an appreciation for long sunsets; and writing a story about fetal alcohol syndrome that won the 1995 South Dakota Associated Press Sweepstakes award for newswriting. During that time she also finally made up her mind to marry a Rapid City man she had known for 11 years.

Since returning to the Black Hills, Barbara worked as a freelance writer and on-call temp in the *Rapid City Journal* newsroom before becoming a full-time copy editor at the *Journal*. Over the years her byline has appeared on stories and photos in the *Chicago Tribune, The Dallas Morning News, The Denver Post, AAA Home & Away* magazine, *Ballooning* magazine and other publications, including a Chinese in-flight magazine. This is her first book but, she predicts, not her last.

When not gazing into a computer monitor, Barbara enjoys playing outdoors, traveling, reading, learning foreign languages, taking pictures, experimenting in the kitchen, and other domestic pursuits, including patchwork quilting. Most of all, she treasures time spent with her husband, Ken, and their blended family of four children. She lives in a handmade house overlooking a creek southwest of Rapid City.

Kimberly Metz

Kimberly Metz was surprised by South Dakota. She grew up in Ohio's rolling farm country, then was struck by an early midlife crisis that compelled her to spend two years traveling around the country. During that adventure she photographed, wrote, planted trees through chilly Southern winters, was flown by hung-over helicopter pilots to remote Minnesota logging country to plant more trees, raked blueberries in Maine, and ran a farm stand on the Massachusetts North Shore. Her first published article, written during these adventures, was hammered out on a rented typewriter propped up on a cardboard box while she sat cross-legged on the ground.

She settled in Santa Fe, New Mexico, and started a word-processing and desktop-publishing business but continued writing articles and editing for clients. After several years of watching sadly as Santa Fe and many other small towns were discovered and forever changed, she looked for an unspoiled region in which to settle. Her then-husband, a South Dakota native, suggested they consider the Black Hills. Seriously misinformed, she expressed doubts about living in a place with roaming cows, wild animals, and no indoor plumbing. Upon her first visit, however, she was terribly embarrassed by these silly misconceptions and immediately fell in love with the beautiful views, friendly mountains, friendlier people, and even the cows, who prefer to stay in their own fields. She is proud to say she suffered ample and instant karma for her misconceptions when every New Mexico friend she informed of her pending move laughed and asked why anyone would move to South Dakota. Secretly pleased, she realized the Hills are still relatively undiscovered, to be enjoyed by the fortunate (and informed) few who take time to discover their natural beauty and opportunities.

After a stint as staff writer for a Rapid City jewelry manufacturer, Kimberly founded Words Unlimited, a freelance writing service. She cranks out ad copy, press releases, bios, resumes, and love letters, but her passion is magazine article writing, which allows her to interview fascinating people and pass along interesting information. She also writes short-short stories and takes photographs; she has won awards for both her fiction and photos. Her articles and short stories have been published in *American Forests, Motorcycle Events, Catholic Digest, Trailer Life, South Dakota Vacation Guide, South Dakota Magazine, New Mexico, Eyes on South Dakota Women, Cigar Lifestyles, Old West Trail Explorer,* Internet publications and elsewhere.

She is renovating her half-century-old home, where affectionate cats walk on the computer keyboard and the barking of a German shepherd named Dakota keeps her from sitting still too long. Her vegetable and flower gardens, lovingly fed by Black Hills rain and sunshine, take up the rest of her time.

About the Revisers

For the past 20 years, Bert Gildart has worked as a writer. Hundreds of his stories have been published in many periodicals including *Smithsonian, Travel & Leisure, Travel Holiday,* and the *Christian Science Monitor*. Ten years ago Jane joined him, and as a husband-and-wife writing team they have produced many books about the outdoors. They also operate their own stock photo agency (GildartPhoto.com), which provides images to publications all over the world.

Updating the second edition of *Insiders' Guide to South Dakota's Black Hills and Badlands* resulted from a love the Gildarts have for the Black Hills, an area they have written about often. Among their titles is *Hiking South Dakota's Black Hills Country* (Falcon Publishing, 1996).